TABLE OF CONTENTS

ARGENTINA - MEASURES AFFECTING THE EXPORT OF BOVINE HIDES AND THE IMPORT OF FINISHED LEATHER

Arbitration under Article 21.3(c) of the Understanding on Rules and Procedures Governing the Settlement of Disputes

Award of the Arbitrator
Florentino P. Feliciano
WT/DS155/10

Circulated to Members on 31 August 2001

I. INTRODUCTION

1. On 16 February 2001, the Dispute Settlement Body (the "DSB") adopted the Panel Report[1] in *Argentina - Measures Affecting the Export of Bovine Hides and the Import of Finished Leather* ("*Argentina - Hides and Leather*").[2] At the DSB meeting of 12 March 2001, Argentina informed the DSB, pursuant to Article 21.3 of the *Understanding on Rules and Procedures Governing the Settlement of Disputes* (the "DSU"), that it would implement the recommendations and rulings of the DSB in this dispute and that it would require a "reasonable period of time" to do so, under the terms of Article 21.3 of the DSU.

2. In view of its inability to reach an agreement with Argentina on the period of time reasonably required for implementation of those recommendations and rulings, the European Communities requested that such period be determined by binding arbitration pursuant to Article 21.3(c) of the DSU.[3]

3. By joint letter of 12 June 2001, Argentina and the European Communities notified the DSB that they had agreed that the duration of the "reasonable period of time" for implementation should be determined through binding arbitration, under the terms of Article 21.3(c) of the DSU, and that I should act as Arbitrator.[4] The parties also indicated in that letter that they had agreed to extend the time-period for the arbitration, which shall be completed no later than 90 days after the date of the appointment of the arbitrator.[5] Notwithstanding this exten-

---

1 WT/DS155/R, WT/DS155/R/Corr.1.
2 WT/DS155/5.
3 WT/DS155/6.
4 WT/DS155/8.
5 *Ibid.*

sion of the time-period, the parties stated that the arbitration award would be deemed to be an award made under Article 21.3(c) of the DSU. My acceptance of this designation as Arbitrator was conveyed to the parties by letter of 12 June 2001.

4. Written submissions were received from Argentina and the European Communities on 3 July 2001, and an oral hearing was held on 18 July 2001.

II. ARGUMENTS OF THE PARTIES

A. Argentina

5. Argentina requests the arbitrator to fix the "reasonable period of time" at forty-six months and fifteen days, so that that period of time will expire on 31 December 2004.

6. Argentina submits that the text of Article 21.3(c) of the DSU makes it clear that the 15-month period provided as a guideline is merely indicative. Article 21.3(c) speaks of the possibility of fixing a period of longer than 15 months for the implementation of the recommendations and rulings of the DSB. According to Argentina, the circumstances in this particular dispute warrant the granting of a period longer than 15 months for the implementation of the DSB recommendations and rulings.

7. Since 1992, Argentina has been working on a programme to combat tax evasion and reform its tax system. The cornerstone of this programme is the system of *percepciones* and *retenciones* applied to the *Impuesto al Valor Agregado* (the "IVA") and the *Impuesto de Ganancias* (the "IG"). This programme ties in, both economically and legally, with the objective of reducing the fiscal deficit. The programme has been explicitly backed by various international financial agencies, in particular, the International Monetary Fund (the "IMF"). The agreements concluded with the IMF set out a number of quantitative targets, notably for the levels of fiscal deficit, primary spending and public debt, that are monitored on a quarterly basis throughout the period covered by the programme. Failure of Argentina to achieve these targets would preclude disbursement of the funds otherwise available under the agreements.

8. Argentina stresses that its fiscal position has seriously deteriorated over the past years, essentially as a result of the fall in tax revenue brought about by the economic recession that began in the third quarter of 1998 in the wake of the 1997 "Asian crisis". In this context of economic recession, Argentina sought to reduce the deficit by increasing taxes, and reducing primary spending. These efforts must continue this year and over the next few years.

9. Under these circumstances, Argentina argues that legal and fiscal difficulties would result from eliminating the extra financial burden imposed on importers as a result of the advances on the IVA and IG at rates higher than those applied to domestic transactions, through a "downward equalization" of the rates applied to imports.

10. Argentina, at the same time, contends that although in theory it would be possible to comply with the findings of the Panel through an "upward equalization" of the rates of the said payments on account, that is, by increasing the rates for domestic transactions, the effects of such a measure on Argentina's current situation, when the country is trying to recover from recession, would make the measures politically and economically unfeasible. Similarly, the introduction of a system of refunding interests to importers, would involve setting up a very complex administrative mechanism to ensure accurate calculation of interest due. Moreover, it would open the door to complaints from the relevant domestic sectors, complicating further the fiscal situation.

11. Argentina submits that the structure of its tax system justifies the requested time-limit. Under Argentina law, there is a set of regulations governing the conditions and time-limits for action by the national authorities in the domestic sphere. In the external sphere, there is a set of payment obligations and commitments assumed by Argentina that can only be honoured by strict compliance with the laws in force: the National Budget Law No. 25,401 of 12 December 2000 and the Fiscal Solvency Law No. 25,152 of 15 September 1999.

12. Argentina describes the process by which its annual budget is enacted as follows. In September of each year, the Executive submits to the Congress of the Nation its draft budget for the following financial year, containing estimated income and expenditure authorizations. First, it is examined by the Budget and Finance Committee of the Chamber of Deputies. Once that Committee has issued its opinion, the draft budget is examined by the Chamber, and upon approval by the Chamber of Deputies, it is passed on to the Budget and Finance Committee of the Senate before final transmission to the Senate. When it has been approved by both Chambers, it is promulgated by the Executive, which has partial veto authority. Once this process has been completed, the National Budget becomes a Law of the Nation, and can be amended only by another national law.

13. The text of the law is accompanied, *inter alia* , by a number of annexed tables providing a breakdown of the budgetary information (income, expenditure, financing, etc.) according to the organization of the national administration and its decentralized bodies. The tax revenue forecast is broken down according to the different taxes (IG, IVA, Personal Property Tax, etc.) and set out in detail in the Executive's annual letter of submission to the National Congress.

14. The projected amounts are then incorporated in the final estimate of income that is ultimately approved by Congress. The specification of these amounts, once they are included in the budget, forms part of the Law and make up the estimate of income for the entire financial year; in other words, they can only be amended by another law, since any change would involve a consequential change in the expenditure/income equation and the deficit level already approved.

15. Argentina further explains that, at the same time, the tax system is tied to the Law on Fiscal Solvency which provides, *inter alia*, for the progressive reduction of the national public deficit with a view to balancing the budget by 2005.

This Law establishes target deficit levels for each year, and any change in the deficit levels indicated would also require a legislative amendment. Because of the relationship between the Law on Fiscal Solvency and the Budget Law, estimated income and expenditure will have to be adjusted in order to reduce the deficit to attain the target prescribed. The procedure will have to be applied by law in each of the succeeding financial years until the process is completed in 2005.

16. The Law on Fiscal Solvency also lays down the obligation to include in the letter of submission of the annual budget a multi-year budget covering at least three years. In other words, the Executive must submit to the Congress, together with the budget for the coming year, a multi-year projection containing estimates of income on the basis of existing tax rates which means calculating the advances in the form of *retenciones* and *percepciones* needed in order to meet the objectives of the Law on Fiscal Solvency for 31 December 2004.

17. As a result, in the view of Argentina, it is not possible to amend the budget currently in force without altering its deficit target as well as the deficit target of the Law on Fiscal Solvency. Nor is it possible, in the current situation, to alter the system of customs levies. That system is not only linked to imports, but is also part of a comprehensive scheme to combat tax evasion which includes levies on purchases in the domestic market and the *retenciones* regime. The system makes it possible to maintain better monitoring of the obligations of taxpayers while providing them with adequate incentives to declare and regularize their operations.

18. Argentina believes that a single and immediate modification of this regime involving a reduction of the rates of levies on imports would clash with the objective of the Law on Fiscal Solvency, since it would involve a significant loss in tax revenue. Moreover, the agreement in force with the IMF provides for reduction in the deficit over the next few years in line with the Law on Fiscal Solvency. This agreement is binding on the Argentine Government, is currently in force, and specifically takes up the deficit reduction commitments contained in the Law on Fiscal Solvency. Any amendment to the IMF agreement would require renegotiation, and the fiscal targets are determined in compliance with the Law on Fiscal Solvency.

19. The Argentine public debt structure includes commitments for short, medium and long-term interest and capital payments. Argentina undertook a major debt equity swap in order to ease the burden imposed by the sequence of debt maturities. Having conducted this swap, it is particularly important in view of the rescheduling of maturities, involving a considerable medium-term fiscal cost, to ensure solvency during the stage covered by the Law on Fiscal Solvency extending up to 2005.

20. Argentina submits that Article 21.2 of the DSU, which speaks of "interests" of developing countries, ties in with the general provisions of Article 21.3(c). The "particular circumstances" of Argentina in this case are a combination of legal obligations that can only be amended through an act of the National

Congress, as in the case of the Budget Law and the Law on Fiscal Solvency, and of international obligations such as the IMF commitments.

21. Argentina recalls that according to past arbitral awards, Article 21.2 of the DSU "... enjoins, *inter alia*, an arbitrator [...] to be generally mindful of the great difficulties that a developing country Member may, in a particular case, face as it proceeds to implement the recommendations and rulings of the DSB."[6] In the present case, Argentina's economic interests as a developing country and its fiscal solvency are at stake. This is clearly reflected in the capital debt maturity schedule throughout the period requested as a reasonable period of time (up to 2005). Likewise, owing to the size of the debt involved, and in particular to the impact of any failure to comply with the IMF Agreement, Argentina would have great difficulty financing an increase in its budget deficit.

22. Argentina maintains that the impact of any change in the rates would be significant. The *retenciones* and *percepciones* are a fundamental element in maintaining an adequate tax collection level. Through this mechanism, $1,600 million were collected in 2000, i.e. more than 18 per cent of the total taxes collected in connection with foreign trade. During the same year, IVA and IG collected at customs accounted for more than 7 per cent and 6 per cent respectively of the total amount collected for each tax. To cushion the impact of this loss of revenue, a procedure involving progressive equalization sector by sector is necessary. Argentina's "interest" as a developing country, therefore, consists in avoiding an abrupt implementation without a transition period, in the space of a single financial year, that would jeopardize the objective of reducing the deficit.

23. Against the foregoing background, Argentina, requests that consideration be given to its "interest" in being granted a period of time that would enable it to implement the recommendations and rulings of the DSB in this dispute "progressively", (i.e., by instalments, as it were) over a period of three financial years beginning in 2002 and ending on 31 December 2004.

B. The European Communities

24. The European Communities notes that the measures in dispute are contained in a series of *Resoluciones Generales* issued by the *Dirección General Impositiva* (the "DGI"). In 1997 the DGI was merged with the *Dirección General de Aduanas* in order to create the *Administración Federal de Ingresos Públicos* (the "AFIP"). The AFIP is an "autarchic entity", which operates autonomously, under the general supervision and control of the Minister of Economy. The Chief of the AFIP is empowered to issue new *Resoluciones Generales* and to amend existing ones.

---

6 Award of the Arbitrator under Article 21.3(c) of the DSU, *Chile - Taxes on Alcoholic Beverages* ("*Chile - Alcoholic Beverages*"), WT/DS87/15, WT/DS110/14, 23 May 2000, DSR 2000:V, 2583, para 45.

25. The European Communities submits that in order to comply with the recommendations and rulings of the DSB, Argentina must take one of the following actions: equalize the rates applied to imports and to internal sales (including the zero rates); and/or provide for the refund to the importers of the additional costs imposed by the higher rates on imports, or establish a similar compensation system. The above actions will require, respectively, amending the existing *Resoluciones Generales* or adopting new ones.

26. The European Communities observes that the adoption or amendment of a *Resolución General* of the AFIP does not have to follow any pre-determined procedural steps, other than the prior consultation (*intervención*) of two administrative units of the AFIP. Nor are they subject to any deadlines, whether mandatory or voluntary. The *Resoluciones Generales* can be enacted or amended within a short time frame and, in practice, are issued very frequently.

27. The latest amendment of *Resolución General* No. 3431/91 is contained in *Resolución General* No. 1021/2001 of 7 June 2001, which lowers the rate of the advance IVA on imports of capital goods to 5 per cent. The reduction of the IVA rate on capital goods was decided for general reasons of economic policy. Nevertheless, according to the European Communities, the ensuing reduction of the advance IVA rate on imports of those products has had the incidental effect of partially removing one of the GATT inconsistent aspects of the measures in dispute. This shows that it is practicable for the AFIP to take the type of measures that would be required for complying with the other DSB's recommendations within an equally short time frame.

28. Article 21.1 of the DSU states the general principle that "prompt compliance with recommendations or rulings of the DSB is essential in order to ensure effective resolution of disputes to the benefit of all Members". This obligation is elaborated in Article 21.3 of the DSU, where it is stipulated that "[i]f it is impracticable to comply immediately with the recommendations and rulings, the Member concerned shall have a reasonable period of time in which to do so". Accordingly, Members should aim to comply "immediately" with the recommendations and rulings of the DSB. Only if it is "impracticable" to do so, is the Member concerned entitled to a "reasonable period of time" for implementation.

29. The European Communities submits that the 15-month period mentioned in Article 21.3(c) of the DSU is a "guideline" for the arbitrator, and not an average, or usual period. As stated in *Australia - Measures Affecting the Importation of Salmon* ("*Australia - Salmon*"), it "does not mean, however, that the Arbitrator is obliged to grant 15 months in all cases."[7] According to the award in *EC Measures Concerning Meat and Meat Products (Hormones)* ("*European Communities - Hormones*"), the "reasonable period of time" should be "the shortest period possible within the legal system of the Member to implement the recommenda-

[7] Award of the Arbitrator under Article 21.3(c) of the DSU, WT/DS18/9, 23 February 1999, DSR 1999:I, 267, para. 30.

tions and rulings of the DSB".[8] Therefore, the "particular circumstances" mentioned in Article 21.3(c) of the DSU are those which can influence what the shortest period possible for implementation may be within the legal system of the implementing Member.

30. Referring to the award in *Canada - Patent Protection of Pharmaceutical Products* ("*Canada - Pharmaceutical Patents*"), the European Communities contends that such "particular circumstances" may include, for example: whether legislative or administrative measures are needed; the complexity of the measures to be adopted; and whether the procedural steps towards implementation, and their respective duration, are mandated by law or are discretionary.[9]

31. The European Communities maintains that the impact of the implementing measures on the domestic industry is not a relevant factor. As noted by the arbitrator in *Indonesia - Certain Measures Affecting the Automobile Industry* ("*Indonesia - Automobile Industry*"), "in virtually every case in which a measure has been found to be inconsistent with a Member's obligations under the GATT 1994 or any other covered agreement, and therefore must be brought into conformity with that agreement, some degree of adjustment by the domestic industry of the Member concerned will be necessary [...] Structural adjustment to the withdrawal or the modification of an inconsistent measure, therefore, is not a 'particular circumstance' that can be taken into account in determining the reasonable period of time under Article 21.3(c)".[10]

32. Similarly, the mere fact that the required implementing measures may be controversial and likely to raise opposition domestically is also not a relevant factor. As the arbitrator in *Canada - Pharmaceutical Patents* noted, there is nothing in Article 21.3(c) to indicate that the supposed domestic contentiousness of a measure taken to comply with a WTO ruling should in any way be a factor to be considered in determining a 'reasonable period of time' for implementation.[11]

33. The European Communities argues that though in accordance with Article 21.2 of the DSU, when assessing the "reasonable period of time" the arbitrator must take into account the "interests" of Argentina as a developing country, this does not mean that the arbitrator must take into account "circumstances" which are "qualitatively different" from those that would be relevant for a developed country. Rather, the arbitrator must apply the same kind of criteria to developing as to developed countries, but bearing in mind the greater difficulties which might be encountered by Argentina as a developing country.

---

[8] Award of the Arbitrator under Article 21.3(c) of the DSU, WT/DS26/15, WT/DS48/13, 29 May 1998, DSR 1998:V, 1833, para. 26.

[9] Award of the Arbitrator under Article 21.3(c) of the DSU, WT/DS114/13, 18 August 2000 .

[10] Award of the Arbitrator under Article 21.3(c) of the DSU, WT/DS54/15, WT/DS55/14, WT/DS59/13, WT/DS64/12, 7 December 1998, DSR 1998:IX, 4029, para. 23.

[11] *Supra*, footnote 9.

34. The European Communities submits that in this case, the implementation of the recommendations and rulings of the DSB does not require any legislative action, but merely administrative measures at the sub-ministerial level, namely the adoption or amendment of *Resoluciones Generales* of the AFIP. Previous practice shows that it is practicable to adopt or amend a *Resolución General* of the AFIP within a matter of months, if not weeks or even days.

35. The European Communities asserts that the "reasonable period of time" proposed in its submission has been generously estimated so as to take into account the "interests" of Argentina as a developing country. Were Argentina a developed country, the "reasonable period of time" would have to be much shorter in the light of the above considerations.

36. The European Communities, therefore, for its part, requests the arbitrator to rule that the reasonable period of time for Argentina to implement the recommendations and rulings of the DSB in this case is eight months from the date of adoption by the DSB of the Panel report.

III. REASONABLE PERIOD OF TIME

37. My task in this arbitration is to determine the "reasonable period of time", as that term is used in Article 21.3 of the DSU, for the implementation of the recommendations and rulings of the DSB in *Argentina - Hides and Leather.*

38. The DSB, as already noted, adopted the Panel's recommendation in *Argentina - Hides and Leather.* That recommendation was that Argentina should bring *Resolución* (ANA) No. 2235/96 and *Resoluciones Generales* (DGI) Nos. 3431/91 and 3543/92 into conformity with Argentina's obligations under Article X:3(a) of the General Agreement on Tariffs and Trade 1994 ("the GATT 1994"), and under Article III:2, first sentence, of the GATT 1994, respectively. At the DSB meeting of 12 March 2001, Argentina informed the DSB that it would require a "reasonable period of time" to implement the recommendations and rulings of the DSB, with respect to *Resoluciones Generales* (DGI) Nos. 3431/91 and 3543/92, and, at the same time, advised that it had already complied with the recommendations and rulings in respect of *Resolución* (ANA) No. 2235/96.[12] The request for arbitration by the European Communities, accordingly, did not include the measures already taken by Argentina to implement its obligations in respect of *Resolución* (ANA) No. 2235/96.[13]

---

[12] Panel Report, para. 12.7.

[13] The European Communities has, however, stated that such exclusion did not mean an admission that the measures already taken by Argentina constituted "adequate implementation" of the DSB recommendations and rulings. The European Communities reserved their right to request recourse to panel proceedings under Article 21.5 of the DSU, should that become necessary. European Communities submission, para. 9.

39. Thus, the present arbitration relates only to the implementation of the DSB recommendations and rulings in respect of *Resoluciones Generales* Nos. 3431/91 and 3543/92.

40. It is useful to go back to basics and perhaps most basic of all considerations is the nature of the act(s) of compliance or implementation that a WTO Member like Argentina, which has engaged in dispute resolution proceedings, is obliged to carry out. Implementation, in essence, consists of bringing the measure held to be inconsistent with the obligations of the WTO Member concerned under particular provisions of a particular covered agreement, into conformity with those same provisions. Article 3.7 of the DSU stresses that "the *first objective* of the dispute settlement mechanism is usually to secure *withdrawal of the WTO-inconsistent measure*". (emphasis added) The DSU goes on to state that compensation may be resorted to only if "the immediate *withdrawal* of the measure is impracticable and then only as "a *temporary* measure *pending the withdrawal of the WTO-inconsistent measure.*" (emphasis added) Suspension of concessions or other obligations under the covered agreements is explicitly designated as a "*last resort*" mode of compliance "subject to authorization by the DSB", but it too remains a "*temporary*" remedy allowed under Article 22.8 of the DSU only until the non-conforming measure is "*removed*" or a "*mutually satisfactory solution*" is achieved. Moreover, and at any rate, Article 22.1 of the DSU cautions that neither compensation nor suspension of concessions or other obligations is to be "preferred to full implementation of a recommendation to bring a measure into conformity with the covered agreements." Clearly, therefore, the non-conforming measure is to be brought into a state of conformity with specified treaty provisions either by *withdrawing* such measure completely, or by *modifying* it by excising or correcting the offending portion of the measure involved. Where the non-conforming measure is a statute, a repealing or amendatory statute is commonly needed. Where the measure involved is an administrative regulation, a new statute may or may not be necessary, but a repealing or amendatory regulation is commonly required.[14]

41. It thus appears that the concept of compliance or implementation prescribed in the DSU is a technical concept with a specific content: the withdrawal or modification of a measure, or part of a measure, the establishment or application of which by a Member of the WTO constituted the violation of a provision of a covered agreement. Compliance within the meaning of the DSU is distinguishable from the removal or modification of the underlying economic or social or other conditions the existence of which might well have caused or contributed to the enactment or application of the WTO-inconsistent governmental measure

[14] The non-conforming measure might also assume other forms: e.g., an executive or administrative practice actually carried out but not specifically mandated or authorized by statute or administrative regulation; or a "quasi-judicial" determination by an administrative body. Since the Argentine measures involved in this arbitration are not of these kinds, it is not necessary to examine the requirements of compliance where those other kinds of measures are concerned.

in the first place. Those economic or other conditions might, in certain situations, survive the removal or modification of the non-conforming measure; nevertheless, the WTO Member concerned will have complied with the DSB recommendations and rulings and with its obligations under the relevant covered agreement. To my mind, it is *inter alia* for the above reason that the need for structural adjustment of the industry or industries in respect of which the WTO-inconsistent measure was promulgated and applied, has generally been regarded, in prior arbitrations under Article 21.3(c) of the DSU, as *not* bearing upon the determination of a "reasonable period of time" for implementation of DSB recommendations and rulings.[15]

42. In the present arbitration, some debate has been generated on the question whether compliance by Argentina with the DSB recommendations and rulings necessitate the enactment of a statute by the federal legislature of Argentina or whether a new *Resolución General* by the AFIP would be sufficient. The European Communities maintains that all that is needed is the adoption of a new *Resolución General* modifying the existing *Resoluciones Generales* (DGI) Nos. 3431/91 and 3543/92 (relating to the advance or withholding payments on IVA and IG on *imports*), or modifying the present *Resoluciones Generales* Nos. 3337/91, 18/97 and 2784/84 (relating to the advance or withholding payments on IVA and IG on *internal sales*). The new *Resolución General* could "equalize" the advance or withholding payment rates with respect to imports and with respect to internal sales, or provide for the refund to importers of the additional costs entailed by the higher rates on imports or for a similar "compensation" scheme. Whether the curative or remedial action adopted provides for "equalization" of rates or for a refund or "compensation" arrangement, the European Communities states that no new Argentine legislation is required.

43. The submissions of Argentina on this point are much more complex. Argentina seems to acknowledge that the *Resoluciones Generales* found to be WTO-inconsistent can be revoked or amended by another *Resolución General* that the AFIP is competent to issue, and that a new legislative enactment by the federal legislature is not, as a matter of public or administrative law, required for that specific purpose. At the oral hearing in this arbitration, Argentina confirmed this. At the same time, however, Argentina underscores its deep concern that so revoking or modifying the *Resoluciones Generales* here involved would set in motion a whole series of financial and fiscal *consequences* which would, in turn, require it to amend its National Budget Law No. 25,401 and its Fiscal Solvency Law, No. 25,152. The inter-relation of these two statutes is such, in the submission of Argentina, that any modification of estimated tax revenues would involve multi-year (at least three years) changes in the specific requirements of both stat-

[15] Award of the Arbitrator under Article 21.3(c) of the DSU, *Indonesia - Automobile Industry*, WT/DS54/15, *supra*, footnote 10 para. 23; and Award of the Arbitrator under Article 21.3(c) of the DSU, *Canada - Pharmaceutical Patents*, *supra*, footnote 9 para. 52.

utes and, as well, changes in the financial ratios and commitments set out in Argentina's present agreements with the IMF.

44. Argentina contends that "equalizing" downwards - that is, lowering the rates of the advance or withholding tax payments on imports to the level of those imposed on internal sales - would result in significant reduction of the IVA and IG tax revenues actually realized. Such decrease in tax revenues would, Argentina maintains, substantially aggravate the current severe liquidity problems of the country. On the other hand, "equalizing" upwards - that is, raising the advances or withholding tax rates imposed on internal sales to the level of those prescribed in respect of imports, would increase the difficulties of controlling the economic recessionary trends the country is presently undergoing. Additionally, it is argued that for Argentina to reimburse importers for the additional costs incurred as a result of the higher advanced or withholding rates on imports would require not only new disbursements from the national treasury and thus affect the estimated level of deficit expenditures, but also the establishment of a complex administrative mechanism to ensure correct and fair reimbursements.

45. Certain considerations need to be brought to mind in respect of the above submissions of Argentina. Firstly, Argentina is not arguing that it needs forty-six months to formulate, draft and put into effect one or more *Resoluciones Generales* to bring its existing WTO-inconsistent *Resoluciones Generales* into conformity with the requirements of Article III(2), first sentence, of the GATT 1994. My understanding is that Argentina, in effect, is contending that it needs forty-six months to control and counter certain economic and financial consequences that it apprehends will follow from putting into legal effect an appropriate amendatory *Resolución General*, to implement the recommendations and rulings of the DSB in this dispute.

46. Secondly, the economic and social consequences of which Argentina is apprehensive, have not been demonstrated to be causally linked to adoption of an appropriate amendatory *Resolución General* in the course of these arbitration proceedings.[16] At least one of the consequences Argentina is anxious about, the decline in revenue collected, is demonstrably *not* linked to an amendatory *Resolución General* that would, for instance, "equalize" downwards the advance or withholding tax rates on imports to the level imposed on internal sales. Since the

[16] The European Communities asserted that the submissions made by Argentina in these arbitration proceedings amount to an effort to re-open issues decided by the Panel in its Report. Argentina at the oral hearing disclaimed any intent to re-open issues decided in the Panel Report. I do not find it necessary to pass upon this particular question. It is clear, on the one hand, that an arbitrator functioning under Article 21.3(c) of the DSU, in principle, lacks jurisdiction to re-open issues decided in a Panel Report which has become final and binding by reason of adoption by the DSB. On the other hand, making factual statements before a panel for the purpose of justifying a measure complained about as WTO-inconsistent need not, in principle, preclude a respondent Member from making the same or similar factual statements before an Article 21.3(c) arbitrator to sustain a claim that particular circumstances exist justifying grant of a certain period as a "reasonable period of time" for implementation purposes.

final or true tax rates remain the same regardless of the level of *advance* or *withholding* rates, any decline in taxes actually collected will be directly attributable to the deficiencies of the revenue collection system in place and to the high levels of tax evasion said to be currently prevailing. Those deficiencies and levels of tax evasion have existed for some years now and certainly long before any amendatory *Resolución General* will have been adopted and put into effect.

47. A third consideration is that there is nothing to prevent Argentina from enacting new legislation or administrative regulations, at the same time that an amendatory *Resolución General* is adopted or soon thereafter, designed, for instance, to strengthen further the existing revenue collection systems and create new incentives for improving voluntary tax compliance among particular sectors of the general community. At the oral hearing in this arbitration, Argentina noted that it already has laws providing for heavy penalties for tax evasion. The kinds of strategies that may be devised for the securing of such objectives are many and varied indeed, and it is the sovereign prerogative of Argentina to determine what strategies are best suited given the actual conditions of the country. It should, however, be borne in mind that the compliance or implementation obligation owed by Argentina by reason of the DSB recommendations and rulings in *Argentina - Hides and Leather*, is not the comprehensive reform of its internal tax system or the elimination or minimization of tax evasion in the general Argentine community. That duty is, as earlier stressed, much more modest and specific in scope: to revoke or modify certain identified *Resoluciones Generales* so as to bring them into conformity with Article III:2, first sentence, of the GATT 1994.

48. A fourth consideration is that while formal adoption of an amendatory *Resolución General* may, as a theoretical matter, require less time than the enactment of a new statute, debate within the Argentine government about the most suitable policies to be embodied in the amendatory *Resolución General* may well involve some additional expenditure of time and administrative resources.

49. A final point that should be made is that to build into the concept of a "reasonable period of time" to comply with DSB recommendations and rulings, time or opportunity to control and manage economic or social conditions which antedate or are contemporaneous with the adoption of the WTO-inconsistent governmental measure, may, in the generality of instances, be to defer to an indefinitely receding future the duty of compliance. The implications for the multilateral trading system as we know it today, of such an interpretation of "reasonable period of time" for compliance are clear and far-reaching and ominous. Such an interpretation would tend to reduce the fundamental duty of "immediate" or "prompt" compliance to a figure of speech.

50. Argentina also emphasizes that it is a developing country for purposes of Article 21.2 of the DSU. In Article 21.2, the DSU, immediately after stressing that "prompt compliance" with the recommendations and rulings of the DSB is essential for the WTO dispute settlement system, provides that

> Particular attention should be paid to matters affecting the interests of developing country Members with respect to measures which have been subject to dispute settlement.

51. Argentina submits that its interests as a developing country Member whose measures have been subjected to dispute settlement proceedings, must be taken into account in determining a "reasonable period of time" for compliance. However, Argentina has not been very specific about how its interests as a developing country Member actually bear upon the duration of the "reasonable period of time" needed to put into legal effect an appropriate amendatory *Resolución General*. Arguably, Argentina is assimilating its "interests" as a developing country Member with the severe economic and financial difficulties it is currently facing. Article 21.2 is cast in exceedingly general terms. Nevertheless, in the arbitral award in *Chile - Alcoholic Beverages,* it is said that "because Article 21.2 is in the DSU, it is not simply to be disregarded." The award goes on to say that "Article 21.2, whatever else it may signify, usefully enjoins, *inter alia*, an arbitrator functioning under Article 21.3(c) to be generally mindful of the great difficulties that a developing country Member may, in a particular case, face as it proceeds to implement the recommendations and rulings of the DSB." In *Indonesia - Automobile Industry*, the arbitrator took into consideration as "very particular circumstances" the status of Indonesia as a developing country and the fact that it was then "currently in a dire economic and financial situation" and its economy "near collapse". The arbitrator then accorded a substantial additional period over and above the "normal" period required for completion of Indonesia's domestic rule-making process. I agree that under Article 21.2 of the DSU in conjunction with Article 21.3(c), account may appropriately be taken of the circumstance that the WTO Member which must comply with the DSB recommendations and rulings is a developing country confronted by severe economic and financial problems. That those problems in the case of Argentina are real is not disputed, although there may be debate as to whether Argentina's economy is "near collapse".

IV. THE AWARD

52. Having regard to the written and oral submissions of the parties, the considerations indicated above and the circumstances constituting this case, my determination is that the reasonable period for Argentina to comply with the recommendations and rulings of the DSB in *Argentina - Hides and Leather* by withdrawing or appropriately amending its *Resoluciones Generales* (DGI) Nos. 3431/91 and 3543/92, or (should Argentina choose to "equalize upwards") its *Resoluciones Generales* Nos. 3337/91, 18/97 and 2784/84, is not more than twelve months and twelve days from 16 February 2001. This period will accordingly expire on 28 February 2002.

UNITED STATES - TRANSITIONAL SAFEGUARD MEASURE ON COMBED COTTON YARN FROM PAKISTAN

Report of the Appellate Body
WT/DS192/AB/R

Adopted by the.Dispute Settlement Body on..5 November 2001

United States, *Appellant*	Present:
Pakistan, *Appellee*	Abi-Saab, Presiding Member
European Communities, *Third Participant*	Ehlermann, Member
India, *Third Participant*	Ganesan, Member

TABLE OF CONTENTS

I. INTRODUCTION

1. The United States appeals from certain issues of law and legal interpretations in the Panel Report, *United States - Transitional Safeguard Measure on Combed Cotton Yarn from Pakistan* (the "Panel Report").[1] The Panel was established on 19 June 2000 to consider a complaint by Pakistan with respect to a transitional safeguard measure imposed by the United States under Article 6.2 of the *Agreement on Textiles and Clothing* (the "*ATC*") on Category 301 imports of combed cotton yarn ("yarn") from Pakistan.

2. On 24 December 1998, the United States filed a request for bilateral consultations with Pakistan, pursuant to Article 6.7 of the *ATC*, on the proposed safeguard measure. The United States attached to this request its Report of Investigation and Statement of Serious Damage or Actual Threat Thereof: Combed Cotton Yarn for Sale: Category 301 (December 1998) (the "Market Statement"), which formed the basis for the proposed safeguard measure. This Market Statement set out the results of the investigation of the conditions prevailing in the United States' market for yarn. It defined the domestic industry to be investigated and concluded that increased imports had caused serious damage, and actual threat thereof, to the domestic industry, and that this damage and threat were attributable to Pakistan.

3. The United States held bilateral consultations with Pakistan in February 1999, which did not result in a mutually agreed solution. Consequently, the United States imposed the transitional safeguard measure at issue in this dispute in the form of a quantitative restriction on Category 301 imports of yarn from Pakistan. The safeguard measure was made effective for one year as of 17 March 1999 and was extended twice, each time for one further year, effective 17 March 2000 and 17 March 2001, respectively.

4. The Textiles Monitoring Body (the "TMB") reviewed the matter, pursuant to Articles 6.10 and 8.10 of the *ATC*, in April and in June 1999. The TMB concluded on both occasions that the United States had not demonstrated successfully that yarn was being imported into its territory in such increased quantities as to cause serious damage, or actual threat thereof, to its domestic industry producing like and/or directly competitive products. Accordingly, the TMB recommended that the safeguard measure introduced by the United States on imports of yarn from Pakistan be rescinded.[2] On 6 August 1999, the United States informed the TMB that it believed its action was justified under the provisions of Article 6 of the *ATC* and that it would maintain the safeguard measure.[3] The United States and Pakistan held a further round of consultations in November 1999 but failed to reach a mutually agreed solution.

---

[1] WT/DS192/R, 31 May 2001.

[2] G/TMB/18, 29 April 1999, para. 32; G/TMB/19, 29 June 1999, para. 36.

[3] G/TMB/R/57, 28 October 1999, para. 5; G/TMB/N/346, 24 September 1999.

5. On 3 April 2000, Pakistan requested the establishment of a panel, pursuant to Article 8.10 of the *ATC*, Article XXIII:2 of the *General Agreement on Tariffs and Trade 1994* (the "GATT 1994") and Article 6 of the *Understanding on Rules and Procedures Governing the Settlement of Disputes* (the "DSU"). The factual aspects of this dispute are set out in greater detail in the Panel Report.[4] The Panel considered Pakistan's claims that, in imposing the transitional safeguard measure, the United States acted inconsistently with Articles 6.2 and 6.4 of the *ATC*. Pakistan also requested that the Panel suggest, in accordance with the second sentence of Article 19.1 of the DSU, that the most appropriate way to implement the Panel's ruling would be to rescind the safeguard measure.[5]

6. In its Report, circulated to Members of the World Trade Organization (the "WTO") on 31 May 2001, the Panel concluded that the transitional safeguard measure imposed by the United States on imports of yarn from Pakistan was inconsistent with the provisions of Article 6 of the *ATC*. Specifically, the Panel found that:

> (a) Inconsistently with its obligations under [Article] 6.2, the United States excluded the production of combed cotton yarn by vertically integrated producers for their own use from the scope of the "domestic industry producing like and/or directly competitive products" with imported combed cotton yarn.
>
> (b) Inconsistently with its obligations under Article 6.4, the United States did not examine the effect of imports from Mexico (and possibly other appropriate Members) individually.
>
> (c) Inconsistently with its obligations under Articles 6.2 and 6.4, the United States did not demonstrate that the subject imports caused an "actual threat" of serious damage to the domestic industry.[6] (footnote omitted)

7. The Panel further concluded that:

> (a) Pakistan did not establish that the US determination of serious damage was not justified based on the data used by the US investigating authority.
>
> (b) Pakistan did not establish that the US determination of serious damage was not justified regarding the evaluation by the US investigating authority of establishments that ceased producing combed cotton yarn.

---

[4] Panel Report, paras. 2.1-2.10.

[5] *Ibid.*, para. 3.1.

[6] Panel Report, para. 8.1.

(c) Pakistan did not establish that the US determinations of serious damage and causation thereof were not justified based upon an inappropriately chosen period of investigation and period of incidence of serious damage and causation thereof.[7]

8. The Panel concluded that the United States' safeguard measure had nullified and impaired the benefits accruing to Pakistan under the *Marrakesh Agreement Establishing the World Trade Organization* (the "*WTO Agreement* "), and in particular, under the *ATC*.[8] Finally, the Panel recommended that the Dispute Settlement Body (the "DSB") request the United States to bring its safeguard measure into conformity with its obligations under the *ATC*, and suggested this could best be achieved by the prompt removal of the safeguard measure.[9]

9. On 9 July 2001, the United States notified the DSB of its intention to appeal certain issues of law covered in the Panel Report and certain legal interpretations developed by the Panel, pursuant to paragraph 4 of Article 16 of the DSU, and filed a Notice of Appeal, pursuant to Rule 20 of the *Working Procedures for Appellate Review* (the "*Working Procedures*"). On 19 July 2001, the United States filed its appellant's submission.[10] On 3 August 2001, Pakistan filed its appellee's submission.[11] On the same day, the European Communities and India each filed a third participant's submission.[12]

10. The oral hearing in the appeal was held on 16 August 2001. The participants and third participants presented oral arguments and responded to questions put to them by the Members of the Division hearing the appeal.

II. ARGUMENTS OF THE PARTICIPANTS AND THIRD PARTICIPANTS

A. *Claims of Error by the United States - Appellant*

1. *Standard of Review*

11. The United States claims that the Panel erred and exceeded the mandate of WTO dispute settlement panels set forth in Article 11 of the DSU by finding that, in assessing the conformity of a transitional safeguard measure with Article 6 of the *ATC*, it could consider evidence that was not in existence at the time of the competent authority's determination.

---

7 *Ibid*., para. 8.2(a), (b) and (c).
8 *Ibid*., para. 8.3.
9 *Ibid*., para. 8.5.
10 Pursuant to Rule 21 of the *Working Procedures*.
11 Pursuant to Rule 22 of the *Working Procedures*.
12 Pursuant to Rule 24 of the *Working Procedures*.

12. In the United States' view, the Panel misinterpreted the standard of review applicable to its assessment of the conformity of the transitional safeguard measure at issue with Article 6 of the *ATC*. In challenges to a transitional safeguard measure, the question before a panel is whether the determination, at the time it was made, was consistent with the requirements of Article 6 of the *ATC*. Such an assessment can be made only on the basis of facts in existence at that time. Examining a Member's determination on the basis of evidence that did not exist at that time would permit panels to strike down the determination of the competent authority for failing to anticipate facts that could emerge in the future. The United States argues that such a review would not be an "objective assessment" of the matter at issue, but would instead constitute a *de novo* review.

13. The United States submits that WTO jurisprudence strongly supports limiting a panel's consideration of evidence to that in existence at the time the competent authority made its determination. For instance, the panel in *United States - Measure Affecting Imports of Woven Wool Shirts and Blouses from India* ("*United States - Shirts and Blouses*"), an *ATC* dispute, found that an objective assessment must be based on facts in existence *at the time of the determination.* [13] The panels that reviewed the consistency of safeguard measures under the *Agreement on Safeguards* in *Korea - Definitive Safeguard Measure on Imports of Certain Dairy Products* ("*Korea - Dairy Safeguard*") and *United States - Definitive Safeguard Measures on Imports of Wheat Gluten from the European Communities* ("*United States - Wheat Gluten Safeguard*") [14] reached a similar conclusion.

14. The United States argues that, contrary to the Panel's reasoning, the finding of the panel in *Argentina - Safeguard Measures on Imports of Footwear* ("*Argentina - Footwear Safeguard*") that a panel may have to consider the raw information from which the data to be scrutinized were compiled, does not support the Panel's conclusion. [15] The Panel sought to distinguish between relying on post-determination evidence to (i) reinvestigate the market situation and (ii) evaluate the "thoroughness and sufficiency" of the "investigation" of the competent authority. Such a distinction might at most, and in limited circumstances, justify consideration of the underlying data used to support a determination. [16]

15. The United States also submits that the Panel implied that "subsequent developments" could be treated differently from post-determination evidence and, unlike post-determination evidence, "subsequent developments" could not

[13] Panel Report, WT/DS33/R, adopted 23 May 1997, as upheld by the Appellate Body Report, WT/DS33/AB/R and Corr.1, DSR 1997:I, 343, para. 7.21.

[14] Panel Report, *Korea - Dairy Safeguard*, WT/DS98/R and Corr.1, adopted 12 January 2000, as modified by the Appellate Body Report, WT/DS98/AB/R, DSR 2000:I, 49, para. 7.30; Panel Report, *United States - Wheat Gluten Safeguard*, WT/DS166/R, adopted 19 January 2001, as modified by the Appellate Body Report, WT/DS166/AB/R, DSR 2001:III, 779, para. 8.6.

[15] Panel Report, WT/DS121/R, adopted 12 January 2000, as modified by the Appellate Body Report, WT/DS121/AB/R, DSR 2000:II, 575, para. 8.126.

[16] United States' appellant's submission, para. 18.

be taken into account by a panel. There is, however, no meaningful distinction between those two categories, as information concerning neither would have been available to the competent authority at the time it made its determination.

16. The United States claims that the Panel further erred in relying on what it perceived to be certain deficiencies in the *ATC*, notably the absence of a right of exporting Members to participate in the national investigation prior to the determination, to justify its consideration of post-determination evidence. Under Article 11 of the DSU, the extent of a panel's review is circumscribed by the text of the agreement it is reviewing. Articles 6.7 and 6.10 of the *ATC* provide exporting Members ample opportunity to contest the fact-finding and determination of the importing Member on a bilateral and multilateral basis.

17. The United States further argues that under the *ATC*, evidence that came into existence after the competent authority's determination may be considered by the TMB pursuant to Article 6.10 of the *ATC*. WTO dispute settlement panels have a more limited mandate than the TMB, as confirmed by the panel in *United States - Shirts and Blouses.* [17]

18. In conclusion, the United States claims that if WTO dispute settlement panels were allowed to review a competent authority's determination on the basis of newly available evidence, competent authorities would be held responsible for facts unknown or unknowable at the time of their determinations. Under such circumstances, the United States submits, it would be impossible for a Member to make a determination that would withstand a panel review and respond in a timely manner to the damaging effects of an import surge, thus seriously impairing the transitional safeguard mechanism guaranteed by Article 6 of the *ATC*.

2. *Definition of the Domestic Industry*

19. The United States claims that the Panel erred in concluding that the United States breached Article 6.2 of the *ATC* by not including in its definition of the domestic industry yarn manufactured and consumed by vertically integrated fabric producers of the United States. According to the United States, the *ATC* permits the importing Member to define the domestic industry as the industry producing a product that was both like *and* directly competitive with the imported product. Vertically integrated fabric producers manufactured yarn that was like, but that was not directly competitive with the imported yarn, because the yarn produced by them was for their own consumption and was not destined "for sale" in the merchant market. Therefore, the United States' identification of the domestic industry, in this case, as the producers of yarn "for sale" in the merchant market, was consistent with the *ATC*.

20. The United States submits that the Panel, in rejecting its domestic industry definition, disregarded the ordinary meaning of the connector "and/or" expressly

[17] Panel Report, *supra*, footnote 13, para. 7.21.

used in Article 6.2 of the *ATC* and, contrary to customary rules of treaty interpretation, reduced the meaning of the term "and" to inutility. The Panel found that the phrase "like and/or directly competitive products" means: (i) every like product; (ii) every directly competitive product; and (iii) any overlap between the two. The Panel interpreted Article 6.2 as if it read "like or directly competitive", completely writing out the word "and" from the Article. The United States contends that the combination of the connectors "and/or" generally means "either together or as an alternative", and allows a range of industry identifications, including the one that it chose in this case.

21. The United States also submits that the Panel ignored customary rules of treaty interpretation by referring first to other WTO agreements rather than to the *ATC* itself in analyzing the context of Article 6.2 of the *ATC*. In accordance with Appellate Body jurisprudence, the Panel should have focused on the particular provision to be interpreted [18] and should have begun its interpretation within the "four corners" of the *ATC*. [19] Specifically, the Panel erroneously relied on jurisprudence pertaining to Article III of the GATT 1994, namely, the panel and Appellate Body reports in *Korea - Taxes on Alcoholic Beverages* ("*Korea - Alcoholic Beverages*"). [20] That dispute involved the interpretation of a different phrase ("directly competitive or substitutable") of a different provision of a different agreement (Article III:2 of the GATT 1994). Therefore, the Panel erred in relying on the Appellate Body statement in *Korea - Alcoholic Beverages* that " 'like products' are, by definition, directly competitive and a subset of 'directly competitive or substitutable products' ". Unlike the present case, *Korea - Alcoholic Beverages* dealt exclusively with products competing in the marketplace, and not with products consumed within a vertically integrated company. When actually in the marketplace, all like products may also be directly competitive. Products consumed captively within vertically integrated companies never reach the marketplace and, therefore, they cannot be regarded as "directly competitive" with like products that are actually in the marketplace.

22. In the United States' view, the Panel failed to properly account for the context provided by Article 6 of the *ATC*. The United States believes that its identification of the domestic industry was consistent with the Preamble and Article 6.1 of the *ATC*. Moreover, the United States does not consider that its definition creates an overly broad authority for an importing Member to take transitional safeguard measures. In this context, the United States points out that the

---

[18] Appellate Body Report, *United States - Import Prohibition of Certain Shrimp and Shrimp Products* ("*United States - Shrimp*"), WT/DS58/AB/R, adopted 6 November 1998, DSR 1998:VII, 2755, para. 114.

[19] Appellate Body Report, *United States - Restrictions on Imports of Cotton and Man-made Fibre Underwear* ("*United States - Underwear*"), WT/DS24/AB/R, adopted 25 February 1997, DSR 1997:I, 11, at 20.

[20] Panel Report, WT/DS75/R, WT/DS84/R, adopted 17 February 1999, as modified by the Appellate Body Report, WT/DS75/AB/R, WT/DS84/AB/R, DSR 1999:I, 44; Appellate Body Report, WT/DS75/AB/R, WT/DS84/AB/R, adopted 17 February 1999, DSR 1999:I, 3.

definition of the domestic industry was only a starting-point and that a WTO Member could take safeguard measures only after fulfilling all the additional conditions set forth in Articles 6.2, 6.3 and 6.4 of the *ATC*.

23. The United States asserts that its identification of the domestic industry is also consistent with the object and purpose of the *ATC*, which carefully balances the interests of exporting and importing Members. In the United States' view, the *ATC* definition of the domestic industry affords Members a certain degree of flexibility to use the transitional safeguard mechanism to address the issue of damaging surges in imports, thereby facilitating any necessary adjustment pending full integration of the textiles and clothing sector into the framework of the GATT 1994.

24. Finally, the United States contends that the Panel's finding that yarn manufactured and consumed by vertically integrated fabric producers is directly competitive with imported yarn, is factually incorrect. The Panel "presumed" that imported yarn was *actually competing* with yarn produced by vertically integrated fabric producers for their internal consumption. However, this is not the case. According to the United States, the consistent *de minimis* nature of yarn purchases and sales of vertically integrated fabric producers over the years is further evidence of the fact that there is no direct competitive relationship between the yarn produced by them and the imported yarn.

3. Attribution of Serious Damage

25. The United States requests that the Appellate Body reverse the Panel's findings concerning the attribution of serious damage under Article 6.4 of the *ATC*. The Panel incorrectly interpreted Article 6.4 to require attribution to *all* Members causing serious damage or actual threat thereof. The Panel, therefore, erred in concluding that the United States' attribution of serious damage and actual threat thereof to Pakistan was inconsistent with Article 6.4 of the *ATC* because it did not examine the effect of imports from Mexico and possibly other Members *individually*. Article 6 does not require identification of, and attribution to, the individual Members from whom imports cause serious damage or actual threat thereof. Causation is determined under Article 6.2 of the *ATC* on the basis of *total* imports and not on the basis of *individual* imports. Article 6.4 does not deal with "causation", but establishes the methodology for determining to which Member(s) to assign the serious damage and actual threat thereof and, in turn, to apply the transitional safeguard measure to such Member(s). The United States claims the Panel misunderstood the two distinct concepts of causation and attribution.

26. The United States points out that the transitional safeguard mechanism envisaged under Article 6 is a *non*-most-favoured-nation safeguard mechanism and that the plain language of Article 6.4 requires the application of a transitional safeguard measure on a Member-by-Member basis. This precludes the requirement that (i) an importing Member attribute serious damage individually to *all* exporting Members that individually cause or contribute to the serious damage,

or (ii) an importing Member attribute serious damage individually to *all* exporting Members that meet the criteria of Article 6.4. The United States adds that the negotiating history indicates that the drafters of the *ATC* rejected such an approach. Article 6.4 of the draft agreement in the *Chairman's Text of the Negotiating Group on Textiles and Clothing*, which had provided that the Member invoking a safeguard measure "shall determine the party or parties contributing to the serious damage ... through a sharp and substantial increase in imports" [21], was not retained.

27. The United States further submits that its interpretation of Article 6.4 is consistent with the context of that provision. For example, Article 6.6 requires the importing Member to account for and provide special treatment to certain Members in applying a transitional safeguard measure. Article 6.1 exhorts importing Members to apply transitional safeguard measures "as sparingly as possible". The United States argues that under the Panel's interpretation, Members would be bound to contravene these requirements by applying the transitional safeguard to *all* those Members meeting the criteria of Article 6.4.

28. According to the United States, the Panel's interpretation of Article 6.4 is inconsistent with the object and purpose of the *ATC*, which is to provide for a safeguard mechanism during the transition period for the integration of the textiles and clothing sector into the GATT 1994. The requirement to attribute serious damage and actual threat thereof to all Members whose imports cause serious damage would increase the burden imposed on importing Members and would undermine the responsiveness and value of the transitional safeguard mechanism. The United States adds that the Panel overlooked how Article 6.4 relates to the carefully negotiated balance of rights and obligations set out in the *ATC*.

29. The United States also argues that the Panel erred in relying primarily on non-transitional WTO agreements in making its findings under Article 6.4 of the *ATC*. Under customary rules of treaty interpretation, the Panel should have first and foremost interpreted the ordinary meaning of the terms of Article 6.4 in the light of their context and the object and purpose of the *ATC*. Appellate Body jurisprudence underscores this requirement [22] as well as the need to remain within the "four corners" of the *ATC*. [23] In contrast, the Panel attempted to impute to the *ATC* words and concepts from the *Agreement on Safeguards* in the guise of "context" and thereby disregarded the unique, *non*-most-favoured-nation transitional safeguard mechanism under Article 6 of the *ATC*. The Panel conducted its analysis as if the textiles and clothing sector was *already* integrated into the GATT 1994 and as if the GATT 1994 rules *already* applied to it. The *ATC* intentionally created a mechanism *different* from Article XIX of the GATT 1994 and the *Agreement on Safeguards* for products not yet integrated into the GATT

[21] MTN.GNG/NG4/W/68, 19 November 1990.

[22] Appellate Body Report, *United States - Shrimp*, *supra*, footnote 18, para. 114.

[23] Appellate Body Report, *United States - Underwear*, *supra*, footnote 19, at 20.

1994. In addition, the *Agreement on Safeguards*, pursuant to its Article 11.1(c), does not apply to transitional safeguard measures taken under Article 6 of the *ATC*.

30. In conclusion, the United States claims that Article 6.4 of the *ATC* requires only a consideration of the factors enumerated therein as it relates to the Member or Members to whom the importing Member attributes serious damage and actual threat thereof. In the present case, the United States attributed serious damage and actual threat thereof to Pakistan based on each of the relevant requirements of Article 6.4. To require more — such as an individual assessment of each exporting Member meeting the criteria of Article 6.4 — would, in the United States' view, impute words and concepts into the *ATC* that are not there.

B. Arguments by Pakistan - Appellee

1. Standard of Review

31. Pakistan submits that the United States' claims and arguments are largely based on a mischaracterization of the Panel's rulings. There is nothing in the Panel's findings to suggest that a panel may conduct a *de novo* review of the determination of the competent authority. On the contrary, the Panel specifically stated that the competent authority's determination under Article 6.2 may *not* be reviewed in the light of subsequent events or developments.

32. According to Pakistan, the Panel ruled that it may, consistently with Article 11 of the DSU, examine evidence not available or submitted to the competent authority at the time of the investigation for the sole purpose of determining whether the substantive conditions for safeguard action were satisfied at that time. Pakistan points out that, in its ruling, the Panel further considered such evidence to be relevant under Article 6 of the *ATC* only if it related to *crucial or decisive facts* that were in existence at the time of the investigation.

33. In Pakistan's view, is not entirely clear whether the United States uses the term "evidence" in a general sense (any fact capable of furnishing a proof) or in a legal sense (statement or document submitted as a means of ascertaining the truth). The United States also does not distinguish clearly between facts that did not exist at the time of the investigation (subsequent developments) and facts that could not be demonstrated at the time of the investigation (for which evidence subsequently emerged). Therefore, when the United States requests the Appellate Body to rule that panels should not consider *evidence that was not in existence at the time of the determination of the competent authority*, one does not know to which category of facts the United States refers. According to Pakistan, the United States' argument implies that a safeguard measure imposed in error need not be brought into conformity with the *ATC*, and may be maintained.

34. Pakistan contends that the United States confuses the question of which evidence a panel must consider pursuant to Article 11 of the DSU with the question of whether the evidence submitted by the complainant supports a finding of inconsistency of a transitional safeguard measure with Article 6 of the *ATC*. The

United States also confuses the question of a panel's *de novo* review of the competent authority's appreciation of the facts with the question of a panel's assessment of whether the facts invoked to justify a safeguard measure ever existed. According to Article 3.2 of the DSU, the dispute settlement system of the WTO "serves to preserve the rights and obligations under the covered agreements". Pakistan, therefore, points out that the ruling the United States is seeking from the Appellate Body would diminish the rights of Members under Article 6 of the *ATC* by curtailing the competence of panels under Article 11 of the DSU.

35. To illustrate its argument, Pakistan submits the following hypothetical example: the United States determined, on the basis of data provided by the American Yarn Spinners Association ("AYSA") (the complainant before the competent authority), that the domestic production of yarn has *declined* by 50 percent. The United States Bureau of Census data, published subsequent to the determination of the competent authority, show that AYSA had provided incorrect data and that the domestic production had in fact *increased* by 50 percent. These newly available data leave no doubt that imports of yarn did not cause serious damage to the domestic yarn industry. Pakistan submits that, according to the contention of the United States, if the United States nevertheless maintains the safeguard measure and Pakistan brings a complaint under the DSU, the panel examining this complaint would be barred from considering the new Census data.

36. In Pakistan's view, the United States' arguments imply that a Member may impose a safeguard measure whenever a competent authority could legitimately conclude, on the basis of the facts before it, that the conditions for taking a safeguard action under Article 6 are met. However, Article 6.2 states that such an action may be taken "when, on the basis of a determination by a Member, *it is demonstrated*" (emphasis added) that increased imports cause serious damage or actual threat thereof. A determination that was based on completely false data does not provide the required demonstration. The role of a panel is not merely to make an objective assessment of the competent authority's investigation. The basic issue is whether the Member invoking Article 6 had the right to take the safeguard action. Therefore, in Pakistan's view, the challenge to an Article 6 safeguard measure does not necessarily call into question the integrity of the original investigation conducted by the competent authority.

37. Finally, Pakistan points out that, in contrast to other WTO agreements providing for safeguards or contingency protection, the *ATC* does not establish any specific requirements for public notice and comment during the investigation. In the case of many safeguard measures under Article 6, there will be evidence that only the exporting Member can furnish (for instance, its own statistics on recent exports) and that is, therefore, not "available" to the competent authority, under the procedures it is permitted to follow under the *ATC*. There will also be evidence that only the exporting Member has an interest in generating (such as precise data on plant closures) and which was, therefore, not "in existence" at the time of the investigation. If the United States' contentions were accepted, such evidence could be submitted, neither before the competent authority, nor before a

panel, even though such evidence may be crucial or decisive in determining the conformity of a safeguard measure with the substantive requirements of Article 6.

2. *Definition of the Domestic Industry*

38. Pakistan submits that the Panel correctly interpreted the phrase "like and/or directly competitive products". According to the ordinary meaning of these words, the domestic industry to be examined includes all domestic manufacturers that produce: (i) a product "like" the imported product; (ii) a product directly competitive with the imported product; or (iii) *both* a product that is "like", *and* a product that is directly competitive, with the imported product. Pakistan contends that with such an interpretation, the term "and" is given meaning and effect and is, contrary to the assertions of the United States, not reduced to inutility.

39. Pakistan also submits that vertically integrated producers manufacturing yarn for internal consumption, rather than for sale on the merchant market, cannot be excluded from the domestic industry. The interpretation of the term "to produce", suggested by the United States, implying that vertically integrated fabric producers are part of the fabric — not yarn — industry, cannot be reconciled with the purpose of Article 6.2 of the *ATC*. An establishment producing yarn for processing into fabric can suffer damage *both* as a result of rising yarn imports *and* as a result of rising fabric imports. Article 6.2 is meant to permit safeguard action in both situations. However, no safeguard measure could be imposed to protect vertically integrated establishments if the yarn they manufacture for internal consumption were not "produced" in the sense of Article 6.2 as contended by the United States. Pakistan adds that the United States' interpretation of the term "producing" would, in effect, as the Panel correctly found, equate "producing" with "selling".[24]

40. In support of its argument that the Panel correctly interpreted Article 6 of the *ATC* in the context of the *WTO Agreement* in its entirety, notably Article III of the GATT 1994, Pakistan submits that the Panel noted the differences in the terms and facts at issue in *Korea - Alcoholic Beverages* and the present case, and based its conclusions only on the common features. The examination of the *ATC*, in the light of other WTO agreements, is called for under customary rules of treaty interpretation and is also required by the terms of the *ATC* itself. In the view of Pakistan, the Panel correctly concluded that captively produced yarn and imported yarn are "directly competitive", even if they are not actually competing with each other for any given sale. In *Korea - Alcoholic Beverages*, the Appellate Body noted that the dictionary meaning of the term "competitive" is "characterised by competition", and concluded therefrom that products are competitive if

[24] Panel Report, footnote 203 to para. 7.40.

they are interchangeable on the market. In examining whether a product is competitive, *both latent and extant demand* must, therefore, be considered.[25]

41. Pakistan further submits that the Panel correctly rejected the contention of the United States that fabric producers which manufacture the yarn they consume are hermetically segregated from the merchant market for yarn. Fabric processed from captively produced yarn is sold on the same market as fabric processed from yarn purchased on the merchant market. A company that owns both a yarn plant and a fabric plant, therefore, cannot ignore the opportunity costs of manufacturing yarn. According to Pakistan, the yarn produced internally and the yarn available on the merchant market are thus, actually, in a competitive relationship.

42. In Pakistan's view, the United States' interpretation of the term "and/or" fails to give meaning and effect to all the terms of the *ATC*. The United States' interpretation would give Members the right to define the domestic industry, *inter alia,* as the producers of "like but not directly competitive products". Pakistan submits that the drafters of the *ATC* would not have provided for such a meaningless alternative under which the requirement of causation could never be met, given the lack of competitive relationship to the surging "like" imports.[26]

43. Pakistan also argues that if Members were permitted to exclude captive yarn producers from the domestic industry within the definition of the domestic industry under Article 6.2 of the *ATC*, the result would be a domestic industry whose size and output would vary according to changes in the ownership and commercial practices of yarn plants. Specifically, the integration of yarn manufacturers, which formerly sold their production on the merchant market, would reduce output of the identified domestic industry and facilitate a finding of serious damage. Pakistan submits that such changes, unrelated to the definition of the domestic industry, should not support a finding of serious damage and permit a Member to impose a transitional safeguard measure on imports.[27]

44. Pakistan argues that the very purpose of the obligation to demonstrate the causation of serious damage to the domestic industry in its entirety is to ensure that the domestic industry is *not* divided into segments supplying different markets. If such segmentation were permitted, Members could focus exclusively on the segment supplying the market in which imports are sold and thereby exclude the producers less exposed to import competition and less likely to suffer serious damage. Pakistan submits that this would create a bias in favour of affirmative determinations of serious damage.

45. Finally, Pakistan points out that vertical integration is one way to adjust to import competition. As the integration of the textiles and clothing sector into the framework of the GATT 1994 proceeds, the discrepancy between the number of producers examined, and the number of producers benefiting from the safeguard

---

25 Appellate Body Report, *supra*, footnote 20, paras. 114-116.

26 Panel Report, para. 7.87.

27 *Ibid.*, para. 7.65.

measure, would increase, in contradiction to the object and purpose of the *ATC*. Pakistan also argues that if the United States were permitted to define the domestic industry as the manufacturers of yarn *for sale*, it would have been required to impose its restraint *only* on imports of yarn *for sale* and not, as it has done, on *all* imports.

3. *Attribution of Serious Damage*

46. Pakistan requests the Appellate Body to uphold the Panel's finding that Article 6.4 of the *ATC* obliges Members to examine the effect of imports from different Members individually. The terms "Member-by-Member" and "attribute" in Article 6.4 do not give the importing Member the right to arbitrarily "pick and choose" the Members included in the attribution analysis. According to its dictionary definition, the term "by" appearing between two nouns indicates a succession of groups, quantities or individuals of the same class, such as in *two-by-two* or *man-by-man*.[28] The requirement that the safeguard "shall be applied on a Member-by-Member basis" means, therefore, that the restrictions shall be imposed on a Member-specific basis. "Member-by-Member" does not mean "any Member", and hence does not suggest that certain exporting Members may be arbitrarily excluded from the attribution of the serious damage. Pakistan adds that the requirement to apply restrictions on a Member-by-Member basis is intended to permit exporting Members to administer the restrictions in accordance with Article 4.2 of the *ATC* and to capture the quota rents. It also permits the importing Member to determine the level of the restrictions individually, in accordance with the criteria set out in the second sentence of Article 6.4.

47. Pakistan points out that "to attribute" means to ascribe an effect to its cause. In the context of Article 6.4, it means to ascribe the effect of the *overall* increase in imports to the imports from particular Members. The attribution thus requires a causation analysis limited to imports from individual Members. The difference in meaning of "cause" and of "attribute" does not, therefore, support the United States' interpretation of Article 6.4 of the *ATC*. This provision requires that the attribution of serious damage to individual Members be made, among other things, on the basis of "the level of imports *compared* with imports from other sources, market share and import and domestic prices". (emphasis added) As the panel in *United States - Underwear* concluded, Article 6.4 requires Members to assess *comparatively* the imports from different sources and their respective effects.[29] In Pakistan's view, the terms "individually" and "compared" found in Article 6.4, leave no doubt that the importing Member must asses all

---

[28] *The New Shorter Oxford English Dictionary*, L. Brown (ed.), (Clarendon Press, 1993), Vol. I, p. 310.

[29] Panel Report, WT/DS24/R, adopted 25 February 1997, as modified by the Appellate Body Report, *supra*, footnote 19, DSR 1997:I, 31, para. 7.49.

potential sources of serious damage and cannot limit its attribution analysis arbitrarily to one Member.

48. Pakistan further argues that Articles 6.1 and 6.6 of the *ATC* do not support the "pick-and-choose" approach advocated by the United States. Article 6.1 exhorts importing Members to apply safeguards as sparingly as possible, not to attribute the damage to as few importing Members as possible. Pakistan stresses that Article 6.6 does not deal with the attribution of damage to Members, but with "the *application* of the transitional safeguard". (emphasis added) It is intended to create benefits for certain Members, not to shift burdens from some Members to others.

49. Pakistan also submits that the Panel correctly analyzed Article 6 of the *ATC* in the context of the entire *WTO Agreement*. Even if one were to regard the GATT 1994 and the *Agreement on Safeguards* as treaties separate from the *ATC*, rather than as elements of a single treaty, they would nevertheless form part of the context of the *ATC* pursuant to Article 31.2(a) of the *Vienna Convention on the Law of Treaties.*[30] In addition, the preamble of the *ATC* specifically states as its purpose the integration of the textiles and clothing sector into the framework of the GATT 1994. Pakistan submits that in the light of this purpose, a panel must consider the basic principles of the GATT 1994, including those reflected in the *Agreement on Safeguards*, when interpreting the terms of the *ATC*.

50. Pakistan further points out that, according to Article 1.6 of the *ATC,* the rights and obligations of Members under the other multilateral trade agreements are not affected "*unless otherwise provided in this Agreement*". (emphasis added) The rules of the GATT 1994 and the *Agreement on Safeguards*, therefore, apply, unless the *ATC* contains a different rule. This does not mean that the *ATC* provisions should be interpreted narrowly as an exception, or that the principles of the GATT 1994 should be imputed to the *ATC*. However, the *ATC* provisions must be understood as temporary departures from the principles of the GATT 1994. If the provisions of the *ATC* are silent on a particular point, the drafters of the *ATC* intended the principles of the GATT 1994 to apply. Given that under the GATT 1994 the most-favoured-nation principle applies, Pakistan asserts that the Panel had to determine to what extent Article 6.4 provides otherwise.

51. In conclusion, Pakistan submits that Article 6.4 of the *ATC* does not allow importing Members to attribute damage to one Member only, because that Member would then suffer a disproportionate share of the effect of the safeguard measure. An appropriate attribution analysis must result in a restraint that is distributed appropriately to all Members whose exports have caused the serious damage. According to Pakistan, the Panel correctly found that an ability to "pick and choose" would be the least consistent with a most-favoured-nation approach

[30] Done at Vienna, 23 May 1969, 1155 U.N.T.S. 331; 8 International Legal Materials 679.

and thus the least conducive to the progressive integration of the textiles and clothing sector into the GATT 1994.

C. *Arguments of the Third Participants*

1. European Communities

52. In its third participant's submission, the European Communities confines itself to the question of permissible evidence and submits that a panel's review concerns the work of the competent authority at the time of its determination.

53. The European Communities argues that panels are not empowered to evaluate the work of the competent authority on the basis of evidence that was *objectively* not available, for example, not in existence, at the time of the determination. This would go beyond the "independent duty of investigation" of the competent authority, which clearly cannot be asked to take into account what is not reasonably available to it while conducting a proper and thorough investigation. However, the European Communities considers that there may be cases where a panel needs to consider evidence that comes into existence after the competent authority's determination, in order to examine the sufficiency and thoroughness of the investigation. As an example, the European Communities refers to a statement from a statistical agency, dated after the investigation, to the effect that it could have produced reliable import statistics if asked, but that it was not.

54. The European Communities emphasizes that, despite the irrelevance of information *objectively not available* at the time of the determination to assess the WTO-consistency of that determination, panels should strictly scrutinize the accuracy of the competent authority's investigation. This scrutiny is all the more necessary for safeguard measures taken under the *ATC*, since that Agreement does not provide for any right to seek removal of a measure that has been adopted without the necessary conditions being fulfilled. In the European Communities' view, this means, for example, that panels should review whether the competent authority seriously tried to verify data which did not come from official sources.

2. *India*

(a) Standard of Review

55. India submits that the Panel correctly concluded that it could "examine any evidence ... for the purpose of evaluating the thoroughness and sufficiency of the ... [determination by the competent] authority." [31] Article 6.2 of the *ATC* states that a safeguard action may be taken "when, on the basis of a determination

[31] Panel Report, para. 7.33.

by a Member, *it is demonstrated* " (emphasis added) that increased imports cause serious damage or actual threat thereof. A determination based on completely incorrect data does not provide this required demonstration. Moreover, under Article 6.3 of the *ATC*, the determination must be based on an examination of changes in specified economic variables. A determination based on an examination in which completely false data on those variables were used, does not meet that requirement. The role of a panel is, therefore, not merely to make an objective assessment of the competent authority's investigation. In India's view, a panel must also assess whether the results of that investigation are capable of demonstrating that the conditions for imposing the safeguard measure were met at the time the determination was made.

56. India submits, therefore, that panels, pursuant to Article 11 of the DSU, may examine evidence not available or submitted to the competent authority at the time of the investigation for the purpose of determining whether the conditions for a safeguard action were satisfied at that time. The Panel further made it clear, in its ruling, that such evidence would be relevant under Article 6 of the *ATC* only if it related to crucial or decisive facts in existence at the time of the investigation. Accordingly, India requests the Appellate Body to find that the Panel's conclusions were consistent with the DSU and the *ATC*.

(b) Definition of the Domestic Industry

57. India requests the Appellate Body to uphold the Panel's finding that the United States' exclusion of captively produced yarn from the definition of the domestic industry is inconsistent with Article 6.2 of the *ATC*. This provision refers to the "domestic industry producing like and/or directly competitive products", not to the domestic industry *selling* those products. In India's view, the *ATC* defines the domestic industry as the *entire* domestic industry producing like and/or directly competitive products.

58. India, therefore, disagrees with the United States' interpretation of the domestic industry definition as allowing a range of different industry definitions. India submits that such flexibility would undermine the objective of the *ATC* of orderly transition and integration of the textiles and clothing sector into the framework of the GATT 1994. India stresses that vertical integration is one form of autonomous industrial adjustment in response to the liberalization of trade in textiles and clothing. The United States' interpretation of Article 6.2 of the *ATC* is prejudicial to meaningful liberalization of trade in textiles and to autonomous industrial adjustment.

(c) Attribution of Serious Damage

59. India also requests the Appellate Body to uphold the Panel's finding that the United States acted inconsistently with Article 6.4 of the *ATC* by not examining the effect of imports from Mexico and other sources, while attributing serious damage of its industry to imports from Pakistan. The Panel correctly pointed out

that the text of Article 6.4 of the *ATC* does not support the United States' interpretation that an importing Member may pick and choose the Member(s) for which it carries out an attribution analysis.

60. India submits that the Panel correctly concluded that the application of safeguards on a "Member-by-Member" basis and the individual attribution of the damage in Article 6.4 of the *ATC* do not enable an importing Member to arbitrarily limit its attribution analysis to the imports of one Member only. India asserts that this Member would then suffer a disproportionate share of the effect of the safeguard measure. That result would also be the least consistent with the most-favoured-nation principle and hinder the progressive integration of the textiles and clothing sector into the framework of the GATT 1994. India submits that the Panel's conclusions are firmly based on the text of Article 6.4, its context and the object and purpose of the *ATC*.

III. ISSUES RAISED IN THIS APPEAL

61. This appeal raises the following issues:

(a) Whether the Panel erred and exceeded the mandate of WTO dispute settlement panels set forth in Article 11 of the DSU by finding that, in examining the conformity of a transitional safeguard measure with Article 6 of the *ATC,* it could consider evidence that was not in existence at the time of the Member's determination;

(b) Whether the Panel erred in finding that the United States acted inconsistently with Article 6.2 of the *ATC* by excluding from the scope of the domestic industry the production of combed cotton yarn by vertically integrated producers for their own internal use; and

(c) Whether the Panel erred in (i) stating that Article 6.4 of the *ATC* requires attribution to all Members whose exports cause serious damage or actual threat thereof, and (ii) finding that the United States acted inconsistently with Article 6.4 by failing to consider the effect of imports from Mexico.

IV. STANDARD OF REVIEW

62. The investigation by the competent authority of the United States leading to the imposition of the transitional safeguard measure on Category 301 imports of combed cotton yarn ("yarn") from Pakistan covered the period from January 1996 until the end of August 1998. The United States relied on data supplied by the American Yarn Spinners Association ("AYSA") and on official data collected by the United States' Bureau of Census for the period up to the end of 1997. For the eight-month period from January to August 1998, the competent authority relied exclusively on AYSA data because official Census data for the calendar

year 1998 ("1998 Census data") were published only in the course of 1999, after the United States had made its determination within the meaning of Article 6.2 of the *ATC*.[32] We note that the participants agree that the date of determination was 24 December 1998, when the United States published its Report of Investigation and Statement of Serious Damage or Actual Threat Thereof: Combed Cotton Yarn for Sale: Category 301 (December 1998) (the "Market Statement") and requested bilateral consultations with Pakistan pursuant to Article 6.7.[33]

63. Pakistan argued before the Panel that the determination made by the United States was based on "unverified, incorrect and incomplete data"[34], and submitted the 1998 Census data in support of its contention. The United States objected to the use of such data by the Panel because that data did not exist when it made its determination. The Panel concluded:

> [W]e shall not examine any evidence for the purpose of reinvestigating the market situation, but we *should examine any evidence, without regard to whether it was available or considered at the time of investigation*, for the purpose of evaluating the thoroughness and sufficiency of the investigation underpinning the decision of the US authority. (footnote omitted, emphasis added)
>
> ...
>
> Accordingly, in our view, the 1998 calendar year US Census data should be examined by the Panel, even though they were not available to the US government at the time of investigation, in order to confirm whether the reliance by the US investigation authority on the AYSA data is justifiable.[35]

64. The Panel, therefore, took into account the 1998 Census data, but concluded that the new data did not vitiate the determination of serious damage by the United States.[36]

65. The United States argues on appeal that the Panel erred and exceeded the mandate of WTO dispute settlement panels set forth in Article 11 of the DSU by finding that, in assessing the conformity of the transitional safeguard measure with Article 6 of the *ATC*, it could examine evidence that was not in existence at the time the United States made its determination of serious damage or threat thereof to the domestic industry.

---

32 Official United States' Census data are published on an annual basis only.

33 Participants' responses to questioning at the oral hearing.

34 Panel Report, para. 7.25.

35 *Ibid.*, paras. 7.33 and 7.94, in relevant part. The Panel made a similar statement at para. 7.35:
> [W]e will examine whether the US fact-finding is justifiable in light of all the facts submitted by the parties, including those which were not considered by, or not available to the US authority at the time of investigation. (footnote omitted)

36 Panel Report, paras. 7.98 and 7.101.

66. The United States' appeal does not concern the question whether a panel may consider *evidence* relating to *facts* that occurred *subsequent* to the determination.[37] Nor does this appeal relate to the question whether a panel may consider *evidence* which existed *before* the date of determination, but which was *not submitted* to the importing Member, or, although *submitted*, was *not considered* by that Member.[38] This appeal also does not concern the question whether the Member, before making its determination, *could have* and *should have taken additional investigative steps* to gather more evidence in order to verify data on all relevant economic variables pertaining to the state of the domestic industry.

67. The issue raised in this appeal is thus limited to whether a panel exceeds its mandate under Article 11 of the DSU by considering, in the context of reviewing a determination under Article 6.2 of the *ATC*, evidence relating to facts which predate the determination, but which was not in existence at the time the determination was made.[39] In other words, the question before us is whether a panel is entitled, in assessing the due diligence of an importing Member in making a determination under Article 6.2 of the *ATC*, to take into account evidence that could not possibly have been examined by that Member when it made that determination.

68. Article 11 of the DSU lays down the standard of review for panels in disputes under the covered agreements[40] in the following terms:

> [A] panel should make an objective assessment of the matter before it, including *an objective assessment of the facts of the case* and the applicability of and conformity with the relevant covered agreements, and make such other findings as will assist the DSB in making the recommendations or in giving the rulings provided for in the covered agreements. ... (emphasis added)

69. We have considered this standard of review on several occasions.[41] In *EC Measures Concerning Meat and Meat Products (Hormones)*, we stated:

---

[37] We note that the participants agree with the Panel that panels cannot consider "developments" subsequent to the determination. (*Ibid.*, footnote 190 to para. 7.33)

[38] The United States stresses that the question "whether a panel may consider evidence that might have been available to the national authority at the time of the determination but was not considered", is not before the Appellate Body. (United States' appellant's submission, para. 9)

[39] In this dispute, we are dealing with evidence in the form of *data* that had not been compiled at the time of the determination and, hence, could not have been known. We do not rule on other kinds of evidence.

[40] Article 1.1, first sentence, of the DSU. For disputes under the *Anti-Dumping Agreement*, Article 17.6 of that Agreement "prevails" over Article 11 of the DSU "[t]o the extent that there is a difference" between these provisions. (Article 1.2, second sentence, of the DSU) *See*, Appellate Body Report, *United States - Anti-Dumping Measures on Certain Hot-Rolled Steel Products from Japan* ("*United States - Hot-Rolled Steel*"), WT/DS184/AB/R, adopted 23 August 2001, paras. 50-62; and, Appellate Body Report, *Thailand - Anti-Dumping Duties on Angles, Shapes and Sections of Iron or Non-Alloy Steel and H-Beams from Poland*, WT/DS122/AB/R, adopted 5 April 2001, paras. 131-138.

[41] Appellate Body Report, *Argentina - Footwear Safeguard*, WT/DS121/AB/R, adopted 12 January 2000, DSR 2000:I, 515, para. 118; Appellate Body Report, *United States - Wheat Gluten Safe-*

> So far as *fact-finding* by panels is concerned, their activities are always constrained by the mandate of Article 11 of the DSU: the applicable standard is *neither de novo review* as such, *nor "total deference"*, but rather the "objective assessment of the facts".[42] (emphasis added)

70. This is the first time we are required to consider a panel's standard of review under Article 11 in a dispute under the *ATC*. We note that the panels in *United States - Underwear* and *United States - Shirts and Blouses* considered this standard of review when examining the consistency of transitional safeguard measures with Article 6 of the *ATC*. The panel in *United States - Underwear* stated:

> [A]n objective assessment would entail an examination of whether the CITA had examined all relevant facts before it ..., whether adequate explanation had been provided of how the facts as a whole supported the determination made, and, consequently, whether the determination made was consistent with the international obligations of the United States.[43]

71. We have, however, examined a panel's standard of review in several cases under the *Agreement on Safeguards*. In *Argentina - Footwear Safeguard*, we reiterated that a panel must not conduct a *de novo* review of the evidence nor *substitute* its analysis and judgment for that of the competent authority.[44] Yet, we emphasized:

> [T]he Panel was obliged, by the very terms of Article 4 [of the *Agreement on Safeguards*], to assess whether the Argentine authorities had examined all the relevant facts and had provided a reasoned explanation of how the facts supported their determination.[45]

72. In *United States - Lamb Safeguard*, we held that, in considering a claim under the *Agreement on Safeguards*, a "panel's objective assessment involves a *formal* aspect and a *substantive* aspect. The formal aspect is whether the com-

---

guard, WT/DS166/AB/R, adopted 19 January 2001, DSR 2001:II, 717, paras. 147-151; Appellate Body Report, *United States - Safeguard Measures on Imports of Fresh, Chilled or Frozen Lamb Meat from New Zealand and Australia* ("*United States - Lamb Safeguard*"), WT/DS177/AB/R, WT/DS178/AB/R, adopted 16 May 2001, paras. 101-116.

42 Appellate Body Report, WT/DS26/AB/R, WT/DS48/AB/R, adopted 13 February 1998, DSR 1998:I, 135, para. 117. We wish to emphasize that, although panels are not entitled to conduct a *de novo* review of the evidence, nor to *substitute* their own conclusions for those of the competent authorities, this does *not* mean that panels must simply *accept* the conclusions of the competent authorities. (Appellate Body Report, *United States - Lamb Safeguard, supra*, footnote 41, para. 106)

43 Panel Report, *supra*, footnote 29, para. 7.13. *See also*, Panel Report, *United States - Shirts and Blouses, supra*, footnote 13, paras. 7.16 and 7.21.

44 Appellate Body Report, *supra*, footnote 41, para. 121.

45 *Ibid.*

petent authorities have evaluated 'all relevant factors'."[46] We stated further that, in reviewing determinations of competent authorities, panels should not simply *accept* the conclusions of that authority:

> Panels must ... review whether the competent authorities' explanation fully addresses the nature, and, especially, the complexities, of the data, and responds to *other plausible interpretations* of that data. A panel must find, in particular, that an *explanation is not reasoned, or is not adequate*, if some *alternative explanation* of the facts is *plausible*, *and if* the competent authorities' explanation does *not seem adequate* in the light of that *alternative* explanation.[47] (emphasis added)

73. In *United States - Wheat Gluten Safeguard*, concerning a claim under the *Agreement on Safeguards*, we considered the duties of competent authorities and stated that an investigation by a competent authority requires a proper degree of activity. Their "duties of investigation and evaluation preclude them from remaining passive in the face of possible short-comings in the evidence submitted".[48] They "must undertake additional investigative steps, when the circumstances so require, in order to fulfil their obligation to evaluate all relevant factors."[49] In describing the duties of competent authorities, we simultaneously define the duties of panels in reviewing the investigations and determinations carried out by competent authorities.

74. Our Reports in these disputes under the *Agreement on Safeguards* spell out key elements of a panel's standard of review under Article 11 of the DSU in assessing whether the competent authorities complied with their obligations in making their determinations. This standard may be summarized as follows: panels must examine whether the competent authority has evaluated all relevant factors; they must assess whether the competent authority has examined all the pertinent facts and assessed whether an adequate explanation has been provided as to how those facts support the determination; and they must also consider whether the competent authority's explanation addresses fully the nature and complexities of the data and responds to other plausible interpretations of the data. However, panels must not conduct a *de novo* review of the evidence nor substitute their judgement for that of the competent authority.

75. Turning to the application of Article 11 of the DSU in the context of the *ATC*, we recall that Article 6.2 of that Agreement provides as follows:

> Safeguard action may be taken under this Article when, *on the basis of a determination by a Member, it is demonstrated* that a particular product is being imported into its territory in such increased

---

46 Appellate Body Report, *supra*, footnote 41, para. 103.

47 *Ibid*., para. 106.

48 Appellate Body Report, *supra*, footnote 41, para. 55.

49 *Ibid*.

quantities as to cause serious damage, or actual threat thereof, to the domestic industry producing like and/or directly competitive products. (footnote omitted, emphasis added)

76. Unlike Article 3 of the *Agreement on Safeguards*, which provides explicitly for an investigation by competent authorities of a Member, Article 6 of the *ATC* does not specify either the organ or the procedure through which a Member makes its "determination". Nevertheless, the above principles concerning the standard of review under Article 11 of the DSU with respect to the *Agreement on Safeguards* apply equally, in our view, to a panel's review of a Member's determination under Article 6 of the *ATC*. We note that Article 6 does not require the participation of all interested parties in the process leading to the determination. We consider, therefore, that the exercise of due diligence by a Member is all the more important in reaching a determination under Article 6 of the *ATC*.

77. The exercise of due diligence by a Member cannot imply, however, the examination of evidence that did not exist and that, therefore, could not possibly have been taken into account when the Member made its determination. The demonstration by a Member that a particular product is being imported into its territory in such increased quantities as to cause serious damage (or actual threat thereof) to the domestic industry can be based only on facts and evidence which existed at the time the determination was made. The urgent nature of such an investigation may not permit the Member to delay its determination in order to take into account evidence that might be available only at a future date. Even a determination on the existence of threat of serious injury must be based on projections extrapolating from *existing* data.[50]

78. In our view, a *panel* reviewing the due diligence exercised by a Member in making its determination under Article 6 of the *ATC* has to put itself in the place of that Member at the time it makes its determination. Consequently, a panel must not consider evidence which did not exist *at that point in time*.[51] A Member cannot, of course, be faulted for not having taken into account what it could not have known when making its determination. If a panel were to examine such evidence, the panel would, in effect, be conducting a *de novo* review and it

[50] See, United States - Lamb Safeguard, where we said as follows:

> *As facts, by their very nature, pertain to the present and the past, the occurrence of future events can never be definitively proven by facts.* There is, therefore, a tension between a future-oriented "threat" analysis, which, ultimately, calls for a degree of "conjecture" about the likelihood of a future event, and the need for a fact-based determination. *Unavoidably, this tension must be resolved through the use of facts from the present and the past to justify the conclusion about the future, namely that serious injury is "clearly imminent".* (emphasis added)
>
> (Appellate Body Report, *supra*, footnote 41, para. 136)

[51] We do not rule upon other forms of evidence, such as an expert opinion submitted to a panel that is based on data which existed when the Member made its determination. (Appellate Body Report, *United States - Lamb Safeguard, supra*, footnote 41, paras. 114-116) *See further, supra*, footnote 39.

would be doing so without having had the benefit of the views of the interested parties. The panel would be assessing the due diligence of a Member in reaching its conclusions and making its projections with the benefit of hindsight and would, in effect, be reinvestigating the market situation and substituting its own judgement for that of the Member. In our view, this would be inconsistent with the standard of a panel's review under Article 11 of the DSU.

79. Moreover, if a Member that has exercised due diligence in complying with its obligations of investigation, evaluation and explanation, were held responsible before a panel for what it *could not have known* at the time it made its determination, this would undermine the right afforded to importing Members under Article 6 to take transitional safeguard action when the determination demonstrates the fulfilment of the specific conditions provided for in this Article.

80. For these reasons, we find that the Panel exceeded its mandate under Article 11 of the DSU by considering United States Census data for the calendar year 1998.

81. There is no need for the purpose of this appeal to express a view on the question whether an importing Member would be under an *obligation*, flowing from the "pervasive" [52] general principle of *good faith* that underlies all treaties [53], to *withdraw* a safeguard measure if post-determination evidence relating to pre-determination facts were to emerge revealing that a determination was based on such a critical factual error that one of the conditions required by Article 6 turns out never to have been met.

V. DEFINITION OF THE DOMESTIC INDUSTRY

82. The United States defined the domestic industry as the producers of yarn who produced it for sale on the merchant market, thereby excluding from the scope of its definition the vertically integrated fabric producers who produce yarn

---

[52] Appellate Body Report, *United States - Tax Treatment for "Foreign Sales Corporations"*, WT/DS108/AB/R, adopted 20 March 2000, DSR 2000:III, 1619, para. 166. *See also*, Appellate Body Report, *United States - Hot-Rolled Steel, supra*, footnote 40, para. 101, where we noted that this principle "informs the provisions of the *Anti-Dumping Agreement*, as well as the other covered agreements."

[53] We recall that in *United States - Shrimp*, we stated:

> This principle, at once a general principle of law and a general principle of international law, controls the exercise of rights by states. One application of this general principle, the application widely known as the doctrine of *abus de droit*, prohibits the abusive exercise of a state's rights and enjoins that whenever the assertion of a right "impinges on the field covered by [a] treaty obligation, it must be exercised bona fide, that is to say, reasonably." An abusive exercise by a Member of its own treaty right thus results in a breach of the treaty rights of the other Members and, as well, a violation of the treaty obligation of the Member so acting. (footnote omitted)
>
> (Appellate Body Report, *supra*, footnote 18, para. 158)

for their own internal use.[54] Pakistan claimed before the Panel that the United States violated Article 6.2 of the *ATC* because it did not investigate the entire domestic industry producing yarn.

83. The Panel found that:

> Inconsistently with its obligations under [Article] 6.2, the United States *excluded* the production of combed cotton yarn by vertically integrated producers *for their own use* from the scope of the "domestic industry producing like and/or directly competitive products" with imported combed cotton yarn.[55] (emphasis added)

84. The United States appeals this finding of the Panel. The United States submits that Article 6.2 permits a definition of the domestic industry on the basis of products that are not only like but also directly competitive with the imported product. According to the United States, yarn sold on the merchant market and yarn produced by vertically integrated fabric producers for their own internal consumption are like, but they are not directly competitive with each other. The United States argues that, by rejecting its definition of the domestic industry, the Panel failed to give full meaning and effect to the term "*and/or*" in Article 6.2 and reduced the word "*and*" to inutility. The United States also argues that the Panel should have interpreted the definition of the domestic industry within the four corners of the *ATC* without having recourse to the wider context of other agreements of the WTO containing a definition of the domestic industry.

85. We begin our analysis of this issue with the definition of the domestic industry as stated in the relevant part of Article 6.2 of the *ATC*, which provides:

> Safeguard action may be taken under this Article when, on the basis of a determination by a Member, it is demonstrated that a particular product is being imported into its territory in such increased quantities as to cause serious damage, or actual threat thereof, to the *domestic industry producing like and/or directly competitive products*. (footnote omitted, emphasis added)

86. A plain reading of the phrase "domestic industry producing like and/or directly competitive products" shows clearly that the terms "like" and "directly competitive" are characteristics attached to the domestic products that are to be compared with the imported product. We are, therefore, of the view that the definition of the *domestic industry* must be product-oriented and not producer-oriented, and that the definition must be based on the products[56] produced by the

---

[54] United States' Market Statement, paras. 1.2-1.3.

[55] Panel Report, para. 8.1(a). *See also*, Panel Report, para. 7.90.

[56] In *United States - Lamb Safeguard,* we also found that the *product* defines the scope of the definition of the domestic industry under the *Agreement on Safeguards*. In that case, the "like" product at issue was lamb *meat*. (Appellate Body Report, *supra,* footnote 41, paras. 84, 86-88 and 95)

domestic industry which are to be compared with the imported product in terms of their being like or directly competitive.[57]

87. We also consider that the term "producing" in Article 6.2 means producing for commercial purposes and that it cannot be interpreted, in itself, to be limited to or qualified as producing for sale on the merchant or any other segment of the market. The definition of the domestic industry, in terms of Article 6.2, is determined by what the industry *produces*, that is, like and/or directly competitive products. In our view, the term "*producing*", in itself, cannot be given a different or a qualified meaning on the basis of what a domestic producer chooses to do with its product.

88. We now turn to the next two components of the definition of the domestic industry under Article 6.2 of the *ATC*, namely, like products and directly competitive products.

89. We note that there is no disagreement between the participants[58] that yarn imported from Pakistan and yarn produced by the producers of the United States, regardless of whether they are vertically integrated fabric producers or independent yarn producers, are like products. The United States has made it clear in its arguments[59] that its exclusion of yarn produced by vertically integrated fabric producers from the definition of the domestic industry was not because they are not producing a like product, but because they are not producing a directly competitive product. It is, therefore, not necessary for us to address the meaning of the term "*like products*" for the purposes of this appeal.

90. Before we examine the term "directly competitive" in the specific context of Article 6.2 and the facts of this particular case, we consider it useful to recall our interpretation of this term on previous occasions.

91. We have interpreted the term "directly competitive " in *Korea - Alcoholic Beverages*[60] and *Japan - Taxes on Alcoholic Beverages.*[61] We are cognizant of the fact that these two reports interpreted this term in the context of the Interpretative Note *Ad* Article III:2 of the GATT 1994. We will refer to this aspect later. The key elements of the interpretation of the term "directly competitive" in our Report in *Korea - Alcoholic Beverages* are:

(a) The word "*competitive*" means "characterised by competition". The context of the competitive relationship is necessarily the marketplace, since that is the forum where consumers choose different products that offer alternative ways of satisfying a particular need

---

57 At this stage, we analyze the terms "like" and "directly competitive" in isolation. For the interpretation of the connectors "and/or" in Article 6.2, *see, infra*, para. 104.

58 Panel Report, para. 7.41.

59 United States' appellant's submission, paras. 33 ff.

60 Appellate Body Report, *supra*, footnote 20, paras. 108-124.

61 Appellate Body Report, WT/DS8/AB/R, WT/DS10/AB/R, WT/DS11/AB/R, adopted 1 November 1996, DSR 1996:I, 97, at 117-118.

or taste. As competition in the marketplace is a dynamic and evolving process, the competitive relationship between products is not to be analyzed exclusively by current consumer preferences[62]; the competitive relationship extends as well to potential competition.[63]

(b) According to the ordinary meaning of the term "directly competitive", products are competitive or substitutable when they are interchangeable or if they offer alternative ways of satisfying a particular need or taste.[64]

(c) In the context of Article III:2, second sentence, the qualifying word "directly" in the *Ad* Article suggests a degree of proximity in the competitive relationship between the domestic and imported products. The word "directly" does not, however, prevent a consideration of both latent and extant demand.[65]

(d) "Like" products are a subset of directly competitive or substitutable products: all like products are, by definition, directly competitive or substitutable products, whereas not all "directly competitive or substitutable" products are "like".[66]

92. The United States argues that the Panel's over-reliance on our Report in *Korea - Alcoholic Beverages* is mistaken for two reasons. First, that dispute involved interpretation of a different phrase ("directly competitive or substitutable"), of a different provision and agreement (Article III:2 of the GATT 1994), and in a different factual setting. In particular, the word "substitutable" is not used in juxtaposition with "directly competitive" in Article 6.2 of the *ATC*. Second, the Appellate Body emphasized, in that case, the importance of the marketplace in judging the competitive relationship between products because that is the forum where consumers choose between different products. According to the United States, a proper reading of the Appellate Body's reasoning reveals that if a domestic product does not enter the marketplace at all, it cannot be regarded as being "directly competitive" with the imported product, even though the two products may admittedly be "like products".

93. We are not persuaded by these arguments of the United States with respect to the relevance and interpretation of our Report in *Korea - Alcoholic Beverages*.

94. With respect to the first argument of the United States, a careful reading of our Report in that case would show that we used the terms "directly competitive" and "directly substitutable" without implying any distinction between them

[62] *Supra*, footnote 20, paras. 114-115.
[63] *Ibid*., paras. 115 and 117.
[64] *Supra*, footnote 20, para. 115.
[65] *Ibid*., para. 116.
[66] *Ibid*., para. 118.

in assessing the competitive relationship between products.[67] We do not consider that the mere absence of the word "substitutable" in Article 6.2 of the *ATC* renders our interpretation of the term "directly competitive" under Article III:2 of the GATT 1994 irrelevant in terms of its contextual significance for the interpretation of that term under Article 6.2 of the *ATC*.

95. We now turn to an examination of the term "directly competitive" in the specific context of Article 6.2 of the *ATC* and the dispute before us. We must bear in mind that Article 6.2 permits a safeguard action to be taken in order to protect a domestic industry from serious damage (or actual threat thereof) caused by a surge in imports, provided the domestic industry is identified as the industry producing "like and/or directly competitive products" in comparison with the imported product. The criteria of "like" and "directly competitive" are characteristics attached to the domestic product in order to ensure that the domestic industry is the appropriate industry in relation to the imported product. The degree of proximity between the imported and domestic products in their competitive relationship is thus critical to underpin the reasonableness of a safeguard action against an imported product.

96. According to the ordinary meaning of the term "competitive", two products are in a competitive relationship if they are commercially interchangeable, or if they offer alternative ways of satisfying the same consumer demand in the marketplace. "Competitive" is a characteristic attached to a product and denotes the *capacity* of a product to compete both in a current or a future situation. The word "competitive" must be distinguished from the words "competing" or "being in actual competition". It has a wider connotation than "actually competing" and includes also the notion of a potential to compete. It is not necessary that two products be competing, or that they be in actual competition with each other, in the marketplace at a given moment in order for those products to be regarded as competitive. Indeed, products which are competitive may not be actually competing with each other in the marketplace at a given moment for a variety of reasons, such as regulatory restrictions or producers' decisions. Thus, a static view is incorrect, for it leads to the same products being regarded as competitive at one moment in time, and not so the next, depending upon whether or not they are in the marketplace.

97. It is significant that the word "competitive" is qualified by the word "directly", which emphasizes the degree of proximity that must obtain in the competitive relationship between the products under comparison. As noted earlier, a safeguard action under the *ATC* is permitted in order to protect the domestic industry against competition from an imported product. To ensure that such protection is reasonable, it is expressly provided that the domestic industry must be producing "like" and/or "directly competitive products". Like products are, nec-

[67] *See*, *ibid*., paras. 114-116.

essarily, in the highest degree of competitive relationship in the marketplace.[68] In permitting a safeguard action, the first consideration is, therefore, whether the domestic industry is producing a like product as compared with the imported product in question. If this is so, there can be no doubt as to the reasonableness of the safeguard action against the imported product.

98. When, however, the product produced by the domestic industry is not a "like product" as compared with the imported product, the question arises how close should be the competitive relationship between the imported product and the "unlike" domestic product. It is common knowledge that unlike or dissimilar products compete or can compete in the marketplace to varying degrees, ranging from direct or close competition to remote or indirect competition. The more unlike or dissimilar two products are, the more remote or indirect their competitive relationship will be in the marketplace. The term "competitive" has, therefore, purposely been qualified and limited by the word "directly" to signify the degree of proximity that must obtain in the competitive relationship when the products in question are unlike. Under this definition of "directly", a safeguard action will not extend to protecting a domestic industry that produces unlike products which have only a remote or tenuous competitive relationship with the imported product.

99. We will now examine whether, in this case, yarn produced by the vertically integrated fabric producers of the United States for their own captive consumption is directly competitive with the imported yarn for the purposes of Article 6.2 of the *ATC*. The United States argues that such yarn is not directly competitive because it is not offered for sale on the market except when the captive production is "out of balance"[69], and even then only in *de minimis* quantities. In addition, vertically integrated fabric producers are not dependent on the merchant market for meeting any of their requirements of yarn except to a *de minimis* extent. In the United States' view, these factors are clearly reflected in the very low and stable rate of yarn sold or purchased by vertically integrated fabric producers to or from the merchant market over the last several years.[70]

100. We are unable to subscribe to this static view which makes the competitive relationship between yarn sold on the merchant market and yarn used for internal consumption by vertically integrated producers dependent on what they choose to do at a particular point in time.

---

[68] Appellate Body Report, *Korea - Alcoholic Beverages, supra,* footnote 20, para. 118; Appellate Body Report, *Canada - Certain Measures Concerning Periodicals*, WT/DS31/AB/R, adopted 30 July 1997, DSR 1997:I, 449, at 473. In these cases, we stated that "like" products are perfectly substitutable and that "directly competitive" products are characterized by a high, but imperfect, degree of substitutability.

[69] United States' response to questioning at the oral hearing.

[70] According to the United States, approximately two percent of captive consumption is purchased from the merchant market and approximately one percent of captive production is sold on the merchant market. (United States' appellant's submission, para. 80)

101. If the competitive relationship between the two products is properly considered, it will be clear that they are "directly competitive" within the meaning of that term in Article 6.2. Our view is illustrated by the following considerations:

(a) The vertically integrated *fabric* producers compete with the independent fabric producers who purchase their requirements of yarn in the merchant market. It is, therefore, unlikely that vertically integrated fabric producers would make their "make-or-buy" decisions with respect to their input of yarn without considering the opportunity cost of doing so.[71] The low and stable rate of their relationship with the merchant market for yarn observed in the past does not imply that the opportunity cost does not enter into their calculations.

(b) Individual vertically integrated fabric producers may enter the merchant market to different degrees for selling their production or buying their requirements of yarn.[72] One may do it for two percent, another for five percent and yet another for 10 or more percent depending on their own individual commercial decisions at a particular point in time. A *force majeure*, or any other serious difficulty, may suddenly compel a vertically integrated fabric producer to rely heavily on the merchant market for its requirement of yarn. Likewise, the competitive conditions in the fabric market may compel a producer to offload a greater part of its yarn production in the merchant market. The low and stable rate of sales and purchases of yarn by vertically integrated fabric producers, observed in the past, is, therefore, not a sufficient reason to conclude that such yarn is not directly competitive with imported yarn sold on the merchant market.

(c) The approach of the United States would lead to constant variations in the size of the domestic industry. In addition to the variations resulting from the *ad-hoc* sale and purchase decisions mentioned above, the size of the domestic industry would depend on ownership or control of yarn plants. The yarn produced by an independent domestic producer would cease to be directly competitive the moment that producer is taken over by a fabric producer, to the extent the latter transforms this yarn into fabric.[73] Likewise, if a vertically integrated fabric producer were to sell its plant producing yarn and that plant were to become an independent producer, the yarn that was previously regarded as non-directly competitive would suddenly become directly competitive.

---

71 Panel Report, para. 7.58.

72 *See also*, *ibid*., para. 7.64(b).

73 *See*, *ibid*., para. 7.64(a).

(d) The approach of the United States would lead to another result which, in our view, cannot be justified. The domestic captive production of yarn by vertically integrated fabric producers would be excluded from the determination of serious damage (or actual threat thereof). However, a safeguard action taken against imported yarn would benefit the vertically integrated fabric producers with respect to the totality of their yarn production, not only with respect to the yarn they sell in the merchant market, but also with respect to yarn they produce for their own consumption.

(e) Finally, the approach of the United States would have major consequences for the justification and scope of the safeguard action. The exclusion of domestic captive production of yarn from the definition of the domestic industry would imply that if a fabric producer imports such yarn from a foreign plant that it owns, such import would also have to be excluded from the calculation of the surge in imports and from the application of the safeguard action. In the case before us, the safeguard action applies to *all* imports. The United States points out that, in this case, this issue does not arise as there are no imports of captively produced yarn from Pakistan; all the imports from Pakistan are destined for the merchant market. This may have been so until now, but the situation may well change in the future. Captively produced imports which had been exempt from the safeguard action could be sold on the merchant market if their prices were lower than those on the merchant market. This would undermine the effectiveness of the safeguard measure.

102. The United States also argues that our ruling in *United States - Hot-Rolled Steel* supports its contention that the captive segment of the market can be separated from the merchant market segment because we observed that captive production was "shielded from direct competition".[74] We did not hold, however, that captive production can be excluded from either the definition of the domestic industry or from the injury analysis. We said that, while an injury analysis can be carried out segment-by-segment before assessing damage to the domestic industry as a whole, an analysis of the captive segment of the market cannot be excluded. Our observation that captive steel production was "shielded from direct competition" did not mean that steel produced in the captive market segment is not directly competitive with imported steel destined for the merchant market. Our ruling in *United States - Hot-Rolled Steel*, therefore, does not support the argument of the United States.

[74] United States' statement at the oral hearing; Appellate Body Report, *supra*, footnote 40, paras. 198 and 207.

103. For all these reasons, we do not accept the contention of the United States that yarn produced by the vertically integrated fabric producers of the United States is not "directly competitive" with yarn imported from Pakistan.

104. We now turn to the interpretation of the connectors "and/or" in Article 6.2, on which the participants disagree.[75] We note that the definition of the domestic industry adopted by the United States in this case would be consistent with Article 6.2 only if we were to find: (i) that captively produced yarn is not directly competitive with imported yarn; and (ii) that the connectors "and/or" in Article 6.2 permit defining the domestic industry on the basis of a product which is not only like but also directly competitive with the imported product. We have reached the conclusion that captively produced yarn *is* directly competitive with imported yarn sold on the merchant market. We, therefore, do not need to address the interpretation of the connectors "and/or" in Article 6.2.

105. For all these reasons, we find that combed cotton yarn produced by vertically integrated fabric producers for their internal consumption is "directly competitive" with combed cotton yarn imported from Pakistan. Accordingly, we uphold the Panel's finding, in paragraph 8.1(a) of its Report, that the United States acted inconsistently with Article 6.2 of the *ATC*, by excluding from the scope of the domestic industry the production of combed cotton yarn by vertically integrated producers for their own internal use.

VI. ATTRIBUTION OF SERIOUS DAMAGE

106. Pakistan claimed before the Panel that the United States acted inconsistently with the requirements of Article 6.4 of the *ATC* because it "attributed serious damage to imports from Pakistan without making a comparative assessment of the imports from Pakistan and Mexico and their respective effects."[76]

107. The Panel stated:

> This does not mean, however, that a Member imposing a safeguard restraint can then pick and choose for which Member(s) it will make an attribution analysis. The attribution cannot be made only to some of the Members causing damage, it must be made to *all* such Members. (emphasis added)
>
> ...
>
> This explicit linking back to the serious damage determination, in our view, requires that *all* the Members causing the serious damage must have it so attributed.[77] (emphasis in the original)

In consequence, the Panel found that:

[75] *See*, *supra*, paras. 19, 20, 38 and 84.
[76] Panel Report, paras. 3.1 and 7.2(a).
[77] Panel Report, paras. 7.126-7.127, in relevant part.

> Inconsistently with its obligations under Article 6.4, the United States did not examine the effect of imports from Mexico (and possibly other appropriate Members) individually.[78] (footnote omitted)

108. On appeal, the United States requests the Appellate Body to reverse (i) the Panel's finding that the United States acted inconsistently with Article 6.4 by failing to consider the effect of imports from Mexico and possibly other Members, and (ii) the Panel's interpretation that Article 6.4 requires attribution to all Members whose exports cause serious damage or actual threat thereof.[79]

109. Before addressing these issues, we have to distinguish three different, but interrelated, elements under Article 6: first, *causation* of serious damage or actual threat thereof by increased imports[80]; second, *attribution* of that serious damage to the Member(s) the imports from whom contributed to that damage; and third, *application* of transitional safeguard measures to such Member(s).[81]

110. We note that the claims made by Pakistan before the Panel[82] related to the question of *attribution* of serious damage or actual threat thereof to the Members the imports from whom contributed to that damage or threat. However, these claims did not relate to the question of *application* of safeguard measures. The Panel did not make a ruling on application *per se,* although, in the course of its reasoning on the question of attribution of serious damage, it interpreted the phrase "shall be applied on a Member-by-Member basis" in the first sentence of Article 6.4[83], an interpretation that has not been appealed. The Panel also found that "Pakistan did not establish that the US determinations of serious damage and causation thereof were not justified based upon an inappropriately chosen period of investigation and period of incidence of serious damage and causation thereof"[84], and this finding has not been appealed either. Hence, the issues raised by the United States in this appeal concern only the *attribution* of serious damage or actual threat thereof to Member(s) imports from whom contributed to that damage.

---

[78] *Ibid.*, para. 8.1(b).

[79] *See*, United States' appellant's submission, paras. 4 and 85, and executive summary, para. 2.

[80] The element of *causation* of serious damage is referred to in para. 2 of Article 6 of the *ATC*. The second sentence of para. 2 provides that serious damage "must demonstrably be caused by such increased quantities in total imports of that product" and not by "*other factors*" such as technological changes or changes in consumer preferences.

[81] The element of *application* of transitional safeguard measures to exporting Member(s) is dealt with in the first and the last sentences of para. 4 of Article 6 of the *ATC*. It is also dealt with in various places in paras. 6 through 16 of that Article. The first sentence of Article 6.4 provides that transitional safeguard measures "shall be applied on a Member-by-Member basis".

[82] In its request for the establishment of a panel, Pakistan claimed, *inter alia*, that the United States failed to comply with Article 6.4 because it attributed the alleged damage, or actual threat thereof, *solely to imports from Pakistan to the exclusion of imports from other sources*, including unrestrained sources. (WT/DS192/1, para. 6, in relevant part)

[83] Panel Report, paras. 7.124, 7.129 and 7.131.

[84] *Ibid.*, para. 8.2(c).

111. The question of attribution is addressed in the following sentence of Article 6.4:

> The Member or Members to whom serious damage, or actual threat thereof, referred to in paragraphs 2 and 3, is attributed, shall be determined on the basis of a sharp and substantial increase in imports, actual or imminent, from such a Member or Members individually, and on the basis of the level of imports as compared with imports from other sources, market share, and import and domestic prices at a comparable stage of commercial transaction; none of these factors, either alone or combined with other factors, can necessarily give decisive guidance. (footnote omitted)

112. Attribution is preceded by three analytical steps which are set forth in Article 6.2: (i) an assessment of whether the domestic industry is suffering serious damage (or actual threat thereof) according to Articles 6.2 and 6.3; (ii) an examination of whether there is a surge in imports as envisaged by Article 6.2; and, (iii) an establishment of a causal link between the surge in imports and the serious damage (or actual threat thereof); according to the last sentence of Article 6.2, "[s]erious damage ... must demonstrably be caused by such increased quantities in *total* imports of that product and not by ... other factors". (emphasis added)

113. Article 6.4 governs the attribution of serious damage to individual Members. This attribution must conform to the two requirements stipulated in Article 6.4, second sentence.

114. The first requirement is that the attribution be confined to only those Members from whom imports have shown a sharp and substantial increase. Such Members will be identified on an individual basis by virtue of the wording in Article 6.4, second sentence, "on the basis of a sharp and substantial increase in imports, actual or imminent, from such a Member or Members individually". (footnote omitted). The Panel interpreted the term "sharp" to refer to the rate of the import increase, and the term "substantial" to the amount of that increase.[85] These interpretations of the Panel have not been appealed and are, therefore, not before us.

115. The second requirement of Article 6.4, second sentence, is a comparative analysis, in the event that there is more than one Member from whom imports have shown a sharp and substantial increase in its imports.[86] The conduct of the

---

[85] Panel Report, para. 7.130.

[86] We note that the panel in *United States - Underwear* stressed that such a comparative analysis of the effects of imports is indispensable in attributing serious damage to a Member. The panel noted that, while there had been a significant increase in imports of underwear from Costa Rica, the position of Costa Rica was not significantly different from that of the other five exporting Members considered in the United States' determination. Nonetheless, the determination failed to undertake a *comparative assessment* of the effects of imports from Costa Rica with those five exporting Members. The panel further reasoned that the United States could not enter into agreements permitting an

comparative analysis is governed by the latter part of the second sentence of Article 6.4, which requires the analysis to address certain specific factors, namely: (i) the level of imports as compared with imports from other sources; (ii) market share; and (iii) import and domestic prices at a comparable stage of commercial transaction. Article 6.4 further specifies that none of these factors, either alone or combined with other factors, can necessarily give decisive guidance.

116. The United States argues that Article 6.4, second sentence, permits a comparative analysis of the effect of imports from a particular Member, without conducting a similar kind of analysis for the other Members from whom imports have also increased sharply and substantially.[87] Pakistan contends that such a comparative analysis requires an assessment of the effect of imports from other such Members taken individually.

117. We note that the wording of Article 6.4, second sentence, does not state expressly how to conduct a comparative analysis of the effects of imports from a particular Member. However, in order to be able to answer this question we have first to address the question *why* a comparative analysis is required.

118. Article 6.4 provides, in relevant part, that "[t]he Member or Members to whom serious damage ... is attributed, shall be *determined on the basis* of a sharp and substantial *increase in imports ... from such a Member or Members*". (emphasis added) The clear inference from this phrase is that the sharp and substantial increase of imports from *such a* Member determines not only the basis, but also the *scope* of attribution of serious damage to that Member.

119. In consequence, where imports from more than one Member contribute to serious damage, it is only that *part* of the total damage which is actually caused by imports from such a Member that can be attributed to that Member under Article 6.4, second sentence. Damage that is actually caused to the domestic industry by imports from one Member cannot, in our view, be attributed to a different Member imports from whom were not the cause of that part of the damage. This would amount to a "mis-attribution" of damage and would be inconsistent with the interpretation in good faith of the terms of Article 6.4.[88] Therefore, the part of the total serious damage attributed to an exporting Member must be proportionate to the damage caused by the imports from that Member. Contrary to the view of the United States, we believe that Article 6.4, second sentence, does not

overall increase of imports of 478 percent over the current import levels from those five Members and, at the same time, claim that an import increase of 22 percent from Costa Rica contributed to serious damage. (Panel Report, *supra*, footnote 29, paras 7.49 and 7.51) The issue of attribution was not appealed in that case.

[87] We note that the United States compared imports from Pakistan only with "total world imports", which included those from Pakistan. *See*, United States' Market Statement, para. 8.9.

[88] *See*, *supra*, footnote 53.

permit the attribution of the totality of serious damage to one Member [89], unless the imports from that Member alone have caused all the serious damage.

120. Our view is supported further by the rules of general international law on state responsibility, which require that countermeasures in response to breaches by states of their international obligations be commensurate with the injury suffered. [90] In the same vein, we note that Article 22.4 of the DSU [91] stipulates that the suspension of concessions shall be equivalent to the level of nullification or impairment. This provision of the DSU has been interpreted consistently as not justifying punitive damages. [92] These two examples illustrate the consequences of breaches by states of their international obligations, whereas a safeguard action is merely a remedy to WTO-consistent "fair trade" activity. [93] It would be absurd if the breach of an international obligation were sanctioned by proportionate countermeasures, while, in the absence of such breach, a WTO Member would be subject to a disproportionate and, hence, "punitive", attribution of serious damage not wholly caused by its exports. In our view, such an exorbitant derogation from the principle of proportionality in respect of the attribution of serious damage could be justified only if the drafters of the *ATC* had expressly provided for it, which is not the case.

121. Finally, and most significantly, if the totality of serious damage could be attributed to only one of those Members the imports from whom have contributed to it, there would be no need to undertake a comparative analysis of the effects of imports from that one Member, once the imports from that Member have been found to have increased sharply and substantially; such an interpretation would reduce a whole segment of Article 6.4 to inutility.

---

[89] This position was clearly stated by the United States in its response to questioning at the oral hearing.

[90] Article 51 of the International Law Commission's draft articles on Responsibility of States reads:

> Proportionality
>
> Countermeasures must be commensurate with the injury suffered, taking into account the gravity of the internationally wrongful act and the rights in question.

(International Law Commission, State Responsibility: Titles and texts of the draft articles on Responsibility of States for internationally wrongful acts adopted by the Drafting Committee on second reading, A/CN.4/L.602/Rev.1, 26 July 2001)

[91] Article 22.4 of the DSU reads:

> The level of the suspension of concessions or other obligations authorized by the DSB shall be equivalent to the level of the nullification or impairment.

[92] The Arbitrators in *European Communities - Regime for the Importation, Sale and Distribution of Bananas - Recourse to Arbitration by the European Communities under Article 22.6 of the DSU* stated that "there is nothing in Article 22.1 of the DSU, let alone in paras. 4 and 7 of Article 22, that could be read as a justification for counter-measures of a *punitive* nature." (Decision by the Arbitrators, WT/DS27/ARB, 9 April 1999, DSR 1999:II, 725, para. 6.3) *See also*, Decision by the Arbitrators, *Brazil - Export Financing Programme for Aircraft - Recourse to Arbitration by Brazil under Article 22.6 of the DSU and Article 4.11 of the SCM Agreement*, WT/DS46/ARB, 20 August 2000, para. 3.55.

[93] Appellate Body Report, *Argentina - Footwear Safeguard*, *supra*, footnote 41, para. 94.

122. We now turn to the question of how to conduct the comparative analysis required by Article 6.4. This analysis is to be seen in the light of the principle of proportionality as the means of determining the scope or assessing the part of the total serious damage that can be attributed to an exporting Member. We recall that Article 6.4 enjoins the importing Member to conduct this comparative analysis on a multi-factor basis including "levels of imports", "market share" and "prices", while specifying that none of these factors alone or in combination with other factors can necessarily give decisive guidance. The comparison is to take place between the effects of imports from the Member in question, on the one hand, and those of imports from other sources, on the other. The comparison must thus be based on a variety of factors, each of which has a different significance and weight, and is to be measured on a different scale.

123. It is of course possible to compare the level of imports of one Member with the level of imports from other sources taken together. Likewise, it is possible to establish the market share of one Member in comparison with all other imports and the output of the domestic industry. However, the full effects of the level of imports from, and the market share of, one Member can only be assessed if this level and this share are compared *individually* with the level of imports from, and the market share of, the other Members from whom imports have also increased sharply and substantially. This conclusion is even more obvious for the comparison of import and domestic prices. The price of imports from one Member can be compared with the average price of imports from other sources and with domestic prices. However, prices of imports from the other Members may vary widely from one another. A fair assessment of the effects of the price of imports from one Member will therefore require a comparison with the price of imports from other Members taken individually. Moreover, these different factors interact in different ways, producing different effects, under different circumstances, not to mention the possible existence of other relevant factors (and their effects) that must be taken into account in the comparison according to the proviso at the end of Article 6.4, second sentence.

124. An assessment of the share of total serious damage, which is proportionate to the damage actually caused by imports from a particular Member, requires, therefore, a comparison according to the factors envisaged in Article 6.4 with all other Members (from whom imports have also increased sharply and substantially) taken individually.

125. In the appeal before us, Pakistan is not the only Member from whom imports have increased sharply and substantially. It is not in dispute that Mexico also falls into this category.[94] We, therefore, consider that the share of the serious damage attributable to imports from Pakistan can be properly assessed only in the light of the effects of the imports from Mexico.

[94] *See*, Panel Report, para. 7.132.

126. Accordingly, albeit for reasons partly different from those given by the Panel, we *uphold* the finding in paragraph 8.1(b) of the Panel Report that the United States acted inconsistently with Article 6.4 by not examining the effect of imports from Mexico (and possibly other appropriate Members) individually when attributing serious damage to Pakistan.

127. We finally turn to the United States' appeal against the Panel's interpretation that Article 6.4 requires attribution to all Members the imports from whom cause serious damage or actual threat thereof. In this respect, we note that the scope of this dispute is defined by Pakistan's claims before the Panel. Pakistan claimed that the United States acted inconsistently with Article 6.4 because it "attributed serious damage to imports from Pakistan without making a comparative assessment of the imports from Pakistan and Mexico and their respective effects".[95] The Panel considered it necessary, in its reasoning, to rule on the broader interpretative question of whether Article 6.4 requires attribution to all Members the imports from whom cause serious damage or actual threat thereof.[96] The United States also appeals the Panel's interpretation on this broader question. However, our findings[97] resolve the dispute as defined by Pakistan's claims before the Panel. We, therefore, do not rule on the issue of whether Article 6.4 requires attribution to all Members the imports from whom cause serious damage or actual threat thereof. In these circumstances, the Panel's interpretation on this question is of no legal effect.

VII. FINDINGS AND CONCLUSIONS

128. For the reasons set out in this Report, the Appellate Body:

(a) concludes that the Panel exceeded its mandate under Article 11 of the DSU by considering United States Census data for the calendar year 1998;

(b) upholds the Panel's finding, in paragraph 8.1(a) of its Report, that the United States acted inconsistently with Article 6.2 of the *ATC*, by excluding from the scope of the domestic industry the production of combed cotton yarn by vertically integrated producers for their own internal use;

(c) upholds the Panel's finding, in paragraph 8.1(b) of its Report, that the United States acted inconsistently with Article 6.4 of the *ATC*, by not examining the effect of imports from Mexico (and possibly other appropriate Members) individually when attributing serious damage to Pakistan; and

---

95 *Ibid.*, paras. 3.1 and 7.2(a).

96 *Ibid.*, paras. 7.126-7.127.

97 *See*, *supra*, paras. 119 and 125-126.

(d) declines to rule on the issue of whether Article 6.4 of the *ATC* requires attribution to all Members the imports from whom cause serious damage or actual threat thereof and concludes that the Panel's interpretation on this issue is of no legal effect.

129. The Appellate Body *recommends* that the DSB request the United States to bring its measure, found in this Report and in the Panel Report as modified by this Report to be inconsistent with the *Agreement on Textiles and Clothing*, into conformity with its obligations under that Agreement.

UNITED STATES - TRANSITIONAL SAFEGUARD MEASURE ON COMBED COTTON YARN FROM PAKISTAN

Report of the Panel
WT/DS192/R

Adopted by the Dispute Settlement Body on 5 November 2001 as modified by the Appellate Body Report

TABLE OF CONTENTS

I. INTRODUCTION

1.1 On 3 April 2000, Pakistan requested the DSB to establish a Panel, pursuant to Article XXIII:2 of GATT 1994, Article 6 of the DSU and Article 8.10 of the ATC[1], to examine a matter involving the application of the transitional safeguard mechanism of the Agreement on Textiles and Clothing by the United States.

1.2 The DSB established a panel at its meeting on 19 June 2000.[2] At that meeting, the parties agreed that the Panel should have standard terms of reference. The terms of reference of the Panel are, therefore, the following:

> "To examine, in the light of the relevant provisions of the covered agreements cited by Pakistan in document WT/DS192/1, the matter referred to the DSB by Pakistan in that document and to make such findings as will assist the DSB in making the recommendations or in giving the rulings provided for in those agreements.".

1.3 On 30 August 2000, the Panel was constituted as follows:

Chairman:	Mr. Wilhelm Meier
Members:	Mr. Carlos Antonio da Rocha Paranhos
	Mr. Virachai Plasai

1.4 The European Communities and India reserved their third-party rights to participate in the Panel proceedings.

1.5 The Panel met with the parties on 16 and 17 November 2000 and with India on 17 November 2000. (The EU did not participate in this meeting, see paragraph 5.1.) The second substantive meeting with the parties was held on 13 December 2000.

II. FACTUAL ASPECTS

2.1 In late 1998, the United States undertook an investigation to determine whether combed cotton yarn for sale, identified as Category 301,[3] was being imported into the territory of the United States in such increased quantities as to cause serious damage or actual threat thereof to the domestic industry producing like and/or directly competitive products.[4]

---

1 Document WT/DS192/1.

2 Document WT/DS192/2.

3 Category 301 refers to the specific U.S. textile category for combed cotton yarn and correlates to partial classifications under the Harmonized Tariff Schedule (HTS) of the United States. Categories serve to identify particular textile and clothing products and represents the basis on which the United States administers its textiles program, including safeguard actions under Article 6 of the ATC. The United States has employed the present category system since 1978.

4 U.S. First Submission Exhibit 3 (Market Statement) para 1.1.

2.2 On 24 December 1998, the United States requested consultations with Pakistan pursuant to Article 6.7 of the Agreement on Textiles and Clothing (ATC) regarding Category 301 imports of combed cotton yarn from Pakistan[5]. The report on this investigation, entitled "Report of Investigation and Statement of Serious Damage or Actual Threat Thereof: Combed Cotton Yarn for Sale: Category 301, December 1998", was presented to Pakistan as the market statement that must be submitted according to Article 6.7 of the ATC in support of the request for consultations on the proposed safeguard action.[6]

2.3 Pursuant to Article 6.7, the United States also communicated this request for consultations, including the relevant factual data, to the Chairman of the Textiles Monitoring Body (TMB).

2.4 Consultations were held between the United States and Pakistan on 10-11 February 1999 which failed to result in a mutual understanding. On 5 March 1999, pursuant to Article 6.10 of the ATC, the United States indicated that it would apply the safeguard, effective 17 March 1999 and notified the TMB of its action.[7]

2.5 The TMB reviewed the matter and heard presentations by the United States and Pakistan on 12-14, 20-22 and 27 April 1999. In its report, the TMB "considered that in view of the serious limitations mentioned above, it was not in a position to assess without doubt whether or not serious damage had been caused to the US' industry producing products like and/or directly competitive with combed cotton yarn by increased imports of combed cotton yarn. Consequently, in the view of the TMB, the United States had not demonstrated successfully that combed cotton yarn was being imported into its territory in such increased quantities as to cause serious damage, or actual threat thereof, to its domestic industry producing like and/or directly competitive products. The TMB, recommended, therefore, that the measure introduced by the United States on imports of combed cotton yarn from Pakistan should be rescinded."[8]

2.6 On 28 May 1999, the TMB received a communication from the United States under Article 8.10 of the ATC informing the TMB that it considered itself unable to conform with this recommendation. At its meeting held on 23-24 June 1999, the TMB examined, in accordance with Article 8:10 of the ATC, the reasons given by the United States for its inability to conform with the rec-

---

5 63 Federal Register 72288 (31 December 1998) (US Exhibit 2).

6 The President of the United States has delegated the authority to implement textile and apparel agreements, including the ATC, to the Inter-agency Committee for the Implementation of Textile Agreements (CITA). For purposes of safeguard actions, the Office of Textiles and Apparel (OTEXA), within the U.S. Department of Commerce, conducts the investigation and produces the statement of serious damage or actual threat of serious damage, and CITA reviews the statements and makes the determination of serious damage or actual threat thereof.

7 Document G/TMB/18, para. 3 and 64 US Federal Register 12290 (12 March 1999) (US Exhibit 4).

8 Document G/TMB/18, para. 32.

ommendation. The TMB concluded that the reasons given in this re-examination did not lead it to change its earlier conclusions and recommendation arrived at during its examination of the measure pursuant to Article 6.10. The TMB recommended, therefore, that the United States reconsider its position and that the measure introduced by the United States on the imports of Category 301 products from Pakistan should be rescinded forthwith.[9]

2.7 On 6 August 1999, the United States informed the TMB that it believed that the US action was justified under the provisions of Article 6 of the ATC and that it would maintain the restraint.[10]

2.8 The United States and Pakistan conducted a further round of consultations on 15-16 November 1999, but no mutual understanding was reached.

2.9 The United States extended the restraint for a further year, effective 17 March 2000, pursuant to Article 6:12 of the ATC.[11]

2.10 Article 8:10 of the ATC provides that if a matter remains unresolved after a further recommendation of the TMB based on that provision, the Members concerned may bring the matter before the Dispute Settlement Body (DSB) and invoke Article XXIII:2 of the General Agreement on Tariffs and Trade 1994 (GATT 1994) and the relevant provisions of the Understanding on Rules and Procedures Governing the Settlement of Disputes (DSU) (see Section I).

III. CLAIMS BY THE PARTIES

Pakistan

3.1 In the light of the facts and arguments put forward, **Pakistan** requests the Panel:

- to find that the United States failed to demonstrate, before taking its safeguard action on combed cotton yarn from Pakistan on 17 March 1999, that imports of combed cotton yarn caused serious damage and actual threat thereof to its domestic industry producing such yarn and that such damage and threat was attributable to Pakistan because the United States
    - did not examine the state of the entire domestic industry producing combed cotton yarn;
    - based its determination on the state of the domestic industry on unverified, incorrect and incomplete data;

9 Document G/TMB/19, para. 36.

10 Document G/TMB/R/57, para. 5 and US communication G/TMB/N/346.

11 65 Federal Register 14544 (17 March 2000) (US Exhibit 6). The restraint was extended for yet a further year as of 17 March 2001 (66 FR 13307, 5 March 2001).

- based its determination on the causal link between imports and serious damage on changes in economic variables during an eight-month period only;
- did not conduct a prospective analysis of the effects of imports to determine whether they were causing a threat of serious damage; and
- attributed serious damage to imports from Pakistan without making a comparative assessment of the imports from Pakistan and Mexico and their respective effects;

- to rule, on the basis of the above findings, that the safeguard action imposed by the United States on combed cotton yarn from Pakistan is inconsistent with the United States' obligations under Article 6 of the ATC;
- to rule further that the United States has nullified or impaired benefits accruing to Pakistan under the ATC since, according to Article 3.8 of the DSU, the infringement of an obligation is considered to constitute a *prima facie* case of nullification or impairment;
- to recommend, in accordance with Article 19.1, first sentence, of the DSU, that the DSB request the United States to bring its safeguard action into conformity with its obligations under the ATC; and
- to suggest, in accordance with Article 19.1, second sentence, of the DSU, that the most appropriate way to implement the Panel's ruling would be to rescind the safeguard action forthwith as has been recommended by the TMB already, in June 1999.

United States

3.2 The **United States** requests the Panel, based on an objective assessment of the facts, to conclude that it acted consistently with the ATC in (i) defining the domestic combed cotton yarn for sale industry, (ii) determining that a sharp and substantial increase in imports of combed cotton yarn caused both serious damage and actual threat of serious damage to the industry, (iii) attributing the serious damage and actual threat of serious damage to the 283.2 per cent surge of low-priced imports of combed cotton yarn from Pakistan, and (iv) relying on the best available and most up-to-date data.

3.3 For these reasons, the United States submits that its transitional safeguard measure applied to imports from Pakistan of combed cotton yarn satisfies U.S. obligations under the ATC. Pakistan's claims to the contrary are without merit and the Panel should reject them.

IV. ARGUMENTS OF THE PARTIES[12]

A. *General Arguments*

Article 6.1 of the ATC: "Members recognize that during the transition period it may be necessary to apply a specific transitional safeguard mechanism (referred to in this Agreement as "transitional safeguard"). The transitional safeguard may be applied by any Member to products covered by the Annex, except those integrated into GATT 1994 under the provisions of Article 2. Members not maintaining restrictions falling under Article 2 shall notify the TMB within 60 days following the date of entry into force of the WTO Agreement, as to whether or not they wish to retain the right to use the provisions of this Article. Members which have not accepted the Protocols extending the MFA since 1986 shall make such notification within 6 months following the entry into force of the WTO Agreement. The transitional safeguard should be applied as sparingly as possible, consistently with the provisions of this Article and the effective implementation of the integration process under this Agreement.".

1. *The Basic Questions Before the Panel*

4.1 **Pakistan** argues that the object of the ATC are the "provisions to be applied by Members during a transition period for the integration of the textiles and clothing sector into the GATT 1994".[13] The basic purpose of these provisions is to ensure that this sector will eventually be integrated.[14] Article 1:5 of the ATC, therefore, calls upon Members to "allow for continuous autonomous industrial adjustment and increased competition in the markets". Raffaelli and Jenkins point out in their book "Drafting History of the Agreement on Textiles and Clothing", that "serious attention needs to be given to this provision, since products representing 49% of total imports in 1990 will be integrated on the last day of the ATC. Autonomous industrial adjustment should be strongly encouraged.".[15]

---

[12] With the agreement of the parties, the Panel decided that the parties to the dispute would provide the Secretariat with a confidential executive summary of the claims and arguments contained in their written submissions, oral presentations and answers to questions, for each substantive meeting of the Panel with the parties. These documents would serve the sole purpose of assisting the Secretariat in drafting a concise arguments section of the Panel report so as to facilitate timely translation and circulation of the Panel report to the Members. They would not serve in any way as a substitute for the written submissions.

[13] Article 1:1 of the ATC.

[14] Preamble to the ATC.

[15] Page 89.

4.2 Pakistan goes on to point out that Article 6 of the ATC provides for a specific transitional safeguard mechanism for products that have not yet been integrated into GATT 1994 and which is to be resorted to "as sparingly as possible" and consistently with the effective implementation of the process of integrating the textiles and clothing sector into GATT 1994. A Member may resort to Article 6 only if it demonstrates that the product subject to the safeguard action is being imported in such increased quantities as to cause serious damage, or actual threat thereof, to the domestic industry producing like and/or directly competitive products, and that such damage or threat is attributable to a sharp and substantial increase in imports from the Member to which the action is applied. According to the jurisprudence of the Appellate Body, all the terms in Article 6 must be given effect and interpreted in the light of the above object and purpose of the ATC.

4.3 Pakistan notes that the United States has applied a safeguard action under Article 6 of the ATC with respect to combed cotton yarn from Pakistan since 17 March 1999. The TMB, which must examine all such actions, noted that the information provided by the United States had "serious limitations". First, the United States failed to provide data on the segment of the domestic industry which was vertically integrated with the fabric industry, which accounted for about one-third of domestic output of combed cotton yarn. Second, the United States provided data on the evolution of the domestic industry for an eight-month period only. And, third, "some aspects concerning the developments in, and the state of its domestic industry remained unclear (such as the evolution of employment, the closure of plants, investment and the restructuring that could have taken place in the domestic cotton yarn industry)".[16]

4.4 Pakistan recalls that the TMB concluded, therefore, that "the United States had not demonstrated successfully that combed cotton yarn was being imported into its territory in such increased quantities as to cause serious damage, or actual threat thereof, to its domestic industry producing like and/or directly competitive products" and recommended that "the measure introduced by the United States on imports of combed cotton yarn from Pakistan should be rescinded".[17] The United States declared itself unable to follow this recommendation and maintained the measure. Pakistan, therefore, exercised its right under Article 8 of the ATC to request the Dispute Settlement Body to establish a panel under the Dispute Settlement Understanding to resolve the matter.

4.5 In the view of the **United States**, this dispute involves an attempt by Pakistan to use the WTO dispute settlement process to force a re-opening of the safeguard investigation conducted by the United States on Category 301 imports of combed cotton yarn from Pakistan. The United States carefully reviewed the information it had collected over a two-year and eight-month period and determined that the domestic industry had experienced a severe downturn, particularly

[16] Document G/TMB/18, para. 3.

[17] Document G/TMB/18, para. 32.

during January-August 1998 when the surge of imports was at its height. That investigation conclusively demonstrated that a surge in Category 301 imports from Pakistan caused serious damage and actual threat of serious damage to the domestic combed cotton yarn for sale industry.[18] During the time of the surge, all relevant indicators of the industry's economic performance deteriorated substantially: production dropped, shipments declined, inventories increased, unfilled orders fell, profitability evaporated, market share contracted, investment stagnated, employment declined, and mills exited the industry. Based on this compelling evidence, the United States acted in full conformity with the ATC and established a transitional safeguard on imports of combed cotton yarn from Pakistan.

4.6 The United States further argues that the situation described above is precisely the kind of situation that the special transitional safeguard of Article 6 of the ATC is designed to cover. In challenging the U.S. action, Pakistan fails to offer legally sufficient evidence and arguments to establish a *prima facie* case that the U.S. transitional safeguard was inconsistent with its obligations under the ATC. Rather, Pakistan would have the Panel believe that its role is to reopen the safeguard investigation, consider new evidence, and even speculate about hypothetical measures not in existence. In the view of the United States, there is no basis in the DSU for Pakistan's request. This would take the Panel well beyond its proper role of considering whether, based on an objective assessment of the facts, the transitional safeguard action on Category 301 imports of combed cotton yarn from Pakistan conforms with Article 6 of the ATC. Pakistan itself concedes that panels are not to engage in *de novo* reviews but rather are to make an objective assessment of the facts surrounding the application of the specific restraint. The Panel in the *United States - Wool Shirts* decision[19] clearly stated that DSU panels do not reinvestigate the market situation or consider developments subsequent to the initial determination but rather limit themselves to the evidence used by the importing Member in making its determination to impose the measure - which in this case is the U.S. Market Statement.

4.7 In response to certain of the above comments of the United States, **Pakistan** claims that it has not asked the Panel to reopen the safeguard investigation but to make an objective assessment of the investigation conducted by the United States. According to Article 11 of the DSU and the jurisprudence of the Appellate Body, the role of the Panel is to examine whether the published report on the investigation contains an adequate, reasoned and reasonable explanation of how the facts in the record support the determinations made.[20] The United States did not object to the application of this standard of review. Pakistan has not asked the

[18] The results of this investigation are set out in *Report of Investigation and Statement of Serious Damage or Actual Threat thereof: Combed Cotton Yarn for Sale: Category 301*, December 1998 ("Market Statement").

[19] Documents WT/DS33/R and WT/DS33/AB/R.

[20] Page 17 of Pakistan's first submission.

Panel to make rulings on "a hypothetical future dispute about measures not even in existence". The legal claims on which Pakistan requests rulings from the Panel relate exclusively to inconsistencies that have already occurred. As the Appellate Body noted, "to provide only a partial resolution of the dispute would be false judicial economy".[21] Pakistan has, therefore, requested the Panel to rule on all inconsistencies that have already occurred.

4.8 The **United States** goes on to state that the single question facing the Panel is whether the transitional safeguard established on Category 301 imports from Pakistan is consistent with the actual terms of Article 6 of the ATC and, based on an objective assessment of the facts before the United States at the time of its investigation, supported by the U.S. analysis. The United States urges the Panel to follow Appellate Body practice and analyze this dispute within the four corners of the ATC. This dispute does not raise any issue that the ATC does not fully answer. Article 6.2 addresses the scope of the domestic industry; Articles 6.2 and 6.3 define the standard for examining whether increased quantities of imports cause serious damage or actual threat of serious damage. Article 6.4 fully addresses attribution, and Articles 6.7 and 6.8 define the requirements and time-period for the information necessary for inclusion in the Market Statement. It would be inappropriate to rely on other agreements whose text, object, and purpose differ fundamentally from the ATC when the ATC itself provides the basis for resolution of these issues. Moreover, the Market Statement reflects the evidence used by the United States in making its determination and, therefore, defines the scope of this Panel's factual review. For that reason, the focus must be on these facts and not on unsupported speculation, misstatements of fact, developments occurring subsequent to the investigation, or facts outside the scope of the U.S. investigation advanced by Pakistan. Further, under Article 11 of the DSU, this Panel is not to engage in a *de novo* review of the market situation or to determine what it would have done with the evidence available to the United States. Rather, Article 11 charges the Panel with reviewing whether the U.S. transitional safeguard measure conforms with Article 6 based on an objective assessment of the matter before it, including the facts of the case and the applicability of and conformity with the relevant provisions of the ATC. When this standard is applied, the United States believes that the Panel will have no choice but to conclude that the U.S. transitional safeguard on imports of combed cotton yarn from Pakistan was appropriate and fully consistent with the ATC.

[21] *Australia - Measures Affecting the Importation of Salmon*, WT/DS18/AB/R, DSR 1998:VIII, 3327, para. 223. The Appellate Body confirmed this jurisprudence in *Canada - Certain Measures Affecting the Automotive Industry*, WT/DS139/AB/R - WT/DS142/AB/R, DSR 2000:VI, 2985, para. 115.

2. *Relevance of Other WTO Jurisprudence*

4.9 The **United States** argues that Pakistan wrongly assumes that Article 6 transitional safeguards must be interpreted using other WTO agreements. The ATC differs significantly from other, non-transitional WTO agreements in terms of its status as a transitional agreement, its purpose of gradually integrating the textiles and clothing sector into GATT 1994, and its language regarding the definition and treatment of "domestic industry". If, for example, there had been no intent to create a difference between the transitional safeguard of the ATC and the Agreement on Safeguards, negotiators would not have included a safeguard provision in the ATC; rather, they would have relied on Article XIX of the GATT and the Agreement on Safeguards. Accordingly, the Panel should look to the text and purpose of the ATC - not other WTO agreements or interpretations of other agreements - to interpret Article 6 for non-integrated textile and clothing products. The United States also refers to Pakistan's view that there is no reason why the issue of market segmentation in the case of a safeguard action under Article 6 of the ATC should be resolved differently than in the cases of safeguard actions under Article XIX of GATT 1994 and countervailing and antidumping measures. It argues that the plain text of Article 6.2 demonstrates Pakistan's error: the ATC differs in key respects from other agreements and the purpose of Article 6 (to provide a transitional safeguard during the integration of the textiles and clothing sector into GATT 1994) differs substantially from the purpose of the non-transitional provisions and agreements. The United States also considers that the object and purpose of the ATC demands an interpretation of Article 6 that will permit Members to utilize the transitional safeguard mechanism to address a damaging surge in imports. The ATC represents a careful balancing of interests between exporting and importing Members to guide the textiles and clothing sector through the delicate ten-year transition from a regime of special quotas to GATT rules. For importing Members, a fundamental aspect of this bargain was the ability to address damaging surges in imports of non-integrated products through a special safeguard provision separate from Article XIX of GATT 1994 and the Safeguards Agreement. Once that transition is over and textiles and clothing products have been integrated into the GATT, the special, transitional safeguard provision will no longer be available, and textile and clothing products will fall under the normal safeguard rules of the GATT and the Safeguards Agreement.

4.10 In respect of the above argument, **Pakistan** explained its position that the interpretations of other WTO agreements may be taken into account in determining the meaning of the terms of the ATC. All the WTO agreements, including the ATC, are integral parts of the WTO Agreement,[22] which was negotiated and con-

[22] See Article II:2 of the WTO Agreement.

cluded as a single undertaking.[23] It is therefore legitimate and common practice for panels to seek guidance for the interpretation of the terms of a WTO agreement from the rulings on similar terms in other WTO agreements. For instance, the recent panel on *Guatemala - Cement* draws on rulings on provisions of the Agreement on Safeguards to substantiate its interpretations of provisions of the Anti-Dumping Agreement. [24] The panel on *Argentina - Footwear Safeguard* referred to the panels on *United States - Underwear* and *United States - Shirts and Blouses* to substantiate its rulings on the issue of standard of review, methods for collecting data and the question of whether all relevant factors affecting the state of the industry must be examined.[25] If the interpretations of the ATC can be invoked to guide the interpretation of other WTO agreements, why should the interpretation of other WTO agreements not guide the interpretation of the ATC?

4.11 The argument of Pakistan is that interpretations of the terms of other agreements are relevant when the specific issue addressed by those terms is similar to the issue addressed by equivalent terms in the ATC. For instance, both the Agreement on Safeguards and the ATC require a demonstration of causality. There is no reason why this issue should be resolved differently in the two agreements merely because they deal with different types of safeguards. Article III of GATT 1994 and Article 6 of the ATC both deal with market access and both use the term "directly competitive" to delineate the range of products to which the provision applies in terms of their relationship in the market. There is no reason why the interpretation of these terms in the ATC should be different from the one adopted under GATT 1994 merely because they deal with different measures curtailing market access. Pakistan, therefore, invites the Panel to seek guidance from other WTO agreements.

B. The Interpretation of Article 6.2 of the ATC

Article 6.2 of the ATC: "Safeguard action may be taken under this Article when, on the basis of a determination by a Member, it is demonstrated that a particular product is being imported into its territory in such increased quantities as to cause serious damage, or actual threat thereof, to the domestic industry producing like and/or directly competitive products. Serious damage or actual threat thereof must demonstrably be caused by such increased quantities in total imports of that product and not by such other factors as technological changes or changes in consumer preference.".* (*Footnote not included.)

[23] See the analysis of the Appellate Body in *Brazil - Measures Affecting Desiccated Coconut*, WT/DS22/AB/R, DSR 1997:I, 167, at pp183-184.

[24] Para. 8.284.

[25] WT/DS/121/R, *supra footnote 15*paras. 8.119 and 8.123.

1. The General Issue

4.12 **Pakistan** states that the core legal issue that gave rise to this complaint is the following: the United States, when evaluating the effect of imports of combed cotton yarn on the state of its domestic industry, did not take into account vertically integrated establishments producing yarn for further processing into fabric (representing about half of the total number of producers of combed cotton yarn and about one-third of total domestic production). The United States does not deny that these establishments produce a product like the combed cotton yarn subject to the safeguard action. It also does not deny that all combed cotton yarn from Pakistan is subject to the restraint, whether sold in the merchant market or shipped to a related fabric producer. However, unsupported by the TMB, the United States argues that these producers were not part of the domestic industry to be examined under Article 6.2 of the ATC because their production did not compete directly with imported yarn in the merchant market for combed cotton yarn.

4.13 Pakistan further argues that the United States fails to explain how its approach could be reconciled with the terms, object and purpose of Article 6.2 of the ATC. This provision defines the domestic industry to be examined as the domestic industry producing products that are like and/or directly competitive with the particular product subject to the safeguard action. Article 6.2, thus, clearly defines the domestic industry in terms of the product it produces, not in terms of the market in which it competes. The terms of Article 6.2 also make clear that the definition of the product subject to the safeguard action controls the definition of the domestic industry. The TMB correctly found (and the United States did not dispute) that, since imported combed cotton yarn sold in the merchant market bore the same physical characteristics as combed cotton yarn produced by vertically integrated plants, the vertically integrated producers were part of the domestic industry producing a product "like" imported combed cotton yarn. Article 6.2, consequently, required the United States to examine the entire domestic industry manufacturing combed cotton yarn and not merely the segment of the industry supplying a particular market.

4.14 The **United States**, however, considers that it acted consistent with the text, object, and purpose of the ATC, in identifying the combed cotton yarn for sale industry as the "domestic industry producing like and/or directly competitive products" and, therefore, excluded vertically integrated producers which manufacture combed cotton yarn for their own consumption in the process of producing a final product (fabric, apparel, or home furnishings). Combed cotton yarn for sale establishments produce combed cotton yarn and sell it in the market. Thus, this yarn competes directly with Category 301 imports. In contrast, vertically integrated producers produce fabric, apparel, or home furnishings and manufacture combed cotton yarn as an input to their production chain. The yarn manufactured by vertically integrated producers is not intended for release onto the market and thus is not "produced" for purposes of the U.S. market and does not compete with Category 301 imports. Hence, combed cotton yarn for sale establishments and vertically integrated producers of fabric and other non-yarn products are not part of the same industry; they "produce" different products. According to Oxford's English Dictionary, "produce" means "bring a thing into existence, bring about, effect or cause an action or result". In other words, the term "produce" turns on the good that the relevant enterprise actually makes, not the input used to make a subsequent product.

2. *Views on the Plain Meaning of Article 6.2*

4.15 **Pakistan** agrees that the ordinary meaning of the term "to produce" is "to bring a thing into existence". Hence, in the view of Pakistan, a plant manufacturing combed cotton yarn brings combed cotton yarn into existence, whether it is owned by a fabric producer or not. There is nothing in the ordinary meaning of the terms of Article 6.2 that would permit the exclusion of an establishment that produces combed cotton yarn solely on the ground that it is owned by a company that also produces fabric. The United States' novel interpretation of the term "to produce" cannot be reconciled with the purpose of Article 6.2. An establishment producing yarn for processing into fabric can suffer damage both as a result of rising yarn imports and as a result of rising fabric imports. Article 6.2 is meant to permit safeguard action in either situation. All WTO agreements providing for safeguard or contingency protection define the domestic industry to be examined in terms of the products it produces. If, as the United States argues, captively consumed production is not "produced", no safeguard measures could be taken to protect a domestic industry that uses a large portion of its production of the domestic like or directly competitive product in the manufacture of downstream articles.

4.16 Pakistan goes on to state that with respect to the United States' argument that, for purposes of an Article 6 analysis, the distinction between the production of an input and that of a final product is critical, the United States provides no evidence demonstrating why the economic viability of a combed cotton yarn plant cannot be determined if a fabric producer owns it. Why should it not be possible to determine the output, inventories and market share of plants producing for a captive market? Most of the establishments that the United States included in its investigation produce not only combed cotton yarn but also other types of yarn. If, in analysing the factors mentioned in Article 6.3, it was possible to segregate combed cotton yarn from other types of yarn, why should it not be possible to segregate combed cotton yarn from fabric? By accepting Article 6.3 as drafted, the United States assumed the obligation to examine the eleven factors mentioned in Article 6.3 in all cases. According to Article XVI:4 of the WTO Agreement, the United States "shall ensure the conformity of its laws, regulations and administrative procedures with its obligations" under Article 6.3. The United States must consequently put its agency conducting the transitional safeguard investigations in a position to examine the eleven factors in all cases.

4.17 In response to Pakistan's assertion that "[t]he terms of Article 6.2 also make clear that the definition of the product subject to the safeguard action controls the definition of the domestic industry." (paragraph 4.13), the **United States** argues that, although the imported product is the starting point for an Article 6 analysis, Article 6.2 identifies the producers of the like and/or directly competitive product as ultimately controlling the scope of the domestic industry. In other words, it is what the domestic industry produces, not what the exporting industry produces, that defines the domestic industry (see paragraphs 4.35 and 4.36).

3. *Identification of the Domestic Industry*

The Views of Pakistan

4.18 **Pakistan** argues that the purpose of the obligation to demonstrate that a rise in imports caused serious damage to the domestic industry in its entirety is to ensure that the importing Member takes into account the state of all producers, including those that are not adversely affected by the rise in imports. The domestic producers that supply a market different from the one supplied by importers may be shielded, temporarily or permanently, from import competition. If there are many such producers, the rise in imports may not cause serious damage to the domestic industry in its entirety and a safeguard action should, therefore, not be taken. If the importing Member could define the "domestic industry" in terms of the market in which it competes rather than the product it produces, it could always exclude the producers less exposed to import competition and, therefore, less likely to suffer serious damage. This would exaggerate the size of imports relative to domestic production and the overall impact of the imports and, therefore, create a bias in favour of affirmative determinations of serious damage. As a result, serious damage determinations would be much more likely, if not almost automatic, and the purpose of the requirement to examine the impact of imports on the entire industry would be completely frustrated.

4.19 Pakistan also considers that the United States' industry definition cannot be reconciled with the object and purpose of the ATC. If Article 6.2 were interpreted to permit Members to divide, for the purposes of their damage investigation, the domestic industry into segments supplying different markets and to base the damage determination exclusively on the segment supplying the market on which imports are sold, the purpose of the ATC could not be achieved. India rightly points out in its oral third-party submission that vertical integration is one way to adjust to import competition. As the integration of the textiles and clothing sector proceeds, more and more fabric producers may, therefore, affiliate with yarn producers. At the end of this process there may only be few independent yarn producers left. In the present case, the United States excluded from examination about half of the producers of combed cotton yarn and about one-third of total domestic production. The proportion of domestic producers and production that it would be able to exclude from the examination under its approach could easily be even more extreme in the future. As a result, the discrepancy between the number of producers examined and the number of producers benefiting from the safeguard action would become greater and greater. This could not be reconciled with the object and purpose of the ATC.

4.20 Recalling its arguments that the terms of Article 6.2 of the ATC make clear that the definition of the product subject to the safeguard action controls the definition of the domestic industry, Pakistan considers that the United States has not offered any arguments that could justify the discrepancy between the definition of the particular product subject to the restraint and the definition of the particular product manufactured by the industry investigated by the United States. Its only reply at the first meeting of the Panel was that there were to its knowledge at present no Pakistani yarn plants that were owned by US fabric producers and that Pakistan was raising a theoretical issue. However, this is not a theoretical issue. As the Appellate Body and numerous panels have recognised, the WTO law governing market access protects competitive opportunities. What is relevant, therefore, is that a fabric producer in the United States is currently not given the opportunity to escape the restraint by purchasing a yarn plant in Pakistan and shipping the yarn directly to its fabric plant in the United States. It is realistic to assume that, if that possibility existed, it would immediately be made use of.

The Views of the United States

4.21 The **United States** considers that its identification of the domestic industry as the combed cotton yarn for sale industry clearly accords with the language of Article 6.2 of the ATC, which requires an analysis of the domestic industry producing like and/or directly competitive products. Combed cotton yarn producers, not vertically integrated establishments, produce a like and directly competitive product to Category 301 imports. The special safeguard provision of Article 6 of the ATC affords importing Members a mechanism to address serious damage and/or actual threat of serious damage to its domestic industry caused by a surge in imports. But, if the products of domestic producers are not directly competitive with imports - such as in the case of yarn manufactured by vertically integrated producers for their own consumption - the need for safeguard action would not arise (see also paragraph 4.51).

4.22 Also in this regard, the United States argues that Pakistan erroneously claims that the United States did not consider the yarn sold by vertically integrated producers on the open market. These amounts are *de minimis*. Nevertheless, the United States considered all yarn sold on the open market - whether it was produced by combed cotton yarn for sale producers or manufactured by vertically integrated producers of another product. With very limited exceptions, vertically integrated producers consume the combed cotton yarn they manufacture in their production of a final product for sale. On rare occasions, vertically integrated producers sell excess production of combed cotton yarn on the open market and also may purchase outside yarn. The United States verified that vertically integrated producers purchase roughly two per cent of their consumption of combed cotton yarn from the market and sell roughly one per cent of their production on the open market. Contrary to Pakistan's assertions, official U.S. Bureau of Census production statistics account for the *de minimis* amount of yarn sold by vertically integrated producers and record all yarn sold into the market - no matter how *de minimis* - as yarn for sale regardless of the identity of the producer.

4.23 The United States also disagrees with the assertion by Pakistan that the failure to account separately for imports of combed cotton yarn purchased by vertically integrated producers, if any, represents a serious flaw in the U.S. analysis. Pakistan provides no factual basis for the contention that vertically integrated producers import combed cotton yarn. However, even if they do, the amount in question would constitute a subset of the already *de minimis* amount of yarn (two per cent) that vertically integrated producers may purchase on the open market (which includes domestic production and imports). Excluding such *de minimis* quantities from the import figures used in the analysis of serious damage would not have affected the results in any statistically significant way.

4.24 In response to the specific comments in paragraph 4.20, the United States pointed out that, to their knowledge, no U.S. fabric plant wishing to purchase a yarn plant in Pakistan would be unable to do so because of the transitional safeguard. When the U.S. conducted its investigation, no such firms existed. To the United States' knowledge, none exist today. Moreover, the mere existence of a transitional safeguard would not prevent a business from purchasing a yarn plant in Pakistan or shipping yarn from that plant to the United States. In the current year, Pakistan is able to ship 5,578,425 kilograms of combed cotton yarn to the United States, a figure which increases six per cent each year of the restraint.

4.25 In sum, the U.S. approach to the identification of the domestic industry is fully consistent with the ATC. Pakistan's belief that Article 6 requires the United States to include vertically integrated producers of fabric, apparel, or home furnishings within the scope of the "domestic industry producing like and/or directly competitive products" amounts to suggesting that Article 6 requires a Member to incorporate separate industries and include products that do not compete with imports. Neither the text nor the purpose of the ATC support Pakistan's claim and the Panel should reject it accordingly.

The Role of Vertically Integrated Fabric Producers

4.26 In relation to the U.S. argument that Article 6 of the ATC does not permit the division of the industry into segments supplying different markets, **Pakistan** claims that this is based on the incorrect assumption that imported yarn and domestic yarn produced by vertically integrated mills for further processing are not competing with one another. According to the United States' own admission, integrated fabric producers do buy combed cotton yarn on the merchant market. Combed cotton yarn offered on the merchant market is, therefore, in fact competing with the yarn produced by the fabric manufacturers themselves. The integrated fabric producers might be buying less than 5 per cent of their needs, but there is, nevertheless, a market for imported combed cotton yarn in which integrated fabric producers participate as buyers of yarn. The United States argues that it could ignore this market because the transactions on it were *de minimis.* However, the small quantity of yarn bought by integrated producers reflects the particular conditions prevailing in this market. If the United States had not imposed the safeguard, these conditions would have changed and no doubt more yarn would have been bought by integrated producers. The United States confuses the issue by claiming that the captive yarn production is not normally destined for the merchant market and, therefore, not competing with imports. Yarn produced for internal use competes with imported yarn even if it is never offered on the merchant market.

4.27 Regarding the above comments, the **United States** responds that Pakistan has attempted to suggest that situation, by introducing hypothetical situations where combed cotton yarn manufactured by vertically integrated fabric producers might theoretically compete with imports of combed cotton yarn. Pakistan has provided no evidentiary support for this speculation; the U.S. investigation did not reveal any such circumstances. Moreover, Pakistan's claim that vertically integrated fabric producers would completely restructure simply to take advantage of low cost imports is based on an overly simplistic view of the initial business decision that led these establishments to produce fabric and fabric products within a vertically integrated structure. Likewise, Pakistan seems to confuse "directly competitive" with "indirectly competitive" in asserting that the transitional safeguard actually benefits vertically integrated fabric producers. *De minimis* purchases and sales of combed cotton yarn by vertically integrated fabric producers are not, as Pakistan suggests, evidence of actual or potential competition. In rare circumstances where yarn production does not match fabric production needs, vertically integrated fabric producers purchase roughly two per cent of combed cotton yarn from the merchant market and sell roughly one per cent. This fact does not mean that the other 99 per cent - which never enters the market - is directly competitive with Category 301 imports.

4.28 The United States refers to Pakistan's claims (paragraph 4.26) that the highly exceptional release onto the market of combed cotton yarn by vertically integrated fabric producers - in those rare instances when they spin too much yarn for their fabric production - means that all combed cotton yarn spun by such producers are directly competitive. This flawed argument has no basis in fact. At the time of the Market Statement, vertically integrated fabric producers were not in the business of spinning yarn for sale for the market, and consumers in the market (such as weavers) did not rely on captive combed cotton yarn as an alternative source of supply. Based on the facts, there was no reason to expect that vertically integrated fabric producers would change their established business practices and production methods and begin to produce substantial quantities of combed cotton yarn for sale in the market. The remote and hypothetical possibility that they would is not enough to convert goods, which are in fact not directly competitive, into those that are.

Could Imports of Combed Cotton Yarn Damage Vertically Integrated Producers

4.29 In this regard, the Panel invited the views of the parties as to whether imports of combed cotton yarn could cause "damage" to producers of that product for their own use. In the view of **Pakistan**, the producers of yarn "for own use" go on to produce fabric from their yarn. These fabric producers compete in the fabric market with the fabric from the "for sale yarn". If, as claimed by the United States, imported yarn causes the price of "for sale yarn" to come down, the fabric made from "for sale yarn" will become cheaper and will begin to damage the profitability of the competing fabric made out of "own use yarn". Thus, by the United States own argument, low priced imports of combed yarn will damage the fabric industry using "own yarn". Similarly, if through transitional safeguard measures or any other measure, imports of yarn can be checked, it will, according to the United States' own argumentation, help raise the price of domestic "for sale yarn". This, in turn, will raise the cost of production of fabric produced from "for sale yarn", which will benefit the competing fabric producers using "for own use" yarn.

4.30 On this question, the **United States** argues that the effect of either increased combed cotton yarn imports or the subject transitional safeguard on vertically integrated producers of fabric, apparel, or home furnishings may be, at best, indirect given that they do not normally enter the marketplace for yarn, either as a buyer or seller. Of course, it is possible that an import surge from Pakistan or a safeguard taken to address this surge could eventually have an indirect effect on vertically integrated producers of fabric just as it could have indirect effects on other industries and businesses in the United States. However, the effects, if any, might differ based on the markets, production methods, capital equipment, and other business considerations involved. Pakistan's view that vertically integrated facilities would completely restructure simply to take advantage of low cost imports is based on an overly simplistic view of the initial business decision that led these establishments to vertically integrate. An establishment that is structured to make its production of fabric independent of the "for sale" market achieves advantages other than merely being in a position to produce low-cost yarn. Vertical integration as to yarn allows fabric producers to control the quality, type, delivery, and supply of the yarn that serves as an input to their fabric in ways that would not be available if the fabric producers were dependent on external supplies. Vertical integration can lead to predictability and efficiencies that, from a business perspective, justify continued vertical integration even if yarn is being sold at very low prices in the market.

Other Aspects of This Discussion

4.31 Continuing the discussion of the definition of the domestic industry, **Pakistan** notes that the issue of industry segmentation by markets has been examined in another recent dispute brought before the DSB. The United States, in a complaint against anti-dumping measures on high fructose corn syrup by Mexico, has vigorously (and successfully) challenged the decision of the Mexican authorities to divide the sugar industry into segments supplying different markets and to base the injury determination on the segment supplying the same market as imports. The position the United States took in that case, as an exporter, is inconsistent with the one it adopts in the present case as an importer.

4.32 In response to a further question by the Panel, the **United States** explained that it does not consider the "domestic industry as a whole" provision of the Antidumping Agreement to be generically broader or narrower than the "domestic industry" provision contained in the ATC. The two provisions are different, both textually and in the context and purpose of the agreements that they serve. The ATC provides no definition for domestic industry, but rather refers to "the domestic industry producing like and/or directly competitive products." The Antidumping Agreement devotes an entire Article to the definition of "domestic industry," reflecting precise concepts agreed in the negotiations. The ATC and the Antidumping Agreement also used different concepts to identify the products produced by the "domestic industry." For the Antidumping Agreement, the products are "like products;" for the ATC, the products are "like and/or competitive products." It is noteworthy that the ATC draws from the phrase "like and/or directly competitive products" in the MFA rather than from terms used in the Antidumping Agreement.

4.33 Also in response to the question from the Panel, **Pakistan** notes that the United States has not contested its claim (and the finding of the TMB) that the term "domestic industry" refers to the entire industry. The United States has consistently claimed that it has investigated the entire industry producing combed cotton yarn for sale. According to Article 4.1(i) of the Anti-Dumping Agreement, the term "domestic industry" shall be interpreted as referring to "the domestic producers as a whole of the like products or to those of them whose collective output of the products constitutes a major proportion of the total domestic production of those products, except that ... when producers are related to the exporters or importers or are themselves importers of the allegedly dumped product, the term "domestic industry" may be interpreted as referring to the rest of the producers ...". By contrast, Article 6.2 of the ATC does not qualify the scope of the domestic industry in terms of a proportion of domestic production. The industry definition for safeguard action under the ATC is, therefore, broader than the industry definition applicable in the case of anti-dumping measures.

4. *The Interpretation of the Term "like and/or directly competitive products"*

(a) Approaches to Identification of the Industry in Terms of "like and/or directly competitive products"

The United States' Position

4.34 The **United States** considers that the ATC requires a focus on the domestic industry "producing like and/or directly competitive products". Read alone, this language would allow a Member to identify an industry producing a product that is: (1) like and directly competitive; (2) like but not directly competitive; or (3) unlike but directly competitive. Accordingly, the U.S. identification of the domestic industry as the combed cotton yarn for sale industry is permissible. Combed cotton yarn for sale is "like and directly competitive" with Category 301 imports from Pakistan.

4.35 In a question to the United States, the Panel sought greater detail on the argument in the above paragraph. In response, the United States explained that the plain language of Article 6.2 of the ATC permits a Member to identify the "domestic industry producing like and/or directly competitive products" as the industry producing like products, the industry producing like and directly competitive products, or the industry producing directly competitive products that are not like. This interpretation does not enable a Member to pick and choose which domestic industry it wants to consider in any manner that is not contemplated by the Agreement itself. Nor does it create an open-ended approach to the identification of the domestic industry. The ATC has set the scope of what can be considered the domestic industry as the domestic industry producing like and/or directly competitive products. The U.S. approach in this case merely accords with that scope by focusing on the domestic industry producing the like and directly competitive product, i.e., the combed cotton yarn for sale industry.

4.36 The United States goes on to explain that it took this approach because it reflected the realities of this particular market and because the United States would otherwise have been unable to consider all the factors set forth in Article 6.3 of the ATC. Nothing about the context or the object and purpose of the ATC would disallow a focus on the industry producing like and directly competitive products. The ATC incorporated this phrase from the MFA and did not draw from other agreements which had defined domestic industry in another manner. In addition, giving the phrase the full range of its ordinary meaning is consistent with the purpose of Article 6 which is to provide assurance that a safeguard mechanism would be available during the transitional period. To disregard the ordinary meaning of that phrase and limit the availability to physically like products would amount to rewriting the carefully negotiated bargain struck in the ATC.

4.37 The United States further sets out its position on the definition of the domestic industry for purposes of the transitional safeguard mechanism, stating that it is the domestic industry producing like and/or directly competitive products which is not an interpretation of the ATC, but are the actual words the Agreement uses. No matter which dictionary is used, this phrase expressly authorizes an importing Member to focus on the domestic industry producing one of three products: (1) like and directly competitive products, (2) like (but not directly competitive) products; and (3) directly competitive (but not like) products. This phrase does not address "directly competitive or substitutable" products; this phrase does not address "indirectly competitive" products; this phrase does not address "hypothetically competitive" products; and this phrase does not address "subsets" of products. On the facts of this case, the United States focuses its identification of the domestic industry on one of the three options in Article 6.2, namely, products which are like and directly competitive with imports. The only domestic mills producing combed cotton yarn like and directly competitive with Category 301 imports are combed cotton yarn for sale establishments. Vertically integrated fabric producers - upon which Pakistan's entire argument turns - spin combed cotton yarn for their internal consumption, not for sale on the market.

The Position of Pakistan

4.38 **Pakistan** sets out its views as follows: the product to which the United States' transitional safeguard applies is combed cotton yarn. According to Article 6.2, the United States, therefore, had to examine its domestic industry producing a product like combed cotton yarn and/or a product directly competitive with combed cotton yarn. The United States confirmed that there are no material differences in the technical specifications of the yarn produced domestically for sale, for internal use and the yarn imported from Pakistan or Mexico. All domestic combed cotton yarn, whether produced for sale or internal use is, thus, identical to the yarn subject to the restraint. Being identical to imported yarn, all domestic yarn is, thus, indisputably both "like" and "directly competitive". The obvious conclusion is, therefore, that the United States had to examine the state of all mills manufacturing combed cotton yarn, including those manufacturing yarn for further processing into fabric. Instead of accepting this obvious fact, the United States presents to this Panel the argument that captively consumed production is not production within the meaning of Article 6 because a vertically integrated industry does not "produce" the captively manufactured inputs but only the downstream articles that it puts on the market. This is a position that cannot be reconciled with the ordinary meaning of the word "producing". The plain fact is that a yarn mill does not stop producing yarn merely because it is bought by a fabric producer. Accepting the United States' interpretation of the term "producing" would have the curious consequence that a Member's right to take safeguard action would depend on the degree of vertical integration of its industry (see also paragraphs 4.18-4.20).

4.39 Pakistan rejects the United States' claim that a domestic product that is physically identical to an imported product and, therefore, capable of satisfying the same need or taste is nevertheless not "directly competitive" with the imported product if it was produced by an vertically integrated establishment for captive consumption. In the view of Pakistan, this is plainly wrong. In the text of Article 6.2 of the ATC, the term "directly competitive" is used to describe the characteristics of a product, not the characteristics of the industry manufacturing it. The plain fact is that the characteristics of the product produced by a combed cotton yarn plant do not vary with the ownership of the plant. The United States claims that the captive yarn production is not normally destined for the merchant market and, therefore, not competing with imports. However, according to the United States' own admission, integrated fabric producers do buy combed cotton yarn on the merchant market. It is an undeniable fact that integrated fabric producers compete with non-integrated fabric producers and must, therefore, constantly compare the cost of producing yarn with the cost of purchasing yarn. Yarn produced for internal use, therefore, competes with imported yarn even if it is never offered on the merchant market. There is, thus, both latent and extant competition between captively produced yarn and yarn offered on the merchant market. Moreover, the United States' definition of cotton yarn "for own use" comprises yarn destined for consumption by legally separate but affiliated companies. Goods are normally exchanged between legally separate companies at market prices.

4.40 Pakistan also refers to an assumption of the U.S. which is that the particular product to which the United States is applying the restraint is combed cotton yarn for sale. In this regard, the United States acknowledges that, according to Article 6.2, the definition of the product subject to the safeguard action controls the definition of the domestic industry (paragraph 4.17). Therefore, even if the United States were permitted to define the domestic industry as the manufacturers of combed cotton yarn for sale, it could have imposed its restraint only on combed cotton yarn for sale. Conversely, having decided to restrict all imports of combed cotton yarn, whether for sale or not, the United States was obliged to examine the domestic industry producing combed cotton yarn, whether for sale or not. The United States does not dispute that the restraint applies to all imports of combed cotton yarn, whether destined for sale in the merchant market or for consumption by a related fabric producer (see also paragraph 4.23).

4.41 Pakistan sums up its arguments on this point saying that the United States has not examined the entire domestic combed cotton yarn industry as required by Article 6.2 of the ATC but only the producers of combed cotton yarn that are members of the AYSA. The industry definition adopted by the United States therefore corresponds to the membership of the lobbying organisation that has asked for the restraint and provided the data for the crucial January-August 1998 period. There is, of course, a gap between the combed cotton yarn producers that must be investigated in accordance with Article 6.2 and the combed cotton yarn producers that are members of the AYSA. To bridge this gap, the United States is now asking the Panel to interpret the term "domestic industry producing like and directly competitive products" to mean "domestic industry producing a like product that actually competes with the imported products". Even if this interpretation was consistent with basic principles of treaty interpretation endorsed by the Appellate Body, the United States' industry definition would be inconsistent with Article 6.2 because internally produced yarn and the yarn offered on the merchant market do compete with one another because they are alternative sources of supply satisfying the same needs of integrated fabric producers. Even if the laws of the market did not apply to the United States' integrated fabric producers, the United States' industry definition would be inconsistent with Article 6.2 because it does not correspond to the definition of the products subject to the restraint.

4.42 In relation to the above comments, the **United States** reiterates its arguments that the plain meaning of "like and/or directly competitive" makes it clear that competition is relevant and is an appropriate factor to consider. The language of Article 6.2 - informed by the market-based factors that Members must consider under Article 6.3 - supports this reading and underscores the importance of competition in the marketplace to the identification of the domestic industry. To disregard the ordinary meaning of "like and/or directly competitive" and limit the availability of an Article 6 safeguard to physically "like" products would amount to rewriting the ATC.

(b) Views on the Term "like but not directly competitive products"

4.43 **Pakistan** notes that the United States does not deny that combed cotton yarn imported from Pakistan is "like" the combed cotton yarn produced by the vertically integrated mills it excluded from its damage investigation. The central argument of the United States is that the term "and/or" in Article 6.2 gives it the option to define the domestic industry as the industry producing a product that is "like and competitive". The combed cotton yarn produced by the vertically integrated mills was "like" Pakistani yarn but not "directly competitive" with it because it was not competing with Pakistani yarn on the merchant market. In the view of Pakistan, the United States' argument rests on incorrect assumptions.

4.44 Pakistan continues this discussion, stating that one of the assumptions underlying the United States argument is that an individual product can be described as "like but not directly competitive". This assumption is logically incorrect. In the Appellate Body Report on *Korea - Alcoholic Beverages* (paragraph 118), the Appellate Body confirmed an earlier ruling according to which: "like" products are a subset of directly competitive or substitutable products: all like products are, by definition, directly competitive or substitutable products, whereas not all "directly competitive or substitutable" products are "like". This has important implications for the interpretation of the term "the domestic industry producing like and/or directly competitive products" in Article 6.2 of the ATC. The fact that directly competitive products are a subset of like products means that it is not logically possible to define products as "like but not directly competitive" because, being alike, they are necessarily also directly competitive. To claim that there is yarn that is like but not directly competitive is equivalent to claiming that there is an animal that is an eagle but not a bird.

4.45 On this aspect, the **United States** observes that the Appellate Body made its findings, not on the phrase "directly competitive products," as Pakistan asserts, but rather on the phrase "directly competitive or substitutable product" found in Ad Article III:2 of GATT 1994. The word "substitutable" - a key term which does not appear in Article 6.2 of the ATC - was central to the Appellate Body's findings. The United States submits that the Panel should, therefore, not impute interpretations of the phrase "directly competitive or substitutable" to an agreement which covers "like and/or directly competitive" products.

4.46 **Pakistan** concludes from its arguments, above, that an individual product cannot logically be described as "like and/or directly competitive". These terms can, therefore, only be interpreted to refer to different products manufactured by the particular domestic industry. It follows that the particular industry to be examined may produce different products of which some might be "like" and others that are "not like but directly competitive". However, the domestic industry cannot produce an individual product that is like but not directly competitive because there are no such products. The United States' interpretation, therefore, does not make sense. Pakistan is not asking the Panel to ignore the words "and/or" in Article 6.2. Pakistan is asking the Panel to recognise that these terms reflect the fact that a domestic industry can produce different products of which some may be like and others directly competitive. The term "and/or" therefore has a function and a meaning even if one recognises that a single product that is physically identical to the imported product cannot be "like but not directly competitive".

(c) Discussion of the Term "directly competitive"

4.47 **Pakistan** refers to the assumption on which the United States' argument rests; namely, that a domestic product is "directly competitive" within the meaning of Article 6.2 of the ATC only if it is actually competing with the product subject to the restraint. The extracts from the Appellate Body report on *Korea - Taxes on Alcoholic Beverages*, as reproduced in the Panel's question, leave no doubt that this assumption is incorrect. The Appellate Body makes clear that the dictionary meaning of the term "competitive" is "characterised by competition" and concludes therefrom that products are competitive if they are interchangeable on the market. In examining whether a product is competitive, both latent and extant, demand must, therefore, be considered. The Appellate Body ruling quoted by the Panel leaves no doubt: "competitive" does not mean "actually competing". The conclusion that must be drawn from the ruling of the Appellate Body is clear: "directly competitive products" are products with common characteristics that give them the potential of satisfying the same need or taste.

4.48 Pakistan notes that the United States, in a third-party submission to the Appellate Body, has argued itself that two products can be demonstrated to be directly competitive, *inter alia*, "through the inherent degree of substitutability evidenced by the products' similar physical characteristics and basic end-uses".[26] Pakistan believes that the Appellate Body ruling sought by the United States inevitably leads to the following conclusion: Combed cotton yarn from Pakistan and combed cotton yarn produced by the vertically integrated mills that the United States excluded from its investigation are "directly competitive" products because they share common characteristics that give them the potential of satisfying the same need or taste. The fact that integrated firms buy, according to the United States' own admission, certain quantities of yarn on the merchant market demonstrates that this yarn has the potential of satisfying the needs of integrated fabric producers. The term "directly competitive" in Article 6.2 does not permit the United States to distinguish, for the purpose of defining the domestic industry, between yarn that is actually being offered and hence competing in the merchant market, and yarn that is not.

4.49 Pakistan recalls that one of the assumptions on which the United States argument rests is that imported combed cotton yarn and domestic combed cotton yarn produced by vertically integrated mills for further processing are not competing with one another. Pakistan considers this to be factually incorrect. If a company owns a yarn plant and a fabric plant, it must treat each of these plants as separate profit centres and constantly compare the costs of producing yarn internally with the cost of purchasing yarn externally. The company must do so because the fabric processed from internally produced yarn is sold on the same market as fabric manufactured by the company's competitors with yarn purchased on the merchant market. The company cannot, therefore, ignore the opportunity costs of manufacturing yarn. The yarn produced internally and the yarn available on the merchant market are, therefore, actually competing with one another. The fact that integrated firms buy, according to the United States' own admission, certain quantities of yarn on the merchant market demonstrates that this yarn is actually competing with the yarn produced by these firms. The restraint imposed by the United States benefits, therefore, all producers of combed cotton yarn: the non-integrated producers benefit because they can sell the combed cotton yarn itself at a higher price and the integrated producers benefit because they can sell the fabric processed from combed cotton yarn at a higher price.

4.50 Pakistan also notes that because of the likeness of the combed cotton yarn exported by Pakistan and the combed cotton yarn produced by the vertically integrated mills, these mills are part of the domestic industry to be examined. The question of whether the yarn produced by vertically integrated mills is directly competitive is, consequently, irrelevant. The United States' claim that "only yarn produced by the combed cotton yarn for sale industry is 'directly competitive'

[26] Para. 72 of the Appellate Body report on *Korea - Alcoholic Beverages*, DSR 1999:I,3

with imported yarn", therefore, does not support its proposition that vertically integrated mills producing combed cotton yarn are not part of the industry to be examined. Pakistan points out that the United States confounds, and therefore confuses, the concepts "directly competitive products" and "directly competing products". Two products are "directly competitive" if there is the potential of a substitution between them and they are consequently capable of directly competing with one another. This is the situation contemplated by the terms of Article 6.2. There is nothing in the terms of Article 6.2 that allows Members to distinguish, for the purpose of defining the domestic industry, between products that are actually being offered, and hence competing in a given market, and those that are not. Pakistan considers it illogical to equate "competitive" and "competing".

4.51 In the view of the **United States**, Pakistan is wrong in arguing that the mere manufacture of a physically like article - even if it is not released onto the market and even if it does not directly compete with the import in question - should determine the scope of a domestic industry for purposes of the ATC. This interpretation denies the relevance of the marketplace for purposes of transitional safeguard action; would make it infeasible for a Member to analyze many of the market based factors listed in Articles 6.2 and 6.3 of the ATC; and, contrary to the object and purpose of the ATC, would render recourse to Article 6 impossible. That was not part of the carefully negotiated balance struck by the ATC. The United States believes that the Panel must analyze the meaning of the term "directly competitive" within the "four corners" of the ATC based on the facts of this case and considered in light of the object and purpose of Article 6 and the ATC. The essential purpose of Article 6 is to allow Members to resort to a transitional safeguard to address a damaging surge in imports that compete with domestic products on the market. The phrase "directly competitive" is in Article 6 for a reason, and the Panel should not accept Pakistan's invitation to read those key words out of the ATC.

4.52 **Pakistan** further notes that in *Korea - Taxes on Alcoholic Beverages*, the Appellate Body ascertained the meaning of "directly competitive" in Article III:2 of GATT 1994 by basing itself on the ordinary meaning of this term. The United States interprets the terms "directly competitive" in Article 6.2 of the ATC to mean "directly competing", which is contrary to the ordinary meaning of the term. The Appellate Body has repeatedly emphasised that all interpretation must be based on the language of the treaty and that the principles of treaty interpretation do not "condone the imputation into a treaty of words that are not there".[27] This principle follows from Article 3.2 of the DSU. The ATC, just as the GATT, is an agreement covered by the DSU. The principles of treaty interpretation that the Appellate Body applied to determine the meaning of "directly competitive" in Article III:2 of the GATT are, therefore, equally applicable to the interpretation of the same terms in Article 6.2 of the ATC.

[27] Appellate Body in *India - Patents* (WT/DS50/AB/R) para. 45.

4.53 Pakistan also recalls that the immediate context in which the term "directly competitive" appears is the requirement to demonstrate that a rise in imports caused serious damage to the domestic industry. The "domestic industry" to be examined is defined in Article 6.2 in terms of the products it produces. The term "domestic industry" is not otherwise qualified and can, therefore, only be interpreted to refer to the domestic industry in its entirety. The purpose of the requirement to investigate the domestic industry in its entirety is to ensure that the importing Member, when assessing the damage caused by imports, takes into account the state of all producers, including those that are not adversely affected by the rise in imports. If there are many domestic producers that are shielded from import competition because they supply a market different from the one supplied by importers, the rise in imports does not cause damage to the domestic industry in its entirety and no safeguard action may be taken. Contrary to the assertions of the United States, the very purpose of the obligation to demonstrate that a rise in imports caused serious damage to the domestic industry in its entirety is to ensure that the domestic industry is not divided into segments supplying different markets. The immediate context in which the terms "directly competitive" appear thus makes clear that they cannot be interpreted in a manner that would permit such market segmentation. If "competitive" were interpreted to mean "actually competing", the domestic industry could be divided into segments supplying different markets and the purpose of the requirement to examine the industry in its entirety could be frustrated. The immediate context in which the term "directly competitive" is used consequently does not support the United States' interpretation.

4.54 Pakistan goes on to argue that the wider context that must be taken into account in interpreting the term "directly competitive" includes Article 6.1 of the ATC, which stipulates that "the transitional safeguard should be applied as sparingly as possible" and consistently with "the effective implementation of the integration process". In *Japan - Alcoholic Beverages* the Appellate Body further ruled that Article III:1 of the GATT, according to which internal measures "should not be applied to imported or domestic products so as to afford protection to domestic production", constitutes part of the context of each of the other paragraphs of Article III. The Appellate Body stated that "any other reading of Article III would have the effect of rendering the words of Article III:1 meaningless, thereby violating the fundamental principle of effectiveness in treaty interpretation".[28] The principle of effective treaty interpretation requires an interpretation of the term "directly competitive" that takes into account that the basic principle enunciated in the first paragraph of Article 6 informs the remaining paragraphs of that Article. In *EC -Bananas* the Appellate Body ruled that, because of

[28] *Japan - Taxes on Alcoholic Beverages*, WT/DS8/AB/R - WT/DS10/AB/R - WT/DS11/AB/R, Section G. DSR 1996:1, 97

their exceptional nature, "waivers should be interpreted with great care".[29] Article 6.2 should be interpreted with similar care. The words "as sparingly as possible" make clear that the drafters of the ATC regarded transitional safeguard actions as measures running counter to the basic purpose of the ATC. Any interpretation of Article 6.2 that expands the possibilities of recourse to transitional safeguards beyond the scope indicated by the ordinary meaning of its terms would be an interpretation that fails to take into account the context in which these terms appear and the object and purpose of the ATC.

4.55 The **United States** re-iterates its view that the Panel should give full meaning to the term "directly competitive" contained in Article 6.2 and should not read these words out of the ATC. The ordinary meaning of "directly competitive" read in light of the object and purpose of the ATC means that products are directly competitive only when, in reality, they compete with each other on the marketplace. The New Shorter Oxford English Dictionary defines "competitive" as "of, pertaining to, involving, characterized by, or decided by competition." The qualifying term "directly" suggests "a degree of proximity in the competitive relationship between the domestic and the imported product." In other words, "directly competitive" reflects the actual state of affairs in the marketplace. In this case, the combed cotton yarn manufactured by vertically integrated establishments is consumed internally, is not intended for release onto the market, and thus does not compete with imports of combed cotton yarn in the real marketplace. Therefore, such yarn is not a "directly competitive product" with imports of combed cotton yarn.

(d) Discussion of the Term "directly competitive or substitutable"

4.56 The **United States** replied to an invitation from the Panel to discuss the Appellate Body's findings in *Korea - Taxes on Alcoholic Beverages* in relation to the use of the term "directly competitive or substitutable"[30]. In the view of the United States, these findings confirm that the ordinary meaning of "directly competitive" turns largely on whether the imported and domestic products compete with each other in the marketplace. However, these findings concern the phrase "directly competitive and substitutable" considered against the object and purpose of Article III of the GATT and rely on the word "substitutable," particularly for findings on potential competition or latent demand. The United States believes that the Panel should be cautious about relying on interpretations of the phrase "directly competitive or substitutable" to analyze the term "like and/or directly competitive" in the ATC, particularly given that the object and purpose

[29] *European communities - Regime for the Importation, Sale and Distribution of Bananas* (WT/DS27/AB/R), DSR 1997:II, 591, para. 185.

[30] Appellate Body Report on *Korea - Alcoholic Beverages*, WT/DS75/AB/R and WT/DS84/AB/R, DSR 1999:I,3, paras. 114-115 and 120.

of Article 6 of the ATC differ significantly from those of Article III of the GATT. Nevertheless, as applied to the facts of this case, the Appellate Body's findings on "directly competitive or substitutable" support the U.S. conclusion that combed cotton yarn manufactured by vertically integrated fabric producers for internal consumption is not "directly competitive" with imports of combed cotton yarn. Unlike combed cotton yarn for sale establishments, vertically integrated fabric producers do not produce combed cotton yarn for the purpose of sale in the marketplace and therefore do not have actual or potential customers for the combed cotton yarn they spin.

4.57 Also in this regard, the United States notes that there are fundamental differences between the text, context, and object and purpose of Article III:2 of the GATT and Article 6 of the ATC which yield a fundamentally different relationship between "like" and "directly competitive." Textually, "like" and "directly competitive" appear separately and refer to separate obligations in GATT Article III. By contrast, Article 6 of the ATC joins in the same sentence the terms "like" and "directly competitive" with the "and/or" function word. In addition, "directly competitive or substitutable" is informed by the term "substitutable" which does not appear in ATC Article 6. The phrase "like and/or directly competitive" is informed by the term "and/or," which does not appear in GATT Article III. Finally, unlike Article III:2, the terms "like" and "directly competitive" are tied to the same legal obligation and identify the range of products within which an importing Member may identify the domestic industry for purposes of Article 6.

(e) The Term "like and/or directly competitive products" as used in the MFA

Relationship to the Concept of Market Disruption

4.58 The **United States** notes that the phrase "like and/or directly competitive products" was central to "market disruption" for safeguard actions taken under the MFA. The relevant MFA provisions (Article 3 and Annex A) based assessment of serious damage on the impact of imports on like and/or directly competitive products. MFA signatories underscored the importance of "directly competitive" to this phrase in paragraph 24 of the 1986 Protocol of Extension of the MFA, which expanded the MFA's fibre coverage from cotton, wool and man-made to include silk blend and non-cotton vegetable fibres. By agreeing to expanded fibre coverage, MFA signatories explicitly acknowledged that textile products made from the so-called "new MFA fibres," while perhaps not identical to textile products made from traditional MFA fibres, nonetheless were directly competitive in the market. The interpretation given to "like and/or directly competitive" as products which compete in the marketplace - along with the prior MFA existence of this phrase - should inform an interpretation of Article 6. The United States believes that the Panel should be guided by the fact that the ATC retains the MFA phrase "like and/or directly competitive products" and does not draw from GATT Article XIX or other non-transitional WTO agreements.

4.59 **Pakistan** observes in this regard that the MFA was based on the concept of "market disruption", while the ATC is based on the concept of "serious damage". Raffaelli and Jenkins point out in their book "Drafting History of the Agreement on Textiles and Clothing" that damage, as defined in the ATC, "has nothing to do with market disruption".[31] According to Annex A of the MFA "market disruption shall be based on the existence of serious damage to domestic producers or actual threat thereof". However, the Annex did not define the domestic producers that must be demonstrated to have suffered serious damage. In particular, the Annex - unlike Article 6.2 of the ATC - does not use the terms "like and/or directly competitive products" to define the domestic industry to be examined.

4.60 Pakistan also points out that Annex A of the MFA stipulated that the serious damage to domestic producers must demonstrably not be caused by changes in technology or consumer preferences "which are instrumental in switches to like and/or directly competitive products made by the same industry." This means that the market disruption provisions of the MFA could not be invoked in respect of a product made of a fibre not specified in Article 12 of the MFA even if it might be directly competitive with a product made of a fibre specified in Article 12. It was only in 1986 that the GATT Textiles Committee acknowledged, "the concern of some importing countries regarding substantially increased imports of textiles made of vegetable fibres, blends of vegetable fibres with fibres specified in Article 12, and blends containing silk, which are directly competitive with fibres specified in Article 12. Accordingly, the Committee agreed that the provisions of Articles 3 and 4 may be invoked with respect to directly competitive imports of such textiles, in which any or all of such fibres in combination represent either the chief value of the fibres or 50 per cent or more by weight of the products, which cause market disruption ... . In examining the case for market disruption, the Textiles Surveillance Body is instructed to pay particular attention to the evidence demonstrating that these products are directly competitive with products of cotton, wool, and man-made fibres manufactured in the importing country concerned.".[32] In 1986 the MFA was extended subject, *inter alia,* to the above conclusion of the Textiles Committee.[33]

4.61 Pakistan continues its explanation, arguing that the approach of the ATC on product coverage is completely different from the MFA: Article 6 may be invoked in respect of the products listed in the Annex to the ATC. In respect of products not listed there, including any product that may be directly competitive

[31] Page 109.
[32] BISD 33S/13-14.
[33] BISD 33S/7.

with a listed product, only Article XIX of the GATT can be invoked.[34] Against this background, it is difficult to see how the industry definition of the MFA could illuminate the industry definition of the ATC. In any case, according to Article 32 of the Vienna Convention on the Law of Treaties, the preparatory work of the treaty and the circumstances of its conclusion can be used to determine the meaning of the terms of the treaty only if the interpretation according to the text-based method set out in Article 31 of that Convention leaves the meaning ambiguous or obscure or leads to a result which is manifestly absurd or unreasonable. However, the text-based method of interpretation does not leave the meaning of Article 6 of the ATC unclear nor does it lead to absurd or unreasonable results.

The Legal Relevance of the MFA in Interpreting the ATC

4.62 In response to a request from the Panel for both parties to clarify their positions regarding the legal relevance of the MFA in interpreting the ATC, the **United States** argues that the MFA is relevant as context for interpreting the ATC and it made reference to the MFA to illustrate that the ATC drew from the MFA's phrase "like and/or directly competitive" rather than from any other agreement. The United States notes the Appellate Body's discussion of the MFA in making its findings on Article 6.10 of the ATC in *United States - Underwear:* "We turn to another element of the context of Article 6.10 of the ATC: the prior existence and demise, as it were, of the MFA ... . We believe the disappearance in the ATC of the earlier MFA provision for backdating the operative effect of a restraint measure, strongly reinforces the presumption that such retroactive application is no longer permissible.".[35] Given this clear statement of the Appellate Body, the United States expresses surprise at Pakistan's assertion that the Appellate Body "did not use the MFA as part of the 'context' relevant for the interpretation of the terms of Article 6"[36] and its contention that "the United States misrepresents the rulings of the Appellate Body".[37] Rather, it appears that Pakistan has misread both the Appellate Body's findings and the U.S. arguments regarding the MFA by suggesting, contrary to the plain language of the Appellate Body's findings, that the prior existence of the MFA does not inform interpretations of the ATC.

4.63 Commenting on this particular point, **Pakistan** states that the United States has misrepresented the Appellate Body statement because it failed to report for which purpose the Appellate Body referred to the demise of the MFA. It

[34] Para. 3 of the Annex to the ATC.

[35] *United States - Restrictions on Imports of Cotton and Man-made Fibre Underwear*, WT/DS24/AB/R, Report of the Appellate Body, 25 February 1997 ("Report of the Appellate Body, *United States - Underwear*"), DSR 1997:I, 11, at p.24

[36] Second written submission of Pakistan, at para. 50.

[37] Second written submission of Pakistan, at paras. 48 and 49.

was true that the Appellate Body had used the word "context" when referring to the prior existence of the MFA. However, it obviously did not use this word within the technical meaning of Article 31:1 and 2 of the Vienna Convention on the Law of Treaties. This clearly follows from the fact that the Appellate Body did not use the MFA to determine the meaning of the terms of Article 6:10 of the ATC in accordance with Article 31 of the Vienna Convention. The Appellate Body referred to the MFA only to confirm the meaning of Article 6.10 that it had already given to this provision without any reference to the MFA in accordance with Article 31. The Appellate Body, after having determined the meaning of the terms of Article 6:10 in accordance with their ordinary meaning in the context provided by the other paragraphs of Article 6, stated: "We believe the disappearance in the ATC of the earlier MFA express provision for backdating the operative effect of a restraint measure strongly reinforces the presumption that such retroactive application is no longer permissible.".[38]

4.64 In the view of Pakistan, a fair reading of the Appellate Body ruling as a whole thus leads to the conclusion that the Appellate Body used the comparison with the MFA merely as a supplementary means of interpretation within the meaning of Article 32 of the Vienna Convention in order to confirm the meaning resulting from the application of Article 31. Article 31:2 of the Vienna Convention on the Law of Treaties provides a clear and exhaustive list of the elements that comprise the context for the purposes of the interpretation of a treaty in accordance with Article 31:1. A former treaty is not among those elements. Therefore, to suggest that the Appellate Body used the MFA as context within the meaning of Article 31:1 of the Vienna Convention, is to suggest that the Appellate Body acted inconsistently with the basic principles of treaty interpretation that it has itself applied in all cases.

The Question of the MFA as Relevant Context of ATC Article 6

4.65 As it has argued during this proceeding (paragraphs 4.56 and 4.57), the **United States** considers as highly relevant the fact that the ATC retains the MFA's phrase "like and/or directly competitive" for non-integrated textile and clothing products and does not draw from GATT Article XIX or any other agreement. The United States submits that just as the Appellate Body in *United States - Underwear* drew strong inferences from the disappearance of the MFA's "backdating" language in the ATC, so this Panel should draw strong inferences from the fact that the ATC retains "like and/or directly competitive" from the MFA, rather than using language from other available agreements. Accordingly, it would be inappropriate to interpret the "domestic industry producing like and/or directly competitive products" in light of WTO agreements - such as the

[38] WT/DS24/AB/R, page 17.

GATT, the Safeguards Agreement, or the Antidumping Agreement - which do not employ this formulation.

4.66 In addition, the United States points out that customary rules of treaty interpretation require giving full meaning to the phrase "domestic industry producing like and/or directly competitive products," whose ordinary meaning permits an identification of the domestic industry producing (1) like and directly competitive products, (2) like (but not directly competitive) products, and (3) directly competitive (but not like) products. In other words, the "and/or" function word gives independent meaning to the term "directly competitive" in options (1) and (3). To support this ordinary meaning, the United States refers to the MFA as relevant context. As the United States explained, "directly competitive" had independent meaning for MFA signatories - including the United States and Pakistan - which explicitly recognized a separate class of "directly competitive" products in paragraph 24 of the 1986 Protocol of Extension of the MFA. Pakistan, however, appears to deny the independent relevance of "directly competitive" for purposes of Article 6.2 and suggests that "directly competitive" is only a secondary inquiry. Pakistan has stated that because combed cotton yarn manufactured by vertically integrated fabric producers may be "like," "the question of whether the yarn produced by vertically integrated mills is directly competitive is consequently irrelevant".[39] This claim appears to run counter to both the ordinary meaning of the "domestic industry producing like and/or directly competitive products" and its context as informed by the "prior existence and demise, as it were, of the MFA".[40]

4.67 The United States explains that it also fails to understand Pakistan's assertion that the U.S. reliance on the MFA as context is an effort to "loosen up the language in Article 6"[41] or impute the MFA's market disruption analysis into the ATC.[42] Contrary to Pakistan's claim, the United States has not argued that the Panel should interpret the serious damage analysis of Article 6 in light of the MFA's market disruption provision. Rather, as discussed above, the United States believes that the ATC's clear retention of the MFA's phrase "like and/or directly competitive products" and the fact that the "directly competitive" element of this phrase had independent meaning under the MFA provide relevant context for interpreting the domestic industry provision of Article 6.2 of the ATC.

4.68 On this same point, **Pakistan** explained its position that, according to the consistent jurisprudence of the Appellate Body, the claims of the United States related to the MFA have to be examined in the light of the principles of interpretation set out in Articles 31 and 32 of the Vienna Convention on the Law of Treaties. According to Article 31 of the Vienna Convention, a treaty is to be inter-

39 Statement of Pakistan at the first meeting of the Panel, at p. 5.
40 Report of the Appellate Body, *United States - Underwear*, DSR 1997:1, 11, at p. 24.
41 Second written submission of Pakistan, at para. 48.
42 Second written submission of Pakistan, at para. 51.

preted in accordance with "the ordinary meaning to be given to the terms of the treaty in their context and in the light of its object and purpose". According to Article 32 of the Vienna Convention, the preparatory work of the treaty and the circumstances of its conclusion can be used for two purposes: First, "to confirm the meaning resulting from the application of Article 31". Second, "to determine the meaning when the interpretation according to Article 31 leaves the meaning ambiguous or obscure or leads to a result which is manifestly absurd or unreasonable". Neither Pakistan nor the United States claims that an interpretation of Article 6 of the ATC in accordance with Article 31 leaves its meaning ambiguous or obscure or leads to a result that is manifestly absurd or unreasonable. The arguments of the United States to which the Panel refers in its question, therefore, give rise only to two issues. The first is whether the Panel, in interpreting the terms of Article 6 of the ATC in accordance with Article 31 of the Vienna Convention, should regard the MFA as part of the context of those terms. The second is whether recourse to the MFA confirms the interpretation of Article 6 of the ATC that the United States requests the Panel to adopt.

4.69 Pakistan argues that the MFA is not part of the context of the terms of Article 6 of the ATC. Article 31:2 of the Vienna Convention clearly defines the "context" that may be taken into account in giving meaning to the terms of a treaty as follows: "The context for the purposes of the interpretation of a treaty shall comprise, in addition to the text, including its preamble and annexes: (a) any agreement relating to the treaty which was made between all the parties in connection with the conclusion of the treaty; (b) any instrument which was made by one or more parties in connection with the conclusion of the treaty and accepted by the other parties as an instrument related to the treaty.". In the view of Pakistan, the MFA does not fulfil the above criteria: it is not part of the text, preamble or annexes of the ATC nor was it concluded in connection with the ATC. There can for this reason be no doubt that the "context" to determine the meaning of Article 6 does not comprise the MFA. Furthermore, Pakistan states that the Appellate Body has not treated the MFA as part of the context of Article 6 of the ATC.

4.70 Pakistan points out that the United States claims that the Appellate Body used the MFA as context of Article 6 of the ATC. It asserts that: "the Appellate Body was very clear in *United States - Underwear* that the "prior existence and demise, as it were, of the MFA" informs the context of Article 6 of the ATC. In that case, the Appellate Body drew strong inferences from the disappearance of certain MFA language in the text of the ATC.".[43] In the view of Pakistan, however, the United States misrepresents the rulings of the Appellate Body. In *United States - Underwear,* the Appellate Body faced the question of whether the practice of "backdating" which was explicitly permitted under the MFA was also permissible under the ATC. The Appellate Body ruled on this as follows: "Arti-

[43] United States' answers to the Panel's questions, para. 26 (footnotes omitted).

cle 6.1 directs that transitional safeguard measures be applied "as sparingly as possible" on the one hand and, on the other, applied "consistently with the provisions of [Article 6] and the effective implementation of the integration process under the [ATC]". It appears to the Appellate Body that to inject into Article 6.10 an authorisation for backdating ... will encourage return to the practice of backdating ... under the regime of the MFA [and] ... loosen up the carefully negotiated language of Article 6.10, which reflects an equally carefully drawn balance of rights and obligations of Members.".[44]

4.71 Pakistan also considers that the United States incorrectly claims that the Appellate Body ruled that "the MFA informs the context of Article 6 of the ATC". The Appellate Body merely stated that "the disappearance in the ATC of the earlier MFA express provision for backdating ... strongly reinforces the presumption that such retroactive application is no longer permissible [because it cannot be assumed that] the disappearance was merely accidental or an inadvertent oversight on the part of either harassed negotiators or inattentive draftsmen".[45] In the *Underwear* case the Appellate Body thus used the MFA only to confirm an interpretation it had already reached in accordance with Article 31 of the Vienna Convention. It did not use the MFA as part of the "context" relevant for the interpretation of the terms of Article 6 of the ATC. The United States' claim to the contrary is plainly incorrect.

4.72 Pakistan further argues that the MFA does not confirm the meaning that the United States has asked the Panel to give to the terms "directly competitive". Pakistan comments that the United States invites the Panel to "draw strong inferences from the fact that the ATC retains the MFA phrase 'like and/or directly competitive products' and does not draw from GATT Article XIX or other non-transitional WTO agreements".[46] It argues that, "nothing about the context or the object and purpose of the ATC suggests that the ordinary meaning of the phrase "like and/or directly competitive" would disallow one or the other of these three possibilities. The ATC could have drawn from other agreements which had defined domestic industry in another manner. Yet the ATC draws directly from the MFA and incorporates its "and/or" phrase. Given this apparently intentional selection of this phrase, it should not be interpreted in a manner that nullifies any part of the meaning of the phrase absent some compelling reason based on the purpose and intent of the ATC.".[47]

4.73 Pakistan stresses that the ordinary meaning of the terms "like and/or directly competitive" is not what the United States claims it to be. In the context of Article 6.2, these words simply confirm that a domestic producer to be examined may not only manufacture like products or directly competitive products but also

---

[44] WT/DS24/AB/R, DSR 1997:I, 11, at p. 23

[45] WT/DS24/AB/R, *supra*, footnote 44, p. 25.

[46] United States' answers to the Panel's questions, para. 26.

[47] United States' answers to the Panel's questions, paras. 70 and 71.

both like and directly competitive products. The terms "like" and "directly competitive" are used in Article 6.2 to define the characteristics of the physical objects manufactured by the domestic industry to be examined, not the characteristics of the producer manufacturing it. For these reasons, it does not follow from the ordinary meaning of the terms "like and/or directly competitive" in their context that a particular product can be like but not directly competitive.

4.74 Pakistan goes on to point out that, contrary to the suggestion of the United States, the MFA does not use the terms "like and/or directly competitive products" to define the domestic industry. These terms appear in a clause in Annex A to the MFA that imposes on participants the obligation to demonstrate that the damage they found to exist was not caused by changes in technology or consumer preferences that "are instrumental in switches to like and/or directly competitive products made by the same industry". In defining the domestic industry, the drafters of the ATC thus clearly did not "retain" the phrases that the drafters of the MFA used to define the domestic producers to be examined for the purposes of a serious damage determination. Moreover, the use of the terms "and/or" is not specific to the MFA or in any way unusual. They appear about 40 times in the WTO agreements. One can, therefore, not readily assume that their use in the ATC reflects an intention to incorporate MFA concepts into the ATC. It is for these reasons inappropriate to suggest that the drafters of the ATC faced a choice between the MFA industry definition and the Article XIX industry definition and selected the MFA definition with the terms "like and/or directly competitive products". There simply was no such industry definition in the MFA.

4.75 It is also the view of Pakistan that the differences in the working of the safeguard provisions of the MFA and the ATC confirm that Article 6 of the ATC should not be interpreted in a manner that encourages a return to practices under the MFA. The United States argues that the Panel should take into account, as the relevant context, that U.S. market disruption analyses and safeguard actions taken on yarn products under the MFA were based on an examination of the yarn for sale industry. However, Pakistan believes that it would be legally incorrect, and inconsistent with the Appellate Body ruling in the *Underwear* case if the Panel were to base its interpretation of Article 6 on the United States' practices under the MFA. Unlike the ATC, the MFA was based on the concept of "market disruption". According to Annex A of the MFA "market disruption shall be based on the existence of serious damage to domestic producers or actual threat thereof". However, Annex A did not define the domestic producers. The absence of any definition of the producers and the focus on the disruption of a market by imports might have given the United States some justification under the MFA to base its determinations of serious damage on the effect of imports in a particular market supplied by imports and the state of domestic producers supplying that market. However, the concept of "market disruption" has been purposefully kept out of the text of the ATC. The serious damage must, therefore, now be caused by increased quantities of imports, not by the situation prevailing in the domestic market supplied by imports. The vague reference to "domestic producers" has been replaced by clear terms defining the producers to be examined as the entire industry producing a particular product. These changes no longer leave any room for an interpretation according to which a serious damage determination may be based on an examination of the state of producers supplying a particular market disrupted by imports. The differences in the drafting of the ATC and the MFA thus confirm, just as in the *Underwear* case, that the carefully negotiated language of Article 6 of the ATC should not be loosened up in a manner that encourages a return to practices under the MFA.

4.76 Also on this topic, Pakistan argues that the 1986 Protocol of Extension of the MFA does not confirm the meaning that the United States has asked the Panel to give to the term "directly competitive". The United States argued that probably the most prominent example of agreement among MFA signatories on the term "like and/or directly competitive" is found in paragraph 24 of the 1986 Protocol of Extension of the MFA, which expanded the MFA's fibre coverage from cotton, wool and man-made fibre textiles and textile products to include silk blend and non-cotton vegetable fibres (such as ramie), and blends thereof. In paragraph 24, MFA signatories underscored the importance and meaning of the term directly competitive for purposes of the MFA's safeguard provision. By agreeing to expanded fibre coverage, MFA signatories explicitly acknowledged that textile products made from the so-called "new MFA fibres," while perhaps not identical to textile products made from traditional MFA fibres, nonetheless were directly competitive on the market.

4.77 In the view of Pakistan, however, contrary to the assertion of United States, paragraph 24 of the 1986 Protocol of Extension of the MFA does not reflect an agreement on the terms "like and/or directly competitive" products. This paragraph simply acknowledges that textiles made of fibres specified in Article 12 of the MFA and textiles made of vegetable fibres (or blends thereof) may be directly competitive. It also permits the invocation of Articles 3 and 4 of the MFA in respect of imports of fibres not covered by Article 12 on the condition that such products are directly competitive with products made of covered fibres. Paragraph 24 of the 1986 Protocol of Extension of the MFA thus essentially redefined the products in respect of which restraint may be applied, not the domestic producers to be examined. It is noteworthy that the term "directly competitive" is used in paragraph 24 to limit the extension of the MFA's market disruption provisions to products made of vegetable fibre. It is for these reasons not clear to Pakistan how paragraph 24 could possibly confirm the contention of the United States that, under the ATC, a particular product can be like but not directly competitive.

4.78 In the negotiation of the ATC a key objective of the developing countries was, thus, to free the multilateral trading system of this concept. They succeeded and Article 6 is worded accordingly. According to Pakistan, the United States requests the Panel to reintroduce this concept by arguing that, because the ATC was preceded by the MFA, Article 6 entitles the importing Member to base its serious damage determination on an examination of the state of producers that actually compete with imports in a particular market. In the view of Pakistan, however, there is no legitimacy in this request and there is no recognised principle of interpretation on which it can be based.

4.79 Commenting on the views of Pakistan set out above, the **United States** observed that Article 6 of the ATC should be interpreted in accordance with its ordinary meaning in light of its object and purpose. Should the Panel look to another agreement to inform its interpretation of "domestic industry producing like and/or directly competitive products", the United States believes that the Panel should focus on the Multifibre Arrangement - the ATC's predecessor - not any other agreement. Pakistan has repeatedly denied the relevance of the MFA to any interpretation of Article 6 of the ATC. Contrary to clear Appellate Body guidance, Pakistan has claimed that the MFA does not inform the context of Article 6. Pakistan has also suggested that the retention in the ATC of the MFA's phrase "like and/or directly competitive products" is inconsequential. Instead, Pakistan appears to believe that it is more appropriate for the Panel to look, not to the MFA, but to other agreements - whose plain text and object and purpose differ significantly from the ATC - to interpret Article 6.

4.80 As the United States discussed earlier, it is noteworthy that Article 6.2 of the ATC drew from the MFA's phrase "like and/or directly competitive products" rather than from GATT Article XIX or any other agreement. While there are specific and important differences between the MFA and the ATC, the ATC - the carefully negotiated successor to the MFA for textile and clothing items not yet integrated into the GATT - is an outgrowth of the MFA's regime, rules and structure. The MFA's phrase "like and/or directly competitive products" is an important example. Pakistan claims that the term "and/or" is "not specific to the MFA or in any way unusual" to suggest that the selection of "and/or" was somehow random. While the use of "and/or" generally may not be unique, the phrase at issue - "like and/or directly competitive products" - is certainly "specific to the MFA" and is, in this respect, "unusual." Other than the MFA and the ATC, no other WTO agreement employs that formulation.

4.81 The United States considers that Pakistan also attempts to trivialise the ATC's reliance on the MFA's phrase "like and/or directly competitive products" by asserting that the MFA did not use this term in the context of the domestic industry. Although there are some differences between the MFA and the ATC, both agreements use the phrase "like and/or directly competitive products" in the context of a finding of serious damage and actual threat thereof, and both agreements use the phrase to refer to goods "made" or "produced" by the relevant domestic producer or domestic industry. Annex A to the MFA, paragraph 1, reads: "The determination of a situation of "market disruption", as referred to in this Arrangement, shall be based on existence of serious damage to domestic producers or actual threat thereof. Such damage must demonstrably be caused by the factors set out in paragraph II below and not by factors such as technological changes or changes in consumer preference which are instrumental in switches to like and/or directly competitive products made by the same industry, or similar factors. The existence of damage shall be determined on the basis of an examination of the appropriate factors having a bearing on the evolution of the state of the industry in question such as: turnover, market share, profits, export performance, employment, volume of disruptive and other imports, production, utilization of capacity, productivity and investments. No one or several of these factors can necessarily give decisive guidance.".

4.82 Similarly, Article 6.2 of the ATC states that "[s]afeguard action may be taken under this Article when, on the basis of a determination by a Member, it is demonstrated that a particular product is being imported into its territory in such increased quantities as to cause serious damage or actual threat thereof, to the domestic industry producing like and/or directly competitive products.". Contrary to Pakistan's suggestion, both Annex A of the MFA and Article 6.2 of the ATC refer to the like and/or directly competitive products produced by the industry in question. Given this clear similarity, it is highly curious for Pakistan to assert that the MFA did not use the phrase "like and/or directly competitive products" in connection with the definition of the domestic industry.[48]

4.83 The United States also clarified that, contrary to Pakistan's claim, it has not invited the Panel to interpret Article 6 of the ATC in a manner that encourages a return to practices under the MFA. Rather, the United States has urged, and continues to urge, the Panel to interpret the ATC according to the ordinary meaning of its carefully negotiated language in light of its object and purpose. As the United States has argued, customary rules of treaty interpretation require giving full meaning to the phrase "domestic industry producing like and/or directly competitive products". The ordinary meaning of this phrase permits an identification of the domestic industry producing (1) like and directly competitive products, (2) like (but not directly competitive) products, and (3) directly competitive (but not like) products. Pakistan challenges this argument and asserts that the ordinary meaning of the terms "like and/or directly competitive" is not what the United States claims it to be. However, Pakistan neither explains why this is the case nor offers any rationale for the ordinary meaning of "like and/or directly competitive" that is any different from that set forth above. In fact, although Pakistan claims that the ordinary meaning is something else, Pakistan appears to agree with the United States regarding the plain meaning of Article 6.2: "[i]n the context of Article 6.2, these words terms simply confirm that a domestic producer to be examined may not only manufacture like products or directly competitive products but also both like and directly competitive products."[49] In other words, like the United States, Pakistan acknowledges that "like and/or directly competitive products" refers to (1) like products, (2) directly competitive products, and (3) like and directly competitive products. However, Pakistan then appears to contradict itself by re-iterating its claim - which runs counter to the plain text of

[48] Answers of Pakistan to additional written questions of the Panel, at para. 10.

[49] Answers of Pakistan to additional written questions of the Panel, at para. 9.

Article 6.2 - that the ordinary meaning of the term "like and/or directly competitive" does not permit the existence of a product that is like but not directly competitive.[50]

4.84 Thus, the United States argues, it is clear that the ordinary meaning of "like and/or directly competitive products" as contained in either the MFA or the ATC permits the U.S. identification of the domestic industry in this case. Pakistan has pointed to nothing about the ordinary meaning or context of the phrase "domestic industry producing like and/or directly competitive products," or the object or purpose of Article 6 and the ATC that would suggest otherwise. Pakistan has also failed to explain why the Panel should not follow the Appellate Body's guidance and consider as relevant the prior existence of the MFA - which used the identical phrase "like and directly competitive products" to refer to the products made by the relevant domestic industry - or why the Panel should instead rely on other WTO agreements with completely different texts, contexts, and purposes.

C. The Determination by the United States of Serious Damage, or Actual Threat Thereof (Article 6.3 of the ATC)

Article 6.3 of the ATC: "In making a determination of serious damage, or actual threat thereof, as referred to in paragraph 2, the Member shall examine the effect of those imports on the state of the particular industry, as reflected in changes in such relevant economic variables as output, productivity, utilization of capacity, inventories, market share, exports, wages, employment, domestic prices, profits and investment; none of which, either alone or combined with other factors, can necessarily give decisive guidance.".

1. The United States Determination of Serious Damage to the Domestic Industry

The United States Explanation of its Determination of Serious Damage

4.85 The **United States** argues that it has satisfied the requirements under Articles 6.2 and 6.3 of the ATC in reaching the conclusion that imports of combed cotton yarn caused serious damage to the domestic industry. The Market Statement clearly documents sharp increases in Category 301 imports and the effect of these soaring levels of imports on the eleven variables enumerated in Article 6.3 of the ATC, as well as additional variables that the United States identified as relevant and material. The U.S. investigation demonstrated that total Category

[50] Answers of Pakistan to additional written questions of the Panel, at para. 9.

301 imports of combed cotton yarn nearly doubled between January-August 1997 and January-August 1998, and imports from Pakistan nearly quadrupled, increasing 283.2 per cent in the same period. The price of imported combed cotton yarn - particularly from Pakistan - was significantly below the average U.S. price of combed cotton yarn for sale.

4.86 The impact of these surges of low-cost imports on the U.S. industry was unmistakably serious damage and the evidence is clear and striking. As these imports were surging during the relevant time period, the economic variables set out in Article 6.3 of the ATC deteriorated substantially: U.S. domestic production dropped 10.2 per cent, shipments declined 14.2 per cent, productivity lagged four per cent, capacity utilization declined, inventories increased 145.9 per cent, the share of the market held by U.S. producers contracted ten percentage points, exports fell by one-third, 6.6 per cent of the production workforce left the industry, profitability was nearly cut in half and investment stagnated. Two mills exited the industry during this eight-month period.

4.87 The United States also demonstrated that increased imports - not other factors - caused serious damage to the domestic industry producing like and/or directly competitive products. While imports were taking a greater share of the U.S. market, the apparent domestic market remained relatively constant during the investigation period, indicating that there was no change in consumer preference. Likewise, technological changes could not account for the serious damage given that there had been no significant new technological changes in the defined industry during the period covered by the investigation.

4.88 Every relevant economic indicator, taken individually, shows an industry irrefutably suffering serious damage resulting from the surge of Category 301 imports. Taken collectively, the indicators reveal a state of serious damage. The United States argues that, with this evidence, it is hard to draw any conclusion other than that the domestic industry was in immediate peril and had suffered serious damage during the period analyzed in the U.S. investigation. In the case before the Panel, Pakistan leaves this clear record of serious damage caused by the import surge unchallenged. In fact, Pakistan asks the Panel to negate this showing based on the fact that a few mills converted their production from combed to carded yarn in the face of serious damage to the industry from imports.

4.89 The United States goes on to state that Pakistan assails the U.S. determination of serious damage using a misplaced reliance on interpretations of other WTO agreements and otherwise fails to establish any violation of the ATC. Pakistan suggests that the Panel should impute interpretations of the Agreement on Safeguards to its causation analysis under the ATC and of the Safeguards and Anti-Dumping Agreements to establish benchmarks for the minimum period for which data must be collected. Pakistan provides no support for either claim other than asserting that interpretations of other agreements are somehow relevant. As is plain from the text, the ATC and non-transitional WTO agreements were drafted in different ways and use different language. The ATC has a fundamentally different purpose from other non-transitional WTO agreements. The United States further states that Pakistan tries to draw attention away from the totality of the data by isolating one small factor after another and speculating about what could have been or might have been the case. The ATC does not allow a Member to isolate one factor in the list of eleven factors in Article 6.3 in reaching its determination of serious damage. Quite the contrary, the ATC states that "none of [these factors], either alone or when combined with other factors, can necessarily give decisive guidance." The United States submits that the Panel should resist Pakistan's efforts to focus exclusively on one particular factor and should instead, as the ATC directs, review whether the U.S. examined all relevant factors in conducting its analysis. When this is done, the U.S. findings must stand.

Interpretation of "Serious Damage" and "Serious Injury"

4.90 In response to a question by the Panel, the **United States** points out that, contrary to Pakistan's suggestion, "serious damage" does not set a higher bar for the invocation of the transitional safeguard than would the term "serious injury." "Serious damage" and "serious injury" are different terms that must be interpreted in light of their context and the object and purpose of the agreements they serve. The ATC does not define "serious damage" but places this determination in the hands of Members, which must carefully consider the factors set forth in Article 6. The use of "serious damage" from the MFA rather than the serious injury contained in other agreements is significant. Although the term "serious injury" of Article XIX of the GATT was available at the time the ATC was drafted, the ATC uses the term "serious damage"- a term that did not carry the connotations that might attach to "serious injury." The purpose of the transitional safeguard in the ATC was not to make safeguard actions more difficult during the transitional period but rather to ease the transition from the MFA to normal GATT rules over a defined period. In fact, "serious damage" - as derived from the MFA - was intended to give Members greater ability to address domestic market disruptions from floods of imports than was available under Article XIX of the GATT or the Safeguards Agreement. The United States also comments that Pakistan has asserted that the ordinary meaning of "serious damage" is "grave injury impairing value or usefulness." While this assertion is questionable, this much is clear: whether or not there is a difference between "serious damage" and "serious injury," "serious damage" under the ATC does not require a Member to go beyond what is required under the Safeguards Agreement. The ATC's transitional safeguard was not intended to make it more difficult to invoke a safeguard during the transitional period than it would be after the transitional period.

4.91 Also in response to this question, **Pakistan** expresses the view that, according to the principles of interpretation followed by the Appellate Body, the term "serious damage" in Article 6 must be interpreted on the basis of its ordinary meaning in its context and in the light of the object and purpose of the ATC. The ordinary meaning of the words " serious damage" is "grave injury impairing value or usefulness".[51] The ordinary meaning of "serious injury" is the same. The United States asserted that a retooling of a combed cotton yarn plant may, for the purposes of a serious damage determination, be deemed to be a "closure" of that plant and the change in activity of the workers involved as "a loss of jobs". However, the fact that a plant retooled in response to a change in the market situation does not demonstrate that imports caused serious damage to that plant. Thus, if a plant produces carded instead of combed yarn, thrives in its new activity and retains its workforce, the increase in imports obviously did not cause any injury that impaired its value or usefulness. The United States' definition of serious damage can, therefore, not be reconciled with the dictionary meaning of serious damage.

4.92 Pakistan also considers that an interpretation of the term "serious damage" in its context and in the light of the purpose of the ATC does not justify the United States' approach. According to Article 6.1 of the ATC, safeguard actions should not frustrate the "effective implementation of the integration process" under the ATC. Article 1.5 of the ATC provides that, in order to facilitate this process, "Members should allow for continuous autonomous industrial adjustment". The terms "serious damage" cannot, therefore, be interpreted to permit safeguard actions in response to autonomous industrial adjustment. If Members were permitted to declare successfully retooled plants to have suffered "serious damage" within the meaning of Article 6.2 merely because they are no longer part of the domestic industry, they would be permitted to invoke the transitional safeguard provisions for the purpose of preventing autonomous industrial adjustment. The United States' approach is, for these reasons, incompatible with the ordinary meaning of the term "serious damage", the context in which this term appears and the objective and purpose of the ATC.

Continuous Autonomous Industrial Adjustment

4.93 In this regard, the **United States** considers that Pakistan misuses the term "continuous autonomous industrial adjustment" in suggesting that it is incompatible with a finding of serious damage or actual threat thereof. Pakistan also implies that this process somehow conflicts with the transitional safeguard mechanism. Continuous autonomous industrial adjustment and serious damage can go hand in hand. For instance, in the case before the Panel, the combed cotton yarn for sale industry was engaged in the process of autonomous adjustment during the period prior to the damaging surge in imports: production was increasing as the number of plants in the industry were decreasing. However, during the investigation period - particularly during the first eight months of 1998 - a dramatic

[51] *The Concise Oxford Dictionary*, Third Edition, Oxford at the Clarendon Press.

surge in imports led to a significant deterioration in the conditions of the industry, as measured by the marked decline in the Article 6.3 factors: production dropped, shipments declined, inventories increased, etc. The fact that the industry was already engaged in adjustment - with some establishments leaving the defined industry and others becoming more efficient - does not minimize the serious damage and actual threat thereof that the industry was experiencing. Pakistan denies the very reality of the deterioration in each and every one of the Article 6.3 factors when it suggests that efforts to convert production from combed to carded yarn or otherwise readjust imply that serious damage or actual threat thereof could not have existed or did not exist.

4.94 The United States argues that the facts of this case - as set forth in the Market Statement and in the various submissions of the United States - clearly establish that the industry was in fact suffering serious damage and actual threat thereof, notwithstanding ongoing efforts to retool, to readjust, and to cope even in the face of the flood of imports. Furthermore, the United States finds it very difficult to understand how Pakistan could suggest that Article 6 is incompatible with continuous autonomous industrial adjustment. Far from being so, the Article 6 transitional safeguard is an essential element of this restructuring process. Article 6 gives Members the ability to act so that industries seriously damaged by increased imports can adjust to the changed circumstances rather than be destroyed by them. The ATC explicitly recognizes this fact by providing a transitional safeguard mechanism during the ten-year restructuring process given to the textiles and clothing sector and contemplates that importing Members might need to resort to Article 6 to provide a temporary limit on imports during the adjustment process. Moreover, the transitional safeguard does not prevent imports; it merely limits imports to current levels and provides for growth in subsequent years.

2. *The Nature of the Data Used and the Data Verification Process*

Arguments of Pakistan

4.95 **Pakistan** argues that the United States failed to base its determination of serious damage on verified, correct and complete data and to provide an adequate, reasoned and reasonable explanation of how the relevant facts support the determinations made. For the Market Statement submitted in 1998, the United States used data on production, shipments, employment, wages, man-hours, capacity utilisation, inventory and unfilled orders provided by the American Yarn Spinners Association (AYSA). The Market Statement declares that the United States "verified and determined that AYSA production data for the defined industry was consistent with official Bureau of the Census production statistics for the subject yarn". However, in December 1998, when the Market Statement was finalised, official statistics for the period ending in August 1998 were not yet available. The United States could, therefore, not have verified the consistency between the AYSA data and official data.

4.96 Thus, for the period January-August 1998, during which most of the unfavourable developments are claimed to have occurred, the United States used exclusively unverified data supplied by AYSA, which had an interest in the safeguard action and which was already known to have previously supplied incorrect data. The Census figures published subsequent to the finalisation of the Market Statement cannot be reconciled with the data provided by AYSA for this period. While AYSA had reported a 10.2 per cent decline in production between January-August 1997 and January-August 1998, Census figures show only a drop of 5 per cent from 1997 to 1998. This confirms that the data provided by AYSA could not be trusted.

4.97 Pakistan also points out that the United States used in its investigation data on profits and investments based on the results of surveys conducted by AYSA among its members. The results of the survey were reported on an aggregate basis. The United States indicates in the Market Statement that it verified that AYSA conducted the surveys and that the firms responded to them, but does not indicate how it verified the accuracy of the information reported by the establishments included in the survey. During its consultation with the United States, Pakistan repeatedly requested details on the AYSA survey, such as the names of the respondents. The United States, however, declined to provide any such details.

4.98 In sum, Pakistan contends that, instead of examining the entire industry producing combed cotton yarn, it examined only those producers that are united in AYSA, the lobbying organisation that had asked for the restraint. However, AYSA's membership comprises only about one half of the domestic producers of combed cotton yarn. For its determination on the changes in economic variables affecting these producers during the first eight months of 1998, the United States relied exclusively on the data supplied by AYSA. It did not verify any of these data even though this organisation had previously supplied the United States government with production data that were incorrect. AYSA informed the United States government that three of its members had closed during the investigation period and 423 jobs were lost. This information turned out to be incorrect because, in fact, the three producers had not closed but switched to the production of carded yarn. As a result, the United States never examined the state of any of the "closed" producers. Nor did it examine whether the workers had actually lost their job or had merely been assigned to another activity in the same plants. The determination of the United States that its combed cotton yarn industry was suffering serious damage during the first eight months of 1998 was, thus, based on unverified information supplied by an interested party that had previously supplied incorrect data. The information was incomplete because it concerned only one half of the producers and, as far as plant closures and job losses are concerned, incorrect.

4.99 Pakistan also notes that the United States combed cotton yarn industry has undergone extensive restructuring in the years prior to the imposition of the restraint. Thus, between 1993 and 1997 the number of units producing combed cotton yarn for sale declined by 37 per cent while production increased by 44 per cent. It was, therefore, far from clear whether the adverse changes in economic variables reported by AYSA could be ascribed to the rise in imports or autonomous adjustment. Nevertheless, the United States made no effort to segregate the various potential causes of the damage reported by AYSA. One way to demonstrate that imports were the cause would have been to demonstrate that there was a consistent relationship between the trends in imports and trends in economic variables. However, there was no such consistent relationship during the investigation period covering two years and eight months. All that the United States was able to show was that a rise in imports coincided with adverse changes in the economic variables reported by AYSA during the last eight months of this investigation period. The United States determined that the rise in imports constituted a threat of serious damage without making any attempt to assess and quantify the size of the expected increase and its impact on the domestic industry. All it did was to extrapolate the present conditions into the future. Finally, it attributed the whole of the damage reported by AYSA to imports from Pakistan, ignoring completely the fact that imports from Mexico had been more substantial and had risen more sharply than those of Pakistan. As a result, it effectively attributed to Pakistan all of the damage reported by AYSA even though Pakistan's could not possibly have been its sole cause.

4.100 While Pakistan fully recognises that the ATC does not impose on the importing Member any specific method for collecting and verifying the data on the relevant economic factors; nevertheless, whatever method the Member has chosen, it must result in a demonstration that the increased quantities of imports are causing serious damage or actual threat thereof.[52] Pakistan's claim is that the method for collecting and verifying data that the United States chose to adopt in this specific case did not result in the demonstration required by Article 6.2. The panel on *United States - Blouses,* while fully recognising the United States' right to determine its methods for collecting data,[53] criticised it for having collected only inadequate data on certain economic factors. Thus, it concluded that the United States should have been able to obtain more reliable data on market shares by data from private surveys "or even directly from the fifteen or so producers in this sector".[54] It is, therefore, clear that the right to choose a method for collecting and verifying the data does not include the right to chose a method that fails to generate reliable and correct data.

---

52 WT/DS33/R, DSR 1997:I, 343, para. 7.24

53 WT/DS33/R, *supra*, footnote 52, para. 7.52.

54 WT/DS33/R, *supra*, footnote 52, paras. 7.37 and 7.51.

4.101 Pakistan believes for these reasons that it has established an unrebutted *prima facie* case that the United States based its damage determination on unreliable and unverified data, that it failed to examine the state of the allegedly "closed" mills that switched to the production of carded yarn and that the United States has, therefore, not provided the required demonstration of serious damage of the industry as it had defined it.

Arguments of the United States

4.102 The **United States** argues that it employed an appropriate and reasonable methodology for collecting and analyzing the data used to support its determination that the surge in imports from Pakistan had caused serious damage and actual threat of serious damage to the U.S. combed cotton yarn for sale industry. The United States conducted its investigation using the best information available and relied on official data to the extent possible. The United Sates relied on official U.S. Bureau of Census Statistics to obtain import and export data for the defined industry and to verify the production data supplied by AYSA. Because official data were not available for shipments, employment, wages, man-hours, capacity utilization, inventories, unfilled orders, productivity, profitability, and investment, the United States utilized AYSA data for these factors and verified them to the extent possible. The United States also relied on published data to the extent that it was available.

4.103 The United States goes on to point out that the ATC sets forth no methodology for the collection and analysis of data and affords the importing Member discretion in establishing its methodology, including relying on data furnished by the private sector. The Panel in the *United States - Wool Shirts* case specifically allowed the importing Member to collect the relevant data from relevant sources, including the private sector. The ATC only requires that the Member accompany its request for consultations with specific, relevant, and current factual information related, as closely as possible, to identifiable segments of production and to the 12-month reference period. As discussed above, the United States fully complied with these requirements. U.S. data - reflecting data for 1996, 1997 and for the first eight months of 1998 - was as up-to-date as possible. The data enabled the United States to evaluate the level of imports and the effect of the increase in imports of combed cotton yarn on the defined domestic industry, as reflected in such economic variables as output, productivity, capacity utilization, inventories, market share, exports, wages, employment, domestic prices, profits and investment.

4.104 The United States verified all data it received from the private sector to the extent possible. None of Pakistan's arguments to the contrary establish a violation of the ATC. Rather, Pakistan makes unfounded allegations and introduces new evidence outside the scope of this dispute in an effort to cast doubt on the reliability of the U.S. data. The United States also states that, contrary to Pakistan's assertions, AYSA data are not "inherently untrustworthy." The United

States verified AYSA data by comparing them with official data and by engaging in direct discussions with individual firms. Also contrary to Pakistan's insinuations, AYSA did not provide "incorrect" production data for 1997 and did not provide "false" and then "unverifiable" data for the first eight months of 1998. AYSA production data for 1996 and 1997 were fully consistent with official U.S. Bureau of the Census data. As the United States explained with respect to data for 1998, official 1998 production data were not available to the United States at the time the Market Statement was prepared. The AYSA data, current through August 1998, were the most up-to-date available at that time, and the United States assessed its accuracy based on the accuracy of other AYSA data and discussions with individual producers. In addition, contrary to Pakistan's completely false claims, the subsequently released 1998 official Census data supported rather than undermined AYSA figures. The United States discussed the consistency of the two sets of data, and pointed out that, while AYSA production data were slightly higher than Census Bureau data, the difference in each year was quite small (only two-tenths of one per cent) and the level of decline was the same for both sets of data.

4.105. The United States also responded to Pakistan's calculations on page 23 of its Second Written Submission, where Pakistan claims to have demonstrated that the AYSA partial year data was necessarily in conflict with full year Bureau of the Census data. The United States claims that its analysis shows Pakistan's computation yields a mathematically impossible result.

4.106 Contrary to assertion by Pakistan, the United States claims that the membership of AYSA fully represents the yarn for sale industry even though five of its members produce fabric in addition to sales yarn. These members produce fabric and sales yarn in separate divisions as separate profit centers and report their production data separately. The separate yarn for sale divisions of these five AYSA members are, therefore, part of the defined yarn for sale industry. Concerning Pakistan's claims that the United States failed to examine the entire industry because it relied on data furnished by AYSA, the United States points out that the membership of AYSA fully represents the yarn for sale industry and the United States verified this information to ensure that it was complete. Pakistan has been unable to advance any argument that contradicts this fact. The Panel requested an explanation for the adoption by the United States of the "best information available" standard, and in reply, the United States explains that it did not intend to imply in its first written submission that the "best information available" was a standard required by the ATC. Rather, in the absence of any specific requirement for the collection of data set out in the ATC, the United States was making the factual statement that it relied on the best and most reliable information available to it in the preparation of the Market Statement. In addition, the United States does not intend to imply that its data collection ended with whatever statistics were available. Rather, the United States verified all data it received from the private sector, to the extent possible, to ensure their accuracy and consistency with official statistics.

4.107 In sum, the U.S. Government employed an appropriate and reasonable methodology for collecting and analyzing the data and conducted its investigation using the best information available relying on official data to the extent possible. Where official data were not available, the United States used information from other sources and conducted ongoing verification of this information. Pakistan's insinuations that the data supplied by the AYSA were "false data" or that the United States failed to verify the accuracy of such data are plainly wrong. Pakistan offers no concrete evidence to support these claims; nor does Pakistan explain how the United States should have acted any differently. Pakistan merely makes and draws inferences from unsupported and inaccurate assertions.

Discussion of the Data Verification Methodology

4.108 In a question to the United States, the Panel notes the above explanations that the United States has verified the data for the Market Statement by (a) comparing them with the US official statistics prepared by the US Bureau of the Census; and (b) direct contact with producers (including vertically integrated firms). The Panel asks the United States to explain this second aspect more fully and to describe how this verification methodology (both in regulation and practice) compared with the methods used in other types of investigation of imports (e.g., in antidumping/countervailing duties/safeguards procedures).

4.109 In its response, the **United States** notes that the ATC sets forth no requirements regarding the data collected and analyzed during an investigation conducted by the importing Member. The United States recalls that Article 6.7 provides: "The Member proposing to take safeguard action shall seek consultations with the Member or Members which would be affected by such action. The request for consultations shall be accompanied by specific and relevant factual information, as up-to-date as possible, particularly in regard to: (a) the factors, referred to in paragraph 3, on which the Member invoking the action has based its determination of the existence of serious damage or actual threat thereof; and (b) the factors, referred to in paragraph 4, on the basis of which it proposes to invoke the safeguard action with respect to the Member or Members concerned. In respect of requests made under this paragraph, the information shall be related, as closely as possible, to identifiable segments of production and to the reference period set out in paragraph 8 ... .". The Panel on *United States - Wool Shirts* did not find that the ATC imposed any specific methodology for the collection and analysis of data. Instead, it underscored that "... we do not interpret the ATC so as to impose on WTO Members any method of collecting data but that it is up to each concerned Member to collect the relevant data from relevant sources, possibly including the private sector.".[55] The United States has fully complied with

[55] United States - Measures Affecting Imports of Woven Wool Shirts and Blouses *from India*, 6 January 1997, WT/DS33/R, DSR 1997:I, 343, at para. 6.4.

these requirements by providing Pakistan with a Market Statement containing specific, relevant, and current information with respect to the economic variables listed in Article 6.3 of the ATC and the attribution factors in Article 6.4. The Market Statement, reflecting data from 1996, 1997, and the first eight months of 1998 and including the most current import data through October 1998, was as up to date as possible and was related, as closely as possible, to identifiable segments of production and to the reference period set out in Article 6.8.

4.110 Commenting on the above response of the United States, **Pakistan** emphasises that it fully recognises that the ATC does not impose on the importing Member any specific method for collecting and verifying the data on the relevant economic factors and that it does not exclude the resort to private sector data. However, whatever method the Member has chosen, it must result in a demonstration that the increased quantities of imports are causing serious damage or actual threat thereof".[56] Pakistan's claim is that the method for collecting and verifying data that the United States chose to adopt in this specific case did not result in the demonstration required by Article 6.2. The panel on *United States - Blouses,* while fully recognising the United States' right to determine its methods for collecting data,[57] criticised it for having collected only inadequate data on certain economic factors. Thus, it concluded that the United States should have been able to obtain more reliable data on market shares by data from private surveys "or even directly from the fifteen or so producers in this sector".[58] It is, therefore, clear that the right to choose a method for collecting and verifying the data does not include the right to chose a method that fails to generate accurate and reliable data and that the Member may have to obtain data directly from the companies involved.

4.111 The **United States** goes on to explain its earlier statements that it has carefully confirmed the accuracy and reliability of the core data in this case. The United States used official Bureau of Census data as source data to the extent possible (e.g., import data) and to verify data provided by the AYSA. AYSA collected data from the industry on production, shipments, employment, man-hours, wages, capacity utilization, inventories, exports, unfilled orders, profits, price, and investment, aggregated the data, and provided aggregate information to the United States. The United States verified all of this data to the fullest extent possible. In addition to relying on official statistics for verification purposes, the United States engaged in direct discussions with individual firms to verify AYSA data. For instance, the United States obtained profit and investment data that were based on the results of two separate surveys conducted by AYSA of the financial performance of its members which produce combed cotton yarn for sale. The surveys were designed to obtain information about the combed cotton

[56] WT/DS33/R, *supra*, footnote 52, para. 7.24
[57] WT/DS33/R, *supra*, footnote 52, para. 7.52.
[58] WT/DS33/R, *supra*, footnote 52, paras. 7.37 and 7.51.

yarn for sale industry and included information specifically with respect to combed cotton yarn for sale. The surveys did not reflect the financial performance of firms that do not produce combed cotton yarn for sale, and reflected only those operations of member firms producing combed cotton yarn for sale.

4.112 **Pakistan** comments on the above paragraph stating that, as far as the data for the crucial period of the first eight months of 1998 were concerned, no official statistics were available that could be used for verification purposes. The AYSA data could not be verified through direct discussions with individual firms because these data had been supplied on an aggregate basis. Notwithstanding the pointed question of the Panel, the United States provided no evidence demonstrating the contrary.

4.113 The **United States** continues its explanation, stating that eight firms, representing 90 per cent of the domestic industry, had participated in both of these surveys. Each of these firms, except one, was privately owned and did not report financial data outside the company. Therefore, data on profitability and investment were collected through surveys conducted by AYSA with the understanding that results would be reported to the United States on an aggregate basis. The United States engaged in individual discussions with these eight firms to confirm that they had participated in the survey and that the aggregate figures reported by AYSA were consistent with their own profitability and investment picture. With respect to profits, the eight firms which responded to the survey reported declining profits of combed cotton yarn for sale. The results of the survey indicated that the industry's profits, as measured by operating income from sales of the combed cotton yarn as a per cent of sales, declined throughout the investigation period. Likewise, the United States verified the results of the AYSA investment survey through individual discussions with these firms with the view to assessing the degree to which investment or lack of investment affected the competitiveness of the U.S. combed cotton yarn for sale industry. Typically, the responses fell into two categories. Investment had been made in either machinery for the production of yarn, or automated materials handling and yarn packaging. In either case, the objective was to cut cost in an effort to become as competitive as possible within the global market. However, according to the survey, as verified by the United States in conversations with individual firms, because of sharply declining returns, the prospects for investment in new capacity in the industry, or even new production or handling methods to improve efficiency, were not good.

4.114 Furthermore, the United States has engaged in separate conversations with individual mills to verify AYSA-supplied data concerning the number of mills that exited the combed cotton yarn for sale industry, the number of jobs lost, and that these job losses were in the production of combed cotton yarn. The United States also engaged in direct discussions with vertically integrated fabric producers to verify the extent to which such firms purchased or sold combed cotton yarn in the open market. In Appendix I to the Market Statement, the United States noted that it "verified that less than five per cent of the integrated sector's yarn consumption was purchased from the 'for sale' market during the period covered by the investigation." The United States based this figure on a poll, conducted by AYSA, of leading manufacturers (both sales yarn and vertically integrated fabric producers), which indicated that vertically integrated fabric producers play a small role in the purchase of combed cotton yarn, estimated to be less than 5 per cent per year of the sales yarn market. The United States verified this information in individual discussions with representatives of large vertically integrated fabric producers. The United States specifically asked these producers what per cent, if any, of their combed cotton yarn requirements were met by yarn that was purchased from the "for sale market" during the period covered by the investigation. In individual discussions with the United States, these vertically integrated fabric producers confirmed that, on average, for the period covered by the investigation, they purchased less than 5 per cent per year of their combed cotton yarn requirements.

4.115 In addition to the above, prior to the TMB review of the transitional safeguard measure, the United States had engaged in additional discussions with vertically integrated fabric producers to determine what per cent of their combed cotton yarn requirements were met by purchases of yarn from the "for sale" market, and what per cent of their production was sold.[59] Based on discussions with these vertically integrated fabric producers, in addition to the information provided by the vertically integrated fabric producers prior to the TMB review, the United States determined that these mills purchase roughly two per cent of their yarn requirements from the "for sale" market and sell roughly one per cent of their output in the "for sale" market.

Comparing the ATC Verification Process with Methods in Other Agreements

4.116 In response to the question by the Panel as to how this verification process compared with the methodology used by the United States in other types of import investigations, the **United States** commented that the President had delegated the authority to implement textile and apparel agreements - including the ATC - to the interagency Committee for the Implementation of Textile Agreements ("CITA").[60] For purposes of safeguard actions taken under Article 6, the Office of Textiles and Apparel ("OTEXA"), within the U.S. Department of Commerce, conducts the investigation and produces the statement of serious damage, actual threat thereof, and attribution, and CITA reviews the statement

[59] The United States asked these mills four separate questions: during the period 1996, 1997 and the first eight months of 1998, have you 1) produced any combed cotton yarn for your own consumption; if so, how much?, 2) have you sold any combed cotton yarn; if so, how much?, 3) have you purchased any combed cotton yarn from the "for sale market"; if so, how much?, and 4) have you purchased any combed cotton yarn from foreign sources; if so, how much?

[60] Section 204 of the Agricultural Act of 1956, as amended, grants the President the authority to regulate imports of textile products. 7 U.S.C. sec. 1854. The President delegated this authority to CITA pursuant to Executive Order 11651 of March 3, 1972.

and makes the final determination of serious damage, actual threat thereof, and attribution. As discussed above, the ATC contains little procedural guidance concerning the investigations or the determinations of serious damage - other than the factors contained in Article 6.3 of the ATC. U.S. law and regulation do not impose any additional requirements.

4.117 The United States explains that antidumping and countervailing duty laws are administered by the U.S. Department of Commerce and the U.S. International Trade Commission ("USITC").[61] The USITC also has responsibility for assessing whether U.S. industries are seriously injured by imports in a global safeguard action. In contrast to transitional safeguards taken in the textile area, U.S. statute and regulation provides extensive guidance with respect to procedures, timeframes, and investigations taken with respect to antidumping and countervailing duty actions[62] and global safeguard actions.[63] With respect to verification, the Department of Commerce verifies information provided by respondents in antidumping and countervailing duty proceedings, in accordance with Article 6.7 and Annex I of the Antidumping Agreement and Article 12.6 and Annex VI of the SCM Agreement, respectively, as well as the pertinent U.S. statutory and regulatory provisions.[64] In each instance, the main purpose of the investigation is to verify information provided or to obtain further details about the information received in the questionnaire response from the responding company or government. In addition to verifying the accuracy of the submitted information, the practice of the Department of Commerce is also to verify that relevant data were not omitted from the response.[65]

[61] Less than fair value price information (used in antidumping determinations) and subsidy information (used in countervailing duty determinations) fall within the jurisdiction of the Department of Commerce. Injury determinations for both antidumping and countervailing duty purposes fall within the jurisdiction of the USITC.

[62] Subtitle IV of the Tariff Act of 1930, 19 U.S.C. sec. 1671-1677n (provides the U.S. statutory requirements for countervailing and antidumping duties). See also 19 C.F.R. Part 351 (provides the federal regulations for antidumping and countervailing duties) and 19 C.F.R. Part 207 (provides the federal regulations for injury determinations in antidumping and countervailing duty cases).

[63] Section 201-204 of the Trade Act of 1974, as amended, 19 U.S.C. sec. 2251-2254 (provides U.S. statutory requirements for safeguard actions). See also 19 C.F.R. Part 206 (provides the federal regulations for investigations relating to safeguard actions).

[64] See 19 U.S.C. sec. 1677m(i) (U.S. statutory requirement that "[t]he administrating authority shall verify all information relied upon in making ... a final determination in an investigation ...") and 19 C.F.R. sec. 351.307 (U.S. federal regulations concerning verification of information in a determination of sales at less than fair value or of a countervailable subsidy).

[65] The verification undertaken by the Department of Commerce in antidumping and countervailing duty investigations involves information relating to foreign respondents (and therefore may be less relevant to the Panel's question, which addresses verification of data provided by the relevant domestic industry). For further details regarding the verification process of the Department of Commerce in anti-dumping actions, see Commerce Anti-dumping Manual, "Verification," Chapter 13 at 2, *www.ita.doc.gov/admanual.* Following the verification, Commerce prepares a report detailing the methods, procedures, and results of the verification. 19 C.F.R. sec. 351.307(c).

4.118 In injury investigations under the antidumping, countervailing duty, and safeguard laws, the USITC may verify data submitted by representative companies in the relevant domestic industry. Although no domestic laws or regulations specifically govern the methodology for verifying such data in injury investigations, the typical USITC verification process is as follows. During the investigation, USITC prepares and sends to the relevant domestic producers questionnaires seeking the types of industry information required by the U.S. statute and the relevant WTO agreement. Responses to the questionnaires are reviewed by the USITC. As considered appropriate, USITC staff may conduct onsite verification of the information submitted by domestic producers in the replies to these questionnaires. Typically, the verification includes a review of all information submitted in the company's questionnaire response. Often, an important aspect of the verification is an examination of the allocation of costs between the product covered by the investigation and other related products produced by the company. Allocations are typically an issue since few antidumping, countervailing duty, or global safeguard investigations cover products that constitute the entire output of the U.S. producers. Unlike OTEXA, the USITC also possess subpoena powers to compel the response of information from outside sources.[66]

4.119 The United States stresses that the practices described above have been developed by the Department of Commerce and the USITC in connection with investigations in antidumping, countervailing duty, and global safeguard cases. While the practices of these two agencies differ from each other and from that of the Department of Commerce in a transitional safeguard case, what is crucial is that each practice comports with the obligations of the relevant WTO agreement and that the practice satisfactorily establishes the reliability of the data on which the decision is based. For example, where the ATC is silent, Article 6.6 of the Antidumping Agreement provides that the "authorities shall during the course of an investigation satisfy themselves as to the accuracy of the information supplied by interested parties upon which their findings are based;"[67] Annex I of the Antidumping Agreement and Annex VI of the SCM Agreement authorize "on-the-spot investigations" for purposes of verifying information provided or obtaining further details; and paragraph 3 of Annex II to the Antidumping Agreement states that "[a]ll information which is verifiable, which is appropriately submitted ... should be taken into account when determinations are made." Practices developed under these agreements accommodate these express provisions. In addition, Article 6.7 of the Antidumping Agreement and Article 12.6 of the SCM Agreement authorize, but do not require, investigations of foreign entities for verification, subject to certain limitations. The Safeguards Agreement does not address

[66] 19 U.S.C. sec. 1333; 19 C.F.R. sec. 207.8.

[67] Article 12.5 of the SCM agreement similarly provides that "... the authorities shall during the course of an investigation satisfy themselves as to the accuracy of the information supplied by interested Members or interested parties upon which their findings are based."

verification, but unlike the ATC, it provides detailed guidance with respect to the investigation procedures of the importing Member.[68] Accordingly, the practices developed under that agreement reflect that guidance.

4.120 The Panel also asked for an explanation of whether and how exporting Members are given the opportunity to present their views and supporting evidence in the US investigation procedures. The United States explained that Article 6.7 of the ATC requires that the Member proposing transitional safeguard action seek consultations with the relevant Member and accompany that request with specific, relevant, and up-to-date factual information, but that it does not set forth requirements for the collection and analysis of data. The ATC allows the importing Member to establish this methodology. Nor does the ATC (unlike non-transitional agreements) contain specific requirements for public notice and comment during the investigation. The United States fulfilled the requirements of the ATC by requesting consultations with Pakistan accompanied by the specific, relevant, and current factual information contained in the Market Statement. Although not required by the ATC, the United States also provided public notice and solicited public comments on its request for consultations with Pakistan regarding Category 301 imports of combed cotton yarn. The United States added that it believes that it would be inappropriate for the Panel, particularly in the absence of such allegations by Pakistan, to impute requirements from non-transitional WTO agreements (e.g. specific notice and comments procedures) into the text of the ATC, particularly in view of the carefully negotiated balance that this agreement struck between importing and exporting Members.

4.121 In sum, the United States explains that, regardless of the agreement under which the need to verify data arises, the objective is in all instances the same, i.e., to satisfactorily establish the reliability of the data on which the decision is based. This could be accomplished using any number of approaches. Accordingly, the question in this case should be whether there was any serious doubt concerning the reliability of the data presented rather than whether the steps taken in this case were the same as or different from the steps that might be taken by another agency, or a different component of an agency, in a different investigation involving separate facts and a different WTO agreement. In this case, the United States has engaged in a careful and thorough verification of the data it received from AYSA to ensure its completeness and accuracy. The United States has relied on official U.S. Bureau of Census statistics, where available, to assess the data provided by AYSA. The United States has also engaged in discussions with individual mills to confirm data in areas where official statistics were unavailable. Therefore, Pakistan's many unfounded and unproven assertions concerning the "unverified," "unverifiable," "untrustworthy, "inaccurate," "incorrect," or "false" AYSA data have no basis in fact and fail to undermine the ines-

---

[68] Safeguards Agreement, art. 3. There is no parallel to this provision in the ATC.

capable conclusion that the U.S. transitional safeguard measure on imports of combed cotton yarn from Pakistan is fully consistent with the ATC.

Further Comments of Pakistan

4.122 **Pakistan** points out that it is not claiming that the United States violated any rules on the collection, verification or evaluation of data. It recognises that there are no such rules. However, Pakistan claims that, by relying exclusively on unverified data supplied by the lobbying organisation that stood to benefit from the safeguard action and that had previously furnished incorrect information, the United States chose a data collection method prone to abuse by an interested party and, therefore, incapable of yielding the required demonstration. Pakistan emphasizes that it does dispute the core data on which the United States relied in making its determinations. The United States reliance on unverified data supplied by an organisation of producers standing to benefit from the safeguard is of great concern to Pakistan. It considers this to be an important issue before this Panel. The decision of the United States to respond to Pakistan's arguments by claiming that Pakistan never made them is regrettable.

4.123 With respect to the above point and in response to a Panel question, Pakistan states that it agrees with the United States that the Panel cannot examine evidence for the purpose of a reinvestigation of the market situation. However, according to the established WTO jurisprudence endorsed by the Appellate Body, the Panel must make an objective assessment in accordance with Article 11 whether the published report on the investigation contains an adequate, reasoned and reasonable explanation of how the facts in the record support the determination made. The *U.S. - Underwear* panel made clear that the task of a panel under Article 11 of the DSU comprises an examination of whether the United States "had examined all relevant facts before it (including facts which might detract from an affirmative determination ...)".[69] Pakistan is, therefore, entitled to submit facts that were available to the United States at the time of the investigation but that it failed to consider in the Market Statement. Otherwise, Pakistan would be prevented from demonstrating that the United States did not consider relevant facts detracting from an affirmative determination.

Further Comments by the United States

4.124 In this regard, the **United States** notes that Pakistan introduced a market statement produced in 1997 on combed cotton ring spun yarn (a subset of Category 301 combed cotton yarn) to suggest that the U.S. data were unreliable. Given that the Panel is limited to the evidence used by the Member in making its determination, this document is outside the scope of the Panel's review and

[69] WT/DS24/R, DSR 1997:I, 31, para. 7.13.

should not be considered. The figures contained in previous market statements are not relevant to this dispute. As the United States explained, the 1997 market statement on ring-spun cotton yarn is not an issue in this case. No safeguard measure was applied as a result of that investigation. Accordingly, it is inappropriate for Pakistan to draw conclusions about the Market Statement at issue in this proceeding from previous documents covering different time periods. Nevertheless, this document - which the United States used to consider transitional safeguard action on imports from Pakistan of combed cotton ring spun yarn - only enhances the integrity of the Market Statement. The United States ultimately decided to drop its Article 6 action after ongoing verification of the data raised questions about the data in the 1997 statement. Thus, far from suggesting that the United States used unreliable data, the circumstances surrounding the U.S. decision not to take transitional safeguard action on combed cotton ring spun yarn demonstrates the extent to which the United States used the best information available, verified the information to the extent possible and continued to monitor the industry to ensure that the information that ultimately formed the basis for the Market Statement was accurate.

4.125 The United States is also concerned that Pakistan is attempting to mislead the Panel into questioning the accuracy of production statistics supplied by AYSA by introducing 1998 data released by the U.S. Bureau of Census subsequent to the preparation of the Market Statement. These data were not available to the United States at the time it prepared the Market Statement and should not be considered. Nevertheless, contrary to Pakistan's assertions, the 1998 Census data support AYSA data. Both AYSA and Census data - which compare two different time periods - showed a sharp decline in production in 1998. The fact that the level of decline was different for the two data sets does not indicate that either is incorrect. Rather, they both confirm that the trend was down during 1998 and imply that the greatest downturn in production occurred during the first eight months. Furthermore, Pakistan's assertions regarding the accuracy of AYSA data on profitability and investment are unfounded. The United States verified the profit and investment information to the extent possible and Pakistan provides no reason to question their accuracy.

4.126 The United States also responds to Pakistan's comments regarding AYSA, stating that AYSA is not a lobbying organization formed for the purpose of securing safeguard action in this case and does not represent half of the producers of the combed cotton yarn for sale industry. The AYSA represents the interests of the entire combed cotton yarn for sale industry and has done so since 1967. Reliance on information supplied by the sole voice of the combed cotton yarn for sale industry - information which was subsequently verified - was, therefore, perfectly reasonable and appropriate.

Information on the Status of Certain Manufacturers

4.127 In questions to the **United States**, Pakistan raised a number of points regarding specific manufacturers in the U.S. yarn and textile industries. First, Pakistan submits information previously provided to the TMB by the United States concerning Avondale Mills, specifically, stating that this firm did not produce combed cotton yarn for its own consumption. Pakistan asked, if Avondale Mills is an integrated fabric producer, would this mean that it "sells" all its own manufactured combed cotton yarn production and that it purchases its requirements of combed cotton yarn, for manufacture of fabrics from the "for sale market"? The United States replies that Pakistan's question relies on the faulty assumption that Avondale Mills both produces combed cotton yarn for sale and manufactures fabric from combed cotton yarn. While one establishment of Avondale Mills' yarn division produces combed cotton yarn for sale, its fabric divisions do not use combed cotton yarn in their manufacture of fabric and, therefore, do not purchase combed cotton yarn from the market. The United States goes on to explain that the TMB document in question is completely accurate and was prepared in response to a question from the TMB by the U.S. delegation in consultation with a representative from AYSA. Because Pakistan has repeatedly called AYSA information into question throughout these proceedings, the United States - in preparing the more complete description of Avondale in response to this question - has made personal contact with representatives of Avondale and has relied on an Avondale submission that is required by the federal government (i.e., Avondale's "10-K" submission to the Securities and Exchange Commission) to reconfirm the understanding of the United States of Avondale's operations. This further inquiry fully supports the information presented to the TMB.

4.128 The United States went on to explain that Avondale Mills was organized into three principal business segments: yarns; greige (woven fabric in an unbleached, undyed state as taken from the loom) and specialty fabrics; and apparel fabrics. These three business segments were separate divisions. As the United States explained in its answers to written questions from Pakistan, "division", as it is typically used to refer to business units within a company, refers to an organizational entity that operates in a distinct business area. Typically, it is self-contained and has its own functional departments (for example, its own finance, purchasing, production, and marketing departments). Avondale's three business segments were self-contained and had their own functional departments. Avondale's yarn division produces various types of yarn at several manufacturing facilities. As reflected in the TMB document in question, one of these facilities produces yarn, chief weight of combed cotton spun, for sale. The TMB document also correctly describes Avondale's yarn segment as a separate sales yarn division with its own management and sales force, operating as an independent sales yarn company. All of this combed cotton yarn is sold on the open market.

4.129 The TMB document referred to above also states that "Avondale Mills does not produce combed cotton yarn for its internal consumption". In response, **Pakistan** asks the United States that if Avondale does not produce combed cotton yarn for its own consumption, then are Avondale's combed cotton yarn requirements for the manufacture of fabric met by the purchase of combed cotton yarn from the market? The United States replied that the answer to this question is no. Neither of Avondale's two fabric divisions have any "combed cotton yarn requirements," and, therefore, neither purchases combed cotton yarn. First, as to the greige and specialty fabric division, none of the fabrics produced by this division uses combed cotton yarn, chief weight of cotton. In fact, virtually all of Avondale's cotton fabric produced within this division is carded cotton fabric. The greige and specialty fabric division manufactures undyed, unfinished cotton and cotton-blend greige fabrics that are marketed to apparel, home furnishing and industrial products manufacturers and a variety of specialty fabrics that are marketed to recreational, industrial and military products manufacturers, including coated fabrics for awnings, tents, boat covers and life vests. Second, the apparel fabric division manufactures fabric for use in jeans, utilitywear, sportswear and other apparel, using carded cotton and carded cotton-blend yarn. That is, these cotton and cotton-blend products are produced using yarns other than combed cotton yarn, chief weight cotton spun. The apparel fabric division does not purchase combed cotton yarn. In the rare circumstance that combed cotton fabric is required, the United States has been advised by representatives of Avondale that the apparel fabric division purchases the unfinished combed cotton fabric (not combed cotton yarn) and finishes it to its customers specifications. These facts were confirmed by the United States through a conversation with Avondale representatives.

4.130 Pakistan also refers to a statement by the United States that the AYSA represents the interests of the entire combed cotton yarn for sale industry and has done so since 1967. Pakistan had found companies listed as offering cotton combed yarn for sale whose name did not appear on the list of members of AYSA and manufacturers offering cotton combed yarn for sale that are not members of AYSA. Pakistan asked, in view of these mills offering cotton combed yarn for sale (many of them integrated mills) how can the United States state categorically that AYSA represents the interest of the entire combed cotton yarn for sale industry?

4.131 In reply to this question, the **United States** provided the following information for the four companies for which Pakistan had obtained information from the On-Line Product Directory of American Textile Manufacturers Institute:

(1) *Dan River Inc.* - Dan River is a vertically integrated fabric producer that, at one time, produced woven and knit fabric. In 1996, Dan River shut down its circular knit fabric operations, and was left with excess yarn spinning capacity. Rather than idle the spinning frames, Dan River disposed of (or sold) whatever output it did not consume in its woven fabric operations through brokers.

Any production of combed cotton yarn that is sold by Dan River was part of the *de minimis* amounts of combed cotton yarn that is sold by vertically integrated fabric producers, which were captured by the United States in its investigation. The President of the company described the volume of these sales as "insignificant", i.e., less than 2 per cent of its total combed cotton yarn production. As the company is not substantially engaged in the production of yarn for sale, it is not eligible for AYSA membership.

(2) *Nisshinbo California, Inc.* - Prior to its sale to Mount Vernon Mills in 1999, Nisshinbo was a vertically integrated operation with relatively small amounts of combed cotton fabric production.

(3) *Saunders Thread Company* is a producer of combed cotton sewing thread, not yarn. Cotton thread is not included in Category 301; rather it is included in Category 200, Yarn For Retail Sale, Sewing Thread.

(4) *Titan Textiles Co., Inc.* - Titan Textiles Company imports combed cotton yarn and offers this yarn on the "for sale" market. In the United States, this firm manufactures textured polyester, nylon filament, spun rayon, and spun polyester yarns, but not combed cotton yarn.

ATMI has confirmed to the United States that the listings of Nisshinbo California Inc., Saunders Thread Company and Titan Textiles Co. Inc. in the ATMI on-line product directory as suppliers of combed cotton yarn were in error.

4.132 The United States also notes that the companies identified by Pakistan in the Cotton Council International website are not, as Pakistan claims, manufacturers of combed cotton yarn. Nor does the website from which the information was obtained represent them as such. Rather, this website is a resource designed to assist overseas buyers in locating sources of products, including yarn manufactured from U.S. raw cotton. These sources can include textile products made outside of the United States from U.S. raw cotton. As to the four entries unearthed by Pakistan from the Cotton Council International website: (1) *American Textile Export Company* (AMTEC) is a yarn export trading company for AYSA members. AMTEC has no production of any kind; (2) *Andrex Industries Corp.* is a producer of circular knit fabric. All of its yarn requirements, including cotton, are purchased from the "for sale" market; (3) *Joe Tisdale & Assoc.* is a yarn sales agent; and (4) *L.P. Muller & Co., Inc.* is a commission broker. It does not sell any combed cotton yarn; rather, it sells carded cotton yarn. In sum, the United States correctly established that AYSA is fully representative of the combed cotton yarn for sale industry. The "facts" offered by Pakistan in this question cast absolutely no doubt on the U.S. reliance on AYSA as representative of the interests of the entire combed cotton yarn for sale industry.

4.133 In its comments on the above responses of the United States, **Pakistan** sums up its views on this aspect of the case, saying that it considered that the following facts remained undisputed between the parties to this dispute:

- AYSA gave the United States government incorrect production figures in 1997. The inaccuracy contributed to a damage determination in 1997 intended to favour the membership of AYSA.
- The information on production supplied by AYSA for the period January-August 1998 was unverifiable by Census figures because it related to an eight-month period for which the Census does not collect statistics. The decision of the United States to base its damage determination on changes during eight-month periods rather than calendar year periods gave AYSA the possibility to submit, once again, false data that could not subsequently be proven incorrect by Census figures.
- AYSA incorrectly reported that three of 22 of its members "closed" and incurred "job losses" during January - August 1998, while in fact they had merely switched to the production of carded yarn.
- The United States did not verify whether the allegedly "closed" establishments that had switched to the production of carded yarn had suffered serious damage. The United States simply assumed that switching from combed to carded yarn production entails serious damage.
- The United States also did not verify any of the data on profitability and investment submitted by AYSA. In particular, it did not request data on financial performance directly from the eight firms that had participated in the surveys conducted by AYSA. The contacts with the member companies merely served to "confirm that they had participated in the survey and the aggregate figures reported by AYSA were consistent with their own profitability and investment picture".[70]
- According to the Market Statement, the United States "verified that the closing of [the three "closed"] establishments were the result of imports in discussions with the companies".[71] In fact, the establishments had not closed at all. The method of verification chosen by the United States, thus, did not reveal the truth.
- The United States domestic law does not impose on the Office of Textiles and Apparel any detailed procedural requirements for the conduct of the investigation for transitional safeguard action. The exporting country is not involved in the investigation. It is, in particular, not given any opportunity to comment on the facts collected by the Office. The Office also does not publicly seek comments on the results of its investigation before making its final determination. The

70 Para. 12 of the answers of the United States.
71 Para. 1.6(b).

Office does not possess subpoena powers to compel the supply of information from outside sources.[72]

4.134 In the view of **Pakistan**, the undisputed facts listed above demonstrate that the data supplied by AYSA, as the sole interested party involved in the investigation, were inherently untrustworthy and that this was known to the United States at the time of the investigation. They further demonstrate that, for the decisive period January-August 1998, the United States relied exclusively on the figures on production, profits, investments, plant closures and job losses that had been supplied by AYSA. Notwithstanding the fact that AYSA had previously supplied incorrect information favouring its members, the United States did not verify these data. The method chosen by the United States to verify AYSA's information on plant closures and job losses - direct telephone discussions with the "closed" companies involved - failed to reveal that the establishments had not closed at all. The domestic law of the United States does not impose any legal requirements on the Office of Textiles and Apparel and the companies or organisations involved in its investigations that are designed to ensure the accuracy and reliability of the data on which its determinations are based. The undisputed facts lead for these reasons to the inescapable conclusion that the Market Statement on which the United States based its safeguard action does not provide the demonstration required by Article 6:2 of the ATC.

3. The Arguments Concerning Plant Closures

4.135 Pakistan argues that, central to the United States' determination of serious damage, was the finding that, during the investigation period, "three of twenty-two producers of the subject yarn closed" due to the adverse impact of imports and that there was "a loss of 423 jobs" in the defined industry. Pakistan's research, however, revealed that the three producers had not been closed during the investigation period but had retooled to produce a different type of cotton yarn and that, therefore, the workers claimed to have lost their job continued to hold jobs in the same plants.

4.136 Pakistan points out that during the TMB examination the United States did not deny the fact that the three producers had not closed but had retooled to produce a different type of cotton yarn and argued that the three plants could be deemed "closed" (and hence presented as having been damaged by imports) because they were no longer part of the defined industry. This argument would be well founded if the purpose of the safeguard investigation was to ascertain whether domestic producers had to restructure in response to a rise in imports. If that were the case, producers that had to switch to alternative activities as a result of import competition could legitimately be deemed to have suffered serious damage. However, in fact, one of the main purposes of the requirement to exam-

[72] See paras. 17 and 20 of the answer of the United States.

ine the effect of the rise in imports on the state of the domestic industry is to oblige the importing Member to ascertain whether or not the industry successfully restructured in response to increased import competition. To the extent that it did, imports did not cause serious damage and there was no reason to impose a safeguard action. Articles 1.5 and 6.1 of the ATC make clear that the transitional safeguard mechanism is not to be used to hinder autonomous industrial adjustment and increased competition. If plants that have successfully adjusted to changes in their competitive environment could be deemed to have suffered serious damage, the objective of these provisions would be frustrated.

4.137 Referring to the above information, the United States considers that Pakistan makes a number of misleading allegations regarding plant closures and employment trends. The United States correctly determined that, during the period of its investigation, three establishments exited the defined industry and that, as a result, 423 production worker jobs left that industry. That two of these plants continue to operate in another capacity and in other markets is not relevant to the existence of serious damage in the defined industry. Rather, what is relevant is that the deteriorating industry conditions (i.e., dropping production, declining profitability, increasing inventories, etc.) faced by the combed cotton yarn industry at the time of the surge of imports from Pakistan directly caused these mills to exit the combed cotton yarn industry. Because of the situation they faced, they were no longer viable industry participants and were forced either to shut down entirely or to produce different products.

Producers Leaving the Industry in the 1994-98 Period

4.138 The Panel raised a question concerning whether there were producers leaving the industry in the preceding five years for restructuring or modernization, including both sales yarn firms and vertically integrated firms who manufacture yarn for their own consumption in the production of fabric. In reply, the United States explains that it did not investigate whether producers had exited the combed cotton yarn for sale industry during the previous five-year period; rather, consistent with the terms of Article 6.7 of the ATC, the United States considered evidence of plant closures during the two-year and eight-month period of its investigation of serious damage and actual threat thereof. Article 6.7 requires that information with respect to the factors in Article 6.3 be "as up to date as possible" and related as closely as possible to the 12-month reference period set out in Article 6.8. The United States considered the information on plant closures to be relevant in the context of Article 6.3, and therefore included in the Market Statement the information that three mills produced combed cotton yarn for sale which had exited the industry during the period 1996, 1997 and January-August 1997/1998.

4.139 Given the requirements of Articles 6.7 and 6.8, the United States did not examine whether additional mills had exited the combed cotton yarn business in the five years prior to the period of investigation. Nevertheless, the United States was aware that additional mills producing combed cotton yarn exited the industry in the lead up to the period of investigation. However, the United States chose to limit its analysis of firms exiting the industry to the period of investigation and, accordingly, did not consider these developments in its determination of serious damage/actual threat thereof. Furthermore, given that the U.S. investigation focused on the sales yarn industry, the United States focused on vertically integrated fabric producers only to establish that these mills purchase and sell *de minimis* amounts of combed cotton yarn. The United States did not specifically investigate whether these vertically integrated mills stopped manufacturing combed cotton yarn.

4.140 On this same topic, Pakistan states that figures for plant closures (i.e. plants exiting from combed cotton yarn manufacture) over the period of 1994-1998 were available to the United States from its own earlier market statements and the figures on combed cotton yarn production during that period from the US Census statistics. The autonomous industrial adjustment that has taken place in the United States combed cotton yarn for sale industry during 1994-1998 is reflected in the figures for the number of combed cotton yarn for sale plants: 1994 (32); 1995 (26); 1996 (22); 1997 (21); and 1998 (19). For these same years, combed cotton yarn for sale production in 1,000 kg was: 1994 (122,785); 1995 (135,985); 1996 (142,346); 1997 (144,401); and 1998 (136,617).

4.141 A comparison of the figures in the above tables indicates that: (a) there were producers leaving the combed yarn industry before 1996, at that time imports from Pakistan were zero (up to 1994) or nominal (in 1995); (b) many of the exiting plants restructured and modernised; (c) the number of plants exiting from combed yarn is meaningless as far as production of yarn is concerned; and (d) production can increase while the number of plants is decreasing for several reasons. These reasons include: (i) through an autonomous industrial adjustment process, different plants are finding different niches for themselves; (ii) some plants are increasing their combed yarn capacity; (iii) some plants switch over to other products like carded, heather dyed, and also from cotton to man-made fibres like polyester or blends; (iv) the same machinery can produce polyester or polyester cotton blend; and (v) some plants are becoming integrated plants through mergers and acquisitions or by adding fabric to their production. All the above phenomena are part of the process of continuous autonomous industrial adjustment referred to in Article 1.5 of ATC. It is worth noting in this context that the total "for sale yarn" (combed carded, heather dyed etc.) showed a growth from 913.45 mkg in 1997 to 975.94 mkg in 1998 (US Census Bureau).

4.142 In commenting on the figures set out above, the United States argues that Pakistan attempts to discredit the U.S. finding of serious damage by introducing tables that purport to show that the events in January-August 1998 in the combed cotton yarn for sale industry were merely part of "continuous autonomous industrial adjustment." These figures reveal that, prior to 1998, the combed cotton yarn for sale industry was engaged in a process of "autonomous adjustment" with some establishments leaving the industry and the remaining establishments becoming more efficient. However, these figures show that the situation changed dramatically in 1998. The number of mills exiting the industry reversed the earlier downward trend, doubling in 1998. And, for the first time since 1994, production decreased, nearly to the 1995 level. In 1998, something significant happened to this industry. As reflected in the facts of this case, something is obvious: the dramatic 91 per cent surge in Category 301 imports during the first eight months of that year. In short, the two concepts - "serious damage" and "continuous autonomous industrial adjustment" - are not, as Pakistan suggests, mutually exclusive. An industry may suffer serious damage or actual threat of serious damage at the same time that it is in the process of readjusting or retooling. The ATC explicitly recognizes this fact by providing a transitional safeguard mechanism during the ten-year restructuring period given to the textiles and clothing sector. Far from being incompatible with continuous autonomous adjustment, the Article 6 safeguard is an essential element in this restructuring process, giving Members the ability to facilitate adjustment in industries seriously damaged or threatened with serious damage by increased imports.

4.143 Pakistan stresses that its argument in respect of the plant closures is straightforward and simple: if a mill switches to the production of a new product and thrives in this new activity, it has engaged in successful autonomous industrial adjustment. In this situation no damage occurred because the plant's value has not declined and the workers have not lost their jobs. This demonstrates that "exiting" a narrowly defined industry is not equivalent to incurring serious damage. The United States could, therefore, not simply assume that the so-called "closed" plants had incurred damage. It had to examine whether the change from combed to carded yarn did, in fact, entail damage. The United States did not conduct such an examination because it had been misinformed by AYSA that the plants no longer existed. Consequently, it failed to demonstrate that the "closed" plants had suffered serious damage. That is the only point the Panel needs to address. How expensive it is to switch from combed to cotton yarn production and how much discretion Members have in determining the seriousness of the damage incurred are issues that need not be decided by this Panel.

4.144 The United States strongly rejects Pakistan's contention that "retooling" (paragraphs 4.135 and 4.136) should somehow mitigate the serious damage done to the industry by the surge in imports and that an Article 6 transitional safeguard measure is inappropriate if an industry is able to successfully restructure in response to an import surge or if an employee in a failing mill is able to find a job in another industry. Restructuring does not require a situation of serious damage. Rather, it is part of the normal evolution of an industry. The case before the Panel is one of forced restructuring which occurred as the direct result of serious damage to the industry caused by a surge in imports. The fact that some mills went on to restructure and retool in no way detracts from the serious damage facing the combed cotton yarn industry when the United States issued its Market Statement in December 1998. These mills and their employees - although lucky to find a new home in another industry - had no choice but to abandon the combed cotton yarn industry.

4.145 The United States considers the evidence of three mills exiting the combed cotton yarn for sale industry as one of the many factors examined in the damage investigation. Evidence of mills leaving the industry may also point to "continuous autonomous industrial adjustment" referred to in Article 1.5 of the ATC. However, "serious damage" and "continuous autonomous industrial adjustment" are not, as Pakistan suggests, mutually exclusive. An industry may suffer serious damage or actual threat of serious damage at the same time that it is readjusting or retooling. The ATC explicitly recognizes this fact by providing a transitional safeguard mechanism during the ten-year restructuring period given to the textiles and clothing sector. Far from being incompatible with continuous autonomous adjustment, as Pakistan suggests, the Article 6 safeguard is an essential element in this restructuring process. Article 6 gives industries seriously damaged by increased imports the ability to adjust.

4.146 The United States further argues that Pakistan's claim that "serious damage" cannot be found if there was any possibility that individual establishments in an industry could have "retooled" and become participants in another industry is wrong and Pakistan's claim confuses the question of the existence or threat of serious damage with the question of the response to that damage or threat. Pakistan's claim assumes that a single factor - which does not even appear in Article 6.3 - can alone preclude a finding of serious damage. It strains reason to suggest that a factor that is not even included among those enumerated in the ATC could alone preclude a finding of serious damage. Contrary to Pakistan's suggestion, the United States did not base its determination of serious damage and actual threat thereof solely on the fact that three mills and their employees exited the combed cotton yarn industry. While important, the data on employees and firms exiting the defined industry constitute one of the many factors that the United States examined. As discussed above, the United States based its determination on a wide range of additional factors, including production, shipments, exports, capacity utilization, inventories, unfilled orders, wages, productivity, profits, investment, market share, import share, prices, and the apparent domestic market.

4.147 In sum, in the view of the United States, these factors, taken alone or together, revealed a domestic industry in peril - with declining production and shipments, deteriorating financial performance, rising inventories and falling unfilled orders, dwindling market share, contracting exports, and stagnating investment. Based on careful consideration of all these factors - not just on the number of employees and firms exiting the industry - the United States concluded that the 283.2 per cent surge in imports from Pakistan had caused serious damage and actual threat of serious damage to the domestic combed cotton yarn for sale industry.

Technical Implication in Switch between Combed and Carded Yarn

4.148 The Panel asked, how difficult (technically or financially) is it to switch a plant producing combed cotton yarn into that producing carded cotton yarn? What measures (e.g. investments, replacement of machines, training of employees) are necessary to successfully convert a plant that produces combed cotton yarn into a plant that produces carded cotton yarn? In response, the **United States** explained that the combing process relies on high grades of cotton, requires specialized machinery, and produces a product which is intended for specified, distinct market niches (i.e., higher quality). Fairchilds' Dictionary of Textiles defines "combing" as a step that is subsequent to the carding process in yarn manufacture. In the cotton spinning system, "combing" is used to produce finer, smoother cotton yarns than merely carding. The combing process physically separates the long, choice, desirable fibres from knots, impurities and shorter, weaker fibres in the cotton before it is spun. As a result of the combing process, the combed cotton yarn produced is finer, cleaner, more lustrous, and stronger than carded cotton yarns. By contrast, carded yarn contains a wider range of fibre lengths and, as a result, are not as uniform or as strong as combed yarns. Only better grades of cotton may be combed. Purchases of these better grades of cotton are contracted for, usually in advance of the new harvest for these fibres, at premium prices, 15 per cent (or more) above prices for cotton grades that are used for carding. The domestic market in the United States for carded cotton yarn is roughly five times larger than the domestic market for combed cotton yarns. Carded cotton yarns are generally used in coarser, heavier-weight fabrics (such as denim, canvas, osnaburg, blanketing and heavy knitwear such as sweaters, tube socks, or fleece). Combed cotton yarns are generally used in thinner, lighter-weight, higher quality fabrics (such as fine gauge jersey knits, broadcloth, percale or lawn/batiste).

4.149 The United States considers that Pakistan overstates the ease with which a plant can convert production from combed cotton yarn to carded cotton yarn. Pakistan fails to take into account the amortization cost of idling equipment, lost plant and equipment facility, and marketing cost required to establish a new customer base. Because of the financial risk involved, such conversions are generally not feasible without a substantial re-engineering of the facility. Specifically, conversion of a plant from the production of combed cotton yarn to the production of carded cotton yarn would engender the following serious financial and technical obstacles: (I) the plant would have incurred higher raw material costs for premium grade cotton, contracted in advance of the new harvest for these fibres, at the same time as the output of the plant was reduced in value; (2) the plant would bear the amortization and opportunity costs of idling of expensive additional equipment required for combing operations (in addition, fixed costs for building, air conditioning, warehouse, office space, and auxiliary service equipment would continue to accrue); (3) in the absence of the combing operations, more of the cotton fibre would be available to be spun. Since the installed spindles are "balanced" (that is, from the opening of raw cotton fibre to the packing of the spun yarn) for the smaller quantity of raw materials that would result from a combing process, the plant would need to either install new spindle capacity to pick up the additional cotton fibre, or idle some of the preparatory machinery, increasing costs in either circumstance; (4) the plant may require new construction in order to maintain operating efficiencies; (5) idled equipment would result in the elimination of production worker jobs; and (6) finally, the plant would need to invest in research and marketing efforts to develop a new customer base in a larger market than combed cotton yarn, subject to greater competitive pressures.

4.150 The conversion from combed to carded yarn offers no assurance of success in the carded yarn market. As the United States noted in its first written submission, one of the three establishments producing combed cotton yarn during the period covered by the U.S. investigation into serious damage and actual threat thereof, China Grove Textiles, attempted the conversion of a plant from combed cotton yarn to carded cotton yarn. The plant was not competitive in the carded yarn market and was closed. The experience of China Grove Textiles exemplifies the point that the attempted conversion from a combed yarn mill to a carded yarn mill is a complicated, expensive and uncertain endeavour, not undertaken lightly or routinely.

4.151 On this question, it was the view of **Pakistan** that, essentially, all spun yarns are carded yarns; combed yarns are a sub-category of carded yarns, that is, carded yarns which have also been combed. For the production of carded yarn, the combing process is by-passed and card sliver goes directly to drawing. There is no re-tooling involved. Most spinning plants produce both carded and combed yarns. In other words, a part of the production goes through combing to produce "combed yarn" and another part does not go through combing and produces "carded yarn". It often happens in the normal course of trade that a mill shuts down all or part of its combers in response to changes in demand. When combers are not in use, their capital cost has to be absorbed. For older mills the capital cost of combers is very small and, therefore, a minor factor in deciding the product mix. For example, the Dixie, Tarboro plant, which was sold to the Pillowtex Corporation, was a very old plant. For this plant the "consumer preference" for carded yarn (the consumer being its new owner) would be a more important factor than the capital costs of idling of old combers whose value had already been written down. For newer plants the capital cost of idling combers may be more important. However, newer plants are efficient and produce good quality. No plant less than 5 to 10 years old has been reported to have exited from combed yarn manufacture. According to Pakistan's research, all the plants claimed to have "closed" or existed from manufacture of combed yarn" were very old plants (more than 30 years old). There are no measures (investment, replacement of machinery, training of employees) required to convert a plant that produces combed cotton yarn into a plant that produces carded cotton yarn or to convert it back into producing combed cotton yarn.

D. *Demonstrating the Causal Link Between Imports and Serious Damage*

4.152 **Pakistan** notes that Article 6.2 of the ATC requires the importing Member to demonstrate that there is a causal connection between the rise in imports and the damage suffered by the domestic industry and that the damage caused is serious. As explained in the recent panel report on *Argentina - Footwear Safeguard*, a proper causation analysis consists of an analysis of the relationship between the trend in imports and the trends in the economic variables affecting the state of the domestic industry, such as output, market share, etc. A causal connection between imports and damage can be assumed if the rise in imports coincides with changes in economic variables. This means that, as a rule, the period during which trends are observed must be sufficiently long to permit the importing Member to convincingly demonstrate that the rise in imports was the cause of adverse changes in economic variables and the damage caused was more than temporary and, hence, serious. In the case before the Panel, the United States determined causality on the basis of unfavourable developments that emerged during the first eight months of 1998. Pakistan requests the Panel to find that this period was too short to permit a proper analysis of trends and that, given the absence of any other supporting evidence, the United States has, therefore, not demonstrated causality.

4.153 Pakistan also points out that a significant amount of restructuring has taken place in the United States combed cotton yarn for sale industry between 1994 and 1998: while the number of plants steadily declined from 32 to 19, production rose from 122 to 136 million kg. Against this background, the United States' claim that the adverse changes in all economic variables affecting the defined industry were attributable to a rise in imports is totally unconvincing. In all likelihood, the changes were in large part a reflection of the process of autonomous industrial adjustment that took place during the 1994-1998 period. This factor, detracting from an affirmative determination of causality, should have been examined and taken into account.

4.154 The **United States** considers that it clearly demonstrated causation, even under the non-ATC framework Pakistan references. The United States examined the relationship between an upward trend in imports and negative trends in economic variables and reasonably concluded, based on this analysis, that the surge in imports of Category 301 combed cotton yarn caused serious damage to the domestic industry. As set forth conclusively in the Market Statement, the United States established that imports from Pakistan were surging at the same time that conditions in the industry were deteriorating and that other factors were not a cause.

4.155 The United States further considers that it has satisfied ATC requirements to provide specific, relevant factual information that is as up-to-date as possible. Pakistan criticizes the U.S. determination claiming that the eight-month time period used by the United States to establish serious damage was too short. Pakistan apparently assumes that, because the United States presented the most current data in an eight-month format, the United States somehow limited its inquiry to eight months. Pakistan is wrong. The Market Statement reflected comprehensive data for two years and eight months - from January 1, 1996 through August 1998, and included import data through October 1998. At the time of the U.S. request for consultations, these data constituted the most up-to-date data available, which for imports were current through October 1998 and for the other variables were current through August 1998. These data revealed that, during the early part of the period under investigation, many industry indicators were relatively flat but others revealed a worrisome trend. Conditions during 1998 - at which time global imports surged 91.3 per cent and imports from Pakistan surged 283.2 per cent - validated early indications of industry distress.

4.156 The United States noted that Article 6.2 of the ATC requires the Member invoking a transitional safeguard to demonstrate that the serious damage or actual threat of serious damage is caused by the increase in imports and not by other causes, such as technological changes or changes in consumer preference. The United States did so, observing that "the market for these yarns has remained constant" during the investigation period, demonstrating that "there has been no change in consumer preference" that could account for the serious damage. The Market Statement also notes that "there has not been any significant new technological changes in the defined industry" during the investigation period. Pakistan makes no effort to challenge the U.S. demonstration that increased Category 301 imports, not other factors, caused damage to the defined domestic industry. Rather, Pakistan claims that causality cannot be established unless the Member undertakes an examination of "the relationship between an upward trend in imports and negative trends in economic variables," without elaborating on how the U.S. failed to do so. Pakistan disregards the Market Statement's clear showing that imports were surging as the economic factors listed in Article 6.3 were deteriorating and has made no attempt to rebut this showing. Similarly, Pakistan did not renew its contention made in its first submission related to causation, namely, that the time period considered by the U.S. was too short to establish causation.

E. Attribution of Serious Damage, or Actual Threat Thereof (Article 6.4 of the ATC)

Article 6.4 of the ATC: " Any measure invoked pursuant to the provisions of this Article shall be applied on a Member-by-Member basis. The Member or Members to whom serious damage, or actual threat thereof, referred to in paragraphs 2 and 3, is attributed, shall be determined on the basis of a sharp and substantial increase in imports, actual or imminent, from such a Member or Members individually, and on the basis of the level of imports as compared with imports from other sources, market share, and import and domestic prices at a comparable stage of commercial transaction; none of these factors, either alone or combined with other factors, can necessarily give decisive guidance. Such safe-*

guard measure shall not be applied to the exports of any Member whose exports of the particular product are already under restraint under this Agreement.".

*Such an imminent increase shall be a measurable one and shall not be determined to exist on the basis of allegation, conjecture or mere possibility arising, for example, from the existence of production capacity in the exporting Members.

1. The Attribution of Serious Damage, or Actual Threat Thereof, to Pakistan

4.157 The **United States** argues that its attribution of serious damage or actual threat of serious damage to a sharp and substantial surge in Category 301 imports from Pakistan was fully consistent with the requirements of Article 6.4 of the ATC - which authorizes the imposition of a transitional safeguard on a Member-by-Member basis.

4.158 For the January-August 1997 and January-August 1998 periods, Pakistan's Category 301 imports were surging by 283.2 per cent compared to 73 per cent from other sources; Pakistan's share of domestic production quadrupled and Pakistan's imports as a percentage of total imports doubled. Moreover, prices of Category 301 imports from Pakistan, in comparison with the rest of the world, were substantially lower - 26.2 per cent below the average U.S. price and 20 per cent below the average world price. For a specific subset of Category 301 (where imports from Pakistan were concentrated), imports from Pakistan entered the United States at a value of 28.3 per cent below the average U.S. price and 12.6 per cent below the average world price.

4.159 In the view of the United States, Pakistan does not dispute that, during January-August 1998, the magnitude of its 283.2 per cent surge was greater than any of the leading suppliers to the U.S. market or that its prices (26.2 per cent lower than the average U.S. price and 20 per cent lower than the average world price of imports) were substantially less than any of the leading suppliers to the U.S. market. Instead, Pakistan asks the Panel to strike down the U.S. attribution analysis because the United States did not comply with obligations that the ATC does not impose.

2. The Question of the Need for a Comparative Assessment of Imports from Mexico

4.160 **Pakistan** notes that the panel in *United States - Underwear from Costa Rica* clarified an important point: Article 6.4 of the ATC requires the importing Member to attribute serious damage to the exports of the Member subject to the action on the basis of a "comparative assessment" of the imports from different sources and their respective effects. The United States, however, attributed serious damage and actual threat thereof to rising imports from Pakistan without comparing those imports and their effects with imports from Mexico. It, therefore, did not take into account that the rise in imports from Mexico had been sharper and more substantial than the rise in imports from Pakistan. Just as in the underwear case, the United States, thus, failed to conduct the comparative assessment required by Article 6.4 of the ATC.

4.161 In this regard, the **United States** claims that Pakistan neither contests the figures nor establishes a violation of Article 6.4 of the ATC. Instead, Pakistan attempts to obfuscate the clear showing of attribution by asserting - without any basis - that Article 6.4 required the United States to undertake a specific comparative analysis between Pakistan and Mexico. Pakistan's suggestion that the United States was required to conduct a specific assessment of another Member's exports has no support in the ATC. Article 6 does not impose such a requirement; rather, Article 6 provides that import levels and trends are one of the several factors to be analyzed. The ATC specifically authorizes Member-by-Member safeguard action based on a sharp and substantial increase in imports from that Member individually and an analysis of imports from other sources generally, as well as market share and price. As the ATC states, no one factor in the attribution analysis "either alone or combined with other factors, can necessarily give decisive guidance".

4.162 Contrary to Pakistan's assertion, the United States argues that it did carefully consider the increase in imports from other sources as a factor in its Article 6.4 attribution analysis. The Market Statement clearly reflects that the U.S. analysis accounted for the increase in imports from its Free Trade Agreement (FTA) partners. The United States concluded that - even though imports from its FTA partners were also increasing - serious damage or actual threat of serious damage was attributable to the 283.2 per cent surge in imports from Pakistan. The Market Statement supports the transitional safeguard related to Category 301 imports from Pakistan, and specific information regarding Mexico was not required. The ATC does not require the Market Statement to include a separate analysis of each exporting Member or of all principal suppliers to the market. Article 6.4 only requires a consideration of the factors enumerated therein, and Article 6.7 requires this information to be as up-to-date as possible.

4.163 In response to a question from the Panel, the United States comments that Article 6.4 of the ATC gives an importing Member the discretion to take a transitional safeguard measure against an exporting Member to whom serious damage is attributable, but simultaneously not to take such measure against another exporting Member whose exports are contributing to the same serious damage. The ATC contemplates that Members will establish transitional safeguard actions only on those Members to whom the safeguard action can be attributed under the strict terms of Article 6.4 and not on all Members whose "exports are contributing to the same serious damage".

4.164 The view of **Pakistan** on this question is that, according to first sentence of Article 6.4 of the ATC, transitional safeguard measures "shall be applied on a Member-by-Member basis". The term "Member-by-Member" needs to be interpreted in its context. Part of its context is Article 4.1, according to which the restrictions applied under Article 6 shall be administered by the exporting Members. The requirement to apply the restrictions on a Member-by-Member basis thus means that the Member invoking Article 6 may not impose a global quota or a quota applicable to imports from several Members because the exporting Members would in that case not be able to administer the restrictions. The Member-by-Member application of restrictions thus means that the restrictions must be country-specific. Another part of the context is the second sentence of Article 6.4, according to which serious damage shall be attributed to Members individually on the basis of a sharp and substantial increase in imports. The Member invoking Article 6 may, therefore, not impose a country-specific restriction on imports from all Members. The restrictions must be applied exclusively on the imports from those Members whose exports increased sharply and substantially. Moreover, the third sentence of Article 6.4 prohibits the application of restrictions to Members already under restraint. This context makes clear that the requirement to impose the restrictions on a "Member-by-Member" basis does not mean that the country-specific restrictions must be imposed on a most-favoured-nation basis.

4.165 Pakistan also considers that, according to Article 1.6 of the ATC, the rights of the exporting Members under Articles I and XIII of the GATT are affected by the ATC only to the extent that the ATC provides otherwise. Nothing in the term "Member-by-Member" and in the context in which it appears, however, implies that an individual exporting Member to whom serious damage is attributable in accordance with the second sentence of Article 6.4 can be exempted from the application of the measure. Pakistan, therefore, disagrees with the United States' claim that the requirement to impose restrictions on a "Member-by-Member" basis constitutes a license to arbitrarily exempt a particular exporting country to which serious damage must be attributed from the application of the transitional safeguard.

4.166 In response to a question from the Panel asking how the United States determined that imports from other sources did not "contribute in a material way" to the serious damage or actual threat thereof found to exist under Article 6.2, the **United States** points out that "contribution" is not the same issue as "attribution". In contrast to Article 6.2 of the ATC, Article 6.4 is not framed in terms of cause or contributing to the serious damage. In the present case, each of the 29 sources listed in Table V of the United States' Market Statement contributed to some greater or lesser degree to the serious damage or actual threat thereof. Article 6.4 is designed to determine to which of the Member or Members - whose imports are a part of the total increase of imports causing serious damage - to assign this serious damage. Article 6.4 defines what must be considered in making this determination. Any requirement that an importing Member go beyond these requirements would be inconsistent with the carefully negotiated balance of the ATC. In this case, the United States carefully considered all these factors - including the increase in imports from other sources - in its Article 6.4 attribution analysis. The United States concluded that - even though imports from other sources were also increasing - serious damage or actual threat of serious damage was attributable to the 283.2 per cent surge in imports from Pakistan. Pakistan's sharp and substantial increase in imports, together with the fact that its imports were priced so much lower than the average world price, made attribution to Pakistan appropriate under the terms of the ATC.

4.167 **Pakistan** addressed a Panel question, "What precautions, if any, should be taken under the ATC in order to assure a transparent and equitable attribution of 'serious damage' or 'actual threat thereof' to a Member or Members?", stating that Article 6.4 of the ATC requires that the attribution of serious damage to individual Members must be made on the basis of "a sharp and substantial increase in imports" and on the basis of "the level of imports compared with imports from other sources, market share and import and domestic prices". The panel on *United States - Underwear from Costa Rica* concluded from this that Article 6.4 requires a "comparative assessment" of the imports from different sources and their respective effects.[73] The importing Member is, therefore, required to assess individually and compare all potential sources of serious damage. Pakistan submits that this follows not only from the terms "compared" and "individually" in Article 6.4 but also from the nature of the attribution determination. To attribute damage to a WTO Member means to ascribe the cause of the damage to the imports from that Member. The attribution thus requires a causation analysis. In any proper causation analysis, all factors relevant to the determination of the cause must be taken into account, including the factors that might detract from an affirmative determination. In the present case, the United States was, therefore, required to determine whether imports from sources other than Pakistan were the cause of the alleged damage. Since Mexico and Pakistan are the two largest suppliers to the United States' market, the attribution to Pakistan could not logically be made without a comparison of imports from these two sources.

4.168 In Pakistan's view, the import statistics annexed to the United States' Market Statement do not indicate the changes in the levels of imports from Mexico but only the total of all imports of combed cotton yarn from countries with which the United States has concluded free trade agreements, that is Canada, Mexico and Israel.[74] The Market Statement, thus, does not indicate that the United States considered the sharp and substantial increase in imports from Mexico as a potential alternative cause in its attribution determination. The United States, thus, failed to take into account a relevant factor detracting from an affirmative determination. Therefore, the United States failed to attribute the alleged damage to Pakistan in a manner consistent with Article 6.4 of the ATC.

[73] *United States - Restrictions on Cotton and Man-made Fibre Underwear,* WT/DS24/R, DSR 1997:I, 31, para. 7.49.

[74] U.S. Market Statement, Table V.

4.169 In summing up its arguments, Pakistan submits that the United States cannot reasonably claim that the facts on the record justified the attribution to Pakistan rather than Mexico if the record does not give any figures on imports from Mexico. As the Panel on *United States - Blouses* stated, it is the public record that must indicate that all relevant factors were considered.[75] It is not sufficient to submit those facts subsequently to the Panel. The plain fact remains that the United States did not conduct the source-specific or Member-by-Member analysis required by Article 6.4. Pakistan submitted statistics on the imports from Pakistan and Mexico in its first submission that have remained undisputed by the United States. These statistics clearly demonstrate that the rise in imports from Mexico had been sharper and more substantial than the rise in imports from Pakistan and that the exclusive attribution of serious damage to imports from Pakistan was, therefore, not justified. What happened was that the United States attributed the whole of the alleged damage to Pakistan, while import statistics clearly showed that there was another much more important potential source of that damage. This is plainly unfair and is plainly not what Article 6.4 permits. The Panel on *United States - Underwear* found that the United States could not attribute serious damage to Costa Rica and leave its market wide open to imports from five other countries.[76] It also found that "the fact that the US underwear industry was able to accept and withstand such a huge inroad of products from five other exporting Members suggests that there was no serious damage to the industry in the first place".[77] In the present case, the Panel should similarly find that the United States could not attribute the whole of the serious damage to Pakistan and leave its market open to a much more important supplier of combed cotton yarn. It should also find that the fact that the United States combed cotton yarn industry was able to withstand the sharper and more substantial rise in imports from Mexico suggests that there was no serious damage in the first place.

4.170 In response to a further Panel question, Pakistan expresses the view that the question of whether the United States was entitled to exempt Mexico from the application of the safeguard under Article XXIV is distinct from the question of whether the United States was required to compare the imports from Mexico with those from Pakistan in order to properly attribute the alleged damage to imports from Pakistan. Pakistan decided not to raise the exemption of Mexico from the safeguard action as an issue because this would have required the Panel to examine the relationship between the ATC and Article XXIV of the GATT and, depending on its conclusions on this issue, the applicability of Article XXIV to discriminatory safeguard actions. According to the ruling of the Appellate Body in the *Turkey - Textiles* case, an invocation of Article XXIV of the GATT by the defendant requires the panel to examine the consistency of the regional trade

75 WT/DS33/R, *supra*, footnote 52, paras. 7.28,7.50 and 7.52
76 WT/DS24/R, *supra*, footnote 44, para. 7.51.
77 WT/DS24/R, *supra*, footnote 44, footnote 24.

agreement with that provision.[78] Pakistan feared that, if these issues formed part of the present Panel proceeding, substantially more time would be required to resolve the dispute.

The Import Data for Mexico

4.171 The Panel invited the United States to provide the data for combed cotton yarn imported from Mexico equivalent to those for imports from Pakistan provided in each of the Tables of the 1998 Market Statement. In response, the United States supplied five tables as set out and explained hereunder. As an introductory comment, the **United States** recalls that Article 6.4 of the ATC does not require an importing Member to conduct a separate analysis of each exporting Member or of all principal suppliers to the market. Rather, Article 6.4 required an importing Member to base attribution on a sharp and substantial increase in imports from the exporting Member and on the basis of the level of imports as compared with imports from other sources, market share, and import and domestic price at a comparable stage of the commercial transaction. As reflected in the Market Statement, the United States carefully considered all such factors in making its attribution to Pakistan. Furthermore, as the United States had discussed in its second written submission, the Market Statement was prepared to support a transitional safeguard action on Category 301 imports from Pakistan. Because Article 6.4 did not require separate and specific information regarding other individual suppliers, the United States did not include a separate analysis of Mexico or any other supplier. However, because Mexico does not appear as a separate heading, this does not mean that the United States did not consider data related to Mexico. As the tables below reveal, the data on Mexico reinforces the U.S. determination to attribute serious damage and actual threat of serious damage to a sharp and substantial increase in Category 301 exports from Pakistan.

4.172 Table I, reprinted from the Market Statement, provides the core economic data regarding the variables listed in Article 6.3 of the ATC and other factors that the United States considers relevant and material to analyze during the two-year and eight-month investigation period. This table demonstrates that during the early part of the period of investigation, many industry indicators were relatively flat, but others (such as imports, inventories, and unfilled orders) revealed a worrisome trend and signaled industry distress. Furthermore, it is clear from the table that the conditions took a dramatic turn for the worse during the January-August 1998 period, at which time global imports surged 91 per cent and imports from Pakistan surged 283.2 per cent.

---

78 WT/DS90/AB/R, DSR 1999:IV, 1763, para. 108.

TABLE I

Economic Data[1] for the Industry Producing Yarn for Sale, Chief Weight Combed Cotton Spun Category 301

	1996	1997	January - August 1997	January - August 1998	Per cent Change 1996/1997	Per cent Change Jan. - Aug. 1997/1998
Total Shipments (1,000 kg.)	142,628	141,984	99,818	85,644	-0.4	-14.2
Production (1,000 kg.)	142,346	144,664	98,371	88,337	1.6	-10.2
Imports (1,000 kg.)	19,045	21,347	10,767	20,595	12.1	91.3
Exports (1,000 kg.)	14,014	14,409	10,690	7,168	2.8	-32.9
Apparent Domestic Market (1,000 kg.)[2]	147,659	148,922	99,895	99,071	0.8	-0.8
I/P (per cent)	13.4	14.8	10.9	23.3	n/a	n/a
Domestic Market Share (per cent)[3]	87.1	85.7	89.2	79.2	n/a	n/a
Employment (production workers)	5,258	5,175	5,175	4,835	-1.6	-6.6
Wages ($ per hour)	8.34	8.67	8.67	9.02	4.0	4.0
Man-hours (1,000 hours)	10,831	10,971	7,425	6,937	1.2	-6.6
Capacity Utilization (per cent)	86.3	82.7	84.3	75.7	n/a	n/a
Inventories, end of period (1,000 kg.)	6,120	8,800	4,673	11,493	43.8	145.9
Unfilled Orders, end of period (1,000 kg.)	64,268	49,628	48,865	41,155	-22.8	-15.8
Productivity (output per man-hour)	13.14	13.19	13.26	12.73	0.4	-4.0
Profits (ratio of operating income to net sales)	4.0	3.5	3.9	2.1	-12.5	-46.2

[1] Data for shipments, production, employment, wages, man-hours, capacity utilization, inventories, unfilled orders, and profits supplied by AYSA. Data supplied by AYSA is based on its members which fully represent the output of the defined industry.

[2] Equal to shipments - exports + imports.

[3] Equal to (shipments - exports)/(shipments - exports + imports).

4.173 Table II compares prices between the United States, Pakistan, and Mexico during January-August 1998 for full Category 301 imports and for those specific yarn products where Category 301 imports are concentrated. The data reveals that Pakistan's prices were significantly lower than those of Mexico. As displayed below, for full Category 301, the price of imports from Mexico ($3.96 per kilogram) was 9.1 per cent higher than the price of imports from Pakistan ($3.63 per kilogram). In the specific product classifications where Category 301 imports are concentrated (representing 54 per cent of Category 301 imports from Pakistan and 77 per cent of Category 301 imports from Mexico), the price of imports from Mexico ($3.96 per kilogram) was 16.8 per cent higher than the price of imports from Pakistan ($3.39 per kilogram). In an industry where profit margins are determined by pennies, the difference in price between imports from Pakistan and Mexico was extremely significant.

TABLE II

Average U.S. Producers' Prices and Average Landed Duty-Paid Value of Imports Yarn for Sale, Chief Weight Combed Cotton Spun Category 301

	January-August 1998 Unit Value ($ per Kilogram)	% Above or Below Average U.S. Producers' Price
Category 301[1]		
Average U.S. Producers' Price	$4.92	
World	$4.54	-7.8
Pakistan	$3.63	-26.2
Mexico	$3.96	-19.5
HTSUSAS WHICH INCLUDE YARNS OF COUNTS 18-38 SINGLES[2]		
Average U.S. Producers' Price	$4.73	
World	$3.88	-18.0
Pakistan	$3.39	-28.3
Mexico	$3.96	-16.3

[1] The U.S. producers' price for full Category 301. The U.S. producers' price represents the average price for U.S. produced subject yarn, and was obtained in consultation with firms in the defined industry. The import price represents the duty paid landed value for Category 301 computed from U.S. import data.

[2] The U.S. price represents the average price for 18 to 38 singles ring spun combed wholly cotton yarns computed from American Textiles International published data. Import prices represent the average landed duty-paid values computed from HTSUSA numbers 5205.22.0020, 5205.23.0020 and 5205.24.0020. The imports entering under these HTSUSA numbers are wholly cotton, ring spun combed cotton singles yarn with yarn counts ranging from 8 to 47 cotton count (14 to 80 metric number). The bulk of the imports in these HTSUSA numbers are of 18 to 38 cotton counts and represent 46 per cent of total Category 301 imports, 54 per cent of Pakistan's imports of Category 301, and 77 per cent of Mexico's imports of Category 301.

4.174 Table III compares the per cent change in imports during the critical January-August 1997 and January-August 1998 periods and reveals that the magnitude of the surge from Pakistan exceeded the per cent change from Mexico. During this period, Category 301 imports from Pakistan surged 283.2 per cent compared with a 212.5 per cent increase in imports from Mexico.

TABLE III

U.S. Imports from Pakistan and the World
Yarn for Sale, Chief Weight Combed Cotton Spun
Category 301 (Kilograms)

			January - August		
	1996	1997	1997	1998	% Change
WORLD	19,044,740	21,346,787	10,766,564	20,595,066	91.3
PAKISTAN	2,279,348	2,709,192	942,756	3,612,652	283.2
MEXICO	2,066,480	3,603,675	1,450,969	4,534,144	212.5

4.175 Table IV compares the share of the market accounted for by imports from Pakistan and Mexico, as measured against production and total imports. Again, the data reveals that, during the critical January-August period, Pakistan's share of the market was growing at a much faster rate than that of Mexico. Category 301 imports from Pakistan as a percentage of production more than quadrupled, while imports from Mexico as a per cent of production increased by a multiple of 3.4. Similarly, as a percentage of total imports, Category 301 imports form Pakistan doubled while imports from Mexico increased by a multiple of 1.6.

TABLE IV

Pakistan's Share of Production and Imports
Yarn for Sale, Chief Weight Combed Cotton Spun
Category 301

	Per cent of Production				Per cent of Imports			
			January - August				January - August	
	1996	*1997*	*1997*	*1998*	*1996*	*1997*	*1997*	*1998*
WORLD	13.4	14.8	10.9	23.3	100.0	100.0	100.0	100.0
PAKISTAN	1.6	1.9	1.0	4.1	12.0	12.7	8.8	17.5
MEXICO	1.4	2.5	1.5	5.1	10.8	16.9	13.5	22.0

4.176 Table V provides import data for after the investigation period. The United States includes the information in Table V to ensure, consistent with Article 6.7, that the data provided in the Market Statement was as up-to-date as possible.[79] Table V demonstrated that the volume of imports from Mexico continued to increase after August 1998 as did the volume of imports from Pakistan. However, at this particular point in time, the rate of increase in imports from Pakistan had slowed relative to that of Mexico, but imports from Pakistan were still surging by 164.3 per cent. Furthermore, Table V is limited to import data only and does not reflect any of the other variables set out in Articles 6.3 and 6.4, notably price. The price of imports from Mexico remained substantially higher than the price of imports from Pakistan, which continued to be the lowest-priced unrestrained supplier to the U.S. market.

TABLE V

Major Suppliers' Report
Yarn for Sale, Chief Weight Combed Cotton Spun
Category 301 (Kilograms)

		Calendar Years		Year-Endings		Y/E 10/1998	
	Country	1996	1997	10/1997	10/1998	% Change	% Share
	WORLD	19,044,740	21,346,787	17,929,878	30,282,677	68.90	100.00
	FTAs[1]	2,719,817	4,008,235	2,683,456	7,687,307	186.47	25.39
	MEXICO	2,066,480	3,603,675	2,311,225	7,241,757	213.33	23.91
	CANADA	650,837	404,494	372,165	445,550	19.72	1.47
	PAKISTAN	2,279,348	2,709,192	1,857,294	4,908,794	164.30	16.21
SL	EGYPT	2,443,227	1,866,402	1,672,623	3,466,952	107.28	11.45
SL	THAILAND	1,691,592	2,125,347	1,562,573	2,886,357	84.72	9.53
SL	INDONESIA	2,252,218	1,884,384	1,674,586	2,739,284	63.58	9.05
SL	MALAYSIA	451,842	1,117,351	880,241	1,818,626	106.61	6.01
	EU15[2]	1,782,298	2,964,098	2,903,903	1,577,397	-45.68	5.21
SL	CHINA TAIWAN	878,262	1,167,230	1,065,616	1,076,588	1.03	3.56
SL	KOREAN REP	532,770	612,589	724,619	969,874	33.85	3.20
	PERU	1,241,386	1,431,693	1,513,055	955,966	-36.82	3.16
SL	TURKEY	491,322	265,458	252,604	453,093	79.37	1.50
	SALVADOR	333,870	236,475	187,329	398,648	112.81	1.32
G	PHILIPPINES	32,660	16,330	16,330	369,296	2161.46	1.22

[79] As discussed, the information presented and analyzed by the United States in the Market Statement was as up-to-date as possible - reflecting data for 1996, 1997, and the first eight months of 1998 and including the most current import data through October 1998. First written submission of the United States, at para. 146.

	Country	Calendar Years 1996	1997	Year-Endings 10/1997	10/1998	Y/E 10/1998 % Change	% Share
	SWITZERLA ND	473,795	335,282	371,404	290,209	-21.86	0.96
	JAPAN	160,980	248,214	247,667	285,593	15.31	0.94
	SRI LANKA	295,413	0	0	128,355	*	0.40
G	INDIA	205,761	199,708	165,989	106,690	-35.72	0.35
SL	CHINA P	40,824	0	0	103,357	*	0.34
SL	BRAZIL	576,046	106,624	85,414	57,737	-32.4	0.19
	CZECH	61	0	0	729	*	0
	LITHUANIA	*	0	0	626	*	0
	TANZANIA	0	0	0	296	*	0
C	RICA	0	46	46	287	523.91	0
	KENYA	0	39,853	39,599	254	-99.36	0
	ARGENTINA	477	37	37	200	440.54	0
	UZBEKISTA N	*	0	0	162	*	0
	COLOMBIA	781	0	0	0	*	0
	AUSTRALIA	21,926	9,533	10,674	0	-100.00	0
	MOROCCO	137,914	0	11,963	0	-100.00	0
	REP SAF	150	2,706	2,856	0	-100.00	0

[1] Free Trade Arrangements: Canada, Mexico and Israel. Israel did not export combed cotton yarn to the United States.

[2] European Community.

4.177 The United States concludes, based on the totality of the factors set out in Article 6.4 - taken alone or in comparison with Mexico - that the U.S. determination to attribute serious damage and actual threat of serious damage to Pakistan was appropriate and fully consistent with the ATC. In the first eight months of 1998:

- Category 301 imports from Pakistan surged 283.2 per cent (compared with a 212.5 per cent increase from Mexico);
- imports from Pakistan as a share of domestic production quadrupled (compared with a 3.4-fold increase from Mexico);
- imports from Pakistan as a share of total imports doubled (compared with a 1.6-fold increase from Mexico);
- the price of Category 301 imports from Pakistan was 26.2 per cent below the average U.S. price (compared with the price of imports from Mexico which was 19.5 per cent below the average U.S. price); and
- for specific yarn products where Category 301 imports were concentrated, the price of imports from Pakistan was 28.3 per cent be-

low the average U.S. price (compared to the price of imports from Mexico which was 16.3 per cent less than the average U.S. price).

4.178 Thus, even if one were to engage in a source-specific analysis - an analysis not required by the ATC - the statistical differences between Pakistan and Mexico were extremely significant and reinforce the appropriateness of attributing serious damage and actual threat thereof to Pakistan and to no other Member.

Pakistan's Comments on the Information in the Tables

4.179 Commenting on the above information provided by the United States, **Pakistan** refers to the following claims made in its first submission: absent altogether from the Market Statement is a comparison of the respective prices and market shares of the imports from Pakistan and Mexico. The Market Statement merely compares Pakistan's imports with total imports and Pakistan's prices with domestic prices and world market prices.[80] During the year ending in October 1997, imports of combed cotton yarn from Pakistan represented 10.4 per cent of total imports. Pakistan's share rose to 16.2 per cent during the year ending in October 1998. However, during the same period Mexico's share in total imports rose by almost twice as much. The Market Statement contains no reference to this fact. The import statistics annexed to the Market Statement do not indicate the changes in the level of imports from Mexico but only the total of all imports of combed cotton yarn from countries with which the United States has concluded free trade agreements, that is Canada, Mexico and Israel.[81] The Market Statement thus does not indicate that the United States considered the sharp and substantial increase in imports from Mexico individually.[82]

4.180 In the view of Pakistan, the facts provided by the United States in response to the Panel's question confirm the accuracy of Pakistan claims. The amendments to Table V in the Market Statement now clearly reveal that imports of combed cotton yarn from Mexico were more substantial and rising more sharply than those from Pakistan. Pakistan draws the Panel's attention in particular to the following elements in the amended Table V:

TABLE V (amended)

Source	Year-Endings		Year-Ending 10/1998	
	10/1997 (kg)	10/1998 (kg)	Change (per cent)	Share (per cent)
World	17,929,878	30,282,677	68.90	100.00
Mexico	2,311,225	7,241,757	213.33	23.91
Pakistan	1,857,294	4,908,794	164.30	16.21

80 Market Statement (Exhibit PAK-1), paras. 7.4 - 7.6.

81 Market Statement (Exhibit PAK-1), Table V.

82 Pages 42 and 43.

The Question of Price

4.181 The Panel also asked the United States if it had determined if there was a long-term price differential between Pakistan and other sources including Mexico. The **United States** replied that Article 6 does not require a Member to conduct an analysis of long-term price differentials between other sources. Rather, Article 6.4 of the ATC requires that a Member examine "import and domestic prices at a comparable stage of commercial transaction" as part of its determination of attribution, and Article 6.7 requires current, relevant and up-to-date information. In complying with these requirements, the United States looked at the average landed duty-paid value of imports of the products in Category 301 from all sources, including Mexico and other FTA partners, and determined that Pakistan was the lowest-priced of the leading, uncontrolled suppliers of Category 301 imports. The Market Statement reflects that the value of Category 301 imports of Pakistan ($3.63 per kilogram) was 26.2 per cent below the average U.S. producers' price ($4.92 per kilogram) and 20 per cent below average world prices ($4.54 per kilogram). As regards Mexico, its statistics reinforced the U.S. determination to attribute serious damage and actual threat of serious damage to a sharp and substantial increase in Category 301 imports from Pakistan. These statistics revealed Mexico's imports over the period of the investigation were also increasing. However, during the first eight months of 1998, the magnitude of Pakistan's surge was greater than Mexico's, and Pakistan's prices were significantly lower than those of Mexico. While imports from Pakistan were surging 283.2 per cent, imports from Mexico increased 212.5 per cent increase. The price of imports from Mexico was 9.1 per cent higher than the price of imports from Pakistan. Where Category 301 imports are concentrated, the price of imports from Mexico was 16.8 per cent higher. In an industry where profit margins are determined by pennies, the difference between imports from Pakistan and Mexico was very significant.

4.182 Pakistan asked the United States what is the reason for higher sales of Mexican cotton combed yarn as compared to Pakistani cotton combed yarn (during year ending in October 1998, Mexican cotton combed yarn was imported into the United States 50% more than Pakistan cotton combed yarn) in spite of the difference in price? The United States responded that, as stated earlier, there could be a variety of reasons why sales of Mexican combed cotton yarn in the U.S. market might be higher than sales from Pakistan, even though combed cotton yarn from Mexico is priced higher than combed cotton yarn from Pakistan. Some of these reasons might include: quickness of delivery, proximity to the U.S. market, reliability, long and established customer relations, and consistent quality. However, as the United States explained when this question was asked previously, any attempt to isolate a particular reason would be speculative.

4.183 Commenting on this response, **Pakistan** states that the United States tried to justify the attribution of the whole of the damage to Pakistan by the fact that Pakistani yarn was less expensive than Mexican yarn. In its answer to an earlier question (paragraph 4.176), the United States had explained that Table V was limited to import data only and did not reflect any of the other variables set out in Articles 6.3 and 6.4, notably price. The price of imports from Mexico remained substantially higher than the price of imports from Pakistan, which continued to be the lowest-priced unrestrained supplier to the U.S. market.[83] The Market Statement, however, did not compare the prices of Mexican and Pakistani yarn nor did it indicate any reason for the difference in the prices of domestic and Pakistani yarn. Pakistan asked the United States twice why imports from Mexico increased more sharply than those from Pakistan in spite of the fact that Pakistan's prices were determined to be lower (paragraph 4.173).

4.184 In its comments, Pakistan submitted that the United States could not conduct a proper attribution analysis without identifying the reason(s) why importers purchased increased quantities of Mexican yarn in spite of its higher price. If, for instance, the price difference could be explained by differences in quality or proximity to the United States' market or the rules of origin applicable in the trade between NAFTA countries, the lower price of Pakistani yarn would merely compensate the importers for the additional costs incurred in purchasing Pakistani rather than Mexican yarn. From the perspective of the importer, the total costs of importing Pakistani yarn and Mexican yarn would then be the same, notwithstanding the price difference. As a result, the price difference, as such, would not be an indication of the superior competitiveness of Pakistani yarn and, therefore, be no ground for attributing the alleged serious damage and threat of serious damage to Pakistan.

Discussion of Technical Aspects of the Yarn

4.185 Pakistan also asked the question, following the second substantive meeting of the Panel, if the United States has determined the average count of ring spun combed cotton yarn imported from Pakistan and that manufactured in the United States? It asserted that the range of counts "18-38" used by the United States in its market statement is a very wide range and yarn prices vary by about 5 cents/count/kg. Thus, in Pakistan's view, if imports from Pakistan are averaged count 20 and the average count manufactured in the United States is count 30, there would be a difference of 50 cents per kg (about 15% of sale price) regardless of other difference, i.e. level of trade, quality, preferential treatment, etc. In response, the **United States** explained that it had established the transitional safeguard measure on combed cotton yarn imports from Pakistan in strict conformity with the ATC and made every effort to ensure that its price comparisons reflected comparable goods. The ATC Annex specifically requires safeguard actions under Article 6 to be taken with respect to particular products, such as combed cotton yarn. Paragraph 2 of the ATC Annex provides that "[a]ctions under the safeguard provisions in Article 6 will be taken with respect to particular

[83] Para. 31 of the answers of the United States.

textile and clothing products and not on the basis of the HS lines *per se*." Thus, the U.S. action was taken with respect to combed cotton yarn for sale. For purposes of administration of quotas, including actions under the Article 6 safeguard, the various Harmonized Tariff Schedule of the United States of America ("HTSUSA") classifications for combed cotton yarn are grouped into a textile quota category, specifically, Category 301. Since the categories serve to identify "particular textile and clothing products," data for domestic production and other Article 6.3 variables for like and/or directly competitive products were collected and analyzed in the same category framework. Nevertheless, the United States made every effort to ensure that the price comparisons in its analysis and Market Statement reflected comparable goods. Category 301 actually comprises a wide variety of yarn counts, ranging from less than or equal to 14 metric number to greater than 120 metric number, which correspond to yarn counts of less than or equal to eight, to 71 and over.[84] As discussed in the Market Statement, the United States identified within this broad category the particular classifications in which imports are concentrated.[85] Once the United States had identified the specific HTSUSA classifications covering the majority of imports from Pakistan, the United States obtained from published data the U.S. producer price corresponding to the same particular "counts," so as to ensure that the price comparison was done on the basis of similar goods. Therefore, as reflected in Table II of the Market Statement, the United States based its price comparisons on the basis of all of Category 301 imports and on those particular yarn counts where imports from Pakistan were concentrated.

4.186 The United States also notes that, in this question, Pakistan makes a number of unsupported suggestions regarding the average yarn count of imports from Pakistan and U.S. domestic production and price variations that may result from differences in yarn counts. Pakistan offers no support, evidentiary or otherwise, for its assertion that the average yarn count of imports from Pakistan is 20 count. Nor does Pakistan offer any substantiation for its assertion that the average U.S.-manufactured yarn is 30 count. Instead, Pakistan asks that we assume that the average yarn count of imports form Pakistan is 20 count and the average yarn count of U.S. domestically produced yarn is 30 count to support its claim related to yarn price. It may assist the evaluation of Pakistan's claim to know that both

---

84 A yarn count is a measure of the fineness of yarn. Lower numbers designate heavier or thicker yarns, while higher numbers refer to finer yarns. Phyllis G. Tortora and Robert S. Merkel, *Fairchild's Dictionary of Textiles*, (7th ed, 1996), p. 143. To go from a cotton count to a metric count number, one would use the conversion factor of cotton count x 1.693. For example, a yarn of cotton count 8 would have a metric number of 13.55. Hoechst Celanese, Yarn Number Conversion Formula, *Dictionary of Fibre & Textile Technology*, (1990), p. 209.

85 Market Statement, at Table II note 2. The United States explained that 46 per cent of total Category 301 imports and 54 per cent of Category 301 imports from Pakistan enter the United States under three HTSUSA classifications (5205.22.0020, 5205.23.0020, and 5205.24.0020). These classifications cover wholly cotton, ring spun combed cotton singles yarn with yarn counts ranging from 8 to 47 count (14 to 80 metric number). The bulk of these imports are of 18 to 38 cotton counts.

yarn counts of 20 and 30 are included in this range of HTSUSA classifications in which imports from Pakistan were concentrated. Thus, as discussed above, the United States made every reasonable effort to ensure that the price comparisons used in the Market Statement analysis reflected, as closely as possible, comparable products in terms of yarn counts. Pakistan has provided no basis in its parenthetical comment to its question to suggest that the U.S. pricing analysis was in any way inappropriate or more importantly, violated the ATC.

4.187 The United States went on to respond to a Panel question concerning quality and technical specifications of domestically produced yarn in relation to imports from Pakistan or Mexico. It noted that some variations in quality are characteristic of goods in the marketplace, whether domestically-produced or imported, although quality is somewhat subjective. Generally, however, combed cotton yarn in the marketplace, whether domestically produced or imported (from any source) is of similar and comparable quality. To the best of their knowledge, there are no material differences in the technical specifications of the yarn produced domestically for sale, for internal use and the yarn imported from Pakistan or Mexico.

4.188 The United States also pointed out, in response to a further question from the Panel, that to the best knowledge of the United States, U.S. manufacturers did not make direct investments in combed cotton yarn production in Mexico during the period of investigation.

F. The Question of the Need for a Prospective Analysis to Determine Actual Threat of Serious Damage

4.189 Pakistan recalled that, according to the panel on *United States - Underwear from Costa Rica,* actual threat of serious damage can only be determined by what it described as a "prospective analysis": "serious damage refers to a situation that has already occurred, whereas "actual threat of serious damage" refers to a situation existing at present which might lead to serious damage in the future. Consequently, in its view, a finding on "serious damage" requires the party that takes action to demonstrate that damage has already occurred, whereas a finding on "actual threat of serious damage" requires the same party to demonstrate that, unless action is taken, damage will most likely occur in the near future".[86]

4.190 It follows from the above that the United States was required to demonstrate in the published record that, unless the restraint on combed cotton yarn was imposed, the domestic combed cotton yarn industry would suffer serious damage. This demonstration required a quantitative analysis of the likely future impact of the imports. It follows from the above that the parameters of a "prospective analysis" to determine whether there was an actual threat of serious damage re-

[86] *United States - Restrictions on Cotton and Man-made Fibre Underwear,* WT/DS24/R, supra, footnote 73, para. 7.55.

quired the United States, as a minimum: (a) to demonstrate that a further sharp and substantial increase in imports was possible and likely; (b) to quantify the level of those imports; and (c) to present an assessment of the impact of this increase in imports on all relevant economic variables affecting the state of the domestic industry, including the factors mentioned in Articles 6.3 and 6.4 of the ATC.

4.191 The United States' Market Statement does not present such a prospective analysis; it first describes under the heading "Actual Threat of Serious Damage" the conditions of the domestic industry with reference to the same data used for the determination of actual threat.[87] It then presents under the heading "Analysis of Actual Threat" again the import data and price data used for the determination of actual threat. The only element of a prospective nature is the following statement: "The increase in global imports and the fact that they are and will continue to be priced below domestic prices leads the USG to conclude that the defined domestic industry is threatened with serious damage or the exacerbation of serious damage from increased imports of the subject product".[88] Pakistan submits that a mere assertion that import and price trends will continue does not meet the requirement of a demonstration of actual threat of serious damage.

4.192 The **United States** points out, in response to a question from the Panel regarding the parameters of a "prospective analysis" required to determine whether there is actual threat of serious damage, that Article 6 of the ATC sets forth no specific requirement regarding whether an importer must conduct a separate analysis of actual threat of serious damage and, if so, what the parameters of that analysis should be. Nevertheless, Article 6 requires a Member to base its assessment of actual threat of serious damage on (1) the eleven economic variables set out in Article 6.3 and (2) specific and relevant factual information that is as up-to-date as possible. The United States clearly fulfilled these requirements by conducting a separate analysis focused on the impact that the surge in Category 301 imports would likely have in the immediate future. The United States examined objective and verifiable data for the factors contained in Article 6.3 - particularly data reflecting the months prior to the safeguard action when the surge of Category 301 imports was at its height and most damaging - reflecting the latest available data. Based on this fact-based, up-to-date information, the magnitude of the most recent surge, the low prices of imports compared to the average U.S. price, the likelihood that combed cotton yarn would continue to enter into the United States at such low prices, and the dire condition of the domestic industry, the United States concluded that the economic variables for the industry would continue to decline and that the industry faced an actual threat of serious damage and an exacerbation of the current serious damage from the increased imports of combed cotton yarn.

---

[87] Market Statement, paras. 8.1 - 8.3.

[88] Market Statement, para. 8.7.

4.193 Accordingly, the United States considers that it has demonstrated, based on a prospective analysis, that imports of combed cotton yarn from Pakistan were causing an actual threat of serious damage to the domestic combed cotton yarn for sale industry. The analysis of the market starkly revealed that every major benchmark of economic performance during 1998 was deteriorating and would likely continue to deteriorate. The data demonstrated that, as imports from Pakistan were surging, output was dropping, productivity was deteriorating, capacity utilization was falling, domestic market share was declining, employment was decreasing, prices were falling, profits were diminishing, investment was stagnating, inventories were increasing, unfilled orders were falling, and mills were exiting the industry.

4.194 In addition, world prices - particularly from Pakistan - were substantially below domestic prices. For all of Category 301, the world price was 7.8 per cent below the average U.S. price; the price from Pakistan was 26.2 per cent below the average U.S. price. In specific areas, where imports were concentrated, the world price was 18 per cent below the average U.S. price and the Pakistan price was 28.3 per cent below the average U.S. price. Because price is a major factor in generating orders, the United States concluded that combed cotton yarn imports - particularly low-priced imports from Pakistan - would continue to rise while domestic production, market share, and return on investment would continue to fall.

4.195 The United States also states that Pakistan neither contests its findings nor advances any arguments that establish a violation of the ATC. Rather, Pakistan confuses the text of Article 6.3 with that of Article 6.4 and attempts, on that basis, to add new unfounded requirements into the analysis of actual threat of serious damage, such as a demonstration of a further sharp and substantial increase in imports and a quantification of that surge. Furthermore, Pakistan introduces highly misleading data regarding Pakistan's import trends subsequent to the investigation which is outside the scope of this proceeding. Developments subsequent to the initial determination were not available to the United States at the time of its investigation and, accordingly, should not be considered. As a footnote to its submission, the United States comments that Pakistan's introduction of new evidence is also highly misleading. Although outside the scope of the Panel's review, the United States notes that a two-month decline in year-ending imports of Category 301 yarn from Pakistan is not a meaningful trend. Imports of Category 301 yarn from Pakistan have a history of high month-to-month volatility, and Pakistan exports the capacity to surge dramatically in a short period of time. Since 1996, monthly imports from Pakistan have ranged from zero to over one million kilograms. As it turned out, imports from Pakistan on a year-ending basis declined through August 1999, but Category 301 imports from Pakistan then surged again to the highest levels ever recorded, and Pakistan ended up actually overshipping the first year limit. The United States goes on to argue that Pakistan also wrongly suggests that the Market Statement did not rely on the most up-to-date information and, therefore, cannot support the U.S. determination of actual threat of serious damage. As discussed above, the United States relied on the most up-to-date information in making its assessment of actual threat of serious damage.

4.196 **Pakistan** also offers comments on the above question, explaining that the text of Article 6.4 makes clear that the threat of serious damage must be "actual" and that it must be determined on the basis of a "sharp and substantial" increase in imports that is either "actual" or "imminent". An "imminent increase shall be a measurable one", according to the footnote to Article 6.4. The Member invoking Article 6.2 must, consequently, demonstrate that the threat is not merely potential or hypothetical and that a sharp and substantial increase in imports from individual Members has already occurred or is threatening to occur immediately. The requirement to limit safeguard actions to situations in which there is "actual" threat and the imminence of increase imports is "measurable" sets a high standard for determinations of actual threat of serious damage.

4.197 In response to the above point, the **United States** comments that without acknowledging that the ATC does not require a Member to conduct a separate analysis of actual threat of serious damage or set forth parameters for that analysis, Pakistan assumes that such an analysis is required and even proposes its own parameters. Without citing any support in the ATC or elsewhere, Pakistan also adds additional requirements of its own to Articles 6.2 and 6.3: "a further sharp and substantial increase" and a requirement to "quantify the level of those [future] imports". Pakistan appears to confuse the text of Articles 6.2 and 6.3 with the text of Article 6.4. Articles 6.2 and 6.3 do not require a showing of a "sharp and substantial increase" for establishing serious damage or actual threat thereof. Rather, a "sharp and substantial increase" is required for attribution to a particular Member under Article 6.4. Articles 6.2 and 6.3 only require a Member to show that a particular product is "being imported into its territory as to cause serious damage or actual threat thereof".

4.198 In the view of the United States, at best, Pakistan has confused the serious damage requirements of Article 6.2 and 6.3 with the attribution requirements of Article 6.4. At worst, Pakistan is inviting this Panel to write into Article 6.2 and 6.3 the different attribution requirement of Article 6.4. It is worth observing that, even though world imports had doubled and Pakistan's own imports had quadrupled in a mere eight months, Pakistan would want to impose on an analysis of actual threat of serious damage a requirement to show a second sharp and substantial surge. As if that were not enough, Pakistan would have the Member invoking the safeguard "quantify" that future surge. If there was already an actual threat to the domestic industry, requiring a Member to demonstrate a second sharp and substantial increase would render a Member's ability to establish actual threat of serious damage a nullity. In addition, to demand, as Pakistan does, that a Member "quantify" that future surge simply invites a Member to engage in speculation, and adds nothing to an analysis of actual threat of serious damage. Pakistan's efforts to question the U.S. analysis of actual threat of serious damage fail.

4.199 The Panel asked if, in the view of the United States, an examination of production capacity in the exporting country would be required for an analysis of actual threat of serious damage. In reply, the United States commented that footnote 6 to Article 6.4 relates to situations when attribution of serious damage/actual threat thereof is made on the basis of an imminent, rather than an actual, increase in imports. In this case, the United States based its attribution of serious damage/actual threat thereof to the domestic industry producing combed cotton yarn for sale on an actual 283.2 per cent increase in imports of Category 301 products from Pakistan, within the meaning of Article 6.4. The United States did not consider available statistics on Pakistan's production capacity at the time that it prepared the Market Statement. Such statistics reveal that Pakistan's production capacity far outstripped that of other exporters and that Category 301 imports from Pakistan have a history of high month-to-month volatility, demonstrating that Pakistan's exports unquestionably had the capacity to surge dramatically in a short period of time.

4.200 The view of **Pakistan** on this question is that the text of the footnote itself does not establish this requirement. However, the exporting Member's production capacity may be a factor relevant to the prospective analysis required under Article 6.4.

G. Discussion of the TMB Review of this Matter

4.201 The **United States** notes that Pakistan has repeatedly claimed that the United States acted improperly by failing to follow the TMB's recommendations in this case, suggesting that the U.S. violated the ATC in this regard. While the TMB has an important overall supervisory role in the implementation of the ATC, TMB recommendations are non-binding and are not dispositive for purposes of these proceedings. The United States did not refer to previous TMB recommendations to suggest that they are binding. Rather, the United States noted that the TMB had previously justified a safeguard, whose identification of domestic industry mirrored that in this case, in order to emphasize that the United States acted reasonably in identifying the domestic industry in a similar manner based on virtually identical facts and circumstances. Article 8.10 of the ATC specifically contemplates that a Member may disagree with the TMB's findings. In this case, the U.S. had a number of serious, substantive concerns about the TMB review and informed the TMB that the U.S. was unable to conform to the TMB's recommendations. Therefore, the U.S. has carefully followed the ATC both in substantive and procedural terms, just as Pakistan has exercised its rights to request that this Panel hear its claims (paragraphs 4.209- 4.210).

H. the Late Submission of Evidence

4.202 In providing answers to the questions of the Panel and of Pakistan in connection with the second substantive meeting of the Panel, the **United States** considers that Pakistan failed to justify its late submission of "evidence" on the basis of paragraph 12 of the Working Procedures for the Panel, which provides that: "Parties shall submit all evidence to the Panel no later than during the first substantive meeting, except with respect to evidence necessary for the purposes of rebuttal submissions, answers to questions, or comments on answers provided by others. Exceptions to this procedure will be granted upon a showing of good cause. In such cases, the other party shall be accorded a period of time for comments, as appropriate.".

4.203 The United States points out that Pakistan attached to its written questions to the United States, dated 14 December 2000, three documents. Under paragraph 12 of the Working Procedures of the Panel, Pakistan was required to submit this evidence to the Panel no later than during the first substantive meeting. This evidence was not necessary for, and was not used for, the purpose of rebuttal submission, answers to the questions from the United States or the Panel, or comments on answers provided by the United States. Rather, Pakistan had introduced this evidence as the basis for new questions to the United States - a circumstance that did not fall within the exception in paragraph 12.

4.204 The United States fails to understand how Pakistan could claim that this new evidence was submitted in rebuttal to arguments made by the United States in its second written submission or during the second substantive meeting of the Panel. The points raised by the United States in its second written submission and during the Panel's second meeting were not new arguments. Rather, the United States was responding to Pakistan's repeated claims, which Pakistan failed to support with credible evidence, that the United States relied on false, unverified, unverifiable, untrustworthy, incorrect, and inaccurate data. Pakistan could have and should have submitted its new so-called "evidence" to support the many unfounded assertions it had made throughout this proceeding at the time it made the assertion. Indeed, each of these documents should have been available to Pakistan since well before the beginning of this proceeding.

4.205 Moreover, given that this new "evidence" did not appear necessary to rebut arguments made by the United States, Pakistan should have justified its unseasonably submitted evidence on a showing of good cause pursuant to paragraph 12 of the Working Procedures of the Panel. However, Pakistan had made no effort whatsoever to do so. Accordingly, the United States does not see how Pakistan could claim to have complied with paragraph 12 of the Working Procedures of the Panel in submitting new evidence at this stage in the proceeding regarding claims its has made and should have supported in its first written submission, the first substantive meeting of the Panel, its answers to written questions from the Panel, its second written submission, and the second substantive meeting of the Panel.

4.206 The United States also notes that the new evidence submitted by Pakistan failed to support the many unfounded assertions that it introduced during the course of this proceeding. As the Panel may recall, Pakistan had orally claimed during the Panel's second substantive meeting to have evidence to support Pakistan's many instances of unsupported speculation that the United States listed in footnote 3 of its second written submission. However, Pakistan failed to provide this evidence for the record and also failed to provide evidence to support other unfounded claims that it made during the Panel's second substantive meeting. The United States also noted that Pakistan had similarly failed to provide any evidence to support many similar groundless assertions made in its second written submission.

4.207 Accordingly, the United States requests that the Panel disregard any so-called "evidence" that Pakistan claims orally to possess but has failed to introduce on a timely basis into the written record. The United States further requests that the Panel disregard all assertions that Pakistan made orally or in its submissions that Pakistan failed to support with actual evidence. Finally, the United States requests that Pakistan should be given no further chances to submit evidence which it should have submitted during the course of this proceeding.

4.208 **Pakistan** provided comments on the views of the United States as set out in the preceding two paragraphs. Pakistan emphasised that it strongly disagreed with each of the United States' claims. In the instances listed by the United States, Pakistan submitted both facts and considerations to establish a *prima facie* case of violation of Article 6 of the ATC. It was for the United States to effectively rebut Pakistan's case. The mere characterisation of these facts and considerations as "speculative" is not an effective rebuttal. In several instances the United States turned a legal argument presented by Pakistan into a factual claim based on unsupported speculation. For instance, in paragraphs 36 and 37 of its second submission, Pakistan argued that the terms of Article 6.2 make clear that the definition of the product subject to the safeguard action controls the definition of the domestic industry. If the United States were permitted to define the domestic industry as the manufacturers of combed cotton yarn for sale, it would consequently have been required to impose its restraint only on combed cotton yarn for sale. However, in fact, the restraint applies to all imports of combed cotton yarn, whether destined for sale in the merchant market or for consumption by a related fabric producer. Therefore, even if the United States industry definition was consistent with Article 6 of the ATC, its safeguard action would not be justified by Article 6. The United States described the above argument in paragraphs 36 and 37 of the second submission as "unsupported speculation concerning the existence of captive imports" and "whether a U.S. fabric producer would want to purchase a yarn plant in Pakistan" even though Pakistan made clear that its argument does not rest on the existence of captive imports but on the current potential for such imports. Pakistan therefore believes that the United States' dismissal of Pakistan's legal claim as unsupported factual speculation does not constitute an effective refutation of that claim.

I. Concluding Comments

4.209 **Pakistan** states that many of the deficiencies in the United States' determinations are similar to those identified by the panels that examined the United

States transitional safeguard actions on underwear from Costa Rica and wool shirts from India. It must, therefore, have been obvious to the United States that its action on combed cotton yarn could not be reconciled with the requirements of Article 6. The successive reviews of a safeguard measure by the TMB, a panel and the Appellate Body take a considerable amount of time and during all this time the domestic industry remains protected. Under the WTO dispute settlement procedures, no compensation is due to the exporting Member suffering the damage corresponding to the benefits enjoyed by the protected industry. It is, therefore, with considerable regret and frustration that Pakistan is now asking a third panel to make essentially the same obvious ruling, namely, that the United States may not invoke the transitional safeguard mechanism unless it can demonstrate on the basis of verifiable, correct and complete data that the requirements set out in Article 6 are met.

4.210 Pakistan also comments that the arguments presented by the United States in these proceedings cannot be reconciled with the most basic principles of interpretation and the rulings of the Appellate Body. Some of the positions defended by the United States are inconsistent with the positions adopted by the United States in other panel proceedings. Others cannot be reconciled with its own practices. It is not clear to Pakistan whether we are hearing in these proceedings a voice expressing the overarching interests of the United States or the voice of the AYSA. The conduct of the United States in these proceedings confirms, in the view of Pakistan, that the United States is using the time-consuming proceedings under the ATC and the DSU not as a means to settle a genuine dispute but to provide protection to the members of AYSA while lengthy proceedings take their course. This is extremely worrisome. If this practice were to continue and to spread to other Members, the WTO dispute settlement procedures would be turned into a mechanism to escape WTO obligations and the ATC would effectively become unenforceable during the last two to three years of its existence. Our hope is that the Panel shares Pakistan's views on the United States' approach and its consequences for the integrity of the WTO dispute settlement system and that it states this in its report.

4.211 In summing up its views, the **United States** observes that this case comes down to two fundamentally different views of Article 6 of the ATC. Like the Appellate Body stated in *United States - Wool Shirts* case, the United States believes that "the transitional safeguard mechanism provided in Article 6 of the ATC is a fundamental part of the rights and obligations of WTO Members concerning non-integrated textile and clothing products covered by the ATC during the transitional period". Accordingly, the United States has urged this Panel throughout this proceeding to focus on and give meaning to the plain words of Article 6 interpreted in light of their object and purpose. In the view of the United States, Pakistan has taken the opposite view of Article 6. For Pakistan, Article 6 is not part of the fundamental rights and obligations of the ATC. Rather, at various points during this proceeding, Pakistan has characterized Article 6 as a "waiver," or an "exception," or an "exception within an exception," or more tellingly, as "counter to the basic purpose of the ATC."

4.212 The United States continues, stating that, informed by its view, Pakistan has advanced arguments whose effect would interpret Article 6 out of the ATC. For each issue in contention, Pakistan has asked the Panel to either ignore words clearly present in Article 6 or add new words and requirements that are not. For instance, under Pakistan's approach, the Panel would ignore Article 6.2's plain words "and/or" and "directly competitive" when interpreting the scope of the domestic industry. The result: importing Members would lose the ability afforded by Article 6.2 to focus on those products directly competitive with imports in the marketplace and industries most affected by an import surge. Under Pakistan's approach, the Panel would ignore the factors set out in Article 6.3 and its clear direction that no one of these factors gives decisive guidance. Instead, Pakistan would have the Panel consider readjustment - a factor that is not even listed in Article 6.3 - to the exclusion of all others. The result: importing Members would never be able to find serious damage if an industry attempts to restructure, notwithstanding clear evidence of serious damage or actual threat of serious damage as reflected in the overall deterioration in the Article 6.3 factors. Also, under Pakistan's approach, the Panel would add the obligation to obtain data for all factors from official sources and to refrain from relying on verified data from the private sector because, in Pakistan's view, such data are inherently self-serving, inaccurate and untrustworthy. The result: importing Members would be unable to obtain data for most of the factors listed in Article 6.3. And for those that it could obtain from official sources, an importing Member would have to wait until such data were collected, analyzed and officially released to resort to the transitional safeguard mechanism, even if evidence of serious damage was clear and compelling. If a Member were required to wait until all data forming the basis of its analysis could be compared to official government statistics, then it would be impossible for a Member to respond to the damaging effects of an import surge in a timely manner, and Article 6 would be severely undermined.

4.213 The United States also considered that, under Pakistan's approach, the Panel would add to Article 6.2 and 6.3 new terms regarding actual threat of serious damage to require importing Members to "demonstrate a further sharp and substantial increase" and "quantify the level of those imports".[89] The result: importing Members would face requirements impossible to meet and, in turn, would never be able to conduct a meaningful analysis of actual threat of serious damage. Under Pakistan's approach, the Panel would add drawn-out time lines into the analysis of causation beyond anything required in the ATC.[90] The result: notwithstanding clear evidence of serious damage, importing Members would have to

[89] See e.g., Answers of Pakistan to Written Questions from the Panel, at p. 24; Second Written Submission of Pakistan, at p. 33.

[90] *See e.g.*, First Written Submission of Pakistan, at p. 37.

postpone safeguard action while imports continue their damaging surge. Under Pakistan's approach, the Panel would add new terms into Article 6.4 to require an importing Member to "assess individually and compare all potential sources of serious damage" and to conduct a new and separate causation analysis (even after causation has already been established) to determine whether imports from other sources caused serious damage.[91] Pakistan also tries to suggest that the volatility of its imports, which even Pakistan characterizes as extreme, should mitigate the effects of a 283.2 per cent surge.[92] The result: importing Members would face an insurmountable attribution burden and would lose the ability to establish a Member-by-Member safeguard even in the face of a clear finding of serious damage or actual threat thereof.

4.214 The United States considered that these are just a few examples of how Pakistan would like the Panel to rewrite through interpretation the text of Article 6 and thereby disrupt the carefully negotiated balance of rights and obligations set out in the ATC. The United States urges the Panel to reject these efforts and to give full effect to the Article 6 transitional safeguard mechanism based on its plain meaning and the object and purpose it serves. Contrary to Pakistan's mistaken view, Article 6 of the ATC is a fundamental right given to importing Members. The United States would urge the Panel to interpret it as such and, as provided in Article 3.2 of the DSU, not to "diminish the rights and obligations provided in the covered agreements".

4.215 The United States also recalled that it was mindful of guidance from previous panels and the Appellate Body regarding past U.S. transitional safeguard investigations and specifically followed this guidance in this instance by examining and explaining its conclusions regarding all relevant economic factors in Article 6.3; considering at least all the factors in Article 6.3; considering and explaining how the totality of factors supported its conclusion of serious damage or actual threat thereof resulting from increased quantities of imports; establishing a causal link between the increased quantities of imports and the declining conditions in the domestic industry; addressing the specific question of whether changes in consumer preferences or technological changes caused serious damage; relating the data to the particular industry damaged; conducting a separate and future oriented analysis of actual threat of serious damage; and applying the restraint after the consultation process had been concluded, with prospective effect.

---

91 *See e.g.*, Second Written Submission of Pakistan, at pp. 34-37.

92 *See* Second Written Submission of Pakistan, at p.38.

V. ARGUMENTS PRESENTED BY THIRD PARTIES

A. *Participation of the European Communities*

5.1 When the DSB established the Panel on 19 June 2000, the European Communities and India reserved their third party rights to participate in the proceedings. Subsequently, on 8 November 2000, the **European Communities** informed the Panel, "in view of the arguments developed in these submissions, the EC considers that the main issues raised in this procedure are inextricably linked with the factual elements of the case. As a third party, the EC is not in a position to effectively intervene on such issues. Accordingly, it wishes to notify you that it does not intend to file a third party submission in this case.".

B. *The Submission of India*

5.2 In its submission, **India** argues that the core legal issue in this dispute is whether the U.S., when evaluating the effect of imports of combed cotton yarn on the state of its domestic industry, could exclude from its consideration the vertically integrated establishments producing yarn for further processing into fabric (representing about half of the total number of producers of combed cotton yarn and about one-third of total domestic production). This involves interpretation of Article 6 of the ATC.

5.3 On the ground that the ATC does not define "domestic industry", the U.S. defines its cotton yarn industry as "combed cotton yarn for sale industry" i.e., establishments producing combed cotton yarn for sale in the market. Excluded from this definition are the vertically integrated producers, which produce cotton yarn for the production of fabric and not for sale in the market. According to the U.S., it should be so defined because of the uniqueness of the ATC. According to the U.S., the wording "domestic industry producing like and/or directly competitive products" in Article 6.2 of the ATC allows it "to identify an industry producing a product that is: (1) like and directly competitive; (2) like but not directly competitive; or (3) unlike but directly competitive". This interpretation would allow a Member invoking a safeguard measure "to address serious damage and/or actual threat of serious damage to its domestic industry caused by sharp and substantial increases in imports. But, if the domestic products are not directly competitive with imports ... the need for safeguard action would not arise.". Therefore, it justifies its action of excluding the vertically integrated producers from the domestic industry.

5.4 India believes that this interpretation is inconsistent with the text and context of Article 6 of the ATC. Article 6.2 of the ATC lays down that a safeguard action could be taken by a Member when "it is demonstrated that a particular product is being imported into its territory in such increased quantities as to cause serious damage, or actual threat thereof, to the domestic industry producing like and/or directly competitive products". Article 6.3 states that in making determination of a serious damage or actual threat thereof, the Member "shall examine the effect of those imports on the state of the particular industry" as reflected in changes in relevant economic variables, such as output, productivity, etc. Here words used are 'particular product' and 'domestic industry producing ... product' and no reference is made to selling or marketing. The like products always compete with each other. The product, which is not like but still competes with the subject product should also be covered by Article 6.2. The use of the term "particular" to define both the imported product and the domestic industry in Articles 6.2 and 6.3 makes it clear that the definition of product subject to the safeguard action controls the definition of the 'domestic industry' and the economic variables that must be examined.

5.5 In this connection, the observation of the TMB may be noted: "whether or not combed cotton yarn was sold or further processed within a vertically integrated company did not affect the product characteristics of such combed cotton yarn. Indeed, combed cotton yarn produced by vertically integrated plants bore the same physical characteristics as combed cotton yarn produced for sale ... therefore, in the view of the TMB the two products can be considered as 'like' products". Thus, the relevant domestic industry consists of all domestic establishments producing combed cotton yarn, including the vertically integrated producers.

5.6 Therefore, the U.S. definition of domestic industry under Article 6.2 is not supported by ATC provisions and thus is not tenable. Accordingly, its determination, based on such a narrow definition, that imports from Pakistan were causing serious injury or actual threat thereof is inconsistent with the ATC.

5.7 Furthermore, it may be noted that while the U.S. distinguishes between products for sale (in the market) and vertically integrated products for producing fabric only in defining its domestic industry, no such distinction is made with respect to imports of cotton yarn.

5.8 Another issue that this dispute raises is attribution of serious damage or actual threat to imports from Pakistan and not from any other comparable source. Article 6.4 of the ATC requires that safeguard measures under Article 6 should be applied on Member-by-Member basis. However, attribution of serious damage should be done "on the basis of a sharp and substantial increase in imports, actual or imminent, from such a Member of Members individually, and on the basis of the level of imports as compared with imports from other sources, market share, and import and domestic prices at a comparable stage of commercial transaction;". The Panel on *United States - Underwear from Costa Rica* (DS24/R) emphasized the importance of comparative assessment under Article 6.4.

5.9 In the present case, Pakistan and Mexico are the largest suppliers of combed cotton yarn to the U.S. The statistics of the U.S. Department of Commerce indicate that during the relevant period, i.e. between January-October 1997 and January-October 1998, while imports of cotton yarn from Pakistan rose from 10.4 per cent of the U.S. total imports to 16.2 per cent (i.e., 1.7 million kg to 3.9 million kg), the imports from Mexico during the same period rose almost twice (i.e., from 2.1 million kg to 5.8 million kg). But the U.S. did not make any comparative analysis as mandated by Article 6.4. Thus, the U.S. action is not consistent with the ATC and the Panel should find violation by the U.S. of its obligations under the ATC and the WTO.

5.10 The U.S. argues that the ATC (and its Article 6) is unique and special. It is different from other non-transitional agreements of the WTO. It "derives" from no other WTO Agreement, rather the ATC is a carefully negotiated successor to the MFA (GATT Multifibre Arrangement). Therefore, the MFA "rather than any other agreement - (should) serve as the model for the ATC.".

5.11 It may be noted that despite its transitory nature and unique provisions of the bilateral safeguard mechanism, the ATC is a "covered agreement". The rules of treaty interpretation as expounded and applied by the Appellate Body in *United States - Gasoline* (DS2) and subsequent cases are applicable to the interpretation of the ATC. Accordingly, Articles 31 and 32 of the Vienna Convention on the Law of Treaties are applicable. Article 31 states that a treaty should be interpreted in "good faith in accordance with the ordinary meaning to be given to the terms of the treaty in the light of its object and purpose". Under Article 32 negotiating history could be resorted to as a secondary means of interpretation, either to confirm the textual meaning or in case the textual interpretation under Article 31 leaves ambiguity or results in absurd and unreasonable meaning.

5.12 As to the claim that the MFA should be the model for interpretation of the ATC, India invites the attention of the Panel to the Appellate Body rulings in *Argentina - Footwear* (DS121) and *Korea - Dairy Products* (DS98) cases, where it refused to consider arguments based on past history that the text (first clause - "unforeseen developments") of Article XIX of GATT 1994 was subsumed into Article 2 of the Agreement on Safeguards.

5.13 Another legal issue is whether the Panel should consider only those facts taken into account by the Member at the time of applying the safeguard measure and refuse to take into account, even in the case of actual threat of serious damage, which requires prospective analysis of the effects imports, the facts emerged subsequent to the application of the safeguard measure. In this connection, India draws the Panel's attention to the finding of the Panel *United States - Import Measures* (DS165), where the events subsequent to the measure at issue were examined to understand and clarify the measure at issue.

VI. INTERIM REVIEW[93]

A. General

6.1 On 30 March 2001, Pakistan and the United States requested an interim review by the Panel of certain aspects of the interim report issued to the parties on 23 March 2001. Neither party requested an interim review meeting, and thus, as provided for in the Working Procedures of the Panel, both parties were permitted to submit further comments on the other party's interim review requests. Pakistan did not submit any further comments, while the United States submitted further comments on 6 April 2001.

B. Comments of Pakistan

1. Standard of Review

6.2 **Pakistan** made the following comments on the standard of review which the Panel had applied to this case: "Pakistan is ... concerned about the 'justifiability' standard that the Panel applied when examining the question of whether the United States had demonstrated serious damage (see in particular paragraphs 7.116, 7.110 and 7.120. The concept of 'justifiability' is a new concept that can be found neither in the text of the ATC nor in the WTO jurisprudence regarding the standard of review to be applied under Article 11 of the DSU. The Panel does not explain what the treaty basis and scope of this standard are. In the view of Pakistan, the Panel applies this standard in a manner that reduces substantially the value of the disciplines set out in Article 6 of the ATC and the practical relevance of Panel's rulings on industry definition, attribution and actual threat. The effect of the Panel's approach is [to] relieve the United States of the obligation set out in Article 6 to demonstrate serious damage and causality and to shift the burden of meeting this obligation to Pakistan."[94]

6.3 **The Panel** would like to emphasize that in the interim report, footnote 127, "[w]e consider th[e] term ["justifiable"] to be *descriptive of the current jurisprudence*, rather than any addition or deletion thereto" (emphasis added), and accordingly, has moved this statement into the text of paragraph 7.35. In contrast to the argument of Pakistan, we do not consider that this standard would reduce the value of the disciplines set out in Article 6 of the ATC. As we explained in subsection VII.D.3, in particular, paragraph 7.32, this standard is not introduced from without the WTO Agreement, but derived from the text of Article 11 of the DSU. As both the DSU and the ATC are integral parts of the WTO Agreement, the standards set out in the DSU are applicable in interpreting the ATC. In addi-

[93] Pursuant to Article 15.3 of the DSU, the findings of a panel report shall include a discussion of the arguments made at the interim review stage. Consequently, the following section entitled Interim Review is an integral part of the Findings of this Panel Report.

[94] Pakistan's comments on the interim report, para. 1.

tion, we disagree with the argument that this standard improperly shifts the burden of proof to Pakistan. As we pointed out, in line with the jurisprudence, it is Pakistan rather than the United States that bears the burden of establishing a *prima facie* case that the United States did not demonstrate serious damage and causality.

2. *Comments Specific to Claims*

(a) General

6.4 **Pakistan** also commented "that some of its legal claims and some of the undisputed facts relevant to its claims were not examined by the Panel in reaching its conclusions on serious damage."

6.5 **The Panel** is of the view that it has properly examined all the legal and factual claims of Pakistan, as indicated in Section VII (in particular, subsection F) below. Nevertheless, for purposes of further clarification, we will discuss several points in greater depth.

(b) Claim on the Reliability of AYSA Data:

6.6 **Pakistan** provided the following comments on the Panel's finding regarding its claim concerning the reliability of AYSA data:

(a) "The Panel reaches its conclusions without discussing the undisputed facts on which Pakistan based its *prima facie* case. Pakistan respectfully requests the Panel to do so in its final report and to indicate how, in its view, the United States had demonstrated that it had verified the data supplied by AYSA.

(b) The Panel states in paragraph 7.95 that the data AYSA supplied in 1997 'might not have been fully accurate', while they were demonstrated to be false. In fact, in the next paragraph the Panel describes these data as "incorrect". The data should in both paragraphs be described as incorrect.

(c) In paragraph 7.96, the Panel notes the authorities' positive reaction to the submission of incorrect data by AYSA in 1997. However, the issue in this paragraph is not the good faith of the authorities but the reliability of the AYSA data. It is therefore not clear to Pakistan why the Panel considers the authorities' reaction to the submission of false data by AYSA to be relevant in this context.

(d) The Panel examines in paragraph 7.95 whether the data provided by AYSA were inherently untrustworthy. It states that the data of interested trade organisations are not *per se* unreliable but that this was a question of verification and judgement. This statement is no doubt correct but does not deal with the facts and arguments submitted by Pakistan. Pakistan had argued that the data of an interested trade association that *had previously supplied incorrect data to obtain a safeguard measure* were inherently untrustworthy. The Panel therefore does not examine the specific facts on which Pakistan had requested findings.

(e) Pakistan had demonstrated that *the United States had failed to verify the data supplied by AYSA*. The Panel, while recognising that the data of interested trade association required verification and judgement, does not examine whether the data had been verified.

(f) The Panel states in paragraph 7.96 that the United States verified the 1996 and 1997 production data supplied by AYSA by comparing them with official statistics. However, as Pakistan had pointed out, this particular verification was completely irrelevant because *the United States based its determination on 1998 production data, which were not verified by comparing them with official statistics* .... This point is not addressed by the Panel."[95]

6.7 Also, with respect to paragraph 7.97, Pakistan commented that "[i]t is not clear from this paragraph under which norm the Panel subsumes which facts and how it distributed the burden of proof."[96] Furthermore, Pakistan claims that the Panel is not required to prescribe methodologies for information gathering and verification, but should find that the US methods did not yield the required demonstration in this case. Pakistan again argues that the United States failed in its demonstration because "the data supplied by AYSA could be used without verification."[97]

6.8 The **United States** responded to Pakistan's argument concerning the burden of proof by stating that "[a]ccording to well settled principles of WTO jurisprudence,[98] Pakistan, as the party claiming a breach of the ATC, must assert and prove its claim and put forward evidence and argument sufficient to demonstrate that the transitional safeguard was inconsistent with the ATC".[99]

6.9 The United States also responded to Pakistan's arguments regarding the reliability of AYSA data by stating the United States had demonstrated throughout this proceeding that it had verified the accuracy and reliability of the data in this case. The United States disputed Pakistan's suggestion that it is "undisputed" that the data supplied by AYSA in 1997 were "incorrect", noting that in the process of conducting ongoing verification of data contained in the 1997 market statement on combed cotton ring spun yarn, the United States had "discovered

95 *See ibid.*, para. 8. (emphasis in original)

96 *Ibid.*, para. 10.

97 *Ibid.*, first bullet.

98 The United States referred to Appellate Body Report on *United States - Measures Affecting Imports of Woven Wool Shirts and Blouses from India*, WT/DS33/AB/R, adopted 25 April 1997, DSR 1997:I, 323, pp. 333-335.

99 US comments on Pakistan's comments on the interim report, para. 1.

evidence that called the 1997 market statement into question." At no point did the United States conclude that AYSA data were false, incorrect, or inherently untrustworthy. Accordingly, the United States objects to Pakistan's request that the Panel refer to this data as incorrect and requests that the Panel strike reference to "incorrect data" in paragraph 7.96 of the interim report.[100]

6.10 First, **the Panel** would like to emphasize that when finding that Pakistan did "not establish" its claim, for example, in paragraph 7.101, it meant that Pakistan had not established a *prima facie* case that the transitional safeguard measure in question is inconsistent with Article 6 of the ATC. This is clear from reading the paragraphs with our finding on the burden of proof, in particular in paragraph 7.23. In this sense, we agree that what Pakistan should do was "the presentation of a *prima facie* case that the United Stated ... failed to [demonstrate serious damage]."[101] We note, however, that exactly because we did not find that Pakistan had presented such a *prima facie* case, we rejected some of Pakistan's claims. In other words, the United States must demonstrate the basis for its safeguard action. The United States presented its 1998 Market Statement for this purpose. Pakistan then has the burden of establishing a *prima facie* case that the United States did not in fact make such a demonstration. The reference to "demonstrated" in Article 6.2 does not refer to a shift of the burden of proof within the context of dispute settlement.

6.11 In this connection, we note that Pakistan claimed that the "question before the Panel was whether the United States had demonstrated serious damage",[102] rather than "whether Pakistan had established that the data supplied by AYSA are inherently untrustworthy."[103] In support of this proposition, Pakistan referred to the language of Article 6.2 of the ATC, which provides that "[s]afeguard action may be taken under this Article when ... it is demonstrated that a particular product is being imported into its territory in such increased quantities as to cause serious damage ... to the domestic industry...".[104] In accordance with the WTO jurisprudence on the burden of proof, we examined whether Pakistan established that the United States had not demonstrated serious damage, as stated above. We do not accept Pakistan's request that "the Panel ... indicate how, in its view, the United States had demonstrated that it had verified the data supplied by AYSA",[105] because this request would mean to shift the burden of proof to the United States, the respondent, in contrast to the WTO jurisprudence on this issue. Rather, as noted in Section VII.D.2 below, in examining the consistency of a transitional safeguard measure with Article 6 of the ATC, the Appellate Body stated that "a party claiming a violation of a provision of the *WTO Agreement* by

[100] *See ibid.*, paras. 2-3.
[101] *See* Pakistan's comments on the interim report, para. 5.
[102] *Ibid.*
[103] *Ibid.*, para. 10, first bullet.
[104] *Ibid.*, para. 4.
[105] *Ibid.*, para. 8, first bullet.

another Member must assert and prove its claim."[106] In this line, we considered that Pakistan, the complainant, bears the burden of proof for establishing a *prima facie* case that the subject transitional safeguard measure is inconsistent with Article 6, and subsequently, found that Pakistan did not discharge this responsibility for its claim on serious damage.

6.12 Second, Pakistan requested that "[t]he data [supplied by AYSA in 1997] should in both paragraphs 7.95 and 7.96 be described as incorrect",[107] as in paragraph 7.96, "the Panel describes these data as 'incorrect'",[108] but we do not accept this request. To the contrary, we did not find the data "incorrect". The evidence before us only shows that the US investigation authority decided not to rely on the data supplied by AYSA in the 1997 proceedings,[109] because it "discovered evidence that called the 1997 statement into question."[110] We accordingly deleted the term "incorrect" in the second sentence of paragraph 7.96.

6.13 Third, we would like to point out that, as opposed to Pakistan's comments, the Panel actually examined "the specific facts on which Pakistan had requested findings"[111], as shown in paragraphs 7.95-7.97 below. There, we concluded that Pakistan did not establish that the data supplied by AYSA in the proceedings for the transitional safeguard measure in question were "inherently untrustworthy", taking into consideration the fact that the data supplied by the AYSA in the 1997 proceedings were called into question, and the other fact that the AYSA is a trade association consisting of domestic producers which are requesting trade remedies.[112]

6.14 Also, we noted that "the United States pointed out that it verified the production data for 1996 and 1997 supplied by AYSA for the transitional safeguard measure at issue by comparing them with the official statistics ...".[113] Further, we point out the following statement of the United States: "In addition to relying on official statistics for verification purposes, the United States engaged in direct discussions with individual firms to verify AYSA data",[114] for example, regarding profit and investment, and "the number of mills that exited the combed cotton yarn for sale industry, and the number of jobs lost."[115] In this connection, Pakistan stated that the verification of the production data for 1996 and 1997 is ir-

---

[106] Appellate Body Report on *United States - Measures Affecting Imports of Woven Wool Shirts and Blouses*, WT/DS33/AB/R, adopted 23 May 1997, *supra*, footnote 98, p. 337. (emphasis in original)

[107] Pakistan's comments on the interim report, para. 8, second bullet.

[108] *Ibid.*

[109] *See* para. 7.87.

[110] US First Submission, para. 158.

[111] *See* Pakistan's comments on the interim report, para. 8, fourth bullet.

[112] *See* para. 7.95.

[113] Para. 7.96.

[114] US Answers to Panel's Questions, 22 December 2000, para. 11. *See also* 1998 Market Statement, US Ex. 3, Section II.

[115] *Ibid.*, para. 14.

relevant because the United States based its determination on 1998 production data.[116] We acknowledge that the United States did not specifically state that it verified the 1998 production data. Nevertheless, we must note that the United States verified a large part of data submitted by AYSA, including 1998 data on profit and investment. In our view, the question is the reliability of the overall data. It is unrealistic to require that every single element of data be verified. Furthermore, this is not required by the treaty language. We however would like to emphasize that we do not mean that the national investigation authority has an unfettered discretion in fact-finding, since this Panel has a mandate under the DSU to make "an objective assessment of the facts of the case".

6.15 Also, it appears that Pakistan's argument incorrectly implies that there is only one method of "verification" and that is matching with official statistics. There is no basis for this implication, for if it were so, questionnaires (either written or verbal) would be irrelevant and investigations would be required to be on the basis of periods for official statistics and only after a time-lag to take account of official statistics.[117]

6.16 Furthermore, in our view, Pakistan's comments in numerous places, in effect, add a new substantive element to Article 6, namely, "verification". Pakistan asked the Panel to explain how the United States "demonstrated that it had verified the data".[118] That is not what the treaty requires. The United States, in its investigation, must demonstrate that there was serious damage caused by increasing imports. The United States is not required to demonstrate that it verified the data. Adequate verification procedures may be part of supporting the demonstration, but they are not themselves what must be demonstrated. There are no treaty standards for verification. Indeed, the word does not appear in the ATC. Moreover, the Panel inquired of the United States how it verified the data underlying the determination. The United States explained its methodology. In light of all the explanations and facts before us, we concluded that, on balance, it was not established that the United States had failed to demonstrate the elements required by Article 6.2.

6.17 Fourth, we disagree with Pakistan's argument that the fact that the aforesaid decision of the US authority in the 1997 proceedings is irrelevant to the issue of the reliability of the data supplied by AYSA in the 1998 proceedings.[119] In our view, this fact suggests, as indicated in paragraph 7.96 below, that in the proceedings for the transitional safeguard measure at issue as well, the US authority tried to make an objective fact-finding, and, thus, did not unquestioningly rely on

---

116 *See* Pakistan's comments on the interim report, para. 8, fifth bullet.

117 In addition, we note that we examined Pakistan's challenge against the US fact-finding based upon a discrepancy with the 1998 official statistics, and found that "this discrepancy is not sufficient for us to conclude that the factual situation was not 'demonstrated' within the meaning of Article 6.2." *See* para. 7.98 below.

118 Pakistan's comments on the interim report, para. 8, first bullet.

119 *See* Pakistan's comments on the interim report, para. 8, third bullet.

the data supplied by AYSA. In addition, as referred to in the preceding paragraph, the United States pointed out that the US authority had made verification; Pakistan provided no major factual argument to counter the US statement. We would like to emphasize that the question before us is not whether the data supplied by AYSA is inherently untrustworthy, but whether the US fact-finding is justifiable, *i.e.* has been "demonstrated" as that term is interpreted in light of the relevant jurisprudence.

6.18 With respect to Pakistan's comments on paragraph 7.97, we must first state that we find Pakistan's premise incorrect. The AYSA data were not used without verification. Pakistan has argued previously that the United States must demonstrate that it verified the AYSA data, that the US treatment of the earlier AYSA data was irrelevant, that Pakistan had demonstrated that the United States failed to verify the AYSA data, and that the 1998 production data used by the United States were not verified by comparing them with official statistics. In fact, the United States verified the data. Pakistan's mere assertion here to the contrary is insufficient to establish otherwise. As discussed above, the US obligation was to demonstrate serious damage and causation, not to demonstrate verification. We have examined all of the facts before us, including the US treatment of the 1998 AYSA data in light of its previous submissions, including the steps taken for verification by the United States, and Pakistan's arguments made in its submissions and restated here. The norm which we use is that Pakistan, in light of *all* the facts before us, did not establish a *prima facie* case that the United States did not demonstrate serious damage and causation thereof. We further note that Pakistan by its claim that verification must be done by comparison with official statistics is indeed asking the Panel to prescribe methodologies. We decline to do so and for the reasons stated in the Findings (inclusive of this Interim Review Section) find that Pakistan did not establish that the methodologies actually used by the United States did not demonstrate serious damage and causality thereof.[120]

3. *Treatment of Establishments Retooled to Produce Other Products*

6.19 **Pakistan** also commented that "[t]he Panel ... does not examine Pakistan's claims that the *United States failed to examine* whether:

(a) the retooling entailed damage,

(b) the retooling was autonomous or forced upon the industry by imports, and

(c) the damage was serious."[121]

[120] We recall that the Findings in regard to this issue must be read, *mutatis mutandis*, with our finding that the United States did not properly identify the domestic industry. *See* para. 7.93.

[121] *See* Pakistan's comments on the interim report, para. 12. (emphasis in original)

6.20 The **United States** responded to Pakistan's claim that the US verification "did not reveal the truth regarding the state and activities of the plants reported to be closed,"[122] and directed the Panel's attention to its submissions.

6.21 **The Panel** would like to emphasize that it stated that "the fact that an establishment changed its products to those which are neither like nor directly competitive products should be treated as an indicator of 'serious damage' to a subject domestic industry".[123] In our view, it is not decisive in this case whether "one plant had not closed at all during the investigation period"; rather, it is more important whether the plant "changed its products to those which are neither like nor directly competitive products". It is not disputed that the establishment at issue was producing carded cotton yarn rather than combed cotton yarn at the time of the US determination. Pakistan has not argued that carded cotton yarn is a like or directly competitive product with combed cotton yarn, which is the subject product in this case.[124] Therefore, we must suppose otherwise (*i.e.* that carded cotton yarn is neither a like product nor a directly competitive product) in evaluating Pakistan's claim, because Pakistan bears the burden of establishing a *prima facie* case. Thus, it might run counter to the common usage and meaning of the terms "close" and "closure" when the US authority found that the three plants "closed" during the investigation period. However, this was not the language used by the Panel, we merely stated that the establishment ceased producing combed cotton yarn and has not been producing any "like and/or directly competitive products".

6.22 With respect to Pakistan's point (b), this of course is a question of causation rather than damage. We examined the evidence of how the United States linked the fact of these establishments ceasing to produce combed cotton yarn to the increased imports. In our view, the United States adequately showed this as part of its overall demonstration of causation. We also listened carefully to Pakistan's arguments that this element of the US investigation was not supportable. On balance, we found that Pakistan did not establish a *prima facie* case that the United States had not demonstrated causation, including this element of the US investigation. We further note that Pakistan, here as elsewhere, has merely restated what it argued in its main submissions and claims that the Panel did not listen. We did listen; we simply did not agree.

6.23 With respect to Pakistan's point (c), we think it is misplaced. The question is not whether the establishments' exit from the industry constituted serious damage. We have re-examined the 1998 Market Statement and cannot find where the United States so claimed. Rather, the exit of these establishments was one element of a broader demonstration of serious damage. We found the evidence to be an appropriate element of such demonstration.

---

[122] *See* US comments on Pakistan's comments on the interim report, para. 4.
[123] Para. 7.105.
[124] *See also* footnote 237 below.

4. *Investigation Period, Including Period for Determining Serious Damage and Causation*

6.24 **Pakistan** provided the following comments on the Panel's finding on its claim concerning the investigation period:

(a) The Panel bases its conclusions in part on factual assertions of the United States that Pakistan has demonstrated to be incorrect, in particular assertions as to the "closure of plant" and "job losses" (see paragraph 7.118(a) and (b) of the report).

(b) The legal claim submitted by Pakistan was not that the United States' choice of the investigation period, as such, was inconsistent with the ATC. The Panel therefore makes a ruling on an issue that Pakistan did not raise in this form.

(c) Pakistan claimed that the United States had not conducted the trend analysis required by the terms of Article 6 of the ATC nor otherwise demonstrated a causal link. The interim report however does not address the questions of whether:

  (i) Article 6.2 requires a trend analysis,

  (ii) such an analysis has been conducted by the United States, and

  (iii) an eight-month period lends itself to such an analysis.

(d) More generally, the interim report does not indicate how the Panel objectively assessed whether the United States has met its obligation under Article 6.2 to demonstrate in its Market Statement that the rise in imports and change in economic variables were not merely coincidental but causally linked.

(e) By stating that Pakistan has not established that the United States failed to demonstrate "serious damage" to the domestic industry, the Panel appears to impose on Pakistan a burden of proof that clearly falls on the United States: It is the United States that must according to Article 6.2 of the ATC demonstrate that there was a causal link. Nowhere in the interim report is there any indication on which basis the Panel concluded that the United States had met this requirement.

(f) The Panel applies the standard of "justifiability", which has no treaty basis.

(g) Panel refers to the "changes in all relevant economic variables between 1996 and 1997" as one of the bases of its conclusions even though these changes did not point to any serious damage. Pakistan recalls that the changes during that period were minimal and provided a chart to that effect.[125]

6.25 The **United States** responded to Pakistan's argument concerning the burden of proof, stating that "[a]ccording to well settled principles of WTO jurisprudence,[126] Pakistan, as the party claiming a breach of the ATC, must assert and prove its claim and put forward evidence and argument sufficient to demonstrate that the transitional safeguard was inconsistent with the ATC".[127]

6.26 The United States also claimed that it "established, based on clear evidence, that the surge of low-priced imports on the domestic industry unmistakably caused serious damage and actual threat thereof."[128] The United States further argued that it "demonstrated that other possible factors - such as changes in consumer preference and technological changes - were not responsible for such serious damage and actual threat thereof."[129]

6.27 First, **the Panel** notes that subsection 3 above addressed Pakistan's claim (a) above.

6.28 Second, with respect to Pakistan's claim (b), we would like to point out that we expressly noted the parties' agreement that "Article 6.2 does not explicitly set forth any specific period of time as the minimum period for investigation, or for determining whether damage is serious or, in turn, is caused by the subject imports."[130] This statement is quite clear that the panel looked at two distinct points: (1) the period of investigation; and (2) the period for determining whether there is serious damage or causation thereof. We included the first point because much of the language in Pakistan's submissions referred to the period of investigation. However, the focus of our discussion and findings was on the second issue as is made quite clear in paragraphs 7.115-7.117. Thus, we cannot accept this argument by Pakistan.

6.29 Third, with respect to Pakistan's claims (c) and (d), we note that our finding on Pakistan's claim concerning the investigation period was in accordance with the following findings of the Appellate Body on *Argentina - Footwear*, under the Safeguards Agreement, to which Pakistan referred in support of its argument:

> "We also agree with the Panel that, in an analysis of causation, 'it is the *relationship* between the *movements* in imports (volume and market share) and the *movements* in injury factors that must be

[125] Pakistan's comments on the interim report, para. 19.

[126] The United States referred to Appellate Body Report on *United States - Measures Affecting Imports of Woven Wool Shirts and Blouses from India*, WT/DS33/AB/R, adopted 25 April 1997, *supra*, footnote 98, pp. 333-335.

[127] US comments on Pakistan's comments on the interim report, para. 1.

[128] *Ibid.*, para. 5.

[129] *Ibid.*

[130] Para. 7.116.

central to a causation analysis and determination.'[131] (emphasis added) Furthermore, with respect to a 'coincidence' between an increase in imports and a decline in the relevant injury factors, we note that the Panel simply said that this should 'normally' occur if causation is present.[132] The Panel qualified this statement, however, in the following sentence:

> 'While such a coincidence by itself cannot *prove* causation (because, *inter alia*, Article 3 requires an explanation - i.e., 'findings and reasoned conclusions'), its absence would create serious doubts as to the existence of a causal link, and would require a *very* compelling analysis of why causation still is present.'[133]".[134]

6.30 Following this statement, the Appellate Body explicitly rejected the appeal of Argentina that the panel erroneously "required that an upward trend in imports must *coincide* with a *downward* trend in the injury factors", stating "Argentina mischaracterized the Panel's interpretation and reasoning."[135]

6.31 Keeping in mind the finding of the Appellate Body as quoted in paragraphs 6.29 and 6.30 above, we consider that the analysis of the relationship between the movement in imports and the movements in injury factors would be "central" to a causation analysis, but not required under Article 6 of the ATC. Pakistan demands a ruling on whether a "trend analysis" is required. Such a term is not contained in Article 6. Therefore, literally speaking, the answer is "no". We have used the test contained in Article 6.2 utilizing the guidance of the Appellate Body cited above. In this line, as indicated in subsection VII.G of the interim report, we evaluated the US analysis contained in the 1998 Market Statement, and consequently, concluded that the US fact-finding on serious damage and causation is justifiable, in light of its factual basis, including the changes in economic variables of the US domestic industry and those in imports from Pakistan and all other sources during the investigation period - from January 1996 to August 1998, for the purpose of injury and causation determination. In the interim report, in support of our conclusion, we put an emphasis on the (negative) direction and magnitude of changes in economic variables of the US domestic industry, and the surge in imports from Pakistan between January-August 1997 and January-August 1998. Thus, we consider that Pakistan's comment (c) has been already addressed in the interim report, but for clarification, we have made changes to subsection VII.G below. We believe that such changes naturally re-

---

[131] (footnote in original) *Ibid.*

[132] (footnote in original) Panel Report., para. 8.238.

[133] (footnote in original) *Ibid.*

[134] Appellate Body Report on *Argentina - Safeguard Measures on Imports of Footwear*, WT/DS121/AB/R, DSR 2000:I, 515, adopted 12 January 2000, para. 144. (emphasis in original)

[135] *Ibid.* paras. 143 and 145. (emphasis in original)

spond to Pakistan's comments (d) and (g) above. In regard to (g), we would specifically point out that we of course took into consideration "changes in all relevant economic variables between 1996 and 1997", to which Pakistan again called our attention, but we must examine the case from a broader perspective. Thus, taking into consideration *not only* these changes *but also* the negative changes in economic variables of the US domestic industry, and increase in imports between January-August 1997 to January-August 1998, we concluded that the US fact-finding is justifiable.

6.32 Fourth, we believe that Pakistan's comments (e) and (f) above have already been addressed in paragraphs 6.10-6.11 above and subsection 1, respectively.

6.33 Lastly, Pakistan requested that we revise the heading of subsection VII.G.[136] We considered this request and have revised the heading as follows: "Investigation Period, including Period for Determining Serious Damage and Causation", in response to Pakistan's request.

5. *Attribution*

6.34 **Pakistan** requested that the Panel not mention "Mexico" in paragraph 8.1(b) because "the Panel's ruling effectively does not concern only Mexico".[137]

6.35 "The **United States** objects to this suggestion. Pakistan's arguments regarding attribution focused entirely on imports from Mexico, not other unrestrained sources. The Panel's findings and conclusions are consistent with these arguments. Accordingly, Pakistan's suggested change could broaden the findings of the Panel beyond the facts of this case."[138]

6.36 **The Panel** notes that in its first submission, Pakistan claimed that the United States "attributed serious damage to imports from Pakistan without making a comparative assessment of the imports from Pakistan and *Mexico* and their respective effects",[139] and did not refer to any other exporting Members. Furthermore, the conclusion is already generalized by the parenthetical in paragraph 8.1(b). Thus, we do not accept the request of Pakistan.

---

[136] *See* Pakistan's comments on the interim report, para. 20. On this point, the United States commented that "[w]hile the United States understands the basis for the suggestion, a more appropriate change to address the concern is to move the text under the title above 7.114 to Section IV.D, not have two sections of the report with the same heading." US comments on Pakistan's comments on the interim report, para. 6, first tiret.

[137] *Ibid.*, para. 22.

[138] US comments on Pakistan's comments on the interim report, para. 6, second tiret. (footnote omitted)

[139] Pakistan First Submission, p. 43. (emphasis added)

6. *Other Drafting Suggestions*

6.37 Pakistan made a drafting suggestion regarding paragraph 7.84,[140] which we decline to accept. Also, Pakistan suggested moving footnote 220 into the text.[141] We agree with this suggestion.

C. *Comments of the United States*

1. *General*

6.38 The Panel accepted some of the US comments, and revised Section VII below, specifically, paragraphs 7.45, 7.83, 7.96, and 7.118 and footnote 132. The following is our response to the other comments.

2. *Issue of Descriptive Part*

6.39 The United States made numerous comments concerning the Descriptive Part of the Panel Report. The primary comment was that the Descriptive Part was unbalanced in that it addressed several portions of Pakistan's arguments in full because the executive summaries provided by Pakistan were not available or were inadequate, while the US arguments were presented only in the summary form drawn from the more complete US executive summaries. The United States therefore proposed that this Panel adopt the practice of other panels and attach the full submissions to the Report. Should the Panel not agree with this suggestion, then the United States offered extensive additions to the existing Descriptive Part.

6.40 We cannot agree with the suggestion that we attach all the submissions to the Report for the reasons discussed in the Findings. We will not elaborate further here. As we say in the Findings, we commend the parties for doing a good job overall on the executive summaries. This is a new process with which parties to disputes as well as panels and the Secretariat will need to gain experience. In this case, we have used the summaries as the basis for the Descriptive Part of the Report, but we have also made adjustments where we thought them necessary.

6.41 We disagree with the overall complaint of the United States that there is an imbalance in the Descriptive Part in favour of Pakistan. While we are reluctant to refer to mere word or paragraph counts, we do note that there are 123 paragraphs of the Descriptive Part discussing the US arguments and 92 discussing Pakistan's arguments. More importantly, we are of the view that substantively the Descriptive Part accurately reflects the arguments of the parties. We continue to disagree with the US argument that it has been prejudiced in any way. As we note in the Findings, the Panel's deliberations Findings and Conclusions were based

---

140 *See* Pakistan's comments on the interim report, para. 21.

141 *See ibid.*, para. 23.

on its assessment of the **full** submissions and oral arguments of the parties, not on the executive summaries.

6.42 The United States has noted that Pakistan's first executive summary was merely the introduction to their submission. This is true and that executive summary was only six pages long. But the separately submitted executive summary of the United States for its first submission was only eight pages. We used both as the bases for that portion of the Descriptive Part and made some additions where necessary.

6.43 The United States also notes that Pakistan did not submit any summary for its first set of answers to panel questions, while the United States did. According to the United States this led to another imbalance because the Panel used the full Pakistan answers while relying on the US summaries. The United States raised this complaint during the proceedings. At that time, we declined the US request that we require Pakistan to submit an executive summary of its answers. We noted that during the first substantive meeting of the Panel with the parties, the Chairman provided guidance to the parties to the effect that they were encouraged to provided summaries if their answers were longer than 20 pages in total. It is the case that Pakistan's answers were somewhat longer than that, but taking into account that they were not much longer and that Pakistan restated the questions each time thereby adding length to their document, Pakistan was not required to make a summary of those answers.

6.44 Deciding how to deal with answers to panel questions is indeed difficult. They are not easily summarized because, unlike the primary and rebuttal submissions, they generally are not woven into a single coherent whole. They tend to be a series of responses to distinct inquiries that may or may not be susceptible to summarization. This is an issue that has caused us some difficulties in writing the Descriptive Part and that panels in future disputes may need to address. In the present dispute, in response to the US request, we have included much fuller accounts of the answers to questions of both parties.

6.45 In its comments on the Interim Report, the United States provided a further explanation of the concerns expressed in its Descriptive Part comments. In light of this most recent explanation by the United States, we have made a large number of changes to this section of the Report. Thus, given the extensive nature of the amendments we will not attempt to identify specific paragraphs of this section of the interim report which have been changed.

3. Standard of Review

6.46 The United States requested the deletion or revision of footnotes 126 and 130 which point out that the ATC does not ensure that exporting Members may participate in the national investigation procedures for transitional safeguard measures, for example, because the United States provided this opportunity to Pakistan in this case. We accepted this point, and revised those footnotes accordingly.

4. Definition of Domestic Industry

6.47 The **United States** requested that the second sentence of paragraph 7.38 be replaced with the following language:

> "Vertically integrated fabric manufacturers spin combed cotton yarn not for sale in the open market but for their internal consumption in the subsequent production of a fabric, apparel, or home furnishing. Consequently, the combed cotton yarn manufactured by these firms is not directly competitive with combed cotton yarn imported from Pakistan."[142]

6.48 **The Panel** accepted this request except for the use of the term "spin". We would like to point out that the United States used the term "manufacture[]" in the relevant paragraph in its First Submission.[143]

6.49 The **United States** argued that its position on the interpretation of the term "like and/or directly competitive products" is consistent throughout this procedure,[144] and accordingly requested a revision of the Panel's finding that "the United states took a different position in its rebuttal submission."

6.50 **The Panel** points out that the US Answers to the Panel's first set of questions indicates as follows: "Therefore, the ordinary meaning of the phrase 'like and/or directly competitive' permits a Member, in analyzing a domestic industry, to choose from three potential definitions of domestic industry. First, the industry producing *like* products. Second, *like and directly competitive* products. Third, the industry producing *directly competitive* products that are not *like*."[145] On its face, it is difficult to definitively conclude that the first category means "products which are like but not directly competitive", which is one of the three categories that the United States clearly presented in its first submission, but we accepted the US request.

6.51 The **United States** requested the deletion of footnote 176 in the interim report, because "[t]he factual record provides no basis to infer that vertically integrated fabric producers were interested in selling or made offers to sell."[146]

6.52 **The Panel** does not accept this request. In that footnote, we do not suggest that "vertically integrated fabric producers were *interested* in selling or made offers to sell." (emphasis added) Instead, we were looking for evidence that there had been an inquiry as to whether there were or were not such offers. It is in the offers where competition occurs. Shipments only serve as an indirect indication of competition. Thus, in our view, in order to determine whether combed cotton yarn produced by those manufacturers is "directly competitive" with combed

---

[142] S comments on the interim report, p. 6.

[143] US First Submission, para. 49.

[144] *See* US comments on the interim report, pp. 7 and 8.

[145] US Answers to Panel's Questions, 28 November 2000, para. 70.

[146] *See* US comments on the interim report, pp. 7-8.

cotton yarn sold in the market, it may be more important whether and how often combed cotton yarn produced for the internal consumption was *offered* for sale in the market, and combed cotton yarn sold in the market was sought by vertically integrated fabric manufacturers as alternatives for combed cotton yarn they produce for their internal use. It is the very lack of evidence of an investigation of offers for sale, and therefore competition, which we noted.

6.53 The **United States** also requested the deletion of footnote 180 in the interim report (footnote 246 in the final report), because it "did not suggest that the concept of *de minimis* sales was treaty based."[147]

6.54 **The Panel** disagrees. We have never indicated that the United States made the aforesaid suggestion. Our point is that the United States argued that vertically integrated fabric manufacturers sell or purchase combed cotton yarn in the open market but only in a *de minimis* amount, and thus, combed cotton yarn produced by them for their internal consumption is not "directly competitive" with combed cotton yarn imported from Pakistan.[148] It is obvious that in this context, the term "*de minimis*" was used not only as a description of the fact, but also as a threshold for determining whether certain domestic products are "directly competitive" with subject imports. We find nothing in Article 6 that includes the concept of "*de minimis*" in determining the scope of "directly competitive products".

5. *Attribution*

6.55 The **United States** contested the summary of its argument contained in paragraph 7.122 regarding the issue of attribution. Among other things, the United States is claiming that it "did not argue that the requirements of Article 6.4 'could be satisfied by a simple comparison of Pakistan to a grouping of all other exporters.'"[149] Also, the United States contested the Panel's summary, stating that "the United States did not argue that a measure may be applied to 'any, but not all, Members that are the cause of serious damage'."[150]

6.56 The **Panel** disagrees with these arguments. First, indeed, the United States pointed out that Article 6.4 of the ATC enumerates a number of factors that should be considered, and provides that "none of these factors - including volume - is dispositive," as the United States argued.[151] However, the central question we are confronted with under Article 6.4 is whether or not that Article requires the analysis of impacts of imports from Mexico (and possibly other suppliers) indi-

[147] *See ibid.*, p. 8.
[148] E.g. US First Submission, para. 69.
[149] US comments on the interim report, p. 11.
[150] *Ibid.*, p. 12.
[151] *Ibid.*, p. 11, referring to US Rebuttal Submission, paras. 74-75.

vidually. In its Oral Statement at the first substantive meeting with the Parties, the United States made the following statement:

> "[T]he ATC specifically authorizes Member-by-Member safeguard action based on a sharp and substantial increase in imports from that Member and *an analysis of imports from all other sources generally* as well as market share and price."[152]

Also, in its First Submission, the United States stated that it had "compared this surge in imports from Pakistan *to imports from other sources*, market share and price." The United States then went on in separate sub-paragraphs to examine: "Imports from Pakistan versus all imports"; "Market share of Pakistan versus market share of all imports", and "Price from Pakistan versus price from other sources".[153] Also, the United States stated in its Rebuttal Submission that "the ATC does not impose on an importing Member such a source-specific analysis."[154]

6.57 Second, we note that the United States stated that "Article 6.4 of the ATC gives an importing Member the discretion to take a transitional safeguard measure against an exporting Member to whom serious damage is attributable, but simultaneously not to take such measure against another exporting Member whose exports are contributing to the same serious damage."[155] We do not find any error in our summary of the US argument that "a safeguard measure may be applied to any, but not all, Member or Members that are a cause of the serious damage."[156] On the other hand, we accept the other comments of the United States on paragraph 7.122, and have revised it accordingly.

6.58 The **United States** contested the finding of the Panel on Pakistan's claim concerning the US attribution analysis, repeating its argument that the US investigation authority assessed data regarding Mexico in conducting its attribution analysis.[157]

6.59 In the view of **the Panel**, the evidence before it reveals that the US investigating authority did not assess the impact of imports from Mexico *individually*, in contrast to the US argument. In this regard, we added explanation to subsection VII.H below. The only mention of Mexico is in one chart that has a line item of "FTA's" that includes Mexico.

---

[152] Oral Statement of the United States at the First Meeting with the Panel, para. 15. (emphasis added)

[153] US First Submission, para. 131. (emphasis added)

[154] US Rebuttal Submission, para. 73.

[155] US Answers to Panel's Questions, 28 November 2000.

[156] Para. 7.122.

[157] *See* US comments on the interim report, p. 10, referring to US Rebuttal Submission, para. 78.

VII. FINDINGS[158]

A. *Claims by the Parties*

7.1 The subject measure is the transitional safeguard (quantitative restriction) imposed by the United States on imports of combed cotton yarn (Category 301[159]) from Pakistan as of 17 March 1999,[160] and extended on 17 March 2000 for a further year.[161] The United States explained that it had taken this action based on an investigation[162] conducted to determine whether the surge in imports from Pakistan had caused serious damage or actual threat of serious damage to its domestic combed cotton yarn for sale industry.[163]

7.2 **Pakistan** requests the Panel:

(a) to find that the United States failed to demonstrate, before taking its safeguard action on combed cotton yarn from Pakistan on 17 March 1999, that imports of combed cotton yarn caused serious damage and actual threat thereof to its domestic industry producing such yarn and that such damage and threat was attributable to Pakistan because the United States:

- did not examine the state of the entire domestic industry producing combed cotton yarn;
- based its determinations on the state of the domestic industry on unverified, incorrect and incomplete data;
- based its determinations on the causal link between imports and serious damage on changes in economic variables during an eight-month period only;
- did not conduct a prospective analysis of the effects of imports to determine whether they were causing a threat of serious damage; and

---

[158] Pursuant to Article 15.3 of the DSU, the findings of a panel report shall include a discussion of the arguments made at the interim review stage. Consequently, the preceding section entitled Interim Review is an integral part of the Findings of this Panel Report.

[159] *See* US Ex. 1.

[160] Committee for the Implementation of Textile Agreement ("CITA"), Establishment of an Import Limit for Certain Cotton Textile Products Produced or Manufactured in Pakistan, 5 March 1999, 64 FR 12290. (US Ex. 4)

[161] CITA, Establishment of an Import Limit for Certain Cotton Textile Products Produced or Manufactured in Pakistan, 14 March 2000, 65 FR 14544. (US Ex. 6) Further, the transitional safeguard was extended again for a further year as of 17 March 2001. CITA, Establishment of an Import Limit for Certain Cotton Textile Products Produced or Manufactured in Pakistan, 5 March 2001, 66 FR 13307.

[162] Report of Investigation and Statement of Serious Damage or Actual Threat Thereof: Combed Cotton Yarn for Sale Category 301, December 1998 (the "1998 Market Statement") (US Ex. 3).

[163] US First Submission, para. 1. *See* CITA, Request for Public Comments on Bilateral Textile Consultations with the Government of Pakistan, 31 December 1998, 63 FR 72288. (US Ex. 2)

- attributed serious damage to imports from Pakistan without making a comparative assessment of the imports from Pakistan and Mexico and their respective effects;

(b) to rule, on the basis of the above findings, that the safeguard action imposed by the United States on combed cotton yarn from Pakistan is inconsistent with the United States' obligations under Article 6 of the ATC;

(c) to rule further that the United States has nullified or impaired benefits accruing to Pakistan under the ATC since, according to Article 3.8 of the DSU, the infringement of an obligation is considered to constitute a *prima facie* case of nullification or impairment;

(d) to recommend, in accordance with Article 19.1, first sentence, of the DSU, that the DSB request the United States to bring its safeguard action into conformity with its obligations under the ATC; and

(e) to suggest, in accordance with Article 19.1, second sentence, of the DSU, that the most appropriate way to implement the Panel's ruling would be to rescind the safeguard action forthwith as has been recommended by the TMB already, in June 1999.

7.3 The **United States** requests the Panel, based on an objective assessment of the facts, to conclude that it acted consistently with the ATC in (i) defining the domestic combed cotton yarn for sale industry, (ii) determining that a sharp and substantial increase in imports of combed cotton yarn caused both serious damage and actual threat of serious damage to the industry, (iii) attributing the serious damage and actual threat of serious damage to the 283.2 per cent surge of low-priced imports of combed cotton yarn from Pakistan, and (iv) relying on the best available and most up-to-date data. For these reasons, the United States submits that its transitional safeguard measure applied to imports from Pakistan of combed cotton yarn satisfies US obligations under the ATC. Pakistan's claims to the contrary are without merit and the Panel should reject them.

B. Descriptive Part Issue

7.4 In its comments on the draft Descriptive Part of the Report, the **United States** has requested that the Panel fundamentally alter its approach to the "Arguments of the Parties" section. Pursuant to paragraph 16 of the Working Procedures of this Panel, the parties were to submit executive summaries of their arguments at each stage of the proceedings. The Panel stated that its intention was to use these summaries as *the basis for* the relevant section of the Report. We have proceeded in this manner by relying on the parties summaries, but making changes as appropriate to more accurately reflect the overall arguments.

7.5 The United States argues that the Descriptive Part is uneven. Among other things, the United States notes that Pakistan did not submit summaries for its answers to questions and used its introduction to its first submission as its summary for that document. The United States complains that, as a result, large portions of the actual submissions by Pakistan were included while only the summaries of US submissions were included. The united States claims that it is prejudiced by the Descriptive Part of the Report.

7.6 The United States then goes on to make several specific arguments concerning flaws it found in the draft Descriptive Part and the Interim Report. Many of these points relate to matters of emphasis that the United States argues were made differently in its full submissions as compared to the executive summaries, or at least that it now appears so in the draft Descriptive Part.

7.7 The **Panel** has reviewed in full the individual points raised by the United States and Pakistan in their comments on the draft Descriptive Part and Interim Report. We have made a number of changes which are reflected in the Final Report. However, in view of the broader issues raised by the United States it is necessary that we address those issues as part of the Findings of the Panel.

7.8 We do not agree with the US argument that the Descriptive Part of the Report results in prejudice to the position of the United States. As the United States was informed when it raised a question earlier in this proceeding, the Panel has reviewed in great detail each and every one of the substantive submissions of the parties. The Panel has analyzed with great care all of the testimony at the two substantive meetings with the parties. Our Findings and Conclusions are based on those full submissions and testimony. Thus, the United States has in no way been prejudiced; all US arguments were fully considered.

7.9 According to the United States, the preferred alternative to using the executive summaries would be to go along with the "practice of attaching submissions to the report".[164] It is the case that several panels have adopted the approach suggested by the United States; however, most other panels have proceeded otherwise and constructed a more conventional Descriptive Part which summarizes the parties' arguments without resorting to verbatim attachments. Furthermore, even where the attachment method has been used, it has only been with the agreement of the parties and no such agreement was reached here.

7.10 In the present dispute, this Panel at the outset declined to follow the attachment method. Using the attachment method would increase the Descriptive Part of the Report to approximately 400 single-spaced pages from the approximately 70 it now is. We do not consider this to be a viable approach. We are aware that the WTO dispute settlement system is struggling under the burden of massive translation requirements arising from the multi-hundred page Reports that result from the attachment method Using such a method here would also

[164] *Ibid.*

result in significant delays in issuing the Final Report.[165] We take note of Article 12.2 of the DSU, which provides that "[p]anel procedures should provide sufficient flexibility so as to ensure high-quality panel reports, while *not unduly delaying the panel process*".[166] Furthermore, while our responsibility is to decide the case before us, we also feel constrained not to take steps that would damage the dispute settlement system as a whole.[167]

7.11 The only actual alternative to the executive summary approach would have been for the Panel to draft its own concise summary of the parties' arguments. Such a summary would most likely have been a shorter summary than what is presently found in the Descriptive Part. It is unclear how this would answer the US complaint. The purpose of the proposal to use executive summaries was to break the dynamic of the litigation process that has caused Descriptive Parts of Reports to grow to elephantine proportions. In the absence of any direct information as to which party will prevail at the point when they first see the Descriptive Part, parties often responded by requesting that the Descriptive Part be a virtual reproduction of their arguments, presumably in order to prevent any later criticism of their argumentation once the substantive results are known. Under this pressure, panels have often opted for increasing the Descriptive Part by adding more and more of the parties' arguments until they reached the extreme situation where the only acceptable "description" for some parties is actual inclusion of every word written or spoken. This has led to Reports of hundreds of pages for relatively straightforward disputes.

7.12 In our view, the Reports of panels that have attached all submissions and testimony unedited to the Findings result in huge documents that are virtually unreadable. We also note that the United States has informed the Panel at the organizational meeting that it intended to make all its submissions public. We are of the view that this is the right way to proceed should the United States be concerned that the full arguments of the parties have not been reflected in the Descriptive Part.[168] For those wishing to read in full detail the US arguments, its

---

[165] In this regard, we take further note of the extraordinarily short time-period provided in Appendix 3 of the DSU for translation of the Final Report prior to circulation to Members. While we are aware that this time-period is seldom met, we are not inclined to accept a procedure which would virtually disregard the provision.

[166] Emphasis added.

[167] The United States has noted its surprise at the Panel's rejection of the attachment method "in light of the fact that this is the approach contained in an amendment to the DSU sponsored by 13 Members and currently under consideration by the General Council." This Panel obviously would follow the requirements of any treaty language. However, no such language now exists in the DSU and this Panel will offer no comment on, nor presume to prejudge, any negotiations for amendment to the DSU text. We also note that the United States is not among those Members sponsoring the amendment.

[168] Pakistan declined the US request that it make its full submissions public and, instead, stated that it would supply non-confidential summaries (which are distinct from the executive summaries which remain confidential). This is the right of Members under the rules of the DSU and we imply no criticism of Pakistan in this regard.

submissions are available for analysis. For those wishing to have a thorough overview of the arguments, the Descriptive Part based on the executive summaries is more manageable. We recall that this section of the Report is still over 70 single-spaced pages. This is hardly a cursory treatment of the issues. The purpose of taking the path we chose was precisely to allow the parties to succinctly express their views themselves because they are the best judges of their own arguments. This is a new approach and it will require adaptation along the way. We commend the parties for their efforts and are of the view that, overall, they have done a good job in making their summaries.

7.13 We must also note that the Descriptive Part of the Report cannot be read and evaluated in isolation; it forms a whole with the Findings part and the full weight and importance of certain facts and arguments advanced by the parties emerges fully only in that section, where the panel returns in detail (and repeats again) the facts and arguments from both sides in order fully to evaluate them, discuss them on their merits and finally decide on them. The present Panel Report, read as a whole, demonstrates that the Panel has fulfilled the standard of Article 11 of the DSU (*i.e.* "an objective assessment of the matter before it, including an objective assessment of the facts of the case and the applicability of and conformity with the relevant covered agreements").

7.14 In summary, we disagree with the US argument that it has somehow been prejudiced by the Panel's approach in using the executive summaries as the basis for the Descriptive Part. However, we have made a number of changes to the Descriptive Part in response to the comments of both parties, although keeping largely within the parameters we originally set out.

C. *Relevant Provisions of the WTO Agreement*

7.15 Articles 6.2 to 6.4 are the major provisions of the ATC which are relevant to our analysis:

> "2. Safeguard action may be taken under this Article when, on the basis of a determination by a Member, it is demonstrated that a particular product is being imported into its territory in such increased quantities as to cause serious damage, or actual threat thereof, to the domestic industry producing like and/or directly competitive products. Serious damage or actual threat thereof must demonstrably be caused by such increased quantities in total imports of that product and not by such other factors as technological changes or changes in consumer preference. (footnote omitted)
>
> 3. In making a determination of serious damage, or actual threat thereof, as referred to in paragraph 2, the Member shall examine the effect of those imports on the state of the particular industry, as reflected in changes in such relevant economic variables as output, productivity, utilization of capacity, inventories, market share, exports, wages, employment, domestic prices, profits and

investment; none of which, either alone or combined with other factors, can necessarily give decisive guidance.

4. Any measure invoked pursuant to the provisions of this Article shall be applied on a Member-by-Member basis. The Member or Members to whom serious damage, or actual threat thereof, referred to in paragraphs 2 and 3, is attributed, shall be determined on the basis of a sharp and substantial increase in imports, actual or imminent[6], from such a Member or Members individually, and on the basis of the level of imports as compared with imports from other sources, market share, and import and domestic prices at a comparable stage of commercial transaction; none of these factors, either alone or combined with other factors, can necessarily give decisive guidance. Such safeguard measure shall not be applied to the exports of any Member whose exports of the particular product are already under restraint under this Agreement.

> (original footnote) [6] Such an imminent increase shall be a measurable one and shall not be determined to exist on the basis of allegation, conjecture or mere possibility arising, for example, from the existence of production capacity in the exporting Members."

D. General Issues of Interpretation

1. Guidelines for Interpretations of the WTO Agreement

7.16 Before addressing the parties' arguments in detail, the **Panel** believes it necessary and appropriate to clarify the general issues concerning the interpretation of the relevant provisions and their application to the parties' claims.

7.17 First, Article 3.2 of the DSU provides that the dispute settlement system of the WTO "serves ... to clarify the existing provisions of those agreements [i.e. the WTO covered agreements] in accordance with customary rules of interpretations of public international law." With respect to the "customary rules of interpretation of public international law", the Appellate Body repeatedly refers to Articles 31 and 32 of the Vienna Convention on the Laws of Treaties (the "Vienna Convention") as interpretative guidelines.[169] Paragraph 1 of Article 31 pro-

[169] For example, in *Japan - Taxes on Alcoholic Beverages*, the Appellate Body stated as follows: "Article 3.2 of the *DSU* directs the Appellate Body to clarify the provisions of GATT 1994 and the other 'covered agreements' of the *WTO Agreement* 'in accordance with customary rules of interpretation of public international law'. Following this mandate, in *United States - Standards for Reformulated and Conventional Gasoline*, we stressed the need to achieve such clarification by reference to the fundamental rule of treaty interpretation set out in Article 31(1) of the *Vienna Convention*. We stressed there that this general rule of interpretation 'has attained the status of a rule of customary or general international law'. There can be no doubt that Article 32 of the *Vienna Convention*, dealing with the role of supplementary means of interpretation, has also attained the same status." Appellate

vides that "[a] treaty shall be interpreted in good faith in accordance with the ordinary meaning to be given to the terms of the treaty in their context and in the light of its object and purpose." In *US - Shrimps*, the Appellate Body accordingly stated as follows:

> "A treaty interpreter must begin with, and focus upon, the text of the particular provision to be interpreted. It is in the words constituting that provision, read in their context, that the object and purpose of the states parties to the treaty must first be sought. Where the meaning imparted by the text itself is equivocal or inconclusive, or where confirmation of the correctness of the reading of the text itself is desired, light from the object and purpose of the treaty as a whole may usefully be sought."[170]

7.18 Paragraphs 2 to 4 of Article 31 of the Vienna Convention, to the extent that may be relevant to this case, are cited below:

> "2. The context, for the purpose of the interpretation of a treaty shall comprise, in addition to the text, including its preamble and annexes:
>
> (a) any agreement relating to the treaty which was made between all the parties in connexion with the conclusion of the treaty;
>
> (b) any instrument which was made by one or more parties in connexion with the conclusion of the treaty and accepted by the other parties as an instrument related to the treaty.
>
> 3. There shall be taken into account, together with the context:

Body Report on *Japan - Taxes on Alcoholic Beverages* ("*Japan - Alcoholic Beverages*"), WT/DS8/AB/R, WT/DS10/AB/R and WT/DS11/AB/R, adopted 1 November 1996, DSR 1996:I, 97, at p. 104. (emphasis in original; footnotes omitted). *See also*, with respect to Article 31, *e.g.* Appellate Body Reports on *United States - Standards for Reformulated and Conventional Gasoline* ("*US - Gasoline*"), WT/DS2/AB/R, adopted 20 May 1996, DSR 1996:I, 3, p. 16; *India - Protection for Pharmaceutical and Agricultural Products*, WT/DS50/AB/R, adopted 16 January 1998, DSR 1998:I, 9, paras. 45-46; *European Communities - Customs Classification of Certain Computer Equipment* ("*EC - Computer Equipment*"), WT/DS62/AB/R, WT/DS67/AB/R and WT/DS68/AB/R, adopted 22 June 1998, DSR 1998:V, 1851, para. 84; and *Argentina - Measures Affecting Imports of Footwear, Textiles, Apparel and Other Items*, WT/DS56/AB/R, adopted 22 April 1998, DSR 1998:III, 1003, para. 42.

[170] Appellate Body Report on *United States - Import Prohibition of Certain Shrimp and Shrimp Products* ("*US - Shrimp*"), WT/DS58/AB/R, adopted 6 November 1998, DSR 1998:VII, 2755, para. 114. *See also* Panel Reports on *United States - Sections 301 - 310 of the Trade Act 1974*, WT/DS152/R, adopted 27 January 2000, DSR 2000:II, 815, para. 7.22; *India - Patent Protection for Pharmaceutical and Agricultural Chemical Products*, WT/DS50/R, adopted 22 September 1998, DSR 1998:I, 41, para. 7.18; *United States - Restrictions on Imports of Cotton and Man-made Fibre Underwear* ("*US - Underwear*"), WT/DS24/R, adopted 25 February 1997, DSR 1997:I, 31, para. 7.18; and Appellate Body Report on *Argentina - Safeguard Measures on Imports of Footwear* ("*Argentina - Footwear*"), WT/DS121/AB/R, adopted 12 January 2000, DSR 2000:I, 515, para. 91.

(a) any subsequent agreement between the parties regarding the interpretation of the treaty or the application of its provisions;

(b) any subsequent practice in the application of the treaty which establishes the agreement of the parties regarding its interpretation;

(c) any relevant rules of international law applicable in the relations between the parties.

4. A special meaning shall be given to a term if it is established that the parties so intended."

7.19 Further, Article 32 of the Vienna Convention provides:

"Recourse may be had to supplementary means of interpretation, including the preparatory work of the treaty and the circumstances of its conclusion, in order to confirm the meaning resulting from the application of Article 31, or to determine the meaning when the interpretation according to Article 31:

(a) leaves the meaning ambiguous or obscure; or

(b) leads to a result which is manifestly absurd or unreasonable."

7.20 On this point, in *EC - Computer Equipment*, the Appellate Body noted as follows:

"The application of these rules in Article 31 of the *Vienna Convention* will usually allow a treaty interpreter to establish the meaning of a term. However, if after applying Article 31 the meaning of the term remains ambiguous or obscure, or leads to a result which is manifestly absurd or unreasonable, Article 32 allows a treaty interpreter to have recourse to:

'... supplementary means of interpretation, including the preparatory work of the treaty and the circumstances of its conclusion.'

With regard to 'the circumstances of [the] conclusion' of a treaty, this permits, in appropriate cases, the examination of the historical background against which the treaty was negotiated."[171]

[171] Appellate Body Report on *EC - Computer Equipment*, op. cit., para. 86. (footnote omitted) *See also* Appellate Body Report on *Japan - Alcoholic Beverages*, op. cit., p. 10.

2. *Burden of Proof*

7.21 With respect to the burden of proof concerning transitional safeguard measures under the ATC, in *US - Shirts and Blouses*, the Appellate Body considered that the burden of proof is incumbent on the complainant, stating as follows:

> "... The *ATC* is a transitional arrangement that, by its own terms, will terminate when trade in textiles and clothing is fully integrated into the multilateral trading system. Article 6 of the *ATC* is an integral part of the transitional arrangement manifested in the *ATC* and should be interpreted accordingly. As the Appellate Body observed in *United States - Restrictions on Imports of Cotton and Manmade Fibre Underwear* with respect to Article 6.10 of the *ATC*, we believe Article 6 is 'carefully negotiated language ... which reflects an equally carefully drawn balance of rights and obligations of Members ... .'[172] That balance must be respected.
>
> The transitional safeguard mechanism provided in Article 6 of the *ATC* is a fundamental part of the rights and obligations of WTO Members concerning non-integrated textile and clothing products covered by the *ATC* during the transitional period. Consequently, a party claiming a violation of a provision of the *WTO Agreement* by another Member must assert and prove its claim. ..."[173]

7.22 The Appellate Body and subsequent panels endorsed this principle that a complainant bears the burden of proof.[174] For example, the Appellate Body, in *EC - Hormones*, states as follows:

> "... The initial burden lies on the complaining party, which must establish a *prima facie* case of inconsistency with a particular provision of the *SPS Agreement* on the part of the defending party, or more precisely, of its SPS measure or measures complained about. When that *prima facie* case is made, the burden of proof moves to the defending party, which must in turn counter or refute the claimed inconsistency. This seems straightforward enough and is in conformity with our ruling in *United*

[172] original footnote) AB-1996-3, adopted 25 February 1997, WT/DS24/AB/R, p. 15.

[173] Appellate Body Report on *United States - Measures Affecting Imports of Woven Wool Shirts and Blouses* ("*US - Shirt and Blouses*"), WT/DS33/AB/R, adopted 23 May 1997, DSR 1997:I, 323, p. 337. (emphasis in original)

[174] *E.g.* Appellate Body Reports on *EC Measures Concerning Meat and Meat Products* ("*EC - Hormones*"), WT/DS26/AB/R and WT/DS48/AB/R, adopted 13 February 1998, DSR 1998:I, 135, paras. 98 and 104; and *Brazil - Export Financing Programme for Aircraft*, WT/DS46/AB/R, adopted 20 August 1999, DSR 1999:III, 1161, paras. 141.

States - Shirts and Blouses, which the Panel invokes and which embodies a rule applicable in any adversarial proceedings."[175]

7.23 In this line, we consider that Pakistan, the complaining party, bears the burden of proof for establishing a *prima facie* case that the subject transitional safeguard measure is in violation of Article 6.[176]

3. *Standard of Review*

7.24 The parties made extensive arguments concerning the standard of review the Panel should use in this case. They agreed that the Panel should not make a *de novo* review, but they are in disagreement on the scope of review that the Panel should exercise.

7.25 With respect to the US fact-finding, **Pakistan** argued that "*[t]he core issue before the Panel is ... whether the Market Statement constitutes a logical proof that the requirements set out in Article 6 were met.*"[177] Pakistan further argued that the US determination was based upon "unverified, incorrect and incomplete data" in a number of respects,[178] and improper methods of evaluation of facts.[179]

7.26 The **United States** argued in support of the correctness and accuracy of its fact-finding contained in the 1998 Market Statement. In addition, the United States contended that Pakistan had attempted to "introduce[] new evidence of Pakistan's import trends *subsequent* to the investigation that is outside the scope of this proceeding."[180] The United States further argued that the Panel is requested to review only whether the US measure was "based on the best available data as contained in the 1998 Market Statement at the time that the United States conducted its determination", citing the panel report on *US - Shirts and Blouses*.[181]

7.27 In response, **Pakistan** agreed that the Panel cannot examine evidence for the purpose of reinvestigating the market situation, but argued that this does not mean that the Panel cannot examine evidence presented by Pakistan for the purpose of determining whether the market situation was investigated consistently with the requirement of Article 6. According to Article 11 of the DSU and the established WTO jurisprudence endorsed by the Appellate Body, the Panel must

---

175 Appellate Body Report on *EC - Hormones*, op. cit., para. 98. (emphasis in original; footnote omitted)

176 *See* Appellate Body Report on *US - Shirts and Blouses*, op. cit., pp. 335. *See also* Appellate Body Report on *EC - Hormones*, op. cit., para. 98.

177 Pakistan First Submission, p. 14. (emphasis in original) (*Also* paras. 4-12-4.13.)

178 *See* Pakistan First Submission, pp. 30-36. (*Also* paras. 3.1 and 4.95-4.101.)

179 *See* Pakistan First Submission, pp. 36-42. (*Also* paras. 4.110 and 4.112.)

180 US First Submission, para. 124. (emphasis in original) *See also ibid.* para. 91, 152 and 155-159. (*Also* paras. 4.8, 4.104, 4.124 and 4.202-4.207.)

181 US First Submission, para. 124. (*Also* para. 4.102.)

make an objective assessment as to whether the published report on the investigation contains an adequate, reasoned and reasonable explanation of how the facts in the record support the determination made. Pakistan is thus entitled to submit facts that were available to the United States at the time of the investigation, but that it failed to consider in the 1998 Market Statement. Pakistan is also entitled to submit facts demonstrating that the data used by the United States were unreliable and incorrect because it would otherwise be prevented from proving that the Market Statement is inconsistent with the requirements of Article 6 of the ATC. In support of its proposition, Pakistan referred to the difference between the ATC and other WTO Agreements; in case of ordinary safeguard measures, countervailing duties or antidumping duties, exporters subject to investigation shall be given an opportunity to present evidence to national investigative authorities, but the ATC does not set forth any such procedural requirement.[182]

7.28 The **Panel** first notes that the ATC does not have any particular provision concerning the standard of review, and thus, Article 11 of the DSU should be used by panels assigned to review measures taken by a Member under the ATC as the basis for their standard of review. Article 11 of the DSU requires panels to "make ... an objective assessment of the facts of the case ...".[183] We further note that the Appellate Body, in *EC - Hormones*, stated that "[m]any panels have in the past refused to undertake *de novo* review, wisely, since under current practice and systems, they are in any case poorly suited to engage in such a review."[184]

7.29 On the issue of the standard of review to be applied in cases involving the ATC, the panel on *US - Underwear* rejected both total deference to the findings of national authorities and a *de novo* review. The panel stated as follows:

> "...a policy of total deference to the findings of the national authorities could not ensure an 'objective assessment' as foreseen by Article 11 of the DSU.
>
> ...
>
> ... the Panel's function should be to assess objectively the review conducted by the national investigating authority, in this case the CITA. We draw particular attention to the fact that a series of panel reports in the anti-dumping and subsidies/countervailing duties context have made it clear that it is not the role of panels to engage in a

182 Pakistan Rebuttal Submission, paras. 8-10. (*Also* para. 4.208.)

183 The Appellate Body has stated that Article 11 of the DSU is applicable to all the WTO Agreements except for the Anti-Dumping Agreement. *See* Appellate Body Reports on *EC - Hormones*, op. cit., *supra* footnote 174, paras. 114-119; *Australia - Measures Affecting Importation of Salmon* ("*Australia - Salmon*"), WT/DS18/AB/R, adopted 6 November 1998, DSR 1998:VIII, 3327, para. 2.67; *Argentina - Footwear*, op. cit., para. 118; and *United States - Definitive Safeguard Measures on Imports of Wheat Gluten from the European Communities* ("*US - Wheat Gluten*"), WT/DS166/AB/R, adopted 19 January 2001, DSR 2001:II, 717, para. 150.

184 Appellate Body Report on *EC - Hormones*, op. cit., para. 117.

de novo review. In our view, the same is true for panels operating in the context of the ATC, since they would be called upon, as in the context of cases dealing with anti-dumping and/or subsidies/countervailing duties, to review the consistency of a determination by a national investigating authority imposing a restriction under the relevant provisions of the relevant WTO legal instruments, in this case the ATC. In our view, the task of the Panel is to examine the consistency of the US action with the international obligations of the United States, and not the consistency of the US action with the US domestic statute implementing the international obligations of the United States. Consequently, the ATC constitutes, in our view, the relevant legal framework in this matter.

We have therefore decided, in accordance with Article 11 of the DSU, to make an objective assessment of the Statement issued by the US authorities on 23 March 1995 (the "March Statement") which, as the parties to the dispute agreed, constitutes the scope of the matter properly before the Panel without, however, engaging in a *de novo* review. In our view, an objective assessment would entail an examination of whether the CITA had examined all relevant facts before it (including facts which might detract from an affirmative determination in accordance with the second sentence of Article 6.2 of the ATC), whether adequate explanation had been provided of how the facts as a whole supported the determination made, and, consequently, whether the determination made was consistent with the international obligations of the United States."[185]

7.30 Further, with respect to the question as to what is included within the scope of the factual examination by panels, in *US - Shirts and Blouses*, the panel stated as follows:

"... Unlike the TMB, a DSU panel is not called upon, under its terms of reference, to reinvestigate the market situation. When assessing the WTO compatibility of the decision to impose national trade remedies, DSU panels do not reinvestigate the market situation but rather limit themselves to the evidence used by the importing Member in making its determination to impose the measure. In addition, such DSU panels, contrary to the TMB, do not consider developments subsequent to the initial determination. In respect of the US determination at issue in the present case, we consider, therefore, that this Panel is requested to make an objective assess-

[185] Panel Report on *US - Underwear*, op. cit., paras. 7.10, 12 and 13. (footnote omitted) This approach has been endorsed by the Appellate Body in *EC - Hormones*, op. cit., paras. 115-117.

> ment as to whether the United States respected the requirements of Article 6.2 and 6.3 of the ATC at the time of the determination."[186]

7.31 Moreover, in *US - Underwear*, the panel restricted its review to an examination of the fact-finding of the national authority on which the subject transitional safeguard measure was proposed. In that case, the United States provided the panel with the Statement issued by the US authorities on 23 March 1995 (the "March Statement") on which it proposed the transitional safeguard measure in question, and another Statement it later provided to the complainant in the TMB review proceedings (the "July Statement"). The panel stated as follows:

> "... we should restrict our review to an examination of the March Statement. We believe that statements subsequent to the March Statement should not be viewed as a legally independent basis for establishing serious damage or actual threat thereof in the present case. A restriction may be imposed, in a manner consistent with Article 6 of the ATC, when based on a determination made in accordance with the procedure embodied in Article 6.2 and 6.4 of the ATC. This is precisely the role that the March Statement is called upon to play. Consequently, to review the alleged inconsistency of the US action with the ATC, we must focus our legal analysis on the March Statement as the relevant legal basis for the safeguard action taken by the United States."[187]

7.32 We agree with the aforesaid finding of the panel on *US - Shirts and Blouses* that panels should not reinvestigate *de novo* the market situation when reviewing decisions made by national investigative authorities. Article 13 of the DSU provides that panels "have the right to seek information and technical advice from any individual or body which it deems appropriate." However, panels are less equipped and might have less expertise in fact-finding than national authorities.[188] In this overall context of the DSU, and in light of the above-quoted jurisprudence, we conclude that "an objective assessment" under Article 11 generally means a more limited factual examination than a *de novo* review.

7.33 We will next consider whether we should examine evidence submitted by Pakistan, which was not examined by, or not available to, the United States at the time of investigation. As the panel on *US - Underwear* indicated, the task of panels is not to determine whether or not to take transitional safeguard measure based upon all facts presented in the panel proceeding in accordance with the national legislation, but to review the consistency of decisions by national au-

---

186 Panel Report on *US - Shirts and Blouses*, WT/DS33/R, adopted 23 May 1997, DSR 1997:I, 343, para. 7.21.

187 Panel Report on *US - Underwear*, op. cit., para. 7.26.

188 *See also* Appellate Body Report on *EC - Hormones*, op. cit., para. 117, as cited in para. 7.28 above.

thorities with the ATC.[189] Thus, we shall not examine any evidence for the purpose of reinvestigating the market situation, but we should examine any evidence, without regard to whether it was available or considered at the time of investigation, for the purpose of evaluating the thoroughness and sufficiency of the investigation underpinning the decision of the US authority.[190] We do not find any provision in the ATC or the DSU that limits the authority of panels to collect factual data in order to review the fact-finding of national authorities in this manner.[191]

7.34 We further recall that in *Argentina - Footwear*, the Appellate Body concluded that the panel had discharged its duties of making an "objective assessment of facts" in accordance with Article 11 of the DSU, stating as follows:

> "... the Panel examined whether, as required by Article 4 of the *Agreement on Safeguards*, the Argentine authorities had considered all the relevant facts and had adequately explained how the facts supported the determinations that were made. Indeed, far from departing from its responsibility, in our view, the Panel was simply fulfilling its responsibility under Article 11 of the DSU in taking the approach it did. ...".[192]

---

[189] Panel Report on *US - Underwear*, op. cit., para. 7.12.

[190] In this connection, we recall that as cited in para. 7.30 above, the panel on *US - Shirt and Blouses* stated that panels shall "not consider developments subsequent to the initial determination". Panel Report on *US - Shirts and Blouses*, op. cit., para. 7.21. Our conclusion is consistent with this statement; it does not mean to take into consideration any development that occurred to the US domestic industry or subject imports, for example, change in sales volume, after the 1998 Market Statement had been made.

[191] We also note that the ATC does not ensure that exporting Members may participate in the national investigation proceedings for transitional safeguard measures, thereby leaving such Members possibly unable to contest the fact-finding of the importing Member at that stage; however, exporting Members have the opportunity to contest the fact-finding of an importing Member prior to the introduction of a transitional safeguard measure, through consultation contemplated by Article 6.7. In addition, we are informed that the United States provided a public notice and accordingly, gave Pakistan and any other interested party an opportunity to comment on its own fact-finding prior to the establishment of the transitional safeguard measure at issue. (See US comments on the interim report, p. 5.)

[192] Appellate Body Report on *Argentina - Footwear*, op. cit., para. 121. *See also* Appellate Body Report on *US - Wheat Gluten*, op. cit., para. 153. *Compare* Panel Report on *US - Shirts and Blouses*, op. cit., para. 7.21, in which the panel stated that panels shall "limit themselves to the evidence used by the importing Member in making its determination to impose the measure", as cited in para. 7.30. We understand that this finding of the panel implies that panels shall examine any evidence not for the purpose of reinvestigating the market situation, but for the purpose of evaluating the thoroughness and sufficiency of the investigation underpinning the decision of the national investigation authority, in light of the finding of the Appellate Body in *Argentina - Footwear*.

7.35 Therefore, we will examine whether the US fact-finding is justifiable[193] in light of all the facts submitted by the parties, including those which were not considered by, or not available to the US authority at the time of investigation. We consider this term "justifiable" to be descriptive of the current jurisprudence, rather than any addition or deletion thereto. Of course, the Appellate Body did not mean that panels should reverse a fact-finding of a national investigation authority if the authority did not consider a marginally relevant fact that was not provided by any party to the authority, or that was not available at the time of investigation. In contrast, it also would not be correct if panels were unable to reverse a fact-finding of a national authority even if the authority overlooked a crucial or decisive fact simply because it was not presented to the authority at the time of investigation[194]; this would mean that the more poorly the investigation procedures are designed, the more likely a deficient fact-finding of a national authority could withstand the scrutiny of panels.[195] Further, it also could not be correct that panels have to uphold a fact-finding of a national authority when the authority "adequately explained how the facts supported [its] determinations ...", however, excluding a crucial or decisive fact from the explanation. Thus, under Article 6 of the ATC, we deem it necessary and appropriate to review whether a national authority's fact-finding and decision was justified in light of the relevant facts before us.

E. Definition of Domestic Industry

1. Identification of Issues

7.36 Article 6.2 of the ATC requires that, in order to take a transitional safeguard measure, a Member must demonstrate that "... a particular product is being

---

[193] We note that the *New Shorter Oxford English Dictionary* defines the term "justifiable" as: "able to be legally or morally justified; able to be shown to be just, reasonable, or correct; defensible". *New Shorter Oxford English Dictionary* (Clarendon Press 1993), p. 1466. By using the term "justifiable", we do not imply that there is a burden on the respondent to justify itself to a panel, thereby incorrectly shifting the burden of proof. Instead, we refer to the requirement that an investigating authority take into consideration the relevant facts and then adequately explain its reasoning. We have recourse to this term also in order to avoid terms such as "reasonableness" or "wide margin of discretion" which are used in national systems of administrative law and which inevitably carry with them many connotations from these national legal systems.

[194] In this connection, we note that the Appellate Body, in *US - Wheat Gluten*, stated that "[t]he competent authorities must, in every case, carry out a full investigation to enable them to conduct a proper evaluation of all of the relevant factors expressly mentioned in Article 4.2(a) of the *Agreement on Safeguards*." Appellate Body Report on *US - Wheat Gluten*, op. cit., para. 55.

[195] We note again that the ATC does not ensure that exporting Members may participate in the investigation proceedings for transitional safeguard measures, thereby leaving such Members possibly unable to contest the fact-finding of the importing Member at that stage; however, exporting Members have the opportunity to contest the fact-finding of an importing Member prior to the introduction of a transitional safeguard measure, through consultation contemplated by Article 6.7. *See also* footnote 191 above.

imported into its territory in such increased quantities as to cause serious damage, or actual threat thereof, to *the domestic industry producing like and/or directly competitive products.*" (emphasis added)

7.37 **Pakistan** argued that Article 6.2 provides that the subject "domestic industry" consists of domestic manufacturers that produce: (a) like products; (b) directly competitive products; or (c) like products and directly competitive products, with subject imports. In violation of this provision, in relation to the transitional safeguard measure on imports of combed cotton yarn from Pakistan, the United States excluded from the scope of the domestic industry the vertically integrated manufacturers that produced combed cotton yarn for their own use. Combed cotton yarn produced by domestic producers, whether for sale in the market or for internal use, is a directly competitive product with combed cotton yarn imported from Pakistan. The US position is inconsistent with the practice on the scope of a domestic industry concerning safeguard measures under GATT Article XIX, countervailing duties or antidumping duties.[196]

7.38 In rebuttal, the **United States** argued that the text of Article 6 would allow a Member to identify an industry producing a product that is (a) like and directly competitive; or (b) like but not directly competitive; or (c) unlike but directly competitive.[197] According to the United States, vertically integrated fabric producers manufacture combed cotton yarn not for sale in the open market but for their internal consumption in the subsequent production of a fabric, apparel, or home furnishing. Consequently, the combed cotton yarn manufactured by these firms is not a directly competitive product with combed cotton yarn imported from Pakistan.[198] Thus, it is proper to exclude this captive production from the scope of the domestic industry. In support of this proposition, the United States argued that the objective of the ATC is to integrate gradually the textile and clothing sector into the disciplines of the GATT, and thus, the MFA rather than the GATT or any other WTO Agreement should serve as the model for the ATC. The United States referred to Annex A to the MFA, which used the term "like and/or directly competitive products".[199]

7.39 **Pakistan** asserted that the US position was illogical in that it resulted in a mismatch between imports and domestic products. "If the United States were permitted to define the domestic industry as the manufacturers of combed cotton yarn for sale, it would consequently have been required to impose its restraint only on combed cotton yarn for sale. However, in fact, the restraint applies to all imports of combed cotton yarn whether destined for sale in the merchant market

---

196 *See* Pakistan First Submission, pp. 21-27. (*Also* paras. 4.10-4.11 and 4.18-4.20.)

197 *See* US First Submission, para. 49. (*Also* paras. 4.34-4.37.)

198 *See* US First Submission, para. 50. (*Also* paras. 4.21-4.25.)

199 *See* US First Submission, paras. 37-43, in particular, para. 41. (*Also* para. 4.58.)

or for consumption by a related fabric producer."[200] Pakistan also argued that the US position is inconsistent with GATT/WTO jurisprudence on the definition of the terms "like" and "directly competitive" wherein "like" is a subset of "directly competitive", in that it presupposes that like but not directly competitive products exist.[201]

7.40 The **Panel** understands that the issue before it is whether the text of Article 6.2 permits the US exclusion of production of combed cotton yarn by vertically integrated fabric manufacturers for their internal use from the scope of "the domestic industry".[202] The issue consists of the following two interpretative questions regarding Article 6.2[203]:

(a) Does the term "directly competitive products" cover those products which are produced by vertically integrated fabric manufacturers for their internal consumption; is the term limited to products that are *actually competing* with subject imports?[204]; and

(b) Should Members examine the "domestic industry" consisting of all manufacturers producing (i) like products, or (ii) directly competitive products, or (iii) both like products and directly competitive products[205]; or are they permitted to identify a "domestic industry" as an industry producing a product that is: (i) like but not directly

---

[200] Pakistan Rebuttal Submission, para. 36. *See also* Pakistan First Submission, pp. 21-22. (*Also* paras. 4.18-4.20 and 4.40.)

[201] *See* Pakistan Rebuttal Submission, para. 31. (*Also* paras. 4.38-4.41 and 4.43-4.44.)

[202] The 1998 Market Statement defined the domestic industry as "domestic establishments (or 'mills') engaged in the production of the subject yarn *for sale* to other firms." US Ex. 3, para. 1.3. (emphasis added) "The USG investigation ... considered only the domestic market combed cotton far sale, chief weight combed cotton spun, as defined by Category 301, and not such yarn produced by vertical integrated firms. The 1998 Market Statement further states that "[v]ertically integrated firms do not sell the yarn they produce in the domestic market, and their production does not compete directly with imports in the U.S. 'yarn for sale' market." *Ibid.* para. 3.1. (footnote omitted)

[203] We note that in addition to those two points, the parties are in disagreement on the interpretation of the term "producing" in Article 6.2; Pakistan argued that the vertically integrated fabric manufacturers "produce" combed cotton yarn while the United States argued that they "produce" not combed cotton yarn, but subsequent products, *e.g.* fabric, apparel or home furnishings for sale, within the context of Article 6.2. *See* Pakistan Rebuttal Submission, paras. 19-25 and US Oral Statement at the First Substantive Meeting, paras. 9-11. In our view, it is obvious that the term "producing", in light of its ordinary meaning, to mean the production not only final products but also intermediary products which are to be used as input for the production of final products. Also, in the WTO Agreement, the term "production" is distinctly used from the term "sale". *See e.g.* GATT Article III:1, which provides as follows: "The Members recognize that internal taxes ... affecting the internal *sale* ... of products ... should not be applied ... so as to afford protection to domestic *production*." (emphasis added) To the contrary, the US interpretation of the term "producing" would in effect equate "producing" with "selling".

[204] With respect to Pakistan's position, *see e.g.* Pakistan Rebuttal Submission, paras. 35-36; with respect to the US position, *see e.g.* US First Submission, paras. 50-51.

[205] This is Pakistan's position. *See e.g.* Pakistan First Submission, pp. 22-23. (*Also* paras. 4.38-4.41.)

competitive; or (ii) unlike but directly competitive; or (iii) both like and directly competitive?[206]

7.41 In addition, it is necessary to examine the factual question of whether combed cotton yarn produced by vertically integrated fabric producers for their own consumption is a directly competitive product with combed cotton yarn imported from Pakistan; both parties agree that these products are "like products".[207]

2. *Interpretation of "directly competitive products"*

(a) Text and Context

(i) Article 6.2 of ATC and the WTO Agreement

7.42 **Pakistan** argued that "'directly competitive products' are products with common characteristics that give them the potential of satisfying the same need or taste."[208] In support of its proposition, Pakistan referred to the Appellate Body's finding in *Korea - Alcoholic Beverages*, which it summarizes as "[i]n examining whether a product is competitive *both latent and extant demand* must therefore be considered."[209] Combed cotton yarn produced by vertically integrated fabric manufacturers for their internal consumption share similar technical specifications with imported combed cotton yarn, and as a result, they are "directly competitive" with each other.[210] "All the WTO agreements, including the ATC, are integral parts of the WTO Agreement, which was negotiated and concluded as a single undertaking. It is, therefore, legitimate and common practice for panels to seek guidance for the interpretation of the terms of a WTO agreement from the rulings on similar terms in other agreements."[211]

7.43 The **United States** responded that "combed cotton yarn spun by vertically integrated fabric producers for their own consumption is not intended for release on the marketplace and is not directly competitive with ... imports [of combed cotton yarn]."[212] The Appellate Body's finding cited by Pakistan concerns the term "directly competitive or substitutable products" in Ad Article III:2 of the GATT, which is different from the term "directly competitive products" in Article 6.2 of the ATC.[213] According to the United States, the term "'directly com-

---

206 This is the US position. *See e.g.* US First Submission, para. 49. (*Also* paras. 4.34-4.37.)

207 Pakistan First Submission, p 23, and US Rebuttal Submission, para. 26. (*Also* para. 4.43.)

208 Pakistan Rebuttal Submission, para. 33. *See also* Pakistan's Answers to Panel's Questions, 28 November 2000, p. 5. (*Also* paras. 4.39 and 4.47-4.50.)

209 Pakistan Rebuttal Submission, para. 32. (emphasis in original) (*Also* para. 4.39.)

210 *See e.g.* Pakistan Rebuttal Submission, para. 33. (*Also* para. 4.39.)

211 Pakistan Rebuttal Submission, para. 13. (*Also* paras. 4.10-4.11.)

212 US Rebuttal Submission, para. 26. (*Also* paras. 4.51 and 4.55.)

213 *See e.g.* US Rebuttal Submission, para. 36. (*Also* paras. 4.56-4.57.)

petitive' reflects the actual state of affairs in the market place."[214] Further, the United States urged "the Panel to remain, as the Appellate Body has discussed, within the 'four corners' of the ATC and interpret Article 6 as it applies to the facts of this case based upon the unique text of Article 6 considered in light of the object and purpose of the ATC."[215]

7.44 **Pakistan** also pointed out that vertically integrated fabric producers purchase combed cotton yarn on the merchant market. Thus, Pakistan argued that combed cotton yarn offered on the merchant market is in fact competing with the yarn produced by the vertically integrated fabric producers for their internal use.[216]

7.45 In response, the **United States** indicated that vertically integrated fabric producers purchase roughly two per cent of their combed cotton yarn from the merchant market and sell roughly one per cent. "*De minimis* purchases of combed cotton yarn made by vertically integrated fabric producers are not, as Pakistan suggests, evidence of actual or potential competition. ... The fact that vertically integrated fabric producers may sell roughly one per cent on the market does not mean that the other 99 percent - which never enters the market - is directly competitive with Category 301 imports."[217]

7.46 The **Panel** first notes that the parties are in disagreement on whether the GATT/WTO jurisprudence on any WTO Agreement other than the ATC is relevant to the interpretation of Article 6 of the ATC; Pakistan cited the finding of the Appellate Body on GATT Article III in support of its argument, while the United States urged "the Panel to remain, as the Appellate Body has discussed, within the 'four corners' of the ATC...". As indicated in Article 31(2) of the Vienna Convention, the "context" within the meaning of Article 31(1) comprises "the text" of the *treaty* itself, including its preamble and annexes. The treaty in question here is the WTO Agreement, of which the ATC is an integral part.[218] Thus, it is the WTO Agreement in its entirety, including GATT Article III, that provides the context of Article 6 of the ATC. As the International Law Commission explained in its commentary to the final set of draft articles on the law of treaties, with regard to Article 31(1) of the Vienna Convention[219]:

> "... the ordinary meaning of a term is not to be determined in the abstract but *in the context of the treaty* and in the light of its object

[214] US Rebuttal Submission, para. 37. (*Also* paras. 4.56-4.57.)

[215] US Answers to Panel's Questions, 28 November 2000, para. 3. (footnote omitted) In support of its argument, the United States referred to Appellate Body Report on *US - Underwear*, WT/DS24/AB/R, adopted 25 February 1997, DSR 1997:I, 11, p. 20

[216] *See e.g.* Pakistan Rebuttal Submission, paras. 34-35. (*Also* para. 4.26.)

[217] US Rebuttal Submission, para. 40. (*Also* paras. 4.22 and 4.27-4.28.)

[218] WTO Agreement, Article II:2.

[219] Article 27(1) of the Final Draft Articles of the International Law Commission.

> and purpose. These principles have repeatedly been affirmed by the [International] Court [of Justice]. ...
>
> ...
>
> And the Permanent Court in an early Advisory Opinion stressed that the context is not merely the article or section of the treaty in which the term occurs, but the treaty as a whole:
>
>> 'In considering the question before the Court upon the language of the Treaty, it is obvious that the Treaty must be read as a whole, and that its meaning is not to be determined merely upon particular phrases which, if detached from the context, may be interpreted in more than one sense.'"[220]

In this case, the "treaty as a whole" is the WTO Agreement and all its annexes; it is not just the ATC.[221] Therefore, we consider that the interpretation on the term "directly competitive or substitutable products" under GATT Article III is relevant in interpreting the term "directly competitive products" under Article 6 of the ATC.

7.47 We note that the United States pointed out that in *US - Underwear*, the Appellate Body rejected certain finding of the panel, indicating that "the Panel went outside the four corners of the *ATC*."[222] In that case, in examining whether or not the retroactive application of transitional safeguard measures is permissible, the panel stated that "[s]ince the ATC is silent on this question, we will first examine how the matter is treated under the provisions of the GATT 1994 ...", and found that "Article X:2 of GATT 1994 is the relevant provision ...".[223] The aforesaid statement of the Appellate Body was made to reject this finding of the panel,[224] however, because as opposed to the panel, the Appellate Body did "*not* ... believe that Article 6.10 [of the ATC] does not substantively address that is-

---

[220] Report of the Commission to the General Assembly, Part I, Report of the International Law Commission on the work of the second part of its seventeenth session, [1966] 2 Y. B. Int'l L. Comm'n 169, U.N. Doc. A/6309/Rev.1., p. 221, citing *Competence of the ILO to Regulate Agricultural Labour, P.C.I.J.* (1922), Series B, Nos. 2 and 3, p. 23. (emphasis added) Doctrinal writings also indicate that the "context" is the treaty as a whole, not merely a para., an article, a section, or a part of the treaty. *See* Sinclair, Sir Ian, KCMG, QC, *The Vienna Convention on the Law of Treaties*, Second edition, 1984, p. 127 ; Jennings, Sir Robert, QC and Watts, Sir Arthur, KCMG QC, *Oppenheim's International Law*, Ninth Edition, 1992, p. 1273 ; Yasseen, Mustafa Kamil, *L'interprétation des traités d'après la Convention de Vienne sur le Droit des Traités, Recueil des Cours*, Tome 151, 1976 - III, p. 34; Nguyen Quoc Dinh, Daillier, Patrick, et Pellet, Alain, *Droit international public*, quatrième edition, 1992, pp. 252-253. *See also* Brownlie, Ian, QC, DCL, FBA, *Principles of Public International Law*, Fourth edition, 1990, p. 629.

[221] Also, the Appellate Body, in *US - Shrimp*, stated that "[t]he preamble of the WTO Agreement ... informs not only the GATT 1994, but also the other covered agreements ...". Appellate Body Report on *US - Shrimp*, op. cit., para. 129.

[222] Appellate Body Report on *US - Underwear*, op. cit., p. 20.

[223] Panel Report on *US - Underwear*, op. cit., para. 7.64.

[224] Appellate Body Report on *US - Underwear*, op. cit., p. 12.

sue."[225] Contrary to the US argumentation, nothing in the Appellate Body Report on *US - Underwear* prevents us from using any WTO covered agreement other than the ATC as the "context" of Article 6 of the ATC within the meaning of Article 31(1) of the Vienna Convention.

7.48 Second, we recall that panels and the Appellate Body have often consulted dictionaries as a starting point in analyzing the ordinary meaning of terms used in the WTO Agreement in accordance with Article 31(1) of the Vienna Convention.[226] In this case, we note that the term "competitive" is defined as "of, pertaining to, involving, characterized by, or decided by competition."[227]

7.49 Our attention is next directed to the most immediate context of the term "competitive" in Article 6.2, *i.e.* the qualifier "directly". In our view, if the term "competitive" were to have only a narrow meaning, for example, *actually competing*, the qualifier "directly" would be rendered meaningless; the function of defining the scope of the term "competitive" has been left to the term "directly".

7.50 Accordingly, we go on to examine the meaning of the term "directly". It is obvious that under Article 6.2, the term "directly" excludes those products which are in remote competition with a subject textile or clothing product, from the scope of a subject domestic industry. In this connection, we note that competition can exist in some sense between any two products. This is particularly obvious in case of consumer products; for example, a number of consumers would make comparison between cashmere sweaters and silk neckties as a birthday present, and in that sense, they are competing with each other. Keeping in mind the aforesaid relevance of the jurisprudence with respect to GATT Article III, we note that in relation to the interpretation of "directly competitive or substitutable products" under GATT Article III, the panel on *Korea - Alcoholic Beverages* stated as follows:

---

225 *Ibid.* p. 14. (emphasis in original)

226 For a few recent examples, Appellate Body Reports on *US - Wheat Gluten*, op. cit., para. 53; *Korea - Measures Affecting Imports of Fresh, Chilled and Frozen Beef*, WT/DS161/AB/R and WT/DS169/AB/R, adopted 10 January 2001, DSR 2001:I, 5, paras. 111 and 120; and *Brazil - Export Financing Programme for Aircraft - Recourse by Canada to Article 21.5 of the DSU*, WT/DS46/AB/RW, adopted 4 August 2000, DSR 2000:VIII, 4067, para. 45.

227 *New Shorter Oxford English Dictionary*, op. cit., p. 459. Further, the term "competitive" is defined in the *New Shorter Oxford English Dictionary* as: (1a) "The action of competing or contending with others"; (1b) "Striving for custom between rival traders in the same commodity"; (2) "An event in which persons or teams compete; a match; a contest; a trial of ability"; (3) "The person or persons competing with one; the opposition in a contest". *Ibid.* The United States also referred to the definition of "competitive" in the *New Shorter Oxford English Dictionary. See* US Rebuttal Submission, fn. 30 and para. 37. *Webster's New Encyclopedic Dictionary* defines the term "competitive" as "relating to, characterized by, or based on competition," and in turn, "competition" as: (1) "the act or process of competing"; (2) "a contest between rivals ..."; (3) "the effort of two or more persons or firms acting independently to secure business by offering the most favorable terms"; (4) "active demand by two or more organisms or kinds of organisms for some environmental resource in short supply." *Webster's New Encyclopedic Dictionary* (Black Dog & Leventhal Publishing Inc. 1994 ed.), p. 201.

> "At some level all products or services are at least indirectly competitive. Because consumers have limited amounts of disposable income, they may have to arbitrate between various needs such as giving up going on a vacation to buy a car or abstaining from eating in restaurants to buy new shoes or a television set."[228]

7.51 The foregoing analysis is suggestive of the role of the term "directly" in qualifying "competitive" under Article 6. Without the qualifier "directly" in Article 6, for example, in order to decide whether a transitional safeguard measure should be imposed on imports of cashmere sweaters, a Member would need to examine the situation of domestic producers of not only cashmere sweaters, but also silk neckties and a wide range of other consumer products. If it were necessary to consider this remote competition under Article 6, the scope of a subject domestic industry would be too broad. Thus, the qualifier "directly" of "competitive" under Article 6 limits the scope of a subject domestic industry by excluding such remote competition.

7.52 The panel on *Korea - Alcoholic Beverages* also found that "an assessment of whether there is a direct competitive relationship between two products or groups of products requires evidence that consumers consider or could consider the two products or groups of products as alternative ways of satisfying a particular need or taste."[229] The Appellate Body agreed with this standard, stating that "according to the ordinary meaning of the term, products are competitive or substitutable when they are interchangeable or if they offer, as the Panel noted, 'alternative ways of satisfying a particular need or taste'."[230] Therefore, we consider that this interpretation of "directly competitive or substitutable products" is of relevance in interpreting the term "directly competitive products" under Article 6 of the ATC, because GATT Article III constitutes part of the "context" of Article 6 of the ATC within the meaning of Article 31(1) of the Vienna Convention, as indicated in paragraphs 7.46-7.47 above.

7.53 We will then recall the factual arguments of the parties on the products in question. First, both parties admitted that imported combed cotton yarn and domestically produced combed cotton yarn, whether for sale or internal use, share basically the same technical specifications.[231] Second, Pakistan claimed and the United States acknowledged that vertically integrated firms are purchasing

---

[228] Panel Report on *Korea - Taxes on Alcoholic Beverages* ("*Korea - Alcoholic Beverages*"), WT/DS75/R and WT/DS84/R, adopted 17 February 1999, DSR 1999:I, 44, para. 10.40.

[229] *Ibid.*

[230] Appellate Body Report on *Korea - Alcoholic Beverages*, WT/DS75/AB/R and WT/DS84/AB/R, adopted 17 February 1999, op. cit., DSR 1999:I,3, para. 115.

[231] *See* US Answers to Panel's Questions, 28 November 2000, para. 91 ("To the best of our knowledge, there are no material differences in the technical specifications of the yarn produced domestically for sale, for internal use and the yarn imported from Pakistan or Mexico."), and Pakistan Rebuttal Submission, para. 33. (*Also* paras. 4.12 and 4.187.)

combed cotton yarn in the market presumably with the same objective.[232] This indicates that the vertically integrated fabric producers recognize combed cotton yarn offered in the open market and combed cotton yarn they produce for their own consumption "as alternative ways of satisfying a particular need ...". Imported combed cotton yarn is also offered for sale in the market, and thus, should be presumed to be actually competing with combed cotton yarn produced by vertically integrated fabric producers for their internal consumption. In our view, it is obviously unreasonable to exclude captive production from the scope of a domestic industry on the ground that it is not "directly competitive products".

7.54 Here, it is necessary to address further arguments of the United States. The United States argued that the Appellate Body's aforesaid finding in *Korea - Alcoholic Beverages* relies on the term "substitutable", which is missing in Article 6 of the ATC. According to the United States, the absence of this term indicates that the relationship between "like products" and "directly competitive products" under Article 6 of the ATC is different from that between "like products" and "directly competitive or substitutable products" under GATT Article III:2.[233] Also, the statement of the Appellate Body is based upon the object and purpose of GATT Article III, which is different from that of Article 6 of the ATC.[234]

7.55 The Panel notes that, indeed, the finding of the Appellate Body appears to rely on the term "substitutable" as well as "competitive". In *Korea - Alcoholic Beverages*, the Appellate Body also stated as follows:

> "The term 'directly competitive or substitutable' describes a particular type of relationship between two products, one imported and the other domestic. It is evident from the wording of the term that the essence of that relationship is that the products are in competition. This much is clear both from the word 'competitive' which means 'characterized by competition', and from the word 'substitutable' which means 'able to be substituted'. The context of the competitive relationship is necessarily the marketplace since this is the forum where consumers choose between different products. Competition in the market place is a dynamic, evolving process. Accordingly, the wording of the term 'directly competitive or substitutable' implies that the competitive relationship between products is *not* to be analyzed *exclusively* by reference to *current* consumer preferences. In our view, the word 'substitutable' indicates that the requisite relationship *may* exist between products that are not, at a given moment, considered by consumers to be substitutes but

232 US Rebuttal Submission, para. 40. (*Also* paras. 4.21-4.23.)

233 US Rebuttal Submission, paras. 30 and 35-37. (*Also* paras. 4.56-4.57.)

234 US Answers to Panel's Questions, 28 November 2000, para. 8. (*Also* paras. 4.56-4.57.)

which are, nonetheless, *capable* of being substituted for one another.

Thus, according to the ordinary meaning of the term, products are competitive or substitutable when they are interchangeable[235] or if they offer, as the Panel noted, 'alternative ways of satisfying a particular need or taste'.[236] Particularly in a market where there are regulatory barriers to trade or to competition, there may well be latent demand.

The words 'competitive or substitutable' are qualified in the *Ad* Article by the term 'directly'. In the context of Article III:2, second sentence, the word 'directly' suggests a degree of proximity in the competitive relationship between the domestic and the imported products. The word 'directly' does not, however, prevent a panel from considering both latent and extant demand."[237]

7.56 Also, in *Korea - Alcoholic Beverages*, the Appellate Body relied on the objective of GATT Article III as follows:

"In view of the objectives of avoiding protectionism, requiring equality of competitive conditions and protecting expectations of equal competitive relationships, we decline to take a static view of the term 'directly competitive or substitutable.' The object and purpose of Article III confirms that the scope of the term 'directly competitive or substitutable' cannot be limited to situations where consumers *already* regard products as alternatives. If reliance could be placed only on current instances of substitution, the object and purpose of Article III:2 could be defeated by the protective taxation that the provision aims to prohibit."[238]

7.57 However, we note that the case on *Korea - Alcoholic Beverages* dealt with questions of substitutability of *unlike* products while in the case at hand we are dealing with the competitiveness of *like* products, and thus, the situation at hand is even clearer than that in the above-quoted case. In *Korea - Alcoholic Beverages*, the subject products, Korean *soju*, and imported products such as gin and whisky, were different in some respects, while our question is whether the like products (*i.e.* captively produced combed cotton yarn and imported combed cotton yarn) are "directly competitive" with each other. In our view, there is no question that these two like products before us are "directly competitive" even if they are not actually competing with each other for any given sale. The defini-

[235] (footnote original) Appellate Body Report on *Canada - Measures Concerning Periodicals*, WT/DS31/AB/R.

[236] (footnote original) Panel Report on *Korea - Alcoholic Beverages*, op. cit., para. 10.40.

[237] Appellate Body Report on *Korea -Alcoholic Beverages*, op. cit., paras. 114-116. (emphasis in original)

[238] Appellate Body Report on *Korea - Alcoholic Beverages*, op. cit., paras. 119-120.

tions of "like products" and "directly competitive products" may vary depending on the provision,[239] but it is worth noting that under GATT Article III, in *Korea - Alcoholic Beverages*, the Appellate Body stated that "'like' products are a subset of directly competitive or substitutable products...."[240] While the precise scope of "directly competitive products" may be different, it is instructive to note the relationship between the terms (*i.e.* one as a subset of another).

7.58 Further, we would like to emphasize again that in the case before us, vertically integrated fabric producers purchase combed cotton yarn and also sell combed cotton yarn they produce, in the market, which includes imported combed cotton yarn, even though their amounts are small. In our view, these facts reveal that combed cotton yarn produced by the integrated producers for their own use is "directly competitive" with imported combed cotton yarn. Manufacturers' decisions as to whether to buy materials in the market or to rely exclusively on internal production, or whether to sell their intermediary products in the market or use them to manufacture downstream products, are an economically driven choice made by individual companies. Such decisions are much more particular in nature than the decision that we have to make as to whether two like products are "directly competitive". Vertically integrated manufacturers make a business decision on these points based primarily on profit maximization. No such decision will be necessary for either the non-integrated purchaser (*i.e.* a fabric producer, which does not have a make/buy decision) or the non-integrated combed cotton yarn producer (which does not have a sell/use decision). Thus, it is arguable that an investigating authority might weigh the evidence differently with regard to the two types of combed cotton yarn producers, but that is a matter of evaluating damage to producers, not whether the products are "directly competitive" with each other.[241]

7.59 In our view, the interpretation to be given of the term "directly competitive" in Article 6 is of a more general and objective nature, without taking account of factors specific to each and every producer or consumer. The focus initially is on the *products*. Thus, the alleged fact that vertically integrated fabric producers do not intend to sell combed cotton yarn in the market would not pre-

---

[239] Cf. Appellate Body Report on *Japan - Alcoholic Beverages*, op. cit., fn. 44, referring to Panel Report on *Japan - Alcoholic Beverages*, op. cit., para. 6.20.

[240] Appellate Body Report on *Korea - Alcoholic Beverages*, op. cit., para. 118.

[241] In addition, we note that the 1998 Market Statement only reflects statistics on actual completed sales. There is no evidence that *offers for sale* were investigated. This latter point would be necessary to be established even under the US method of defining "directly competitive". It would be reasonable to infer that there must be offers for sale several times as many as actual completed sales, even assuming that vertically integrated fabric manufacturers do not purchase or sell combed cotton yarn in the open market for business. It would be rather unreasonable to consider that they are always able to purchase or sell combed cotton yarn whenever they wish. Taking this into consideration, the US general statement that the vertically integrated manufacturers did not intend to sell their products in the market would appear to be conjecture rather than a fact demonstrated in the 1998 Market Statement.

vent us from finding that captively produced combed cotton yarn and imported combed cotton yarn are "directly competitive" with each other. In other words, the US interpretation would require an unacceptably novel reading of Article 6 to permit the definition of *products*, in terms of *producers* rather than the reverse, which is the natural reading of the language and that most consistent with GATT/WTO practice.

(ii) Article 6.2 within the ATC

7.60 **Pakistan** argued that the US interpretation of "directly competitive products" would run counter to the exceptional nature of the transitional safeguard, and in its support, referred to Article 6.1, which provides that "[t]he transitional safeguard should be applied as sparingly as possible, consistently with ... the effective implementation of the integration process...".[242] Also, in a further support of its argument, Pakistan referred to the Appellate Body Report on *US - Underwear*, which used Article 6.1 as a basis for rejection of retroactive application of transitional safeguard measures.[243]

7.61 The **United States** responded that "Article 6 exists for the purpose of providing importing Members meaningful recourse to a safeguard mechanism during the transition period in which the textiles and clothing sector is integrated into the GATT. Accordingly, this provision is a fundamental aspect of the carefully negotiated balance struck in the ATC. It is not, as Pakistan claims, a measure 'running counter to the basic purpose of the ATC.' To disregard the ordinary meaning of 'domestic industry producing like and/or directly competitive products' and limit the availability of an Article 6 safeguard only to physically 'like' products would prevent the Panel from giving meaning to words clearly in the text and would amount to rewriting the ATC's carefully negotiated balance of rights and obligations."[244]

7.62 On this point, **the Panel** agrees that Article 6.1 is part of the immediate context of Article 6.2. The last sentence of Article 6.1 reads as follows:

> "The transitional safeguard should be applied as sparingly as possible, consistently with the provisions of this Article and the effective implementation of the integration process under this Agreement."

7.63 Indeed, we acknowledge that the last sentence of Article 6.1 could be interpreted as an exhortation that Members exercise restraint in the frequency with which they *apply* transitional safeguard measures, rather than limiting the scope of the interpretation of the language itself. However, it is more natural to read

---

[242] *See* Pakistan Rebuttal Submission, paras. 38-42, in particular, para. 41. (*Also* paras. 4.2, 4.54 and 4.70.)

[243] Pakistan referred to Appellate Body Report on *US - Underwear*, op. cit., p. 15. (*Also* para. 4.70.)

[244] US Rebuttal Submission, para. 23. (footnote omitted) (*Also* para. 4.36.)

Article 6.1 as encouraging Members to restrict transitional safeguard measures in a more general manner. The Preamble of the ATC notes that "negotiations in the area of textile and clothing shall aim to formulate modalities that would permit the eventual integration of this sector into GATT/WTO on the basis of strengthened GATT rules and disciplines, thereby also contributing to the objective of further liberalization of trade". It would be inconsistent with this Preamble if Article 6 were to set forth an overly broad authority of Members to take transitional safeguard measures.

7.64 Moreover, in this connection, we note that the US interpretation of the term "directly competitive" would also permit transitional safeguard measures to be taken to address the following cases:

(a) A US manufacturer of combed cotton yarn had been acquired by a vertically integrated fabric producer during the investigation period but continues to produce the same product, but now only for the internal use of the integrated firm. According to the US interpretation, even if the acquired manufacturer had maintained the same number of employees and facilities and the same level of production (or even increased them), it should be deemed to have "exited" the industry merely because of the change in ownership, and, among other things, could be an indicator of "serious damage" to the domestic industry.[245]

(b) The integrated fabric producers sell more combed cotton yarn in the market, thereby achieving a market share greater than *de minimis*[246] (say, 10%) before the investigation period. Then the integrated firms maintain the same level of production during the investigation period, but switch a significant amount to their own internal use sufficient to drop below the *de minimis* threshold. According to the US interpretation, the integrated firms should be deemed to have "exited" the industry to the extent that they ceased to sell their products in the market in order to use them for their internal consumption, and hence, their resulted loss of shares in the sales market, among other things, could be an indicator of "serious damage" to the domestic industry.[247]

---

[245] This is not an extravagant hypothesis. See US First Submission, para. 162, 3rd bullet. (*Also* paras. 4.144-4.148.)

[246] We further note that an illustration of the artificiality of the US definition is that the United States has had recourse to the concept of *de minimis* sales which has no basis in the treaty language.

[247] In response to the Panel's question as to whether the United States would find "damage" to the domestic industry in these cases, the United States did not provided any clear-cut answer, but did not deny the possibility of finding serious damage based upon the given set of facts. US Answers to Panel's Questions, 28 November 2000, paras. 75-82. (*Also* paras. 4.144-4.148.)

7.65 It would be manifestly absurd to find serious damage to a domestic industry in these situations, and therefore, to impose a transitional safeguard measure when the domestic production of combed cotton yarn has been maintained at the same level. It is difficult to see how a mere change of ownership or a transitory change in make/buy decisions could support a finding of "serious damage",[248] and permit the Member to impose a transitional safeguard measure on imports. In our view, the language encouraging general restraint in Article 6.1, which constitutes part of the context of Article 6.2, supports the interpretation of the term "directly competitive products" as including combed cotton yarn produced by vertically integrated fabric manufacturers for their internal consumption, in order to avoid unjustifiable use of the safeguard mechanism as illustrated by the situations in the preceding paragraph.

(b) Object and Purpose of the ATC

7.66 We recall that Article 31(1) of the Vienna Convention provides that "[a] treaty shall be interpreted in good faith in accordance with the ordinary meaning to be given to the terms of the treaty in their context and in the light of its *object and purpose*." (emphasis added) We will thus examine whether the aforesaid product-based (as opposed to producer-based) interpretation of the term "directly competitive products" is consistent with the object and purpose of the ATC.

7.67 **Pakistan** argued that the object and purpose of the ATC is to ensure that the textiles and clothing sector will eventually be integrated into the GATT 1994, in response to the Panel's question as to how the object and purpose of the ATC demands Pakistan's interpretation of the scope of a subject domestic industry under Article 6, and excludes the US interpretation. In this line, Pakistan claimed that this leads to Article 1.5, which requests Members to "allow for continuous autonomous industrial adjustment and increased competition in the markets", and further, Article 6.1, which provides that "the transitional safeguard should be applied as sparingly as possible...". Further, the US definition of the subject domestic industry cannot be reconciled with the object and purpose of the ATC, because it allows Members to take transitional safeguard measures to protect domestic producers that are most likely to suffer serious damage from competition with imports. This would greatly facilitate the use of transitional safeguard measures, which would seem contrary to the whole purpose of progressively integrating the textiles and clothing sector into the GATT/WTO.[249]

7.68 In response to a similar question, the **United States** indicated that "[t]he ATC sets forth a careful balancing of interests between exporting and importing

[248] Further, it would be improper to adopt any interpretation that would lead to absurd results. *See* Appellate Body Report on *EC - Computer Equipment*, op. cit., para. 86.

[249] *See* Pakistan Answers to Panel's Questions, 28 November 2000, pp. 8-10, and Pakistan Rebuttal Submission, paras. 44-46. (*Also* paras. 4.92 and 4.54.)

Members to guide the textiles and clothing sector through the delicate ten-year transition from a regime of special quotas to GATT rules."[250] Further, it claimed that "[f]or importing Members, a fundamental aspect of this bargain was the ability to address damaging surges in imports of non-integrated products through a special safeguard provision *separate from* Article XIX of GATT 1994 and the WTO *Agreement on Safeguards* ...."[251] Also, the United States criticized Pakistan's interpretation in that it "denies the relevance of the marketplace for purposes of transitional safeguard action."[252]

7.69 In a further rebuttal, **Pakistan** claimed that the United States attempts to turn an "exception in the ATC into the expression of the basic object and purpose of the ATC."[253]

7.70 The **United States** further stated that "[t]he Article 6 transitional safeguard mechanism represents a fundamental part of the ATC's carefully negotiated text; it is *not* ... a measure running counter to the basic purpose of the ATC."[254]

7.71 In **the Panel**'s view, in order to address the issues at hand, it is not necessary to answer the general question of whether or not transitional safeguard measures are *exceptionally* permitted under the ATC. We believe that in the final analysis the parties do not disagree that integration of the trade in textile and clothing into GATT/WTO system is the object and purpose of the ATC as stated in its Preamble. This object and purpose is referred to again in the last sentence of Article 6.1. As indicated above, the interpretation of the term "directly competitive products" in the light of this sentence and also the object and purpose of the ATC would rather favour the traditional product-based interpretation[255] as is usual under the GATT/WTO, *inter alia*, in GATT Articles III and XIX.[256] This is

---

250 US Answers to Panel's Questions, 28 November 2000, para. 16. (*Also* para. 4.9.)

251 US Answers to Panel's Questions, 28 November 2000, para. 16. (emphasis in original) *See also* US Rebuttal Submission, para. 13. (*Also* para. 4.9.)

252 US Answers to Panel's Questions, 28 November 2000, para. 18. (*Also* para. 4.51.)

253 Pakistan Rebuttal Submission, para. 44. (*Also* para. 4.54.)

254 US Rebuttal Submission, para. 13. (emphasis in original) (*Also* paras. 4.211-4.215.)

255 We recall our discussion in para. 7.59 above, where we noted that traditionally the domestic producers are defined in term of directly competitive products rather than defining the products in terms of who produces them.

256 The panel on *United States - Safeguard Measures on Imports of Fresh, Chilled or Frozen Lamb Meat from New Zealand and Australia* ("*US - Lamb*") recently touched on this issue. In relation to Article 4.1(c) of the Agreement on Safeguards, which defines a "domestic industry" as "the producers as a whole of the like or directly competitive products ... or those whose collective output of the like or directly competitive products constitutes a major proportion of the total domestic production of those products", the panel found that it is inconsistent with this provision to include input producers (growers and feeders of live lamb) in the scope of the domestic industry producing lamb meat. Panel Report on *US - Lamb*, WT/DS177/R and WT/DS178/R, circulated 21 December 2000 and appealed 31 January 2001, section 4(a), in particular, para. 7.118. In support of this finding, the panel referred to GATT Panel Reports on *United States - Definition of Industry Concerning Wine and Grape Products*, adopted 28 April 1992, SCM/71, BISD 39S/436; *New Zealand - Imports of Electrical Transformers from Finland*, adopted 18 July 1985, BISD 32S/55; *Canada - Imposition of*

consistent with our finding in paragraph 7.46 above that GATT Article III constitutes part of the context of the term "directly competitive" in Article 6.2 of the ATC.[257]

(c) Issue of the MFA

7.72 The **United States** argued that the MFA constitutes part of the context of Article 6 of the ATC, with reference to the Appellate Body Report on *US - Underwear*,[258] which states that "[w]e turn to another element of the context of Article 6.10 of the ATC: the prior existence and demise ... of the MFA."[259]

7.73 In contrast, **Pakistan** argued that "[i]n the *Underwear* case the Appellate Body used the MFA *only to confirm* an interpretation it had reached in accordance with Article 31 of the Vienna Convention."[260]

7.74 **The Panel** first notes that Article 31(2) of the Vienna Convention sets forth as follows:

> "The context for the purpose of the interpretation of a treaty shall comprise, in addition to the text, including its preamble and annexes:
>
> (a) any agreement relating to the treaty which was made between all the parties in connexion with the conclusion of the treaty;
>
> (b) any instrument which was made by one or more parties in connexion with the conclusion of the treaty and accepted by the other parties as an instrumented related to the treaty."

This clearly indicates that the MFA cannot be part of the "context" of the ATC within the meaning of Article 31(2) of the Vienna Convention. The MFA is not an integral part of the WTO Agreement, and was not made "in connexion with the conclusion of" this treaty. We further note that the Appellate Body Report on *US - Underwear* mentioned as part of the "context" of Article 6.10 of the ATC, not the MFA itself, but "the prior existence and demise ... of the MFA".[261] They are occurrences rather than "any agreement" or "any instrument". Clearly, in our view, the Appellate Body used the MFA not as part of the "context" of the ATC

Countervailing Duties on Imports of Manufacturing Beef from the EEC, dated 13 October 1987, SCM/85. *See* Panel Report on *US - Lamb*, op. cit., paras. 7.78-7.109.

[257] We note that our interpretation of Article 6 of the ATC is consistent with the object and purpose of the WTO Agreement, as described in its Preamble, as well as the object and purpose of the ATC.

[258] US Answers to Panel's Questions, 28 November 2000, paras. 26-28, stating that "[t]he MFA is relevant as providing context for the interpretation of "like and/or directly competitive products" for the purpose of Article 6." (*Also* para. 4.62.)

[259] Appellate Body Report on *US - Underwear*, op. cit., p. 24.

[260] Pakistan Rebuttal Submission, para. 47-51, in particular, para. 50. (emphasis in original) (*Also* para. 4.63.)

[261] Appellate Body Report on *US - Underwear*, op. cit., p. 24.

within the meaning of Article 31(1) of the Vienna Convention, but as part of the circumstances of the conclusion of the ATC.[262]

7.75 In any event, the US position would not be supported by referring to the fact that the same term "like and/or directly competitive products" was used in the MFA. This reference was made to support its proposition that in interpreting the term under Article 6 of the ATC, the Panel should not apply the interpretation of similar terms used elsewhere in the WTO Agreement (*e.g.* "like or directly competitive products" under GATT Article XIX and the Safeguards Agreement). Also, the United States argued that, in light of MFA practices, the term under Article 6 should refer to products which compete in the marketplace.[263]

7.76 The United States is correct that the term "and/or" does not appear elsewhere in the WTO Agreement for the purpose of determining the producers of products in question. Nevertheless, this would not necessarily support the US justification for the exclusion of captive production from the scope of "directly competitive products" under the proper interpretation of the language of the ATC as discussed above.

7.77 We further note that the MFA required a finding of "market disruption ... based on the existence of serious damage to domestic producers", as distinct from "serious damage to the domestic industry producing like and/or directly competitive products" under the ATC. Also, under the MFA, "and/or" referred to "technical changes or changes in consumer preference which are instrumental in switches" in production.[264] This is different terminology from Article 6.2, which adopts the forms used elsewhere in the WTO (*i.e.* defining an industry based upon products and then assessing the impact of the imports on such an industry), albeit with somewhat different wording. Further, we do not accept the relevance of the MFA pursuant to Article 32 of the Vienna Convention because the interpretation under Article 31 of the Vienna Convention is enough, but even if we had, for the United States, to merely point out that the MFA used the term "and/or" does not help support the US interpretation of the ATC in light of the other more significant distinctions between the treaties' texts.

---

[262] *See* para. 7.20 above. In this connection, please also note that in its Rebuttal Submission, the United States did not specifically argued that the MFA constitute part of the "context" of the ATC, as that term is used in the Vienna Convention. *See* US Rebuttal Submission, para. 31, in particular, fn. 22. The US answer to the Panel's question about the legal relevance of the MFA does not specifically characterize the MFA as such. The US Answers to Panel's Question, dated 22 December 2000, paras. 1-6.

[263] *See* US Answers to Panel's Questions, 28 November 2000, paras. 26-28. (*Also* para. 4.58.)

[264] Both parties agreed that Annex A to the MFA, which used the term, clarified that safeguard measures could be invoked to protect domestic producers of certain textile products, *e.g.* cotton fibres, from imports of not identical but directly competitive products, *e.g.* non-cotton vegetable fibres such as ramie. The text of Annex A and the materials the parties cited seem to support their arguments. Pakistan Answers to Panel's Questions, 28 November 2000, p. 14 and US Answers to Panel's Questions, 28 November 2000, para. 25. (*Also* paras. 4.59-4.61.)

(d) Practicability

7.78 The **United States** pointed out that it is difficult to examine the factors enumerated in Article 6.3 in respect of vertically integrated producers.[265]

7.79 **Pakistan**, however, responded that it is possible to do so under the ATC as under the Anti-Dumping Agreement, and that the United States did so under its antidumping law.[266]

7.80 **The Panel** notes that under the Anti-Dumping Agreement, the importing Member is required to examine all relevant economic variables of the domestic industry, "including actual and potential decline in sales, profits, output, market share, productivity, return on investments, or utilization of capacity; factors affecting domestic prices ...; actual and potential negative effects [of dumping] on cash flow, inventories, employment, wages, growth, ability to raise capital or investments",[267] which cover almost all the economic variables that are required to be examined under Article 6.4 of the ATC. It may be the case that some factors, such as profits, may be difficult to assess for captive producers. However, other factors such as labour, productivity, inventory, wages, capacity utilization, production levels, etc. would be very similar to assess.[268] Thus, the examination of the captive producers may be somewhat different and the weighting of such assessment may require further analysis on a case-by-case basis, but that certainly does not mean that it cannot be done.[269]

3. *Interpretation of "and/or"*

7.81 The interpretations of the parties are also in a sharp contrast with each other regarding the meaning of "and/or" in Article 6.2. As noted above, according to **Pakistan**, a subject domestic industry consists of producers of (i) like products, or (ii) directly competitive products, or (iii) both like products and directly competitive products.[270] In contrast, the **United States** argued that Members are permitted to identify a "domestic industry" as an industry producing a

---

[265] *See* US First Submission, para. 48 and US Rebuttal Submission, para. 22. (*Also* paras. 4.21-4.23 and 4.25.)

[266] Pakistan Rebuttal Submission, paras. 22-25. (*Also* para. 4.16.)

[267] Antidumping Agreement, Article 3.4.

[268] In this connection, we note that the United States did not contest Pakistan's argument that the United States has done this successfully with respect to vertically integrated producers in the antidumping proceedings. *See* Pakistan Rebuttal Submission, para. 24 and fn. 25.

[269] Further, we note that the US interpretation would not remove its alleged difficulties; if vertically integrated fabric manufacturers had sold in the market combed cotton yarn in the amount greater than *de minimis*, the United States presumably would have had to examine these factors only for the production of such combed cotton yarn, as distinct from all the establishment's production.

[270] *See* Pakistan First Submission, pp. 22-23. (*Also* para. 4.39.)

product that is: (i) like but not directly competitive; or (ii) unlike but directly competitive; or (iii) both like and directly competitive.[271]

7.82 **Pakistan** rebuts the US argument by arguing that the category "like but not directly competitive products" is inconceivable in light of the jurisprudence concerning GATT Article III that like products are a subset of directly competitive products.[272]

7.83 The **United States** further responded that the connecting word "and/or" between "like" and "directly competitive products" suggests that the "like products" should not be constructed as a subset of the "directly competitive products". If "like products" is a subset of "directly competitive products" under Article 6 of the ATC, Pakistan's interpretation would contravene the principle of effectiveness in treaty interpretation, because the words "like and/or" would be unnecessary to define a domestic industry under Article 6.2.[273]

7.84 In **the Panel**'s view, it is difficult to envisage products that are like but not directly competitive and as a factual matter we have found the products in this dispute to be both. However, we cannot ignore the existence of the term "and" in Article 6.2. It may be the unintended result of unfortunate drafting, but the term "and" is there nonetheless. Thus, we shall carry our analysis through on this basis.

7.85 The following diagram might help illustrate the position of Pakistan.[274] In the view of Pakistan, the category of "like products" (A) is always a subset of "directly competitive products" (B); therefore, "like products" plus "directly competitive products" = "directly competitive products" ($A \cup B = B$). Consequently, the choice is, in effect, limited to two possibilities: "like" or "directly competitive".

Diagram 1

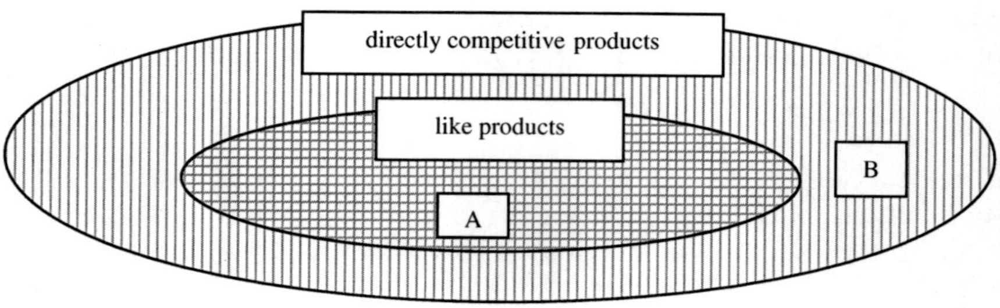

[271] *See* US First Submission, para. 49. *See also* the discussion in paras. 7.38-7.40 above. (*Also* paras. 4.34-4.35.)

[272] *See* Pakistan Answers to Panel's Questions, 28 November 2000, p. 4. (*Also* paras. 4.43-4.44.)

[273] *See* US Rebuttal Submission, paras. 31-34. (*Also* para. 4.45.)

[274] This and the following diagrams are illustrative only and not according to scale.

7.86 Also, the following diagrams help illustrate our understanding of the US position. The category of "like but not directly competitive products" is A; the category of "unlike but directly competitive products" is B; therefore, products that are both "like and directly competitive" is C. As mentioned in paragraph 7.83 above, the United States contended that the category of "like products" is not a subset of "directly competitive products", and hence, it must presuppose that illustration in Diagram 3.

Diagram 2

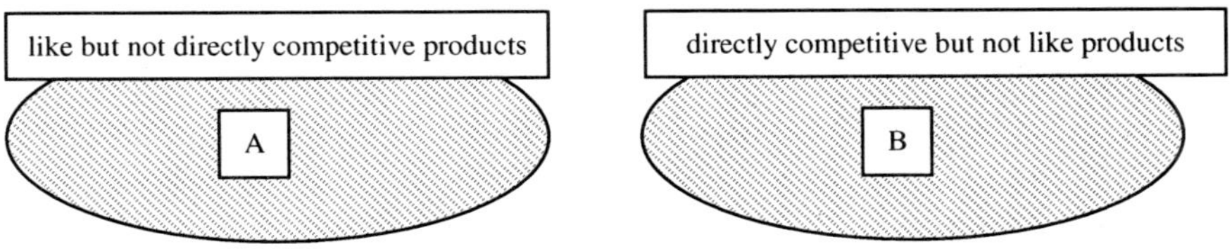

Diagram 3

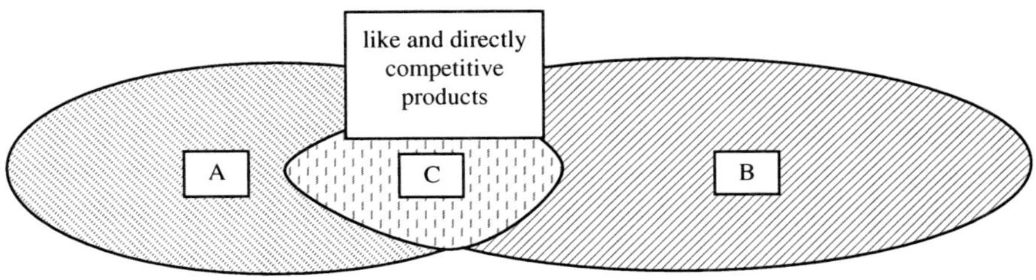

7.87 Both of the parties' interpretations of the term "and/or" are grammatically possible. However, in our view, the chart shows that the US interpretation is flawed in that among other things, one of the categories of a domestic industry, *i.e.* the producers of product A in the chart above, is a meaningless alternative. Imports of any textile product cannot damage producers of "like but not directly competitive products" through market competition. The United States itself conceded that "if the products of domestic producers are *not* directly competitive with imports - such as in the case of yarn manufactured by vertically integrated producers for their internal consumption - the need for safeguard action would not arise."[275] Indeed, not only would the need not arise, but the case could not be made because causation could not be demonstrated. Thus, the treaty would give a meaningless right. In this respect, the US interpretation is inconsistent with the principle of effectiveness in treaty interpretation.[276]

---

[275] US First Submission, para. 50. (emphasis in original) (*Also* para. 4.21.)

[276] Appellate Body, in *US - Gasoline*, stated as follows:

7.88 In the case, which would be difficult to envision, where "like products" (A) is not a subset of "directly competitive products" (B), the more logical description of the category of "like and directly competitive products" would be A $\cup$ B (A plus B), *i.e.* the broader grouping, rather than the narrow US suggestion of A $\cap$ B (both A and B, which is shown in the previous illustration as "C"). This is the more logical reading of the language and is consistent with the usage everywhere else in the WTO Agreements. In our view, the correct illustration of "like and directly competitive" is as follows:

> "... One of the corollaries of the 'general rule of interpretation' in the *Vienna Convention* is that interpretation must give meaning and effect to all the terms of the treaty. An interpreter is not free to adopt a reading that would result in reducing whole clauses or paras. of a treaty to redundancy or inutility."

Appellate Body Report on *US - Gasoline*, op. cit., p. 21. *Also* Appellate Body Reports on *Japan - Alcoholic Beverages*, op. cit., pp. 104-105; *US - Underwear*, op. cit., p. 22; *Argentina - Footwear*, op. cit., para. 95; and *Korea - Dairy*, op. cit., para. 81.

Diagram 4

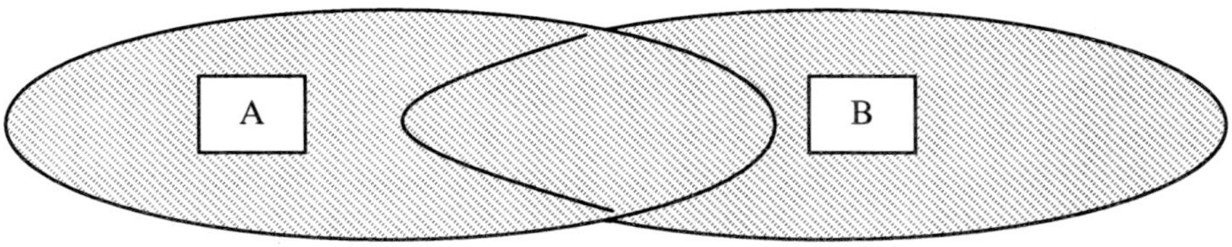

Thus, the category "like *and* directly competitive products" should consist of A *plus* B ($A \cup B$), rather than the mere overlap of the two ($A \cap B$).[277]

7.89 Further, in our view, the US interpretation is problematic in permitting Members to impose transitional safeguard measures for domestic producers of "unlike but directly competitive products". This means that "serious damage" would be found based upon the examination of the situation regarding these producers, without taking into consideration the situation regarding producers of "like and directly competitive products", which are *core* products competing with subject imports. To give an example of the absurdity of the potential result from the US formulation, take the following example of an investigation with respect

277 We note that the term "and/or" is used in the following places in the WTO Agreements: (i) DSU: Article 8.1; (ii) TRIPS: Articles 45.2 and 61; (iii) GATS: Articles V:1, XXVII(b)(ii) and XXVIII(f)(i); Annex on Air Transport, para. 6(d); (iv) SCM: Articles 8.2(c) and 25.3; Illustrative List, item (k); Annex V, para. 6; (v) Licensing: Articles 3.3, 3.5(a)(iv), and 3.5(b); (vi) Rules of Origin: Articles 9.2(c)(iii) and 9.3(a); (vii) Agriculture: Annex 5, Section A, para. 1; (viii) Textiles: Articles 5.1, 5.2, 5.3, 5.6, 6.2 and 6.13; (ix) Antidumping: Articles 2.2.1.1 and 9.5; (x) Preshipment Inspection: Articles 1.3 and 2.17; and (xi) Valuation: Articles 2.1(b) and 3.1(b); Annex I, Note to Article 2, para.3 and Note to Article 3, para. 3.

In the instances enumerated above, the items linked by the "and/or" are discrete factors not dependent on each other for their definitions. The "and/or" term allows the person applying it flexibility as to which of the factors to include. Either one may be used individually or both may be included collectively. A useful example may be found in Annex I to the Customs Valuation Agreement. It is provided there as a note to Article 2 as follows:

> "2. Having found a sale under any one of these three conditions adjustments will then be made, as the case may be, for:
>
> (a) quantity factors only;
>
> (b) commercial level factors only; or
>
> (c) both commercial level and quantity factors.
>
> 3. The expression 'and/or' allows the flexibility to use the sales and make the necessary adjustments in any one of the three conditions described above."

While the use of the term "only" might superficially seem to support the US position, a closer look shows that, among others, the third category is constructed with "and" as a broad, inclusive meaning rather than referring to a narrow overlap.

to an industry producing directly competitive but unlike products. In such a case the imported products could be combed cotton yarn as in the present case, but the domestic industry would not be the cotton yarn industry; rather, it could be the synthetic yarn industry if such products were found to be directly competitive. But because the chosen category is unlike but directly competitive, then the combed cotton yarn producers would be excluded from the investigation.[278] This would leave open the possibility of finding serious damage and causation thereof even where the domestic combed cotton yarn industry was flourishing, but the synthetic yarn industry was in trouble. This would seem to be in direct conflict with the requirement of the treaty language in Article 6.2 that "Serious damage or actual threat thereof must demonstrably be caused by such increased quantities in total imports of that product *and not by such other factors as technological changes or changes in customer preferences.*" (emphasis added)

7.90 Therefore, in our view, we agree with Pakistan's interpretation on "and/or", and find that the United States is in violation of Article 6.2 of the ATC in excluding the captively produced combed cotton yarn from the scope of the domestic industry.

F. Finding of Serious Damage

1. Reliability of AYSA Data

7.91 **Pakistan** claimed that the United States based its determination on the state of the domestic industry on the data supplied by the American Yarn Spinners Association (AYSA), which data, however, were unverified, incorrect and incomplete. Pakistan claimed that the data supplied by AYSA were inherently untrustworthy because this organization had previously supplied incorrect data. Pakistan recalled that combed cotton yarn, ring spun, from Pakistan had been subject to a request for restraint by the United States in 1997, and that the Market Statement[279] presented on that occasion included data supplied by AYSA which turned out to be inconsistent with official data that were subsequently published. The US official statistics had not been available when the 1998 Market Statement

---

278 While the United States did not explain the full functioning of their proposed system of applying the categories of domestic production, it could be argued that this category of directly competitive but unlike would only be applied if there were no like products. First, there is no basis in the treaty language for such an assertion. Second, this interpretation would mean that there would be no option of examining an industry producing directly competitive products when, as a factual matter, the like products were found to be a subset of directly competitive products (which as we have stated is by far the most common, if not the exclusive case). Thus, instead of the treaty language presenting options to the importing Member, the US approach would *dictate* which of the three possibilities must be used in a particular factual situation. And the most common factual situation where like products are a subset of directly competitive would be eliminated as one of the options.

279 Report of Investigation and Statement of Serious Damage or Actual Threat Thereof: Yarn for Sale, 85 Per cent or More by Weight Combed Cotton Ring Spun Category 301 Part, April 1997 (the "1997 Market Statement"), PAK Ex. 2.

was finalized in December 1998, and thus, without verification using any official statistics, the United States relied the data supplied by the AYSA, which is composed of domestic producers of combed cotton yarn, and thus, has an interest in the safeguard measure in question.[280] The Census figures published subsequent to the finalization of the Market Statement cannot be reconciled with the data provided by AYSA for the period January-August 1998. While AYSA had reported a 10.2 per cent decline in production between January-August 1997 and January-August 1998, the Census figures show only a drop of 5 per cent between the calendar years 1997 and 1998. According to Pakistan, this confirms that the data provide by AYSA could not be trusted.[281]

7.92 In response, the **United States** first argued that the Census data were not available to the US authority at the time of investigation, and as such, should be disregarded. Further, the aforesaid 1997 Market Statement is for ring spun yarn which is additional evidence outside the scope of our review. Should it be deemed relevant, it would enhance the integrity of the data contained in the 1998 Market Statement, because in the case of combed cotton ring spun yarn, the United States discovered evidence that called the 1997 Market Statement into question, and consequently, did not impose a transitional safeguard measure at that time.[282] Further, the United States stated that it decided on the reliability of the AYSA data by confirming that the 1996 and 1997 production data supplied by the AYSA were consistent with its official statistics;[283] both the AYSA data and the official statistics showed a decline in domestic production despite the alleged discrepancy between them.[284] Further, the United States pointed out that it verified the AYSA data not only by comparing them with official data but also by engaging in direct discussions with individual firms.[285]

7.93 On the issue of the reliability of the AYSA data, the **Panel** first notes that in Section E above, we already found that the United States excluded the captive production of combed cotton yarn from the scope of the domestic industry, and the measure at issue is inconsistent with Article 6.2. This is enough to recommend that the DSB find the US measure at issue inconsistent with the ATC. However, in order to provide the full explanation to the parties, we have declined to exercise judicial economy and have proceeded to examine the other claims of Pakistan.

7.94 Next, we have to decide, based on the correct standard of review, whether certain evidence submitted by Pakistan should be disregarded or not. Our conclu-

---

[280] *See* Pakistan First Submission, pp. 30-31, and Rebuttal Submission, paras. 52-53. (*Also* paras. 4.95-4.98.)

[281] *See* Pakistan First Submission, p. 31. (*Also* para. 4.96.)

[282] *See* US First Submission, paras. 157-158, and US Oral Statement at the Second Substantive Meeting with the Panel, para. 10. (*Also* para. 4.124.)

[283] *See* US First Submission, para. 150. (*Also* para. 4.125.)

[284] *See* US First Submission, paras. 152-153. (*Also* para. 4.125.)

[285] *See* US First Submission, paras. 150 and 154. (*Also* para. 4.121.)

sion, in paragraph 7.33 above, was that we can and should examine any evidence, not for the purpose of reinvestigating the market situation, but only for the purpose of reviewing the thoroughness and sufficiency of the decision of the US authority. Accordingly, in our view, the 1998 calendar year US Census data should be examined by the Panel, even though they were not available to the US government at the time of investigation, in order to confirm whether the reliance by the US investigation authority on the AYSA data is justifiable. Pakistan presented the data in order to contest the reliability of the AYSA data, rather than to claim that the decision of the US authority is unjustifiable in light of "developments subsequent to the ... determination."[286]

7.95 First, keeping this in mind, we will proceed to examine the parties' arguments, and we note that data supplied by AYSA in the 1997 investigation proceeding for a transitional safeguard measure on combed cotton ring spun yarn might not have been fully accurate. However, it would be exaggerated to conclude that because of that, data supplied by AYSA in the proceeding for the transitional safeguard measure at issue were "inherently untrustworthy." If evidence is supplied by a party which has interest in the proceeding, such evidence should be more carefully examined for reliability. However, this does not lead to a generalization that evidence supplied by trade associations consisting of domestic producers which are requesting trade remedies such as transitional safeguard measures is *per se* unreliable. It becomes then a question of verification and judgement by the investigating authority.

7.96 Second, we note that there is evidence the US investigation authority did seek to make an objective fact-finding in this regard. This is exemplified by the reaction of the United States to data supplied by AYSA in the 1997 proceeding; the United States pointed out as follows: "In the process of conducting ongoing verification of the data, the United States discovered evidence that called the 1997 statement in question. As a result, ... the United States did not impose an Article 6 safeguard with respect to combed cotton ring spun ...".[287] Further, we note that the United States pointed out that it verified production data for 1996 and 1997 supplied by AYSA for the transitional safeguard measure at issue by comparing them with the official statistics, as shown in paragraph 1.4(b) of the 1998 Market Statement.[288]

7.97 In light of the foregoing, we consider that Pakistan has not established that data supplied by AYSA are inherently untrustworthy. It is not for panels to prescribe precise methodologies for information gathering and verification. In our view, the US methods used in this proceeding are not unjustifiable, even though we recognize that there may be other approaches.

---

[286] Panel Report on *US - Shirts and Blouses*, op. cit., para. 7.21.

[287] US First Submission, para. 158. (*Also* para. 4.124.)

[288] US Ex. 3, para. 1.4(b). *See also* US Answers to Panel's Questions, 28 November 2000, para. 84 and fn. 64. (*Also* paras. 4.104, 4.107 and 4.106.)

7.98 With respect to Pakistan's challenge to data supplied by AYSA for January-August 1998, we do not agree that the US fact-finding based upon the data supplied by AYSA is unjustifiable. Pakistan pointed out that there is a discrepancy between the data and the official statistics, but in light of the difference for the subject period (*i.e.* AYSA data - the eight-month period for January-August 1998 and the Census data - the one-year period for 1998), in our view, this discrepancy is not sufficient for us to conclude that the factual situation was not "demonstrated" within the meaning of Article 6.2.

7.99 On this point, **Pakistan** further argued that if both sets of data were correct, monthly production by domestic producers during the period from September to December 1998 was nine per cent higher than the average monthly production during the period from January to August 1998 despite the fact that there were fewer establishments operating during the September to December period.[289]

7.100 The **United States** responded that this shows a decline in domestic production in 1998 and that the decline was most severe in the earlier part of the year, and accordingly, supports its position.[290]

7.101 In **the Panel**'s view, Pakistan's calculation does not establish that AYSA data were incorrect, because a nine per cent increase in monthly production does not necessarily sound unrealistic, and Pakistan has not so proven. Thus, we do not find the US determination unjustifiable in this regard.

2. *Treatment of Establishments Retooled to Produce Other Products*

7.102 **Pakistan** also argued that the United States should not have treated as indicia of damage to the domestic industry the fact that establishments producing combed cotton yarn had been retooled to produce carded cotton yarn or any other products. In support of this proposition, Pakistan referred to Article 1.5 of the ATC, which provides that, in order to facilitate the process of integration of the textiles and clothing sector into the GATT disciplines, "... Members should allow for continuous autonomous industrial adjustment...".[291] In this connection, Pakistan argued that in the 1998 Market Statement, the United States erroneously mentioned that "three establishments which are producers of the subject yarn *closed*," because these establishments had not ceased operation during the investigation period.[292]

---

[289] Pakistan Rebuttal Submission, paras. 55-57, as corrected later by Pakistan's Answers to Panel's Questions, 14 December 2000, p. 4.

[290] US Letter dated 15 December 2000 to the Chairman of the Panel.

[291] Pakistan First Submission, pp. 31-35. (*Also* para. 4.92.)

[292] Pakistan First Submission, pp. 32-34 (emphasis in original), and Rebuttal Submission, para. 64. (*Also* paras. 4.98, 4.101 and 4.133.)

7.103 In rebuttal, the **United States** argued that the retooled establishments were now producing entirely different products, and thus, had exited the combed cotton yarn industry. Accordingly, this can be used as an indicator of "serious damage" to the domestic industry. In support, the United States pointed out that the ATC allows the textiles and clothing sector to restructure over a ten-year period.[293] Also, in response to Pakistan's claim that the 1998 Market Statement is erroneous in stating that three establishments ceased operation during the investigation period, the United States noted that they ceased producing combed cotton yarn, and then switched to carded cotton yarn.[294]

7.104 In the **Panel**'s view, this issue concerns the interpretation of the term "damage" under Article 6.2. Transitional safeguard measures are permitted to protect the domestic industry producing - rather than individual companies which are producers of - "like and/or directly competitive products" from import competition. Pakistan itself argues that the scope of the domestic industry is determined not by producers but by products.[295] Otherwise, changes in ownership of domestic enterprises producing "like and/or directly competitive products" could be deemed as an indicator of "serious damage" to the "domestic industry".

7.105 In this connection, we recall that Pakistan argued that "if a plant produces carded instead of combed yarn, thrives in its new capacity and retains its workforce, the increase in imports obviously did not cause *grave injury that impaired its value or usefulness*."[296] However, we disagree with this argument. Assume that, in reaction to import surge, domestic producers of certain textile products merged into companies in another industry; and the establishments of the acquired producers, after retooling to produce totally different products, achieved the same level of production, sales, profit, employment, etc. In this situation, indeed, the "value" of the retooled establishments may not have been impaired in some overall sense, but it would be obviously unreasonable that no transitional safeguard measure would be permitted since the "domestic industry" producing the textile products was driven out by the import surge. In our view, the fact that an establishment changed its products to those which are neither like nor directly competitive products should be treated as an indicator of "serious damage" to a subject domestic industry.[297]

---

[293] *See* US First Submission, paras. 163-166. (*Also* paras. 4.142 and 4.144-4.146.)

[294] US First Submission, paras. 161-162. (*Also* para. 4.137.)

[295] Pakistan First Submission, pp. 4-5. (*Also* paras. 4.18-4.20.)

[296] Pakistan Rebuttal Submission, para. 65. (emphasis in original) (*Also* para. 4.91.)

[297] We note that in support of its proposition, Pakistan emphasized that it is not difficult to switch from the production of combed cotton yarn to that of carded cotton yarn. *See* Pakistan Rebuttal Submission, para. 67. In our view, it might be relevant to the determination on "serious damage" how easy it is for establishments retooled to produce carded cotton yarn or any other product to resume the production of combed cotton yarn. However, the arguments of the parties on this point suggest that it costs more or less to switch from the production of combed cotton yarn to that of carded cotton yarn, and *vice versa*. *See* Pakistan's Answers to Panel's Questions, 28 November 2000,

7.106 This is a corollary to our findings regarding the relevance of ownership in paragraphs 7.63-7.65 above. If the industry is defined by the *producers* of the *products*, then it follows that if the producers change products, they are no longer in the industry, and accordingly, the fact can be treated as indicia of "damage" to the industry.[298]

7.107 We further note that this conclusion is consistent with Article 1.5, in contrast to Pakistan's argument. Indeed, it might be a good example of "autonomous industrial adjustment" that plants were retooled to produce different products. However, Article 6.2 provides that Members may take transitional safeguard measures in order to react to "serious damage" to a domestic industry. Insofar as damage experienced by a domestic industry is not "serious", no transitional safeguard measure will be permitted and, accordingly, the importing Member must allow for "autonomous industrial adjustment" which the domestic industry will make to deal with the damage. In other words, it is a matter of degree. If a limited number of establishments exit the industry, that might be an indicator of some sort of damage, but of an amount consistent with "autonomous industrial adjustment." But if a larger number of establishments exit, it can be an indicator of serious damage. Thus, the exit of establishments is a relevant factor as long as properly weighted, and we do not find the US determination here to be unjustifiable in this regard.

3. *Other Factual Claims*

7.108 **Pakistan** contested the US fact-finding on employment and investment. First, according to Pakistan, the employment and production figures concerning combed cotton ring spun yarn for the year 1996 contained in the 1997 Market Statement seem inconsistent with those concerning combed cotton yarn for the same year contained in the 1998 Market Statement. Second, the 1998 Market Statement erroneously states that "investment in recent years has been to update and replace equipment rather than to create new productive capacity,"[299] in light of the fact that between 1993-1997, the units producing combed cotton yarn decreased by 37 per cent, but combed cotton yarn production rose by 44 per cent.[300]

7.109 Initially, **the Panel** recalls that the 1998 Market Statement found that the US industry suffered serious damage based primarily on the comparison of rele-

pp. 17-20 and US Answers to Panel's Questions, 28 November 2000, paras. 41-47. We further note that the US finding of "serious damage" does not rely exclusively on the fact that the two establishments ceased to produce combed cotton yarn. *See* US Ex. 3, para. 8.3. Thus, in our view, Pakistan has not established that the US finding of "serious damage" is unjustifiable in this respect.

298 In this connection, we further note that Pakistan did not include in the terms of reference a claim that the other products in question (*e.g.* carded cotton yarn) are like or directly competitive products.

299 US Ex. 3, para. 5.15.

300 *See* Pakistan First Submission, pp. 35-36. (*Also* paras. 4.99-4.153.)

vant economic variables between the period of January-August 1997 and that of January-August 1998.[301] Pakistan's figures regarding employment and production in the 1997 and 1998 Market Statements are not based on equivalent segments; in the 1997 Market Statement, for ring spun combed cotton yarn for sale while in the 1998 Market Statement, for all combed cotton yarn for sale.[302] The figures are not sufficient for us to conclude that the US fact-finding is unjustifiable. We also note that there are many ways of explaining changes in production; new machinery may be more efficient; labour may be employed more effectively, etc. In order to reach the conclusion Pakistan requests, we would need to engage in a *de novo* review of the factual situation.

7.110 In our view, Pakistan's aforesaid factual claims described in this section are not enough to sustain a challenge to the overall justifiability of the US fact-finding.

G. *Investigation Period, Including Period for Determining Serious Damage and Causation*

7.111 **Pakistan** contested the US causation analysis.[303] The correlation of an upward trend in imports and negative trends in the relevant economic variables of the domestic industry must be central to the causation analysis. But such correlation can be found only in the comparison of relevant economic variables on an eight-month basis, *i.e.* between the period of January-August 1997 and that of January-August 1998. Pakistan argued that the analysis on an eight-month basis is not enough, referring to the recommended guidelines adopted at the Committee on Anti-Dumping Practices for time period for investigation, which states that "the period of data collection for injury investigation normally should be *at least three years*." Pakistan also pointed out that "five-year investigation periods are common" under Article XIX of the GATT.[304]

7.112 In response, the **United States** pointed out that the ATC does not provide for a specific minimum time period for investigation. Article 6.7 of the ATC only requires that the Member proposing to take safeguard action provide "specific and relevant factual information, as up-to-date as possible...", which "shall be related, as closely as possible ..." to the 12-month period to be referenced under

[301] *See* US First Submission, paras. 81-82. (*Also* paras. 4.5 and 4.85-4.88.)

[302] *See* Pakistan First Submission, p. 35. (*Also* para. 4.124.) The 1997 Market Statement indicates that the US investigation authority "excluded from its investigation other combed cotton yarn for sale, including ... yarn produced by the open-ended spinning method", because it "distinguished ring spun from open-end because such products are not like and/or directly competitive products with the subject yarn due to their physical characteristics, commercial applications and price structure." 1997 Market Statement, PAK Ex. 2, para. 1.2. In contrast, the 1998 Market Statement does not exclude ring spun from the scope of the investigation. *See* 1998 Market Statement, US Ex. 3, paras. 1.1-1.2.

[303] We note that this issue also included the proper period for assessing serious damage and we have considered it in this sense, as well.

[304] Pakistan First Submission, pp. 36-39. (*Also* para. 4.152.)

Article 6.8 to determine the level of restraints. When the United States made a request for consultation in December 1998, the data for the period of January-August 1998 was the best available data. Also, the United States based its determination on the comparison of relevant economic variables between 1996 and 1997 as well, and as a result, on the two year and eight month investigation.[305]

7.113 **The Panel** first notes that Article 6.2 does not explicitly set forth any specific period of time as the minimum period for investigation, or for determining whether damage is serious or, in turn, is caused by the subject imports. The parties agreed on this point.[306]

7.114 Second, Article 6.7 of the ATC requires that when the Member invoking a transitional safeguard measure seeks consultations with the Member or Members which would be affected by such action, it shall provide the Member or Members with "specific and relevant factual information, as up-to-date as possible, particularly in regard to: (a) the factors ... on which the Member invoking the action has based its determination of the existence of serious damage or actual threat of damage; and (b) the factors ... on the basis of which it proposes to invoke the safeguard action with respect to the Member or Members concerned." Also, that Article provides that "the information shall be related, as closely as possible, to identifiable segments of production and to the reference period set out in paragraph 8", which period is defined under paragraph 8 as "the 12-month period terminating two months preceding the month in which the request for consultation was made." In our view, Article 6.7 does not address, directly or indirectly, the length of either investigation periods or periods during which damage occurs. For example, the requirement that the information to be provided to the exporting Member or Members "be related, as closely as possible, to the [12-month] reference period" does not give any guidance as to how long the investigation period should be or how long damage should continue in order to constitute "serious damage" and causation thereof.

7.115 In this respect, we recall Pakistan's argument that "since the damage must be determined to be 'serious', the period must be adequately long to discern that the effect of imports was more than just temporary."[307] However, it is unclear how this general consideration demands that the period during which the serious damage occurred must be longer than the eight months utilised by the United States. In our view, whether or not the chosen period is justifiably long would depend on, at least partly, the extent of the damage suffered by a subject domestic industry during that period. Thus, we deem it inappropriate to set out a general guideline on the length of the period during which damage or causation occurs, when there is no specific treaty language in the ATC.

---

[305] US First Submission, paras. 101-107. (*Also* para. 4.103.)

[306] *See* Pakistan First Submission, p. 37 and US First Submission, para. 101. (*Also* para. 4.103.)

[307] Pakistan First Submission, p. 37. (*Also* para. 4.152.)

7.116 In light of this, we interpret Pakistan's claim as requesting the Panel to examine the factual question of whether the US fact-finding on serious damage and causation is accurate, rather than to address the legal issue of whether Article 6 of the ATC requires that the period during which the damage occurs be longer than the period the United States focused on in this particular case.[308] Thus, we will make an "objective assessment of facts" on this point using the "justifiability" standard discussed in Section 0 above.

7.117 We further note that Pakistan also contested the US focus on the eight-month period in finding serious damage and causation, based on the specific set of facts in this case. Pakistan argued that economic variables of the domestic industry during a longer period would present a much more positive picture of the US domestic industry, noting that the domestic production declined only between 1997 and 1998 after having reached unprecedented heights in 1997.[309] Pakistan also claimed that the "focus on the evolution during an eight-month period only made it impossible to segregate the effect of rapidly declining exports from the effect of imports"; the decline in exports between 1997 and 1998 "is due to the fact that Mexico, which as recently as 1996 had accounted for two-thirds of United States exports of combed cotton yarn, is now producing this yarn itself."[310]

7.118 We note that in support of its conclusion that "the increase in imports in 1998 has caused serious damage to the industry," the 1998 Market Statement found and considered, among others, the following changes in the situation of the US domestic industry, the domestic market and imports from all sources, between the calendar years 1996 and 1997, and between January-August 1997 and January-August 1998:

(a) Three out of twenty-two establishments had closed since 1996, and two of them closed during January-August 1998;

(b) there was a loss of 423 jobs in the domestic industry from 1996 through August 1998, of which 340 jobs were lost in January-August 1998;

(c) US production increased by 1.6 per cent between 1996 and 1997, and decreased from 98,371,000 kilograms to 88,337,000 kilograms (10.2 per cent lower) between January-August 1997 and January-August 1998;

(d) US shipments decreased by 0.4 per cent between 1996 and 1997, and also decreased from 99,818,000 kilograms to 85,644,000 kilo-

[308] In this respect, we recall that Pakistan indicated that "Article 6 of the ATC does not explicitly impose a specific minimum period for which data must be collected, nor has such a period been established by jurisprudence." Pakistan First Submission, p. 37. (*Also* para. 4.100.)

[309] Pakistan First Submission, pp. 38-39. (*Also* paras. 4.96-4.98.)

[310] Pakistan First Submission, p. 39. (*Also* para. 4.169.)

grams (14.2 per cent lower) between January-August 1997 and January-August 1998;

(e) US exports increased by 2.8 per cent between 1996 and 1997, and decreased from 10,690,000 kilograms to 7,168,000 kilograms (32.9 per cent lower) between January-August 1997 and January-August 1998;

(f) Capacity utilization decreased by 3.6 per cent between 1996 and 1997, and also decreased from 84.3 per cent to 75.7 per cent (8.6 percentage points lower) between end of August 1997 and end of August 1998;

(g) End-of-period inventories increased by 43.8 per cent between 1996 and 1997, and also increased by 145.9 per cent between January-August 1997 and January-August 1998;

(h) Unfilled orders increased by 22.8 per cent between the year-end 1996 and the year-end 1997, but decreased 15.8 per cent between the end of August 1997 and the end of August 1998;

(i) The average number of employees decreased by 1.6 per cent between 1996 and 1997 and also decreased by 6.6 per cent between January-August 1997 and January-August 1998; the number of hours worked increased by 1.2 per cent between 1996 and 1997, and decreased by 6.6 per cent between January-August 1997 and January-August 1998; and hourly wages increased from $8.34 to $8.67 between 1996 and 1997 and also increased from $8.67 in January-August 1997 to $9.02 in January-August 1998[311];

(j) Profitability ratio decreased from 4 per cent to 3.5 per cent between 1996 and 1997, and also decreased from 3.9 per cent to 2.1 per cent between January-August 1997 and January-August 1998;

(k) New investment in productive capacity was stagnant;

(l) Imports from all sources increased 12.1 per cent between 1996 and 1997, and also increased by 9,828,000 kilograms or 91.3 per cent between January-August 1997 and January-August 1998, to 20,595,000 kilograms;

(m) The apparent domestic market remained relatively constant during the period increasing by 0.8 per cent between 1996 and 1997, and decreasing by 0.8 per cent in January-August 1998 from the January-August 1997 level;

---

[311] The 1998 Market Statement explains that "[t]he increase in the average hourly wage rate was attributed to the upward pressure exerted by exogenous factors outside the control of the companies in this industry including the influence of the mandated rise in the US minimum wage, ...". US Ex. 3, para. 5.10.

(n) US producers' market share decreased from 87.1 per cent to 85.7 per cent (1.4 percentage points lower) between 1996 and 1997, and also decreased from 89.2 per cent to 79.2 per cent (10 percentage points lower) between January-August 1997 and January-August 1998;

(o) The ratio of imports to domestic production increased from 13.4 per cent to 14.8 per cent between 1996 and 1997, and also increased from 10.9 per cent to 23.3 per cent between January-August 1997 and January-August 1998; and

(p) The average landed duty-paid value of imports was $4.54 per kilogram during the period January-August 1998, 7.8 per cent below the average US producers' price.[312]

7.119 Further, in support of its conclusion that "serious damage to this industry is directly attributable to a sharp and substantial increase in imports of the subject yarn from Pakistan,"[313] the 1998 Market Statement found and considered, among others, the following changes in imports from Pakistan of combed cotton yarn between January-August 1997 and January-August 1998:

(a) Imports from Pakistan, in volume, increased from 942,756 kilograms to 3,612,652 kilograms (283.2 per cent higher);

(b) Pakistan is the second largest supplier;

(c) Imports from Pakistan, as a percentage of total imports, increased from 8.8 per cent to 17.5 per cent, and as a percentage of US production, increased from 1.0 per cent to 4.1 per cent, between January-August 1997 and January-August 1998; and

(d) The average landed duty-paid value of imports from Pakistan was $3.63 per kilogram during the period January-August 1998, 26.2 per cent below the average US producers' price.[314]

7.120 In light of the magnitude of the aforesaid changes in economic variables of the US domestic industry,[315] the surge in imports from Pakistan between January-August 1997 and January-August 1998, and the price-undercutting of imports from Pakistan, together with changes in all relevant economic variables between 1996 and 1997, in our view, Pakistan has not established that the US choice of the period is unjustifiable. The "period of investigation" was sufficiently compre-

[312] 1998 Market Statement, US Ex. 3, Sections V and VI. *See also* US First Submission, para. 115. (*Also* Table 2, para. 4.173.)

[313] 1998 Market Statement, US Ex. 3, para. 7.1. (*Also* paras. 3.2, 4.5 and 4.157-4.159.)

[314] 1998 Market Statement, US Ex. 3, paras. 7.2-7.5. *See also* US First Submission, para. 131. (*Also* para. 4.158.)

[315] In light of the specific data set out here, we wish to recall our finding that the United States did not properly identify the domestic industry. The specific facts would thus be different if a proper definition were used.

hensive, and the question of whether an eight-month period of damage caused by imports was sufficiently long to find serious damage and causation is a case-by-case determination.

7.121 In this case, for the reasons discussed above, we conclude that in respect of the length of the investigation period and the period in which serious damage occurred, Pakistan has not established that the United States failed to demonstrate "serious damage" to the domestic industry, and the causal link between the serious damage and imports from Pakistan.[316]

H. Attribution

7.122 The **United States** argued that Article 6.4 of the ATC authorizes Members to apply safeguard measures on a Member-by-Member basis. According to the United States, this is consistent with the requirement that a sharp and substantial increase in imports be assessed on an individual Member basis. The requirement is only that a Member subject to investigation have its exports compared to "all other sources", that is, to the basket of other exporters. The United States asserted that the breakdown of exporters, as done in Table V of the 1998 Market Statement, goes further than is required by Article 6.4, which requirements could be satisfied by a simple comparison of Pakistan to a grouping of all other exporters. It then follows that a safeguard measure may be applied to any, but not all, Member or Members that are a cause of the serious damage.[317]

7.123 **Pakistan** responded that a proper attribution analysis cannot be done if the largest exporter, in this case Mexico, is simply ignored. Mexico's exports of the subject product had increased rapidly and from a higher base. It is inconceivable that the United States could do a proper attribution analysis without also individually examining Mexico's exports.[318]

7.124 In **the Panel**'s view, it is clear from Article 6 of the ATC that safeguard measures need not be applied on an MFN basis. They are to be applied only to those imports causing serious damage, not to all imports. Furthermore, they are not to be imposed on imports already subject to restraint. However, we do not agree that this means that restraints can be imposed only on some of the imports which may be responsible for causing serious damage. We think that that approach stretches both the logic and the language of Article 6.4 too far.

7.125 In our view, the analysis should proceed in the following manner. First, there is an assessment of the state of the domestic industry. This can be seen as

[316] We recall that this must be read *mutatis mutandis* with our conclusion that the United States did not properly define the domestic industry.

[317] *See* US First Submission, paras. 125-141 and Rebuttal Submission, paras. 73-79. (*Also* paras. 4.161-4.163.)

[318] *See* Pakistan First Submission, pp. 41-42 and Rebuttal Submission, paras. 85-94. (*Also* paras. 4.160, 4.164, 4.165 and 4.167.)

determining the level of actual damage caused to the industry. Next, it must be determined if this actual damage constitutes "serious damage". If there is serious damage to the domestic industry, the next step is to determine pursuant to paragraphs 2 and 3 of Article 6 whether imports are causing such damage. Damage from other factors such as technological changes or changes in consumer preferences must not be attributed to imports in assessing whether such imports have caused serious damage.

7.126 However, unlike other safeguard investigations, and resulting applications of measures, which are done on an MFN basis, the analysis cannot stop there. The Member imposing a safeguard under the ATC must then do a further attribution analysis and narrow the causation down to only those Members whose exports are causing the serious damage. This does not mean, however, that a Member imposing a safeguard restraint can then pick and choose for which Member(s) it will make an attribution analysis. The attribution cannot be made only to some of the Members causing damage, it must be made to all such Members. The language of Article 6.4 leads to this conclusion. The first sentence contains a requirement that safeguard measures shall be applied on a Member-by-Member basis. However, this is a reference to the *application* of the measure, not the attribution analysis of which Members are subject to such measure(s). That is covered by the second sentence which specifically speaks of "attribution" of causation of serious damage in contrast to the first sentence which describes how the measure is to be "applied". The second sentence reads:

> "The Member or Members to whom serious damage, or actual threat thereof, referred to in paragraphs 2 and 3, is attributed, shall be determined on the basis of a sharp and substantial increase in imports, actual or imminent, from such a Member or Members individually, and on the basis of the level of imports as compared with imports from other sources, market share, and the import and domestic prices at a comparable stage of commercial transaction ...."

7.127 Obviously, we first look to this language of the treaty itself. The reference is to the Member or Members to whom serious damage is attributed and it refers specifically back to the previous two paragraphs which describe the obligations in making such a determination of serious damage. This explicit linking back to the serious damage determination, in our view, requires that *all* the Members causing the serious damage must have it so attributed.[319] Thus the question is which Member(s)' exports caused the serious damage as determined pursuant to paragraphs 2 and 3, rather than identifying some new sub-group that is not specified by the treaty language. The rest of the sentence merely describes a method-

[319] This is supported by the French and Spanish texts of the agreement which use definite articles in referring to the serious damage determination, namely "le préjudice grave" and "el perjuicio grave", respectively, both of which refer directly to the earlier determination.

ology. It does not permit a reading to the effect that only one of such Member or Members to whom causation of serious damage is attributed may be subjected to restraints. As a factual matter, it may end up being only one to whom causation is properly attributed, but that can only be determined *after* a proper attribution analysis is done, not *before* as the United States has done in the present investigation.

7.128 As always, we should examine the context and the object and purpose of this language for guidance in interpreting its meaning. We recall that the four corners of the treaty is the WTO Agreement as a whole. As we discussed above, we do not agree with the US argument that the ATC should be interpreted in isolation from the rest of the GATT/WTO.[320] It is distinct where it specifically states that it is such in the treaty language, but it must be interpreted in the context of the WTO Agreement as a whole when there is a question as to its meaning. We also recall that the Preamble of the ATC provides that the ATC is meant to be an agreement embodying the progressive integration of the sector into GATT/WTO on the basis of strengthened GATT/WTO rules and disciplines. In our view the method most consistent with the WTO Agreement', including the Safeguards Agreement's, requirements of MFN treatment and with the ATC's object and purpose is to require attribution to *all* Members found to be causing serious damage, not just one or some of such Members. Such an ability to pick and choose Members as proposed by the United States would be the least consistent with an MFN approach and, therefore, would be the least conducive to the progressive integration of the sector into the WTO system.

7.129 A further review of the context of applying safeguards measures under Article 6, even on a non-MFN basis, supports this conclusion. Article 5.1 of the Safeguards Agreement provides that: "A Member shall apply safeguard measures only to the extent necessary to prevent or remedy serious injury and facilitate adjustment." While we recognize the distinction between general safeguard actions and safeguard measures applied pursuant to the ATC, we consider this particular statement one of general applicability. Applying this logic to Article 6 of the ATC implies that a safeguard restraint will be imposed at such a level presumably to alleviate the serious damage. If this were not the case, *i.e.* a solution sufficient to cure the problem, it would hardly make sense to impose any restraint. However, if the restraint could be imposed on only one Member contributing to the serious damage, then such a Member would suffer a disproportionate level of the pain for the remedy. If, however, an appropriate attribution analysis is undertaken, then the restraint will be spread appropriately to all Members whose exports have caused the serious damage.

7.130 Thus, the correct interpretation of Article 6.4 requires an analysis of the imports from individual Members, but it does not mean that such analysis may be

[320] *See* the discussion in paras. 7.46-7.47 above.

limited to only some of the Members of those which are the cause of the serious damage. The treaty language of the second sentence of Article 6.4 provides the method for proceeding; compliance with this method is mandatory, as indicated by the term "shall" used in this provision. The first step is that there must be an examination of the imports from all the Members which have shown the characteristics of a sharp and substantial increase. We take the term "sharp" to refer to the percentage increase and the term "substantial" to refer to the absolute increase. Thus, for example, it would not be necessary to examine the imports from a Member which showed a sharp percentage increase if such imports were from a low base because they would not then represent a substantial increase in imports. This obviously must be done on an individual Member basis or there could be a blurring of the two criteria and it could result in sweeping in Members whose exports possibly met one but not both of the criteria. But to say it needs to be done individually does not imply that it can be limited only to some individual Members. Then the required second step of the attribution analysis is to take all the Members whose exports have met the criteria of the first step and examine them according to the other listed criteria in Article 6.4, namely, a comparative assessment of levels of imports from other sources, market share and import and domestic prices at a comparable stage of commercial transaction. Only at this point can the investigating authority come to a justifiable conclusion as to which Member or Members the causation of serious damage can be attributed. To simply stop after finding that one Member is contributing to serious damage does not satisfy the obligations of Article 6.4.

7.131 Thus, there are three categories of exporters in each case: (1) those causing the serious damage and not subject to existing restraints; (2) those to which the serious damage is not attributable; and (3) those already subject to restraints. New restraints may only be imposed on individual Members in the first group.[321] Identifying that first group means certain examinations on an individual Member basis, as discussed above. It also means imposing the restraint on a Member-by-Member basis, as restraints in this sector are administered by the exporting Member, not by the importing Member. However, it does not mean that only some of the Members in the first category will be subject to the restraint while others in that same category are excluded from the restraint.

7.132 In the 1998 Market Statement, the United States compared the impact of Pakistan's exports only to those of the rest of the world, which included Mexico. However, the United States clearly did not assess the impact of Mexico's exports individually in such a manner.[322] In this case, we do not see how that can be

---

[321] We note that the United States grouped Mexico in a category labelled "FTA's". The United States did not assert that Mexico was exempt from investigation based on its membership of an FTA with the United States, so we do not need to reach that issue here.

[322] We note the US argument that it assessed imports from Mexico. US Rebuttal Submission, para. 78. However, the 1998 Market Statement does not state that the US investigation authority assessed

avoided. Imports from Mexico showed a signficant percentage increase in shipments during the period of investigation and, therefore, the increase appeared to be sharp. Mexico was also the largest exporter and, therefore, the increase could reasonably be considered substantial. There was also some evidence that Mexico met the criteria of the second step. We must be clear, however, that we are not suggesting that the serious damage[323] must also be attributed to imports from Mexico because panels are not to make *de novo* reviews of that sort. It may be the case that Mexico did not contribute to serious damage to a properly defined domestic industry. It may not always be the case that the largest exporter will be found to be contributing to the serious damage. However, there is adequate evidence in the record to show that this assessment of imports from Mexico (and any other appropriate assessments of imports from other Members) must be done by the investigating authority and it was not done in the present case.[324]

I. Actual Threat of Serious Damage

7.133 **Pakistan** argued that the United States should have made a "prospective analysis" of relevant economic variables in order to find "actual threat of serious damage, referring to the finding of the panel on *US - Underwear*, which required a prospective analysis. Pakistan also argued that the United States should have considered the prospective increase in imports from Mexico in order to find actual threat of serious damage. In particular, "a mere assertion that import and price trend will continue does not meet the requirement of a prospective analysis."[325]

7.134 In response, the **United States** contended that it is not clear whether "serious damage" and "actual threat of serious damage" are distinct concepts, and that the panel on *US - Underwear* did not require a prospective analysis in all cases.[326] Further, the United States conducted a prospective analysis by considering the correlation between the increase in imports from Pakistan in 1998 and negative trends in relevant economic variables of the domestic industry, and the price differences between imports from Pakistan and domestically produced products.[327]

---

the impact of imports from Mexico *individually*, where no specific reference is made to the import amount or price from Mexico. *See* US Ex. 3.

323 Once again, we must note that this statement must be read in light of our finding that the United States did not properly demonstrate the existence of serious damage due to the incorrect definition of the industry.

324 It is not the case that *each and every* exporter necessarily needs to be examined individually in such a comparative manner. For example, some Members' exports may be low or dropping and, therefore, may not meet the criteria in the first step of the Article 6.4 analysis.

325 Pakistan First Submission, p. 39. (*Also* paras. 4.189-4.191.)

326 US First Submission, paras. 109-112. (*Also* paras. 4.192-4.195.)

327 US First Submission, paras. 113-117. (*Also* paras. 4.192-4.195.)

7.135 **The Panel** notes that on these issues, the panel on *US - Underwear* stated as follows:

> "Article 6.2 and 6.4 of the ATC make reference to 'serious damage, or actual threat thereof'. The word 'thereof', in our view, clearly refers to 'serious damage'. The word 'or' distinguishes between 'serious damage' and 'actual threat thereof'. In our view, 'serious damage' refers to a situation that has already occurred, whereas 'actual threat of serious damage' refers to a situation existing at present which might lead to serious damage in the future. Consequently, in our view, a finding on 'serious damage' requires the party that takes action to demonstrate that damage has already occurred, whereas a finding on 'actual threat of serious damage' requires the same party to demonstrate that, unless action is taken, damage will most likely occur in the near future. The March Statement contains no elements of such a prospective analysis. In our view, even if the mention of 'actual threat' in the Diplomatic Note accompanying the March Statement were to be considered, the fact that the March Statement made no reference to actual threat and contained no elements of such a prospective analysis was dispositive *per se*. Consequently, we do not agree with the US argument that the March Statement supports a finding on actual threat of serious damage."[328]

7.136 Also, we note that Article 6.4, second sentence, reads as follows:

> "The Member or Members to whom serious damage, or actual threat thereof, referred to in paragraphs 2 and 3, is attributed, shall be determined on the basis of a sharp and substantial increase in imports, actual or imminent, from such a Member or Members individually ..."

The footnote to this sentence refers to "imminent" and states as follows:

> "Such an imminent increase shall be a measurable one and shall not be determined to exist on the basis of allegation, conjecture or mere possibility arising, for example, from the existence of production capacity in the exporting Members."

7.137 In our view, the US finding on actual threat of serious damage contained in the 1998 Market Statement is essentially a finding that the existing "serious damage" to the domestic industry would continue if imports were to continue as before.[329] It would seem a reasonable inference to assume that if the trend in imports were to continue, the trend in domestic sales would continue, and conse-

[328] Panel Report on *US - Underwear*, op. cit., para. 7.55. (footnote omitted)

[329] *See* US First Submission, paras. 115-116, and the 1998 Market Statement, US Ex. 3, paras. 8.1-8.2. (*Also* paras. 4.192-4.195 and 4.197-4.199.)

quently, the existing "serious damage" would continue. Under the terms of Article 6.4, there seems to be no basis for demanding any further "prospective analysis" than taking into consideration the prospect that the price-undercutting of imports from Pakistan would likely continue, in contrast to Pakistan's argument.

7.138 However, this US finding of "actual threat of serious damage" in the 1998 Market Statement is totally dependent on the finding of serious damage. It is based on a finding that there is current serious damage and extrapolates to a conclusion that there is an actual threat of the serious damage continuing. This means that it does not serve as an independent (or alternative) determination of actual threat of serious damage. It is a redundant exercise and that means that if there is a fatal flaw in the serious damage determination, the actual threat determination necessarily falls, too. If the United States were to make an independent finding of actual threat of serious damage, further analysis would need to be done to substantiate the finding. In other words, a prospective analysis is required if an independent finding of actual threat is to be made rather than a redundant and dependant one as was effectively made by the United States in the 1998 Market Statement.

7.139 As an example of what we mean, Article 6.4, and footnote thereto, indicate that it is insufficient to look only at foreign production capacity to determine actual threat. Specifically, Articles 6.4 contains a reference to "a sharp and substantial increase in imports, actual or *imminent*" (emphasis added). The footnote is to the word "imminent" and it reads as follows:

> "Such an imminent increase shall be a measurable one and shall not be determined to exist on the basis of allegation, conjecture or mere possibility arising, for example, from the existence of production capacity in the exporting Members."

7.140 It is a clear implication that a determination of production capacity in exporting Members would normally be a useful step, albeit an insufficient one. Other steps to substantiate the possibility of continuation or increased magnitude of increasing import trends could also be done, such as determining the likelihood of continued or increased price undercutting by imports (perhaps through a forward review of offers for sale). We do not mention these points to suggest there is a prescribed manner of doing a prospective analysis to substantiate an independent finding of actual threat of serious damage. The treaty language does not provide a specific list of factors that must be addressed; therefore, it is left to a case-by-case assessment of what is a justifiable determination. Instead, we are merely highlighting what was not done in the present case.

7.141 A review of the 1998 Market Statement makes it clear that the United States did not demonstrate the existence of an actual threat of serious damage from imports of combed cotton yarn. An adequate prospective analysis could serve as the basis for such an independent determination,[330] but no such analysis was done here. Therefore, because the finding of serious damage has been found to be flawed, we also conclude that the US determination of "actual threat" was not justifiable.

VIII. CONCLUSIONS AND RECOMMENDATIONS

8.1 In light of the findings made in Section I above, the Panel concludes that the transitional safeguard measure (quantitative restriction) imposed by the United States on imports of combed cotton yarn from Pakistan as of 17 March 1999, and extended as of 17 March 2000 for a further year is inconsistent with the provisions of Article 6 of the ATC. Specifically, we find that:

(a) Inconsistently with its obligations under 6.2, the United States excluded the production of combed cotton yarn by vertically integrated producers for their own use from the scope of the "domestic industry producing like and/or directly competitive products" with imported combed cotton yarn.

(b) Inconsistently with its obligations under Article 6.4, the United States did not examine the effect of imports from Mexico (and possibly other appropriate Members) individually.[331]

(c) Inconsistently with its obligations under Articles 6.2 and 6.4, the United States did not demonstrate that the subject imports caused an "actual threat" of serious damage to the domestic industry.

8.2 With respect to the other claims, we find that Pakistan did not establish that the measure at issue was inconsistent with the US obligations under Article 6 of the ATC.[332] Specifically, we find that:

(a) Pakistan did not establish that the US determination of serious damage was not justified based on the data used by the US investigating authority.

(b) Pakistan did not establish that the US determination of serious damage was not justified regarding the evaluation by the US investigating authority of establishments that ceased producing combed cotton yarn.

---

[330] We specifically note in this regard that the industry must be properly defined before a justifiable determination can be demonstrated. We do not wish to imply that a prospective analysis in this case could have salvaged a determination of actual threat without first properly defining the relevant industry.

[331] The findings in Items (b) and (c) in this para. are provided on the basis that the United States defined the domestic industry in conformity with Article 6.2 of the ATC. *See* para. 7.93 above.

[332] As discussed in the relevant sections of our findings, these conclusions must be read in light of our findings that the United Stated did not properly define the domestic industry.

(c) Pakistan did not establish that the US determinations of serious damage and causation thereof were not justified based upon an inappropriately chosen period of investigation and period of incidence of serious damage and causation thereof.

8.3 Pursuant to Article 3.8 of the DSU which provides that "In cases where there is an infringement of the obligations assumed under a covered agreement, the action is considered *prima facie* to constitute a case of nullification and impairment", we conclude that the said US measure nullified and impaired the benefits of Pakistan under the WTO Agreement, in particular under the ATC.

8.4 We note that Pakistan requested that the Panel suggest in accordance with Article 19.1, second sentence, of the DSU that the most appropriate way to implement the Panel's ruling would be to rescind the safeguard action forthwith. Article 19 reads as follows:

> "Where a panel or the Appellate Body concludes that a measure is inconsistent with a covered agreement, it shall recommend that the member concerned bring the measure into conformity with that agreement. In addition to its recommendations, the panel or Appellate Body may suggest ways in which the member concerned could implement the recommendations."

8.5 In this case, we recommend that the Dispute Settlement Body request that the United States bring the measure at issue into conformity with its obligations under the ATC. We suggest that this can best be achieved by prompt removal of the import restriction.

ARGENTINA - DEFINITIVE ANTI-DUMPING MEASURES ON IMPORTS OF CERAMIC FLOOR TILES FROM ITALY

Report of the Panel

WT/DS189/R

Adopted by the Dispute Settlement Body on 5 November 2001

TABLE OF CONTENTS

Page

Page

Page

I. INTRODUCTION

1.1 On 26 January 2000, the European Communities (the "EC") requested consultations with Argentina regarding the definitive anti-dumping measures on imports of ceramic floor tiles from Italy imposed by Argentina on 12 November 1999.[1] The EC made its request pursuant to Article 4 of the Understanding on Rules and Procedures Governing the Settlement of Disputes ("DSU") and Article 17.3 of the Agreement on Implementation of Article VI of the General Agreement on Tariffs and Trade 1994 (the "AD Agreement"). The EC and Argentina held consultations on 1 March 2000, but failed to reach a mutually satisfactory solution.

1.2 On 7 November 2000, the EC requested the establishment of a panel with the standard terms of reference set out in Article 7 of the DSU.[2] The EC made its request pursuant to Article 6 of the DSU and Article 17 of the AD Agreement. In that request, the EC identified the measures at issue as the definitive anti-dumping measures on imports of ceramic floor tiles (*"porcellanato"*) from Italy imposed by Argentina on 12 November 1999.

1.3 At its meeting on 17 November 2000, the Dispute Settlement Body ("DSB") established a Panel pursuant to the above request.[3] At that meeting, the parties to the dispute agreed that the Panel should have standard terms of reference. The terms of reference were:

> To examine, in the light of the relevant provisions of the covered agreements cited by the European Communities in document WT/DS189/3 the matter referred to the DSB by the European Communities in that document, and to make such findings as will assist the DSB in making the recommendations or in giving the rulings provided for in those agreements.

1.4 On 12 January 2001, the parties agreed to the following composition of the Panel:

---

[1] WT/DS189/1.

[2] WT/DS189/3.

[3] WT/DS189/4.

1.5 Chairman: Mr. Hugh McPhail

Members: Mr. Gilles Gauthier

Mr. Stephen Powell

1.6 Japan, Turkey and the United States reserved their rights to participate in the Panel proceedings as third parties.

1.7 The Panel met with the parties on 18-19 April 2001 and 1 June 2001. It met with the third parties on 19 April 2001.

1.8 The Panel submitted its interim report to the parties on 25 July 2001. The Panel submitted its final report to the parties on 14 September 2001.

II. FACTUAL ASPECTS

2.1 This dispute concerns the imposition of definitive anti-dumping measures by the Argentine Ministry of the Economy on imports of ceramic floor tiles from Italy.

2.2 On 30 January 1998, Cerámica Zanon ("Zanon") filed an application for an anti-dumping investigation with the Dirección de Competencia Desleal ("DCD" - Directorate of Unfair Trade) of the Argentine Ministry of the Economy alleging that imports of ceramic tiles were being exported to Argentina at dumped prices.[4] On 25 September 1998, the Ministry of the Economy published a public notice announcing the initiation of an anti-dumping investigation on imports of ceramic tiles from Italy.

2.3 On 30 November 1998, Assopiastrelle, the association of Italian producers of ceramic tiles, requested the DCD to limit the calculation of individual dumping margins to four or five exporters accounting for around 70 per cent of the exports of the subject product from Italy to Argentina.[5] On 12 December 1998, the DCD accepted this request.[6] On 10 December 1998, four Italian exporters filed responses to the investigation questionnaire: Ceramica Bismantova "(Bismantova"), Ceramiche Casalgrande ("Casalgrande"), Ceramiche Caesar ("Caesar"), and Marazzi Ceramiche ("Marazzi"). On 24 March 1999, the DCD issued an affirmative preliminary determination ("Preliminary Dumping Determination").[7] In that determination, the DCD disregarded the questionnaire replies

[4] The DCD was responsible for conducting the dumping investigation. The injury investigation was conducted separately by the Comisión Nacional de Comercio Exterior (CNCE - National Foreign Trade Commission). As the EC did not make any injury claims, no reference is made here to the injury aspects of the investigation.

[5] See Exhibit EC-3A.

[6] See Exhibit EC-3B.

[7] *Informe Relativo a la Determinación Preliminar del Margen de Dumping en la Investigación por Presunto Dumping en Operaciones de Exportación hacia la República Argentina de Placas y Baldosas de Cerámica, sin Barnizar ni Esmaltar, para Pavimentación o Revestimiento, de Gres Fino, "Porcellanato", en todas sus Medidas, Originarias de la República Italiana,* Exhibit ARG-8.

submitted by the above-mentioned exporters. The DCD proceeded to determine the dumping margin on the basis of the information available on the record, other than that presented by the exporters.[8] As the DCD applied the same set of "facts available" to the four exporters concerned, they all were assessed the same dumping margin.

2.4 On 23 September 1999, the DCD issued an affirmative final determination ("Final Dumping Determination").[9] In this determination, the DCD relied predominantly on the information available on the record, other than that presented by the exporters.[10] As the DCD applied the same set of "facts available" to the four exporters concerned, an identical dumping margin was assessed for all of them.

2.5 On 12 November 1999, the Ministry of the Economy, based upon the affirmative final determination regarding the existence of dumping issued by the DCD on 23 September 1999, and the affirmative final determination regarding the existence of injury and causality issued by the CNCE on 3 September 1999,[11] imposed definitive anti-dumping measures on imports of ceramic tiles originating in Italy for a period of three years.[12] Such measures took the form of specific anti-dumping duties to be collected as the absolute difference between the FOB price invoiced in any one shipment and a designated "minimum export price" also fixed in FOB terms, whenever the former price is lower than the latter. Each of the three size categories used for the dumping margin calculations was assigned its own "minimum export price".

III. PARTIES' REQUESTS FOR FINDINGS AND RECOMMENDATIONS

A. *The European Communities*

3.1 The EC requests that the Panel finds that the anti-dumping measures applied by Argentina with respect to imports of *porcellanato* originating in Italy are inconsistent with Article 6.8 and Annex II, and Articles 6.10, 2.4, and 6.9 of the AD Agreement.

---

[8] The DCD calculated three separate dumping margins for the subject product, on account of three different size-categories: tiles of 20 cm by 20 cm, tiles of 30 cm by 30 cm, and tiles of 40 cm by 40 cm

[9] *Informe Relativo a la Determinación Definitiva del Margen de Dumping en la Investigación por Práctica Comercial Desleal en Operaciones de Exportación hacia la República Argentina de Placas y Baldosas de Cerámica, sin Barnizar ni Esmaltar, para Pavimentación o Revestimiento, de Gres Fino, "Porcellanato", en todas sus Medidas, Originarias de la República Italiana*, Exhibit EC-2.

[10] As in the preliminary determination, the DCD calculated the dumping margin by size category.

[11] *Acta de Directorio No. 547,* Comisión Nacional de Comercio Exterior.

[12] *Resolución 1385/99 del Ministerio de Economía y Obras y Servicios Públicos* ("Notice of Imposition of Definitive Anti-Dumping Measures"), Exhibit EC-1.

B. *Argentina*

3.2 Argentina requests that the Panel rejects the EC's claims with respect to the alleged breaches of Article 6.8 and paragraph 6 of Annex II, and Articles 6.10, 2.4 and 6.9 of the AD Agreement.

IV. ARGUMENTS OF THE PARTIES AND THIRD PARTIES

A. *Claim under Article 6.8 of the AD Agreement*

1. *The EC*

(a) Arguments of the EC in its First Written Submission in Support of its Claim under Article 6.8 of the AD Agreement

4.1 In its first written submission, the EC made the following arguments regarding its claim under Article 6.8 of the AD Agreement.

4.2 The EC submits that in its Final Dumping Determination the DCD disregarded all the information on normal value and on export prices provided by the four exporters included in the sample and relied instead upon the petitioner's allegations and import statistics.

4.3 By disregarding the exporters' information without any valid justification, the DCD violated Article 6.8 and Annex II of the AD Agreement, which only allow the investigating authorities to resort to "facts available" in those cases where the exporters do not provide timely necessary information or significantly impede the investigation.

4.4 The EC presented first a number of facts relevant to its claim under Article 6.8.

4.5 All the four exporters included in the sample submitted complete responses to the questionnaires received from the DCD within the prescribed deadline (at the request of the exporters, the DCD agreed to extend the deadline to submit the questionnaire responses from 30 November 1998 until 9 December 1998; see Final Dumping Determination, Section III.4, p. 9. The four exporters included in the sample filed their responses on 9 December 1998. At a meeting held at the DCD on 10 May 1999, the case-handlers requested that Casalgrande and Bismantova submit copies of invoices covering at least 50 per cent of their sales in Italy and for export, both to Argentina and to third countries, during the period of investigation. The requested invoices were submitted by those two exporters within the deadline of 31 May 1999 set by the DCD. The submission of these invoices is mentioned expressly in the Final Dumping Determination; see Section V.1.3, page 26, paragraphs 6 and 7. The DCD made no further request for additional information). Moreover, the exporters agreed in advance to the verification of their responses, should the DCD consider it necessary (Final Dumping Determination, Section III.6, pp. 15-17).

4.6 Although the exporters timely provided all the necessary information, the DCD disregarded their responses and resorted to the petitioner's allegations, for the normal value, and to official import statistics, for the export price.

(i) Normal Value

4.7 According to the table included in page 30 of the Final Dumping Determination (reproduced below as Table I), the DCD calculated three different normal values.

Table I

Source of Information	**Supplied by**	**US$/m2**
20 cm x 20 cm		
Price list	Petitioner	8.65
Invoices (weighted average)	Italian Firms	5.54
30 x 30 cm		
Price list	Petitioner	9.89
Invoices (weighted average)	Petitioner	10.16
Invoices (weighted average)	Italian Firms	6.70
40 cm x 40 cm		
Price lists	Petitioner	11.04
Invoices (weighted average)	Petitioner	10.83
Invoices (weighted average)	Italian Firms	7.10

4.8 The first normal value was derived by the DCD from a series of price lists submitted by Zanon (although the precise method used by the DCD to derive the normal value from these lists is explained nowhere in the Final Dumping Determination), namely:

(i) the "Prezzi Informativi delle Opere Edili in Milano 1997" (reference prices in the building industry in Milan 1997);

(ii) the "Prezzi Informativi dell'Edilizia - febbraio 1997" (information prices in the Building Industry);

(iii) a price list of Bismantova;

(iv) a price list of Casalgrande;

(v) a price list of Floor Gres (an Italian producer not included in the sample);

(vi) a price list of Mirage (an Italian producer not included in the sample); and

(vii) a price list of Cooperativa Ceramica d'Imola (an Italian producer not included in the sample).

4.9 The producers' list prices supplied by Zanon provide a rough indication of the prices paid by the end-users of *porcellanato*. But they bear little resemblance to the prices actually charged to distributors and wholesalers, who normally receive large discounts (of up to 75 per cent of the list price). Thus, they are not comparable to the prices for the export sales to Argentina, which are made to distributors and wholesalers and not to final users.

4.10 Similarly, the reference prices shown in the other two documents supplied by Zanon are also prices to end-users. Moreover, they are prices for February and August 1997, i.e., for a period not covered by the dumping investigation.

4.11 The second normal value in Table I is described by the DCD as a weighted average of the prices shown in the invoices supplied by the petitioner. Yet, according to the information available in the public file, Zanon provided to the DCD only seven invoices. In contrast, the four exporters included in the sample reported in their responses several hundred transactions.

4.12 The third normal value in Table I is the weighted average of the invoice prices reported in their responses by the four exporters included in the sample. As explained below, this normal value was not used subsequently by the DCD in order to calculate the dumping margin. Indeed, as shown in Table V below, had the DCD used this normal value, it would have found no dumping.

(ii) Export Price

4.13 The export prices compared by the DCD to the normal value are shown in the table included on page 37 of the Final Dumping Determination (reproduced here below as Table II).

Table II

Size	Unit FOB price in US$
20 cm x 20 cm	6.43
30 cm x 30 cm	7.00
40 cm x 40 cm	9.84

4.14 The export prices in Table II have been derived from the Summary Table (*Cuadro Resumen*) included in the Annex to the Final Dumping Determination, which in turn appears to be a weighted average of the import statistics collected by the *Delegación II - Unidad Informática* within the *Secretaría de Industria, Comercio and Minería* and of the data supplied by two importers: Quadri y Cia. and Canteras Cerro Negro S.A ("Cerro Negro").

(iii) Dumping Margin

4.15 The DCD calculated two different dumping margins for each size category of *porcellanato*. The details of the calculation are set out in two tables included on page 45 of the Final Dumping Determination (reproduced here below as Tables III and IV).

Table III

Product	Normal Value. US$/m2	FOB Export price US$/m2	Dumping Margin
Porcellanato 20 cm x 20 cm	8.65	6.43	34.52 per cent
Porcellanato 30 cm x 30 cm	10.02	7.00	43.14 per cent
Porcellanato 40 cm x 40 cm	10.94	9.84	11.18 per cent

Table IV

Product	Normal Value. US$/m2	FOB Export priceUS$/m2	Dumping margin
Porcellanato 20 cm x 20 cm	7.10	6.43	10.42 per cent
Porcellanato 30 cm x 30 cm	8.92	7.00	27.43 per cent
Porcellanato 40 cm x 40 cm	9.66	9.84	--

4.16 The export prices in Table III and in Table IV are the same: those shown in Table II. The difference in the level of the dumping margins results exclusively from the use of higher normal values in Table III than in Table IV.

4.17 The normal values in Table III are a simple (i.e. non-weighted) average of the first two normal values in Table I, i.e. the normal value based on the price lists supplied by Zanon, and the normal value based on the seven invoices provided by Zanon.

4.18 In turn, the normal values in Table IV are the simple average of the three normal values in Table I, i.e. of the two normal values based on Zanon's information and the normal value based on the data reported by the exporters included in the sample.

4.19 Thus, neither of the two dumping margins calculated by the DCD are based on the normal value data provided by the exporters. Such data was not used at all in the first calculation and was arbitrarily averaged with the petitioner's data in the second calculation.

4.20 As evidenced by Table V, had the DCD compared the export prices in Table II to the normal value determined by the DCD itself on the basis of the exporters' responses, it would have found no dumping.

Table V

Product	A) Normal Value US$/m2	B) FOB Export price US$/m2	C) Dumping margin (A - B))
Porcellanato 20 cm x 20 cm	5.54	6.43	- 0.89
Porcellanato 30 cm x 30 cm	6.70	7.00	- 0.30
Porcellanato 40 cm x 40 cm	7.10	9.84	- 2.74

4.21 In the Final Dumping Determination, the DCD appears to have regarded the two dumping calculations reproduced in Tables III and IV as being equally relevant. Similarly, *Resolución 1385/99* makes no express choice between them. As a result, it is unclear on which of the two dumping margins the anti-dumping measures in place are based.

4.22 The EC presented next its legal arguments concerning its claim under Article 6.8 of the AD Agreement.

4.23 The EC recalled that Article 6.8 of the AD Agreement provided that:

> In cases in which any interested party refuses access to, or otherwise does not provide, necessary information within a reasonable period or significantly impedes the investigation, preliminary and final determinations, affirmative or negative, may be made on the basis of the facts available. The provisions of Annex II shall be observed in the application of this paragraph.

4.24 Therefore, when making a dumping determination, the investigating authorities may resort to facts available only to the extent that the exporter concerned:

(a) refuses access to necessary information; or

(b) otherwise fails to provide necessary information within a reasonable period of time; or

(c) significantly impedes the investigation.

4.25 None of those three circumstances was present in this investigation. The four exporters included in the sample cooperated fully in the investigation. They provided all the information requested by the DCD within the prescribed time limits and volunteered their agreement to receive a verification visit, should it be considered necessary by the DCD.

4.26 The DCD did at no point during the investigation suggest that the exporters failed to provide necessary information or that they impeded in any other way the investigation. Indeed, during the consultations, Argentina did not argue that the exporters' responses had been disregarded on any of the grounds mentioned in Article 6.8. Instead, Argentina argued that the exporters' responses had been "considered" by the DCD "on an equal footing" with the information provided by the petitioner, but eventually the investigating authorities decided to rely on the latter.

4.27 However, the export prices reported by the exporters were totally ignored by the DCD. In turn, the exporters' normal value information was not used at all in calculating one of the two dumping margins calculated by the Argentinean authorities and was arbitrarily averaged with the petitioner's data in order to calculate the other dumping margin. Thus, it is beyond question that the DCD effectively rejected the information supplied by the exporters.

4.28 The position taken by Argentina during the consultations reflects a gross misunderstanding of the requirements imposed by the AD Agreement. Argentina seems to consider that, when making a dumping determination, the investigating authorities have complete discretion to pick and choose data from different sources, including the petitioner, provided that, previously, they have "considered" all of them. That view is manifestly mistaken.

4.29 The information supplied by each exporter is, in principle, the most direct and reliable source of evidence of that exporter's normal value and export price (with respect to cost of production data, Article 2.2.1.1 provides expressly that: "For the purpose of paragraph 2, costs shall normally be calculated on the basis of records kept by the exporter or producer under investigation, provided that such records are in accordance with the generally accepted accounting principles of the exporting country and reasonably reflect the costs associated with the production and sale of the product under consideration". This provision is but an expression of the principle underlying the AD Agreement that dumping determinations should be based, in principle, on the normal value and export price information provided by the exporter). The investigating authorities may not disregard such information and substitute information from other sources, including the petitioner, except in the well defined circumstances enumerated in Article 6.8.

4.30 Argentina's interpretation would render totally redundant Article 6.8 and Annex II. If the investigating authorities were free to choose between the information provided by the exporters and that supplied by the petitioner, the restrictions imposed by Article 6.8 and Annex II on the use of facts available would become meaningless.

4.31 Consider, for example, paragraph 1 of Annex II, which provides that:

> [...] The authorities should also ensure that the party is aware that if information is not supplied within a reasonable period of time, the authorities will be free to make determinations on the basis of the facts available, including those contained in the application for the initiation of the investigation by the domestic industry.

4.32 The warning mandated by paragraph 1 of Annex II would be totally unnecessary if, as argued by Argentina, the investigating authorities were entitled to use information provided by the petitioner also where, as in the present case, the exporters have provided timely all the necessary information.

4.33 Further confirmation is provided by paragraph 7 of Annex II, which states that:

> If the authorities have to base their findings, including those with respect to normal value, on information from a secondary source, including the information supplied in the application for the initiation of the investigation, they should do so with special circumspection [...].

4.34 Paragraph 7 evidences that the investigating authorities are not allowed to consider all sources of information "on an equal footing". Paragraph 7 recognises a hierarchy between "primary" and "secondary" sources. For the purposes of establishing whether an exporter is dumping, the "primary source" of information is the normal value and export price information supplied by that exporter. Paragraph 7 confirms that investigating authorities are not free to substitute secondary sources, such as the information provided by the petitioner, to the primary sources. In accordance with Paragraph 7, investigating authorities may resort to secondary sources only when they "have to", i.e. where the relevant primary sources cannot be used as a result of one of the circumstances described in Article 6.8.

4.35 For the above reasons, the EC submits that, by substituting the information provided by the petitioners and import statistics to the normal value and export price data supplied by the exporters, respectively, the DCD acted inconsistently with Article 6.8 and Annex II.

(b) Arguments of the EC in its First Oral Statement in Support of its Claim under Article 6.8 of the AD Agreement

4.36 In its first oral statement, the EC presented the following arguments with respect to its claim under Article 6.8 of the AD Agreement.

4.37 The main claim submitted by the EC in this case is based on Article 6.8 and Annex II of the AD Agreement.

4.38 The DCD disregarded the normal value and export price information provided by the exporters and substituted information from other sources, including the petitioners. This allowed the DCD to find a high margin of dumping where there was none.

4.39 The AD Agreement only allows the use of "facts available" in one of the three situations specified in Article 6.8, i.e. where the exporters:

(a) refuse access to necessary information; or

(b) otherwise fail to provide necessary information within a reasonably period of time; or

(c) significantly impede the investigation.

4.40 None of those circumstances was present in this investigation. By disregarding the information provided by the exporters without any valid justification, the DCD violated Article 6.8 and Annex II of the AD Agreement.

4.41 During the consultations, Argentina argued that the exporters' responses had not been rejected. Rather, according to Argentina, they had been considered on an "equal footing" with the petitioners' information.

4.42 That position is, of course, legally untenable. In its first written submission, Argentina changes its line of defence and argues that that the exporters' responses were in fact rejected pursuant to Article 6.8.

4.43 The grounds invoked by Argentina for rejecting the exporters' responses are either factually inaccurate, or insufficient as a matter of law, or both. Moreover, all of them are *ex-post facto* justifications. The DCD did not inform the exporters during the investigation of the reasons why their responses had been rejected. Nor are those reasons stated in the Final Dumping Determination. Indeed, the Final Dumping Determination does not even say expressly that the exporters' responses have been rejected. This has to be inferred from the fact that the exporters' data are not used at all in one of the two dumping margin calculations made by the DCD and are arbitrarily averaged with the petitioners' data in the other calculation.

4.44 It is not possible to address in an oral statement all the inaccurate, misleading or irrelevant assertions made in Argentina's submission. The EC will attempt, nevertheless, to respond to the main ones, starting with Argentina's contention that the exporters' responses were submitted late.

(i) Alleged Late Submission of the Questionnaire Responses

4.45 The original deadline for the submission of the responses was 30 November 1998. At the request of the exporters, that deadline was extended until 9 December 1998. The responses were submitted in the early morning of 10 December 1998.

4.46 Article 25 of *Decreto 1.759/72*, which implements the *Ley de Procedimientos Administrativos No. 19.549*, allows the filing of documents within the first two working hours of the day following that in which a deadline expires. The questionnaire responses were filed at 10.00 AM of 10 December 1998 (the hour of reception of the responses is stamped on the cover letters). In view of that, the EC understands that, in accordance with Article 25 of *Decreto 1759/72*, the responses must be deemed submitted within the prescribed deadline. It may be added that the representatives of the exporters had informed in advance the DCD that they would make use of the possibility provided in Article 25 of *Decreto 1.759/72*. The DCD raised no objections. The Panel should ask Argentina to clarify this issue.

4.47 One could assume for the sake of argument that the responses were in fact submitted one day late. No provision of the AD Agreement allows the investigating authorities to resort to "facts available" simply because the party concerned has missed a deadline. Article 6.8 provides that the investigating authority may resort to "facts available" when necessary information is not submitted "within a reasonable period of time", while paragraph 3 of Annex II requires that all information which is submitted "in a timely fashion" should be taken into account.

4.48 Interpreting these two provisions, the recent panel report on *US - Hot Rolled Steel* concluded that:

> What is a 'reasonable period' will not, in all instances be commensurate with pre-established deadlines ... a rigid adherence to such deadlines does not in all cases suffice as the basis for a conclusion that information was not submitted within a reasonable period and consequently that facts available may be applied.
>
> Particularly, where information is actually submitted in time to be verified, and actually could be verified, ... it should generally be accepted, unless to do so would impede the ability of the investigating authority to complete the investigation within the time limits established by the Agreement (Panel Report on *United States -*

Anti-Dumping Measures on Certain Hot Rolled Steel Products from Japan, WT/DS184/R, circulated on 28 February 2001, at paras 7.54 and 7.55 respectively).

4.49 The EC agrees. A mere one-day delay, especially at the very outset of the investigation, is clearly an insufficient ground for resorting to "facts available".

4.50 Argentina also alleges that one of the exporters (Casalgrande) missed the deadline for submitting some supporting invoices. Nevertheless, the delay was, once again, very short: at most three days. Moreover, the invoices were submitted in time to be verified and used by the DCD, and were indeed used in one of the dumping calculations (the invoices were filed on 10 June 1999, and the Final Dumping Determination was not issued until 23 September 1999).

4.51 More generally, Argentina complains about "repeated request for extensions" of deadlines (*"reiteradas solicitudes de prórrogas"*). In reality, however, the exporters requested only two extensions: one for filing the responses and another for submitting additional non-confidential summaries and supporting invoices. The DCD agreed to both requests and is estopped from complaining now that, as a result, the information was not submitted "within a reasonable period" or that the extensions impeded the investigation.

(ii) Alleged Failure to Submit Adequate Non-Confidential Summaries

4.52 Argentina invokes as an additional ground for rejecting the responses that the exporters failed to provide adequate non-confidential summaries.

4.53 This allegation is, to say the least, ironic. The actual fact is that the DCD's relentless demands forced the exporters to waive all its confidentiality claims and to disclose to their Argentinean competitors highly sensitive price and cost information.

4.54 The EC recalls briefly the relevant facts.

4.55 Together with the questionnaire responses, the exporters submitted non-confidential summaries. In preparing those summaries, the exporters applied the following principles:

(a) non-sensitive information was left unchanged in the summary;

(b) sensitive information covering several years/months was expressed in indexed form (Annexes IV, V and VI); and

(c) other sensitive information was omitted from the summary (Annexes III, VII, VIII, IX, X and XI).

4.56 The DCD gave no indication to the exporters that the non-confidential summaries were inadequate until the Preliminary Dumping Determination of 24 March 1999, i.e more than three months after the filing of the responses.

4.57 By letters dated 30 April 1999, the DCD requested the exporters to waive their confidentiality requests or to supply more detailed non-confidential summaries. Specifically, these letters referred to Annexes III, VII,VIII, IX, X and XI, i.e. to the Annexes for which no confidential summary had been provided by the exporters.

4.58 Argentina now complains that the non-confidential summaries of Annexes IV, V and VI containing indexed figures were insufficient. But this issue was not raised by the DCD in the Preliminary Dumping Determination, or in the letters of 30 April 1999, or indeed at any stage of the investigation.

4.59 Following the letters of 30 April 1999, the representatives of the exporters met with the case-handlers on 11 May 1999. At that meeting, it was agreed that the exporters would submit non-confidential summaries of Annexes VII (exports to Argentina), VIII (sales in Italy) and IX (export to third countries), in which the names of the customers and the models would be replaced by "virtual codes".

4.60 On 4 June 1999 the four exporters submitted non-confidential summaries of Annexes VII, VIII and IX in the format agreed at the meeting of 11 May. A "Conversion Table" indicating the correspondences between each code number and the customer and model was submitted to the DCD on a confidential basis.

4.61 One should emphasize that the summaries submitted on 4 June contained the same information as the confidential responses, with the only difference that the name of the model and of the customer had been replaced by a code number. Thus, the summaries allowed the petitioners to calculate by themselves the dumping margins by comparing the actual prices in the domestic and the export market. Clearly, this is more than enough to permit "a reasonable understanding of the substance of the information submitted in confidence" as required by Article 6.5.1.

4.62 In spite of that, on 22 June 1999, the DCD sent a letter to the exporters requesting them to waive the confidentiality of the product code. Within two days, the exporters agreed to that request.

4.63 By way of justification, the letter of 22 June asserted that the disclosure of the product code was necessary so that the DCD "can make a precise comparison" ("*... a fin de que la [DCD] pueda realizar una precisa comparación en su informe de determinación final del margen de dumping...*"). This suggests that the Argentinean authorities thoroughly misunderstood the purpose of the non-confidential summaries. Article 6.5.2 provides that information provided on a non-confidential basis may be disregarded if the party concerned does not provide a confidential summary. But this does not mean that the investigating authorities must base their findings on the information contained in the non-confidential summaries. If so, the submission of information on a confidential basis would be totally redundant. The non-confidential summaries serve exclusively to inform the other interested parties, so that they can defend adequately their interests.

4.64 By letter of 3 August 1999, the DCD requested the exporters to waive the confidentiality of the cost of production data contained in Annexes X and XI. On 10 August, the exporters agreed to that request (rather misleadingly, the exporters' response of 10 August is omitted in Argentina's first written submission).

4.65 Contrary to Argentina's contentions, this sequence of events does not evidence lack of co-operation on the part of the exporters, but rather the opposite.

4.66 Although the non-confidential summaries submitted by the exporters on 10 December 1998 might not have been sufficiently detailed, the DCD did not inform the exporters of this until more than three months later. Thus, the DCD acted inconsistently with paragraph 6 of Annex II, which requires that "if evidence or information is not accepted, the supplying party should be informed *forthwith* of the reasons therefor..." (emphasis added by the EC).

4.67 Once the exporters were advised by the DCD that the non-confidential summaries were not considered adequate, they agreed promptly to each of the successive, and increasingly exacting demands made by the DCD.

4.68 Eventually, the exporters were led by the DCD's demands to disclose to their Argentinean competitors all the price and cost-of-production data for the investigation period included in their responses, a type of information which is clearly entitled to confidential treatment in accordance with Article 6.5. The EC is not aware of any other investigating authority in the world that requires the exporters to disclose that type of information, except under a narrowly drawn protective order (see footnote 17 of the AD Agreement), a system which is not available in Argentina.

(iii) Alleged Failure to Provide Supporting Documents

4.69 Yet another ground invoked by Argentina for rejecting the exporters' responses is their alleged failure to provide "supporting documents", and more particularly to provide copies of a "sufficient" number of invoices for the sales made in the Italian market.

4.70 Paragraph 1 of Annex II provides that the investigating authorities "should specify *in detail* the information required" (emphasis added by the EC). The DCD's questionnaire did not require the exporters to provide copies of a "sufficient" number of invoices. Therefore, Argentina cannot complain now if the exporters did not do so in their questionnaire responses.

4.71 The only reference to invoices is found in Section B of the questionnaire ("Exports to Argentina"), which requests the exporters to provide "probatory documents which help to better understand the transactions" (*"documentación probatoria que ayude a una mejor comprensión de la operación"*), including invoices. This suggests that the DCD was interested in receiving only a few examples of invoices. This would accord with the practice of most investigating authorities, which is to ask for invoices during the subsequent on-the-spot verification, and not as part of the questionnaire response.

4.72 Argentina argues now that one of the introductory paragraphs to the questionnaire stated that the respondents should supply "supporting documents" (*"documentación respaldatoria"*). But that reference is too vague to meet the requirements of paragraph 1 of Annex II. Moreover, taken literally, it would have required the exporters to provide copies not only of the invoices, but of all the accounting and cost records that are usually examined in the course of an on-the-spot verification.

4.73 Even though, with the sole exception just mentioned, the questionnaire did not require specifically to provide copies of invoices, the exporters did provide, by way of example, some copies of invoices.

4.74 At any rate, the Preliminary Dumping Determination did not mention the alleged failure to provide "supporting documents" as a reason for rejecting the responses. Rather, as mentioned before, the Preliminary Dumping Determination suggested that the responses were rejected because the non-confidential summaries were deemed inadequate.

4.75 Nor did the letters of 12 April 1999 mention specifically the alleged failure to provide "supporting documents", contrary to what is repeatedly asserted in Argentina's first written submission. Those letters referred exclusively to alleged deficiencies of the non-confidential summaries.

4.76 It was only at the meeting of 11 May 1999 that the case-handlers requested specifically for the first time that Casalgrande and Bismantova, the two main exporters, provide copies of invoices covering an "important" volume of sales. The case-handlers justified that request on the grounds that they could not conduct on-the-spot verifications in Italy and, therefore, needed to check the responses "from their offices".

4.77 In response to the request made at the meeting of 11 May, the exporters concerned submitted copies of invoices covering approximately 50 per cent of the sales in Italy and of the exports to Argentina and third countries (together with a translation into Spanish of each invoice!).

4.78 The DCD made no further request for "supporting documents" during the remainder of the investigation. The exporters, therefore, assumed that the DCD was satisfied with the documents submitted.

(iv) Alleged Lack of Representativeness of the Sample of Exporters

4.79 Argentina also invokes the lack of representativeness of the sample of exporters as a reason for resorting to "facts available".

4.80 The EC rejects the contention that the sample was not representative. What matters is whether the exports made by the selected exporters were representative of the exports to Argentina covered by the investigation, and not whether the domestic sales made by the selected exporters were representative of the domestic sales made by all the Italian producers of *porcellanato* (including those made by the more than 100 producers which did not export to Argentina).

4.81 From that perspective, it is beyond question that the sample was sufficiently representative since the four selected exporters accounted for more than 70 per cent of all the Italian exports to Argentina during 1997.

4.82 Article 6.10 confirms that this is the relevant criterion. It provides that the examination may be limited to a reasonable number of exporters by using statistically valid samples or, as an alternative, to "the largest percentage of the volume of exports from the country in question which can reasonably be investigated".

4.83 Furthermore, even assuming that the sample were in fact not sufficiently representative, that would still not justify the DCD's decision to resort to "facts available". Article 6.10 contains no provision authorising the investigating authorities to resort to "facts available" in such circumstances. The only options available under Article 6.10 would be: (1) to enlarge the sample; (2) to choose a new sample; or (3) to extend the examination to all the exporters.

4.84 Argentina suggests that the alleged lack of representativeness of the sample amounts to a refusal to provide necessary information in the sense of Article 6.8. However, the decision to limit the examination to a sample of exporters was a decision taken by the DCD itself. Argentina cannot fault now the non-selected exporters for failing to provide information that they were not requested to provide.

4.85 Moreover, the DCD did at no point during the investigation inform the exporters or Assopiastrelle that the sample was not considered representative. It was only in the Final Dumping Determination that the DCD made for the first time some vague remarks in that sense. Nevertheless, even at that late stage, the DCD refrained from drawing any conclusions. Thus, once again, this is but an *ex post* justification.

4.86 Argentina further suggests that the lack of representativeness of the sample could be established by the DCD only at a late stage of the investigation because of the delay in providing "supporting documents". This is not true. As explained before, the "supporting documents" in question were supplied as soon as they were requested by the DCD. Moreover, nothing prevented the DCD from checking the representativeness of the sample on the basis of the confidential information contained in the questionnaire responses filed on 10 December 1998.

4.87 Furthermore, given Argentina's view that the percentage of domestic sales, and not the percentage of exports, is the decisive criterion, the DCD could, and indeed should have requested that information from Assopiastrelle before taking any decision on the sampling.

(v) Other Alleged Deficiencies

4.88 Argentina also alleges in passing a series of miscellaneous deficiencies in the questionnaire responses. The EC submits that some of them were not such, while the others were minor omissions which did not warrant the DCD's decision to reject the responses.

4.89 First, Argentina alleges that Caesar and Marazzi did not provide information with respect to their export sales to third countries. This is true. But Argentina misleadingly omits to mention that the questionnaire allowed the exporters not to provide such information if the domestic sales were sufficiently representative. Caesar and Marazzi relied expressly upon that possibility.

4.90 Second, Argentina contends that Marazzi did not provide cost-of-production data for the models exported to Argentina. However, Marazzi explained in its response that the models exported to Argentina were the same as those sold in Italy and had the same cost of production, except for the differences in selling expenses.

4.91 Third, Argentina complains that three of the exporters did not provide a Spanish translation of their balance sheet. Again, this is correct but cannot justify the rejection of the responses. The requested translation cannot be considered as "necessary information" in the sense of Article 6.8, given that the essential content of the document in question were figures, that Italian and Spanish are closely related and that, in particular, the accounting terminology is very similar in both languages. Moreover Italian is widely understood in Argentina.

4.92 It is worth noting that the DCD accepted as good the "translation" provided by Marazzi. Yet Marazzi limited itself to translate one word in the front page, namely the word "esercicio", which Marazzi rendered somewhat inaccurately as "año", the precise translation being "ejercicio". This confirms that the requested translations were by no means necessary.

4.93 Finally, Argentina complains that Bismantova provided the information requested in Annex VI (a summary table of the sales made during the last four years in different markets) in Italian Lire instead of in US$. With respect, it is simply ridiculous to pretend that this minor omission impeded significantly the investigation.

(c) Replies of the EC to the First Set of Questions by the Panel Relating to the EC's Claim under Article 6.8 of the AD Agreement

4.94 The EC replied to the first set of questions by the Panel relating to the EC's claim under Article 6.8 of the AD Agreement as follows.

4.95 The Panel asked the parties whether, in their view, the DCD rejected the information from the exporters for one of the reasons set out in Article 6.8 AD Agreement. The Panel further asked whether reference was made in the record to one of these reasons and, if so, where. The Panel also asked under what circumstances an investigating authority may resort to secondary source information outside the specific circumstances of Article 6.8 AD Agreement.

4.96 To this question, the EC provided the following reply.

4.97 As explained in the EC's first written submission, during the consultations Argentina did not argue that the information submitted by the exporters had been rejected on any of the grounds set out in Article 6.8. Instead, Argentina argued that the exporters' information had been "considered" on an "equal footing" with the information supplied by the petitioner. This suggests that the DCD based its final determination on the erroneous premise that the investigating authority is free to use secondary sources of information, such as import statistics or data supplied by the petitioner, even if the circumstances specified in Article 6.8 are not present.

4.98 As discussed in the EC's first written submission, that position is untenable under the AD Agreement. Predictably, in its first written submission Argentina invokes a misunderstanding on the part of the EC and argues that the DCD did in fact reject the exporters' information for the reasons set out in Article 6.8.

4.99 Argentina's new position is not supported by the record of the investigation. The Final Dumping Determination does not mention anywhere that the exporters' information had to be rejected for any of the reasons set out in Article 6.8. Moreover, the DCD did at no point during the investigation inform the exporters that their responses had been rejected for the reasons set out in Article 6.8, contrary to the requirement imposed by paragraph 6 of Annex II.

4.100 Argentina's new position also is contradicted by the fact that the DCD did use the exporters' information in one of the two dumping margin calculations contained in the Final Dumping Determination, albeit arbitrarily averaged with secondary source information. Obviously, this would not have been possible if the exporters had failed to provide necessary information, or if such information had been deemed unreliable by the DCD.

4.101 The Panel recalled that Argentina's first written submission alleged that the exporters' questionnaire responses were deficient in many ways. In particular, that such questionnaire responses were submitted late, were not fully translated, lacked public summaries of confidential information sufficiently detailed, lacked some currency conversions, failed to report data on exports to third countries and costs of the product exported, and lacked supporting documentary evidence. The Panel asked Argentina which of these deficiencies, if any, were relied upon by the DCD for its final determination. The Panel further asked if Argentina could provide the Panel with the relevant references in either the report accompanying the final determination or in the administrative record.

4.102 To this question, the EC provided the following reply.

4.103 The DCD's Final Dumping Determination does not say anywhere that the exporters' information had to be rejected for any of the reasons stated in Article 6.8. Nor did the DCD inform the exporters that their responses had been rejected, as required by paragraph 6 of Annex II.

4.104 The following is a summary of the references made in the record to the grounds invoked now by Argentina in order to reject the responses.

(i) Late Submission of the Questionnaire Responses and of Supporting Evidence

4.105 The Preliminary Dumping Determination and the Final Dumping Determination record the dates on which the exporters' submissions were made. But they make no suggestion to the effect that information was submitted late or that it was rejected for that reason.

(ii) Non-Confidential Summaries

4.106 The Preliminary Dumping Determination suggests that the information on normal value provided by the exporters was disregarded for reasons related to the confidentiality requests, but such reasons are not specified. No similar suggestion is found in the export price section of the Preliminary Dumping Determination.

4.107 The DCD's letters of 30 April 1999 requested the exporters to waive their confidentiality requests or supply more detailed non-confidential summaries of Annexes III, VII, VIII, IX, X, and XI. Those letters make no reference to the non-confidential summaries of Annexes IV, V and VI.

4.108 The letter of 22 June 1999 requested the exporters to disclose the "product code" included in the non-confidential summaries of Annexes VII and VIII submitted on 4 June 1999.

4.109 The letter of 3 August 1999 requested the exporters to waive the confidentiality requests or supply more detailed non-confidential summaries of Annexes X and XI.

4.110 The Final Dumping Determination records the above letters and the exporters' replies. It does not mention anywhere that the information submitted by the exporters in response to the DCD's requests was deemed insufficient or that the exporters' normal value and export price information was rejected because the exporters failed to disclose confidential information or provide adequate non-confidential summaries.

(iii) Supporting Evidence

4.111 The Preliminary Dumping Determination did not mention the lack of supporting evidence, and in particular of invoices. Nor was this supposed deficiency mentioned in the letters of 30 April 1999. This issue was raised for the first time by the DCD at the meeting of 11 May 1999.

4.112 The letters of 22 June 1999 and of 3 August 1999 contain no reference to this alleged deficiency.

4.113 The Final Dumping Determination records that Bismantova and Casalgrande submitted the requested invoices on 7 and 11 June 1999, respectively. It makes no suggestion to the effect that the exporters failed to provide sufficient supporting invoices (or any other supporting evidence), or that the normal value and export price information supplied by the exporters was disregarded for that reason.

(iv) Representativeness of the Domestic Sales

4.114 The supposed lack of representativeness of the domestic sales reported by the exporters was mentioned for the first time in the Final Dumping Determination. Moreover, the DCD did not draw any conclusions from this.

(v) Currency Conversions

4.115 The Preliminary Dumping Determination records that the exporter Bismantova completed the tables in Annex VI in Italian lire and provided exchange rates between that currency and the US$, but attaches no consequences to this. This issue was not raised again until Argentina's first written submission to the Panel.

(vi) Export Sales to Third Countries

4.116 The Preliminary Dumping Determination records that Marazzi and Caesar did not report export sales to third countries in Annex IX, together with the explanations given by both exporters to the effect that such information was not provided in accordance with the instructions contained in the questionnaire, which only required to complete Annex IX in the event that the volume of domestic sales was not sufficiently representative. The Preliminary Dumping Determination attaches no consequences to this. This issue was not raised again by the DCD and is not mentioned in the Final Dumping Determination.

(vii) Cost-of-Production Data for the Exported Merchandise

4.117 The Preliminary Dumping Determination records that Marazzi did not report cost of production data for the exported merchandise in Annex XI, together with Marazzi's explanation that the cost of production of the exported merchandise was the same as that of the merchandise sold in Italy. The Preliminary Dumping Determination attaches no consequences to this. The issue was not raised again by the DCD during the investigation and is not mentioned in the Final Dumping Determination.

(viii) Translation of Accounting Documents

4.118 The Preliminary Dumping Determination mentions that Bismantova, Casalgrande and Caesar did not provide a Spanish translation of their balance sheet, but attaches no consequences to this. The issue was not raised again by the DCD during the investigation.

4.119 The Panel recalled that Argentina, in paragraph 39 of its first written submission, states that "the submission of information and documentation for which confidential treatment is requested constitutes a *limiting factor* with respect to the analysis and public conclusions of the implementing authority" (emphasis added by Argentina). The Panel asked Argentina whether, in its opinion, the confidential nature of the information submitted constituted a constraint on the investigating authority's ability to base its determination on that information. The Panel further asked Argentina to explain in which way it considered that confidentiality limited the DCD's analysis in this case. The Panel also asked the EC to comment on the above-quoted statement from Argentina.

4.120 To this question, the EC provided the following reply.

4.121 Argentina's interpretation is mistaken. Articles 6.5.1 and 6.5.2 of the Anti-Dumping Agreement do not require the investigating authority to base its findings on non-confidential information. Indeed, if so, the submission of confidential information by the parties would be totally redundant.

4.122 Article 6.5.2 provides that the investigating authority may, subject to certain requirements, disregard confidential information. This provision would be unnecessary if the investigating authority had to use always non-confidential information.

4.123 Further confirmation is provided by Articles 12.2.1 and 12.2.2, which stipulate that the notice or the report of the imposition of provisional and definitive measures, respectively, shall pay due regard to the requirement for the protection of confidential information. Again, this would have been unnecessary if the dumping and injury determinations had to be based exclusively on non-confidential information.

4.124 Dumping and injury determinations require necessarily the use of information which is confidential by nature, including information which is not capable of summarization. Argentina's interpretation would make it impossible for the investigating authority to make an accurate dumping or injury determination without violating its duties under Article 6.5. The present case proves this point. The DCD was able to make a dumping determination (partially) based on non-confidential information supplied by the exporters only because the exporters had been forced previously to relinquish virtually all their confidentiality claims.

4.125 The Panel asked the Parties whether they drew a distinction between the obligation of authorities to protect confidential information from disclosure, on the one hand, and the obligation of authorities to use for their determinations exporter data that meets the requirements of the Agreement.

4.126 The EC replied that the investigating authority must base its determination of dumping on information provided by the exporter, including that for which confidential treatment has been requested. The investigating authority may not disregard the information provided in confidence by the exporter and resort to "facts available" except in the circumstances specified in Article 6.5.2.

4.127 The Panel recalled Argentina's statement that, according to the DCD, the non-confidential summaries submitted by the exporters were insufficient under Article 6.5.1 AD Agreement, since this provision required that such summaries permit a "reasonable understanding of the substance of the information provided in confidence". The Panel asked the parties how did they interpret the objective of Article 6.5.1, that is, whose "reasonable understanding" was being addressed - that of the public or that of the investigating authorities?

4.128 The EC replied that the non-confidential summaries provided for in Article 6.5.1 serve exclusively to inform the other interested parties. They constitute a compromise between the conflicting objectives of protecting the confidentiality of the information supplied by each party and of allowing the other parties to defend adequately their interests.

4.129 The Panel asked the parties whether the following summary of relevant facts was correct. The exporters requested confidentiality for most of the information provided in their questionnaire reply. On 30 April 1999, the DCD sent letters to the exporting firms requesting them to consider providing a more detailed non-confidential summary than that already provided in the questionnaire replies, to elaborate on the information supplied, or to remove the requested confidentiality that had been granted by the investigating authority. More specifically, information on sales in the Italian market (Annex VIII) and the cost structure of the goods in the domestic Italian market (Annex X) was requested. On 4 June 1999, the exporting firms submitted public and confidential information concerning domestic sales of the product concerned, with conversion tables that were submitted as confidential information. On 7 June 1999, Bismantova and Casalgrande further submitted as confidential information sales invoices relating to the Italian domestic market. By its letters of 22 June 1999 and 3 August 1999, the DCD requested the exporting firms to reconsider the requested confidentiality of the information concerning product codes and the production costs. The DCD's report acknowledged that the exporting firms agreed by letters of 23 and 24 June that the product code item could be made non-confidential. On 10 August 1999, the exporting firms further agreed to remove the confidentiality of the item concerning cost of production provided that the names of the companies relating to each cost structure were not revealed.

4.130 To this question, the EC provided the following reply.

4.131 The above summary of the facts is generally correct. Nevertheless, some additional clarifications were in order:

(a) The letters of 30 April 1999 did not request the exporters to provide "information on sales in the Italian market (Annex VIII) and the cost structure of the goods in the domestic Italian market (Annex X)". Those letters mentioned exclusively the supposed deficiencies of the non-confidential summaries. Moreover, the letters addressed to Bismantova and Caesar did not mention Annex X.

(b) The EC recalls that on 11 May 1999 representatives of the exporters held a meeting with the case-handlers, in which the DCD specified its requests.

(c) On 4 June 1999, the four exporters did not submit "public and confidential information concerning domestic sales", but rather a non-confidential summary of both their domestic and export sales as previously reported in their questionnaire responses. In addition, as indicated correctly in the summary, they submitted in confidence conversion tables, with the product and customer codes.

(d) On 7 and 10 June 1999, Casalgrande and Bismantova submitted not only invoices of domestic sales, but also invoices of export sales to Argentina and to third countries.

(e) The letter of 22 June 1999 requested exclusively the disclosure of the "product code" used in the non-confidential summaries of Annexes VII and VIII submitted on 4 June 1999. The disclosure of the cost of production tables (Annexes X and XI) was requested for the first time in the letter of 3 August 1999.

4.132 The Panel asked the parties to clarify whether, in light of the exporters' agreement to re-classify the information as requested, the concerns the DCD raised with regard to the confidential nature of the information at the time of the preliminary determination (recorded on page 23 of the DCD's Final Dumping Determination) had been resolved by the time of the final determination. The Panel further asked the parties to indicate which of the exporters' information, if any, was still confidential at the time of the final determination. If certain information had remained as confidential, the Panel also asked the parties to clarify whether non-confidential summaries were provided for this confidential information.

4.133 To this question, the EC provided the following reply.

4.134 In response to the DCD's requests, the exporters were forced to waive virtually all their confidentiality requests. Thus, they assumed that all the concerns of the DCD with respect to this issue had already been resolved by the time of the final determination. Indeed, as mentioned above, the Final Dumping Determination does not say anywhere that that the information submitted by the exporters in response to the DCD's requests was deemed insufficient or that the exporters' normal value and export price information was rejected because the exporters failed to disclose confidential information or provide adequate non-confidential summaries.

4.135 More specifically, at the time of the final determination, the exporters maintained the following confidentiality requests:

(a) Annex III (list of customers): the exporters did not provide a non-confidential summary for this Annex. The EC considers that this information is not capable of summarization (see Panel Report on *Guatemala - Definitive Anti-Dumping Measures on Grey Portland Cement from Mexico,* WT/DS156/R, adopted 17 November 2000, at para. 8.211).

(b) Annex IV (information on the exporter's market situation), Annex V (summary of sales in different markets - quantity) and Annex VI (summary of sales in different markets - value): the exporters provided non-confidential summaries together with their questionnaire responses of 10 December 1998, in which the actual figures had been replaced by indexes. Argentina raised no objections with respect to the non-confidential summaries of these Annexes until its first written submission in these proceedings.

(c) Annex VII (export sales to Argentina), Annex VIII (domestic sales) Annex IX (export sales to other markets): following the DCD's requests of 30 April 1999 and of 22 June 1999, the exporters maintained their confidentiality requests only with respect to the customer code.

(d) Annexes X and XI (cost of production tables): in response to the DCD's request of 3 August 1999, the exporters accepted to disclose these Annexes, provided that the name of the exporter was kept confidential.

(e) Invoices: the exporters requested confidential treatment for the invoices submitted on 7 and 10 June 1999. Nevertheless, the contents of these invoices are summarised in the non-confidential summaries provided on 4 June 1999.

4.136 The Panel asked Argentina to explain the relevance of the DCD's finding that the four exporters included in the sample only represented 1.92 per cent of the total volume of sales in the home market. In particular, did the 1.92 per cent refer to all sales made by Italian producers, including those with no exports to Argentina? If this was the case, the Panel asked the parties whether they were of the view that, as a legal matter, companies selected for an individual determination have to account collectively for a large percentage of all home market sales made.

4.137 To this question, the EC provided the following reply.

4.138 Article 6.10 allows the investigating authority to limit the examination to (1) a statistically valid sample of exporters; or (2) the largest percentage of the volume of exports from the country in question which can reasonably be investigated. The question posed by the Panel may arise only where the investigating authority resorts to the first method.

4.139 In the present case, it is unclear which of the two methods permitted by Article 6.10 was followed by the DCD, even if both parties have been referring, without too much precision, to a "sample" of exporters. The following comments are, therefore, based on the assumption that the DCD intended to select a "statistically valid sample".

4.140 The purpose of an anti-dumping investigation is to establish whether the exports under investigation are dumped. The existence of dumping does not require the existence of domestic sales. Therefore, there is no reason why a sample should include a large percentage of domestic sales.

4.141 This interpretation is supported by the second method provided in Article 6.10. If the percentage of domestic sales is irrelevant for the purposes of that method, why should it be considered as decisive when applying the first method?

4.142 At any rate, assuming that the percentage of domestic sales were in fact relevant in assessing whether a sample is statistically valid for the purposes of Article 6.10, Argentina disregards that, as noted by Japan in its third party submission, a sample covering a relatively small percentage of the relevant universe may nevertheless be "statistically valid".

4.143 The Panel asked the parties to confirm whether that the four exporters included in the sample accounted, in quantity terms, for around 70 per cent of all exports made.

4.144 The EC replied that this had been the case.

4.145 The Panel asked the parties to comment on the relevance of the fact that the DCD initially accepted the sampling methodology suggested by the exporters' association, although the sampled firms were later found by the DCD to cover too few home sales.

4.146 The EC replied that the decision to limit the examination to the four exporters concerned was a decision of the DCD, even if it was suggested by Assopiastrelle. The DCD could and should have verified in advance the representativeness of the sample. Consequently, the DCD is estopped from claiming now that the sample was not representative.

4.147 The Panel recalled that the exporters' questionnaire made reference to the provision of supporting documentation in two places. In the introductory section, while indicating that supporting documentation must be provided, it also allowed exporters the possibility to identify instead the source of the information reported. In addition, Section B requested the submission of any supporting documentation that would help the DCD to better understand the mechanics of the reported transactions. The Panel asked Argentina whether it was of the view that, according to the specifications of the questionnaire used by the DCD, respondents were obliged to provide full documentary evidence of each and every sale reported. The Panel further asked Argentina to clarify whether any of the exporters chose to comply with the requirement set out in the introductory section of the questionnaire by identifying the source of its information. If no exporters took advantage of that option, the Panel asked Argentina whether it was of the view that the DCD was entitled to require the submission of "additional" supporting documentation without specifying what that information should consist of.

4.148 The EC replied that the exporters' replies to Annexes VII, VIII and IX include the number and the date of the sales invoices from which the information reported in those Annexes was derived. Thus, in any event, those Annexes would satisfy the requirement to indicate the "source of the information".

4.149 The Panel recalled that, on page 14 of the EC's first written submission, the EC argued that the Argentine authority acted inconsistently with paragraph 6 of Annex II of the AD Agreement, by failing to inform the exporters that their responses had been rejected and by failing to state the reasons therefor. The Panel asked the EC whether this is not a separate claim of the EC but rather an additional argument in support of the EC's claim that the DCD disregarded the normal value and export price information of the exporters inconsistently with Article 6.8 and Annex II.

4.150 The EC replied that this was the case.

(d) Replies of the EC to the Questions Made by Argentina, Following the First Meeting of the Panel with the Parties, that Relate to the EC's Claim under Article 6.8 of the AD Agreement

4.151 The EC replied to the questions made by Argentina relating to the EC's claim under Article 6.8 of the AD Agreement as follows.

4.152 Argentina asked the EC why it considers irrelevant the legal requirement to provide translations set forth in article 28 of Decree 1759/72, when the EC regards as mandatory article 25 of that same Decree, regarding deadlines for submitting documents in administrative proceedings conducted in Argentina.

4.153 To this question, the EC replied as follows.

4.154 The two situations can be easily distinguished.

4.155 The interpretation of the obligations imposed upon the investigating authority by the AD Agreement cannot be left to the discretion of each Member. Thus, the definition of what constitutes "necessary information" or a "reasonable period" made in the domestic law of each Member is subject to review by Panels.

4.156 Nonetheless, each Member's own interpretation of those notions creates legitimate expectations for the interested parties. The investigating authority is estopped from claiming that information submitted within the deadline which it has prescribed (computed according to the applicable domestic rules) has not been submitted within a "reasonable period".

4.157 Argentina asked the EC what value the EC attaches to non-confidential summaries, bearing in mind the obligations arising from Article 6.5.1, if, as argued by the EC in its first oral statement, "the non confidential summaries serve exclusively to inform the other interested parties, so that they can defend adequately their interests".

4.158 The EC replied that its answer to this question was reflected in its answers to questions 3, 4 and 5 made by the Panel following the first meeting.

4.159 Argentina asked the EC why it believed there would not be a justification for resorting to the "facts available" even in situations where samples turn out to be admittedly not representative.

4.160 The EC replied that the decision to limit the examination to a sample of exporter is taken by the investigating authority, which must satisfy itself in advance that the sample is sufficiently representative. Thus, the situation described in the question might arise only as a result of the investigating authority's own fault. Exporters should not be penalized for the lack of diligence of the investigating authority.

4.161 The circumstances in which the investigating authority may resort to facts available are enumerated exhaustively in Article 6.8. Neither that provision, nor Article 6.10 authorise the investigating authority to use facts available in the event that the sample turns out not to be sufficiently representative in the course of the investigation.

4.162 Argentina asked the EC how one check the veracity of the pricing information regarding home-market sales in the absence of supporting documentation relating to those sales. Argentina further asked the EC how one can check the veracity of this kind of information in cases where the investigating authorities are unable to conduct an on-site verification. Argentina also asked the EC why it gave greater value to an on-site verification than to the provision of supporting documentation.

4.163 The EC replied that its point was simply that the questionnaire did not request the exporters to provide copies of all invoices and that, moreover, this would have been a most unusual request in light of the verification methods usually followed by most investigating authorities.

4.164 Argentina asked the EC why it considered "ridiculous" the issue of currency conversions, even through Article 2.4 of the AD Agreement specifically dealt with the way in which those conversions shall take place. Argentina further asked the EC whether it considered that exchange rates did not have an impact in the calculation of dumping margins. Argentina also asked the EC whether it was of the view that it was unreasonable to request the submission of exchange rate data in order to avoid assigning staff to calculate the value of each of the sales falling within the period of investigation.

4.165 The EC replied that the alleged deficiency concerned exclusively Annex VI, which contains a summary of the sales by market. The 24 amounts reported in that Annex were not used in the dumping calculation. In any event, they can be easily converted into US$ by using the exchange rates provided by Bismantova or other publicly available rates.

(e) Arguments of the EC in its Second Written Submission in Support of its Claim under Article 6.8 of the AD Agreement

4.166 In its second written submission, the EC made the following arguments in support of its claim under Article 6.8 of the AD Agreement.

4.167 During the consultations, Argentina argued that the information submitted by the exporters had not been rejected. Rather, according to Argentina, that information was "considered" by the DCD on an "equal footing" with the information supplied by the petitioner.

4.168 That position is clearly untenable under the AD Agreement. Thus, predictably, in its first written submission Argentina invokes a misunderstanding on the part of the EC and argues that the DCD did in fact reject the exporters' information for the reasons set out in Article 6.8 of the AD Agreement.

4.169 The grounds invoked now by Argentina for resorting to "facts available" are either wrong as a matter of fact, or clearly insufficient as a matter of law, or both.

4.170 Furthermore, Argentina's new position is not supported by the record of the investigation. The DCD did at no point during the investigation inform the exporters that their responses had been rejected for the reasons set out in Article 6.8, contrary to the requirement imposed by paragraph 6 of Annex II. Moreover, the Final Dumping Determination does not mention anywhere that the exporters' information had to be rejected for any of those reasons, contrary also to paragraph 6 of Annex II.

(i) Alleged Late Submission of the Questionnaire Responses

4.171 In its first written submission, Argentina contended that the exporters filed their responses to the questionnaire one day after the expiry of the deadline imparted by the DCD.

4.172 Nevertheless, in its first oral statement Argentina qualified this by noting that:

> Esto no implica de nuestra parte afirmar que la presentación efectuada por las empresas exportadoras el 10 de diciembre fuera considerada una falta procesal, pero de todos modos, destacamos con esto la buena fe de la Autoridad de Aplicación en considerar la presentación efectuada a pesar de ser tardía (Argentina's first oral statement, at para. 11).

4.173 Thus, Argentina seems to admit that the alleged delay in submitting the questionnaire responses is not a sufficient ground for resorting to "facts available" or, at least, that it was not considered as such by the DCD. In view of that, it is difficult to understand what is the relevance, if any, of this argument.

4.174 At any rate, it is not true that the responses were submitted late by the exporters. Article 25 of *Decreto 1.759/72*, which implements the *Ley de Procedimientos Administrativos No. 19.549*, allows the filing of documents within the first two working hours of the day following that in which a deadline expires. The questionnaire responses were filed at 10.00 AM of 10 December 1998 (the hour of reception of the responses is stamped on the cover letters) and, therefore, within the prescribed deadline. It may be added that the representatives of the exporters had informed in advance the DCD that they would make use of the possibility provided in Article 25 of *Decreto 1.759/72*. The DCD raised no objections.

4.175 Argentina also alleges that one of the exporters (Casalgrande) missed the deadline for submitting some supporting invoices. Nevertheless, the delay was short: at most three days. Moreover, the EC recalls that no provision of the Anti-Dumping Agreement allows the investigating authorities to resort to "facts available" simply because the party concerned has missed a deadline. Article 6.8 provides that the investigating authority may resort to "facts available" when necessary information is not submitted "within a reasonable period of time", while paragraph 3 of Annex II requires that all information which is submitted "in a timely fashion" should be taken into account.

4.176 Interpreting these two provisions, the recent panel report on *US - Hot Rolled Steel* concluded that:

> What is a 'reasonable period' will not, in all instances be commensurate with pre-established deadlines ... a rigid adherence to such deadlines does not in all cases suffice as the basis for a conclusion that information was not submitted within a reasonable period and consequently that facts available may be applied.
>
> Particularly, where information is actually submitted in time to be verified, and actually could be verified, ... it should generally be accepted, unless to do so would impede the ability of the investigating authority to complete the investigation within the time limits established by the Agreement (Panel Report on *United States - Anti-Dumping Measures on Certain Hot Rolled Steel Products from Japan*, WT/DS184/R, circulated on 28 February 2001, at paras. 7.54 and 7.55).

4.177 Casalgrande submitted the requested invoices in time to be used by the DCD (the invoices were filed on 10 June 1999, and the Final Dumping Determination was not issued until 23 September 1999). And, indeed, the DCD did use them in one of the dumping calculations. Therefore, the DCD cannot pretend now that this delay impeded the investigation. Moreover, the DCD did not inform Casalgrande that the evidence filed on 10 June 1999 had been rejected. Nor is the rejection of that evidence mentioned in the Final Dumping Determination.

4.178 More generally, Argentina complains about "repeated request for extensions" of deadlines (*"reiteradas solicitudes de prórrogas"*). In reality, however, the exporters requested and obtained only two extensions: one for filing the responses and another for submitting additional non-confidential summaries and supporting invoices. The DCD agreed to both requests and cannot complain now that, as a result, the information was not submitted "within a reasonable period" or that the extensions impeded the investigation.

4.179 Finally, the EC rejects the contention made by Argentina in its oral statement, according to which the deadline for submitting the questionnaire responses would have been successively "extended" by the DCD from 30 November 1998 until 10 August 1999, i.e. until the date were the exporters responded to the DCD's letter of 3 August 1999. The letters of 30 April 1999, 22 June 1999 and 3 August 1999 did not grant any "extensions" for answering to the questionnaire responses. They contained additional requests to remedy the alleged deficiencies of the non-confidential summaries, which were promptly and satisfactorily answered by the exporters.

(ii) Alleged Failure to Submit Adequate Non-Confidential Summaries

4.180 Argentina invokes as an additional ground for rejecting the responses that the exporters failed to provide adequate non-confidential summaries.

4.181 This allegation is, to say the least, ironic. The actual fact is that the DCD's relentless demands forced the exporters to waive all its confidentiality claims and to disclose to their Argentinean competitors highly sensitive price and cost information.

4.182 Together with the questionnaire responses, the exporters submitted non-confidential summaries. In preparing those summaries, the exporters applied the following principles:

(a) non-sensitive information was left unchanged in the summary;

(b) sensitive information covering several years/months was expressed in indexed form (Annexes IV, V and VI); and

(c) other sensitive information was omitted from the summary (Annexes III, VII, VIII, IX, X and XI).

4.183 The DCD gave no indication to the exporters that the non-confidential summaries were inadequate until the Preliminary Dumping Determination of 24 March 1999, i.e. more than three months after the filing of the responses.

4.184 By letters dated 30 April 1999, the DCD requested the exporters to waive their confidentiality requests or to supply non-confidential summaries. Specifically, the letters addressed to Bismantova and Marazzi referred to Annexes III, VII,VIII, IX, X and XI, whereas those addressed to Bismantova and Caesar mentioned only Annexes III, VII, VIII and IX.

4.185 Argentina now complains that the non-confidential summaries of Annexes IV, V and VI containing indexed figures were insufficient. But this issue was not raised by the DCD in the Preliminary Dumping Determination, or in the letters of 30 April 1999, or indeed at any stage of the investigation.

4.186 Following the letters of 30 April 1999, the representatives of the exporters met with the case-handlers on 11 May 1999. At that meeting, it was agreed that the exporters would submit non-confidential summaries of Annexes VII (exports to Argentina) and VIII (sales in Italy), in which the names of the customers and the models would be replaced by "virtual codes". No requests were made with respect to the other Annexes for which the exporters had requested confidential treatment.

4.187 On 4 June 1999 the four exporters submitted non-confidential summaries of Annexes VII and VIII in the format agreed at the meeting of 11 May 1999. A "Conversion Table" indicating the correspondences between each code number and the customer and model was submitted to the DCD on a confidential basis.

4.188 It bears emphasising that the non-confidential summaries submitted on 4 June 1999 contained the same information as the confidential responses of 10 December 1998, with the only difference that the name of the model and of the customer had been replaced by a code number. Thus, the summaries allowed the petitioners to calculate by themselves the dumping margins by comparing the actual prices in the domestic and the export market. Clearly, this is more than enough to permit "a reasonable understanding of the substance of the information submitted in confidence" as required by Article 6.5.1 of the AD Agreement.

4.189 In spite of that, on 22 June 1999, the DCD sent a letter to the exporters requesting them to waive the confidentiality of the product code. Within two days, the exporters agreed to that request.

4.190 By way of justification, the letter of 22 June 1999 asserted that the disclosure of the product code was necessary so that the DCD "can make a precise comparison" (*"... a fin de que la [DCD] pueda realizar una precisa comparación en su informe de determinación final del margen de dumping ..."*). Thus, the DCD appears to have taken the position that the investigating authority can only make a final determination of dumping based on non-confidential information. Argentina's first written submission reflects the same position. For the reasons explained in the EC's answers to some of the questions made by the Panel following the first meeting, that view has no basis on the Anti-Dumping Agreement and is clearly mistaken.

4.191 By letter of 3 August 1999, the DCD requested the exporters to waive the confidentiality of the cost of production data contained in Annexes X and XI. On 10 August 1999, the exporters agreed to that request (although rather misleadingly, the exporters' response of 10 August 1999 is omitted in Argentina's first written submission).

4.192 Contrary to Argentina's contentions, the above sequence of events does not evidence lack of co-operation on the part of the exporters, but rather the opposite. Once the exporters were advised by the DCD that the non-confidential summaries submitted together with the questionnaire responses on 10 December 1998 were not considered adequate, they responded promptly to each of the successive and increasingly exacting demands made by the DCD.

4.193 Eventually, the exporters were led by the DCD's demands to relinquish virtually all their confidentiality requests (while it is true that the EC "never lifted the confidentiality" of the items listed therein, the degree of disclosure accepted by the EC had essentially the same result), and to disclose to their Argentinean competitors all the price and cost-of-production data for the investigation period included in their responses, a type of information which is clearly entitled to confidential treatment in accordance with Article 6.5 of the AD Agreement.

4.194 Having answered promptly and satisfactorily to all the DCD's requests, the exporters assumed that all the concerns of the DCD with respect to this issue had already been resolved by the time of the final determination. And, indeed, the Final Dumping Determination does not mention anywhere that the exporters' normal value and export price information was rejected because the exporters failed to disclose confidential information or provide adequate non-confidential summaries.

(iii) Alleged Failure to Provide Supporting Documents

4.195 Another ground invoked by Argentina for rejecting the exporters' responses is their alleged failure to provide "supporting documents" (*"docu-*

mentación respaldatoria"), and more particularly to provide copies of a "sufficient" number of invoices of the sales made in the Italian market.

4.196 Paragraph 1 of Annex II of the AD Agreement provides that the investigating authorities "should specify *in detail* the information required" (emphasis added by the EC). The questionnaire did not require the exporters to provide copies of a "sufficient" number of invoices for verification purposes. Therefore, Argentina cannot complain now if the exporters did not do so in their questionnaire responses.

4.197 The only reference to invoices made in the questionnaire is found in Section B ("Exports to Argentina"), which requests the exporters to provide "probatory documents which help to better understand the transactions" (*"documentación probatoria que ayude a una mejor comprensión de la operación"*), including invoices. This suggests that the DCD was interested in receiving only a few examples of invoices.

4.198 Moreover, the questionnaire requested the exporters' consent for carrying out on-the-spot verifications, something to which all of them agreed. Thus, the exporters could assume legitimately that the DCD would verify the responses by conducting on-the-spot investigations, rather than through the unusual method of asking the exporters to supply, together with their responses, the invoices of all the reported transactions.

4.199 Argentina argues now that one of the introductory paragraphs to the questionnaire stated that the respondents should supply "supporting documents" (*"documentación respaldatoria"*). But that reference is too vague to meet the requirements of paragraph 1 of Annex II. Moreover, taken literally, it would have required the exporters to provide copies not only of the invoices, but of all the accounting and cost records that are usually examined in the course of an on-the-spot verification. That demand would be clearly unreasonable.

4.200 The AD Agreement envisages that the information provided by interested parties will be verified by means of on-the spot investigations (see Article 6.7 and Annex I of the AD Agreement). An investigating authority may chose not to conduct such investigations. But, if so, it cannot impose upon the exporters the burden of supplying all the supporting documents that might have been requested in the course of an on-the-spot verification (and, in addition, translated into the authority's official language!).

4.201 Furthermore, the introductory paragraph of the questionnaire cited by Argentina allows the exporters to indicate the "source of the information" (*"fuente de la información")* as an alternative to supplying the supporting documents. Annexes VII, VIII and IX mentioned the number and the date of the invoices from which the information reported in those Annexes was derived. Thus, the exporters' responses would in any event have satisfied this requirement.

4.202 At any rate, the Preliminary Dumping Determination did not mention the alleged failure to provide "supporting documents" as a reason for rejecting the responses. Rather, as mentioned before, the Preliminary Dumping Determination suggested that the responses were rejected because the non-confidential summaries were deemed inadequate.

4.203 Nor did the letters of 30 April 1999 mention the alleged failure to provide "supporting documents", contrary to what is repeatedly asserted in Argentina's first written submission and in its first oral statement. Those letters referred exclusively to alleged deficiencies of the non-confidential summaries.

4.204 It was only at the meeting of 11 May 1999 that the case-handlers requested for the first time that Casalgrande and Bismantova, the two main exporters, provide copies of invoices covering an "important" volume of sales.

4.205 In response to the request made at the meeting of 11 May 1999, the exporters concerned submitted copies of invoices covering approximately 50 per cent of the sales in Italy and of the exports to Argentina and third countries (together with a translation into Spanish of each invoice!).

4.206 The DCD made no further request for "supporting documents" during the remainder of the investigation. The exporters, therefore, could assume legitimately that the DCD was satisfied with the documents submitted.

4.207 The Final Dumping Determination comforts that assumption. It confirms that the exporters submitted the requested invoices. It makes no suggestion to the effect that the exporters failed to provide sufficient supporting invoices (or any other supporting evidence) or that the normal value and export price information supplied by the exporters was disregarded for that reason.

(iv) Alleged Lack of Representativeness of the Domestic Sales Reported by the Selected Exporters

4.208 Argentina also invokes the supposed lack of representativeness of the domestic sales reported by the selected exporters as a reason for resorting to "facts available".

4.209 As noted by the Panel in its questions to the parties, it is unclear whether Argentina complains that the sample of exporters was not representative or, rather, that the domestic sales reported by the selected exporters were not sufficient for the purposes of establishing the normal values (the EC has not been able to establish how the percentages mentioned by Argentina at paragraphs 43 and 50 of its first written submission have been calculated).

4.210 For the reasons already explained in its first oral statement and in the answers to the questions made by the Panel following the first meeting, the EC rejects the contention that the sample of exporters was not representative.

4.211 Likewise, the EC rejects the allegation that the domestic sales reported by the selected exporters were insufficient. As explained in the EC's answer to a question by the Panel, the exporters reported in Annex VIII of their responses all the domestic transactions of each of the models exported to Argentina in significant quantities (the total volume and value of the sales of all models made in Italy is reported in Annexes V and VI, respectively, of the questionnaire responses).

4.212 The domestic sales of the other models were not reported in that Annex because that information was not required in order to make a model-to-model comparison of the normal value with the export price. Contrary to Argentina's assertions, this approach was clearly explained in the questionnaire responses and was never contested by the DCD.

4.213 The reported domestic transactions of each model represented more than 5 per cent of the volume of the exports sales of the same model. Moreover, taken together, the reported domestic sales represented more than 5 per cent of the overall export sales of each exporter (the Final Dumping Determination states, on page 29, that the volume of the domestic sales reported by Caesar represented 4.46 per cent of its exports to Argentina during 1998. That figure is incorrect. According to the EC's own calculations, the correct figure is 7.35 per cent for 1998 and 10.6 per cent for the whole investigation period, which included also 1997). Therefore, the reported sales were sufficient for the purposes of establishing the normal values (see footnote 2 of the AD Agreement). They were certainly more "representative" than the seven invoices supplied by the petitioner and relied upon by the DCD.

4.214 Furthermore, the DCD did at no point during the investigation inform the exporters that the reported domestic transactions were insufficient. It was only in the Final Dumping Determination that the DCD made for the first time some remarks in that sense. Nevertheless, even at that late stage, the DCD refrained from drawing any conclusions.

4.215 Argentina argues that the lack of representativeness of the reported domestic transactions could be established by the DCD only at a late stage of the investigation because of the delay in providing "supporting documents". This is not true. The "supporting documents" in question (i.e. the non-confidential summaries submitted on 4 June 1999) were supplied by the exporters as soon as they were requested by the DCD. In any event, the DCD did not need those summaries in order to establish whether the sales reported in the questionnaire responses were sufficient for the purposes of establishing the normal values. Argentina makes again the error of assuming that the determination of dumping must be based on non-confidential information.

4.216 At any rate, this alleged deficiency would concern only part of the information supplied by the exporters. Even if the domestic sales reported by the exporters had in fact been insufficient for establishing the normal values, that would not provide a valid justification for disregarding also the export price information supplied by the exporters in the questionnaire responses.

(v) Other Alleged Deficiencies

4.217 Argentina also alleges in passing a series of deficiencies of the questionnaire responses. As explained below, some of those alleged deficiencies were not such, while the others were minor omissions which did not warrant the DCD's decision to reject all the information contained in the responses.

(vi) Export Sales to Third Countries

4.218 Argentina alleges that Caesar and Marazzi did not provide information with respect to their export sales to third countries.

4.219 This is true. But Argentina misleadingly omits to mention that the questionnaire allowed the exporters not to provide such information if the volume of domestic sales was sufficiently representative. Caesar and Marazzi relied expressly upon that possibility.

4.220 At any rate, the DCD never informed Marazzi and Caesar that their responses had been rejected for this reason. The Preliminary Dumping Determination records that Marazzi and Caesar did not report export sales to third countries in Annex IX, together with the explanations given by both exporters to the effect that such information was not provided in accordance with the instructions contained in the questionnaire, but attaches no consequences to this omission. This issue was not raised again by the DCD during the investigation and is not mentioned in the Final Dumping Determination.

(vii) Cost of Production Data for the Exported Merchandise

4.221 Argentina also alleges that Marazzi did not provide cost-of-production data for the models exported to Argentina.

4.222 Again, this allegation is misleading. Marazzi explained in its response that the models exported to Argentina were the same as those sold in Italy and had the same cost of production, except for the differences in selling expenses.

4.223 Moreover, the DCD never informed Marazzi that its response had been rejected for this reason. The Preliminary Dumping Determination records that Marazzi did not report cost of production data for the exported merchandise in Annex XI, together with Marazzi's explanations, but draws no consequences from this. The issue was not raised again by the DCD during the investigation and is not mentioned in the Final Dumping Determination.

(viii) Currency Conversions

4.224 Argentina complains that Bismantova provided the information requested in Annex VI in Italian Lire instead of in US$.

4.225 This is clearly a minor deficiency which, contrary to Argentina's allegations, could not have impeded significantly the investigation. Annex VI is a summary table of the sales turnover by market. Bismantova reported in that Annex a total of 24 amounts. Those amounts can be easily converted into US$ by using the exchange rates provided by Bismantova or other publicly available rates.

4.226 In any event, the DCD never informed Bismantova that it would reject the response for this reason. The Preliminary Dumping Determination mentions that Bismantova completed the tables in Annex VI in Italian Lire and provided exchange rates between that currency and the US$, but attaches no consequences to this. This issue was not raised again during the investigation and is not mentioned in the Final Dumping Determination.

(ix) Translation of Accounting Documents

4.227 Finally, Argentina complains that three of the exporters did not provide a Spanish translation of their balance sheet.

4.228 Again, this is correct but cannot justify the rejection of the responses. The requested translation cannot be considered as "necessary information" in the sense of Article 6.8, given that the essential content of the document in question were figures, that Italian and Spanish are closely related and that, in particular, the accounting terminology is very similar in both languages. Moreover Italian is widely understood in Argentina.

4.229 It is worth noting that the DCD accepted as good the "translation" provided by Marazzi. Yet Marazzi limited itself to translate one word in the front page, namely the word "esercicio", which Marazzi rendered somewhat inaccurately as "año", the precise translation being "ejercicio". This confirms that the requested translations were by no means necessary.

4.230 At any rate, once again, the DCD did not inform the exporters concerned that their responses had been rejected on this ground. The Preliminary Dumping Determination mentions that Bismantova, Casalgrande and Caesar did not provide a Spanish translation, but draws no consequences from this. The issue was not raised again by the DCD during the investigation and is not mentioned in the Final Dumping Determination.

(x) Paragraph 6 of Annex II

4.231 The DCD failed to comply with the requirements imposed by paragraph 6 of Annex II. It did not inform forthwith the exporters of the rejection of their responses and it failed to give the reasons for such rejection in the Final Dumping Determination.

4.232 Argentina contends that it complied with the requirement to inform the exporters in the letters of 30 April, 22 June and 3 August 1999. However, those letters were concerned exclusively with the alleged deficiencies of the non-confidential summaries, which were in any event remedied by the exporters well before the final determination. Those letters make no reference to any of the other grounds for rejecting the responses now invoked by Argentina.

4.233 Argentina also failed to comply with the requirement to explain in the final determination the reasons for rejecting the evidence provided by the exporters. In its first oral statement, Argentina raises the extraordinary argument that the DCD's decision to resort to facts available is "reflected" on page 39 of the Final Dumping Determination, where the DCD "incorporates" the allegations ("*alegatos*") of the petitioner. There is, however, an obvious difference between the allegations made by an interested party and the findings of the investigating authority. The mere fact that the Final Dumping Determination reproduces the allegations of the petitioner cannot be taken to mean that those allegations were upheld by the investigation authority. The Final Dumping Determination also "incorporates" the allegations made by the exporters, including the allegation that the sales were not made at dumping prices. Yet the EC would not mistake those allegations for the DCD's findings.

(f) Arguments of the EC in its Second Oral Statement in Support of its Claim under Article 6.8 of the AD Agreement

4.234 In its second oral statement, the EC made the following arguments relating to its claim under Article 6.8 of the AD Agreement.

(i) Information on Export Sales

4.235 In Annex VII of the questionnaire responses the exporters reported all the sales made to Argentina of all the models exported in significant quantities. Moreover, the exporters provided to the DCD copies of invoices covering approximately 50 per cent of those sales. Yet that information, and the supporting invoices, were totally disregarded by the DCD.

4.236 In response to a question from the Panel, Argentina mentions, for the very first time, that the export price information supplied by the exporters was disregarded because it could not be "cross-checked" ("*cruzada*") with the official import statistics and the questionnaire responses of some importers.

4.237 This "revelation" leaves us astonished. The exporters were at no point during the investigation informed of the discrepancies now alleged by Argentina. Nor are such discrepancies mentioned anywhere in the Final Dumping Determination or, indeed, in any of Argentina's previous submissions to this Panel.

4.238 Argentina's explanations not only arrive too late, but are also insufficient. Argentina does not bother to specify what were the alleged discrepancies. Moreover, Argentina does not explain why the secondary sources used by the DCD were deemed more reliable than the information supplied by the exporters regarding their own sales, including the invoices.

4.239 The EC is convinced that the alleged discrepancies could have been satisfactorily explained by the exporters, if only they had been given a chance to do so. By denying such opportunity to the exporters, the DCD acted inconsistently, once again, with paragraph 6 of Annex II and, consequently, with Article 6.8 of the Anti-Dumping Agreement.

(ii) Confidentiality

4.240 In response to a question from the Panel, Argentina asserts that the concerns expressed by the DCD with respect to this issue in the preliminary determination had not been resolved by the time of the final determination because "the essential information in order to determine the normal value, the export price and the dumping margin continued to be confidential until the final determination (and still remains so)" ("... *la información sustancial a fin de determinar el valor normal, el valor de exportación y el margen de dumping continuó siendo confidencial hasta la determinación final (y aún subsiste)"*.

4.241 Argentina appears to disregard, once again, that, under Article 6.5 of the AD Agreement, interested parties have a right to request confidential treatment. Thus, the mere fact that the exporters maintained some of their confidentiality requests would not, in itself, be a sufficient justification for disregarding their responses. Rather, Argentina would have to demonstrate that all the requirements for resorting to Article 6.5.2 were met.

4.242 Moreover, Argentina makes again the fundamental mistake of considering that the determination of dumping can be based only on non-confidential information.

4.243 In any event, Argentina's contentions are totally unsupported. Argentina does not say what "essential" information remained undisclosed by the time of the final determination.

4.244 Furthermore, Argentina's contentions are unfounded. It is undisputed that the exporters disclosed all the information on domestic prices and on export prices contained in Annexes VII and VIII, with the only exception of the customer codes. It is also undisputed that the exporters disclosed all the cost of production data reported in Annexes X and XI, except the name of the producers. Those Annexes do contain the "essential" information for calculating the dumping margin.

4.245 Finally, if the DCD remained unsatisfied with the non-confidential summaries by the time of the final determination, why is the Final Dumping Determination silent on this issue?

(iii) Supporting Documents

4.246 The EC rejects once again Argentina's contention that the questionnaire required the exporters to provide a "sufficient" number of invoices for verification purposes.

4.247 The new arguments made by Argentina in its second written submission, like those made in earlier submissions, are contrived and unconvincing. The AD Agreement requires the investigating authority to specify "in detail" the information requested from the exporters (see Annex II, paragraph 1). The DCD failed to do so. It would be unreasonable to read into a vague instruction to provide the "documentación correspondiente", without any further specification, a requirement to supply copies of a "sufficient" number of invoices of the domestic sales listed in Annex VIII (whatever Argentina means now by "sufficient").

4.248 Moreover, on Argentina's own interpretation, the questionnaire would be internally contradictory:

(a) the section entitled *Objetivos y Alcances* requires to provide supporting documents or, alternatively, to cite the source of information;

(b) yet, point 1 of the *Instrucciones Generales* requires to provide the "documentación correspondiente", which would suggest that it is not sufficient to cite the source of information;

(c) finally, Section B (exports to Argentina), but not sections C (sales in Italy) and D (export sales to third countries), requires to provide invoices with the purpose of helping the DCD to "achieve a better understanding of the transactions" (*"... que ayude a una mejor comprensión de la operación"*). That request, however, would have been totally redundant if, as argued now by Argentina, the *Objetivos y Alcances* section and the *Instrucciones Generales* already required to provide copies of a "sufficient" number of invoices with verification purposes.

4.249 The EC also rejects Argentina's assertions that a request to provide supporting documents was made in the letters of 30 April 1999. Argentina quotes selectively from those letters.

4.250 The letters of 30 April 1999 did not request the exporters to supply "nuevos elementos probatorios ...". Rather, the letters allude to:

> ... la incorporación de nuevos elementos probatorios *o bien* la adecuación de la información obrante en las actuaciones (emphasis added by the EC).

4.251 It is also misleading to suggest that the letters requested from the exporters "una ampliación de la información adjuntada". The relevant passage requests the exporter to evaluate:

> ... la posibilidad de incorporar a las actuaciones un resumen no confidencial más detallado *o bien* una ampliación de la información adjuntada *o, en su defecto,* proceda a habilitar la incorporación de dicha documentación a las actuaciones de referencia, levantando el carácter de confidencial oportunamente solicitado (emphasis added by the EC).

4.252 The letters of 30 April 1999 reflect the DCD's erroneous view that only non-confidential information can be used in the dumping calculation and, therefore, that the information covered by a confidentiality request cannot be "*incorporada a las actuaciones*". The letters do not request the exporters to supply any "supporting documents", but rather to waive their confidentiality requests with respect to information already contained in the questionnaire responses of 10 December 1998, so that such information can be "*incorporada a las actuaciones*". Thus, the "*elementos probatorios*" mentioned in the letter of 30 April 1999 were "new" only in the sense that they had not been "incorporados a las actuaciones" yet by the DCD, because they were covered by a confidentiality request.

4.253 Furthermore, the letters of 30 April 1999 refer expressly to Article 6.5 of the *Ley No. 24.425*, which is the equivalent provision of Article 6.5 of the AD Agreement, and not to the equivalent provision of Article 6.8, thus confirming that those letters are concerned exclusively with the issue of the confidentiality requests made by the exporters.

4.254 For those reasons, the EC reiterates its position that the provision of supporting invoices with verification purposes was requested for the first time at the meeting with the case-handlers of 11 May 1999.

4.255 In any event, the EC considers that this issue is ultimately irrelevant, since it is not disputed that the requested invoices were submitted by the exporters on 7 and 11 June 1999 and, thus, could, and indeed were used by the DCD in the final determination, albeit arbitrarily averaged with the petitioner's information.

4.256 Argentina contends that the invoices were not representative of the exporters' domestic sales. However, the invoices covered approximately 50 per cent of the domestic sales reported in the questionnaire responses. Therefore, they were clearly representative of those transactions. Thus, in reality, Argentina's argument appears to be that the transactions reported in the questionnaire responses, rather than the invoices, were not representative, which leads me to the next point of our statement.

(iv) Representativeness of Domestic Sales

4.257 As already explained by the EC, the exporters reported in Annex VIII of their responses all the domestic transactions of each of the models exported to Argentina in significant quantities. The domestic sales of the other models were not reported in that Annex because that information was not required in order to make a model-to-model comparison of the normal value with the export price. This approach was clearly explained in the questionnaire responses and was never contested by the DCD in the course of the investigation.

4.258 The domestic sales reported by the exporters in Annex VIII were certainly more "representative" than the eight invoices supplied by the petitioner and relied upon by the DCD. Moreover, of those eight invoices, four correspond to sales of polished tiles (which according to Argentina's explanations were not used in the dumping calculation) and another to a sale of tiles of 12.5 cm x 25 cm.

4.259 Furthermore, the DCD never informed the exporters that the domestic sales reported in the questionnaire responses were insufficiently representative. It was only in the Final Dumping Determination that the DCD made for the first time some remarks in that sense. Nevertheless, even at that late stage, the DCD refrained from drawing any conclusions.

(g) Replies of the EC to the Second Set of Questions by the Panel Relating to the EC's Claim under Article 6.8 of the AD Agreement

4.260 The EC replied to the second set of questions by the Panel regarding the EC's claim under Article 6.8 of the AD Agreement as follows.

4.261 The Panel recalled that, with respect to Annexes IV-VI, the exporters provided information for which they requested confidential treatment, as well as a non-confidential summary of the information concerned. The Panel recalled further that this summary was prepared by way of indexing all the figures provided in those Annexes. The Panel asked the parties why the DCD was of the view that indexation did not permit a "reasonable understanding of the substance of the information submitted in confidence".

4.262 The EC replied that this issue was not raised by the DCD in the Preliminary Dumping Determination, or in the letters of 22 April 1999, or indeed at any stage of the investigation. Furthermore, this issue was nowhere mentioned by the DCD in the Final Dumping Determination. It was no more than an *ex-post facto* justification and, as such, should be rejected by the Panel.

4.263 The Panel recalled that, with respect to Annexes III and VII-XI of the investigation questionnaire, the exporters provided information for which they requested confidential treatment, although they did not provide a non-confidential summary of the information concerned. The Panel asked the parties whether the exporters provided a justification as to why such information was not capable of summarization (that is, a justification separate from the statement that the information in question required confidential treatment). If this was so, the Panel asked the parties to provide it with copies of the relevant evidence in the record.

4.264 To this question, the EC gave the following reply.

4.265 In the EC's view, the Panel need not reach the issue of whether the information contained in Annexes VII-XI was capable of summarization.

4.266 The EC recalls that on 4 June 1999 the exporters submitted non-confidential summaries of Annexes VII-IX in the format agreed with the case-handlers at the meeting of 11 May 1999. Those summaries contained the same information as the confidential responses of 10 December 1998, with the only difference that the name of the model and of the customer had been replaced by a code number. On 24 June 1999, the exporters agreed to a further request from the DCD to waive the confidentiality of the product code. At the request of the DCD, the exporters also agreed to waive the confidentiality of all the cost of production data contained in Annexes X and XI, on condition that the identity of the producer was kept confidential.

4.267 Thus, contrary to what is suggested in the question, the only Annex for which the exporters did not provide a non-confidential version was Annex III (list of customers). The type of information contained in that Annex (a list of names) is clearly not capable of summarization. And, indeed, the DCD appears to agree since it did not request the exporters to disclose the customer names in the non-confidential summaries of Annexes VII and VIII submitted on 4 June 1999.

4.268 If the exporters did provide a justification as to why the information for which confidential treatment was requested was not capable of summarization, the Panel asked whether the parties were of the view that under Article 6.5.1 of the AD Agreement investigating authorities have the right to contest such justifications. If so, the Panel asked further, did the DCD conclude, contrary to the exporters, that the information in question could in effect be summarized? If the DCD made this conclusion, could Argentina explain the DCD's reasoning?

4.269 The EC replied that its answer to this question was the same as its answer to the previous question.

4.270 The Panel asked the parties to comment on the following statement in the report of the Appellate Body in *Thailand - H-Beams*, in which the Appellate Body addressed the question of the use of confidential information by the investigating authority as a basis for an authority's final determination:

> An anti-dumping investigation involves the commercial behaviour of firms, and, under the provisions of the Anti-Dumping Agreement, involves the collection and assessment of both confidential and non-confidential information. An injury determination conducted pursuant to the provisions of Article 3 of the Anti-Dumping Agreement must be based on the totality of that evidence. We see nothing in Article 3.1 which limits an investigating authority to base an injury determination only upon non-confidential information (Appellate Body Report, *Thailand - Anti-Dumping Duties on Angles, Shapes and Sections of Iron or Non-Alloy Steel and H-Beams from Poland*, WT/DS122/AB/R, adopted 5 April 2001, at para. 107).

4.271 The EC replied that Argentina's position in this case reflects the erroneous assumption that only non-confidential information can be used in a dumping determination. The ruling of the Appellate Body in *Thailand - H Beams* confirms that such view is thoroughly mistaken.

4.272 The Panel recalled that Exhibit EC-10 was a report of the meeting with the case-handlers on 11 May 1999 from the representatives of the exporters in Argentina to the exporters' lawyers in Brussels. The report reflected the discussions with the case handlers, concerning the non-confidential information that needed to be provided, in the following manner:

> Additionally, this information must cover an "important" part of total sales in the domestic market (you said 50 per cent - I don't know, I guess that is largely enough), the coverage must be Sep-

> tember 1997 - October 1998, and we have to present invoices (with confidential status) supporting this non-confidential version.

4.273 The Panel asked Argentina whether this was an accurate reflection of what was said during that meeting and of the requests for information that were made. Further, the Panel asked Argentina whether the case-handlers at the 11 May meeting requested invoices from two exporters only (Casalgrande and Bismantova). The Panel asked the parties next whether the 50 per cent coverage mentioned in this paragraph related to the provision of non-confidential information, or to the documentation supporting the information provided. The Panel also asked the parties whether the 50 per cent related to all sales made in the home market, or only to the sales reported by the exporters.

4.274 To this question, the EC provided the following reply.

4.275 During the meeting of 11 May 1999, the case-handlers made two requests:

(a) first, that all the four exporters provide a non-confidential summary of the domestic and export sales reported in their questionnaire responses in accordance with the agreed format described in Exhibit EC-10; and

(b) second, that the main two exporters (Bismantova and Casalgrande) provide copies of a "sufficient" number of supporting invoices for the domestic and export transactions reported in the questionnaire responses.

4.276 The case-handlers explained that the invoices were requested in order to verify the transactions reported in the confidential version of the questionnaire responses. According to the case-handlers, it was necessary to resort to this method of verification because the DCD could not pay verification visits to Italy. The case-handlers made no suggestion to the effect that the transactions reported in the confidential version of the questionnaire responses were insufficient.

4.277 During the meeting, Mr. Di Gianni (of the law firm Van Bael & Bellis of Brussels), asked whether it would be sufficient to provide invoices covering 50 per cent of the sales reported in the questionnaire responses. The case-handlers agreed.

4.278 The above is confirmed by another report sent by Mr. Di Gianni to the Italian exporters on 19 May 1999, in which it was explained that:

> ... we have decided ... to co-operate with [the DCD] and to include in the non-confidential reply a list of sales in Italy and in Argentina. From such a list, the names of the supplier and customers should be eliminated. The other information, including the prices and quantities should be kept.
>
> Moreover, it would be advisable to submit a copy of the invoices concerning the sales reported in the reply for the period September 1997 to September 1998. The Dumping Team would appreciate it receiving at least 50 per cent of the sales reported for that period (free translation from the Italian language by the EC).

4.279 As a final remark, the EC would recall that Annex II, paragraph 1, provides that the investigating authority must "specify in detail" the information requested from the exporters. The fact that it has become necessary to engage into the exegesis of internal reports of the exporters in order to ascertain what "supporting documents" were actually requested by the DCD is in itself sufficient evidence that the DCD failed to comply with that requirement.

2. *Argentina*

(a) Arguments of Argentina in its First Written Submission Relating to the EC's Claim under Article 6.8 of the AD Agreement

4.280 In its first written submission, Argentina made the following arguments relating to the EC's claim under Article 6.8 of the AD Anti-Dumping Agreement.

4.281 Argentina first laid out the facts relevant for the presentation of its arguments.

(i) General Facts

4.282 The record of the case, File No. 061-000794/98 of the Registry of the Ministry of the Economy and Public Works and Services, incorporated by reference in Resolution 1385/99 introducing the anti-dumping measures in question, demonstrates that the claims of the EC are erroneous. The above-mentioned file explains clearly that Argentina had valid recourse to Article 6.8 of the AD Agreement.

4.283 Argentina considers that the exporting firms significantly impeded the investigation, refused access to necessary information and did not provide it within a reasonable period. This assertion is based on the facts contained in the record of the case.

4.284 By Note SSCE No. 945/98 of 9 October 1998, the implementing authority sent a certified copy of the Resolution initiating this investigation to the Counsellor of the European Commission in Argentina, informing him that "... under Article 6.1 of Law 24.425 (the Argentine law approving the Uruguay Round Agreements, duly notified to the WTO), all interested parties in an anti-dumping investigation shall be given notice of the information which the authorities require and ample opportunity to submit in writing all evidence which they consider relevant ...".

4.285 The then Secretary for Industry, Trade and Mining of Argentina informed the Government of Italy, by its note of 10 November 1998, that "... the fullest transparency will be ensured at every stage of the proceedings, and pursuant to the appropriate legal provisions, all relevant technical and formal requirements will be respected ...". The note went on to state that "... we repeat that the institutions involved in these proceedings are ready at any time to provide both the Government of Italy and the firms and entities concerned with technical advice regarding the various stages of the investigation and the particular features of the case".

4.286 These notes reflect the willingness of the Argentine Government to give the exporters every opportunity to defend their interests in conformity with Articles 6.1 and 6.2 of the AD Agreement.

(ii) Lack of Cooperation from the Exporters in the Light of Article 6.8 of the AD Agreement

4.287 Despite having been invited to an information meeting, the exporters did not attend. Argentina draws the Panel's attention to the note dated 28 October 1998, sent by Assopiastrelle to the DCD (File No. 061-009413 - folio 1), which states "... we regret to inform you that, owing to the distance and our business commitments, it will be impossible for us to attend ...".

4.288 The information meeting was held on 30 October 1998. DCD officials answered all the participants' questions in order to dispel their doubts regarding the procedures and the required information, and supplied them with the questionnaires. The record of that hearing, which lists the participating entities and shows that the exporting companies and/or their representatives were absent, has been attached to the record. Because the exporters were present at that meeting, the Italian Embassy agreed to send them the questionnaires.

4.289 It should be pointed out that the explanatory section of each questionnaire sets out the general and specific instructions for each of the required items, so that the parties could respond properly, in such a way as to enable the implementing authority to use the data supplied by the exporters and importers at the time of the preliminary and definitive determination.

4.290 In addition, the instructions emphasize that "producers and/or exporters from the respondent country must answer this questionnaire with the greatest possible precision, attaching documentation to support its replies, or, if this is impossible, indicating the source of the information". In other words, in no case was it sufficient to state, for example, for determining the normal value, that a certain number of sales had been made, without backing up that information with a sufficient number of sales invoices for the domestic market. The sample evidence in support of the replies needed to be sufficiently extensive to allow a precise evaluation of the information submitted. Argentina submits that the attached replies did not fulfill the time, quality and quantity requirements that would have enabled the DCD to use them as a basis for reaching a determination. Nevertheless, the DCD took the trouble to consider the information supplied on the basis of the standard of review of the AD Agreement. That standard recognizes the principle of deference to the implementing authority, in the context of anti-dumping investigations, as regards the analysis of the facts and definition of the scope of the obligations of the Agreement (Article 17.6 of the AD Agreement).

4.291 The period originally granted for the submission of the forms and replies to the questionnaires expired on 30 November 1998. In response to the requests for extension sent by the foreign exporting firms and national importers concerned, and in conformity with Article 6.1.1 of the AD Agreement, the DCD granted an additional non-extendable period for all submissions, expiring on 9 December 1998, so that the participating firms could duly complete their respective questionnaires, including sufficient supporting documentation, and appropriate evidence (Notes DCD Nos. 273-000414/98, 273-000429/98 and 273-000430/98 of 19 and 27 November 1998 stated that, in view of the request for an additional period for submission of the questionnaire for foreign producers/exporters, duly completed and with the necessary supporting documentation, "... it has been decided to grant the extension, setting 9 December 1998 as the final deadline for submission ...").

(iii) Qualitative, Quantitative and Time-Related Deficiencies in the Information Submitted

4.292 Article 6.8 of the AD Agreement states as follows:

> In cases in which any interested party refuses access to, or otherwise does not provide, necessary information within a reasonable period or significantly impedes the investigation, preliminary and final determinations, affirmative or negative, may be made on the basis of the facts available. The provisions of Annex II shall be observed in the application of this paragraph (emphasis added by Argentina).

4.293 As regards the information supplied in the replies to the questionnaires for producers/exporters, this submission will only highlight the points in which Argentina considers that the producing/exporting companies impeded the investigation, by failing to comply with required formalities in the general and specific instructions of the questionnaires, by not providing the necessary information within a reasonable period, even when granted repeated extensions, by not supplying, with the questionnaires, sufficient supporting documentation (requested for verification purposes), by not providing enough information in the confidential summaries, by not providing any summary in certain cases, and also by the delay and reluctance they displayed in removing the confidentiality of the information supplied, a step which was absolutely necessary to enable the DCD to take account of that information and make it public as an element considered in its decisions.

Replies to the questionnaires

4.294 The four exporting companies making up the sample submitted the following documentation through their representatives on 10 December 1998:

(a) Completed questionnaire for producers/exporters.

(b) Report on procedural deficiencies.

(c) Report on the methodology for selection of the sample.

4.295 The extension granted by the DCD for submitting the forms and replies expired on 9 December 1998. The companies concerned were late in submitting the information, there were a number of formal breaches, and the summaries of the information were insufficient to permit the use of the data supplied, or in some cases were missing altogether.

4.296 As regards the accounting statements submitted by the sample companies, it is important to point out that they were not accompanied by any Spanish translation (except in the case of Marazzi), as required by the general instructions (item 2 of the questionnaire) which refer to the Law on Administrative Procedures No. 19.549, Regulatory Decree No. 1759/72, as harmonized in 1991 by Decree No. 1883/91.

4.297 In this regard the DCD stated, by Notes DCD Nos. 273-000404/99, 273-000405/99, 273-000406/99 and 273-000407/99 of 30 April 1999 to Bismantova, Casalgrande, Caesar and Marazzi (Section 25 of File No. 061-000794/98), that "it is of the utmost importance that all the information and/or documentation presented should be in Spanish or translated into Spanish by a certified translator (Articles 15 and 28, in accordance with the Law on Administrative Procedures No. 19.549, Regulatory Decree No. 1759/72, as harmonized in 1991 by Decree No. 1883/91) in order to be considered in the present proceedings".

4.298 In the case of information requested by the DCD and submitted by the four representative companies in Annex III - List of importers in Argentina and third countries of the goods under investigation, Annex IV - Information on the producer/exporter market, Annex V - Summary of producer/exporter sales (physical volume) and Annex VI - Summary of producer/exporter sales (estimated volume), the information was presented as confidential, and for reasons of competition, a non-confidential summary was supplied.

4.299 With respect to the said documentation and given the importance of the information supplied, classified as confidential, Argentina considers that the lack of non-confidential summaries "in sufficient detail to permit a reasonable understanding of the substance of the information submitted in confidence" (Article 6.5.1 of the AD Agreement) shows a failure to cooperate in clarifying during the investigation whether there was dumping or not.

4.300 The fact that the DCD considered that the summaries were not sufficiently detailed to permit a reasonable understanding of the substance of the information, in particular, the information corresponding to Annexes V and VI without whose supporting documentation it could not validly be considered for the purposes of reaching a determination of the normal value, is apparent from the repeated requests to provide further supporting documentary evidence and to remove the confidentiality or provide sufficiently detailed non-confidential summaries, as can be seen from the DCD Notes to the four exporting companies concerned on 30 April 1999, 22 June 1999 and 3 August 1999.

4.301 In the particular case of the information presented in Annex VI by Bismantova, the latter supplied the information in Italian lire, adding a note with the exchange rates for the years 1995, 1996 and 1997 and January-October 1998. Here it should be emphasized that point 6 of the specific instructions to the questionnaire clearly states that the table in Annex VI must be in US$. Providing this information in Italian lire shows a lack of cooperation and an effort to impede the investigation, as well as a failure to comply with a formal requirement of the procedure established in respect of the implementing authority.

4.302 Similarly, Bismantova stated that Rondine S.p.A. was its controlling company, holding a 60 per cent share, and that these companies were separate legal entities, with independent accounting records.

4.303 The DCD was thus obliged to handle this information separately in reaching the final determination, in view of the high percentage of unpolished *porcellanato* sales on the Italian domestic market between related companies. It was therefore necessary for the DCD to separate sales made to the controlling company, Rondine, from those made to the remaining customers on the said market. In particular, folios 27 and 28 of the Final Dumping Determination state that:

> In the specific case of the manufacturing export company Ceramica Bismantova S.p.A., it should be stated that the sample documentation supplied with respect to its sales on the Italian market showed a high percentage of transactions involving the sale of unpolished *porcellanato* in that market between related companies. Thus, approximately 50 per cent of the documentation submitted by the said company involved sales to its controlling company, Rondine S.p.A., from which it in fact buys its inputs for the production of *porcellanato*. The reply to the questionnaire for exporters originally submitted (Company Structure - File No. 061-10307/98 of 10 December 1998, included in Section XXI, folio 881, sheet 10) reveals that Rondine S.p.A. has a 60 per cent share in Ceramica Bismantova S.p.A.
>
> In accordance with the procedures set forth above, the Directorate of Unfair Competition divided the documentation submitted by Ceramica Bismantova S.p.A. in respect of domestic market sales into those made to its controlling company, Rondine S.p.A., and those made to the remaining customers on the said market, designated as 'other customers'.
>
> This procedure revealed that taking the total samples submitted to the Directorate, the share of 'other customers' in the sales of unpolished 20 cm x 20 cm *porcellanato* was 71 per cent, while Rondine S.p.A.'s share was 29 per cent. In the case of 30 cm x 30 cm tiles, the respective shares were 39 per cent and 61 per cent, while in the case of 40 cm x 40 cm tiles, the shares were 7 per cent for 'other customers' and 93 per cent for the controlling company Rondine S.p.A.
>
> Moreover, in the specific case of prices relating to transactions with 'other customers', there were price differences of some 13.69

per cent for 20 cm x 20 cm *porcellanato* tiles, 26.87 per cent for 30 cm x 30 cm tiles and 30.08 per cent in the 40 cm x 40 cm segment. These differences were not justified by the exporting company.

4.304 As regards Annex VII - Actual exports to Argentina, Annex VIII - Sales in the Italian domestic market, Annex IX - Exports to third countries, Annex X - Cost structure of the goods under investigation in the Italian domestic market and Annex XI - Cost structure of the exported goods, the companies supplied the data as confidential information, attaching a brief note regarding its confidential status and citing reasons of competition as justification.

4.305 As reflected in File No. 061-000794/98 incorporated by reference in Resolution 1385/99, the DCD considered that, in the case of the information contained in the above-mentioned Annexes, the grounds given for confidentiality were somewhat thin. Nevertheless, the implementing authority was quite willing to accept the confidentiality, even where the companies had not so much as provided a sufficiently detailed non-confidential summary to permit a reasonable understanding of the substance of the information submitted in confidence, or offered any justification as to why this was not done, ignoring the provisions of Article 6.5.1 of the AD Agreement.

4.306 Notwithstanding the above, the DCD repeatedly requested further supporting documentation, removal of the confidentiality or at least the submission of sufficiently detailed summaries (Notes of 30 April 1999, 22 June 1999 and 3 August 1999). On the one hand, this shows the willingness of the implementing authority to use all the information supplied and, on the other hand, the importance attached to such information, even though the latter proved to be insufficient as supporting documentation.

4.307 In particular, it should be emphasized that Caesar and Marazzi did not submit any information on exports to third countries (Annex IX), nor did the latter submit any information referring to the cost structure of the exported goods (Annex XI). In Argentina's view, this failure to submit information constitutes at the very least an impediment to the investigation, if not a refusal to provide access to information that is essential in itself.

4.308 Finally, it should be emphasized that, during the evidence-gathering period, none of the exporters offered any evidence, but merely replied to the questionnaire without furnishing sufficient supporting documentation.

Requests to elaborate on the insufficient supporting documentation, to remove the confidentiality or, where appropriate, to provide sufficiently detailed non-confidential summaries

4.309 In its preliminary determination, the DCD stated that the fact that the foreign companies had asked most of the information they supplied to be declared confidential implied differential and restricted treatment in processing that information. The final determination shows that the implementing authority was restricted in its handling of the information, and therefore requested a review of the status of that documentation and the incorporation in the proceedings - during the next stage - of evidence of interest that would enable the Technical Department to present, in its conclusions, the technical and documentary evidence on which they were based from all the firms involved.

4.310 Here it is appropriate to cite Notes DCD Nos. 273-000404/99, 273-000405/99, 273-000406/99 and 273-000407/99 of 30 April 1999 to Bismantova, Casalgrande, Caesar and Marazzi (section 25 of File No. 061-000794/98). In these Notes, the DCD states that it undertook **a** comprehensive and detailed analysis of all the information submitted by the firms and requested their cooperation in incorporating already requested evidence or adapting information in the record of the proceedings in order to ensure that the DCD had the information it needed to reach a public conclusion with respect to the matter at issue. In this regard it states that, although it is conceivable that for reasons of competition certain items of business information supplied by the companies may have to be safeguarded (hence the requested confidentiality that was accepted by the implementing authority), for the purposes of reaching objective and meaningful conclusions, the DCD had to have information that enabled it to do so. Consequently, it requested that the possibility should be considered of including in the record of the case a more detailed non-confidential summary or of elaborating on the information supplied or, failing this, of allowing the said documentation to be incorporated in the record, removing its confidentiality. This would give the parties concerned and their representatives access to the information in question, remembering that only duly accredited parties would be allowed to consult the information, for the purposes of issuing an opinion.

4.311 The Notes go on to list the documents of particular interest for full incorporation in the record as follows:

- List of importers in Argentina and third countries of the goods under investigation - Annex III;
- Actual exports to Argentina - Annex VII;
- Sales in the Italian domestic market - Annex VIII;
- Exports to third countries - Annex IX;
- Cost structure of the goods under investigation in the Italian domestic market - Annex X;
- Cost structure of the exported goods - Annex XI.

4.312 By File No. 061-004097/99 of 14 May 1999, included as folio 1315 in the record of the case, and in response to DCD's requests in the Notes mentioned above, the representatives of the Italian firms requested an extension of the time-limit for the submission of the required information. In Note DCD No. 273-000617/99 of 19 May 1999, the DCD states that "... the implementing authority has decided to grant an extension up to 7 June 1999".

4.313 By File No. 061-004809/99 of 4 June 1999, the representative of Assopiastrelle, Bismantova, Casalgrande, Marazzi and Cesar wrote to the DCD listing the information submitted and stating that, for each of the Annexes corresponding to each of the exporting firms included in the sample, there was a corresponding confidential Annex containing "conversion tables" so that the implementing authority could analyse the information. In other words, information was submitted from the four Italian firms of both a public and a confidential nature, separated into different Annexes.

4.314 By File No. 061-004860/99 of 7 June 1999, the representatives of Bismantova further submitted, as confidential information, Annex IC *bis* containing copies of sales invoices relating to the Italian domestic market.

4.315 On expiry of the extension on 10 June 1999, by File No. 061-005002/99 of 10 June 1999, the representatives of the Italian exporting firm Casalgrande further submitted, as confidential information, Annex IIC *bis* containing copies of sales invoices relating to the Italian domestic market.

4.316 Once again the Italian firms alleged that the confidentiality of all this information was based on strict reasons of competition. Once again, without responding to the DCD's concerns regarding the lack of supporting documentation, when they added a further sample thereof to the record, they asked for it to be treated as confidential information without providing non-confidential summaries "in sufficient detail to permit a reasonable understanding of the substance of the information submitted ..." (Article 6.5.1 of the AD Agreement).

4.317 Consequently, by means of Note No. 273-000768/99 of 22 June 1999, the DCD had to repeat the need for further supporting documentation, since what it had was insufficient:

> ... The DCD repeats the statement made on other occasions concerning the need for information that would enable the implementing authority to reach public conclusions in its technical reports. To that end, and to enable the DCD to make a precise comparison in its report on the final determination of the margin of dumping, the companies Ceramica Bismantova S.p.A., Ceramica Casalgrande Padana S.p.A., Marazzi Ceramiche S.p.A. and Ceramiche Caesar S.p.A are therefore asked to remove the confidentiality requirement for the information concerning the product code so that the said information can be incorporated in the record of the proceedings, or to submit a sufficiently detailed non-confidential summary of the information. This requirement must be met within five days after the receipt of this note ...

4.318 As stated during the proceeding in question, the submission of information and documentation for which confidential treatment is requested constitutes a limiting factor with respect to the analysis and public conclusions of the implementing authority.

4.319 Hence, the DCD sought, during the investigation, to obtain elements that were not subject to that condition so that it could make proper estimates with respect to the product under investigation. The removal of the confidentiality of the product code would enable the goods to be categorized according to their dimensions. In other words, without the product code it was very difficult to make out which product the information submitted applied to.

4.320 By File No. 061-005427/99 of 24 June 1999, the Italian firms, through their representatives, stated that they would remove the confidentiality of the product code item.

4.321 Moreover, by Note DCD No. 273-000890/99 of 3 August 1999, the DCD informed the representative of Assopiastrelle, Bismantova, Casalgrande, Marazzi and Caesar that "... the implementing authority is currently engaged, at this final stage of the investigation, in the analysis of all the information in the record of the case in order to arrive at a final determination in these proceedings. To do so, it must take into account all the information in these proceedings, and considers that it is important to ask you to remove the confidentiality of the information concerning production costs of the product at issue, or to prepare a non-confidential summary that would enable the information to be processed. Given the time-limit for the final determination, we would be grateful if this request could be met within five days following the receipt of this communication ...".

Particular quantitative aspects of the sample

4.322 It is important to emphasize that the sample documentation relating to sales on the Italian domestic market supplied by all of the manufacturing export companies concerned in the case - major representatives of the *porcellanato* production market - in conformity with the supplied sample methodology, covers no more than approximately 1.92 per cent of the physical volume (m^2) and 1.35 per cent of the total estimated value (Italian lire) of sales in the domestic market according to the information duly supplied.

4.323 Argentina would like to stress that the DCD accepted without reservation the sample methodology presented by Assopiastrelle (i.e. the four exporting companies Bismantova, Marazzi, Caesar and Casalgrande) because the association itself said that this would facilitate the work of the investigators. As is apparent from the record of the case, the alleged facilitation of the work did not materialize in practice in view of the lack of sufficiently detailed non-confidential summaries, the absence of such summaries in cases where the information was absolutely necessary, the delay in removing the confidentiality and the limited supply of supporting documentation.

4.324 The Italian companies concerned had to be requested by the DCD to expand on the inadequate supporting documentation (Notes of 30 April, 22 June and 3 August 1999), and even after it had been supplied, it continued to be meaningless for the purposes of an objective valuation.

4.325 Finally, the implementing authority pointed out the shortcomings in the accompanying documentation, as well as the impact of those shortcomings on the investigation. The statements by the DCD in the Notes mentioned above correspond exactly, in the authority's view, to the situation described in Article 6.8 of the AD Agreement. That is to say, this is a situation where the investigation was significantly impeded since the DCD was obliged to continue requesting additional evidence, what it had being insufficient. As a result of the repeated requests for supporting documentary evidence, the DCD was obliged to grant repeated extensions to facilitate the pursuit of the investigation, which was impeded by the attitude of the exporters. The combination of these elements placed the authority in a situation in which it did not have the necessary information because the exporting firms were refusing access to that information.

4.326 Argentina presented then its legal arguments concerning the EC's claim under Article 6.8 of the AD Agreement.

4.327 The EC asserts, in paragraph 48 of its first written submission, that none of the three circumstances required by Article 6.8 to make a determination on the basis of the facts available was present in this case.

(iv) Significant Impeding of the Investigation

4.328 Argentina submits that the exporters did significantly impede the investigation in that they failed to carry out the formalities required in the general and specific instructions accompanying the questionnaires. Nor did they provide sufficient supporting documentation with the information supplied, and the DCD had to request further evidence. Finally, the scant information provided in the confidential summaries also represented a significant impediment to the investigation, particularly as regards information needed to determine the normal value and the export value, where no direct summary was provided at all.

(v) Refusal of Access to Necessary Information

4.329 At the same time, the fact that the DCD accepted, without reservations, the "sample methodology" proposed by Assopiastrelle because the association itself said that this would facilitate the work of the investigators shows that the implementing authority was favourably disposed to consider such information as that party might submit.

4.330 Having accepted this sample methodology, the DCD discovered, upon examining the supporting documentation, supplied belatedly at the specific request of the authority, that it only covered approximately 1.92 per cent of the physical volume (m^2) and 1.35 per cent of the total estimated value (Italian lire) of domestic market sales, based on the information previously received.

4.331 Much of the information supplied by the companies was confidential. This information included data concerning total volumes and amounts of sales in the Italian domestic market by the participating firms. The firms also subsequently provided information concerning some of their sales transactions which enabled the implementing authority to establish average values in accordance with the above-mentioned method. However, it was felt that certain considerations should be highlighted with respect to the supporting sample. Its representativeness was mentioned as a factor to be taken into account, given that the percentages were fairly insignificant in comparison to the total for the period analysed.

4.332 This falls within the scope of Article 6.8 of the AD Agreement as significantly impeding the investigation by refusing access to necessary information.

(vi) Failure to Provide the Information within a Reasonable Period

4.333 With respect to the requirement to provide necessary information within a reasonable period, Argentina submits that the repeated requests for extensions together with the delay in removing the confidentiality of the information and the unwillingness to do so even though absolutely necessary for the DCD to be able to take it into account, in fact reflect the situation described in Article 6.8 in which the party does not provide necessary information within a reasonable period.

4.334 It should therefore be stressed that the two situations described above (significant impeding of the investigation and refusal of access) in themselves reflect the circumstances described in Article 6.8 justifying a determination by the authority on the basis of the facts available as the only possible alternative.

4.335 In the light of the above considerations, the implementing authority could only base its determination on the facts available, and was indeed forced to do so, since it could not, on the basis of a sample as unrepresentative as the one provided, make a correct determination of the normal value.

(vii) Rebuttal of the EC's Supplementary Arguments Concerning Article 6.8 of the AD Agreement

4.336 The Notes of 30 April, 22 June and 30 August 1999 provide confirmation that exporters were informed of the insufficiency of the information, and rebut the assertion in paragraph 54 of the first written submission of the EC that the Argentine interpretation of Article 6.8 renders paragraph 1 of Annex II null and void, since in this case the exporters did not submit all of the information within a reasonable period, nor was the information submitted of the kind required by the authorities to enable them to make a determination on the basis thereof.

4.337 With respect to the information contained in the record, the EC has taken the alleged Argentine terms "considered on an equal footing" - used in the informal context of consultations - out of their context, claiming that according to Argentina, Article 6.8 enables the investigating authorities to "pick and choose" from the data submitted. Argentina had all of the information before it and duly examined it, following the sequence set forth in Article 6.8, but found that it had to opt for a determination on the basis of the facts available because the information from the exporters turned out to be insufficient, as explained above.

4.338 At the same time, while the authority accepted the sample put forward by the exporters, it asked that the confidentiality of the supporting information be removed and granted a series of extensions to the importers, even accepting late answers to the questionnaires (10 December 1998). How can the EC contend that Argentina has deviated from paragraph 7 of Annex II and that it has relied on a secondary source of information without the special circumspection required by that paragraph?

4.339 The DCD was so meticulous that when forced to resort to secondary information, although aware that the supporting documentation for the determination of the normal value was insufficient, it nevertheless took account of that information and averaged the figures out in order to reduce the margin of dumping. This is ultimately what Table 4 in the first written submission of the EC.

4.340 Thus, contrary to the EC's assertion, Argentina followed the sequence of Article 6.8 of the AD Agreement and finding that the circumstances described therein had been met, resorted to a secondary source which provided more extensive information within a reasonable period.

4.341 Argentina addressed next the EC's claim under Paragraph 6 of Annex II of the AD Agreement.

4.342 Argentina first laid out the facts relevant for the presentation of its arguments.

4.343 With respect to the EC's claim in paragraph 49 of its first written submission that the DCD at no point during the investigation suggested that the exporters failed to provide necessary information, Argentina refers the Panel to the Notes DCD Nos. 273-000404/99, 273-000405/99, 273-000406/99 and 273-000407/99 of 30 April 1999 to Bismantova, Casalgrande, Caesar and Marazzi (Section 25 of File No. 061-000794/98), in which the DCD requests the cooperation of the said enterprises in supplying new evidence or adapting the information pertaining to the proceedings so that the implementing authority would have the information it needed to reach a public conclusion with respect to the matter at issue.

4.344 In this connection, the DCD points out that while it is possible that for reasons of competition, certain items of business information supplied by companies must be safeguarded (hence the requested confidentiality that was accepted by the implementing authority), for the purposes of reaching objective and meaningful conclusions the DCD must have information that enables it to do so. This is why it requested the companies to consider the possibility of including in the record of the case a more detailed non-confidential summary or of elaborating on the information supplied or, failing this, to allow the said documentation to be incorporated in the record, removing its confidentiality. This would expressly give the parties concerned and their representatives access to the information in question, remembering that only the duly accredited parties would be allowed to consult the information, for the purposes of issuing an opinion.

4.345 Consequently, by Note No. 273-00768/99 of 22 June 1999, the DCD had to repeat the need for further supporting documentation, since what it had was insufficient:

> ... The Directorate of Unfair Competition repeats the statement made on other occasions concerning the need for information that would enable the implementing authority to reach public conclusions in its technical reports. To that end, and to enable the Directorate of Unfair Competition to make a precise comparison in its report on the final determination of the margin of dumping, the companies Ceramica Bismantova SpA., Ceramica Casalgrande Padana SpA., Marazzi Ceramiche SpA., and Ceramiche Caesar SpA., are therefore asked to remove the confidentiality requirement for the information concerning the Product Code so that the said information can be incorporated in the record of the proceedings, or to submit a sufficiently detailed non-confidential summary of the information. This requirement must be met within five days after the receipt of this note ... .

4.346 Moreover, by Note DCD No. 273-000890/99 of 3 August 1999, the DCD informed the representative of Assopiastrelle, Bismantova, Casalgrande, Marazzi, and Caesar, that "... the implementing authority is currently engaged, at this final stage of the investigation, in the analysis of all of the information in the record of the case in order to arrive at a final determination in these proceedings. To do so, it must take account of all of the information in these proceedings, and considers that it is important to ask you to remove the confidentiality of the information concerning production costs of the product at issue, or to prepare a non-confidential summary that would enable the information to be processed. Given the time-limit for the final determination, we would be grateful if this request could be met within five days following the receipt of this note ...".

4.347 Argentina presented next its legal arguments concerning the EC's claim under Paragraph 6 of Annex II of the AD Agreement.

4.348 The EC's argument in paragraph 49 of its first written submission that the implementing authority "did at no point during the investigation suggest that the exporters failed to provide necessary information" is unfounded in view of the above-mentioned Notes. Moreover, it is clear that the reason why the DCD requested - through these Notes - further information from the exporters, was that the information supplied by them was not sufficient.

4.349 In any case, even if it were to be assumed that Argentina had violated paragraph 6 of Annex II, this would be a harmless error (an error committed in the progress of the trial "..., but which was not prejudicial to the rights of the party assigning it, and for which, therefore, the court will not reverse the judgment ..."; see *Blacks Law Dictionary*, Revised Fourth Edition, West Publishing Company, 1968, p. 638) that did not cause any injury, since its effect would be formal and procedural; in other words, what the EC would be demanding is a separate notification with a special format setting out the conclusion that the

DCD had reached. As concluded in the previous paragraph, that conclusion was in fact implicit in the mentioned Notes (see Annexes ARG-7, 10 and 11) and would in no way have signified a change of position on the part of the implementing authority.

(b) Arguments of Argentina in its First Oral Statement Relating to the EC's Claim under Article 6.8 of the AD Agreement

4.350 In its first oral statement, Argentina made the following arguments relating to the EC's claim under Article 6.8 of the AD Agreement.

(i) Treatment of the Information in the Record

4.351 Argentina submits that it had valid recourse to Article 6.8 of the AD Agreement, as shown by the record of the case (File No. 061-000794/98 of the Registry of the Ministry of the Economy and Public Works and Services, incorporated by reference in Resolution No. 1385/99 introducing the anti-dumping measures in question). The above-mentioned file explains clearly that the exporting firms significantly impeded the investigation, refused access to necessary information or did not provide that information within a reasonable period.

4.352 Consequently, Argentina was fully justified in resorting to the information available.

4.353 Argentina considers that the producing/exporting firms significantly impeded the investigation for the following reasons:

(a) They failed to provide information, or they did so without sufficient supporting documentation;

(b) they did not provide the necessary information within a reasonable period, even when granted repeated extensions;

(c) ©©they were late and displayed reluctance in removing the confidentiality of the information that was absolutely necessary so that the DCD could take it into account and make it public;

(d) they provided little information in the non-confidential summaries;

(e) in some cases they did not provide any non-confidential summary at all;

(f) they failed to comply with some of the required formalities in the general and specific instructions of the questionnaires.

Lack of information or information without sufficient supporting documentation

4.354 Firstly, the information requested from the exporters in the questionnaires was the information that the implementing authority considered absolutely necessary to reach a reasoned and public conclusion. Moreover, it was not enough simply to reply to the questionnaires: the replies needed to be backed by sufficient supporting documentation.

4.355 To allow a precise evaluation of the information submitted, the documentation in support of the replies needed to be sufficiently extensive. Indeed, the general and specific instructions accompanying the questionnaires emphasize that "producers and/or exporters from the respondent country must answer this questionnaire with the greatest possible precision, attaching documentation to support their replies, or if this is impossible, indicating the source of the information".

4.356 This is reflected in the repeated Notes sent by the DCD to the exporters requesting more extensive information, since what they had provided was not sufficient to make a correct determination of the normal value, the export value and the margin of dumping (see DCD Notes of 30 April, 22 June and 3 August 1999. The last of these Notes is the one in which the DCD merely requested that the confidentiality of the information be removed).

4.357 Moreover, some exporting firms failed to provide any information at all for certain Annexes to the questionnaires. In particular, Caesar and Ceramiche failed to provide any information concerning exports to third countries (Annex IX), and the latter failed to provide any information concerning the cost structure of the exported goods (Annex XI).

4.358 Nor did Caesar and Marazzi supply any information or supporting documentation concerning sizes 20 cm x 20 cm and 30 cm x 30 cm. The latter, did not even provide any information or supporting documentation concerning size 40 cm x 40 cm. Therefore, one of the four sample enterprises failed to provide any information on any of the size categories established by DCD for the product, although this segmentation was accepted by the firms even before Assopiastrelle presented the sampling methodology and the questionnaires were answered.

4.359 In the view of Argentina, this failure to supply information at the very least constitutes an impediment to the investigation, if not a refusal to provide access to information that is essential in itself.

Information within a reasonable period

4.360 Further evidence that the investigation was impeded can be found in the failure by the exporters to supply the requested information within a reasonable period, in spite of the fact that the implementing authority responded favourably to their repeated requests for extensions.

4.361 The exporters were originally given until 30 November 1998 to reply to the questionnaires, and in response to the requests for extension, it was decided to "grant the extension, setting 9 December 1998 as the final deadline for submission". This does not mean that Argentina submits that the submission of the information by the exporting firms on 10 December was considered a procedural error, but whatever the case, Argentina emphasizes the goodwill shown by the implementing authority in considering the information despite the fact that it was late.

4.362 In any case, Argentina considers the argument made by Japan in its third party submission that a delay of one day should have led the authority to conclude that the information had nevertheless been submitted within a reasonable period to be wrong. Technically, the reasonable period is established by the authority in conformity with its anti-dumping laws and regulations (Article 1 of the AD Agreement). Consequently, it is those laws and regulations which govern the matter at issue. In other words, while the implementing authority was willing to grant extensions for the purposes of gathering the information supplied by the exporters, the limit to that willingness was determined by the statutory deadlines provided for in the AD Agreement (Article 5.10) and Decree 2121/94.

4.363 In the end, the period actually used by the exporters for completing the requirements of the questionnaire ran from 30 November 1998 to 10 August 1999. Indeed, the DCD, in its Note of 30 April 1999, granted 15 days to definitively fulfil the requirements of the questionnaire in view of the shortcomings it had already noted in the replies. Similarly, in its Note of 22 June 1999, the DCD granted a new extension of five days, and finally, in its Note of 3 August, granted another five-day extension. Argentina considers that these successive extensions of the period for submitting the necessary information reflect, in fact, a lack of cooperation by the exporters that is contrary to Article 6.8 of the Agreement.

4.364 It is questionable whether a period running from 30 November 1998 to 10 August 1999 is in fact "reasonable" for the purposes of Article 6.8.

Delay and reluctance in removing the confidentiality of the information; lack of information in the non-confidential summaries; and absence of summaries in certain cases

4.365 The exporting firms were effectively impeding the investigation by completing the required information only at the request of the implementing authority. The authority considered the information to be insufficient without non-confidential summaries or sufficiently detailed summaries, and considered the removal of the confidentiality to be essential. This was finally done on 10 August 1999, that is eight months after the period accorded.

4.366 Argentina recalls in this connection that the DCD repeatedly requested further information, stressing that what had been received was insufficient. Argentina cites, for example, Notes DCD Nos. 273-000404/99, 273-000405/99, 273-000406/99 and 273-000407/99 of 30 April 1999 to Bismantova, Casalgrande, Caesar and Marazzi (Section 25 of File No. 061-000794/98), in which the DCD requested the cooperation of these firms in incorporating already requested evidence or adapting information in the record of the proceedings in order to ensure that the DCD had the information it needed to reach a public conclusion with respect to the matter at issue, granting them a period of 15 days for the purpose.

4.367 In these Notes, the DCD points out that for the purposes of reaching objective and meaningful conclusions, it had to have the information that enabled it to do so. Consequently, to ensure that the parties concerned and their representatives had access to the information in question, it requested that the possibility should be considered of including in the record of the case a more detailed non-confidential summary or of elaborating on the information supplied, or, failing this, of allowing the said documentation to be incorporated in the record, removing its confidentiality.

4.368 Exhibit ARG-19 contains a complete list of the confidential information submitted by each one of the firms with respect to each one of the Annexes, and identifies the information that was accompanied by non-confidential but incomplete summaries. The non-confidential summaries provided by the four sample firms with respect to Annexes III, VII, VIII, IX, X and XI, provided to the Panel in Exhibit ARG-20, are completely irrelevant in that they lack substance and hence could not be used by the implementing authority. Thus, the EC's comment to the effect that Argentina's allegation concerning the inadequacy of the non-confidential summaries is ironic seems out of place.

4.369 The exporters were aware that, as indicated in the general instructions for completing the questionnaire (point 5), " ... 'confidential' information that is not accompanied by a summary or an explanation of why it is impossible to provide such a summary will not be considered as such". Argentina asks the Panel to make an objective evaluation of whether the summaries provided in Exhibit ARG-20 are "in sufficient detail to permit a reasonable understanding of the substance of the information submitted in confidence" (Article 6.5.1 of the AD Agreement).

4.370 Moreover, the DCD had to repeat its request for further supporting documentation, since what it had was insufficient (see paragraphs 38 and 42 of Argentina's first written submission).

Failure to comply with the required formalities in the general and specific instructions of the questionnaires

4.371 Yet another example of the investigation being impeded within the meaning of Article 6.8 of the AD Agreement is, in our view, the fact that the accounting statements submitted by the sample companies were not accompanied by any Spanish translation (except in the case of Marazzi) as required by the general instructions (item 2 of the questionnaire) which refer to the Law on Administrative Procedures No. 19.549, Regulatory Decree No. 1759/72, as harmonized in 1991 by Decree No. 1883/91. In this regard, Argentina recalls that Exhibit ARG-7 cites the DCD Notes of 30 April 1998 in which the DCD states that "it is of the utmost importance that all the information and/or documentation presented should be in Spanish or translated into Spanish by a certified translator (Articles 15 and 28, in accordance with the Law on Administrative Procedures No. 19.549, Regulatory Decree No. 1759/72, as harmonized in 1991 by Decree No. 1883/91) in order to be considered in the present proceedings".

4.372 Likewise, point 6 of the specific instructions to the questionnaire clearly states that the table in Annex VI (Summary of producer-exporter sales - physical volume) must be in US$. And yet, in the particular case of Bismantova, the information relating to Annex VI was provided in Italian lire, accompanied by a note with the exchange rates for 1995, 1996, 1997 and January-October 1998. Argentina considers that providing this information in Italian lire shows a lack of cooperation and an effort to impede the investigation, as well as a failure to comply with a formal procedural requirement. Moreover, in view of the EC's comments concerning the legal value of other Argentine legislative provisions (paragraph 12 of its first oral statement), Argentina does not understand why it describes this requirement as ridiculous (paragraph 59).

(ii) Treatment of the Information as Reflected in the Final Determination

Impeding of the investigation and refusal of access to the necessary information

4.373 The impeding of the investigation and the refusal of access to the necessary information is also reflected in the final determination, folio 29, which states that: "The sample documentation relating to sales on the Italian domestic market supplied by all of the manufacturing export companies concerned in the case - and as affirmed at the time of their participation in the proceedings by Assopiastrelle, of which these firms are members, they are major representatives of the Italian *porcellanato* production market - covers no more than approximately 1.92 per cent of the physical volume (m^2) and 1.35 per cent of the total estimated value (Italian lire) of sales in the domestic market according to the information duly supplied".

4.374 Argentina therefore wonders how it is possible to make a correct determination of the normal value of the goods on the basis of a sample of market sales invoices that is so unrepresentative of the total for domestic sales given by the exporting firms. Indeed, the implementing authority had no alternative but to base its determination on the facts available.

4.375 Finally, Argentina stresses that the implementing authority pointed out the shortcomings in the accompanying documentation, as well as the impact of those shortcomings on the investigation. The statements by the DCD in the notes appearing in Annexes ARG-7, ARG-10, ARG-11 and ARG-18 to Argentina's first written submission correspond exactly to the situation described in Article 6.8 of the AD Agreement. That is to say, this is a situation where the investigation was significantly impeded since the DCD was obliged to continue requesting additional evidence, what it had being insufficient.

4.376 As a result of the repeated requests for supporting documentary evidence, the DCD was obliged to grant repeated extensions to facilitate the pursuit of the investigation, which was impeded by the attitude of the exporters. The combination of these elements placed the authority in a situation in which it did not have the necessary information because the exporting firms were refusing access to that information.

4.377 This was reflected in the final determination, folio 39, where the implementing authority includes the paragraphs of the argument submitted by Zanon, in that these paragraphs introduce the reasoning which led the implementing authority to use the best information available: "As regards the margins of dumping, we submit that the preliminary determination of the Directorate of Unfair Competition (folios 1131 *et seq*) should be endorsed in that the information on which it was based, i.e. 'information and documentation supplied by the domestic manufacturing firm Ceramica Zanon S.A.C.I. y M. and by the domestic importing company Canteras Cerro Negro S.A. (from its Italian supplier ITS S.p.A.)', is the best information available in view of the lacunae and inconsistencies in the information submitted both by the Italian exporting companies and by Ceramica San Lorenzo (...)."

Rebuttal of various paragraphs of the EC's first written submission

4.378 In paragraph 60 of its first written submission, the EC claims that the DCD did not inform the exporters at any time during the investigation that the information on export prices and normal value contained in their questionnaire responses had been disregarded.

4.379 Argentina does not consider this to be the case, since the DCD repeatedly asked for more extensive information, stressing that the information submitted was insufficient. One only needs to mention, in this connection, the Notes of 30 April, 22 June and 3 August 1999, in which the DCD requests the cooperation of the exporting firms in incorporating already requested evidence or adapting information in the record of the proceedings in order to ensure that the DCD had the information it needed to reach a public conclusion with respect to the matter at issue. Similarly, in its Note of 22 June 1999, the DCD had to repeat the need for further supporting documentation, since what it had was insufficient.

4.380 The EC is also mistaken when it states, in paragraph 61, that the DCD did not explain in the final dumping determination the reasons why such information was rejected. Indeed, the DCD, in its determinations, pointed out that the information supplied was not sufficient to enable it to reach a reasoned and public conclusion.

4.381 Firstly, already in its preliminary determination the DCD stated that the fact that the exporting firms had asked most of the information they supplied to be declared confidential implied differential and restricted treatment in processing that information.

4.382 Likewise, the final determination shows that the implementing authority was restricted in its handling of the information, and therefore requested a review of the status of that documentation and the incorporation in the proceedings of evidence of interest that would enable the Technical Department to present, in its conclusions, the technical and documentary evidence on which they were based from all the firms involved.

4.383 At the same time, the final determination also shows that as stated before, the lack of representativeness of the sample was a determining factor in forcing the implementing authority to use the best information available.

4.384 It is well known that a sample of some 2 per cent is not valid in statistical terms. In this case, the exporters submitted as the universe of their sales in the domestic market precisely what is usually considered to be the margin of error, and even worse, they did so without indicating the criterion on which they based their sample.

4.385 Argentina submits therefore that the DCD used the facts available because it considered that the exporters had acted in a manner that fit the description in Article 6.8, that is to say they refused access to the necessary information, did not supply such information within a reasonable period and significantly impeded the investigation.

4.386 In its first oral statement, Argentina also presented a series of arguments relating to the EC's claim under Paragraph 6 of Annex II of the AD Agreement.

4.387 In Argentina's view, the EC is mistaken in paragraph 60 of its first written submission when it claims that the DCD did not inform the exporters at any time during the investigation that the information on export prices and normal value contained in the questionnaire responses had been disregarded. Similarly, the EC is mistaken when, in paragraph 61 of its first written submission, it states that the DCD did not explain in the final dumping determination the reasons why such information was rejected.

4.388 On the contrary, the DCD, in its determinations, showed that the information submitted was not sufficient to enable it to reach at a reasoned and public conclusion.

4.389 Indeed, Argentina considers that the implementing authority was explicit enough in the notes provided in Annexes ARG-7, ARG-10 and ARG-11 in which it explained to exporters the situation that was developing in the investigation owing to the lack of necessary information within a reasonable period. In other words, Argentina is of the view that sufficient notice was given to exporters that they were involved in the situation described in 6.8 of the AD Agreement.

4.390 As required in paragraph 6 of Annex II, Argentina informed the exporters of the insufficiency of the information provided and the lack of sufficiently detailed summaries, and granted a series of extensions. Since the requirements had not been met, i.e. since not enough supporting information had been submitted to enable the authority to arrive at a reasoned and public conclusion, the DCD gave the reasons, in its final determination, why the information was disregarded (see paragraphs 61 to 65 of Argentina's first written submission and folios 29 and 39 of the final determination, incorporated by reference in Resolution No. 1385/99 introducing the measure.

(c) Arguments of Argentina in its Oral Statement at the Third-Party Session of the First Meeting of the Panel with the Parties, Relating to the EC's Claim under Article 6.8 of the AD Agreement

4.391 In its oral statement at the third-party session of the first meeting of the Panel with the parties, Argentina made the following arguments relating to the EC's claim under Article 6.8 of the AD Agreement.

4.392 Japan's submission (at paragraph 2) proceeds from certain assumptions that do not apply to this case:

(a) Firstly, that information submitted within a reasonable period and not contested is automatically valid. In fact, this was not the case, since a series of extensions were granted and, above all, the information submitted was insufficient.

(b) Secondly, that the authorities did not point out that the information would not be accepted. This is also wrong: the authority at least pointed out that the information was insufficient, asked for more extensive information, and requested that the confidentiality be removed. Consequently, Japan's conclusion that in this case "the respondent is reasonably entitled to assume that the investigating authority is satisfied with the information" is false. On the contrary, the authority expressed its dissatisfaction in its notes dated 30 April 1999, 20 June 1999 and 3 August 1999 and gave these reasons in its final determination to justify its decision to use the best information available.

4.393 Moreover, the authority, in conformity with paragraph 6 of Annex II, notified that it would not consider the information that was not accompanied by a non-confidential summary. Exhibit ARG-20 containing a series of summaries from the four exporting firms with respect to the different annexes in the record: Annex III - List of importers in Argentina and third countries of the goods under investigation; Annex VII - Actual exports to Argentina; Annex VIII - Sales in the Italian domestic market; Annex IX - Exports to third countries; Annex X - Cost structure of the goods under investigation in the Italian domestic market; and Annex XI - Cost structure of the exported goods. Exhibit ARG-20 should help the Panel to appreciate the technical weakness of the non-confidential summaries and confirm that in the circumstances, the authority had no alternative but to resort to the best information available.

4.394 Thus, Japan's statement that the exporters did cooperate in the investigation is false. In fact, the contrary is true.

4.395 Japan is also mistaken in asserting that the authority considered the issue of the date to be the determining factor in its decision to use the best information available. It was the combination of various elements, delays in submitting information, successive extensions, delay in removing the confidentiality of the information, and insufficient non-confidential summaries that meant that the authority had to resort to the best information available, since in fact, the exporting firms were to all intents and purposes refusing access to the information.

(d) Replies of Argentina to the First Set of Questions by the Panel Relating to the EC's Claim under Article 6.8 of the AD Agreement

4.396 Argentina replied to the first set of questions by the Panel relating to the EC's claim under Article 6.8 of the AD Agreement as follows:

4.397 The Panel asked the parties whether, in their view, the DCD rejected the information from the exporters for one of the reasons set out in Article 6.8 AD Agreement. The Panel further asked whether reference was made in the record to one of these reasons and, if so, where. The Panel also asked under what circumstances an investigating authority may resort to secondary source information outside the specific circumstances of Article 6.8 AD Agreement.

4.398 To this question, Argentina replied that the DCD proceeded the way it did because it found that the combination of different circumstances set out in Article 6.8 of the AD Agreement had been satisfied. Only the circumstances laid down in Article 6.8 could justify recourse to Annex II of the AD Agreement.

4.399 The Panel recalled that Argentina's first written submission alleged that the exporters' questionnaire responses were deficient in many ways. In particular, that such questionnaire responses were submitted late, were not fully translated, lacked public summaries of confidential information sufficiently detailed, lacked some currency conversions, failed to report data on exports to third countries and costs of the product exported, and lacked supporting documentary evidence. The Panel asked Argentina which of these deficiencies, if any, were relied upon by the DCD for its final determination. The Panel further asked if Argentina could provide the Panel with the relevant references in either the report accompanying the final determination or in the administrative record.

4.400 To this question, Argentina provided the following reply.

4.401 For its final determination, the DCD did not rely on the deficiencies only, but on all of the facts contained in the record.

4.402 Paragraphs 7 to 60 inclusive of Argentina's first written submission and paragraphs 2 to 35 inclusive of Argentina's first oral statement provide a full explanation of where, in the preliminary and final determinations, each one of the different ways in which the exporters impeded the investigation is recorded: failure to supply information within a reasonable period and refusal of access to the necessary information.

4.403 In the report on the final determination of the margin of dumping in the investigation at issue, the items identified as V.1.3 and V.2.3 (final determination of normal value and final determination of the f.o.b. export price, respectively) explain both the deficiencies and the limitations that the DCD encountered in analysing the information and documentation supplied by the participating firms.

4.404 Regarding the last part of the question, Argentina provided a detailed account of the documentation submitted by the firms concerned as an indication of the information to which the DCD had access.

4.405 The Panel recalled that Argentina, in paragraph 39 of its first written submission, states that "the submission of information and documentation for which confidential treatment is requested constitutes a *limiting factor* with respect to the analysis and public conclusions of the implementing authority" (emphasis added). The Panel asked Argentina whether, in its opinion, the confidential nature of the information submitted constituted a constraint on the investigating authority's ability to base its determination on that information. The Panel further asked Argentina to explain in which way it considered that confidentiality limited the DCD's analysis in this case.

4.406 Argentina replied that confidentiality imposes a limit on the authority by preventing it from relying on public elements that can be invoked against the parties or third parties, particularly when the information in question is not accompanied by non-confidential summaries in sufficient detail to permit a reasonable understanding of the substance of the information submitted in confidence and hence to allow the determination reached, which must be public, to be backed.

4.407 The Panel asked the Parties whether they drew a distinction between the obligation of authorities to protect confidential information from disclosure, on the one hand, and the obligation of authorities to use for their determinations exporter data that meets the requirements of the Agreement.

4.408 Argentina replied that the above were two different concepts. On the one hand, there was the generic obligation of the authority to protect the confidentiality of information provided in confidence by the exporters and importers during the investigation, information which must be accompanied by non-confidential summaries in sufficient detail to permit a reasonable understanding of its substance. On the other hand, there was another obligation relating to the treatment which the authority must give to the information provided by exporters as an element in calculating the normal value and the export value and determining the margin of dumping. The implementing authority tried to do both things, i.e. to protect the confidentiality of the information submitted in confidence while using the information furnished by the exporters.

4.409 The Panel recalled Argentina's statement that, according to the DCD, the non-confidential summaries submitted by the exporters were insufficient under Article 6.5.1 AD Agreement, since this provision required that such summaries permit a "reasonable understanding of the substance of the information provided in confidence". The Panel asked the parties how did they interpret the objective of Article 6.5.1, that is, whose "reasonable understanding" was being addressed - that of the public or that of the investigating authorities?

4.410 Argentina replied that the implementing authority considers that the non-confidential summaries must enable the authorities to arrive at reasoned and public conclusions and enable the parties concerned to exercise their right of defence by participating in the investigation and commenting on the submissions of the other parties involved.

4.411 In Argentina's view, additionally, the non-confidential summaries must meet the requirements of Article 6.5.1 by permitting a reasonable understanding of the substance of the information submitted so that the authority can make them public.

4.412 The Panel asked the parties whether the following summary of relevant facts was correct. The exporters requested confidentiality for most of the information provided in their questionnaire reply. On 30 April 1999, the DCD sent letters to the exporting firms requesting them to consider providing a more detailed non-confidential summary than that already provided in the questionnaire replies, to elaborate on the information supplied, or to remove the requested confidentiality that had been granted by the investigating authority. More specifically, information on sales in the Italian market (Annex VIII) and the cost structure of the goods in the domestic Italian market (Annex X) was requested. On 4 June 1999, the exporting firms submitted public and confidential information concerning domestic sales of the product concerned, with conversion tables that were submitted as confidential information. On 7 June 1999, Bismantova and Casalgrande further submitted as confidential information sales invoices relating to the Italian domestic market. By its letters of 22 June 1999 and 3 August 1999, the DCD requested the exporting firms to reconsider the requested confidentiality of the information concerning product codes and the production costs. The DCD's report acknowledged that the exporting firms agreed by letters of 23 and 24 June that the product code item could be made non-confidential. On 10 August 1999, the exporting firms further agreed to remove the confidentiality of the item concerning cost of production provided that the names of the companies relating to each cost structure were not revealed.

4.413 Argentina replied that the notes contained in Exhibit ARG-7 not only requested further information concerning Annex VIII and Annex X, but also, in the case of Marazzi y Casalgrande, requested additional information with respect to the following:

List of importers in Argentina and third countries of the goods under investigation (Annex III);

- Actual exports to Argentina (Annex VII);
- Sales in the Italian domestic market (Annex VIII);
- Exports to third countries (Annex IX);
- Cost structure of the goods under investigation in the Italian domestic market (Annex X);
- Cost structure of the exported goods (Annex XI).

4.414 In the case of Bismantova and Caesar, the notes requested additional information with respect to:

List of importers in Argentina and third countries of the goods under investigation (Annex III);

- Actual exports to Argentina (Annex VII);
- Sales in the Italian domestic market (Annex VIII);
- Exports to third countries (Annex IX).

4.415 The Panel asked the parties to clarify whether, in light of the exporters' agreement to re-classify the information as requested, the concerns the DCD raised with regard to the confidential nature of the information at the time of the preliminary determination (recorded in p. 23 of the DCD's Final Determination Report, Exhibit EC-2) had been resolved by the time of the final determination. The Panel further asked the parties to indicate which of the exporters' information, if any, was still confidential at the time of the final determination. In certain information had remained as confidential, the Panel also asked the parties to clarify whether non-confidential summaries were provided for this confidential information.

4.416 To this question, Argentina provided the following reply.

4.417 The DCD's concern with regard to the confidential nature of the information during the preliminary investigation persisted even after the confidentiality of the product code and costs of production was removed, since the substantial information needed to determine the normal value, the export value and the margin of dumping remained confidential until the final determination (and is still confidential).

4.418 Regarding the information submitted in response to the various requests from the implementing authority, Argentina referred the Panel to its past comments on the merits thereof and the limitations encountered by the implementing authority in treating the said information.

4.419 Argentina referred back, in this reply, to the DCD's explanations concerning the exporters' submissions of 4 June 1999.

4.420 A detailed look at the information supplied by the exporters and their submissions of 4 June 1999 shows that not only did they not provide any information regarding the Annexes listed in the DCD's Note of 30 April, as recognized by the EC in paragraph 25 of its first oral submission, but they never in fact furnished sufficient supporting documentation relating to the information provided regarding Annex V (confidential), nor did they provide non-confidential summaries in conformity with Article 6.5.1 or remove the confidentiality with respect to the Annexes that were essential to determining the normal value, the export value and the margin of dumping.

4.421 The Panel asked Argentina whether it agreed with the EC's statement that the submission of questionnaire replies within the first two hours of the morning of the working day following the specified deadline cannot be regarded as late as it is consistent with the provisions of *Decreto 1759/72*, as amended by *Decreto 1883/1991*. If so, the Panel asked Argentina to clarify which, if any, of the exporters' submissions were not covered by this grace period.

4.422 Argentina replied that it agreed with the EC regarding the possibility of using the first two hours of the day following a specified deadline, and indeed all of the parties to the procedure have that right. Argentina had only mentioned this subject as yet another example of the uncooperative attitude of the exporters. What Argentina wanted to stress was the fact that the period actually used by the exporters to complete the questionnaire requirements ran from 30 November 1998 to 10 August 1999.

4.423 The Panel asked Argentina to explain what the concern of the DCD was with respect to the alleged lack of "representativeness" of the exporters' home sales. In particular, was this a concern relating to the sampling method, or did this concern relate to the "sufficiency" of the exporters' home sales for the purpose of establishing normal values?

4.424 Argentina replied that the DCD's concern related to the lack of representativeness of the sales on the Italian domestic market, as stated on page 29, Section V.1.3, of the report on the final determination of the margin of dumping, and not the sampling methodology itself, since this was accepted by the DCD in the Note of 22 December 1998 (DCD No. 273-000471/98).

4.425 The Panel asked Argentina to explain the relevance of the DCD's finding that the four exporters included in the sample only represented 1.92 per cent of the total volume of sales in the home market. In particular, did the 1.92 per cent refer to all sales made by Italian producers, including those with no exports to Argentina? If this was the case, the Panel asked the parties whether they were of the view that, as a legal matter, companies selected for an individual determination have to account collectively for a large percentage of all home market sales made.

4.426 Argentina replied that the sample documentation on domestic market sales, which covered only 1.92 per cent of the physical volume and 1.35 per cent of the total estimated value in Italian lire, refered to the domestic market sales reported by the four companies participating in the investigation. The relevance of this weakness in the sample documentation was that it prevented the implementing authority from understanding precisely the transactions that took place in the domestic market during the investigation period and hence from making an accurate determination of the normal value. In other words, the supporting documentation was not statistically valid for the purposes of reaching an accurate determination of the normal value. Additionally, as noted earlier, this supporting documentation was submitted in confidence.

4.427 The Panel asked the parties to confirm whether that the four exporters included in the sample accounted, in quantity terms, for around 70 per cent of all exports made.

4.428 Argentina replied to this question by citing Exhibit ARG-23, which contains a note from Assopiastrelle to the DCD, dated 30 November 1998, stating that: " ... Based on our information the exports of the 4 to 5 largest exporting companies would account for approximately 70 per cent of the overall exports from Italy to Argentina of the products under investigation ... ".

4.429 The Panel asked the parties to comment on the relevance of the fact that the DCD initially accepted the sampling methodology suggested by the exporters' association, although the sampled firms were later found by the DCD to cover too few home sales.

4.430 Argentina replied that Exhibit ARG-12 shows that the sampling methodology was proposed on 1 December 1998, before the replies to the questionnaires were received. On 22 December 1998, the DCD, by Note DCD No. 273-000471/98, accepted the said methodology on the understanding that Assopiastrelle had suggested it with a view to cooperating in, and simplifying the investigation. It would have been impossible for the DCD, in the space of 12 days, to evaluate the replies to the questionnaires and the supporting documentation and to assess whether the information provided was sufficient to arrive at a reasoned and public conclusion.

4.431 In short, Argentina said, the DCD accepted the sampling methodology on the understanding that the companies making up the sample would fill out the questionnaires properly, and provide all of the information that the implementing authority needed to arrive at a proper determination of dumping.

4.432 The Panel recalled that the exporters' questionnaire made reference to the provision of supporting documentation in two places. In the introductory section, while indicating that supporting documentation must be provided, it also allowed exporters the possibility to identify instead the source of the information reported. In addition, Section B requested the submission of any supporting documentation that would help the DCD to better understand the mechanics of the reported transactions. The Panel asked Argentina whether it was of the view that, according to the specifications of the questionnaire used by the DCD, respondents were obliged to provide full documentary evidence of each and every sale reported. The Panel further asked Argentina to clarify whether any of the exporters chose to comply with the requirement set out in the introductory section of the questionnaire by identifying the source of its information. If no exporters took advantage of that option, the Panel asked Argentina whether it was of the view that the DCD was entitled to require the submission of "additional" supporting documentation without specifying what that information should consist of.

4.433 Argentina replied that the exporters' questionnaire clearly establishes the obligations of the exporters interested in participating in the investigation. In the introductory section, they are asked to provide supporting documentation, and only when this is not possible, to identify the source. The supporting documentation requested in Section B must be sufficiently representative to enable the implementing authority to better understand the transactions carried out on the domestic market. This clearly does not mean that it must include, for example, all of the invoices for the domestic market - but it should include a statistically valid percentage thereof.

4.434 Additionally, the implementing authority was entitled to ask exporters to elaborate on the information provided. The need for the implementing authority to impose such a requirement was duly established. As mentioned throughout the investigation, the authority was trying all along to obtain information that would enable it to make individual determinations for each exporter.

4.435 The Panel recalled that Argentina argued that, by means of the notes that have been provided to the Panel as Annexes ARG-7, ARG-10 and ARG-11, the DCD duly informed the exporters that it was necessary for them to provide additional documentary evidence. The Panel asked Argentina in what ways, other than by requesting the information to be re-classified, did Annexes ARG-7, ARG-10 and ARG-11 draw the exporters' attention to the need to provide additional documentary evidence?

4.436 Argentina replied that, clearly, the note of 30 April 1999 requested further evidence and the submission of non-confidential summaries in sufficient detail to permit a reasonable understanding of the substance of the information submitted in confidence. Thus, the DCD was not merely asking for the confidentiality to be removed. The notes of 22 June and 3 August (Annexes ARG-10 and ARG-11) requested that the confidentiality of the product code and production costs be removed so that the information supplied on 4 June following the first request could be used, since the said information was not accompanied by non-confidential summaries.

(e) Arguments of Argentina in its Second Written Submission Relating to the EC's Claim under Article 6.8 of the AD Agreement

4.437 In its second written submission, Argentina made the following arguments relating to the EC's claim under Article 6.8 of the AD Agreement.

(i) Significant Impeding of the Investigation

4.438 Argentina reiterates that the exporters significantly impeded the investigation by failing to comply with the required formalities in the general and specific instructions of the questionnaires provided by the implementing authority, by not providing enough supporting documentation with the information supplied and by providing little information in the non-confidential summaries.

Failure to comply with the formalities

4.439 With respect to point (e) of the EC's first oral statement, Argentina would like to stress that according to Article 1 of the AD Agreement, "The following provisions govern the application of Article VI of the GATT 1994 insofar as action is taken under anti-dumping legislation or regulations." This Article concerns the rules governing the implementation of the Agreement which, it stipulates, are valid to the extent that they are consistent with its provisions.

4.440 Argentine legislation implements the AD Agreement and stipulates that the submissions of the parties must be translated into the national language, and that values must be expressed in US$. It is unacceptable that the EC should play down rules governing a procedure conducted in Argentina in accordance with Argentine legislation while at the same time invoking that legislation in its own favour and considering it valid when it comes to justifying the delay in submitting documentation - specifically, the provision allowing documentation to be provided during the first two hours of the day following the deadline.

Insufficient supporting documentation

4.441 Argentina reiterates that, in its Note of 30 April 1999, the DCD specifically asked the companies to "... supply further evidence ..." and "... elaborate on the information supplied ...". In Argentina's, what was being requested was supporting documents, since the supporting documentation provided with the replies to the questionnaires was insufficient.

4.442 Moreover, a meeting was held on 11 May 1999 between the DCD and the representatives of the exporters for the purposes of informing the latter of the shortcomings in their supporting documentation, and the result of the meeting was the Note provided by the EC in Exhibit EC-10. This Note clearly shows the DCD's concern - understood by the representative of the exporters - regarding the insufficiency of the documentation submitted. Indeed, the representative states that at least 50 per cent of the exporters' sales invoices for the Italian domestic market should be provided.

Insufficient non-confidential summaries

4.443 Argentina recalls Exhibit ARG-19, which contains a complete list of the confidential information submitted by each one of the firms with respect to each one of the Annexes, and identifies the information that was accompanied by non-confidential but incomplete summaries. Moreover, the non-confidential summaries provided by the four sample firms with respect to Annexes III, VII, VIII, IX, X and XI are completely irrelevant in that they lacked substance and hence could not be used by the authority.

4.444 Argentina also reiterates that the exporters were aware that, as indicated in the general instructions for completing the questionnaire (point 6), "... 'confidential' information that is not accompanied by a summary or an explanation of why it is impossible to provide such a summary will not be considered as such".

(ii) Refusal of Access to Necessary Information

4.445 The EC cannot reasonably claim, as it does in paragraph 37 of its first oral statement, that the questionnaires only required invoices for exports to Argentina. Argentina draws the Panel's attention to page 2, Title 1 of the questionnaire:

OBJECTIVES AND SCOPE

> The Agreement on Implementation of Article VI of the General Agreement on Tariffs and Trade 1994 (GATT Uruguay Round) was implemented by Argentina through Law No. 24.425, published in the Official Bulletin of 5 January 1995, and Regulatory Decree No. 2121/94 of 30 November 1994, published in the Official Bulletin of 5 December 1994.
>
> *The purpose of this questionnaire* is to enable the Secretary of Industry, Trade and Mining of the Republic of Argentina to obtain *necessary and sufficient information* for investigations of unfair international trade practices.
>
> The producer and/or exporter of the respondent country *shall answer this questionnaire as accurately as possible, accompanying its replies with supporting documentation or, where this is not possible, identifying the source of the information.*
>
> All of the information supplied shall be subject to possible verification by the implementing authority. Where it is not possible to verify *the replies in a satisfactory manner or if they are incomplete or submitted after the time-limit has elapsed, determinations shall be made on the basis of the best information available* (emphasis added by Argentina).

4.446 Argentina considers that anyone participating in an anti-dumping procedure should be able to appreciate that the implementing authority's requirements as set forth in the "Objectives and Scope" section form a fundamental part of the instructions, in that they include the essential requirements for fulfilling the legal obligation and describe the consequences of failing to do so.

4.447 Similarly, Argentina draws the Panel's attention to point 1 of the general instructions for completing the questionnaire, which appear on page 4:

> The four sections ... [Section A: General Information; Section B: Exports to Argentina; Section C: Sales in the domestic market and to third countries; Section D: Production cost structure. Manufacturing process] ... include Annexes and detailed information. The producer/exporter is asked to indicate the file number on each of the sheets it submits, answering each question in detail and identifying the sources used, *adding, as a necessary condition for certifying the validity of the source, the corresponding documentation* (emphasis added by Argentina).

4.448 This clearly shows that contrary to what the EC claims in paragraphs 35 to 39 of its first oral statement, the DCD had stated precisely its requirements in the way of supporting documentation and the conditions under which such submissions as were made in this respect could be considered valid.

4.449 In other words, the documentation required by the authority is that which can reasonably be requested in any anti-dumping investigation, and the EC's far-fetched claim that the implementing authority required copies not only of all the invoices, but of all the accounting and cost records, is unacceptable.

4.450 Regarding the EC's claim in paragraph 41 of its first oral statement concerning the DCD's Note of 30 April 1999, Argentina would like to point out that its request to the firms to "... supply further evidence ..." and "... elaborate on the information supplied ..." refers to none else than "supporting documents".

4.451 It is clear from the above that it was not only at the meeting held on 11 May between the DCD and the representatives of the exporters that the latter were informed of the shortcomings in the supporting documentation submitted, as the EC asserts. Following this meeting, as shown by Exhibit EC-10, the exporters clearly could no longer have any doubts as to DCD's requirements.

4.452 In Argentina's view, the clearest evidence that the accompanying documentation was not sufficient appears in the Note provided by the EC as Exhibit EC-10, in which the representative of the exporters, following the above meeting, states that "... this information must cover an 'important' part of total sales in the domestic market (you said 50 per cent ...)".

(iii) Lack of Representativeness of the Sample of Domestic Market Sales

4.453 In paragraph 46 of its first oral statement, the EC asserts that what matters is whether the exports made by the selected exporters were representative of exports to Argentina, and not whether the domestic sales made by the selected exporters were representative of the domestic sales made by all the Italian producers. This statement is out of context and refers to a point against which Argentina did not argue. It was precisely because the four sample firms were representative in terms of their exports to Argentina - "more than 70 per cent" - that the DCD accepted the sampling methodology proposed by Assopiastrelle on 22 December 1998.

4.454 What Argentina did argue in paragraphs 43-46 and 49-52 of its first written submission and in paragraphs 23 and 24 of its oral submission was that the lack of representativeness of the documents provided by the exporters in respect to their sales (those of the four sample exporters) in the Italian domestic market, and not in respect of all sales by all producers of *porcellanato* in the Italian market.

4.455 The Panel will appreciate the relevance of the fact that the sales invoices in the domestic market included in the record by the exporters for the totality of their sales on the Italian domestic market were not sufficient from a statistical point of view to determine the normal value, and hence, the margin of dumping.

4.456 It is odd that the EC should argue, in discussing Article 6.8, that "... even assuming that the sample were in fact not sufficiently representative, that would still not justify the DCD's decision to resort to 'facts available'. Article 6.10 contains no provision authorizing the investigating authorities to resort to 'facts available' in such circumstances". It is a bit confusing that in this context the EC should refer to Article 6.10, claiming that it contains no provision authorizing the investigating authorities to resort to the facts available. Perhaps the EC is thinking of its own regulations, which do in fact entitle it to do what it seems to want to prevent Argentina from doing.

4.457 In fact, the provision that enables the authority to rely on the facts available is Article 6.8, which is at the centre of the discussion on the insufficiency of supporting documentation. Ultimately, what links Article 6.8 and 6.10 of the AD Agreement is the fact that in normal circumstances, Article 6.10 applies, whereas if the authority does not have sufficient information, Article 6.8 applies.

4.458 Argentina reiterates that upon examining the supporting documentation - submitted late and at the DCD's specific request - the authority found that the firms making up the sample proposed by Assopiastrelle itself only represented approximately 1.92 per cent of the physical volume (m^2) and 1.35 per cent of the total estimated value (in Italian lire) of sales on the domestic market.

(iv) Failure to Provide the Information within a Reasonable Period

4.459 Argentina stresses once again that the repeated extensions and the delay and reluctance displayed in removing the confidentiality of the information supplied without sufficiently detailed non-confidential summaries in fact reflect the situation described in Article 6.8 as regards the failure to provide the necessary information within a reasonable period.

4.460 Specifically, with respect to paragraph 52 of the EC's first oral statement, the supporting documentation was not submitted as soon as it was requested as the EC contends, since it was in fact requested in the questionnaires of 30 October 1998, and the deadline for submitting replies and documentation, once it had been extended, was 9 December (within the first two hours of 10 December, as the EC has pointed out).

4.461 As the EC also correctly states in paragraph 25 of its oral statement, following the Note of 30 April 1999, the exporters, on 4 June, submitted information on Annexes VII, VIII and IX. Consequently, the EC itself recognizes that the information was not submitted as soon as it was requested. Argentina reiterates that the information was insufficient.

4.462 Argentina also reiterates its conviction that the exporters were warned of the shortcomings in the information supplied, as illustrated by the Notes sent by the DCD to the exporters on 30 April, 22 June and 3 August 1999.

4.463 Since the exporters did not provide the requested information within a reasonable period and since the information provided did not meet the authority's requirements for reaching a determination based thereon, Argentina submits that the investigating authority acted within the legal framework of Annex II, paragraph 1.

4.464 Consequently, Argentina considers that the situations described (significant impeding of the investigation and failure to provide access, added to the failure to provide the information within a reasonable period) reflect the circumstances described in Article 6.8, the combination of which enables the authority to make a determination on the basis of the facts available as the only remaining alternative.

(v) Other Claims by the EC

4.465 The EC is mistaken when it claims in paragraph 7 and 8 of its oral statement that Argentina changed its line of defence. In paragraph 57 of its first written submission, Argentina explains the meaning of the expression "considered on an equal footing", which the EC had taken out of its context.

4.466 In other words, far from changing a line of defence, the paragraph in question merely sets out the facts, i.e. that Argentina had all of the information before it, the information submitted by the exporters and that submitted by the complainant. In the case of the former, which - and Argentina does not dispute this - should form the basis for calculating the normal value and the export value, the authority did try to use it. However, in view of the considerations mentioned with respect to the shortcomings in the information, its late submission, and the incomplete and insufficient supporting documentation submitted by the sample firms (that is, the exporters submitted supporting documentation concerning their own insufficient sales on the domestic market: 1.35 per cent in value and 1.92 per cent in volume), the authority had no alternative but to resort to the "facts available".

4.467 This is very different from the distorted version of the facts according to which the authority placed both sets of information (the information submitted by the exporters and the rest of the information) on an equal footing when considering them from the legal point of view and picked only the data which it found the most convenient.

4.468 Argentina had all of the information before it, and only opted for a determination on the basis of the facts available when it had concluded, in the light of the situation described above, that the information from the exporters was insufficient. The mention of Folio 29 was more than a "vague remark": it concerned a finding under point V.I.3 of the authority's final determination. The conclusion that the DCD drew from this is reflected in that final determination in Folio 39, which was cited by Argentina in paragraph 27 of its first oral statement.

4.469 Thus, Argentina did not deviate from paragraph 7 of Annex II, since the authority accepted the sample proposed by the exporters and requested sufficiently detailed non-confidential summaries. It also asked for supporting documentation and granted a series of extensions, finally having to resort to secondary information because the supporting documentation was insufficient.

4.470 In this respect, Argentina is convinced that it acted in conformity with the sequence laid down in Article 6.8. Making sure that the circumstances described in Article 6.8 existed, the implementing authority resorted to a secondary source which provided more ample information, and within a reasonable period, only when forced to do so.

(f) Arguments of Argentina in its Second Oral Statement Relating to the EC's Claim under Article 6.8 of the AD Agreement

4.471 In its second oral statement, Argentina made the following arguments relating to the EC's claim under Article 6.8 of the AD Agreement.

(i) Refusal of Access to Necessary Information Concerning the Lack of Supporting Documentation

4.472 Firstly, contrary to what the EC argued in a reply to a question by the Panel following the first meeting, Argentina never argued that the investigating authority was free to use secondary sources of information. On the contrary, Argentina reaffirms that the DCD was forced to do so when it found that the information submitted by the exporters was insufficient.

4.473 This is clearly reflected in the record of the investigation. Suffice it to mention once again, for example, the meeting held on 11 May 1999 between the DCD and the representatives of the exporters, one of the essential purposes of which was to remind the exporters of the shortcomings in the supporting documentation submitted. This meeting resulted in the Note provided by the EC in Exhibit EC-10, which shows the DCD's concern regarding the insufficiency of the documentation submitted. Indeed, the representative of the exporters states that at least 50 per cent of the exporters' sales invoices for the Italian domestic market should be provided, stressing the particular importance of including invoices for all sizes (20 x 20, 30 x 30 and 40 x 40).

4.474 Argentina submits that in accordance with the facts described and as reflected in Exhibit ARG-7, the DCD explicitly requested exporters to " ... supply further evidence" and " ... elaborate on the information supplied ...". With due respect, Argentina would like to ask the Panel: does this not constitute a request for supporting documents, given the insufficiency of the supporting documentation provided in the replies to the questionnaires?

4.475 From the beginning of this case, the EC has maintained, both in its first written submission and in a reply to a question by the Panel following the first meeting, that Argentina went back on the position it held during the consultations on how the DCD proceeded in relation to the information supplied by the exporters. Argentina quotes Article 4.6 of the DSU in this respect: "Consultations shall be confidential, and without prejudice to the rights of any Member in any further proceedings."

4.476 In its statements before the Panel, the EC has distorted the meaning of an informal exchange during the consultations, and is trying to pass this off as a legal interpretation by Argentina when it is no such thing. "Equal footing" can only mean that value is given to a secondary source when the circumstances set forth in Article 6.8 are met in a specific case and in accordance with the particular nature of that case.

4.477 Once again, Argentina points out that the DCD never considered that the sampling methodology put forward by Assopiastrelle was not representative; on the contrary, the DCD accepted it, precisely because the four sample companies were representative in respect of their exports to Argentina - "more than 70 per cent". Argentina maintains that the supporting documentation provided by the four sample firms in respect of their sales in a Italian domestic market was insufficient to constitute a statistically valid sample for the purposes of determining the normal value of sales in that market. This was reflected in the final determination, folio 29 1967, page 29.

4.478 Argentina trusts that the Panel will understand the importance in the context of the investigation of the fact that the sales invoices in the domestic market were not sufficient from a statistical point of view for the purposes of determining normal value and hence the margin of dumping.

(ii) Lack of Representativeness of the Sample Owing to the Insufficiency of the Information Provided

4.479 Once again, the EC is confusing the issue when it states, in its reply a question by the Panel, that the implementing authority should have verified in advance the representativeness of the sample suggested by Assopiastrelle. Obviously, in accepting the sample, the DCD took account of what the exporters had said, i.e. the Note from Assopiastrelle of 30 November 1998, according to which the four selected firms represented 70 per cent of exports to Argentina. However, although the sample was representative, the information provided by the selected companies was not. The DCD never doubted the representativeness of the sample. Clearly, however, no implementing authority can verify, in the space of seven working days, whether information provided in replies to questionnaires is sufficient as supporting documentation (note that the replies to the questionnaires were submitted on 10 December 1998, while the DCD accepted the sampling methodology on 22 December 1998). Consequently, the DCD reaffirms that although the sample was representative, the information supplied by the sample firms in respect of normal value was not statistically valid.

4.480 Regarding the EC's claim in paragraph 38 of the replies to the questions of the Panel that the exporters reported in their responses "all" the domestic sales of each of the models that were exported to Argentina in significant quantities, Argentina reiterates that, as stated in Argentina's reply to question 15 by the Panel, the questionnaire responses were incomplete since they did not contain sufficient information, in particular concerning domestic market sales.

(iii) Impeding of the Investigation by Refusing Access to Necessary Information

4.481 Likewise, Argentina would like to refute the EC's reply to a question by the Panel in which it states that the DCD Notes of 30 April did not request the exporters to provide information on Annexes VIII and X. Argentina reiterates that these Notes make it clear that information on Annex VIII was requested of all the firms, while information on Annex X was requested of Marazzi and Casalgrande, although these were not the only Annexes on which information was requested. Argentina refers the Panel to its reply to question 6 of the Panel.

(iv) Impeding of the Investigation by Failing to Comply with the Formalities Required under Argentine Law

4.482 As regards the EC claims in paragraphs 59-65 of its second written submission concerning the formalities required in the questionnaires, Argentina repeats what it said in paragraphs 6 and 7 of its second written submission: since Article 1 of the AD Agreement provides that domestic legislation or regulations implementing the Agreement must be respected, and Argentine legislation implementing the AD Agreement provides that submissions of the parties must be translated into the national language and values expressed in US$, it is unacceptable that the EC should play down the rules governing a procedure conducted in Argentina in accordance with Argentine legislation.

(v) Lack of Cooperation

4.483 Argentina does not share either the EC's assertion that there was no evidence of lack of cooperation on the part of the exporters. Suffice it to mention that they were late in submitting the information and failed to comply with certain formalities, and that the information was supplied with non-confidential summaries that were insufficient for the purposes of using the data supplied, or without any summaries at all.

(vi) Three New EC Claims

Qualitative analysis of the documentation supplied

4.484 As regards the EC's assertion that the questionnaire did not require the exporters to provide copies of a sufficient number of invoices, Argentina reiterates that the instructions emphasized that "Producers and/or exporters from the respondent country must answer this questionnaire with the greatest possible precision, attaching documentation to support their replies, or if this is impossible indicating the source of the information".

4.485 In other words, it clearly was not enough to state that a given number of sales had been made without providing a sufficient number of sales invoices in the domestic market to back the reply to the question. Indeed, the sample backing the replies had to be sufficiently extensive to allow a precise evaluation of the information submitted, and although the actual word "invoices" was not mentioned, it was implicitly included in the type of information requested.

4.486 Similarly, Argentina refutes the EC's assertion that the reference to the fact that the respondents should supply supporting documents was too vague to meet the requirements of paragraph 1 of Annex II. Argentina does not agree, since the documentation supporting the replies was requested from the exporters in the general and specific instructions for each one of the items required in each questionnaire, in its explanatory part. Thus, Argentina considers that the implementing authority specified the information required in detail. Moreover, the EC's statement that the said reference was too vague is an interpretation, and in any case, would fall within the realm of the implementing authority's discretion.

Article 2.2 and its footnote as a flawed defence by the EC

4.487 Argentina does not understand why the EC has brought in a new claim - in paragraph 48 of its second written submission - with respect to Article 2.2 and footnote 2, as a argument in defence of the contention that the supporting documentation provided with respect to Annex VIII to the questionnaire was sufficient.

4.488 Article 2.2 lays down the methodology to be used for establishing the margin of dumping when there are no sales of the like product in the ordinary course of trade in the domestic market of the exporting country or when, because of the particular market situation or the low volume of the sales in the domestic market of the exporting country, such sales do not permit a proper comparison. It then goes on to establish how the margin of dumping is to be determined in such situations, i.e. by comparison with a comparable price of the like product when exported to an appropriate third country, or with the cost of production in the country of origin, subject to certain conditions in both cases.

4.489 The 5 per cent referred to in footnote 2 is an exception which, if applicable, entitles the authority to use, as evidence of normal value, the comparable price of the like product when exported to an appropriate third country, or to use the cost of production. But footnote 2 nowhere refers to the supporting documentation for sales in the domestic market. Consequently, the said Article does not say that it is enough for exporters to provide supporting documentation on domestic market sales when such sales constitute 5 per cent or more of the sales of the importing Member.

4.490 In other words, what the footnote does not say is that 5 per cent can be considered as sufficient supporting documentation to back the validity of a sample.

4.491 The EC's claim should cause the Panel to have serious doubts with respect to its assertion that it provided sufficient supporting documentation.

Article 6.8 and a mistaken link with Article 6.10

4.492 The EC has also stated in its defence that the circumstances provided for in Article 6.8 were not met, claiming that Article 6.10 does not allow the authority to base its determination on the facts available.

4.493 Its argument focuses on the alternatives offered by Article 6.10, which assume that there is such a great number of exporters and producers that it is impossible to carry out a determination. Thus, it allows the authority to limit the examination to a reasonable number of interested parties using (1) a statistically valid sample of exporters; or (2) the largest percentage of the volume of exports.

4.494 In the present case Assopiastrelle offered a sample which was, in fact, valid for the investigation (four exporting enterprises which, as stated by Assopiastrelle, represented 70 per cent of exports to Argentina). However, the EC appears to interpret Article 6.10 to imply that once the sample is limited to a reasonable number of interested parties, the implementing authority cannot weigh the quantity and quality of the information supplied.

4.495 Nor does Argentina agree with the EC's interpretation in paragraph 49 of its first oral statement - among the claims with respect to Article 6.8 - according to which Article 6.10 establishes the possibility of (1) enlarging the sample; (2) choosing a new sample; or (3) extending the examination to all exporters.

4.496 This raises a question: if the DCD accepts a sample methodology, at the request of the exporters, because it considers the sample to be representative of the exporters, and the sample companies do not provide sufficient information to enable it to arrive at a reasoned conclusion - refusal of access to information - does the EC maintain that at this point in the investigation (almost eight months after its initiation) the implementing authority should enlarge the sample, choose a new sample or extend the examination to cover all exporters, to request what they failed to request?

4.497 In any case, what led the implementing authority to use the facts available was precisely that the four companies in question supplied documentation for approximately 1.35 per cent of the value of domestic market sales. Clearly, as Argentina said in paragraph 34 of our first oral statement, the exporters submitted as the universe of their sales in the domestic market precisely what is usually considered to be the margin of error - which cannot exceed two or three per cent of the sample - in any statistical data.

4.498 In short, Argentina submits that the scant information provided in the way of supporting documentation relates to Article 6.8 in that it implies a refusal of access to necessary information. When the parties act in accordance with the circumstances described in Article 6.8, the authority may use the facts available to reach a determination.

4.499 Indeed, as Argentina stated in paragraph 24 of its second written submission, what links Article 6.8 and 6.10 of the AD Agreement is the fact that in normal circumstances, Article 6.10 applies, whereas if the authority does not have sufficient information, Article 6.8 applies. In other words, if the implementing authority had had the said information at its disposal in order to make a dumping determination in accordance with Article 6.10, it would not have had to apply Article 6.8 to Article 6.10.

(g) Replies of Argentina to the Second Set of Questions by the Panel Relating to the EC's Claim under Article 6.8 of the AD Agreement

4.500 Argentina replied to the second set of questions by the Panel relating to the EC's claim under Article 6.8 of the AD Agreement as follows:

4.501 The Panel recalled that, in its reply a question by the Panel following the first meeting, Argentina argues that "As stated in Exhibit ARG-19, the confidentiality requested in the submission contained in File No. 061-010305/98 of 10 December 1998 was maintained throughout the proceedings. Although in the last submission of 4 June 1999, the company provided information on exports to Argentina, it could not be used, since the information provided in the lists could not be checked against the information in the official registers or against that submitted by the importers in their questionnaire responses. This prevented the implementing authority from checking the accuracy of the information provided." The Panel asked Argentina to clarify why it believed that this information could still not be used by DCD. Could the information still not be used for reasons relating to the confidentiality of the information or does this remark relate to Argentina's argument concerning lack of supporting documentation? The Panel further asked Argentina to explain why the DCD felt it was necessary to cross-check the information and documentation provided by the exporters with information from the official registers.

4.502 To this question, Argentina provided the following reply.

4.503 Throughout the proceedings, Argentina was faced with two different situations. On the one hand, the confidentiality of much of the documentation supplied was maintained. On the other hand, there was a failure to comply with the formal requirements for the supporting documentation relating to export transactions. More specifically, the documentation in question was submitted without the consular certification required under Article 28 of the Argentine Law on Administrative Procedures (Law No. 19549).

4.504 To illustrate this pointed, Argentina quoted the relevant part of the instructions to exporters' questionnaire:

GENERAL INSTRUCTIONS FOR COMPLETING THE QUESTIONNAIRE:

> 2. The replies and documentation attached hereto must be submitted in Spanish. Where other languages are used, a translation by a registered translator must be provided. Documents issued by foreign authorities must be authenticated by consular or diplomatic officials of the Republic. The signatures must, in turn, be authenticated by the Ministry of Foreign Affairs, International Trade and Worship of Argentina (Article 28 and related articles of the System of Administrative Procedures - Law No. 19.549, Regulatory Decree No. 1759/72, Regulatory Enactment of 1991 by Decree No. 1883/91).

4.505 In spite of the above, and given that it was not the intention of the investigating authority to reject the information submitted, the DCD proceeded to cross-check the information with the documentation in the record obtained from the official registers and from the other parties involved in the proceedings, specifically the importers. It is all of this information that made up the 30 sets of documentation in these proceedings and thus constituted the essential facts of the investigation which determined the conclusions reached.

4.506 In fact, this cross-checking revealed differences. For example, the implementing authority found information that had been submitted by the importer, in this particular case Quadri y Cia. S.A., which had not been supplied by the exporter, as well as the information on exports from the exporter that was not supplied by the importer. In other cases, the implementing authority detected export and import transactions that had not been notified by any of the parties, but that appeared in the official Argentine customs registers.

4.507 Cross-checking of information from different sources enables the implementing authority to bring together elements with a view to providing a full picture of trade operations with the participation of the exporting firm, the importers and the official Argentine registers. Thus the authority is able to double check every aspect of the facts and weed out the conjectures, contributing to the reliability of its conclusions as to what actually took place.

4.508 The Panel recalled that Argentina replied to a question by the Panel following the first meeting as follows: "The DCD's concern with regard to the confidential nature of the information during the preliminary investigation persisted even after the confidentiality of the product code and costs of production was removed, since the substantial information needed to determine the normal value, the export value and the margin of dumping remained confidential until the final determination (and is still confidential)". The Panel asked Argentina to explain which substantial information remained confidential until the final determination.

4.509 To this question, Argentina gave the following reply.

4.510 In its reply to a question by the Panel following the first meeting, Argentina provided an exhaustive list of information submitted by the exporters making up the sample and of the accompanying Annexes for which confidentiality was requested, indicating for each case whether a non-confidential summary was provided.

4.511 However, as it regards normal value, Argentina wished to explain that the supporting information was not only confidential, and remained that way throughout the proceedings, but in fact it was inappropriate and ill-suited for the purposes of determining the normal value. In other words, in this specific case, the most important problem was the lack of representativeness of the supporting documentation provided for the purposes of determining the normal value.

4.512 As regards the export price, the supporting documentation supplied did not enable the authority to carry out the task mentioned in the preceding question. This explains why the implementing authority proceeded the way it did.

4.513 The Panel recalled that, with respect to Annexes IV-VI, the exporters provided information for which they requested confidential treatment, as well as a non-confidential summary of the information concerned. The Panel recalled further that this summary was prepared by way of indexing all the figures provided in those Annexes. The Panel asked the parties why the DCD was of the view that indexation did not permit a "reasonable understanding of the substance of the information submitted in confidence".

4.514 In replying to this question by the Panel, Argentina recalled that Exhibit ARG-20 contained, as an illustration, the non-confidential summaries submitted by the exporting firms for Annexes III, VII, VIII, IX, X and XI to the questionnaires. In addition, Argentina wished to submit Exhibit ARG-24, containing the non-confidential summaries for Annexes IV, V and VI. Thus, in the opinion of Argentina, the Panel had before it all of the relevant non-confidential summaries provided by the exporting firms and would be able to appreciate that it was impossible, in view of their nature, to arrive at any public conclusions on the basis thereof.

4.515 The Panel recalled that, with respect to Annexes III and VII-XI of the investigation questionnaire, the exporters provided information for which they requested confidential treatment, although they did not provide a non-confidential summary of the information concerned. The Panel asked the parties whether the exporters provided a justification as to why such information was not capable of summarization (that is, a justification separate from the statement that the information in question required confidential treatment). If this was so, the Panel asked the parties to provide it with copies of the relevant evidence in the record.

4.516 Argentina replied that it had dealt with this question exhaustively before, but for the purposes of further clarification it wished to refer the Panel to the documentation provided in Annexes ARG-20 and ARG-24.

4.517 Argentina added that, as could be seen in Annexes III, IV, V, VI, VII, VIII, IX, X and XI, the request was justified in the following terms: "The request for confidentiality of this information is based on reasons of competition".

4.518 If the exporters did provide a justification as to why the information for which confidential treatment was requested was not capable of summarization, the Panel asked whether the parties were of the view that under Article 6.5.1 of the AD Agreement investigating authorities have the right to contest such justifications. If so, the Panel asked further, did the DCD conclude, contrary to the exporters, that the information in question could in effect be summarized? If the DCD made this conclusion, could Argentina explain the DCD's reasoning?

4.519 Argentina replied to this question by saying that it was understood that the parties concerned must do their utmost to provide the implementing authority with the elements it needed to reach public conclusions (as required in investigations such as this one to avoid further consultations such as those that took place subsequently because the confidential nature of the information made it impossible for the authority to provide a full report of how it had proceeded - for example, in the case of the 1.92 per cent).

4.520 The Panel asked the parties to comment on the following statement in paragraph 107 of the report of the Appellate Body in the case *Thailand - H-Beams*, in which the Appellate Body addressed the question of the use of confidential information by the investigating authority as a basis for an authority's final determination:

> An anti-dumping investigation involves the commercial behaviour of firms, and, under the provisions of the Anti-Dumping Agreement, involves the collection and assessment of both confidential and non-confidential information. An injury determination conducted pursuant to the provisions of Article 3 of the Anti-Dumping Agreement must be based on the totality of that evidence. We see nothing in Article 3.1 which limits an investigating authority to base an injury determination only upon non-confidential information (Appellate Body Report, *Thailand - Anti-Dumping Duties on Angles, Shapes and Sections of Iron or Non-Alloy Steel and H-Beams from Poland*, WT/DS122/AB/R, adopted 5 April 2001, at para. 107).

4.521 Argentina replied that the DCD had proceeded in accordance with the legislation in force for the investigation of alleged dumping. This was reflected in the comprehensive survey conducted by the DCD with respect to the documentation in the record of the proceedings and to its status.

4.522 The impossibility of reflecting all of the information supplied in the technical reports did not imply that the implementing authority ignored the information. However, it was the status of the information and the possibility of arriving at conclusions on the basis thereof that determined whether it could be considered.

4.523 The Panel recalled that Exhibit EC-10 was a report of the meeting with the case-handlers on 11 May 1999 from the representatives of the exporters in Argentina to the exporters' lawyers in Brussels. The report reflected the discussions with the case handlers, concerning the non-confidential information that needed to be provided, in the following manner:

> Additionally, this information must cover an "important" part of total sales in the domestic market (you said 50 per cent - I don't know, I guess that is largely enough), the coverage must be September 1997 - October 1998, and we have to present invoices (with confidential status) supporting this non-confidential version.

4.524 The Panel asked Argentina whether this was an accurate reflection of what was said during that meeting and of the requests for information that were made. Further, the Panel asked Argentina whether the case-handlers at the 11 May meeting requested invoices from two exporters only (Casalgrande and Bismantova). The Panel asked the parties next whether the 50 per cent coverage mentioned in this paragraph related to the provision of non-confidential information, or to the documentation supporting the information provided. The Panel also asked the parties whether the 50 per cent related to all sales made in the home market, or only to the sales reported by the exporters.

4.525 To this question, Argentina provided the following reply.

4.526 The meeting held on 11 May 1999 was in fact an information meeting held at the request of the Italian exporting firms for the purpose of clarifying, for the legal representatives of the exporting firms, the points they considered to be of interest to them. Thus, the results and exact terms used in this meeting were not recorded in writing in the record of the proceedings.

4.527 Although it is impossible to be certain of the actual terms used, the terms reflected in the quoted statement correspond fairly closely to what would be in the interests of any anti-dumping proceeding. Thus, it is helpful in all anti-dumping proceedings to have supporting documentation corresponding to a high percentage of trade transactions in respect of the goods under investigation. In this case, it would be understood that what the investigating authority wanted was to have information corresponding to sales transactions in the Italian domestic market, and in view of the proposal submitted with respect to the Italian producing firms, this would mean documentation in respect of the four firms making up the sample.

4.528 As regards the question of whether the information was requested from Bismantova and Casalgrande only, the answer is that it was requested for the four firms making up the sample.

4.529 In other words, the sample having been accepted, the high percentage of supporting information to be provided concerned the exporters making up the sample.

4.530 In this connection, while Argentina recognized the possibility of requesting confidentiality for documentation that warrants such treatment, such requests could only be considered, and taken into account in conjunction with the overall treatment of the other elements in the proceedings, provided an adequate non-confidential summary was supplied.

4.531 Regarding the volume of the supporting documentation requested (required percentage), this applies to the totality of information concerning trade in the product under investigation, and domestic market sales of the four firms making up the sample, with full details of the transactions carried out during the period defined and where they are reflected. The non-confidential summary requested refers to the totality of sales of the product at issue during the period in question, with a reservation as to the publication of data which might be sensitive for the firms concerned.

4.532 The Panel recalled that, in replying to a question by the Panel following the first meeting, Argentina stated that the 1.92 per cent figure mentioned on page 29 of the DCD's Final Determination, referred to the supporting documentation covering domestic market sales reported by the four companies participating in the investigation. The Panel asked Argentina to explain how this figure was calculated. Specifically, the Panel wished to know whether the total home market sales (the denominator in this calculation):

included sales by all producers in Italy, independently of whether they exported to Argentina?

included sales by exporters not in the sample?

included sales of models not exported in significant quantities to Argentina?

included all of the sales made of any given model? (that is, they did not refer to a sample of sales)

4.533 Likewise, the Panel wished to know if the sales for which invoices were provided (the numerator in the calculation):

- related to all four companies?
- excluded sales to related parties and sales at prices below cost?

4.534 The Panel asked Argentina to provide it, if possible, with the figures that went into the calculation.

4.535 Argentina replied that, as already stated on several occasions, the DCD interrelated the information available in the questionnaires provided in the course of the proceedings, and concluded that the documentation supplied covered that percentage in relation to total sales on the Italian domestic market.

4.536 Unfortunately, this was a good example of the limitations facing the implementing authority as a result of the request for confidentiality of the information provided. In this case, the Argentine authority was limited in the reply it could give to the question, in that it could not reveal the numerical calculation made, but for the purposes of that calculation, it considered the information corresponding to the aggregate total amount of sales reported for the Italian domestic market by the four firms in relation to the total obtained from the documentation contributed by those firms during the proceedings.

3. *Third Parties: Japan*

(a) Arguments of Japan in its Written Submission Relating to the EC's Claim under Article 6.8 of the AD Agreement

4.537 In its written submission, Japan made the following arguments relating to the EC's claim under Article 6.8 of the AD Agreement.

4.538 The EC claimed that the DCD disregard the normal value and export price information provided by the exporters inconsistently with Article 6.8 and Annex II. The relevant legal provisions are those in AD Agreement Article 6.8:

> In cases in which any interested party refuses access to, or otherwise does not provide, necessary information within a reasonable period or significantly impedes the investigation, preliminary and final determinations, affirmative or negative, may be made on the basis of the facts available. The provisions of Annex II shall be observed in the application of this paragraph.

4.539 Article 6.8 must be read in context with the other provisions on evidence in Article 6 and the provisions of Annex II. When so read, it is clear that Article 6 as a whole establishes a strong preference for using actual information collected from interested parties in an antidumping investigation. Article 6.1, for instance, provides the right for interested parties to submit information and to obtain the information submitted by other interested parties. Article 6.7 provides for the investigations in the territory of other Members to verify the information submitted. Article 6.8 provides for recourse to "the facts available," but only in limited circumstances when an interested party has failed to cooperate. Annex II further develops conditions on the use of such "best information available." All of these provisions are premised on a preference for real information collected during the investigation and determined to be accurate. It follows that antidumping authorities can only rely on the allegations in an antidumping petition or other "facts available" when real information is simply not available. Where real information has been submitted within a reasonable period and found to be accurate during the course of an investigation, antidumping authorities must rely on it, and cannot give preferential treatment, or even equal treatment to unverified allegations by the petitioner.

4.540 The practical reasons for this hierarchy of factual sources in the AD Agreement are well illustrated by the DCD's final dumping determination in the ceramic tiles investigation. Rather than rely on real, verifiable information about actual prices paid for ceramic tile in the Italian market, DCD appears to have relied wholly or in part on published lists of prices to end-users supplied by the petitioner. According to the EC written submission, these prices to end-users bear little resemblance to the prices actually charged to distributors and wholesalers, who normally receive large discounts of up to 75 per cent of the list price. These end-user prices were compared not to end-user prices in the Argentine market but to prices for export sales to distributors and wholesalers in Argentina. Apparently there was no on-the-spot verification of these price list data.

4.541 Paragraph 7 of Annex II provides that "if an interested party does not cooperate and thus relevant information is being withheld from the authorities, this situation could lead to a result which is less favourable to the party than if the party did cooperate." As the panel noted in the recent dispute on *United States - Hot-Rolled Steel,* "any 'less favourable' result under paragraph 7 of Annex II may only be appropriate in the case of an interested party who does not cooperate" (Panel Report, *United States - Anti-Dumping Measures on Certain Hot-Rolled Steel Products from Japan,* WT/DS184/R, circulated on 28 February 2001, at para. 7.71). The facts as presented by the EC indicate that the four Italian respondent tile exporters did cooperate; if this is in fact the case, the use to any extent of "facts available" was inconsistent with Argentina's obligations under Article 6.8 of the AD Agreement.

4.542 Article 6, and the information collection exercise it provides for, must be interpreted in a manner that gives them meaning. If antidumping authorities were free to disregard the information collected, then this information collection exercise would be pointless. The provisions of Article 6.1 would be a nullity, and the limitations specified in Article 6.8 would be meaningless as well. Article 6, and Annex II, reflect the concept that the legal regime of antidumping is based on an investigative process in which respondents cooperate with the investigating authority to produce real data, relating to verifiable facts, so as to arrive at an antidumping margin that reflects as closely as possible the actual degree of dumping that may or may not have taken place. If investigating authorities can simply disregard with no explanation the data collected from respondents, respondents have no incentive to cooperate, and the purposes of this regime are frustrated.

4.543 The DCD final determination indicates that the deadline set for receipt of information from the four responding firms was 9 December 1998, and the information was received only on 10 December 1998. A similar situation occurred in the antidumping investigation examined in *United States - Hot-Rolled Steel.* In that case, certain information requested was supplied after the deadline set by the US Department of Commerce (DOC) but well before the time of verification; DOC then rejected this information and applied the "facts available" instead. The panel in that case noted that the AD Agreement:

> establishes that facts available may be used if necessary information is not provided within a reasonable period. What is a 'reasonable period' will not, in all instances be commensurate with pre-established deadlines ... a rigid adherence to such deadlines does not in all cases suffice as the basis for a conclusion that information was not submitted within a reasonable period and consequently that facts available may be applied (Panel Report, *United States - Anti-Dumping Measures on Certain Hot-Rolled Steel Products from Japan,* WT/DS184/R, circulated on 28 February 2001, at para. 7.54).

4.544 Noting the provisions in paragraph 3 of Annex II, the panel went on to find:

> Particularly where information is actually submitted in time to be verified, and actually could be verified, we consider that it should generally be accepted, unless to do so would impede the ability of the investigating authority to complete the investigation within the time limits established by the Agreement (Panel Report, *United States - Anti-Dumping Measures on Certain Hot-Rolled Steel Products from Japan,* WT/DS184/R, circulated on 28 February 2001, at para. 7.55).

4.545 The panel then determined that an unbiased and objective investigating authority could not have reached the conclusion that the company concerned had failed to provide necessary information within a reasonable period. On this basis, the panel concluded that DOC had acted inconsistently with Article 6.8 in applying facts available in making its dumping determination.

4.546 In the ceramic tiles investigation, the DCD final dumping determination states that DCD received responses from the four firms in the agreed sample of respondent exporters on 10 December 1998. While this was one day later than the deadline, the information was clearly submitted within a "reasonable period" in terms of Article 6.8. Since the purpose of timely submission is to enable the authorities to verify the information and complete their investigation in a timely manner, if DCD did not conduct any verification then Argentina cannot now claim that it had a right to disregard this information, to give equal status to unverified allegations by the petitioner or to give such allegations any status at all in its investigation. In consequence, it appears that Argentina's treatment of information on normal values was inconsistent with Article 6.8 and Annex II of the AD Agreement.

4.547 The EC first written submission notes that paragraph 6 of Annex II of the AD Agreement provides that if evidence or information is not accepted, the party supplying it should be informed "forthwith" of the reasons for the refusal to accept, and should be given an opportunity to provide further explanations within a "reasonable period;" if the authorities consider these explanations as not being satisfactory, the reasons for the rejection of such evidence or information should be given in any published determination.

4.548 According to the EC, the DCD never informed the exporters at any time during the investigation that the information they had supplied on normal value and export prices had been disregarded. In this case, if DCD did not verify this information, in spite of the fact that the four firms had consented in advance to verification, the firms were reasonably entitled to assume that DCD was satisfied with the information and would rely entirely on it in its dumping calculations. The DCD final dumping determination provides no explanation of why DCD failed to rely entirely on the information submitted when it computed the normal values in this case. Moreover, *Resolución* 1385/99 provides no explanation at all of the basis on which the normal values therein were derived, what factors were taken into account or what treatment was accorded to the information received from the four exporters in the agreed sample.

4.549 Article 6.8 of the AD Agreement specifically requires that the provisions of Annex II be observed. Respect for the provisions of Annex II is not only an obligation itself, since (under Article 18.7) Annex II is an integral part of the AD Agreement; it is also a limiting condition on recourse to Article 6.8. If the facts are as alleged by the EC, then DCD's failure to inform the four exporters that their information would not be taken into account, its failure to accord them opportunities to supply more information, and its failure to publish any explanation why DCD did not wholly rely on the submitted information would therefore appear to constitute not only violations of Annex II, but additional reasons why this determination was in violation of Article 6.8.

(b) Arguments of Japan in its Oral Statement Relating to the EC's Claim under Article 6.8 of the AD Agreement

4.550 In its oral statement, Japan made the following arguments relating to the EC's claim under Article 6.8 of the AD Agreement.

4.551 The parties to this dispute disagree concerning whether the Italian respondents cooperated fully with Argentina's investigation. It is for the Panel to determine the facts of this case and to apply the appropriate burden of proof. However, Japan has a few further legal points on Annex II and Article 6.8.

(i) Information Requested in the Questionnaire

4.552 Argentina claims that the questionnaire responses received by DCD were non-responsive because the Italian producers did not provide supporting documentation for their home market sales. However, if DCD requested that respondents submit complete documentation for each such sale reported, this request goes well beyond any reasonable demand on the respondent. Checking documentary proof for transactions is for the verification process, not for the questionnaire. Submissions are verified by reviewing a sample of invoices during an on-the-spot investigation.

4.553 Paragraph 3 of Annex II requires the investigating authority to take into account "all information which is verifiable." As the panel in *Guatemala - Cement (II)* found, "'best information available' should not be used when information is 'verifiable,' and when 'it can be used in the investigation without undue difficulties'" (Panel Report, *Guatemala - Definitive Anti-Dumping Measures on Grey Portland Cement from Mexico*, WT/DS156/R, adopted 17 November 2000, at para. 8.252).

4.554 Respondents' alleged failure to provide supporting documentation in questionnaire responses does not mean the information they submitted was not verifiable, since the sales information could have been verified by conducting an on-the-spot investigation in Italy under Article 6.7. If Argentina chose not to conduct such an investigation, for reasons that did not relate to any action by the respondents unreasonably impeding the investigation, Argentina cannot now claim the information was not "verifiable." Moreover, under paragraph 5 of Annex II, if the EC provides a prima facie case that the Italian respondents did act to the best of their ability, then Argentina was not justified in rejecting the information that the respondents did supply, unless Argentina can rebut that prima facie case.

(ii) Demands to Waive Claims of Confidential Status

4.555 Argentina's first written submission discusses in paragraphs 20-21, 25-27 and 30-42 correspondence in which DCD appears to have demanded that Italian respondents waive claims of confidential status for certain sensitive information. Argentina appears to have taken the position that DCD could only make a final determination based on non-confidential information, and if DCD did not have the respondents' information in non-confidential form, then DCD was entitled to proceed on the basis of the "facts available."

4.556 This position is legally unfounded (and unusual). Antidumping authorities in many Members reach and announce final dumping determinations based strictly on information submitted in confidence. The provisions on public notice in Article 12.2 of the AD Agreement specifically defer to the "requirement for the protection of confidential information"(see Articles 12.2.1, 12.2.2, and 12.2.3). Article 6.5 of the AD Agreement recognizes that antidumping investigations necessarily concern issues and data deeply sensitive to interested parties from a business standpoint, and requires authorities to keep such information confidential. A recent Appellate Body report on *Thailand-H Beams* also made clear that the AD Agreement "permits an investigating authority making an injury determination to base its determination on all relevant reasoning and facts before it", inclusive of the confidential information (Appellate Body Report, *Thailand - Anti-Dumping Duties on Angles, Shapes and Sections of Iron or Non-Alloy Steel and H-Beams from Poland,* WT/DS122/AB/R, adopted 5 April 2001, at para. 111).

4.557 Article 6.5.1 requires the investigating authority to require interested parties submitting confidential information to furnish non-confidential summaries or to provide a statement of the reasons why summarization is not possible (Panel Report, *Guatemala - Definitive Anti-Dumping Measures on Grey Portland Cement from Mexico*, WT/DS156/R, adopted 17 November 2000, at para. 8.213). However, it only requires that the non-confidential summary must "be in sufficient detail to permit a reasonable understanding of the substance of the information submitted in confidence" (for instance, if a respondent submits a series of prices, its non-confidential summary could present the numerical information in grouped form, or in terms of indices or ranges, or approximate figures). If an investigating authority demands that the respondent submit a summary disclosing the essence of what is confidential in the information submitted, the investigating authority is not requesting a non-confidential summary under Article 6.5.1, but is violating its duties under Article 6.5.

4.558 Article 6.5.1 also recognizes that some information is not susceptible of summary. For instance, customer lists may well not be susceptible of summary, whether submitted by a respondent in a dumping investigation, or by a petitioner in an injury investigation. In *Guatemala - Cement (II)*, at para. 8.211, the panel found that information of the following sort is "not generally capable of summarization 'in sufficient detail to permit a reasonable understanding of the substance": technical information on Cementos Progreso's principal equipment, a contract between Cementos Progreso and F.L. Smith & Co., and tables used to prepare questionnaires and reconcile the cost structure calculated for production of grey portland cement with the accounting statements.

4.559 Article 6.5.2 provides that if the authorities find that a request for confidentiality is not warranted, *and* if the supplier is unwilling either to make the information in question public or to authorize its disclosure in generalized or summary form, the authorities may disregard the information unless it is demonstrated that the information is correct. However, footnote 18 provides that Members may not act in an arbitrary manner with regard to requests for confidentiality, and Article 6.5.1 recognizes that some requests for confidentiality are genuinely warranted, in situations where information is "by nature confidential" under Article 6.5, and the information submitted to the authorities is genuinely not capable of summary. In such a case, an unbiased and objective investigating authority could not find that a request for confidentiality is not warranted, and it could not force a respondent to choose between disclosing company secrets to its competitors and being subjected to "best information available." As the panel in *Guatemala - Cement (II)* found, "the Antidumping Agreement does not require cooperation by interested parties at any cost. Although there are certain consequences (under Article 6.8) for interested parties if they fail to cooperate with an investigating authority, in our view such consequences only arise if the investigating authority itself has acted in a reasonable, objective and impartial manner" (Panel Report, *Guatemala - Definitive Anti-Dumping Measures on Grey Portland Cement from Mexico* (WT/DS156/R), adopted 17 November 2000, at para. 8.251).

(iii) Consequences Following from Article 6.5.2

4.560 Argentina also mischaracterizes the legal consequences when investigating authorities may disregard information under Article 6.5.2. The authorities may not disregard the information if it can be "demonstrated to their satisfaction from appropriate sources that the information is correct," and they remain subject to Article 6.6 of the AD Agreement, which applies except in circumstances provided for under Article 6.8 (on Article 6.6, see Panel Report, *Guatemala - Definitive Anti-Dumping Measures on Grey Portland Cement from Mexico* (WT/DS156/R), adopted 17 November 2000, at para. 8.172).

4.561 Argentina appears to argue in paragraph 20 that failure to submit a non-confidential summary *ipso facto* impedes the antidumping investigation, creates circumstances provided for in Article 6.8, and thereby authorizes the investigating authority to make determinations on the basis of the "facts available". This argument must be rejected.

4.562 Failure to submit a non-confidential summary does not impede an investigation by the antidumping authorities in the meaning of Article 6.8. The antidumping authorities are fully capable of drawing conclusions based on the confidential information if it can be demonstrated to their satisfaction from appropriate sources that it is correct. Therefore, even if lack of a non-confidential summary impedes access to information by other interested parties, this is still not a basis for finding that the investigation has been impeded in the sense of Article 6.8.

4.563 Thus, an investigating authority cannot automatically go to "facts available" even if an interested party failed to comply with Article 6.5.1 (though such is not the case with the Italian respondents in this investigation). That argument dangerously confuses two different concepts within Article 6, and compromises the rights of respondents under the AD Agreement. The panel must reject it.

4.564 It is for the Panel to probe the facts of this case, which appear so differently in the presentations of the two parties. However, the Panel might raise the following issues:

- Argentina argues in paragraph 22 that failure to supply information in US$ constitutes a lack of cooperation. Historical US dollar and Italian lira exchange rates are a matter of public record. Why was Argentina unable to perform this calculation on its own? Does a failure to provide data converted into US$ justify use of entirely different data?
- In paragraph 50, Argentina seems to imply that because the sales in a sample were less than 2 per cent of total Italian domestic market sales, the sample was *ipso facto* unreliable for determining normal value. This argument is wrong. The AD Agreement recognizes that there may be some antidumping investigations with very large numbers of exporters and importers (such as cases involving horticultural products). Article 6.10 provides for use in such situations of "samples which are statistically valid on the basis of information available to the authorities at the time of the selection." The legal requirement is that the sample must be statistically valid, not that it must meet or exceed some arbitrary minimum percentage of the universe sampled.

4. *Third Parties: Turkey*

(a) Arguments of Turkey in its Written Submission Relating to the EC's Claim under Article 6.8 of the AD Agreement

4.565 In its written submission, Turkey made the following arguments relating to the EC's claim under Article 6.8 of the AD Agreement.

(i) Facts Available

4.566 The EC submits that Argentina acted inconsistently with Article 6.8 and Annex II of the AD Agreement by disregarding the normal value and export price information provided by the Italian exporters and substituting information from other sources, including the petitioner. The EC, further contends that, Article 6.8 and Annex II of the AD Agreement, only allow the investigating authorities to resort to "facts available" in those cases where the exporters do not provide timely necessary information or significantly impede the investigation.

4.567 Turkey submits that the wording of Article 6.8 makes clear the circumstances under which an investigating authority may have resort to the "facts available" provisions of the AD Agreement. If an interested party "refuses access to" necessary information within a reasonable period, "otherwise does not provide" necessary information within a reasonable period, or "significantly impedes the investigation" the investigating authority may make determinations on the basis of the facts available.

4.568 Turkey considers that, taking into account the above mentioned conditions, the investigating authorities shall avoid the discretionary implementation of "facts available" and given the provisions of paragraph 5 of Annex II, shall refrain from disregarding the information of the parties, provided that it is timely and the interested party had acted to its best ability. Recourse to facts available should not be punitive, instead the authorities should implement it with due caution to supply the lacking information not made available to them by the interested parties.

4.569 Turkey further submits that, investigating authorities are not free to choose between information supplied by the parties without giving any reason and any opportunity to respondents to provide explanations. On the contrary, the authorities may use information other than that supplied by the interested parties, only if they "have to" and "with special circumspection" as required by the provisions of paragraph 7 of Annex II. Thus, this Article does not give the authority the right to choose between the primary and secondary source of information, contrariwise limits the usage of information from a secondary source.

4.570 Moreover, it is also worth noting that paragraph 3 of Annex II, provides that, "All information which is verifiable, which is appropriately submitted so that it can be used in the investigation without undue difficulties, which is supplied in a timely fashion, (...) should be taken into account when determinations are made." Particularly, as stated clearly in this Article, where information is actually submitted in a timely fashion and is verifiable, Turkey considers that it should be accepted, unless doing so prevents the timely completion of the investigation.

(ii) Failure to Inform the Interested Parties that their Information Was Rejected

4.571 The EC submits that, the Argentinean authorities had acted inconsistently with paragraph 6 of Annex II of the AD Agreement by failing to explain the reasons of rejection of the information provided by the respondents.

4.572 Turkey submits that paragraph 6 of Annex II clearly sets forth the obligation of the investigating authority to inform the interested party of the reasons of rejection and grant them an opportunity to provide further explanations within a reasonable period.

4.573 In Turkey's view failure to do so, should be deemed to impair the right of defence of respondents and be inconsistent with the provisions of the paragraph 6 of Annex II.

(b) Arguments of Turkey in its Oral Statement Relating to the EC's Claim under Article 6.8 of the AD Agreement

4.574 In its oral statement, Turkey made the following arguments relating to the EC's claim under Article 6.8 of the AD Agreement.

(i) Facts Available

4.575 Considering the first issue, Turkey's submission, in general, covered Turkey's understanding of the requirements of Article 6.8 and Annex II.

4.576 In this respect, Turkey submits that, although conditions for recourse to facts available is mentioned in Article 6.8 in connection with Annex II, rising number of members are using this provision in many cases to create artificial dumping margins.

4.577 Turkey considers that, the wording of Article 6.8, puts forward the only cases where the investigating authorities may make use of the facts available.

4.578 Only where, the interested parties, "refuses access to" or "doesn't provide necessary information" "within a reasonable period" or "significantly impedes the investigation", authorities may recourse to "facts available" and preliminary and final determinations affirmative or negative may be made on such basis. This explicit wording in Article 6.8 and other paragraphs of both Article 6 and Annex II, leave no room for misinterpretations and they actually demonstrate that the preference should be given by the authorities to make use of "actual information" obtained in the course of the investigation and determined to be accurate.

4.579 In this respect, in accordance with paragraph 3 of Annex II, the investigating authorities, when making determinations are required to take into account all information which is verifiable and supplied in a timely fashion, appropriately submitted so that it can be used in the investigation without undue difficulties.

4.580 Likewise, paragraph 7 of Annex II, explicitly puts forward the conditions "have to" and "special circumspection" referring to the usage of information from a secondary source which, in other words, limits the freedom of substitution of the information supplied by the respondents.

4.581 Furthermore, paragraph 1 of Annex II, for use of "facts available" and in particular, information in the application, puts forward the condition if information is not supplied within a "reasonable time".

4.582 To sum up, generally speaking, authorities recourse to "facts available" in an investigation should not be of punitive feature. Thus, Turkey submits that, in any given case where information submitted is not lacking or misleading and timely submitted so that it can be verified, should be dealt with.

4.583 Nevertheless, considering the EC's submission, it appears to Turkey in this case that the investigating authorities' recourse to "facts available" is not justified, taking into account the above mentioned reasons and EC's submission which states that the responses of the parties concerned were sufficient, verifiable and timely submitted.

(ii) Failure to Inform the Interested Parties that their Information Were Rejected

4.584 Turkey views the provisions of paragraph 6 of Annex II as an important element for proper conduction of anti-dumping investigations. It is deemed essential for proper functioning of a healthy decision making process by the authorities and, on part of interested parties, for predictability and transparency of decisions taken. Considering the growing number of new investigations initiated, the vitality of the very function of this provision becomes even more important.

4.585 In this regard, Turkey submits that this paragraph clearly sets forth the obligation of the investigating authority to inform the interested party of the reasons of rejection and grant them an opportunity to provide further explanations within a reasonable period.

4.586 Turkey considers that, failure to inform the interested parties that their information were rejected may be deemed to be violation of right of defence of the respondent. As a matter of fact, this provision should be dealt together with Article 6.8, since in many cases recourse to facts available comes along with such practice.

4.587 From the respondent's point of view, having not received any notice of rejection, one may consider that, its own information was deemed sufficient for the purposes of investigation, thus may not necessarily be in need of supplying further explanatory information or supporting evidence to the authority. Eventually, the respondent might be informed about the rejection of its information at the final disclosure stage, at the earliest, which would significantly limit its right to defend.

4.588 Turkey concludes that, as alleged by the EC, if the exporters own information was not used and exporters were not timely informed of such practice and reasons thereby, this behavior may well be deemed inconsistent not only with paragraph 6 of Annex II but also with Article 6.8 of the Agreement.

5. *Third Parties: The United States*

(a) Arguments of the United States in its Written Submission Relating to the EC's Claim under Article 6.8 of the AD Agreement

4.589 In its written submission, the US made the following arguments relating to the EC's claim under Article 6.8 of the AD Agreement.

4.590 The EC claims that, by disregarding the exporters' information without valid justification, Argentina acted inconsistently with Article 6.8 and Annex II of the AD Agreement, which only allows the use of "facts available" in those cases where an interested party does not provide timely information or significantly impedes the investigation. Argentina asserts that it fully complied with Article 6.8 of the AD Agreement because its application of "facts available" in this case was justified by the exporters' failure to provide necessary information in the time and form required.

4.591 Paragraph 6 of Annex II of the AD Agreement places an obligation on the investigating authority to inform an interested party in a timely manner when the investigating authority intends to reject the party's information and to provide the reasons therefor. Paragraph 6 of Annex II also states that the investigating authority should allow the party an opportunity to provide further explanations, due account being taken of the time limits of the investigation.

4.592 The United States is not familiar with the underlying facts of this case and, therefore, cannot comment on whether the letters to the exporters cited by Argentina in its first written submission satisfy Argentina's obligations under Annex II, paragraph 6. However, in the view of the United States, the purpose of the requirement that parties be informed if their information is not accepted is the same as the purpose behind Article 6.9, namely, to ensure that parties are able to defend their interests. Thus, any notice informing the parties of the reasons their information is not accepted must be sufficiently explicit to put the parties on notice that they must provide further explanation as contemplated by paragraph 6 of Annex II.

4.593 The United States did not address in its oral statement the EC's claim under Article 6.8 of the AD Agreement.

B. *Claim under Article 6.10 of the AD Agreement*

1. The EC

(a) Arguments of the EC in its First Written Submission in Support of its Claim under Article 6.10 of the AD Agreement

4.594 In its first written submission, the EC made the following arguments relating to its claim under Article 6.10 of the AD Agreement.

4.595 The EC first presented the facts relevant to its claim under Article 6.10.

4.596 In spite of agreeing to the sampling proposed by Assopiastrelle, the DCD did not determine an individual margin of dumping for each of the four exporters included in the sample.

4.597 Instead, as explained earlier, the DCD calculated two dumping margins for each size category of *porcellanato* by using mainly data supplied by the petitioner and official import statistics. *Resolución* 1385/99 then imposed the same duty rate on all imports of *porcellanato* falling within each size category, irrespective of the exporter.

4.598 The EC then presented its legal arguments relating to this claim.

4.599 The EC recalled that Article 6.10 of the AD Agreement requires that:

> The authorities shall, as a rule, determine an individual margin of dumping for each known exporter or producer concerned of the product under investigation. In cases where the number of exporters, producers, importers or types of products involved is so large as to make such determination impracticable, the authorities may limit their examination either to a reasonable number of interested parties or products by using samples which are statistically valid on the basis of information available to the authorities at the time of the selection, or to the largest percentage of the volume of the exports from the country in question which can be reasonably investigated.

4.600 Thus, in accordance with Article 6.10, the investigating authorities must, "as a rule", determine an individual dumping margin for each known producer or exporter concerned. By way of exception to that rule, where the number of producers and exporters concerned is so large as to make such determination "impracticable", the investigating authorities may limit their examination to some of them. In such case, nevertheless, the investigating authorities must determine an individual dumping margin for each of the producers or exporters included in the examination.

4.601 Where the investigating authorities have made a selection of producers/exporters in accordance with the second sentence of Article 6.10, they cannot pretend that the determination of individual margins for each of those producers/exporters would be "impracticable". Indeed, the very purpose of the selection is to make "practicable" such determination. Therefore, in those circumstances, there can be no valid justification to depart from the general rule set out in the first sentence of Article 6.10 with respect to those exporters.

4.602 The above is confirmed by Article 6.10.2 of the AD Agreement, which provides that:

> In cases where the authorities have limited their examination, as provided for in this paragraph, they shall nevertheless determine an individual dumping margin of dumping for any exporter or producer *not initially selected* who submits the necessary information in time to be considered during the course of the investigation, except where the number of exporters or producers is so large that individual examinations would be unduly burdensome to the authorities and prevent the timely completion of the investigation. Voluntary responses shall not be discouraged (emphasis added by the EC).

4.603 This presupposes that the investigating authorities are required to determine individual margins for each of the producers/exporters "initially selected". Otherwise, it would have been illogical to allow the "not initially selected" producers/exporters to request the determination of individual dumping margins in accordance with Article 6.10.2, and not to give the same opportunity to the "initially selected" producers/exporters.

4.604 Further confirmation is provided by Article 9.4, which stipulates that, where the investigating authorities have limited their examination in accordance with the second sentence of paragraph 10 of Article 6, any anti-dumping duty applied to imports from exporters not included in the examination shall not exceed:

> (a) the weighted average margin of dumping established with respect to the selected exporters or producers, or
>
> (b) where the liability for payment of anti-dumping duties is calculated on the basis of prospective normal values, the difference between the weighted average normal value of the selected exporters or producers and the exporters not individually examined.

4.605 The calculation of a weighted average dumping margin or of a weighted average [prospective] normal value presupposes necessarily that individual dumping margins or individual prospective normal values, respectively, have been determined first for each of the selected producers/exporters.

4.606 Article 9.4 further states that:

> ... the authorities shall disregard for the purposes of this paragraph any zero and *de minimis* margin*s* and margin*s* established under the circumstances referred to in paragraph 8 of Article 6 (emphasis added by the EC).

4.607 Again, this presupposes that individual dumping margins have been determined previously for each selected producer/exporter.

4.608 The Argentinean authorities agreed to make a selection of exporters in accordance with Article 6.10. Therefore, they were required to determine an individual margin of dumping for each of the four selected exporters. By failing to do so, and by calculating instead a single dumping margin for all the Italian producers/exporters, the Argentinean authorities acted inconsistently with Article 6.10.

(b) Arguments of the EC in its First Oral Statement in Support of its Claim under Article 6.10 of the AD Agreement

4.609 In its first oral statement, the EC made the following arguments in support of its claim under Article 6.10 of the AD Agreement.

4.610 The EC recalls that Article 6.10 provides that the investigating authorities must, "as a rule", determine an individual dumping margin for each known producer or exporter concerned. By way of exception, where the number of exporters is so large as to make such determination "impracticable", the investigating authorities may limit their examination to some exporters. In such case, nevertheless, the investigating authorities must still determine an individual dumping margin for each of the exporters included in the examination.

4.611 In the present case, the DCD decided to limit the examination of dumping to four Italian exporters. Therefore, the DCD was required by Article 6.10 to determine an individual margin of dumping for each of the four selected exporters. Yet the DCD calculated a single dumping margin for all the Italian producers/exporters, including those in the sample. By doing so, the DCD acted inconsistently with Article 6.10.

4.612 In its first written submission, Argentina argues that the information supplied by the exporters included in the sample did not allow the DCD to calculate individual dumping margins for those exporters. This is simply not correct.

4.613 Argentina does not say why the DCD could not have calculated an individual dumping margin for Casalgrande.

4.614 In the case of Bismantova, Argentina alleges that part of its domestic sales were made to a related party (Rondine). But this is not a valid ground for resorting to "facts available". At most, it could have been a reason for calculating Bismantova's normal value on the basis of the constructed value or of the export prices to third countries (see Article 2.2 of the AD Agreement).

4.615 It is true that Caesar only made export sales to Argentina of 40 cm x 40 cm tiles. But the product under investigation was ceramic tiles and not each of the three size categories defined by the DCD. Accordingly, the DCD was required to establish the existence of dumping for the product under investigation as a whole, and not for each single size category (Appelate Body Report, *EC-Anti-Dumping Duties on Imports of Cotton Type Bed Linen from India*, WT/DS141/AB/R, adopted 12 March 2001, at para. 53). Thus, the DCD could, and indeed should have calculated an individual dumping of margin for Caesar in respect of the product under investigation as a whole based on Caesar's export sales of 40 cm x 40 cm tiles.

4.616 Finally, it is not correct that Marazzi submitted no price information.

4.617 The point which Argentina tries to make at paragraphs 115-122 of its first written submission is difficult to grasp. Argentina appears to be arguing, once again, that the sample was not representative. However, this argument is clearly irrelevant in this context. Assuming that the sample were in fact not representative, that could not justify to resort to "facts available" for the exporters included in the sample.

4.618 Finally, Argentina contends that the violation of Article 6.10 would be a "harmless error" (*error inocuo*) since the EC has not demonstrated that it caused a prejudice to the exporters concerned. For the reasons set out by the panel in *Guatemala - Cement (II)*, the EC considers that this is not a valid defence under the WTO Agreement (Panel Report, *Guatemala - Definitive Anti-Dumping Measures on Grey Portland Cement from Mexico*, WT/DS156/R, adopted 17 November 2000, at para. 8.22.). In accordance with Article 3.8 of the DSU, all violations of the WTO Agreement are presumed to cause nullification or impairment. It is for Argentina to rebut that presumption.

(c) Replies of the EC to the First Set of Questions by the Panel Relating to the EC's Claim under Article 6.10 of the AD Agreement

4.619 The EC replied to the first set of questions made by the Panel relating to the EC's claim under Article 6.10 of the AD Agreement as follows.

4.620 The Panel recalled that Argentina argued that the questionnaire responses submitted by the exporters were incomplete since in many cases the exporters failed to report home sales of certain size categories. The Panel asked Argentina to clarify which exporters failed to provide what kinds of home sales? The Panel further asked Argentina to explain whether the exporters concerned made home sales in every size category during the period of investigation. If they did not, the Panel asked whether Argentina contended that the calculation of dumping margins for the product under investigation required the calculation of dumping margins for every size category devised by the DCD.

4.621 To this question, the EC provided the following reply.

4.622 Many models sold in Italy were not exported to Argentina, or only so in small quantities. The exporters reported in their responses all the domestic sales of each of the models that were exported to Argentina in significant quantities.

4.623 In a few cases where a model exported to Argentina was not sold profitably in Italy or where the domestic sales represented less than 5 per cent of the export sales to Argentina, the exporters reported the export sales of that model to third countries, as required by the questionnaire. In addition, the exporters supplied the cost of production for each of the reported models.

4.624 All the models exported to Argentina by Caesar were of 40 cm x 40 cm. Caesar did not report the domestic sales of other models, since that information was not required in order to make a model-to-model comparison. The other exporters reported domestic sales for models of the three size categories.

4.625 The Panel asked the parties whether there was a legal link between Article 6.8 of the AD Agreement and Article 6.10 AD Agreement. Assuming that an investigating authority was justified in using facts available, the Panel further asked whether in the view of the parties Article 6.10 of the AD Agreement nevertheless required an investigating authority to always determine an individual margin of dumping for each exporter included in the sample.

4.626 The EC replied that it was obvious that if the dumping margins for all the exporters included in the sample were based entirely on "facts available", and if those facts were the same for all the exporters concerned, the dumping margin would also be the same.

(d) Replies of the EC to the Questions Made by Argentina, Following the First Meeting of the Panel with the Parties, that Relate to the EC's Claim under Article 6.10 of the AD Agreement

4.627 Argentina made one question to the EC in connection to the EC's claim under Article 6.10 of the AD Agreement. In particular, Argentina asked the EC to clarify its statement to the effect that the DCD "was required to establish the existence of dumping for the product under investigation as a whole and not for each single size category", in spite of the fact that the EC recognized that Caesar had exported tiles corresponding to the 40x40 category.

4.628 The EC replied that the existence of dumping must be established for the product under investigation as a whole. The product under investigation in this case was ceramic tiles, and not each of the size categories. Caesar's dumping margin for the product under investigation could have been calculated by comparing the export price for its exports of models of 40 cm x 40 cm to the domestic prices for the same models.

(e) Arguments of the EC in its Second Written Submission in Support of its Claim under Article 6.10 of the AD Agreement

4.629 In its second written submission, the EC made the following arguments in support of its claim under Article 6.10 of the AD Agreement.

4.630 In its first written submission, Argentina argues that the information supplied by the selected exporters did not allow the DCD to calculate individual dumping margins for those exporters. This argument is totally unfounded.

4.631 Argentina does not explain why it was not possible to calculate an individual dumping margin for Casalgrande.

4.632 As regards Bismantova, Argentina alleges that part of its domestic sales were made to a related party (Rondine). But this is not a valid ground for resorting to "facts available". At most, it could have been a reason for calculating Bismantova's normal value on the basis of the constructed value or of the export prices to third countries using the information provided by that exporter (see Article 2.2. of the AD Agreement).

4.633 All the models exported to Argentina by Caesar were of 40 cm x 40 cm. For that reason, Caesar did not report domestic sales of models of 20 cm x 20 cm or of 30 cm x cm. But this did not prevent the DCD from calculating an individual dumping margin for Caesar. The product under investigation were ceramic tiles and not each of the three size categories defined by the DCD. Accordingly, the DCD was required to establish the existence of dumping for the product under investigation as whole, and not for each single size category (Appellate Body Report, *EC - Anti-Dumping Duties on Imports of Cotton Type Bed Linen from India*, WT/DS141/AB/R, adopted 12 March 2001, at para. 53). Thus, the DCD could, and indeed was required to calculate an individual dumping of margin for Caesar in respect of the product under investigation as a whole based on Caesar's export sales of 40 cm x 40 cm tiles.

4.634 Finally, it is not correct that Marazzi submitted no price information.

4.635 Argentina further contends that the violation of Article 6.10 would, in any event, be a "harmless error" ("*error inocuo*") since the EC has not demonstrated that it caused a prejudice to the exporters concerned. For the reasons set out by the panel in *Guatemala - Cement (II)*, the EC considers that this is not valid defence under the WTO Agreement (Panel Report, *Guatemala - Definitive Anti-Dumping Measures on Grey Portland Cement from Mexico* (WT/DS156/R), adopted 24 October 2000, at para. 8.22). In accordance with Article 3.8 of the DSU, all violations of the WTO Agreement are presumed to cause nullification or impairment. It is for Argentina to rebut that presumption.

4.636 In its second oral statement, the EC did not address its claim under Article 6.10 of the AD Agreement.

4.637 The Panel did not ask the EC any questions following the second meeting relating to the EC's claim under Article 6.10 of the AD Agreement.

2. *Argentina*

(a) Arguments of Argentina in its First Written Submission Relating to the EC's Claim under Article 6.10 of the AD Agreement

4.638 In its first written submission, Argentina made the following arguments relating to the EC's claim under Article 6.10 of the AD Agreement.

4.639 Argentina first presented a number of facts relevant for its arguments.

4.640 The EC argument concerning the failure to calculate an individual dumping margin for each producer is based on the erroneous hypothesis that the authority was in a position to make such a calculation using the elements at its disposal. To a certain extent the EC would seem, on the one hand, to be demanding what its own producers requested, i.e. that the authority work on the basis of the sample provided, while on the other hand blaming Argentina when the information contained in the sample was insufficient and it was impossible to determine an individual margin of dumping for each exporter.

4.641 In discussing Article 6.8, Argentina explained at length that Assopiastrelle itself had asked that the sample should be considered as representative of the Italian ceramics industry. In the same chapter, it pointed out the shortcomings of the sample as a valid tool to calculate normal value. The sample also suffered from shortcomings as a basis for calculating the margin of dumping for each firm.

4.642 The most notorious shortcomings which made it impossible to calculate an individual margin of dumping for each firm are as follows:

(a) 30 x 30 ceramic tiles:

Two companies in the sample (Caesar and Marazzi) failed to provide any information on average prices for this category.

In the case of Bismantova, it was found that 56 per cent of sales on the domestic market were to its controlling company, Rondine.

(b) 20 x 20 ceramic tiles:

The same two companies failed to provide any information for this category.

(c) 40 x 40 ceramic tiles:

The company Marazzi failed to provide any information for this category either.

In the case of Bismantova, it was found that 91 per cent of sales on the domestic market were to its controlling company, Rondine.

4.643 This lack of information in itself makes it impossible to calculate the individual margin of dumping for the company Marazzi in any of the three categories and for Caesar in categories 30 x 30 and 20 x 20. In the case of Bismantova, the high percentage of sales in abnormal trading conditions made it impossible to calculate the margin of dumping for the categories 30 x 30 and 40 x 40.

4.644 In other words, the sample, as such, could not serve to determine the margins of dumping for each company either.

4.645 Argentina presented next a number of legal arguments concerning the EC's claim under Article 6.10 of the AD Agreement.

4.646 Firstly, due account should be taken, as stressed throughout the investigation, of the large number of exporters involved. Indeed, Assopiastrelle listed 205 producers, of which 78 were apparently exporters of the product investigated.

4.647 This justifies, under Article 6.10 of the Agreement, the decision to make a determination on the basis of the sample procedure. Moreover, the sample used was put forward by Assopiastrelle, acting as representative of the Italian manufacturing firms, in view of the large number of manufacturing enterprises involved. In this connection, the presentation by Assopiastrelle of the "methodology for the selection of samples" states, *inter alia*, that "On behalf of the Italian manufacturers of *porcellanato,* Assopiastrelle suggested limiting the supply of information on dumping and injury to a sample considered representative of all of the companies". It goes on to state that "The purpose of Assopiastrelle's proposal was to ensure greater cooperation by the Italian industry concerned and at the same time to simplify the task of the authorities investigating the Italian producers".

4.648 This statement by the Association clearly shows that for the purposes of calculating the margin of dumping, the sample is claimed to be a valid methodology.

4.649 In reply to the proposal submitted by Assopiastrelle, the DCD, by Note No. 273-000471/98, wrote to the Economic and Trade Advisor of the Italian Embassy in Argentina as follows:

> However, according to the information received, we are faced with an investigation involving a large number of Italian exporters, and would therefore like to limit the procedure to the few Italian companies representing most of Italian exports to Argentina.

4.650 In this connection it was pointed out that:

> ... the implementing authority, pursuant to Article 6.10 ... may resort to statistically representative samples for the purposes of determining the margin of dumping in the investigation. Similarly, in order to apply this procedure, the consent of the exporters concerned is needed as long as the conclusions reached would have to be extended to the other firms that were not included in the selection.
>
> While the investigation should extend to all firms which have exported to Argentina from the investigated origin during the period concerned, for purely methodological purposes, the analysis should be confined to a representative number of exporters of the goods involved.

4.651 The note concluded by stating that "having received the express consent of the firms, we shall proceed as stated, subject to the relevant legislation in force".

4.652 Thus, there is on the one hand a recognition by the EC of the validity of a selection or sample as a basis for determining the margin of dumping. It cannot be inferred from the acceptance of the sample that if the sample did not serve the proposed purpose, the authority had no alternative. In other words, either the authority calculates a margin of dumping for all of the companies exporting to Argentina beyond the sample, which would clearly be unreasonable since the very purpose of the sample was to avoid such a situation, or it uses another alternative to make up for the shortcoming.

4.653 The sample did not, as such, serve the purpose, and the authority therefore warned of the possibility of "using samples which are statistically valid on the basis of information available to the authorities at the time of the selection" (Article 6.10). This became necessary in order to complete the missing information. The exporting firms were certainly not left defenceless and could have protested against the note or asked the authority to reconsider its approach; or they could have provided the missing information, thereby enabling the authority to determine a margin of dumping for each firm on the basis of the sample. The exporters did none of this, and legally consented to the approach the authority said it would use in calculating the margin of dumping. It is difficult to see how the situation that the exporters themselves contributed to creating can now be invoked against the DCD, proposing a sample that could not be used for the purpose put forward.

4.654 In any case, even if despite the above considerations Argentina is deemed to have deviated from the requirements of Article 6.10 of the AD Agreement, *quod non*, this would be a case of harmless error, since Argentina could not apply Article 6.10 of the AD Agreement with the supporting information provided by the sample. The error would have been harmless, since the EC did not demonstrate how this situation injured the companies by producing a higher margin of dumping for its exports. In fact, the EC did not even claim that this was the case, but confined itself to arguing that Article 6.10 of the AD Agreement had been violated, thereby tacitly acknowledging that it did not happen.

(b) Arguments of Argentina in its First Oral Statement Relating to the EC's Claim under Article 6.10 of the AD Agreement

4.655 In its first oral statement, the EC made the following arguments relating to the EC's claim under Article 6.10 of the AD Agreement.

4.656 Pursuant to Article 6.10, in particular paragraph 1 thereof, the DCD selected the enterprises that would be the subject of the investigation. To that end, it accepted Assopiastrelle's proposal, as explained in paragraphs 115 and 116 of Argentina's first written submission.

4.657 At the same time, when the implementinng authority, upon opening the investigation, chose as a "homogenization" criterion the segmentation of the tiles on the basis of their size, it distributed the questionnaires prepared accordingly. The firms involved replied to these questionnaires without raising any objections, showing that they accepted the validity of segmentation by size. Nevertheless, a vast majority of the sample documentation provided by the exporting firms did not correspond to the segmentation used by the implementing authority.

4.658 Thus, when the implementing authority had to decide on the elements necessary for the determination of dumping, it found, as explained below, that it did not have the required documentation from the selected companies corresponding to the segmentation of the tiles on the basis of their size.

(i) Characteristics of the Sample

4.659 The fact that the sample companies represented a majority of exports to the Argentine market does not in itself imply that the supporting documentation was representative for each one of the segments selected (20 cm x 20 cm, 30 cm x 30 cm and 40 cm x 40 cm) for the purposes of determining their normal value and export price.

4.660 How could an individual margin of dumping be calculated when the domestic market sales invoices represented only some 1.35 per cent of the value and 1.92 per cent of the physical volume (m^2), as stated earlier on?

4.661 How, also, could the DCD have calculated the margin of dumping for 30 cm x 30 cm tiles from Caesar and Marazzi when these companies failed to submit any information on average prices in the Italian domestic market for that category?

4.662 At the same time, as stated in paragraph 112 of Argentina's first written submission, in the case of Bismantova, 56 per cent of sales on the domestic market were to its controlling company, Rondine; so that without the remaining 44 per cent of the invoices, the calculation would have been somewhat dubious.

4.663 The same doubts arise in the case of Caesar and Marazzi for size 20 cm x 20 cm tiles, for which the firms also failed to provide any information.

4.664 Similarly, Marazzi failed to provide any information concerning the 40 cm x 40 cm. category, while 91 per cent of Bismantova's domestic market sales in that category were made to its controlling company, Rondine. How, then, could the EC have expected the DCD to establish an individual margin of dumping in these cases?

4.665 All this shows that although the DCD had hoped, through the sample methodology, to be able to determine a margin of dumping for each exporter, this proved impossible because the information from the exporters that was available to the DCD when it issued its final determination did not enable it to do so.

4.666 In short, Argentina considers that the EC proceeds from an erroneous hypothesis when it states that the authority was in a position to make the said calculation on the basis of the elements at its disposal, since the only elements that were in fact available were those which the companies had asked to be considered as a sample, and they turned out to be totally insufficient.

4.667 Argentina submits therefore that it did not deviate from the requirements set forth in Article 6.10 of the AD Agreement.

(c) Arguments of Argentina in its Oral Statement at the Third-Party Session of the First Meeting of the Panel with the Parties, Relating to the EC's Claim under Article 6.10 of the AD Agreement

4.668 In its oral statement at the third-party session of the first meeting of the Panel with the parties, and in connection to the EC's claim under Article 6.10 of the AD Agreement, Argentina recalled Japan's statement that the DCD was required to determine individual dumping margins for each of the four selected exporters, since it had accepted the selection of exporters. Argentina argued that this statement failed to recognize the fact that the information in question was insufficient for such a calculation.

(d) Replies of Argentina to the First Set of Questions by the Panel Relating to the EC's Claim under Article 6.10 of the AD Agreement

4.669 Argentina replied to the first set of questions by the Panel relating to the EC's claim under Article 6.10 of the AD Agreement as follows:

4.670 The Panel recalled that Argentina argued that the questionnaire responses submitted by the exporters were incomplete since in many cases the exporters failed to report home sales of certain size categories. The Panel asked Argentina to clarify which exporters failed to provide what kinds of home sales? The Panel further asked Argentina to explain whether the exporters concerned made home sales in every size category during the period of investigation. If they did not, the Panel asked whether Argentina contended that the calculation of dumping margins for the product under investigation required the calculation of dumping margins for every size category devised by the DCD.

4.671 Argentina argued that the questionnaire responses were incomplete since they did not contain sufficient information, as stated in the report on the final determination of the margin of dumping. One thing that was missing was sufficiently detailed supporting documentation on domestic market sales.

4.672 To this question, Argentina provided the following reply.

4.673 To help the Panel understand what domestic market sales information according to size was presented by each exporter, Argentina refers the Panel to the Annex to the Final Determination Report.

4.674 At the same time, Argentina reiterates what was explained in paragraphs 112 and 113 of Argentina's first written submission:

(a) 30 x 30 ceramic tiles:

Two companies in the sample (Caesar and Marazzi) failed to provide any information on average prices for this category.

In the case of Bismantova, it was found that 56 per cent of sales on the domestic market were to its controlling company, Rondine.

(b) 20 x 20 ceramic tiles:

The same two companies failed to provide any information for this category.

(c) 40 x 40 ceramic tiles:

The company Marazzi failed to provide any information for this category.

In the case of Bismantova, it was found that 91 per cent of sales reported for the domestic market were to its controlling company, Rondine.

4.675 This lack of information in itself makes it impossible to calculate the individual margin of dumping for the company Marazzi in any of the three categories and for Caesar in categories 30 x 30 and 20 x 20. In the case of Bismantova, the high percentage of sales in abnormal trading conditions made it impossible to calculate the margin of dumping for the categories 30 x 30 and 40 x 40.

4.676 The implementing authority decided to analyse the product in accordance with the adopted segmentation, 20 x 20, 30 x 30 and 40 x 40, taking account of the elements it had at its disposal. There was no objection to this. The implementing authority expected the selected sample companies to be representative, in terms of their exports, under Article 6.10 of the AD Agreement, and that they would also provide information that would enable it to make a determination of dumping on the basis of the above categories. It is impossible to establish, from the information they supplied, whether or not they in fact sold all the sizes in question on the domestic market. But based on the information in the record of the case, the implementing authority understood that the criterion which would enable it to make a proper determination of dumping was the segmentation of the product under investigation by size.

4.677 Consequently, the DCD had to calculate the margin of dumping of the product under investigation for each one of the size categories analysed.

(e) Arguments of Argentina in its Second Written Submission Relating to the EC's Claim under Article 6.10 of the AD Agreement

4.678 In its second written submission, Argentina made the following arguments relating to the EC's claim under Article 6.10 of the AD Agreement.

4.679 The EC's claim concerning the failure to calculate individual margins of dumping for the exporting firms is based on an erroneous analysis of the elements making up the record which inevitably leads to a mistaken conclusion concerning compliance with Article 6.10.

4.680 Firstly, the EC claims that Article 6.10 has been violated, but analysing the content of the obligation that it claims was violated (" ... determine an individual margin of dumping for each known exporter or producer concerned ..."), it disregards other provisions of the AD Agreement which necessarily condition the interpretation of that provision.

4.681 In other words, the EC speaks of a violation of Article 6.10 that did not occur - since the calculation of the margin of dumping could not take place on the basis of the characteristics of the sample - while at the same time disregarding the determination of the margin of dumping for the product that ultimately served as a basis for adopting the measure, which, for its part, did comply with Article 2 of the AD Agreement. Furthermore, the product was adjusted in order to arrive at a "fair" comparison in conformity with Article 2.4.

4.682 Regarding the first element, i.e. the calculation of the margin of dumping for the product, which is highly relevant to the analysis of the Article 6.10 obligation, in Argentina's view the individual margin of dumping cannot be analysed for each firm outside the context of the calculation of the margin of dumping for the product under investigation. This calculation of the margin of dumping for the product is related to the definition of dumping in Article 2.1 which matches the definition of the product given by the Appellate Body (Appellate Body Report, *European Communities - Anti-Dumping Duties on Imports of Cotton-Type Bed Linen from India*, WT/DS141/AB/R, adopted 12 March 2001, at para. 51).

4.683 This finding of dumping must be made with respect to the product under investigation, i.e. the "product" that is introduced into the commerce of another country at less that its normal value on the market of the exporting country.

4.684 In broaching the subject of Article 6.10, the EC disregards Argentina's argument that the sample proposed by Assopiastrelle being a valid methodology for calculating the margin of dumping, it could not be claimed that when the documentation provided by the sample exporting companies turned out to be insufficient, the Authority was left without any alternative for determining a margin of dumping according to the duly adopted segmentation.

4.685 In this case, the product under investigation was ceramic tiles from Italy, "in all sizes", which includes, specifically, sizes 20 x 20, 30 x 30 and 40 x 40. This type of *porcellanato* makes up 99.29 per cent of imports from the investigated origin comparable to the like domestic product.

4.686 Since the Authority had thus defined the like product, the EC's assertion in paragraph 66 of its oral statement that "the product under investigation was ceramic tiles and not each of the size categories defined by the DCD" is erroneous. It is on the basis of its own definition that the DCD calculated the margin of dumping for each one of the three categories of the product based on the adopted segmentation.

4.687 Having made a calculation of the margin of dumping which was in keeping with its definition of the like product, the authority would have been in a position to proceed with the calculation of the margin for each exporter - Article 6.10 - if it had had the necessary information from the sample that the exporters themselves proposed.

4.688 The sample provided be Assopiastrelle was claimed to be a valid methodology for calculating the margin of dumping. However, as already mentioned on many other occasions, the sample presented a number of shortcomings that made it impossible to calculate an individual margin of dumping for each firm, among which the most significant were the following:

(a) 30 x 30 ceramic tiles: Two companies in the sample (Caesar and Marazzi) failed to provide any information on average prices for this category. In the case of Bismantova, it was found that 56 per cent of sales on the domestic market were to its controlling company, Rondine.

(b) 20 x 20 ceramic tiles: The same two companies failed to provide any information for this category.

(c) 40 x 40 ceramic tiles: The company Marazzi failed to provide any information for this category either. In the case of Bismantova, it was found that 91 per cent of sales on the domestic market were to its controlling company, Rondine.

4.689 This lack of information in itself made it impossible to calculate the individual margin of dumping for the company Marazzi in any of the three categories and for Caesar in categories 30 x 30 and 20 x 20. In the case of Bismantova, the high percentage of sales in abnormal trading conditions made it impossible to calculate the margin of dumping for the categories 30 x 30 and 40 x 40.

4.690 Thus, Argentina does not think that the DCD can be blamed for not having calculated the individual margins of dumping for each exporting firm, since the firms in question did not provide the information needed for that purpose.

4.691 Similarly, Argentina would like to point out that in response to the questionnaires of 30 October 1998, the Argentine representative of Assopiastrelle sent a note dated 12 May 1999 to its principal in which it states that "regarding non-confidential invoices, I suggest to select the same invoices of each segment (20 x 20, 30 x 30, etc.) with prices closer to the weight average of the segment ... ". This note shows once again that the exporters were aware of, and indeed agreed with, the segmentation in question.

(f) Arguments of Argentina in its Second Oral Statement Relating to the EC's Claim under Article 6.10 of the AD Agreement

4.692 In its second oral statement, Argentina made the following arguments relating to the EC's claim under Article 6.10 of the AD Agreement.

4.693 As explained in paragraph 112 of Argentina's first written submission, the information on domestic market sales by size submitted by each exporter was as follows:

(a) 30 x 30 ceramic tiles: two companies in the sample (Caesar and Marazzi) failed to provide any information on average prices. In the case of Bismantova, it was found that 56 per cent of sales on the domestic market were to its controlling company, Rondine.

(b) 20 x 20 ceramic tiles: the same two companies failed to provide any information.

(c) 40 x 40 ceramic tiles: the company Marazzi failed to provide any information for this category either, while in the case of Bismantova, it was found that 91 per cent of sales on the domestic market were to its controlling company, Rondine.

4.694 As stated in paragraph 113 of Argentina's first written submission, this lack of information in itself made it impossible to calculate the individual margin of dumping for the company Marazzi in any of the three categories and for Caesar in categories 30 x 30 and 20 x 20. In the case of Bismantova, the high percentage of sales in abnormal trading conditions made it impossible to calculate the margin of dumping for the categories 30 x 30 and 40 x 40.

4.695 With respect to paragraph 72 of the EC's second written submission and paragraph 66 of its second oral statement, Argentina reiterates that the product under investigation was ceramic tiles from Italy, "in all sizes" which includes, specifically, sizes 20 x 20, 30 x 30 and 40 x 40. As already mentioned, this type of *porcellanato* makes up 99.29 per cent of imports from the investigated origin comparable to the like domestic product.

4.696 Argentina therefore repeats that since the authority had thus defined the like product, the EC's assertion that "the product investigation was ceramic tiles and not each of the size categories defined by the DCD" is erroneous. It is on the basis of its own definition that the DCD calculated the margin of dumping for each one of the three categories of the product based on the adopted segmentation.

4.697 In its reply a question by the Panel following the first meeting, the EC agrees with Argentina's statement that if the implementing authority has to resort to the facts available, the margin of dumping determined will depend on those facts.

4.698 The Panel did not ask Argentina any questions following the second meeting relating to the EC's claim under Article 6.10 of the AD Agreement.

3. *Third Parties: Japan*

(a) Arguments of Japan in its Written Submission Relating to the EC's Claim under Article 6.10 of the AD Agreement

4.699 In its written submission, Japan made the following arguments relating to the EC's claim under Article 6.10 of the AD Agreement.

4.700 The EC submission claims that the Argentine authorities violated Article 6.10 of the AD Agreement by first agreeing to make a selection of exporters and then not determining individual margins of dumping for those four companies which had been selected. Article 6.10 reads as follows:

> The authorities shall, as a rule, determine an individual margin of dumping for each known exporter or producer concerned of the product under investigation.
>
> In cases where the number of exporters, producers, importers or types of products involved is so large as to make such a determination impracticable, the authorities may limit their examination either to a reasonable number of interested parties or products by using

> samples which are statistically valid on the basis of information available to the authorities at the time of the selection, or to the largest percentage of the volume of the exports from the country in question which can reasonably be investigated.

4.701 This provision consists of two sentences. The first sentence requires, as a rule, that the national authorities of a WTO Member calculate individual dumping margins for all producers and exporters of merchandise who are subject to an anti-dumping investigation. The second sentence provides that when there are so many exporters, producers, importers or types of product that calculation of individual margins for each known exporter or producer is impracticable, the national authorities can limit their examination to those firms that account for the largest volume of exports, or alternatively employ statistically valid sampling techniques.

4.702 If national authorities rely on the second sentence of Article 6.10, they are still required to calculate an individual dumping margin for those firms which had been selected for examination. The rate applied to the firms that were not selected for examination must conform to the requirements of Article 9.4 of the AD Agreement.

4.703 The Argentine authorities in the present case did not calculate individual margins of dumping for each of the four selected exporters. Instead, they calculated two dumping margins for each of three tile sizes, which applied to all exporters without exception. Japan agrees that if the EC's factual allegations are correct, this action by the Argentine authorities appears to be inconsistent with Article 6.10 of the AD Agreement, for the following reasons.

4.704 First, nothing in the second sentence of Article 6.10 requires that the general *rule* set out in the first sentence of that provision should be disregarded. The Argentine authorities should therefore have calculated individual margins of dumping for the limited number of companies under investigation.

4.705 Second, Argentina's interpretation would nullify the possibility explicitly created in Article 6.10.2 of the AD Agreement for those exporters that were not initially selected. This provision requires that the national authorities "*shall [...] determine* an individual margin of dumping for any exporter or producer not initially selected who submits the necessary information in time" (emphasis added by Japan). Like those initially selected, exporters submitting information at a later stage have the advantage - as a result of Article 6.10.2 - of also having their individual dumping margins determined. If, as Argentina assumes, national authorities would be allowed to calculate dumping margins for different sizes of a product without considering the situation of those initially or subsequently selected, the content of Article 6.10.2 would be in direct contradiction with this option.

4.706 Japan agrees with the EC that DCD, by agreeing to limit its examination to a selection of exporters, was required to determine individual dumping margins for each of the four selected exporters. By failing to do so, Argentina violated Article 6.10 of the AD Agreement.

4.707 In addition, the DCD calculated the dumping margin of the exporters which were not selected for the investigation based on the "facts available." As was found by the recent Panel on *United States - Anti-Dumping Measures on Certain Hot-Rolled Steel Products from Japan,* Japan believes that the rate applied to the firms not selected for examination ("all others rate") must conform to the requirements of Article 9.4, including the requirement that such a rate not be derived from any calculation in which any element was established on the basis of "facts available."

4.708 Japan did not address in its oral statement the EC's claim under Article 6.10 of the AD Agreement.

4. Third Parties: Turkey

4.709 Turkey did not address the EC's claim under Article 6.10 of the AD Agreement either in its written submission nor in its oral statement.

5. Third Parties: The United States

4.710 The United States did not address the EC's claim under Article 6.10 of the AD Agreement either in its written submission nor in its oral statement.

C. Claim under Article 2.4 of the AD Agreement

1. The EC

(a) Arguments of the EC in its First Written Submission in Support of its Claim under Article 2.4 of the AD Agreement

4.711 In its first written submission, the EC made the following arguments in support of its claim under Article 2.4 of the AD Agreement.

4.712 The EC submits that the DCD did not make "due allowance" for all the differences in physical characteristics between the models of *porcellanato* exported to Argentina and those sold in Italy, thereby violating Article 2.4 of the AD Agreement.

4.713 The EC presented first the facts relevant for its arguments concerning its claim under Article 2.4.

4.714 Porcellanato is a very heterogeneous product. Each of the exporters included in the sample produces many different models, the prices of which may vary considerably. Since the mix of models exported to Argentina is not the same as that sold domestically, the exporters requested to the DCD that the export price for each model be compared, where possible, to the normal value for the same model.

4.715 The DCD rejected that request. Instead, the DCD grouped all the models in three broad categories according to their size (20 x 20 cm, 30 x 30 cm and 40 x 40 cm) and calculated a normal value and an export price for each of those categories. The DCD made only one adjustment to the normal value in order to reflect the differences between polished and unpolished *porcellanato*. No further adjustments were made to take into account the other differences in physical characteristics. Thus, the DCD erroneously disregarded that the prices of *porcellanato* may vary considerably according to factors other than the size, or whether it is polished or unpolished.

4.716 For example, the price list of Casalgrande relied upon by the DCD shows that the list price of unpolished *porcellanato* of 30 cm x 30 cm may range from 25,000 Lit/m2 to more than 50,000 Lit/m2, i.e. more than a 100 per cent price difference (by way of comparison, the dumping margins determined by the DCD for this size category were 43.14 per cent and 27.43 per cent).

4.717 The DCD's failure to make due allowance for all the differences in physical characteristics is all the more unjustifiable in view of the fact that, in its Final Dumping Determination, the DCD itself acknowledged that there were significant prices differentials between models of unpolished *porcellanato* of the same size:

> Del análisis de la información de ventas en el mercado interno italiano (listado de precios) se ha observado una gran disparidad de precios del producto de iguales medidas y precios de venta inferiores en las medidas de mayor tamaño. Así, se pudo observar casos en que el 'porcellanato' sin pulir de 40 cm x 40 cm presenta precios de venta inferiores a los precios de venta del 'porcellanato' de 20 cm x 20 cm, o al de 30 cm x 30 cm; como también precios de venta de la medida 30 cm x 30 cm inferiores a los de la medida 20 cm x 20 cm (Final Dumping Determination, Section V.1.3, at p. 28).

4.718 The EC presented next its legal arguments concerning its claim under Article 2.4.

4.719 The EC recalls that Article 2.4 of the Anti-dumping Agreement provides in pertinent part that:

> A fair comparison shall be made between the export price and the normal value [...]. Due allowance shall be made in each case, on its merits, for differences which affect price comparability, including differences in [...] physical characteristics [...].

4.720 The DCD acknowledged in the Final Dumping Determination that, in addition to the differences in size and the differences between polished and unpolished *porcellanato*, other differences in physical characteristics could have also a significant impact on the price and, consequently, "affect price comparability" in the sense of Article 2.4. Therefore, the DCD was under the obligation to make "due allowance" for such differences.

4.721 In spite of that, the DCD rejected, without advancing any justification, the exporters' request to make the comparison between normal value and export price on a model-to-model basis. Instead, the DCD lumped together very different models with very different prices, thereby grossly distorting the comparison.

4.722 Admittedly, the terms "due allowance" leave some discretion to the investigating authorities. Thus, arguably, the DCD could have chosen to make "due allowance" for the differences at issue by using a different method from that suggested by the exporters. For example, by making adjustments a *posteriori* to the normal value or to the export price. Nevertheless, the DCD also failed to apply any such alternative method. As explained above, the DCD limited itself to make an adjustment for the differences between polished and unpolished *porcellanato*.

4.723 Moreover, had the DCD considered that a different method would be more appropriate to make "due allowance" for the differences in physical characteristics than the model-to-model comparison proposed by the exporters, it should have informed the exporters thereof and indicated to them what evidence was required in accordance with the last sentence Article 2.4, which provides that:

> [t]he authorities shall indicate to the parties in question what information is necessary to ensure a fair comparison and shall not impose an unreasonable burden of proof on those parties.

4.724 In conclusion, by failing to make "due allowance" for all the differences in physical characteristics affecting price comparability, the DCD violated Article 2.4, third sentence. Furthermore, as a result, the DCD also failed to make a "fair comparison" between normal value and export price, contrary to the first sentence of Article 2.4.

(b) Arguments in the EC's First Oral Statement in Support of its Claim under Article 2.4 of the AD Agreement

4.725 In its first oral statement, the EC made the following arguments concerning its claim under Article 2.4 of the AD Agreement.

4.726 *Porcellanato* is a very heterogeneous product. Each of the exporters concerned produces many different models, the prices of which can vary considerably according to factors such as the size, the shape, the thickness, whether they are polished ("polito") or unpolished, the colour of the surface, the pigmentation of the clay, the quality or choice ("scelta"), the resistance, the water absorption, etc.

4.727 Since the mix of models exported to Argentina was not the same as that sold domestically, the exporters requested to the DCD that the export price for each model be compared, where possible, to the normal value for the same model.

4.728 The DCD did not follow that method. Instead, the DCD grouped all the models in three broad categories according to their size (20 cm x 20 cm, 30 cm x 30 cm and 40 cm x 40 cm) and calculated a normal value and an export price for each of those categories.

4.729 As a result, the DCD failed to make "due allowance" for all the differences in physical characteristics affecting price comparability, thereby violating Article 2.4 of the AD Agreement.

4.730 Argentina admits, and indeed even stresses, the existence of numerous differences in physical characteristics, in addition to those relating to the size of the tiles. Nevertheless, it argues that to take them into account would have complicated "enormously" the task of the investigating authorities.

4.731 This defence is clearly without merit. Article 2.4 does not allow investigating authorities to disregard differences in physical characteristics that affect price comparability simply because it would be too complicated to take them into account. Moreover, the difficulties invoked by Argentina could have been easily avoided if the DCD had made a model-to-model comparison.

4.732 Argentina further contends that the DCD's decision to make "due allowance" only for the differences in size is reasonable and within the limits of the "deference" accorded to the investigating authorities by Article 17.6, because size is the most "universal" characteristic of tiles.

4.733 The EC disagrees. As noted in our written submission, Article 2.4 leaves some discretion to the investigating authorities with respect to the choice of the precise method for making "due allowance" for differences in physical characteristics affecting price comparability.

4.734 In contrast, Article 2.4 leaves no discretion to the investigating authorities for choosing whether or not to make "due allowance". The only "permissible" interpretation of Article 2.4 is that it requires to make "due allowance" for all the differences in physical characteristics that affect price comparability. The investigating authorities cannot limit themselves to make "due allowance" only for the differences concerning a certain characteristic of their choice, even if that characteristic is the most "universal".

(c) Replies of the EC to the First Set of Questions by the Panel Relating to the EC's Claim under Article 2.4 of the AD Agreement

4.735 The EC replied to the first set of questions by the Panel relating to the EC's claim under Article 2.4 as follows.

4.736 The Panel asked the parties to clarify whether the exporters that replied to the questionnaire requested the DCD at some point to calculate the dumping margin on the basis of model-based comparisons. If so, the Panel further asked, what specific model-matching methodology was proposed? Could the parties provide the Panel with the relevant references either in the report or in the administrative record? The Panel also asked the EC to comment on the relevance in this respect of Exhibit EC-10.

4.737 To this question, the EC provided the following reply.

4.738 In their questionnaire responses, the exporters requested that the export price for each model exported to Argentina be compared to the normal value based on domestic prices for the same model and, where this was not possible, to the export price to third countries or the constructed value for the same model.

4.739 This request was reiterated by the representatives of the exporters at the meeting of 11 May 2001 with the case-handlers. The representatives of the exporters understood that the DCD would make a model-to-model comparison on the basis of the information provided by the exporters if the exporters supplied the requested additional non-confidential summaries and supporting invoices.

4.740 Casalgrande, Caesar and Marazzi sold their models under the same name in Italy and for export (including to Argentina). Accordingly, no model-matching methodology was necessary.

4.741 Bismantova sold the models for export to Argentina and third countries under a different name. In order to allow the DCD to make a model-to-model comparison, Bismantova provided in its response a "conversion table". As agreed at the meeting of 11 May 1999, that table was disclosed to the other interested parties in Bismantova's submission of 4 June 1999.

4.742 If the exporters did request the DCD to do its margin calculations on the basis of models, the Panel asked the parties to clarify what was the DCD's response to that request.

4.743 The EC replied that the DCD did at no point during the investigation inform the exporters that it would not make a model-to-model comparison. To the contrary, the representatives of the exporters drew the conclusion from the meeting of 11 May 1999 that the DCD would make a model-to-model comparison on the basis of the information provided by the exporters if the exporters supplied the requested additional non-confidential summaries and supporting invoices.

4.744 The Panel recalled that, independently of whether the exporters asked for a model-based comparison of normal value and export prices, the record suggested that prices of tiles varied significantly, even within a single size category, on account of differences in processing (polished/unpolished), quality, and colour (for instance, Bismantova's price list submitted as Exhibit EC-5C). The DCD itself recognized (see page 28 of its Final Dumping Determination) that the exporters' sales information revealed considerable price differences in products of equal size and lower sales prices for the larger sizes than for the smaller sizes. On account of this situation, the Panel asked the parties whether they were of the view that the requirement to adjust for physical differences affecting price comparability could be met in this investigation by comparing normal values and export prices corresponding to the same size category.

4.745 The EC replied to this question in the negative. In accordance with Article 2.4, the DCD was required to make due allowance for all the differences in physical characteristics affecting price comparability, and not only for the differences in size.

4.746 The Panel asked Argentina whether it was of the view that the infinite number of physical differences made adjustment beyond size impracticable, and that Article 2.4 would recognize an exception in this respect. Additionally, was Argentina's view that the exporters failed to support such an adjustment by not providing sufficient data? The Panel further asked Argentina, if the data were considered inadequate, to what extent was such inadequacy based on the confidential nature of the information supplied, and were the exporters informed thereof?

4.747 To this question, the EC provided the following reply.

4.748 In theory, in an investigation involving a large number of different models with many different features, the investigating authority could ensure a "fair comparison", as required by Article 2.4, by using two different methods.

4.749 The first method involves two steps: (1) comparing the export price for each model to the normal value for the same model (or for a similar model, after adjustments if necessary); and (2) averaging the resulting price differentials into a dumping margin for the product under investigation as a whole. This is the most accurate method and also the easiest to apply.

4.750 The second method involves also two steps: (1) making adjustments for all the differences between a "benchmark" model and all the other models; and (2) comparing the adjusted normal value and export price on a product basis. This method would be extremely cumbersome and, in any event, much less accurate in practice than a model-to-model comparison. Moreover, assuming that all the necessary adjustments could be accurately estimated, the result should not differ from that obtained by using the first method. For those reasons, in practice no investigating authority uses this method.

4.751 Since the exporters had requested, and expected, that the DCD would make a model-to-model comparison (the first method), they did not request the DCD to make adjustments for differences in physical characteristics (the second method).

4.752 Argentina argues now that the second method would have been very difficult to apply in this case. The EC would agree. However, this did not entitle the DCD to make allowance only for the differences in size. Rather, Argentina should have made a model-to-model comparison, something for which the exporters had provided all the necessary information.

4.753 The Panel recalled Argentina's statement to the effect that the exporters did not object to the DCD's adjusting only for size, and not for quality or other physical differences affecting price comparability. The Panel asked the EC whether it agreed with this characterization of the evidence. The Panel further asked the parties to comment on the relevance this fact could have under Article 2.4. In other words, the Panel asked, if the investigating authorities have reason to believe that certain physical differences, in fact, affect price comparability, and if the record contains evidence sufficient to make such an adjustment, would the acceptance by the exporters of the adjustments actually made relieve the authorities of the need to make further adjustments?

4.754 To this question, the EC provided the following reply.

4.755 Contrary to Argentina's unsupported assertions, the DCD never informed the exporters that it would make allowance only for differences in size. Nor, consequently, could the exporters have acquiesced to that decision. In particular, it is not correct that the DCD's decision to make allowance only for differences in size was reflected in the questionnaire sent to the exporters. The questionnaire required the exporters to supply normal value and export price information by "model/type/code", and not by size category.

4.756 The Preliminary Dumping Determination was based on "facts available", and not on the exporters' data. The facts available used by the DCD did not allow to make a model-to-model comparison. Thus, the fact that the DCD did not make such comparison in the Preliminary Dumping Determination was not interpreted by the exporters as implying a rejection of that approach.

4.757 The exporters expected that, since the issue of the non-confidential summaries had been resolved in the meantime, the DCD would make a model-to-model comparison in the Final Dumping Determination, based on the information supplied by them, which would take due account of all the differences in physical characteristics. As mentioned before, the meeting of 11 May 1999 with the case-handlers reinforced this expectation. Due to the DCD's failure to make a disclosure of "essential facts" prior to the final determination, the EC exporters were unaware that the DCD would not make a model-to-model comparison and could not object to the DCD's decision to make allowance only for differences in size.

4.758 The Panel recalled that the EC argued in its first written submission (at para. 77) that the DCD did adjust normal value in order to reflect the physical differences between polished and unpolished tiles. However, the DCD's report raised this issue exclusively in the context of margin calculations for one of the exporters (Caesar), and, even in this case (see page 29 of the Final Determination Report), it suggested that the information on home prices provided by the exporter concerned was rejected by the DCD on the grounds that that home sales of polished tiles could not be compared to export sales of unpolished tiles. The Panel asked the parties to clarify whether the adjustment concerned was made.

4.759 To this question, the EC provided the following reply.

4.760 As noted by the Panel, the Final Dumping Determination is unclear about whether the requested adjustment was granted. During the consultations, the Argentinean authorities informed the EC that the adjustment had been granted, but did not disclose the details of the calculation.

4.761 Caesar was the only exporter which requested an adjustment for differences in physical characteristics between polished and unpolished tiles. Caesar made this request because one of the models exported to Argentina was unpolished, while the model sold under the same name in Italy was polished.

4.762 Exhibit EC-17 contains a copy of the relevant section of Caesar's questionnaire response where the adjustment was requested. The amount of the adjustment estimated by Caesar was omitted in the non-confidential version. The EC considers that this amount was not capable of summarization.

4.763 The other exporters did not request an adjustment for differences between polished and unpolished tiles because the models sold in Italy were identical in all respects to those exported to Argentina. Thus, a model-to-model comparison would have been sufficient to ensure a fair comparison.

(d) Replies of the EC to the Questions Made by Argentina, Following the First Meeting of the Panel with the Parties, that Relate to the EC's Claim under Article 2.4 of the AD Agreement

4.764 The EC replied to the questions made by Argentina relating to the EC's claim under Article 2.4 of the AD Agreement as follows.

4.765 Argentina asked the EC how it could make an argument for undertaking price comparisons by model and at the same time express the view that "fair comparison" requires taking into consideration every physical characteristic.

4.766 The EC replied that there was no contradiction. In the present case, a model-to-model comparison would have been the most accurate and the simplest method to make due allowance for all the differences in physical characteristics. The EC referred Argentina to the EC's answer to a question made by the Panel (question No. 2) following the first meeting.

4.767 Argentina asked the EC whether it was of the view that a "fair comparison" could be made on the basis of the information contained in the catalogues that the exporters submitted and were provided to the Panel as Exhibit ARG-22.

4.768 The EC replied that its answer to this question was reflected in paragraphs 82-83 of its second written submission.

(e) Arguments of the EC in its Second Written Submission in Support of its Claim under Article 2.4 of the AD Agreement

4.769 In its second written submission, the EC made the following arguments supporting its claim under Article 2.4 of the AD Agreement.

4.770 Argentina admits, and indeed emphasises, the existence of numerous differences in physical characteristics, in addition to those relating to the size of the tiles. Nevertheless, it argues that to take them into account would have complicated "enormously" the task of the DCD.

4.771 This defence is clearly without merit. Article 2.4 does not allow investigating authorities to disregard differences in physical characteristics that affect price comparability simply because it would be too difficult to take them into account. Moreover, the difficulties invoked by Argentina could have been easily avoided if the DCD had made a model-to-model comparison, as requested by the exporters.

4.772 Argentina further contends that DCD's decision to make "due allowance" only for the differences in size is reasonable and within the limits of the "deference" accorded to the investigating authorities by Article 17.6 of the AD Agreement, because size is the most "universal" characteristic of tiles.

4.773 This argument is thoroughly misguided. Article 2.4 leaves some discretion to the investigating authorities with respect to the choice of the precise method for making "due allowance" for differences in physical characteristics affecting price comparability. Thus, in particular, the investigating authority can choose whether to make "due allowance" by making a model-to-model comparison, or by making adjustments to the normal value and/or the export price prior to the comparison. In practice, nevertheless, the authority's discretion is limited by the fact that the second method is extremely cumbersome where the investigation concerns a product which is sold in many different, multi-featured models.

4.774 In contrast, Article 2.4 leaves no discretion to the investigating authorities for choosing whether or not to make "due allowance". The only "permissible" interpretation of Article 2.4 is that it requires to make "due allowance" for all the differences in physical characteristics that affects price comparability.

4.775 In its first oral statement, Argentina implies that the exporters agreed in advance, or at least did not object, to the DCD's decision to make allowance exclusively for the differences in size. That is not true.

4.776 Argentina also argues in its first oral statement that the exporters failed to provide the necessary information to make adjustments for other differences in physical characteristics. More specifically, Argentina contends that, when answering the questionnaire's request to supply the technical specifications of the products, it was not sufficient for the exporters to refer to the specifications contained in the brochures attached to the response (Argentina also argues, at para. 71 of its first oral statement, that the DCD could not make adjustments because the exporters failed to provide the information requested in Annex IV on a "model/code/type" basis. That Annex, however, requested information on production, production capacity, stocks, exports and imports. That information is not directly relevant for making adjustments for differences in physical characteristics. At any rate, this is the first time that this supposed deficiency is raised by the Argentinean authorities). Argentina, nevertheless, does not explain why. Moreover, this is the first time that the Argentinean authorities complain that the exporters' response to that section of the questionnaire was not complete.

4.777 In any event, it must be recalled that the exporters did not request the DCD to make adjustments (with the exception, in the case of Caesar, of the differences between polished and unpolished models) but rather to make a model-to-model comparison. That comparison would have made unnecessary to make any adjustments before comparing the normal value with the export price. Had the DCD informed the exporters that it would not make a model-to-model comparison, the exporters could have submitted requests for adjustments and supplied supporting evidence.

(f) Arguments of the EC in its Second Oral Statement in Support of its Claim under Article 2.4 of the AD Agreement

4.778 In its second oral statement, the EC made the following arguments in support of its claim under Article 2.4 of the AD Agreement.

4.779 Argentina contends that the decision to calculate the dumping margin by comparing the normal value of each of the three size categories defined by the DCD to the export price for the same category was taken by the DCD at the opening of the investigation ("*a la apertura de la investigación*").

4.780 However, if such decision was taken, it was never communicated to the exporters. It is not mentioned in the Resolution opening the investigation. Nor is there any trace of that decision in the questionnaire. As already explained, the questionnaire required the exporters to provide the information on a "model/type/code" basis, and not by size category.

4.781 Argentina asserts repeatedly that the "segmentation" made by the DCD (to borrow the term used by Argentina) was "accepted" or at least "not objected" by the exporters. This is simply untrue, and Argentina has provided no evidence whatsoever to support those assertions.

4.782 In their questionnaire responses the exporters made a clear request to the DCD to make a model-to-model comparison. That request was renewed at the meeting with the case-handlers of 11 May 1999. The DCD never informed the exporters that such request had been rejected.

4.783 Argentina cites the report of the meeting with the case-handlers of 11 May 1999 as evidence that the exporters would have acquiesced to the segmentation decided by the DCD. However, the passage cited by Argentina is no more than a suggestion made by the representative of the exporters in Argentina to the effect that the sample of invoices requested by the DCD should include examples of the three size categories. The exporters have never questioned that size is an important differentiating characteristic, or that the main size categories are those defined by the DCD. In view of that, it was sensible to suggest that the sample of invoices, so as to be comprehensive, should include examples of each of those size categories. But from this it does not follow that the exporters had renounced to the model-to-model comparison requested in the responses. The exporters understood that the sample of invoices had been requested by the DCD with the exclusive purpose of verifying the information reported in the responses, and that the dumping calculation would be made by using all the transactions reported in the responses. Furthermore, the report of the meeting also alludes to the need to provide non-confidential versions of the conversion tables between models. Yet the submission of those tables would have been totally unnecessary if the exporters had not envisaged that the DCD would make a model-to-model comparison.

4.784 Argentina further argues that the request to make a model-to-model comparison was first "suggested" by the EC before this Panel. But this assertion is contradicted in the very next paragraph of Argentina's second written submission, where Argentina is forced to admit that, in fact, the questionnaire responses showed the "interest" ("*interés*") of the exporters in a model-to-model comparison.

4.785 Argentina goes on to argue that the DCD could not make the requested model-to-model comparison because the exporters failed to provide necessary information. However, this is mere assertion: Argentina nowhere specifies what additional information was required for this purpose.

4.786 Moreover, the exporters were never informed during the investigation of these alleged deficiencies. Nor were these deficiencies mentioned in the Final Dumping Determination.

(g) Replies of the EC to the Second Set of Questions by the Panel Relating to the EC's Claim under Article 2.4 of the AD Agreement

4.787 The EC replied to the second set of questions by the Panel relating to the EC's claim under Article 2.4 of the AD Agreement as follows.

4.788 The Panel asked the EC to confirm that all the information submitted by the exporters related to first-quality, unpolished tiles.

4.789 To this question, the EC provided the following reply.

4.790 The EC can confirm that all the sales reported in the exporters' responses related to first-quality, unpolished tiles, with the exception of some of the domestic sales made by Caesar, which related to polished tiles.

4.791 On the other hand, the EC is not in a position to confirm whether the petitioners' information and import statistics relied upon by the DCD related also to unpolished, first quality tiles. As already explained, of the eight invoices submitted by the petitioner, four correspond to sales of polished tiles, and another to a sale of tiles of 12.5 cm x 25 cm. It is still unclear to the EC whether those five invoices were included by the DCD in the dumping calculation.

4.792 If so, the Panel asked the EC to explain what other physical differences affecting price comparability the EC believed existed for which adjustments should have been made.

4.793 To this question, the EC provided the following reply.

4.794 The following was a non-exhaustive list of other factors affecting price comparability (the EC stated that all the prices mentioned below were for models of 30 x 30 cm of first quality shown in Casalgrande's Price List for October 1998 attached to Casalgrande's questionnaire response).

4.795 Colour: tiles of darker colours such as black, green, blue and red are more expensive to produce than those of lighter colours and are sold at higher prices. By way of example, according to Casalgrande's Price List for October 1998, the price for the model UNICOLOR BIANCO A was 33.000 Lit/m2, whereas the list price of the model UNICOLOR BLU, which is identical in all respects to the

BIANCO A except the colour, was 47.000 Lit/m2 (i.e. 42 per cent more expensive).

4.796 Thickness: thicker tiles require more materials and manufacturing work and are more expensive. Thus, for instance, Casalgrande's list price for the model SAHARA of 9 mm (of the series GRANITO I) was 33.000 Lit/m2, while the list price for the SAHARA of 11/12 mm was 46.000 Lit/m2 (i.e. a 39 per cent difference).

4.797 Raw material and production process: some models undergo further manufacturing processes, often involving the addition of special raw materials (e.g. special salts), in order to acquire an appearance resembling that of certain types of stone, such as granite or marble (e.g. the series GRANITO I, GRANITO II, MARMORIZZATO, ARDESIA, VENATI or TIBURTINO in Casalgrande's catalogue). These models are generally more expensive than the basic ones. Thus, by way of example, the list price of the marble-looking model ARDESIA BIANCO is 42.000 Lit/m2 (27 per cent more than the price of the basic model UNICOLOR BIANCO A). However, a basic model of an expensive colour (e.g. UNICOLOR BLU) can be more expensive than a non-expensive model of one of the special series (e.g. the model SAHARA, of the series GRANITO I).

4.798 Surface: many models are available in versions with special surfaces (e.g. anti-slip) presenting small reliefs. In Casalgrande's catalogue these surfaces are designated with names such as SECURE, ROCCIA, CARBO, PAVE or PROFIL. Those versions are more expensive. Thus, for example, the price list of Casalgrande's model SAHARA ROCCIA is 35.000 Lit/m2, i.e. 6 per cent more expensive than the standard version of SAHARA.

4.799 If the adjustments for physical differences are only granted upon good cause shown, the Panel asked the parties whether the calculation of the dumping margin by model should not be subject to the same requirement.

4.800 To this question, the EC provided the following reply.

4.801 The application of Article 2.4 is subject to the same requirements regarding the burden of proof, regardless of the method followed by the investigating authority to make "due allowance".

4.802 The evidence before the DCD demonstrated beyond doubt that the differences in physical characteristics between models (other than in size) had an impact on their price and, therefore, affected price comparability.

4.803 The DCD has never disputed this. Thus, in the Preliminary Dumping Determination, the DCD noted that:

> ... se debe mencionar que cada empresa posee una gran variedad de líneas de modelos del producto en estudio, con significativas variaciones de precios entre ellos. Esta circunstancia determina una complejidfad adicional en el análisis en curso.

4.804 Similarly, in the Final Dumping Determination stressed that:

> Del análisis de la información de ventas en el mercado interno italiano (listados de ventas) se ha observado una gran disparidad del

> producto de iguales medidas y precios de venta inferiores en las medidas de mayor tamaño en relación a las de menor tamaño. Así, se pudo observar casos en que el "procellanto" sin pulir de 40 cm x 40 cm presenta precios de venta inferiores a los precios de venta del "porcellanato" de 20 cm x 20 cm, o al de 30 cm x 30 cm., como también precios de venta de la medida 30 cm x 30 cm inferiores a los de la medida 20 cm x 20 cm.

4.805 Before this Panel, Argentina has not argued that the physical differences between models (other than in size) do not affect price comparability, but rather that there are so many differences that to take all of them into account would have complicated "enormously" the task of the DCD.

4.806 Thus, in the EC's view, the issue before the Panel is not a factual one (i.e. whether the differences between the models affect price comparability), but rather one of legal interpretation, namely whether, as alleged by Argentina, the "deference" to which the investigating authoirty is entitled under Article 17.6(ii) means that the investigating authority can, for reasons of administrative convenience, limit itself to make "due allowance" for just one of the differences affecting price comparability.

4.807 Furthermore, the EC would recall that the last sentence of Article 2.4 provides that:

> The authorities shall indicate to the parties in question what information is necessary to ensure a fair comparison and shall not impose an unreasonable burden of proof on those parties.

4.808 In its second written submission, Argentina suggested that the DCD could not make a model-to-model comparison because the exporters failed to provide necessary information. However, this was mere assertion. Three of the exporters sold the exported models under the same name and product code in both markets. Thus, no additional information was required in order to make a model-to-model comparison. The other exporter, Bismantova, used different names in each market. Nevertheless, it submitted a *tabla de comparación* in order to allow the DCD to make a model-to-model comparison.

4.809 At any rate, the exporters were never informed during the investigation of the alleged deficiencies. Nor are those deficiencies mentioned anywhere in the Final Dumping Determination.

4.810 If this was so, the Panel asked the parties whether the calculation of the dumping margin by model would be necessary when the same models are sold in both markets in the same proportions.

4.811 To this question, the EC provided the following reply.

4.812 If the normal value is calculated by comparing the weighted average normal value to the weighted average export price (see Article 2.4.2 of the AD Agreement), and if the same models happened to be sold in both markets in precisely the same proportions, there would be no need to make due allowance for differences in physical characteristics, either by making a model-to-model comparison, or by way of adjustments. However, in practice, the model-mix of the export sales is very unlikely to coincide exactly with that of the domestic sales in any given investigation.

4.813 In the case at hand, the information contained in Annexes VII and VIII evidences that the model mix of the export sales was not the same as that of the domestic sales, which rendered it necessary to make due allowance for the differences in physical characteristics between models.

4.814 The Panel recalled that in a reply to question posed by the Panel following the first meeting, Argentina stated that: "Upon opening the investigation, the DCD decided on the segmentation of the product according to the universal criterion that offered the greatest homogeneity, i.e. *porcellanato* in its different sizes, establishing three categories: 20 x 20, 30 x 30 and 40 x 40". The Panel asked Argentina to direct the Panel to the evidence on the record showing that the DCD had made this determination from the moment of initiating the investigation. In addition, the Panel recalled that, in its reply to the same question, the EC argued that the exporters requested that a model-to-model comparison be made. The Panel also asked the EC to direct the Panel to the evidence on the record that demonstrated that the exporters explicitly requested such a comparison.

4.815 To this question, the EC provided the following reply.

4.816 The EC refers the Panel to the relevant sections of Casalgrande's and Bismantova's questionnaire responses provided as Annexes EC-15 and EC-16, respectively, which describe the approach followed by those exporters in responding to Annexes VII and VIII. A model-to-model comparison is inherent in that approach.

4.817 Moreover, as explained above, Bismantova submitted a *tabla de comparación* between the exported and domestic models, with the express indication that it was provided in order to "facilitate the comparison of identical types with different names" (the original Spanish reads as follows: "facilitar la comparación de los tipos idénticos con nombres diferentes").

4.818 Casalgrande sold the exported models under the same name and product code in both markets. Thus, the submission of a *tabla de comparación* was not required. Nevertheless, Casalgrande provided a table comparing the weighted average export price to the weighted average domestic price for the same model. That table evidences clearly that the exporters envisaged that the DCD would make a model-to-model comparison.

4.819 The exporters reiterated their request for a model-to-model comparison at the meeting of 11 May 1999. The case-handlers seemed to agree. Indeed, as recorded in Exhibit EC-10, they requested that Bismantova waive the confidentiality of the *tabla de comparación* between domestic and export models included in Bismantova's questionnaire response. On 4 June 1999 Bismantova agreed to that request. Ecolatina's cover letter recalled expressly that "by using that table [the DCD] can make the necessary comparisons".

4.820 Finally, the EC would recall that in its second written submission Argentina admits that the questionnaire responses showed the "interest" ("*interés*") of the exporters in a model-to-model comparison.

4.821 The Panel recalled that, according to Exhibit EC-10 (at page 2), the local counsel to the exporters in Argentina suggested to the counsel to the exporters in Brussels to provide the DCD invoices with prices "closer to the weight average of the segment". The Panel asked the parties whether this statement suggested that the representatives of the exporters were aware of the fact that the DCD would calculate the normal value for any size category on the basis of all of the home prices available for that size category, irrespective of the model to which those prices referred to. The Panel further asked the parties to comment on the implications of this statement, if any. Did this suggest that the exporters were aware of the fact that their information was going to be compared per size rather than per model?

4.822 To this question, the EC provided the following reply.

4.823 The EC reiterates that the DCD never informed the exporters of the alleged decision to compare the normal value and export price information per size rather than per model. Exhibit EC-10 does not prove the contrary.

4.824 Rather, the opposite is true. Exhibit EC-10 confirms that, after the meeting of 11 May 1999, the exporters continued to expect that the DCD would make a model-to-model comparison. Exhibit EC-10 mentions that Bismantova should waive the confidentiality of the conversion table (*tabla de comparación*) between domestic and export models and that the other exporters should submit similar tables (Mr. Cyrulnik, the author of the document provided as Exhibit EC-10, made an error when he suggested that the other three exporters should submit also conversion tables between domestic and export models. As already explained, the other exporters sold all the models under the same name and code in both markets. Thus, unlike in the case of Bismantova, a conversion table was not necessary in order to allow the DCD to make a model-to-model comparison). Yet the submission of those tables would have been totally pointless if the exporters had acquiesced to the DCD's alleged decision not to make a model-to-model comparison.

4.825 The passage quoted by the Panel contains a personal suggestion of Mr. Cyrulnik, the author of the document, and not something that was discussed, let alone agreed, with the case-handlers. Mr. Cyrulnik's suggestion is not mentioned in Mr. Di Gianni's report to the exporters of 19 May 1999 and was not followed by the exporters.

4.826 The meaning of Mr. Cyrulnik's suggestion is, in any event, rather obscure. To begin with, the quoted passage refers to the selection of "non-confidential invoices". Yet the preceding paragraph correctly states that the supporting invoices had to be provided on a confidential basis only.

4.827 Also, it is far from clear to which "segments" alludes Mr. Cyrulnik. The EC recalls that each model is sold in different sizes. In their responses, the exporters reported separately the sales of each size category within a given model.

Casalgrande went even further by calculating itself the weighted average domestic price and the weighted average export price for each size category within each model. Thus, Mr. Cyrulnik could have been referring to the weighted average for the size "segment" within each model rather than to the weighted average for all the tiles of the same size, regardless of the model, as implied in the Panel's question.

4.828 A misunderstanding on the part of Mr. Cyrulnik cannot be ruled out either. Ecolatina was little else than a mail box for Van Bael & Bellis. Mr. Cyrulnik was not involved in the preparation of the responses, which was carried out exclusively by Van Bael & Bellis. Therefore, he had only a superficial knowledge of the information contained in the responses and of the issues raised by the investigation.

4.829 At any rate, even if the exporters had become aware at a certain point in time of the DCD's alleged decision to make the comparison "per size", it would not follow from this that they acquiesced to such decision, nor that such decision was consistent with the AD Agreement.

2. *Argentina*

(a) Arguments of Argentina in its First Written Submission Relating to the EC's Claim under Article 2.4 of the AD Agreement

4.830 In its first written submission, Argentina made the following arguments relating to the EC's claim under Article 2.4 of the AD Agreement.

4.831 Argentina first presented a number of facts relevant to its legal arguments.

4.832 To begin with, when considering the differences which affect price comparability, account was taken, essentially, of the dimensions of the product in question.

4.833 The implementing authority had to establish some kind of criterion for facilitating a fair comparison of different products which, because they were designer products, were very difficult to compare. The task was made even more difficult by the fact that there were 78 manufacturers of *porcellanato*, each of which produced dozens of different varieties which, in their turn, could be discontinued at any time or replaced by similar articles with a different product code or trade name. This applies to each supplier. Since these circumstances made the implementing authority's job infinitely more difficult, it decided to establish as a basis for comparison the only variable that applied to all of the articles from all of the suppliers and that was not affected by market considerations from one supplier to the other as could be the case with the other variables, such as colour or design. Since the sizes 20 cm x 20 cm, 30 cm x 30 cm and 40 cm x 40 cm were the most representative, it was these sizes that were considered according to the volume exported.

4.834 Once the investigation had been initiated, all of the parties concerned were given ample opportunity to supply as much information as possible so that the implementing authority could rely on homogeneous data in order to make a fair comparison.

4.835 Moreover, the exporting firms did not submit, during the procedure, any evidence to invalidate the product breakdown applied at the opening of the investigation and maintained in the final determination.

4.836 It should be stressed that the DCD always tries to put some order into its investigations by seeking a criterion for ensuring the homogeneity of the products under analysis. In this case, Argentina stresses that there was no objection by the parties to the use of product size as a criterion. Thus, Argentina considers that the implementing authority acted properly and objectively on the basis of a criterion agreed upon by the parties.

4.837 Argentina presented next its legal arguments concerning the EC's claim under Article 2.4.

4.838 The EC has argued that there has been an infringement of Article 2.4, which states that:

> A fair comparison shall be made between the export price and the normal value … . Due allowance shall be made in each case, on its merits, for differences which affect price comparability, including differences in conditions and terms of sale … physical characteristics … .

(i) The Standard of Review Applicable to the Case

4.839 The obligation to make a "fair comparison", an obligation qualified by the words "on its merits", is inspired by the standard of review applied in the framework of the AD Agreement as defined in Article 17.6 thereof.

4.840 This peculiarity of the AD Agreement, the only agreement to contain a specific standard for the review of provisional or definitive anti-dumping measures or price undertakings when they are questioned under the DSU, has been recognized in a number of precedents, such as *United States - Underwear*: "We note that the ATC does not establish a standard of review for panels, contrary, for example, to the WTO Agreement on Implementation of Article VI of the General Agreement on Tariffs and Trade 1994, where Article 17.6 defines the standard of review that panels have to apply when reviewing cases arising under that Agreement. We further note that the DSU does not contain a provision mandating a specific standard of review" (Panel Report, *United States - Restrictions on Imports of Cotton and Man-Made Fibre Underwear*, WT/DS24/R, adopted 25 February 1997, at para. 7.8).

4.841 This same point, that the only exception to the general standard of review set forth in Article 11 of the DSU is the AD Agreement, was also made in *EC - Hormones* with reference to the treatment that should be given to the facts ("Only

Article 17.6(i) of the Anti-Dumping Agreement has language on the standard of review to be employed by panels engaged in the 'assessment of the facts of the matter". We find no indication in the SPS Agreement of an intent on the part of the Members to adopt or incorporate into that Agreement the standards set out in Article 17.6(i) of the Anti-Dumping Agreement. Textually, Article 17.6(i) is specific to the Anti-Dumping Agreement". Appellate Body Report, *EC - Measures Concerning Meat and Meat Products,* WT/DS26/AB/R, adopted 13 February 1998, at page 49), and in a general sense both with respect to the facts and the standards of the Agreement, in *Argentina - Footwear* ("We have stated, on more than one occasion, that, for all but one of the covered agreements, Article 11 of the DSU sets forth the appropriate standard of review for panels. The only exception is the Agreement on Implementation of Article VI of the General Agreement on Tariffs and Trade 1994, in which a specific provision, Article 17.6, sets out a special standard of review for disputes arising under that Agreement". Appellate Body Report, *Argentina - Safeguard Measures on Imports of Footwear,* WT/DS121/AB/R, adopted 12 January 2000).

4.842 Ultimately, these precedents reflect the principle of "deference" towards the methodology applied by the investigating authorities in anti-dumping cases in accordance with Article 17.6(i) and 17.6(ii) of the AD Agreement.

4.843 Indeed, the second sentence of Article 17.6(ii) states that "Where the Panel finds that a relevant provision of the Agreement admits of more than one permissible interpretation, the Panel shall find the authority's measure to be in conformity with the Agreement if it rests upon one of those permissible interpretations." The wording of this provision suggests that it requires the principle of deference to be subjected to a sort of double test before it can be invoked to defend an interpretation of the Agreement, i.e.:

- There should be several permissible interpretations;
- The measure should rest upon one of those permissible interpretations.

4.844 This had been described by Jackson as follows in his book *The Jurisprudence of GATT and the WTO*: "subsection (ii) seems to establish a two-step process ... First, the Panel must consider whether the provisions of the agreement in question admit of more than one interpretation. If not, the Panel must vindicate the provision's only permissible interpretation. If, on the other hand, the Panel determines that the provisions indeed admit of more than one interpretation, the Panel shall proceed to the second step of the analysis and consider whether the national interpretation is within the set of permissible interpretations. If so, the Panel must defer to the interpretation given to the provision by the national government" (Jackson, page 148).

4.845 The concept of deference refers to the existence of various permissible interpretations that may arise from the text of the Agreement, in this case Article 2.4 which calls for a "fair" comparison taking account of the "merits" of each case, inter alia, physical characteristics.

4.846 The permissibility of the interpretation made by the Authority, in this case of the criterion used as a basis for making a "fair" comparison, according to the standard of "deference" established in Article 17.6, is precisely what enables the authority, as a matter of law, to rely, within the limits of the Article, on its own discretion in choosing a method for making the comparison.

4.847 In other words if two different approaches or methodologies are reasonable, and derive from an interpretation of the text, then both are permitted under the Agreement, even if they result in totally different conclusions.

4.848 Generally speaking, and originally in connection with the weighing of the facts, this concept of "deference" towards the national authority forms part of GATT/WTO jurisprudence and has been addressed on a number of occasions in the past, in particular in the case *United States-Salmon*:

> ... the mere fact that in a given case reasonable, unprejudiced minds could differ as to the weight to be accorded to certain facts was not a sufficient ground to find that a determination of material injury based on such facts was not based on positive evidence ... The question of whether a determination of injury was based on positive evidence therefore was distinct from the question of the weight to be accorded to the facts before the investigating authorities ... (GATT Panel Report, *United States - Imposition of Anti-Dumping Duties on Imports of Fresh and Chilled Atlantic Salmon from Norway*, ADP/87, adopted 28 April 1994, at para. 494).

(ii) Deference to the Investigating Authority

4.849 The EC states that it recognizes the discretion of the investigating authorities or the margin available to them in applying Article 2.4: "Admittedly, the terms 'due allowance' leave some discretion to the investigating authorities ... the DCD could have chosen to make 'due allowance' for the differences at issue by using a different method from that suggested by the exporters ...". The problem arises when the EC goes on to suggest an alternative method of adjustment - "by making adjustment a posteriori to the normal value or the export price" - and argues that the fact that the DCD did not apply the alternative method proposed by the EC in itself invalidates the DCD's option of making an adjustment on the basis of differences in size.

4.850 This begs the question of why an a posteriori adjustment of the normal value would be a valid way of complying with the obligation of making a "fair" comparison.

4.851 As indicated, the authority developed the idea of "homogenization" which ultimately amounts to a standardization based on certain parameters which by their nature reflect a certain universality within the product investigated.

4.852 Why, then, should one consider that whereas an adjustment of the kind proposed by the EC would be consistent with Article 2.4, the fact that the authority should base its comparison on a factor such as "physical characteristics" invalidates the comparison?

4.853 What the DCD did, in keeping with Article 2.4, was to use the physical characteristics as a basis and to make a fair comparison. This unquestionably resulted in an adjustment which ultimately produced lower final margins of dumping than those relied upon to initiate the investigation.

4.854 In the end, the authority chose to interpret the scope of the obligation contained in the Agreement on the basis of a physical characteristic of the product, i.e. its size (20 x 20, 30 x 30 or 40 x 40), which was the most universal feature. This factor, applicable to the greatest quantity of imports of the product investigated, would permit the authority, on the basis of the greatest quantity of elements in common, to make the most comprehensive fair comparison "on the merits" of the case (infinite number of models according to colour, design etc.).

4.855 The DCD made a fair comparison taking account of the diversity of the ceramic tiles investigated and chose to use a factor which, in its view, established a "reasonable" basis for comparison and met the Article 2.4 requirement. Thus the DCD made a "reasonable" analysis of the facts, applying to them the obligations set forth in the Agreement, in accordance with the text thereof, and without having to resort to procedures such as the a posteriori adjustment, which does not appear in the text of Article 2.4. To follow the approach suggested by the EC would have meant sacrificing some of the "deference" owed to the investigating authority and specifically recognized in Article 17.6 of the AD Agreement. This double standard involving acceptance of what can reasonably be inferred from the facts available and the interpretation of the obligations arising from the text of the Agreement has been recognized by GATT panels, in particular the *United States - Salmon* Panel cited above.

4.856 In that case, the Panel first examined whether the Agreement imposed an obligation on the United States to use the methodology put forward by Norway: "The Panel noted ... that ... it had specifically requested Norway to present arguments as to why ... the text of Article 2.4 *mandated* the use of acquisition prices paid by exporters ... " (GATT Panel Report, *United States - Imposition of Anti-Dumping Duties on Imports of Fresh and Chilled Atlantic Salmon from Norway*, ADP/87, adopted 28 April 1994, at para. 406, emphasis added by Argentina). Similarly: "the Panel ... found that ... the United States was not under an *obligation* to first consider the use of export prices to third countries as a basis for the establishment of normal values before resorting to the use of constructed normal values" (GATT Panel Report, *United States - Imposition of Anti-Dumping Duties on Imports of Fresh and Chilled Atlantic Salmon from Norway*, ADP/87, adopted 28 April 1994, at para. 393, emphasis added by Argentina). This required an analysis of the text, which included ascertaining whether it contained criteria which the Panel could review to determine whether the Department had used the methodology correctly. Otherwise, the Panel review was limited to examining whether the methodology used could "reasonably ... be sufficient to serve its stated purpose" (GATT Panel Report, *United States - Imposi-*

tion of Anti-Dumping Duties on Imports of Fresh and Chilled Atlantic Salmon from Norway, ADP/87, adopted 28 April 1994, at para. 414) or whether the Department of Commerce had acted reasonably in the light of the information before it (GATT Panel Report, *United States - Imposition of Anti-Dumping Duties on Imports of Fresh and Chilled Atlantic Salmon from Norway*, ADP/87, adopted 28 April 1994, at para. 442) Similarly, in the case at issue, the Panel should assess whether the "homogenization" criterion selected by the implementing authority for the purposes of making a fair comparison was, first of all, reasonable, and whether in addition, the Argentine interpretation of the obligations arising from Article 2.4 was consistent with the requirements of the Agreement, regardless of whether there existed another permissible interpretation.

4.857 In this case, the EC submits that its interpretation of the obligations of the Agreement should be substituted for those of the national authorities in a specific context such as the AD Agreement, Article 17.6 of which refers both to the assessment of the facts and to the scope of the interpretations of the Agreement. Thus, even though an interpretation of the obligation different from that made by Argentina may be permissible, provided the "fair comparison" methodology used is in keeping with Article 2.4 - and here the EC does not disagree, but maintains that the methodology should be replaced by its own - the comparison made by Argentina must be considered consistent with that Article.

(b) Arguments of Argentina in its First Oral Statement Relating to the EC's Claim under Article 2.4 of the AD Agreement

4.858 In its first oral statement, Argentina made the following arguments relating to the EC's claim under Article 2.4 of the AD Agreement.

4.859 Particularly relevant with respect to the analysis of compliance with the obligation set forth in Article 2.4 of the AD Agreement is the standard of review contained in Article 17.6 thereof.

4.860 In its first written submission, Argentina discussed the various elements of that article as regards both the interpretation of the scope of the Agreement (Article 17.6(ii)) and the assessment of the facts on the basis of the above provision (Article 17.6(i)).

4.861 The determination of whether the "fair comparison" made by the authority was consistent with the AD Agreement should be based on the definition of the content or scope of the obligation, without having to resort to Article 17.6(ii) (legal interpretations).

4.862 In paragraph 83 of its first written submission, the EC specifically stated that it recognized that the Agreement left some discretion to the investigating authorities ("Admittedly, the terms 'due allowance' leave some discretion to the investigating authorities"). This being the case, the discussion concerns not so much the scope of the obligation laid down in the Agreement regarding the content of the "due allowance" as the assessment of the facts (differences in the ceramic tiles) requiring an adjustment in order to make a "fair comparison", a process which should make it possible to evaluate the facts in an "unbiased" and "objective" manner.

4.863 Having confirmed this, i.e. that the authority evaluated the facts in an "unbiased" and "objective" manner in conformity with the principle of deference contained in Article 17.6(i), the Panel must respect the authority's evaluation even though it could reach a different conclusion.

4.864 Can the fact that the authority opted for the common parameter which reflected the greatest universality, i.e. the size, a physical characteristic, as a criterion on which to base the fair comparison, be qualified as "biased" or "unobjective"? It would be difficult to find a more universal criterion on which to base an adjustment than the physical characteristics of the product, i.e. the size of the tiles. The authority's final determination, following the market segmentation duly established by the authority and accepted by the exporting firms, states that the volume of 30 cm x 30 cm tiles exported to Argentina represented 70.04 per cent of the total, while 40 cm x 40 cm tiles represented 16.17 per cent and 20 cm x 20 cm tiles 13.08 per cent. Argentina wonders whether the EC actually expected the DCD to make the adjustment for the 0.71 per cent that was not included in any of these categories.

(i) Information Requested

4.865 It is important, at this point, to refer to the information duly requested by the authority. It must be borne in mind that Annex II of the questionnaire for producers/exporters is entitled "Identification of the product at issue". One of the questions in that Annex refers to "technical specifications for each model/type/code of goods sold in the domestic market and those exported to Argentina".

4.866 The answer given to this question by some of the exporting firms was the following: "The technical characteristics of the *porcellanato* are specified in detail in the catalogues annexed hereto." However, Annex II also asks for general catalogues and/or brochures and/or plans. In other words, it seems clear that the submission of catalogues or brochures could not make up for the lack of information referring to the technical specifications for each model/type/code, no matter what the producing/exporting firms may erroneously have understood.

4.867 Moreover, the EC's questions suggesting that the segmentation of the product by the DCD represented a breach of Article 2.4 is incomprehensible. The only way in which the DCD could have carried out an a posteriori adjustment once the investigation had been opened would have been on the basis of new information submitted by the interested parties, more specifically the producers/exporters.

4.868 However, even accepting the hypothesis that a posteriori adjustment was the way to make the fair comparison (and the text of Article 2.4 does not suggest this), as stated above with respect to the information from the producers/exporters relating to the technical specifications for the product under investigation, the producers/exporters did not provide the documentation the DCD would have needed to carry out a new analysis in this connection.

4.869 This attitude of the producers/exporters during the investigation is consistent with the fact that at no time during the proceedings did these interested parties raise any objections to the segmentation of the product and the adjustments made.

(ii) The Authority's Decision

4.870 One wonders how the DCD could have obtained technical characteristics of the product under investigation, without prejudice to the segmentation applied at the opening of the investigation, on the basis of catalogues containing an infinite number of models, designs, uses, etc.: not only is this not the DCD's responsibility, but it would have been impossible to do.

4.871 Perhaps Annex IV (Information on the producer/exporter market) would have helped, since it contains an item referring to "model/code/type". However, the reply given by all of the producers/exporters to this question was: "This type of information is not available by model, code or type. The information provided refers to *porcellanato* in general".

4.872 What other parameter could have provided a common standard on which to base the adjustment? There are an infinite number of colours, for example. The same applies to designs, not to mention the other characteristics listed in Article 2.4 of the Agreement. What other non-confidential criterion supplied during the investigation could the authority rely on?

4.873 How could the EC require an undefined a posteriori adjustment without specifying the parameters on which it should be based? Indeed, Argentina is certain that, as with Article 6.8, the EC itself recognizes the difficulties involved in making an adjustment on the basis of information on which the DCD could not rely. In other words, even if, for instance, the methodology used by the EC (a code by which its sales in its domestic market would be made comparable to export sales) had been adopted for the purpose, the exporters did not supply any quantification of the adjustments to be made either to the normal value or to the export price. Consequently, making an adjustment was not feasible.

4.874 This being so, the Panel should confirm that in this case, as in the case of *US - Salmon from Norway*, the DCD "acted reasonably in the light of the information before it".

4.875 In the end, the DCD was inhibited by the confidential and incomplete nature of the information submitted. In the circumstances, what the DCD had to do was to reach a factual determination in the light of the information available (non-confidential summaries), in which connection Article 17.6(i) prescribes the standard of deference to the national authorities ("That standard provides that panels shall ask only whether the authority's factual determinations were 'proper' and whether an authority's evaluation of those facts was 'unbiased and objective'". John Jackson, *The Jurisprudence of GATT & the WTO*, at page 154).

4.876 It is clear from the above that the DCD did not have the possibility of carrying out a new segmentation of the product under investigation and making the corresponding adjustments, since the information needed to do so was not provided. The DCD unquestionably acted in good faith and on good advice, using, in its determination of dumping, all of the information submitted. In the case of the segmentation of the product and the corresponding adjustments, the producers/exporters, i.e. the parties in possession of the information, did not provide any alternative to the DCD's analysis, nor did they object to that analysis.

4.877 If, as the EC claims, there was any other way of making the adjustment, the elements required for doing so should have been included in the record of the case as non-confidential summaries. Argentina is not aware of the existence of any other summaries in connection with this question of "due allowance". Consequently, there was no other information that could be taken into account.

4.878 Furthermore, if there had been any other information submitted as confidential information that would refute this and the EC wanted to prove its point, it should have removed the confidentiality and contributed it to this Panel. Since no further non-confidential summaries were provided and the confidentiality was not removed, it can only be inferred that there was insufficient information and that the DCD's conclusion was reasonable.

(c) Replies of Argentina to the First Set of Questions by the Panel Relating to the EC's Claim under Article 2.4 of the AD Agreement

4.879 Argentina replied to the first set of questions by the Panel relating to the EC's claim under Article 2.4 of the AD Agreement as follows.

4.880 The Panel asked the parties to clarify whether the exporters that replied to the questionnaire requested the DCD at some point to calculate the dumping margin on the basis of model-based comparisons. If so, the Panel further asked, what specific model-matching methodology was proposed? Could the parties provide the Panel with the relevant references either in the report or in the administrative record? The Panel also asked the EC to comment on the relevance in this respect of Exhibit EC-10.

4.881 To this question, Argentina provided the following reply.

4.882 Upon opening the investigation, the DCD decided on the segmentation of the product according to the universal criterion that offered the greatest homogeneity, i.e. *porcellanato* in its different sizes, establishing three categories: 20 x 20, 30 x 30 and 40 x 40. This segmentation not only met with no objection at any time during the investigation, but in fact, as shown by point 2 of Exhibit EC-10, it was suggested in the note sent by the representative of Assopiastrelle to its principal on 12 May 1999: "... Regarding non-confidential invoices, I suggest to select the some invoices of each segment (20 x 20, 30 x 30, etc.), with prices closer to the weight average of the segment." The first time the EC suggested that model-based comparisons could have been used was during the formal consultations under the DSU.

4.883 With respect to model-based determinations, Argentina submits the following: although certain submissions by some of the participating firms suggest that they were interested in model-based comparisons for the goods previously segmented according to their physical dimensions (30 x 30, 20 x 20 and 40 x 40), the documentation and information supplied for that purpose did not enable the implementing authority to carry out the required analysis with any accuracy. Moreover, the implementing authority was not in a position to conduct a comprehensive analysis of all of the information and documentation in the record of the proceedings since it did not have at its disposal all of the documentation to back the assertions of the interested parties and to permit a correlation with the information contained in the official registers.

4.884 If the exporters did request the DCD to do its margin calculations on the basis of models, the Panel asked the parties to clarify what was the DCD's response to that request.

4.885 Argentina answered that its reply to this question was implicit in its reply to the previous question.

4.886 The Panel recalled that, independently of whether the exporters asked for a model-based comparison of normal value and export prices, the record suggested that prices of tiles vary significantly, even within a single size category, on account of differences in processing (polished/unpolished), quality, and colour (for instance, Bismantova's price list submitted to the Panel as Exhibit EC-5 C). The DCD itself recognized (in page 28 of the Final Dumping Determination) that the exporters' sales information revealed considerable price differences in products of equal size and lower sales prices for the larger sizes than for the smaller sizes. On account of this situation, the Panel asked the parties whether they were of the view that the requirement to adjust for physical differences affecting price comparability could be met in this investigation by comparing normal values and export prices corresponding to the same size category.

4.887 Argentina replied to this question in the affirmative. In the circumstances of this case, the only way in which a price comparison could be made was to take the size as a basis for comparison.

4.888 The Panel asked Argentina whether it was of the view that the infinite number of physical differences made adjustment beyond size impracticable, and that Article 2.4 would recognize an exception in this respect. Additionally, was Argentina's view that the exporters failed to support such an adjustment by not providing sufficient data? The Panel further asked Argentina, if the data were considered inadequate, to what extent was such inadequacy based on the confidential nature of the information supplied, and were the exporters informed thereof?

4.889 Argentina replied that, while the physical differences made it almost impossible to carry out an adjustment, this is not an exception to Article 2.4, but a reasonable application in a specific case of the obligation contained therein, particularly given the irrelevance of the information supplied to that end by the exporters. However, the fact that the exporters did not provide sufficient information also contributed to the impossibility of making other adjustments for physical characteristics. The inadequacy of the information was not due to its confidentiality, but to its insufficiency.

4.890 The Panel recalled Argentina's statement to the effect that the exporters did not object to the DCD's adjusting only for size, and not for quality or other physical differences affecting price comparability. The Panel asked the EC whether it agreed with this characterization of the evidence. The Panel further asked the parties to comment on the relevance this fact could have under Article 2.4. In other words, the Panel asked, if the investigating authorities have reason to believe that certain physical differences, in fact, affect price comparability, and if the record contains evidence sufficient to make such an adjustment, would the acceptance by the exporters of the adjustments actually made relieve the authorities of the need to make further adjustments?

4.891 Argentina replied that the relevance of that fact under Article 2.4 is that the criterion used was the only possible criterion for analysing the like product in all of its sizes, and this is why the exporters accepted the DCD's approach. Moreover, given the facts of this case, the question is a hypothetical one, since the record did not contain evidence sufficient to make other adjustments that would permit a fair comparison.

4.892 Argentina addressed the three questions by the Panel transcribed below at once.

4.893 The Panel recalled that the EC argued in its first written submission (at para. 77) that the DCD did adjust normal value in order to reflect the physical differences between polished and unpolished tiles. However, the DCD's report raised this issue exclusively in the context of margin calculations for one of the exporters (Caesar), and, even in this case (see page 29 of the Final Dumping Determination), it suggested that the information on home prices provided by the exporter concerned was rejected by the DCD on the grounds that that home sales of polished tiles could not be compared to export sales of unpolished tiles. The Panel asked the parties to clarify whether the adjustment concerned was made.

4.894 The Panel recalled that, for initiation purposes, it appeared that the DCD calculated normal value according to price quotations for unpolished, first quality tiles and that this estimate of normal value, adjusted on account of the evidence provided during the course of the proceedings, was also used for calculating normal value for the final determination. The Panel asked Argentina to indicate whether the pricing data used for calculating normal value for the final determination corresponds in effect to unpolished, first quality tiles, or was this pricing data expanded at some point to cover all kinds of tiles. In either case, the Panel further asked Argentina, could the Panel be provided with the relevant references in either the report or in the administrative record?

4.895 The Panel also recalled that it appeared that the DCD calculated the export price for the final determination on the basis of unit prices, drawn from official import records. The Panel asked Argentina whether this export price referred to unpolished, first quality tiles or rather to all kinds of tiles. In either case, the Panel further asked Argentina, could the Panel be provided with the relevant references in either the report or in the administrative record?

4.896 To these questions, Argentina provided the following reply.

4.897 To begin with, it should be pointed out that during the investigation at issue, the implementing authority always considered, in its various determinations, the unpolished product.

4.898 Evidence of this can be found in the administrative record in the various technical reports referring to the determinations, which reveal that the implementing authority considered information relating to the unpolished product and discarded any information relating to flags and paving tiles of fine earthenware *porcellanato*, polished.

4.899 Regarding the recognition of the differences in value, in order to illustrate precisely how the documentation supplied to the implementing authority was treated, specific reference is made to the case of the Italian manufacturing export company Caesar. As stated in the report on the final determination of the margin of dumping in the relevant Annex, in that case information was provided on the relevant adjustment to be made and, as stated, it was considered in the treatment of the information.

4.900 At the same time, Argentina reiterates that the export price considered in the various determinations corresponds to the unpolished product only, whether the analysis was conducted on the basis of the information provided by official sources or on the basis of information provided by the various firms involved in the proceedings.

4.901 Thus, the entire dumping analysis was conducted on the basis of the information in the record of the proceedings in respect of unpolished *porcellanato*.

4.902 Finally, the fact that the product considered was the unpolished product is reflected in the decision contained in the final resolution introducing the definitive anti-dumping measure.

(d) Arguments of Argentina in its Second Written Submission Relating to the EC's Claim under Article 2.4 of the AD Agreement

4.903 In its second written submission, Argentina made the following arguments relating to the EC's claim under Article 2.4 of the AD Agreement.

4.904 Argentina submits that it acted in accordance with Article 2.4, since the DCD made a fair comparison taking account of the physical characteristics (the diversity of the investigated tiles) in the light of the "particular circumstances" (infinite number of models, colours, designs etc.) and opted for a factor, size, which reflected the greatest universality and applied to the greatest quantity of imports of the product under investigation.

4.905 Indeed, the size is the element which provided the best possibility of making the adjustments, since it formed part of the segmentation decided upon at the opening of the investigation and, as stated in paragraphs 103 *et seq.* of Argentina's first written submission, it enabled the authority to make the most comprehensive "fair comparison on the merits of the case" (infinite number of models, colours, etc.).

4.906 At the same time this "fair comparison" on the basis of the size of the tiles is consistent with the Article 2.4 obligation, which mentions "physical characteristics". Or are the differences in size perhaps not a physical characteristic of the tiles that should be taken into consideration?

4.907 Moreover, this reasoning on the part of the authority is consistent with the definition of the like product that includes the different sizes of tiles, and at the same time makes it possible to carry out the adjustment for 99.29 per cent of the imports. It is difficult to see how it would be possible to carry out a more comprehensive "fair comparison" using a different criterion, one which covers the remaining 0.71 per cent of the imports that do not fall within any of these three size categories.

4.908 It should be stressed that what the DCD in fact did was to make a fair comparison on the basis of the physical characteristics of the models in keeping with the obligation to carry out a "fair comparison" on the basis of the physical characteristics which the Appellate Body understands as an essential obligation under Article 2.4 ("Article 2.4 sets forth a general obligation to make a 'fair comparison' between export price and normal value. This is a general obligation that, in our view, informs all of Article 2, but applies, in particular, to Article 2.4.2 which is specifically made 'subject to the provisions governing fair comparison in [Article 2.4]'. Moreover, Article 2.4 sets forth specific obligations to make comparisons at the same level of trade and at, as nearly as possible, the same time. Article 2.4 also requires that 'due allowance' be made for differences affecting 'price comparability'. We note, in particular, that Article 2.4 requires investigating authorities to make due allowance for 'differences in ... physical characteristics'. Moreover, Article 2.4 contains the specific obligation to make the comparisons at the same level of trade and at as nearly as possible the same time. It adds that 'due account shall be made ... for differences which affect price comparability'. We note, in particular, that Article 2.4 *requires the investigating authority to make due allowance for 'differences in ... physical characteristics'* ". Appellate Body Report, *European Communities - Anti-Dumping Duties on Imports of Cotton-Type Bed Linen from India*, WT/DS141/AB/R, adopted 12 March 2001, at para. 59, emphasis added by Argentina).

4.909 Additionally, Argentina would ask the panel, in considering this point, to consider the standard of review applied within the framework of the AD Agreement, as stipulated in Article 17.6 thereof.

4.910 As the Agreement speaks of deference to the investigating authority, the evaluation of the facts that the authority conducted cannot be considered inconsistent with the Agreement. The conclusion reached in the light of the facts of the case (diversity of models, colours, etc.) that the size of the tiles was the main physical characteristic that permitted the segmentation of the product for the purposes of making a fair comparison cannot be qualified as "biased" or "unobjective".

4.911 As stated in paragraphs 96 to 101 of Argentina's first written submission, it is the standard of deference established in Article 17.6(i) and 17.6(ii) of the AD Agreement that gives the authority the discretion to decide on the method by which it makes the comparison. This has been recognized in a number of past cases which upheld the "principle of deference" with respect to the methodology applied by the investigating authorities in anti-dumping cases (" ... the Panel was not faced with a choice among multiple 'permissible' interpretations which would have required it, under Article 17.6(ii), to give deference to the interpretation relied upon by the by the European Communities", Appellate Body Report, *European Communities - Anti-Dumping Duties on Imports of Cotton-Type Bed Linen from India*, adopted 12 March 2001, WT/DS/141/AB/R, at para. 65).

4.912 In this case, the authority's criterion for making a "fair" comparison was "homogenization" which, as mentioned, ultimately amounts to a standardization based on certain parameters which by their nature reflect a certain universality within the product investigated.

4.913 As mentioned in paragraph 87 of Argentina's first written submission, there were 78 manufacturers of *porcellanato*, each of which produced dozens of different varieties which, in their turn, could be discontinued at any time or replaced by similar articles with a different product code or trade name. The above applied to each supplier. This is why the implementing authority decided to establish as a basis for comparison the most representative dimensions in terms of the volume exported, since this was the only variable that applied to all of the articles from all of the suppliers and was not affected by market considerations from one supplier to the other.

4.914 On this basis, the DCD "reasonably" analysed the facts, applying to them the obligations set forth in the actual text of the agreement and without having to introduce criteria such as a posteriori adjustment which are not specifically provided for in the text of Article 2.4.

(e) Arguments of Argentina in its Second Oral Statement Relating to the EC's Claim under Article 2.4 of the AD Agreement

4.915 In its second oral statement, Argentina made the following arguments relating to the EC's claim under Article 2.4 of the AD Agreement.

4.916 Argentina refutes the EC's statement in paragraph 76 of its second written submission, since Exhibit ARG-22 makes it clear that the supporting documentation provided by the exporters was not sufficiently explanatory for the authority to be able to make a fair comparison owing to differences in the physical characteristics of the different models.

4.917 Similarly, the differences revealed by Exhibit ARG-22 illustrate the diversity of models and colours. Taking account of the information supplied during the proceedings with respect to the physical characteristics, the investigating authority, in conformity with Article 17.6(i), concluded that the size of the tiles was the prevailing factor - physical characteristic - for the purposes of making a fair comparison. This cannot be qualified as a "biased" or "unobjective" evaluation in the light of the facts of the case.

4.918 Hence Argentina has argued, and continues to argue, that the difference in size is a physical characteristic which has real effects on prices.

4.919 This is consistent with the Appellate Body's statement in *European Communities - Anti-Dumping Duties on Imports of Cotton-Type Bed Linen from India* that Article 2.4 requires that "due allowance" be made for differences affecting price comparability. The size of the tiles is precisely the difference which has a great impact on price comparability. The implementing authority is required to make due allowance for these differences, and the DCD did so in the present case on the basis of the duly adopted segmentation.

4.920 The EC apparently does not accept that a comparison should have been made on the basis of size, as if this were not a physical characteristic of the tiles.

4.921 As stated in one of Argentina's reply to a question by the Panel following the first meeting, and in confirmation of what has already been said, the implementing authority examined information relating to the unpolished product and discarded any information relating to flags and paving tiles of fine earthenware *porcellanato*, polished.

4.922 As regards Caesar, which only sold polished *porcellanato* on its domestic market, a fair adjustment was duly made, as recorded in the report on the final determination of the margin of dumping, and this was considered during the investigation.

4.923 Argentina does not understand why the EC asserts, in paragraph 79 of its second written submission, that due allowance must be made for all the differences in physical characteristics when the Article 2.4 obligation is subject to or limited by the particular circumstances surrounding the subject of the investigation. Indeed, the relevant part of the article stipulates that "... Due allowance shall be made in each case, on its merits, for differences which affect price comparability ..." .

(f) Replies of Argentina to the Second Set of Questions by the Panel Relating to the EC's Claim under Article 2.4 of the AD Agreement

4.924 Argentina replied to the second set of questions by the Panel relating to the EC's claim under Article 2.4 of the AD Agreement as follows:

4.925 The Panel asked Argentina whether it was of the view that were other physical differences affecting price comparability apart from size. The Panel further asked Argentina what was the basis for the DCD's assumption that, by adjusting for size, it had adjusted for other physical differences affecting price comparability.

4.926 Argentina replied that the DCD's approach was to resort to the basic and elementary physical characteristic of product size (20 x 20, 30 x 30, 40 x 40, etc.). This classification was not questioned at any time during the proceedings and it enabled the implementing authority to make a proper and irrefutable comparison.

4.927 There were probably other physical differences that affected price comparability, but the implementing authority, on the basis of the evidence in the record of the proceedings, considered that the physical characteristic that affected price comparability was the physical size or dimensions.

4.928 If the adjustments for physical differences are only granted upon good cause shown, the Panel asked the parties whether the calculation of the dumping margin by model should not be subject to the same requirement. If this was so, the Panel further asked the parties whether the calculation of the dumping margin by model would be necessary when the same models are sold in both markets in the same proportions.

4.929 Argentina replied that the investigation of adjustments, for example, for physical characteristics, involves evaluating whether such adjustments, if they affect price comparability, should be made. If so, they should only be made where the implementing authority has evidence. With respect to the calculation by model, when the same models are sold in both markets in the same proportions, no adjustments are necessary.

4.930 The Panel recalled that in a reply to question posed by the Panel following the first meeting, Argentina stated that "Upon opening the investigation, the DCD decided on the segmentation of the product according to the universal criterion that offered the greatest homogeneity, i.e. *porcellanato* in its different sizes, establishing three categories: 20 x 20, 30 x 30 and 40 x 40". The Panel asked Argentina to direct the Panel to the evidence on the record showing that the DCD had made this determination from the moment of initiating the investigation. In addition, the Panel recalled that, in its reply to the same question, the EC argued that the exporters requested that a model-to-model comparison be made. The Panel also asked the EC to direct the Panel to the evidence on the record that demonstrated that the exporters explicitly requested such a comparison.

4.931 Argentina replied that the classification applied by the DCD on the basis of the mentioned criterion was defended during the various stages of the investigation and is based on a technical report on the feasibility of initiating an investigation which was provided to the Panel as Exhibit ARG-25. Moreover, the report in Exhibit EC-10 by the representative of the Italian exporting firms in Argentina recognizes this segmentation:

Regarding non-confidential invoices, I suggest to select some invoices of each segment (20 x 20, 30 x 30, etc.) with prices closer to the weight average of the segment.

4.932 The Panel recalled that, according to Exhibit EC-10 (at page 2), the local counsel to the exporters in Argentina suggested to the counsel to the exporters in Brussels to provide the DCD invoices with prices "closer to the weight average of the segment". The Panel asked the parties whether this statement suggested that the representatives of the exporters were aware of the fact that the DCD would calculate the normal value for any size category on the basis of all of the home prices available for that size category, irrespective of the model to which those prices referred to. The Panel further asked the parties to comment on the implications of this statement, if any. Did this suggest that the exporters were aware of the fact that their information was going to be compared per size rather than per model?

4.933 To this question, Argentina provided the following reply.

4.934 The meeting held by the DCD technical staff was not a formal meeting, and the report by the legal representatives of the Italian exporting firms in Argentina falls outside this technical sphere.

4.935 Argentina notes, however, that the Argentine authority does not know what is behind the thinking of the exporting firms. Argentina reiterates that any comparison made must be based on technical criteria, supported by documentation which reflects the arguments made during the proceedings.

4.936 During the investigation, the authority communicated its conclusions through a series of technical reports reflecting the technical criteria used. Thus, the comparison and classification criteria were duly examined by the authority, and the parties involved had the opportunity to familiarize themselves with them and contribute evidence in support of their respective positions. In other words, the classification used throughout the investigation did not give rise to any comments, and as the investigation proceeded, the classification was effectively endorsed.

4.937 As stated in the previous reply, it has been clearly shown that the exporters were informed that the criterion that the implementing authority would continue to use for the purposes of calculating the margin of dumping, based on the information supplied, would be the physical dimensions of the product at issue.

4.938 Finally, it would have been inconceivable for the DCD to have used another criterion, considering that the exporters themselves, in their replies to the questionnaire (in the different Annexes) stated that the information was not available according to code, model or type. What kind of adjustment did the EC expect the DCD to make?

4.939 Argentina refers the Panel to Exhibit ARG-24 which contains the following documentation.

4.940 Casalgrande: File No. 061-010304/98 of 10 December 1998 - folio 876.

- Annex IV. Information on producer/exporter market. "Information not available by model, code or type, but overall information is available concerning gres porcellanato."
- Annex V. Summary of producer/exporter sales. "Information not available by model, code or type, but overall information is available concerning gres porcellanato."
- Annex VI. Summary of producer/exporter sales. "Information not available by model, code or type, but overall information is available concerning *gres porcellanato*."

4.941 Caesar: File No. 061-010305/98 of 10 December 1998 - folio 879.

Annex IV. Information on the producer/exporter market. "This type of information is not available by model, code or type. The information provided refers to porcellanato in general."

- Annex V. Summary of producer/exporter sales. "This type of information is not available by model, code or type. The information provided refers to porcellanato in general."
- Annex VI. Summary of producer/exporter sales. "This type of information is not available by model, code or type. The information provided refers to *porcellanato* in general."

4.942 Marazzi: File No. 061-010306/98 of 10 December 1998 - folio 880.

Annex IV. *Information on the producer/exporter market.* "This type of information is not available by model, code or type. The information provided refers to *porcellanato* in general."

- *Annex V. Summary of producer/exporter sales.* "This type of information is not available by model, code or type. The information provided refers to *porcellanato* in general."
- *Annex VI. Summary of producer/*exporter sales. "This type of information is not available by model, code or type. The information provided refers to *porcellanato* in general."

4.943 Bismantova: File No. 061-010307/98 of 10 December 1998 - folio 881.

- Annex IV. Information *on the producer/exporter market.* "This type of information is not available by model, code or type. The information provided refers to *porcellanato* in general."
- *Annex V. Summary of producer/exporter sales.* "The description of the model/code/type is provided in Sections B and C. The information provided in this table corresponds to the total amounts of sales made."

4.944 Casalgrande: File No. 061-010304/98 of 10 December 1998 - folio 876.

- Annex III. List of importers in Argentina and third countries of the goods under investigation.
- Annex IV. Information on the producer/exporter market.

- Annex V. Summary of producer/exporter sales.
- Annex VI. Summary of producer/exporter sales.
- Annex VII. Actual exports to Argentina (1997 and 1998).
- Annex VIII. Sales in the Italian domestic market (1997 and 1998).
- Annex IX. Exports to third countries.
- Annex X. Cost structure of the goods under investigation in the Italian domestic market in 1997 and 1998.
- Annex XI. Cost structure of the exported goods.

4.945 Caesar: File No. 061-010305/98 of 10 December 1998 - folio 879.

Annex III. List of importers in Argentina and third countries of the goods under investigation.

- Annex IV. Information on the producer/exporter market.
- Annex V. Summary of producer/exporter sales.
- Annex VI. Summary of producer/exporter sales.
- Annex VII. Actual exports to Argentina (1997 and 1998).
- Annex VIII. Sales in the Italian domestic market.
- Annex IX. Exports to third countries.
- Annex X. Cost structure of the goods under investigation in the Italian domestic market.
- Annex XI. Cost structure of the exported goods.

4.946 Marazzi: File No. 061-010306/98 of 10 December 1998 - folio 880.

- Annex III. List of importers in Argentina and third countries of the goods under investigation.
- Annex IV. Information on the producer/exporter market.
- Annex V. Summary of producer/exporter sales.
- Annex VI. Summary of producer/exporter sales.
- Annex VII. Actual exports to Argentina (1997 and 1998).
- Annex VIII. Sales in the Italian domestic market.
- Annex IX. Exports to third countries.
- Annex X. Cost structure of the goods under investigation in the Italian domestic market.
- Annex XI. Cost structure of the exported goods.

4.947 Bismantova: File No. 061-010307/98 of 10 December 1998 - folio 881.

Annex III. List of importers in Argentina and third countries of the goods under investigation.

- Annex IV. Information on the producer/exporter market.
- Annex V. Summary of producer/exporter sales.

- Annex VI. Summary of producer/exporter sales.
- Annex VII. Actual exports to Argentina (1997 and 1998).
- Annex VIII. Sales in the Italian domestic market.
- Annex IX. Exports to third countries.
- Annex X. Cost structure of the goods under investigation in the Italian domestic market.
- Annex XI. Cost structure of the exported goods.

3. Third Parties: Japan

4.948 Japan did not address the EC's claim under Article 2.4 of the AD Agreement either in its written submission nor in its oral statement.

4. Third Parties: Turkey

4.949 Turkey did not address the EC's claim under Article 2.4 of the AD Agreement either in its written submission nor in its oral statement.

5. Third Parties: The United States

(a) Arguments of the United States in its Written Submission Relating to the EC's Claim under Article 2.4 of the AD Agreement

4.950 In its written submission, the United States made the following arguments relating to the EC's claim under Article 2.4 of the AD Agreement.

4.951 The EC submits that Argentina violated Article 2.4 of the AD Agreement by not making a fair comparison between the export price and normal value because Argentina did not make "due allowance" for certain differences in physical characteristics between the models of the subject merchandise exported to Argentina and those sold in Italy. Argentina replies that it made a reasonable adjustment for differences in physical characteristics which is entitled to deference under Article 17.6(i).

4.952 Article 2.1 and 2.2 of the AD Agreement establish that the essence of the determination of dumping is a comparison of export sales with sales of the like product in the home market or third country. Article 2.6, in turn, defines "like product" as "a product which is identical, i.e. alike in all respects to the product under consideration" or, in the absence of such a product, one which "has characteristics closely resembling those of the product under consideration." Finally, Article 2.4 lists differences in physical characteristics as differences for which adjustment may be warranted.

4.953 The United States submits that determining whether the obligation in Article 2.4 has been met is very fact-sensitive. For example, in this case, the United States does not know which differences in physical characteristics of ceramic floor tiles are sufficiently important that adjustments would need to be made. Therefore, the United States cannot comment on whether Argentina made reasonable adjustments. Instead, the United States urges the Panel, in reviewing such a fact-intensive issue, to pay particular attention to the mandate of Article 17.6(i): if the establishment of the facts is proper, and their evaluation unbiased and objective, the Panel should not overturn that evaluation even if the Panel would have reached a different conclusion (see, Panel Report, *Mexico - Anti-Dumping Investigation of High Fructose Corn Syrup (HFCS) from the United States*, WT/DS132/R, adopted 24 February 2000, at para 7.94).

4.954 The United States did not address in its oral statement the EC's claim relating to Article 2.4 of the AD Agreement.

D. Claim under Article 6.9 of the AD Agreement

1. The EC

(a) Arguments by the EC in its First Written Submission in Support of its Claim under Article 6.9 of the AD Agreement

4.955 In its first written submission, the EC made the following arguments in support of its claim under Article 6.9 of the AD Agreement.

4.956 According to the EC, the DCD did not inform the exporters of the "essential" facts concerning the existence of dumping which would form the basis for the decision whether to apply definitive measures. As a result, the exporters were prevented from defending adequately their interests. By not disclosing those "essential facts" to the exporters before the imposition of the definitive anti-dumping measures, the DCD violated Article 6.9 of the AD Agreement.

4.957 The EC presented first a number of facts relevant for its legal arguments.

4.958 By letter dated 28 August 1999, the DCD informed the exporters that the "*etapa probatoria*" of the investigation had been concluded and invited them to examine the public file and, should they consider it necessary, to submit their final allegations ("*alegato final*") no later than 10 September.

4.959 On 3 September 1999, representatives of the exporters inspected the public file. Unlike the Final Injury Determination, the Final Dumping Determination was not available in the public file. Nor did the public file contain any other document prepared by the DCD which identified the "essential facts" that would form the basis of the Final Dumping Determination.

4.960 On 6 September 1999, the exporters addressed a letter to the DCD in which they requested the DCD to disclose the essential facts under consideration which would form the basis for the DCD's final determination of dumping. The request invoked expressly Article 6.9 of the AD Agreement.

4.961 By letter dated 9 September 1999, the DCD informed the exporters that, as far as the dumping determination was concerned, the Argentinean authorities considered that the disclosure requirements imposed by Article 6.9 were fully complied with by granting to the interested parties access to the public file.

4.962 Specifically, the DCD attempted to justify its refusal to disclose the "essential facts" concerning dumping as follows:

> ... el procedimiento habitual implementado por la SUBSECRETARIA DE COMERCIO EXTERIOR en lo referente at tratamiento de este aspecto del Acuerdo Relativo a la aplicación del Articulo VI del Acuerdo General sobre Aranceles Aduaneros y Comercio de 1994 en su artículo 6.9, recogido en la legislación argentina por la Ley No. 24.425, queda absolutamente cumplimentado por parte de la Autoridad de Aplicación al momento que la DIRECCION DE COMPETENCIA DESLEAL de la SUBSECRETARIA DE COMERCIO EXTERIOR ha comunicado for medio fehaciente a todas las partes intervienientes en el procedimiento el cierre de la etapa probatoria, conjuntamente con la invitación a tomar vista de todo lo actuado en el expediente en cuestión a fin de informarse de todos los hechos esenciales producidos a esa fecha y presentar en base a toda la información recabada en ese momento y, si lo desean, su correspondiente alegato.

4.963 The EC presented next its legal arguments relating to its claim under Article 2.4 of the AD Agreement.

4.964 The EC recalled that Article 6.9 of the AD Agreement provides that:

> The authorities shall, before a final determination is made, inform all interested parties of the essential facts under consideration which form the basis for the decision whether to apply definitive measures. Such disclosure should take place in sufficient time for the parties to defend their interests.

4.965 Article 6.9 imposes upon the investigating authorities a duty "to inform" the interested parties. The ordinary meaning of that term ("to give knowledge of something", "to tell", "to acquaint with", *Webster's New World Dictionary*, Third College Edition) demands a positive action from the investigating authorities, which goes beyond merely granting access to the file.

4.966 The public file of an anti-dumping investigation consists essentially of questionnaire responses and allegations submitted by the different interested parties, which are often contradictory. Thus, the mere examination of the public file does not, as such, allow the interested parties to identify the "essential facts" on the basis of which the authorities intend to impose definitive measures. Indeed, it is precisely for that reason that Article 6.9 requires the investigating authorities to indicate to the interested parties which, of all the facts contained in the file, are the "essential facts" that will form the basis for their decision, so that the interested parties can defend their interests adequately.

4.967 If, as contended by the DCD, the disclosure requirements imposed by Article 6.9 could be fulfilled simply by granting access to the file, that provision would become redundant, since the requirement to provide access to the file is already stipulated in very comprehensive terms in Article 6.4, which provides that

> The authorities shall whenever practicable provide timely opportunities for all the interested parties to see all information that is relevant to the presentation of their cases, that is not confidential as defined in paragraph 5, and that is used by the authorities in an anti-dumping investigation, and to prepare presentations on the basis of this information.

4.968 On Argentina's interpretation, Article 6.9 would add nothing to the requirements already imposed by Article 6.4. Argentina's reading of Article 6.9, therefore, must be rejected in accordance with the basic principle of interpretation that requires to give effective meaning to all the terms of a treaty ("An interpreter is not free to adopt a reading that would result in reducing whole clauses or paragraphs of a treaty to redundancy or inutility", Appellate Body Report, *United States - Standards for Reformulated and Conventional Gasoline*, WT/DS2/AB/R, adopted 20 May 1996. See also the Appellate Body Report, *Japan - Taxes on Alcoholic Beverages*, WT/DS8/AB/R, WT/DS10/AB/R, WT/DS11/AB/R, adopted 1 November 1996, at page 12; and Appellate Body Report, *US - Restrictions on Imports of Cotton and Man Made Fibre Underwear*, WT/DS24/AB/R, adopted on 25 February 1997, at page 16).

(b) Arguments in the EC's First Oral Statement in Support of its Claim under Article 6.9 of the AD Agreement

4.969 In its first oral statement, the EC made the following arguments in support of its claim under Article 6.9 of the AD Agreement.

4.970 There is no disagreement between the parties with respect to the relevant facts. The only issue before the Panel is one of legal interpretation, namely whether the investigating authorities can fulfil the obligation imposed by Article 6.9 simply by giving access to the file to the interested parties.

4.971 This issue has been settled by the Panel on *Guatemala - Cement II*, which rejected in rather categorical terms the position maintained by Argentina in this case (Panel Report, *Guatemala - Definitive Anti-Dumping Measures on Grey Portland Cement from Mexico*, WT/DS156/R, adopted 17 November 2000, at para. 8.22). In its submission, Argentina seeks to distinguish the two cases by arguing that the Guatemalan authorities offered to provide a copy of the public file, while the DCD allowed the exporters access to the file. With respect, the EC fails to see the relevance of this distinction.

4.972 Argentina also argues that, at any rate, the violation of Article 6.9 would be a "harmless error". As mentioned before, the EC considers that this is not a valid defence under the WTO Agreement.

4.973 The EC is concerned by Argentina's extraordinary assertion that a violation of Article 6.9 is "by its own nature" a harmless error, because "it lacks the necessary importance to vary the conclusions of the investigating authority" (the original Spanish text states: *"un error que, por su propia naturaleza, carece de la entidad sufficiente como para variar las conclusiones de la Autoridad de Aplicación"*. This suggests that, not only in this case but also as a matter of general practice, the DCD regards the disclosure of essential facts as an empty formality and pays no attention to the comments submitted by interested parties. The EC believes that, quite to the contrary, the disclosure provided in Article 6.9 constitutes an essential procedural safeguard, the omission of which vitiates necessarily the final determination.

(c) Replies of the EC to the First Set of Questions by the Panel Relating to the EC's Claim under Article 6.9 of the AD Agreement

4.974 The EC replied to the first of questions by the Panel relating to the EC's claim under Article 6.9 of the AD Agreement as follows.

4.975 The Panel asked the parties what was, in their view, the object and purpose of the requirement of Article 6.9 AD Agreement to disclose "the essential facts under consideration".

4.976 The EC replied that the essential purpose of Article 6.9 was to allow the parties to defend adequately their interests.

4.977 If the purpose of Article 6.9 was to enable parties better to defend their interests, the Panel asked the parties whether this interpretation suggested that a Party claiming a violation of Article 6.9 also should present information to the Panel on how its exporters were impeded in their defence.

4.978 The EC replied to this question in the negative. The wording of Article 6.9 was unqualified. It required the investigating authority to make always disclosure of the "essential facts". This reflected the assumption that the omission of this essential procedural safeguard will necessarily prejudice the rights of defence of interested parties.

4.979 According to the EC, the violation of the obligation imposed by Article 6.9, like the violation of any other obligation imposed by the WTO Agreement, is presumed, in accordance with Article 2.3 of the DSU, to cause nullification or impairment. It is for Argentina to rebut that presumption.

4.980 The Panel recalled that, in paragraph 79 of its first written submission, Argentina distinguished the DCD's practice from that of the Guatemalan authority which the Panel in the *Guatemala - Cement (II)* case found to be inconsistent with Article 6.9 AD Agreement. Argentina asserted that "it should be stressed that although "*dar copia*" ("providing a copy") was not sufficient to comply with the Article 6.9 obligations, the scope of the expression "*dar vista*" ("give sight") is different, since contrary to the expression "*dar copia*", it implies notifying the interested parties of the record of the proceedings". The Panel asked the parties to comment on the importance of this difference, if any.

4.981 The EC replied that it failed to see the relevance of the distinction drawn by Argentina. If anything, the attitude of the Guatemalan authorities seemed to be more advantageous to the exporters, since by providing the exporters with copies of the file, instead of simply allowing them to inspect it in situ, they gave the exporters the possibility to study the file more carefully

4.982 The Panel asked the parties what, if any, were the essential facts under consideration that the exporters were not informed of.

4.983 The EC replied that, as a minimum, the DCD should have disclosed which "facts available" would be relied upon for establishing the normal value and the export price.

4.984 The Panel asked the parties whether, in their view, the fact that the information from the exporters was disregarded for the calculation of normal value and export price was an essential fact of which the exporters should have been informed under Article 6.9 AD Agreement.

4.985 The EC replied that this question in the affirmative and stated that this was without prejudice to the specific requirements imposed by paragraph 6 of Annex II.

(d) Arguments in the EC's Second Written Submission in Support of its Claim under Article 6.9 of the AD Agreement

4.986 In its second written submission, the EC made the following arguments in support of its claim under Article 6.9 of the AD Agreement.

4.987 There is no disagreement between the parties with respect to the relevant facts underlying the EC's claim under Article 6.9. The only issue before the Panel is one of legal interpretation, namely whether the investigating authorities can fulfil the obligation imposed by Article 6.9 simply by giving access to the file to the interested parties.

4.988 This issue has been settled by the panel on *Guatemala - Cement (II)*, which rejected in categorical terms the position maintained by Argentina in this case (see Panel Report, *Guatemala - Definitive Anti-Dumping Measures on Grey Portland Cement from Mexico*, WT/DS156/R, adopted 17 November 2000, at para. 8.22). In its first written submission, Argentina seeks to distinguish the two cases by arguing that the Guatemalan authorities offered to provide a copy of the public file, while the DCD allowed the exporters access to the file. The EC fails to see the relevance of this distinction.

4.989 The EC agrees with Argentina, and with the United States, that Article 6.9 does not prescribe any particular method of disclosure. Thus, for instance, the investigating authority may choose to make the disclosure at a "disclosure conference", as suggested by Japan in its third party submission, or in a written document sent to the parties (the usual practice in the EC). This does not mean, however, that Article 6.9 leaves complete discretion to the investigating authority for choosing the method of disclosure. For the reasons explained by the Panel in *Guatemala - Cement (II)*, merely granting access to the file is *per se* an inapt method to achieve the result mandated by Article 6.9 and, therefore, incompatible with that provision.

4.990 The textual analysis of Article 6.9 made by the United States is selective and flawed. Contrary to the US assertion, Article 6.9 does not "describe the facts of which interested parties must be informed as the 'essential facts under consideration'". The United States gloss over the terms "which form the basis for the decision whether to apply definitive measures". Those terms qualify the phrase "essential facts under consideration" and are of crucial importance for the correct interpretation of Article 6.9. They indicate clearly that the investigating authority is required to identify which facts will be relied upon in the decision whether to impose measures.

4.991 The United States contends that the EC's interpretation would prevent interested parties from defending their interests, because they would not be informed of those facts that do not support the determination that the authority intends to make. According to the United States, "if a party is not informed of a fact under Article 6.9, it may never know that fact exists at all". This is not correct. The United States overlook that other provisions of Article 9 already ensure that the parties are informed of all relevant facts. In particular, the United States disregard that Article 6.4 requires the investigating authorities to give access to all "information that is relevant for the presentation of their cases ... and that is used by the authorities in an anti-anti-dumping investigation".

4.992 As noted correctly by the panel in *Guatemala - Cement (II)*, the interpretation of Article 6.9 made by Argentina and the United States in this case would render redundant that provision (Panel Report, *Guatemala - Definitive Anti-Dumping Measures on Grey Portland Cement from Mexico*, WT/DS156/R, adopted 17 November 2000, at para. 8.230). The contorted arguments advanced by the United States in order to distinguish its reading of Article 6.9 from the requirements imposed by Article 6.4 are contrived and unconvincing. In light of those arguments, it is ironic that the United States accuses the EC and Japan of engaging in a "tortured" interpretation of Article 6.9.

4.993 Furthermore, in order to give meaning to Article 6.9, the United States is forced to make an unduly narrow interpretation of Article 6.4. According to the United States, Article 6.9 would address the situation where an investigating authority may legitimately refuse access to the file on the grounds that it would be "impracticable" to do so. However, Article 6.4 does not say that interested parties will be given access to the file only "if practicable", but rather that they will do so "whenever practicable" (this difference comes even clearer in the French version, which reads *"chaque fois que cela sera réalisable"*). The terms "whenever practicable" do not address the question of "whether" the investigating authority must grant access to the file, but exclusively the question of "when" to do so. Those terms reflect the assumption that it will always be "practicable" for the investigating authority to grant "timely opportunities" for seeing the file. They do not carve out an exception to the obligation imposed by Article 6.4, but rather reinforce such obligation. They make clear that, although the investigating authority is not required to make the file permanently accessible to the public, it must do so every time that it is practicable, rather than, for example, once at the end of the investigation.

4.994 The United States themselves recognise that a Member claiming that access to the record is not practicable "faces a heavy burden". Furthermore, at the third party session, the representatives of the United States admitted that the instances where a Member could refuse legitimately access to the file would be "exceptional". Thus, on the United States' own interpretation, Article 6.9 would be no more than a safeguard of last resort, which would become operational only in the exceptional situation where the investigation authority is not required to give access to the file pursuant to Article 6.4.

4.995 However, the interpretation of treaty provision cannot start from the unsupported premise that it is intended to apply only in exceptional circumstances. There is simply no indication in Article 6.9, or elsewhere in the AD Agreement, or in its drafting history, that Article 6.9 was designed to address only the very exceptional situation described by the United States (indeed, so exceptional that it is likely to remain purely hypothetical), or that the obligation imposed by Article 6.9 is subsidiary in any manner to that imposed by Article 6.4.

4.996 Argentina also argues that, at any rate, the violation of Article 6.9 is "by nature" a "harmless error". As mentioned above, the EC considers that this is not a valid defence. In any event, the EC believes that the disclosure provided for in Article 6.9 constitutes an essential procedural safeguard, the omission of which, "by nature", prejudices the rights of defence of interested parties and, therefore, vitiates necessarily and irreparably the final determination.

4.997 In its second oral statement, the EC did not address its claim under Article 6.9 of the AD Agreement.

4.998 The Panel did not ask the EC any questions following the second meeting relating to the EC's claim under Article 6.9 of the AD Agreement.

2. *Argentina*

(a) Arguments in Argentina's First Written Submission Relating to the EC's Claim under Article 6.9 of the AD Agreement

4.999 In its first written submission, Argentina made the following arguments relating to the EC's claim under Article 6.9 of the AD Agreement.

4.1000 Argentina first presented a number of facts relevant for its legal arguments.

4.1001 In its first written submission, the EC states as its fourth claim that contrary to the requirements set out in Article 6.9 of the AD Agreement, the DCD failed to inform exporters of the "essential facts" concerning the existence of dumping which would form the basis for the decision whether to apply the definitive measures.

4.1002 Article 6.9 of the AD Agreement stipulates that:

> The authorities shall, before a final determination is made, inform all interested parties of the essential facts under consideration which form the basis for the decision whether to apply the definitive measures. Such disclosure should take place in sufficient time for the parties to defend their interests.

4.1003 By Notes DCD No. 273-000586/99, 273-000587/99, 273-000588/99, 273-000589/99, 273-000590/99, 273-000591/99 and 273-000592/99 of 11 May 1999, the DCD informed the representatives of Canteras Cerro, Casalgrande, Caesar, Bismantova, Marazzi and Assopiastrelle, respectively, that " ... the judicial decision concerning the evidence duly provided by the firms involved in this investigation has been taken, so that those that so wish may consult the corresponding document and familiarize themselves with the decision contained therein ...".

4.1004 On 18 June 1999, the representative of Assopiastrelle confirmed that she had consulted file No. 061-000794/98 consisting of 25 sections with 7,368 folios and taken full note of the proceedings.

4.1005 The EC's first written submission cites a Note of 28 August 1999 in which the DCD informs exporters that the evidence-gathering stage of the investigation has terminated and invites them to consult the record and, where they deem necessary, submit their final pleadings before 10 September.

4.1006 On 3 September 1999, representatives of the exporters consulted the record, as recorded in Note DCD No. 273-001040/99. According to the EC submission, the Final Dumping Determination was not available in the record, nor did the record contain any other document prepared by the DCD which identified the "essential facts" that would form the basis of the Final Dumping Determination.

4.1007 As stated in the EC submission, by letter dated 9 September 1999, the DCD informed the exporters that, as far as the dumping determination was concerned, the Argentine authorities considered that the disclosure requirements imposed by Article 6.9 were fully complied with by granting to the interested parties access to the record.

4.1008 Indeed, in Note DCD No. 273-001040/99 of 9 September 1999 to Assopiastrelle, Bismantova, Casalgrande, Caesar and Marazzi, the DCD pointed out that "... the usual procedure applied by the Undersecretariat for Foreign Trade when addressing this aspect of Article 6.9 of the Agreement on Implementation of Article VI of the General Agreement on Tariffs and Trade of 1994, incorporated into Argentine legislation through Law No. 24.425, was respected in full by the implementing authority when the DCD clearly notified all of the parties concerned in the procedure of the termination of the evidence-gathering stage, inviting them to consult the full record of the proceedings in order to acquaint themselves with all of the essential facts to date and to submit, on the basis of all of the information gathered thus far, and providing they so wished, their final pleadings."

4.1009 On 21 September 1999, the representative of Assopiastrelle confirmed that she had consulted File No. 061-000794/98 consisting of 28 sections and taken full note of the proceedings.

4.1010 Argentina presented next its legal arguments relating to the EC's claim under Article 6.9 of the AD Agreement.

4.1011 Article 6.9 does not specify in what way the authorities shall inform all interested parties of the essential facts under consideration which form the basis of the decision whether to apply definitive measures. It stipulates that the authorities "... shall inform all interested parties of the essential facts". The obligation in the Article is to inform; the text does not specify how, but simply imposes a minimum standard (to inform) and leaves it up to the authority to choose the means. This is what would be defined as an obligation of results, as opposed to an obligation of means.

4.1012 The EC submission cites (in a footnote) the recent Panel on *Guatemala - Cement (II)*, in which the Panel concluded that Guatemala did not comply with Article 6.9 by offering to provide interested parties with copies of all information in the file.

4.1013 In that case, Guatemala argued that the Ministry had revealed the "essential facts" by placing a copy of the file at the disposal of the interested parties. However, in the case of Argentina, the DCD did not merely offer to provide the interested parties with a copy of all of the information contained in the record, but expressly invited them to consult the full record of the proceedings.

4.1014 In this connection it should be stressed that although "*dar copia*" ("providing a copy") was not sufficient to comply with the Article 6.9 obligations, the scope of the expression "*dar vista*" ("give sight") is different, since contrary to the expression "*dar copia*", it implies notifying the interested parties of the record of the proceedings.

4.1015 In this specific case, the entire record of the proceedings was being made available, which implies that the essential facts on which the implementing authority would base its final decision in the subsequent stage were also being made available.

4.1016 Indeed, the fact of having made available the record of the proceedings implies that the requirements set forth in Article 6.9 of the AD Agreement were met. The parties, through this procedural step, were informed of the record of the proceedings "in toto". In other words, since no single fact considered by the implementing authority remained unknown to the interested parties, their rights were not impaired.

4.1017 Nor did the exporters at any time demonstrate that they had suffered injury as a result of this interpretation. Thus, it is clear that the requirements of Article 6.9 of the AD Agreement were met by the implementing authority, and that exporters had access to all of the information on the basis of which the said authority reached its conclusions.

4.1018 In any case, even if one were to assume that the procedure followed by the implementing authority was not in keeping with Article 6.9 of the AD Agreement, *quod non*, Argentina considers that this would be a case of "harmless error". In other words, an error which, by its nature, is not sufficiently important to alter the implementing authority's conclusions.

4.1019 Also important with respect to the content of the Article 6.9 obligation is the work carried out by the Ad Hoc Group on Implementation of the AD Agreement (see Documents G/ADP/W/401 and G/ADP/W/400) created by the Committee on Anti-Dumping Practices to prepare recommendations on issues on which the Agreement is more lax and on issues where agreement among Members seems possible.

4.1020 At its meeting of 29 and 30 April 1997, the Ad Hoc Group on Implementation of the Committee on Anti-Dumping Practices, analysing the question of the information making up the essential facts under consideration before making a final determination, addressed the practical issue of how such information should be provided, recognizing that the specific nature of the investigation and decision-making processes in the systems of the different Members also implied differences as to the way in which this obligation was met. On the one hand, it was suggested that the information should be supplied at as early as possible a stage of the process; on the other hand, it was considered important that the information should be supplied once all of the various stages of the investigation process had been completed and the investigating authority was in a position to make a determination. In fact, this is a provision of the Agreement which leaves WTO Members a certain amount of room for interpretation of the obligation involved. So much so that the Ad Hoc Group tried to find a solution that would conciliate the different positions within the WTO - all of them permissible under the Agreement, owing in particular to Article 17.6. The fact that the Ad Hoc Group did not adopt a recommendation implies that the Member countries still differ on the matter on how to notify the essential facts. In other words, the text of Article 6.9 does not specify a means of fulfilling the obligation.

4.1021 In short, Argentina considers that its interpretation of Article 6.9 did not cause any injury to the exporters concerned. Moreover, the said exporters at no time demonstrated that they had suffered any prejudice as a result of that interpretation. Thus, even if one were to accept that Argentina's application of Article 6.9 was erroneous, this would be, *quod non*, a harmless error.

(b) Arguments of Argentina in its First Oral Statement Relating to the EC's Claim under Article 6.9 of the AD Agreement

4.1022 In its first oral statement, Argentina made the following arguments relating to the EC's claim under Article 6.9 of the AD Agreement.

4.1023 Argentina submits that the DCD acted in conformity with Article 6.9 in that it informed the exporters of the "essential facts" concerning the existence of dumping.

4.1024 While Article 6.9 lays down the obligation to inform the interested parties of the essential facts, it does not specify the way in which this should be done. In other words, the implementing authority has the discretion to choose the way in which it informs the parties.

4.1025 Thus, the text of the article simply lays down a minimum standard (to inform) and leaves it up to the authority to choose the means. This is what would be defined as an obligation of results, as opposed to an obligation of means, as stated in Argentina's first written submission, a view which is also shared by other WTO Members.

4.1026 Since the article in question, in laying down the obligation to inform, does not lay down a method or means for doing so, Argentina considers that the DCD met that obligation when it duly notified all the parties concerned in the procedure of the termination of the evidence - gathering stage, inviting them to consult the full record of the proceedings in order to acquaint themselves with all of the essential facts to date and to submit, on the basis of all the information gathered thus far, their final pleadings.

4.1027 As stated in Argentina's first written submission, this is reflected in Notes DCD Nos. 273-000586/99, 273-000587/99, 273-000588/99, 273-000589/99, 273-000590/99, 273-000591/99 and 273-000592/99 of 11 May 1999, and Note DCD No. 273-001040/99 of 9 September 1999.

4.1028 No single fact considered by the implementing authority remained outside the knowledge of the interested parties: they were invited to consult the record of the proceedings, and thus, the requirements of Article 6.9 of the AD Agreement were met. In other words, the parties, through this procedural step, were informed of what had taken place in the proceedings.

4.1029 Moreover, the implementing authority, in reaching its conclusion, analysed all of the elements of the case, which implies that every action taken was important. Thus, by inviting the parties to consult the full record, the implementing authority complied with the obligation contained in Article 6.9 of the AD Agreement, the purpose of which is to ensure that the parties are informed of the essential facts so that they can defend their interests.

(c) Arguments of Argentina in its Oral Statement at the Third-Party Session of the First Meeting of the

Panel with the Parties, Relating to the EC's Claim under Article 6.9 of the AD Agreement

4.1030 In its oral statement at the third-party session of the first meeting of the Panel with the parties, Argentina made the following arguments relating to the EC's claim under Article 6.9 of the AD Agreement

4.1031 Like the EC, Japan sees in Article 6.9 a requirement that it does not contain, ie. the obligation to produce a special, separate publication containing the essential facts, or to conduct a so-called "disclosure conference".

4.1032 Moreover, Japan appears to meld the obligation in Article 6.8 and paragraph 6 of Annex II with Article 6.9 when it states that "The DCD never informed the exporters at any time during the investigation that the information they had supplied on normal value and export prices had been disregarded". This statement appears to confuse the obligations set forth in Article 6.8 and paragraph 6 of Annex II with the provisions of Article 6.9 requiring that the parties be informed of the essential facts. If this interpretation were correct, Annex II, paragraph 6 would be meaningless. And neither the text itself nor its context warrants such an interpretation.

4.1033 The DCD met its obligation under Article 6.9 by duly notifying the interested parties in writing of the closure of the investigation and inviting them to inspect the file containing all of the essential facts and to submit their pleadings. Argentina reiterates that there was a notification with all of the legal consequences implied by something different from merely allowing the interested parties to "inspect" the file in the sense suggested by Japan.

4.1034 Article 6.9 imposes a result, i.e. to enable the parties to defend their interests in the knowledge of the essential facts. The same point is made in Turkey's submission and in the United States' submission. This is exactly what Argentina did by duly notifying the parties.

(d) Replies of Argentina to the First Set of Questions by the Panel Relating to the EC's Claim under Article 6.9 of the AD Agreement

4.1035 Argentina replied to the first set of questions by the Panel relating to the EC's claim under Article 6.9 of the AD Agreement as follows.

4.1036 The Panel asked the parties what was, in their view, the object and purpose of the requirement of Article 6.9 AD Agreement to disclose "the essential facts under consideration".

4.1037 Argentina replied that the purpose of this provision is to enable the parties, in full knowledge of the essential facts, to fully defend their interests prior to the final determination by the implementing authority.

4.1038 If the purpose of Article 6.9 was to enable parties better to defend their interests, the Panel asked the parties whether this interpretation suggested that a

Party claiming a violation of Article 6.9 also should present information to the Panel on how its exporters were impeded in their defence.

4.1039 Argentina replied that its answer to the previous question did not imply that the parties must prove that they were unable to defend their interests. This was not an obligation under Article 6.9. The Article 6.9 obligation was to disclose the essential facts. Thus, a party claiming violation of Article 6.9 had to prove that this obligation of the AD Agreement was violated.

4.1040 The Panel recalled that, in paragraph 78 of its first written submission, Argentina distinguished the DCD's practice from that of the Guatemalan authority which the Panel in the *Guatemala - Cement (II)* case found to be inconsistent with Article 6.9 AD Agreement. Argentina asserted that "it should be stressed that although *"dar copia"* ("providing a copy") was not sufficient to comply with the Article 6.9 obligations, the scope of the expression *"dar vista"* ("give sight") is different, since contrary to the expression *"dar copia"*, it implies notifying the interested parties of the record of the proceedings". The Panel asked the parties to comment on the importance of this difference, if any.

4.1041 Argentina replied that, as pointed out in paragraph 75 of its first written submission, Article 6.9 contained an obligation of results, i.e. to inform the parties of the essential facts, and not an obligation of means, i.e the means by which the parties are informed of the facts and hence duly notified thereof.

4.1042 Similarly, paragraph 78 of Argentina's first written submission should not be taken out of its context: it forms part of the Argentine counter-argument developed in paragraphs 76 to 80 to the EC's argument concerning the Panel's interpretation in the *Guatemala - Cement (II)* case.

4.1043 The Panel asked the parties what, if any, were the essential facts under consideration that the exporters were not informed of.

4.1044 Argentina replied that the parties were informed of all of the essential facts.

4.1045 The Panel asked the parties whether, in their view, the fact that the information from the exporters was disregarded for the calculation of normal value and export price was an essential fact of which the exporters should have been informed under Article 6.9 AD Agreement.

4.1046 Argentina replied that it was of the view that all of the facts in the record were essential.

4.1047 The Panel recalled that, on several occasions in its first written submission, Argentina referred to the concept of "harmless error". The Panel asked Argentina to define this concept in international law and explain what, in its view, the role of this concept was in WTO dispute settlement proceedings.

4.1048 Argentina replied that a harmless error was an error which did not cause injury or adversely affected the rights of one of the parties - in other words, it was irrelevant as regards the consequences of the challenged act. The concept of harmless error has been accepted in a number of different WTO cases.

4.1049 This was confirmed, for example, in *Korea-Dairy Products* in which the Appellate Body maintained that " *...the European Communities' request should have been more detailed.* However, Korea failed to demonstrate to us that the mere listing of the Articles asserted to have been violated has prejudiced its ability to defend itself in the course of the Panel proceedings. *Korea did assert that it had sustained prejudice, but offered no supporting particulars in its appellant's submission nor at the oral hearing ...*" (emphasis added by Argentina). (Appellate Body Report, *Korea - Definitive Safeguard Measures on Imports of Certain Dairy Products*, WT/SD98/AB/R, adopted 12 January 2000, at para. 131).

4.1050 Clearly, to arrive at these conclusions, the Appellate Body accepted the concept of "harmless error". Otherwise, the Appellate Body's ruling would be without foundation.

4.1051 Thus, as part of the WTO's legal precedent with respect to disputes under the DSU, the concept of harmless error is relevant to the legal settlement of a dispute.

(e) Arguments of Argentina in its Second Written Submission Relating to the EC's Claim under Article 6.9 of the AD Agreement

4.1052 In its second written submission, Argentina made the following arguments relating to the EC's claim under Article 6.9 of the AD Agreement.

4.1053 Argentina reaffirms that it complied with the obligation arising from the text of paragraph 6.9 of the AD Agreement, which stipulates that the authorities "... shall inform all the interested parties of the essential facts", without indicating the method by which the authorities must fulfil that obligation.

4.1054 Argentina submits that the implementing authority informed the exporters of the "essential facts" concerning the existence of dumping, which would form the basis for the decision to apply definitive measures.

4.1055 In paragraph 68 of its first written submission, Argentina mentioned the notes sent to the representatives of Cerro Negro, Casalgrande, Caesar, Bismantova, Marazzi and Assopiastrelle, in which it stated that "... the judicial decision concerning the evidence duly provided by the firms involved in this investigation has been taken, so that those that so wish may consult the corresponding document and familiarize themselves with the decision contained therein ...".

4.1056 Argentina then went on, in paragraphs 69 and 71 of its first written submission, to state that the representative of Assopiastrelle had confirmed that she had consulted the file, consisting of 25 sections with 7,368 folios, on 18 June 1999, and taken full note of the proceedings, and again on 3 September 1999, as recorded in Note DCD No. 273-001040/99.

4.1057 Similarly, paragraph 70 of the said submission cites a note of 28 August 1999 in which the DCD informs exporters that the evidence-gathering stage of the investigation has terminated and invites them to consult the record and, where they deem necessary, submit their final pleadings before 10 September.

4.1058 At the same time, paragraph 72 cites a letter from the EC stating that "... the DCD informed the exporters that, as far as the dumping determination was concerned, the Argentine authorities considered that the disclosure requirements imposed by Article 6.9 were fully complied with by granting to the interested parties access to the record" (Note DCD No. 273-001040/99 of 9 September 1999 to Assopiastrelle, Bismantova, Casalgrande, Caesar and Marazzi).

4.1059 It is clear from the above notes that the exporters were given access to the entire record of the proceedings, and hence, to the essential facts on which the implementing authority would base its final decision, which Argentina considers to be all of the facts making up the record. It should be stressed on the basis of the above that no single fact considered by the implementing authority remained unknown to the interested parties, since the exporters were given access to all of the information on the basis of which the authority reached its conclusions.

4.1060 Similarly, the EC argues in paragraph 69 of its first oral statement that "Finally, Argentina contends that the violation of Article 6.10 would be a "harmless" error since the EC has not demonstrated that it caused a prejudice to the exporters concerned. For the reasons set out by the Panel in *Guatemala - Cement (II)*, the EC considers that this is not a valid defence under the WTO Agreement. In accordance with Article 3.8 of the DSU, all violations of the WTO Agreement are presumed to cause *nullification or impairment*. It is for Argentina to rebut that presumption" (emphasis added by the EC).

4.1061 Apart from its importance in international law and the WTO, the concept of "harmless error" has clearly not been overlooked by the WTO in resolving specific issues, especially those relating to concepts such as "nullification or impairment".

4.1062 This is confirmed, for example, in the report of the Appellate Body in *Korea - Dairy Products* of 14 December 1999 in which the Appellate Body maintained that " ... the European Communities' request should have been more detailed. However, Korea failed to demonstrate to us that the mere listing of the Articles asserted to have been violated has prejudiced its ability to defend itself in the course of the Panel proceedings. Korea did assert that it had sustained prejudice, but offered no supporting particulars in its appellant's submission nor at the oral hearing ... " (see Appellate Body, *Korea - Definitive Safeguard Measure on Imports of Certain Dairy Products*, WT/DS98/AB/R, adopted on 12 January 2000, at para. 131). Clearly, to arrive at these conclusions, the Appellate Body accepted the concept of "harmless error" - i.e. an error which, by its nature, cannot change the result. In other words, the fact that the EC's request "should have been more detailed" did not cause Korea "nullification or impairment". This is precisely what makes this particular situation harmless. Otherwise, the Appellate Body's ruling would be without foundation.

4.1063 In this particular case, even if one assumed that the procedure followed by the implementing authority contained an error, *quod non*, the EC did not suffer nullification or impairment of any kind as a result.

4.1064 A harmless error is an error which does not cause injury or adversely affect the rights of one of the parties - in other words, it is irrelevant as regards the consequences of the challenged act. In this context, the concept of harmless error has implicitly been accepted in a number of WTO cases (Appellate Body Report, *Korea - Definitive Safeguard Measures on Imports of Certain Dairy Products*, WT/SD98/AB/R, adopted 12 January 2000, at para. 131).

4.1065 As a part of WTO's case history relating to the dispute settlement procedure, the concept of harmless error forms part of the Organization's "*acquis*", and is therefore of considerable importance in connection with GATT/WTO disputes.

4.1066 The interpretation of the obligations contained in Article 6.9 must be based on an adjusted definition of its content, i.e. the content of what Article 6.9 describes or specifies as an obligation of results and not of means (a position shared by Argentina and other WTO Members).

4.1067 In other words, the definition of an obligation as being one of results is a definition which may contemplate different means but which is only in fact met when the objective has been reached: informing the parties of the essential facts.

4.1068 It should be noted that an interpretation whereby the Article 6.9 obligation is an obligation of means, i.e. an obligation which prescribes one of the forms of disclosure presented by the EC or Japan - a separate report in the case of the EC, or the so-called "disclosure conference" in the case of Japan - could result in a situation where the parties are informed only partially of the facts, since either the authority may be restricted as regards what is defined or considered, under the methodology, as an essential fact, or a party may be deprived access to a particular fact that is essential.

4.1069 At the same time, a restrictive interpretation would mean that the separate report, as proposed by the EC, would ultimately only contain such essential elements as support the authority's decision whether to apply a measure. What would happen, in this case, with the essential facts that did not support the decision to apply a measure and that, following the EC's logic, should not form part of the report on the essential facts supporting the determination? Should a fact lose its essential character just because it does not support the decision to apply a measure? And do such facts therefore cease to be part of the essential facts which must be disclosed? Other delegations have also argued that this is not the case.

4.1070 The United States makes an interesting point in its oral submission as a third party on the question of how to reconcile the object and purpose of Article 6.9, i.e. to permit parties to defend their interests, with the result that would be obtained through a report containing only the essential facts which supported a determination, when there could very well be cases in which certain facts which support another conclusion were of particular importance to a party in defending its interests.

4.1071 Argentina's approach as regards the particular case at issue was to consider that all of the facts forming part of the record were essential for the purposes of the determination. For example, would it have made any sense, following the EC's logic, for Argentina to refer to the samples of models which it submitted as Exhibit ARG-22, which certainly did not constitute any kind of basis for making an adjustment by model? Indeed, this information did not permit the authority to make the necessary adjustment, so that it would not have formed part of the essential facts that led to an affirmative determination for which only an adjustment by size was made. As this information was not relevant for the purposes of the adjustment by size, it would not have formed part of the essential facts to be disclosed under Article 6.9. Nevertheless, this information is included in the record and was relevant in a negative sense, since it was not relied upon for the purposes of the determination. How, following the EC's definition of the essential facts, should Argentina have treated this information? Should it have included it in a separate report or not?

4.1072 Ultimately, by considering the entire record to be made up of the essential facts, the implementing authority places the parties in a better position to defend their interests.

(f) Arguments of Argentina in its Second Oral Statement Relating to the EC's Claim under Article 6.9 of the AD Agreement

4.1073 In its second oral statement, Argentina made the following arguments relating to the EC's claim under Article 6.9 of the AD Agreement.

4.1074 Argentina reaffirms that it complied with the Article 6.9 obligation to inform the interested parties of all of the essential facts.

4.1075 In its reply a question by the Panel following the first meeting, the EC recognizes that the Article 6.9 obligation is an obligation of results and not of means when it states that "... the essential purpose of Article 6.9 is to allow the parties to defend adequately their interests".

4.1076 Indeed, the text of this provision does not establish an obligation to inform by any particular means: as revealed by the discussions of the Ad Hoc Group of the Anti-Dumping Committee on this subject, the means are left to the discretion of Members.

4.1077 Similarly, Argentina does not agree with the EC's reply to a question by the Panel following the first meeting to the effect that Article 6.9 "... requires the investigating authority to make always disclosure of the essential facts ..." Argentina submits, in reply, that according to the text of Article 6.9, "The authority shall ... inform all interested parties of the essential facts under consideration which form the basis for the decision whether to apply definitive measures ...".

4.1078 It is Argentina's understanding, and the text of the provision does not contradict this, that the essential facts are above all those which are included in the record of the investigation, since all of these facts would be weighed by the authority in arriving at an affirmative or negative determination of dumping.

4.1079 Argentina therefore submits that there was no violation of Article 6.9, and that hence, there is no *prima facie* nullification or impairment under Article 3.8 of the DSU.

4.1080 In any case, Argentina considers that even if it is assumed that there was prima facie nullification or impairment under Article 3.8 of the DSU, and Argentina does not accept that there was in this case, several WTO precedents, in connection with the concept of "harmless error", have pointed to the importance of the existence of injury (see Appellate Body Report, *Korea - Definitive Safeguard Measure on Imports of Certain Dairy Products*, WT/DS98/ABR, adopted 12 January 2000, at para. 162 and Appellate Body Report, *Thailand - Anti-Dumping Duties on Angles, Shapes and Sections of Iron or Non-Alloy Steel and H-Beams from Poland*, WT/DS122, adopted 5 April 2000, at paras. 95 and 96).

4.1081 In its reply to a question by the Panel following the first meeting, the EC states that the DCD should have disclosed which facts available would be relied on for establishing the normal value and the export price. In Argentina's view, the implementing authority is under no obligation to anticipate its decision, which is made once the evidence-gathering stage is concluded and the pleadings submitted.

4.1082 The Panel did not ask Argentina any questions following the second meeting relating to the EC's claim under Article 6.9 of the AD Agreement.

3. *Third Parties: Japan*

(a) Arguments of Japan in its Written Submission Relating to the EC's Claim under Article 6.9 of the AD Agreement

4.1083 In its written submission, Japan made the following arguments relating to the EC's claim under Article 6.9 of the AD Agreement.

4.1084 The account in the EC first written submission indicates that DCD failed to conduct a disclosure conference with exporters or their representatives, as required by Article 6.9 of the AD Agreement. According to the EC, DCD invited the exporters to inspect the public file, which did not include the final dumping determination or any other document prepared by DCD which identified the "essential facts" that would form the basis of that determination. In response to a request by the exporters for a disclosure conference, DCD took the position that the requirements of Article 6.9 are fully fulfilled by allowing interested parties to inspect the public file.

4.1085 Every investigating authority is required under Article 6.4 of the AD Agreement to maintain a file for each antidumping investigation of all information that is relevant and that the authority uses in the investigation, and to provide timely opportunities for interested parties to have access to this information. Japan fully supports the EC position that the provisions of Article 6.9 must be read as imposing obligations that go beyond those in Article 6.4; otherwise Article 6.9 would be rendered mere surplusage.

4.1086 The issue of what Article 6.9 requires has already been settled in the recently- adopted panel report on *Guatemala - Cement (II)*. In that case, Guatemala simply offered to provide interested parties with copies of the information in the file. As the panel noted, the public file typically contains large amounts of information that will not be relied on; the key obligation in Article 6.9 is the requirement that the antidumping authority disclose the essential facts that it will actually rely on, in time for interested parties to defend their interests (Panel Report, *Guatemala - Definitive Anti-dumping Measures on Portland Cement from Mexico,* WT/DS156/R, adopted 17 November 2000, at paras. 8.229-8.230).

4.1087 The requirements of Article 6.9 are not satisfied by merely opening for inspection a file that includes both facts that will be relied upon and facts that will not.

4.1088 If Argentina's position were accepted, then an antidumping authority could simply provide a voluminous file of relevant and irrelevant facts, refuse to identify which facts it will actually rely on, and inform the interested parties of its reasoning as a surprise, only when it is too late to defend their interests. The panel must reject this position.

4.1089 In addition, Japan we would like to point out the logical consequence of this violation. The Argentine authority, by violating the requirements of the Article 6.9, nullifies the provisions which require the Panel to determine whether the authorities' establishment of the facts was proper and whether their evaluation of those facts was unbiased and objective, pursuant to the Article 17.6 of the AD Agreement, or to make an objective assessment of the matter pursuant to the Article 11 of the DSU.

(b) Arguments of Japan in its Oral Statement Relating to the EC's Claim under Article 6.9 of the AD Agreement

4.1090 In its oral statement, Japan made the following arguments relating to the EC's claim under Article 6.9 of the AD Agreement.

4.1091 Article 6.9 of the AD Agreement requires national authorities to inform all interested parties of the "essential facts" under consideration. Japan has already stated in its third party submission that the provisions of Article 6.9 must be read as imposing obligations that go beyond those in Article 6.4 of the Agreement. Japan wishes to further respond to the arguments on Article 6.9 in Argentina's first written submission.

4.1092 Japan agrees with Argentina's argument in paragraph 75 that the AD Agreement does not impose a particular methodology by which national authorities should "inform" interested parties of the key facts that will be relied upon in the decision whether to apply definitive measures. The relevant question before the Panel in the present case is: have the interested parties actually been informed of the "essential facts" under consideration, by the methodology chosen by Argentina? In Japan's view, the answer to this question would appear to be no.

4.1093 Argentina states in paragraph 77 that it did not even provide a copy ("*dar copia*") of the file, as Guatemala did in *Guatemala - Cement (II)*. Instead, DCD simply invited interested parties to examine the contents of the file, by a mere viewing ("*tomar vista*") of the entire file. Argentina argues in paragraphs 77-80 that Article 6.9 is complied with if the entire administrative file is made available for inspection, since the essential facts are by definition included in the entire file. Thus, according to Argentina, no fact considered by the authorities was unknown to the interested parties, including the essential facts.

4.1094 The Panel should reject this method as insufficient under Article 6.9. As the *Guatemala - Cement (II)* panel found, the administrative file in an anti-dumping investigation usually contains large amounts of information that will not be relied on. The key obligation in Article 6.9 is the requirement that the anti-dumping authority disclose the essential facts that it will actually rely on, in time for interested parties to defend their interests (Panel Report, *Guatemala - Definitive Anti-dumping Measures on Portland Cement from Mexico,* WT/DS156/R, adopted 17 November 2000, at paras. 8.229-8.230).

4.1095 Argentina also argues in paragraph 81 that the exporters never indicated they had been injured by Argentina's interpretation of Article 6.9. If Argentina argues that the rights of a WTO Member under the WTO Agreement are (or could be) diminished because of actions taken or not taken by private parties during an antidumping investigation, this argument must be rejected. WTO Members have rights under the WTO Agreement as a matter of international law (see Panel Report, *Guatemala - Definitive Anti-dumping Measures on Portland Cement from Mexico,* WT/DS156/R, adopted 17 November 2000, at para. 8.24, rejecting Guatemala's arguments alleging acquiescence and estoppel). In the past the United States argued that a government should be legally barred from making a legal argument to a panel if (private) respondents had not previously made the same argument to the investigating authority during the underlying antidumping investigation. That US argument was squarely rejected both by panels (see GATT Panel Report, *United States - Imposition of Anti-Dumping Duties on Imports of Fresh and Chilled Atlantic Salmon from Norway*, ADP/87, adopted 28 April 1994, at paras. 347-351. See also GATT Panel Report, *United States - Imposition of Countervailing Duties on Imports of Fresh and Chilled Atlantic Salmon from Norway*, SCM/153, adopted 28 April 1994, at paras. 216-220), and in the Uruguay Round negotiations on antidumping.

4.1096 Even if Argentina's argument is that the EC as a litigant has failed to identify during this dispute any prejudice to EC exporters from denial of Article 6.9 rights, this argument must be rejected. The right to information under Article 6.9 is absolute, not conditional. Requiring a showing of damage to exporters would impose a new condition not provided for by the AD Agreement, in a manner inconsistent with of Article 3.2. of DSU.

4.1097 Moreover, Argentina argues in paragraph 84 that because Article 6.9 is under consideration in the Ad Hoc Group on Implementation of the Committee on Anti-Dumping Practices, Argentina has acted in conformity with this provision by merely making the entire file available for inspection by interested parties. However, the fact that a matter or an interpretation is under consideration by a WTO body, or has been under consideration by a WTO body that was deadlocked, does not mean that a panel cannot make a ruling on the matter or interpret the relevant provisions of the WTO Agreement (see also Appellate Body Report, *India - Quantitative Restrictions on Imports of Agricultural, Textile and Industrial Products*, WT/DS90/AB/R, adopted 22 September 1999, at para. 102).

4.1098 The US third party submission of March 23 makes certain statements regarding Article 6.9 of the AD Agreement, on which Japan has the following comments. The United States argues in paragraph 10 that the Panel should interpret Article 6.9 in such a way as to allow Members to "choose to establish an investigative process which allows interested parties to be presented with all of the facts as they are presented to the authority, as well as all arguments made about those facts." The United States finds support for this broad interpretation of Article 6.9 in some of the findings in *Guatemala - Cement (II)* (Panel Report, *Guatemala - Definitive Anti-dumping Measures on Portland Cement from Mexico,* WT/DS156/R, adopted 17 November 2000, at para 8.228.) .

4.1099 The US account of the *Guatemala - Cement (II)* panel findings is too selective. That panel found in paragraph 8.228 that disclosure of the "essential facts" forming the basis of a preliminary determination is clearly inadequate when the factual basis of the preliminary determination differs substantially from the factual basis of the final determination. Japan agrees, and apparently so does the United States. However, in the present case, DCD never provided anything more than "*dar vista*" of the file at any point during the antidumping investigation. The United States dismisses the key findings in paragraphs 8.229-8.330 of *Guatemala - Cement (II)* with a footnote noting that it "does not understand the basis for the Panel's conclusion". But these findings are still valid and strongly support the argument that the method Argentina has applied in the present case would fall outside the range of possible methodologies that could have been applied under Article 6.9 (Panel Report, *Guatemala - Definitive Anti-dumping Measures on Portland Cement from Mexico,* WT/DS156/R, adopted 17 November 2000, at para. 8.228).

4.1100 Finally, the United States argues in paragraph 20 for an interpretation of Article 6.4 and 6.9 that would allow for a situation where there would be little, if any, practical difference between the two provisions. Japan cannot accept the US interpretation, as the Panel on *Guatemala - Cement (II)* observed that Article 6.9 imposes more substantive requirements than Article 6.4 (Panel Report, *Guatemala - Definitive Anti-dumping Measures on Portland Cement from Mexico,* WT/DS156/R, adopted 17 November 2000, at para. 8.230).

4. *Third Parties: Turkey*

(a) Arguments by Turkey in its Written Submission Relating to the EC's Claim under Article 6.9 of the AD Agreement

4.1101 In its written submission, Turkey made the following arguments relating to the EC's claim under Article 6.9 of the AD Agreement.

4.1102 The EC submits that, Argentina infringed Article 6.9 of the AD Agreement, by failing to inform the exporters of the "essential facts" underlying the dumping determination before imposing definitive measures.

4.1103 Turkey considers that Article 6.9 is very clear in wording and leaves no room for misinterpretations. It puts the investigating authorities under obligation of informing all interested parties of the essential facts which form the basis for the decision whether to apply definitive measures.

4.1104 Furthermore, it specifies that such disclosure should take place before a final determination is made and in sufficient time for the parties to defend their interests.

4.1105 Turkey further considers that, if the intention of Article 6.9 was no more than providing timely opportunities for all interested parties to see information, there would be no need for Article 6.9 when Article 6.4 stood for such intention.

4.1106 In Turkey's view, it is clear that this Article requires the authorities to inform the interested parties and grant them the right to defend their interests before the final determination is made.

(b) Arguments of Turkey in its Oral Statement Relating to the EC's Claim under Article 6.9 of the AD Agreement

4.1107 In its oral statement, Turkey made the following arguments relating to the EC's claim under Article 6.9 of the AD Agreement.

4.1108 Turkey is of the view that, as Article 6.8 and paragraph 6 of Annex II, Article 6.9 also contributes to conduction of fair investigations and predictable results.

4.1109 In this respect, Turkey submits that, the purpose of Article 6.9, in the very essence, is to permit the interested parties to fully defend their interests. To that end, provisions of Article 6.9 are obligatory taken the ordinary meanings of the words. It obliges the investigating authorities to inform the interested parties of the essential facts before the final determination is made. The "essential facts under consideration" in Turkey's understanding refers to all the factual information that the authority had at this hand and considered in deciding whether or not to take anti-dumping action. Moreover, the Article requires such disclosure of essential facts to take place at an appropriate time so that the respondents should be provided and not be deprived of their right of defence.

4.1110 This two basic requirements brings us to a point where authorities, under any given condition, are obliged to inform the interested parties of the essential facts with the aim to provide them an opportunity to make a possible final statement, if any, before the final determination is made.

4.1111 Given such explicit obligations, authorities providing opportunities for interested parties only to see relevant information, where practicable, shall not be deemed to satisfy the requirements of Article 6.9.

4.1112 Furthermore, Turkey also wishes to note that, the problem addressed by the EC in its first written submission, considering the inconsistency with Article 6.9 was not solely on means of disclosure. The EC appears to allege that the public file provided by DCD did not include the "final dumping determination". If that is the case, Turkey is of the view that this panel should also address this matter.

5. *Third Parties: The United States*

(a) Arguments of the United States in its Written Submission Relating to the EC's Claim under Article 6.9 of the AD Agreement

4.1113 In its written submission, the United States made the following arguments relating to the EC's claim under Article 6.9 of the AD Agreement.

4.1114 The EC claims that the DCD failed to inform the exporters of the "essential facts" concerning the existence of dumping, contrary to the requirements of Article 6.9 of the Agreement. The brief of the EC states that the Argentinian authority did not include in the public file a "document prepared by the DCD which identified the 'essential facts' that would form the basis of the final determination". The EC also states that "Article 6.9 requires the investigating authorities to indicate to the interested parties which, of all the facts contained in the file, are the "essential facts" that will form the basis for their decision".

4.1115 The United States does not take a position on whether, under the facts of this case, the measure in question is consistent with Article 6.9. However, in the view of the United States the EC has read requirements into Article 6.9 which simply are not there, and which are inconsistent with the language as well as the object and purpose of that provision. As Argentina observes, Article 6.9 requires only that interested parties be "informed" of the essential facts, and that this requirement does not impose a particular means of disclosure.

4.1116 Article 6.9 permits a Member wide discretion in choosing the manner in which it will inform interested parties of the essential facts under consideration which form the basis for the Member's decision regarding an antidumping measure. Contrary to the argument of the EC, Article 6.9 does not require a document setting out essential facts. It does not establish any other particular means of disclosure which must be followed or define the parameters of "essential facts under consideration." Article 6.9 only requires that, as applied, the selected method actually discloses to interested parties the facts which may be necessary for a defence of their interests. Thus, when a panel is considering whether the obligation in Article 6.9 has been breached, the analysis must turn on whether, under the specific facts of the dispute, the objective set out in Article 6.9 has been met, not on whether any particular mechanism or approach has been used by the Member.

4.1117 Article 6.9 reads as follows:

> The authorities shall, before a final determination is made, inform all interested parties of the essential facts under consideration which form the basis for the decision whether to apply definitive measures. Such disclosure should take place in sufficient time for the parties to defend their interests.

4.1118 As the Appellate Body has stated, the Agreement must be interpreted based on the ordinary meaning of its terms, in context, and in light of the object and purpose of the Agreement (see, e.g., Appellate Body Report, *United States - Standards for Reformulated and Conventional Gasoline*, WT/DS2/AB/R, adopted 20 May 1996, at 23; Appellate Body Report, *Japan - Taxes on Alcoholic Beverages*, WT/DS8/AB/R, WT/DS10/AB/R, WT/DS11/AB/R, adopted 1 November 1996, at 12; and Panel Report, *Australia - Subsidies Provided to Producers and Exporters of Automotive Leather - Recourse to Article 21.5 of the DSU by the United States*, WT/DS126/RW, adopted 16 June 2000, at para. 6.25. See also Article 31 of the *Vienna Convention of the Law of Treaties* providing that, when examining the meaning of a treaty's terms, one must consider those terms "in light of the treaty's object and purpose." The United States' interpretation of Article 6.9 is supported by the ordinary meaning of the text of Article 6.9, as well as the object and purpose of this particular provision).

(i) Article 6.9 Obligates Members to "inform" Interested Parties; it does not Prescribe Any Particular Means of Disclosure

4.1119 As pointed out by Argentina in its submission, Article 6.9 requires that the investigating authority "inform" interested parties of the essential facts under consideration, but it does not prescribe the method by which this obligation must be fulfilled. Thus, while Article 6.9 establishes a required result, it leaves the method of achieving that result to individual Members.

4.1120 The ordinary meanings of the word "inform" include to "make a fact or occurrence known" (*The New Shorter Oxford English Dictionary,* Clarendon Press Oxford 1993). Thus, the word "inform" defines a result, not how that result is achieved. Furthermore, nothing elsewhere in the AD Agreement dictates or suggests any particular method for how parties are to be informed (A panel may not "add to or diminish the rights and obligations provided in the covered agreements." *Understanding on Rules and Procedures Governing the Settlement of Disputes*, Article 19.2. See also Panel Report, *Australia - Measures Affecting Importation of Salmon - Recourse to Article 21.5 by Canada*, WT/DS18/RW, adopted 20 March 2000, at p. 7.69). The AD Agreement only requires that parties, in fact, be informed in a timely manner so they are able to defend their interests.

4.1121 This understanding of the ordinary meaning of the language of Article 6.9 is reinforced by the object and purpose of Article 6.9. The object and purpose are clear from Article 6.9 itself: "Such disclosure should take place in sufficient time for the parties to defend their interests." Regardless of the means of disclosure chosen, as long as the object and purpose are achieved, the obligation in Article 6.9 is satisfied (the object and purpose of Article 6.9 are further informed by the discussions of Members on the predecessor provisions under the former Anti-Dumping Code. In 1983, the Committee on Anti-Dumping Practices recognized that "the right of parties to defend their interests during the course of an anti-dumping proceeding can only be guaranteed if they have the right to see all the information that is relevant to their case providing that it is not confidential". Committee on Anti-Dumping Practices, *Recommendation concerning transparency of anti-dumping proceedings*, 15 November 1983, ADP/17, GATT B.I.S.D. (30th Supp.) 1984, at 24).

4.1122 Thus, Members may implement their obligations under Article 6.9 in a variety of ways. Some Members may choose to implement Article 6.9 by requiring the investigating authority to prepare a separate document of essential facts under consideration, as the EC has suggested. Other Members may choose to establish an investigative process which allows interested parties to be presented with all of the facts as they are presented to the authority, as well as all arguments made about those facts. Other Members may choose some combination of these two approaches, or some other method entirely.

4.1123 It is critical, however, to bear in mind that whether the obligation in Article 6.9 has been satisfied cannot be determined by looking in the abstract at the means of disclosure used. In reviewing a challenge under Article 6.9, the question before the panel is this: under the facts of this case, were the essential facts under consideration made known to interested parties in a timely manner? Because Article 6.9 requires a result rather than a particular method, a claim that Article 6.9 has been violated must be assessed based on the facts of the particular case and whether the particular means of disclosure used, as applied in that instance, satisfied the objective behind Article 6.9. In the case at hand, the Panel must assess whether the Italian exporters were informed of the facts they needed to defend their interests, not whether the Argentinian authorities prepared a particular type of document.

4.1124 The only prior case in which a panel has been directly called upon to interpret the requirements of Article 6.9 provides a good example of why review of a claim under Article 6.9 must be made on a case-by-case basis. In *Guatemala - Cement (II),* the panel found that disclosing the essential facts in an interim determination was insufficient to fulfill Guatemala's obligations with respect to Article 6.9 in an investigation where: (1) the basis of the interim determination was threat of material injury, whereas the basis of the definitive determination was actual material injury; (2) the period of investigation was different for the interim determination and the definitive determination; and (3) much of the evidence was obtained after the interim determination (Panel Report, *Guatemala - Definitive Anti-Dumping Measures on Grey Portland Cement from Mexico*, WT/DS156/R, adopted 17 November 2000, at para. 8.228). The panel also found that providing access to the authority's file was insufficient to fulfill Guatemala's obligations under Article 6.9 because an authority's file is "likely" to contain vast amounts of information, some of which may not be relied upon by the authority in making its definitive determination. *Id.* at para. 8.229. Admittedly, the United States does not understand the basis for the panel's conclusion that such a situation is "likely." In any event, as discussed below, this Panel should not interpret this statement from *Guatemala - Cement (II)* to mean that facts which do not ultimately support the determination reached are not essential to that determination and to a party's ability to defend its interests).

4.1125 Thus, the panel in *Guatemala - Cement (II)* focused on the facts of the case before it. For example, disclosing facts in the interim determination could not satisfy Article 6.9 in that case because, after the interim determination, the period of investigation changed. The parties were given no notice of this change. This meant that they did not even know which sales were being examined for dumping. The *Guatemala - Cement (II)* panel might have reached a different conclusion had there been no change in the period of investigation or injury determination, and had all of the facts been gathered before the interim determination. Thus, the same procedures may satisfy Article 6.9 in some cases, but not in others, demonstrating the need for the Panel to undertake a case-by-case analysis, rather than attempting to enunciate a general rule.

(ii) The Scope of "essential facts under consideration" should not be Interpreted in a Restrictive Manner

4.1126 The Panel should evaluate compliance with Article 6.9's obligation to "inform" by focusing on the facts of the particular case, rather than adopting the EC's suggestion that a particular means of disclosure is required. However, in interpreting Article 6.9, the Panel also must address the scope of the term "essential facts under consideration" in determining whether Article 6.9 has been violated. In the view of the United States, the language as well as the object and purpose of Article 6.9 argue that the Panel not adopt a restrictive interpretation of the scope of "essential facts under consideration." Thus, not only is the methodology suggested by the EC not required by Article 6.9, the EC's statement that authorities should be required to select certain "essential facts" for disclosure could defeat the object and purpose of that provision.

4.1127 Article 6.9 describes the facts of which interested parties must be informed as the "essential facts under consideration." To understand what that phrase means, one must examine the ordinary meaning of the individual terms. Ordinary meanings of the word "essential" include "of or pertaining to a thing's essence" and "absolutely indispensable or necessary" (*The New Shorter Oxford English Dictionary,* Clarendon Press Oxford 1993).

4.1128 In the context of the AD Agreement, the essential facts are those that are necessary to the determination of whether definitive measures are warranted. This may include all the facts before the investigating authority. In such a situation, the EC's suggestion that an authority had to designate certain facts as the essential facts has no meaning. For example, in identifying material injury, the authority must necessarily weigh all of the facts submitted, which typically includes some contradictory information. Similarly, in determining whether dumping has taken place, every sale considered, every adjustment made, and every issue addressed influences whether the ultimate margin found is above the *de minimis* threshold (see AD Agreement, Article 5.8) and definitive measures warranted. Accordingly, the Panel should not adopt a restrictive interpretation of "essential facts under consideration" since that would have the potential to improperly circumscribe the facts disclosed under Article 6.9.

4.1129 Additionally, Article 6.9 refers to the essential facts "under consideration". The term "consideration" has been defined, *inter alia,* as "the action of taking into account" (*The New Shorter Oxford English Dictionary,* Clarendon Press Oxford 1993). With respect to any specific issue, the investigating authority may have conflicting information, all of which is weighed, i.e., "taken into account," in reaching its final determination (this understanding of "essential facts under consideration" is further supported by the use of the phrase "the decision *whether* to apply definitive measures." The word "whether" is used to express two alternatives. *The New Shorter Oxford English Dictionary,* Clarendon Press Oxford 1993. Consequently, the facts referred to are those which support both alternatives). Thus, all such evidence is under consideration in the determination (the *Guatemala - Cement (II)* panel seem to suggested that Article 6.9 might function to reveal, *inter alia,* information not relied upon because it has been "shown to be inaccurate upon verification". Panel Report, *Guatemala - Definitive Anti-Dumping Measures on Grey Portland Cement from Mexico,* WT/DS156/R, adopted 17 November 2000, at para. 8.229. However, Article 6.7 independently provides for disclosure of the results of verification, and Article 6.9 should not be interpreted in a manner redundant of Article 6.7).

4.1130 Further, the scope of "essential facts under consideration" must be interpreted in a manner consistent with the object and purpose of Article 6.9. As discussed above, the object and purpose of Article 6.9 are to permit interested parties to defend their interests. To allow for a proper defence, that provision must be interpreted to require that interested parties be informed of all essential facts under consideration, including those that militate against the decision ultimately reached.

4.1131 The interpretation of Article 6.9 suggested by the EC, which would require authorities to select certain facts for disclosure as the "essential facts" would permit authorities only to designate the facts which supported their ultimate findings as "essential." Such an interpretation would work against the object and purpose of this provision. It would permit an authority to disclose all of the facts supporting its decision, while not disclosing facts which would support a contrary decision (even assuming an authority is acting in good faith to inform parties of all facts it believes would be necessary for their defence, such an authority will not necessarily know which facts the party would consider necessary). Such an interpretation of Article 6.9 would prevent interested parties from defending their interests. In order to defend its interests, a party must be informed of those facts which militate against that decision, as well as any other facts which would permit an affirmative defence. Thus, limiting the facts of which parties are informed under Article 6.9 to those which support one particular outcome would defeat the expressed purpose of that provision.

4.1132 Additionally, if Article 6.9 only addresses facts in support of the determination ultimately reached, then an authority which changed its determination as a result of an argument presented late in the proceeding would have to provide a new disclosure of essential facts. This amounts to a requirement of multiple interim determinations. However, the AD Agreement does not *require* an interim determination at all. Even where a Member chooses to issue such a determination in order to apply provisional measures under Article 7, Articles 7.1 and 12.2 only contemplate a single interim determination (further, reading Article 6.9 to require disclosure only of those facts relied upon in support of the ultimate decision would amount to a requirement that parties be provided with information to defend their interests only after the authorities have decided on the outcome of the case - a plainly absurd result. The object and purpose of Article 6.9 being to allow parties to defend their interests, those parties must be permitted to mount such a defence before the authority has decided whether to impose definitive measures. Moreover, reading a requirement of multiple disclosures under Article 6.9 into the AD Agreement runs the risk of preventing an authority from meeting the deadlines for completion of an investigation set forth in Article 5.10).

4.1133 Finally, the interaction of Article 6.9 and 6.4 does not dictate a restrictive interpretation of the facts of which interested parties must be informed under Article 6.9. Article 6.4 is not mandatory, but specifies a procedure: parties must be allowed to "see" the public information, but only if the authorities determine that it is "practicable." On the other hand, as discussed above, Article 6.9 is mandatory, but does not specify a procedure. In other words, whether or not an authority determines that it is practicable to let the parties see the record under Article 6.4, in every case interested parties must be informed of the "essential facts under consideration". Thus, it may be in a particular case that liberal disclosure under Article 6.4 also satisfies Article 6.9 (this does not necessarily mean that every disclosure under Article 6.4 will satisfy Article 6.9. For example, allowing parties to see a very large record for a very short time may not be sufficient. On the other hand, allowing parties to have unrestricted access to the record, including all arguments about the facts in that record, as it is being developed throughout the investigation, will inform those parties of the essential facts under consideration in accordance with Article 6.9. The Panel must determine under Article 6.9 whether the parties were actually informed).

4.1134 This does not mean that Article 6.9 is redundant of Article 6.4. Article 6.9 requires that interested parties be informed of the essential facts under consideration regardless of whether the authorities have found it practicable to allow those parties to see the public record under Article 6.4.

4.1135 In conclusion, Article 6.9 does not prescribe a particular means of disclosure. Rather, that provision requires a reviewing panel to determine, on a case-by-case basis, whether the method employed, in fact, informed the interested parties of all of the "essential facts under consideration" in sufficient time to allow for a defence of their interests.

(b) Arguments of the United States in its Oral Statement Relating to the EC's Claim under Article 6.9 of the AD Agreement

4.1136 In its oral statement, the United States made the following arguments relating to the EC's claim under Article 6.9 of the AD Agreement.

4.1137 The United States addressed first the arguments regarding the proper interpretation of Article 6.9. Article 6.9 of the AD Agreement furthers the goal of transparency in dumping proceedings by requiring that investigating authorities inform interested parties of all essential facts under consideration prior to making a final determination of dumping. Both the United States and Argentina have argued in their written submissions that Article 6.9 is concerned with a particular result, and does not prescribe the process for reaching that result. By contrast, the EC, joined in some respects by Japan and Turkey, has suggested that Article 6.9 requires the preparation and issuance of a single document prior to the final determination that contains all the supporting facts that the investigating authority will actually rely on when it makes the final determination.

4.1138 In considering the arguments the United States are presenting regarding the proper interpretation of Article 6.9, the United States wishes the Panel to keep in mind a single important consideration apparently overlooked by the EC and Japan: if a party is not informed of a fact under Article 6.9, it may never know that fact exists at all. Article 6.9 is the only guarantee in the Agreement that a party will be informed of all the facts it might need to mount its defence. Under the interpretation advanced by the EC and Japan, parties may find themselves in a situation where the only facts of which they have been informed are those which support the determination the authority intends to reach.

4.1139 Why is this the case? With respect to facts gathered by the authority (and thus not subject to a service requirement under Article 6.1), the only provisions of Article 6 which address disclosure to the parties are Articles 6.4 and 6.9. Note, however, that the language of Article 6.4 holds out the possibility that, in a particular case, and given the appropriate circumstances, an authority could find that it is only practicable to permit interested parties to view the public record for a very brief period of time, or that it is only practicable to permit them to view it at a stage before all of the information has been gathered. Thus, the disclosure under Article 6.4 may be very limited.

4.1140 Article 6.9, on the other hand, guarantees that parties have access to all facts relevant to the final determination. If the more limited interpretation of Article 6.9 offered by the EC and Japan were adopted, the authority would reach its conclusions and inform the parties only of the facts on which it actually intends to rely in support of those conclusions. The parties would then be permitted to defend their interests, informed of only the facts which support one determination and facing an authority which has already made a decision on the outcome of the case.

4.1141 The United States finds it difficult to believe that any interpretation of Article 6.9 which would permit the goal of transparency to be thwarted in this manner is a proper interpretation. Fortunately, as discussed in our written submission, a careful examination of the language, including the express object and purpose of that provision, reveals that the interpretation offered by the EC and Japan is not correct. Rather, Article 6.9 permits a Member wide discretion in choosing the manner in which it will inform interested parties of the essential facts under consideration which form the basis for the Member's decision regarding an antidumping measure. Moreover, the facts addressed by Article 6.9 are all those which are relevant to the determination of whether definitive measures are warranted - facts which argue for, as well as those which argue against, application of such measures.

4.1142 The language of Article 6.9 does not support the interpretation advanced by the EC and Japan. First, as Argentina also pointed out, Article 6.9 only requires that interested parties be informed, and does not specify a means of disclosure. Article 6.9 makes no mention of the disclosure document discussed by the EC, or the disclosure conference discussed by Japan. Second, Article 6.9 requires that parties be informed of the "essential facts under consideration." As discussed in the United States' submission, those words cannot be read as limited to the facts which will be actually relied upon in support of a particular outcome.

4.1143 In interpreting Article 6.9, the Panel must also bear in mind the object and purpose of that provision. The object and purpose is expressed in the provision itself: to permit parties to defend their interests. This object and purpose would not be served if parties were only informed of the facts which support one outcome of the case.

4.1144 The object and purpose of Article 6.9 is further informed by the purpose of the other provisions of Article 6. The provisions of Article 6 of the AD Agreement are aimed at ensuring that parties know what is required of them, and have a full opportunity to be informed of the evidence presented by other parties and gathered by the authorities. For example, Article 6.1.2 requires that "evidence presented in writing by one interested party shall be made available promptly to other interested parties participating in the investigation." Article 6.2 requires authorities to "provide opportunities for all interested parties to meet those parties with adverse interests, so that opposing views may be presented and rebuttal arguments offered." Article 6.3 requires that oral information only be taken into account "insofar as it is subsequently reproduced in writing and made available to other interested parties." Thus, the provisions of Article 6 appear to reflect a concern that parties be given as much information as possible, so that they may be fully in control of their own defence.

4.1145 By contrast, the arguments advanced by the EC and Japan with respect to Article 6.9 appear to reflect a concern that parties may be given too much information, and that the authority conducting the investigation must be required to sort through that information and inform the parties only of the facts on which it will rely. Such an argument is paternalistic and an invitation for mischief. It might be possible that an authority, acting in bad faith, could fill the record with such vast amounts of irrelevant information that parties would be effectively precluded from defending their interests. However, in the view of the United States, the danger posed by this unlikely scenario is vastly outweighed by the very real concern, reflected in the rest of Article 6, that parties must receive all of the information about the investigations to which they are subject in order to adequately defend their interests.

4.1146 In light of this concern, the United States does not understand Japan's suggestion that a dumping file is likely to contain large amounts of irrelevant information. The very purpose of Article 6 is to allow parties to judge for themselves in the first instance whether they believe a particular fact is relevant to arguments they wish to raise, rather than leaving such a judgment to the authority. Recall that if a party is not informed of a fact under Article 6.9, it may not know the fact exists at all, and thus will have no way of determining whether that fact would be relevant to its arguments.

4.1147 In reviewing the arguments raised by the EC and Japan, in this respect joined by Turkey, that Article 6.9 must be interpreted to "go beyond" the requirements of Article 6.4, the source of this misunderstanding of Article 6.9 becomes clear. Because these parties have interpreted Article 6.4 in an excessively broad manner, and have not recognized the limitations of that provision, they are forced into a tortured reading of Article 6.9 in order to avoid a redundancy. However, a proper reading of the language of Article 6.4 reveals that it is not redundant of Article 6.9, and that these Articles can operate independently of and harmoniously with each other.

4.1148 The misunderstanding of Article 6.4 is best summarized by the following sentence from Japan's submission: "[e]very investigating authority is required under Article 6.4 of the AD Agreement to maintain a file for each antidumping investigation of all information that is relevant and that the authority uses in the investigation, and to provide timely opportunities for interested parties to have access to this information". While the United States finds this a laudable ideal, the fact is that the language of Article 6.4 is not quite so broad.

4.1149 Article 6.4 is not mandatory in all circumstances: the requirement to allow parties to see the record under Article 6.4 could be limited by a finding by the authority that such disclosure is not practicable. Thus, while a Member claiming that access to the record is not practicable faces a heavy burden, it is possible that this burden could be met in certain cases such that disclosure under Article 6.4 may be very brief, or occur at a time before all of the information has been gathered. Article 6.9 ensures that, even if the authority is able to support a finding that it is not practicable under Article 6.4 to allow parties to see the full record, that authority must still find a way to inform those parties of the facts contained in that record. Of course, in the view of the United States, allowing liberal access to the record under Article 6.4 goes a long way toward satisfying the requirements of Article 6.9. However, the key point for the Panel to bear in mind is that only Article 6.9, and not Article 6.4, guarantees that parties will be informed of all of the facts they need to defend their interests in every case.

4.1150 On the other hand, Article 6.4 does "go beyond" Article 6.9 in that it requires a particular means of disclosure. When an authority implements Article 6.4, it can only do so by allowing parties to see the original source documents in the record. This firsthand access may be of particular value to parties in assuring them of the completeness and accuracy of the information. Although the United States believes that this also may be the best method of implementing Article 6.9, as the United States has frequently stated, Article 6.9 does not prescribe a particular means of disclosure. To sum up, Article 6.9 is mandatory, but does not prescribe a means of disclosure, whereas Article 6.4 is conditional, but does prescribe a means of disclosure.

4.1151 Thus, the concern that Article 6.9 not be interpreted as redundant of Article 6.4 flows from a misreading of Article 6.4. Article 6.4 and Article 6.9 simply address different concerns, and represent different obligations. The fact that an authority can devise a single means of disclosure which satisfies both provisions does not mean that it is interpreting those provisions in an improper manner.

4.1152 Japan also argues that the logical consequence of not adopting its interpretation of Article 6.9 is that it would nullify a panel's ability to determine whether the authority's establishment of the facts was proper and whether the authority's evaluation of the facts was unbiased and objective, in accordance with Article 17.6 of the AD Agreement. The United States respectfully disagrees. As long as the investigating authority has chosen a method which informs the interested parties of the essential facts under consideration and the authority sets forth in its final determination its reasoning in support of its decision, a reviewing panel should be able to make the necessary determinations under Article 17.6.

4.1153 The United States also addressed certain arguments by Japan which go well beyond what the EC and Turkey have argued with respect to Article 6.9. First, Japan states that Article 6.9 requires authorities to conduct a so-called "disclosure conference" with exporters or their representatives. However, Article 6.9 makes no mention of "disclosure conferences." Indeed, as discussed previously, Article 6.9 does not require any particular method for informing parties of the essential facts under consideration.

4.1154 Second, Japan also appears to argue that in addition to requiring that parties be informed of the essential facts under consideration, Article 6.9 requires that interested parties be informed of the authority's reasoning prior to its final determination. However, the language of Article 6.9 only addresses facts and not legal reasoning. Moreover, this argument would, in essence, require the investigating authorities to make multiple interim determinations, contrary to what is contemplated by Articles 7 and 12.

V. INTERIM REVIEW

5.1 On 20 August 2001, the EC submitted a written request for review by the Panel of particular aspects of the interim report issued on 25 July 2001. Argentina did not provide any comments on the interim report. Argentina commented on the EC's request for interim review on 28 August 2001. Neither party requested an additional meeting with the Panel.

5.2 We have reviewed the comments presented by the EC and the reaction thereto by Argentina and have finalized our report, taking into account these comments which we considered justified.

5.3 The EC notes that the second sentence of paragraph 6.30 of the Panel's interim report does not accurately reflect its position and suggests certain language to the Panel for completing the text. We are of the view that paragraph 6.30 is an accurate reflection of the EC's position on this issue. We note that the language suggested by the EC in its interim review comments was not used by the EC in its submissions to the Panel. Accordingly, we saw no reason to amend the text as requested by the EC.

5.4 The EC states that the exporters had provided the evidence specifically requested by the DCD and that therefore the Panel's statement in paragraph 6.62 of the interim report that "no documentary evidence of any kind was submitted" is inaccurate. Argentina comments that the Panel's statement is correct in so far as it refers to supporting documentation for the information supplied. We decided to amend the text of this paragraph taking into account the comments made.

5.5 The EC notes, in respect of footnote 89, that in *United States - Anti-Dumping Measures on Certain Hot Rolled Steel Products from Japan*, the Appellate Body has confirmed that in Article 9.4 the words "margins" means the individual margin determined for each investigated exporter. The EC makes no suggestion as to how the Panel should use the ruling cited. Argentina comments that the EC should not be allowed to rely on this decision in support of its argument since this decision was issued well after the time for presentation of arguments by the parties. We considered that since footnote 89 refers to the arguments presented by the EC on this issue, it would not be appropriate to incorporate any reference to this decision which was not and could not have been part of the EC's argument as it was issued only days before the issuance of the interim report. Accordingly, we decided to leave footnote 89 unchanged.

5.6 The EC suggests that the Panel completes the last sentence of paragraph 6.89 by adding language used by the EC in its first submission to the Panel. Argentina comments that it is up to the Panel to decide on the language chosen to represent a party's position. In light of the EC's comments, we decided to amend the report as suggested by the EC in order to fully reflect the EC's position on this issue.

5.7 The EC notes that the first sentence of paragraph 6.90 should refer to exporters who are selected for examination under the second *sentence* of Article 6.10, rather than the second paragraph. We considered it was appropriate to amend the text as suggested by the EC.

5.8 The EC requests the Panel to redraft the last sentence of paragraph 6.118. The EC proposes specific language which it believes more accurately reflects its arguments. We have in response to this comment modified the text of this paragraph.

5.9 The EC notes that, in its view, the interpretation of the Panel of the requirements of Article 6.9 as offered in paragraph 6.125 is incorrect. Argentina comments that it sees no problem with the Panel's interpretation of the language of this provision, and requests the Panel to reject the EC's comments and leave the text unchanged. In light of the EC's comments, we decided it was appropriate to briefly clarify our interpretation of Article 6.9 and we amended paragraph 6.125 accordingly.

VI. FINDINGS

A. *Standard of Review*

6.1 Article 17.6 of the AD Agreement sets forth the special standard of review applicable to anti-dumping cases. With regard to factual issues, Article 17.6(i) provides:

> "(i) in its assessment of the facts of the matter, the panel shall determine whether the *authorities' establishment of the facts was proper* and whether their *evaluation of those facts was unbiased and objective*. If the establishment of the facts was proper and the evaluation was unbiased and objective, even though the panel might have reached a different conclusion, the evaluation shall not be overturned"; (emphasis added).

6.2 We note that the Panel in the case *United States - Anti-Dumping Measures on Stainless Steel Plate in Coils and Stainless Steel Sheet and Strip from Korea* considered that Article 17.6(i):

> "speaks not only to the establishment of the facts, but also to their evaluation. Therefore, the Panel must check not merely whether the national authorities have properly established the relevant facts but also the value or weight attached to those facts and whether this was done in an unbiased and objective manner. This concerns the

> according of a certain weight to the facts in their relation to each other; it is not a legal evaluation".[13]

6.3 Accordingly, it is not our role as a panel to perform a *de novo* review of the evidence which was before the investigating authority at the time it made its determination. Rather, we must review the determination the investigating authority made on the basis of the information before it in order to determine whether the establishment of the facts was proper and the evaluation of the facts was unbiased and objective. With respect to the latter aspect of our review, we consider that the task before us is to examine whether, on the basis of the information before it, an unbiased and objective investigating authority evaluating that evidence could have reached the conclusions it did.[14]

6.4 With respect to questions of the interpretation of the AD Agreement, Article 17.6(ii) provides:

> "(ii) the panel shall interpret the relevant provisions of the Agreement in accordance with customary rules of interpretation of public international law. Where the panel finds that a relevant provision of the Agreement admits of more than one permissible interpretation, the panel shall find the authorities' measure to be in conformity with the Agreement if it rests upon one of those permissible interpretations".

6.5 We consider the first part of this subparagraph to be a clear reference to the customary rules of interpretation as laid down in Articles 31-32 of the Vienna Convention on the Law of Treaties. Article 31 of the Vienna Convention provides that a treaty shall be interpreted in accordance with the ordinary meaning to be given to the terms of the treaty in their context and in light of its object and purpose. Article 17.6(ii) of the AD Agreement provides that in the case where this method leads the panel to the conclusion that the provision in question admits of more than one permissible interpretation, the panel shall find the measure in conformity if it is based on one such permissible interpretation.

---

[13] Panel Report, *United States - Anti-Dumping Measures on Stainless Steel Plate in Coils and Stainless Steel Sheet and Strip from Korea*, WT/DS179/R, adopted 1 February 2001, DSR 2000:IV, 1537, para. 6.18.

[14] We note that this is the same standard as that applied by the Panel in *Mexico - Anti-Dumping Investigation of High Fructose Corn Syrup (HFCS) from the US ("Mexico - HFCS")*, which, in considering whether the Mexican investigating authorities had acted consistently with Article 5.3 in determining that there was sufficient evidence to justify initiation, stated: "Our approach in this dispute will ... be to examine whether the evidence before SECOFI at the time it initiated the investigation was such that an unbiased and objective investigating authority evaluating that evidence could properly have determined that sufficient evidence of dumping, injury and causal link existed to justify initiation." Panel Report, *Mexico - HFCS*, WT/DS132/R, adopted 24 February 2000, DSR 2000:III, 1345, para. 7.95.

B. *Burden of Proof*

6.6 We recall that the burden of proof in WTO dispute settlement proceedings rests with the party that asserts the affirmative of a particular claim or defence.[15] It implies that the complaining party will be required to make a *prima facie* case of violation of the relevant provisions of the WTO AD Agreement, which is for the defendant, in this case Argentina, to refute.[16] In this regard, the Appellate Body has stated that "... a *prima facie* case is one which, in the absence of *effective refutation* by the defending party, requires a panel, as a matter of law, to rule in favour of the complaining party presenting the *prima facie* case".[17] Our role as a panel is not to make the case for either party, but we may pose questions to the parties "in order to clarify and distill the legal arguments".[18]

C. *Factual Introduction*

6.7 This dispute concerns the imposition of definitive anti-dumping measures by the Argentine Ministry of the Economy on imports of ceramic floor tiles ("*porcellanato*") from Italy. The European Community raises claims with respect to several aspects of those measures. In particular, the European Community considers that the measures concerned are inconsistent with Articles 6.8 (in conjunction with Annex II), 6.10, 2.4 and 6.9 of the AD Agreement.

6.8 On 30 January 1998, Cerámica Zanon filed an application for an anti-dumping investigation with the Dirección de Competencia Desleal (DCD - Directorate of Unfair Trade) of the Ministry of the Economy alleging that ceramic tiles were being exported to Argentina at dumped prices.[19] On 25 September 1998, the

---

[15] Appellate Body Report, *United States - Measure Affecting Imports of Woven Wool Shirts and Blouses from India*, WT/DS33/AB/R, adopted 23 May 1997, DSR 1997:I, 323, at 335.

[16] We note that the Appellate Body stated in *Korea - Definitive Safeguard Measures on Imports of Certain Dairy Products ("Korea - Dairy Safeguards")*: "We find no provision in the DSU or in the Agreement on Safeguards that requires a Panel to make an explicit ruling on whether the complainant has established a *prima facie* case of violation before a panel may proceed to examine the respondent's defence and evidence." Appellate Body Report, *Korea - Dairy Safeguards*, WT/DS98/AB/R, adopted 12 January 2000, DSR 2000:I, 3, para. 145. The Appellate Body confirmed this view in the *Thailand - Anti-Dumping Duties on Angles, Shapes and Sections of Iron or Non-Alloy Steel and H-Beams from Poland* (*"Thailand - H-Beams"*) case: "In our view a panel is not required to make a separate and specific finding in each and every instance that a party has met its burden of proof in respect of a particular claim, or that a party has rebutted a prima facie case." Appellate Body Report, *Thailand - Anti-Dumping Duties on Angles, Shapes and Sections of Iron or Non-Alloy Steel and H-Beams from Poland ("Thailand - H-Beams")*, WT/DS122/ABR, adopted 5 April 2001, DSR 2001:VII, 2701, para. 134.

[17] Appellate Body Report, *European Communities - Measures Concerning Meat and Meat Products ("EC - Hormones")*, WT/DS26/AB/R - WT/DS48/AB/R, adopted 13 February 1998, DSR 1998:I, 135, para. 104.

[18] Appellate Body Report, *Thailand - H-Beams*, para. 136.

[19] The DCD was responsible for conducting the dumping investigation. The injury investigation was conducted separately by the Comisión Nacional de Comercio Exterior (CNCE - National Foreign Trade Commission). As the EC did not make any injury claims, no reference is made here to the injury aspects of the investigation.

Ministry of the Economy published a public notice announcing the initiation of an anti-dumping investigation on imports of ceramic tiles from Italy. The DCD selected the years 1997 and 1998 as the period of investigation. At initiation, as in the subsequent stages of the investigation, the DCD divided the subject product into 3 size categories (tiles of 20 x 20 cm, tiles of 30 x 30 cm and tiles of 40 x 40 cm), and determined a dumping margin specific to each size category.[20] For the purposes of initiation, the DCD calculated normal values for each size category by averaging several estimates of domestic prices taken from price lists and specialized publications submitted by the petitioner.[21] In turn, the DCD determined the export price for each size category according to two sources: a unit price calculated by the petitioner on the basis of import documents, and a unit price calculated by the DCD itself on the basis of official import statistics.[22]

6.9 On 30 November 1998, Assopiastrelle, the association of Italian producers of ceramic tiles, requested that the DCD limit the calculation of individual dumping margins to 4 or 5 exporters accounting for around 70 per cent of the exports of the subject product from Italy to Argentina.[23] On 12 December 1998, the DCD accepted this request.[24] On 10 December 1998, four Italian exporters (Ceramica Bismantova, Ceramiche Casalgrande, Ceramiche Caesar, and Marazzi Ceramiche) filed responses to the investigation questionnaire. On 24 March 1999, the DCD issued an affirmative preliminary determination.[25] In that determination, the DCD disregarded the questionnaire replies submitted by the abovementioned exporters.[26] The DCD determined the dumping margin on the basis of the information available on the record, other than that presented by the exporters. In particular, for each size category, the DCD calculated normal value on the basis of an average domestic price drawn from price lists (i.e., the price lists submitted by the petitioner in the complaint, and supplementary price lists submitted by the petitioner and by one of the importers following initiation) and sale invoices (submitted by the petitioner following initiation).[27] In turn, for each size-category, the DCD calculated the export price according to the unit price derived from official import statistics.[28]

---

[20] Final Dumping Determination, p. 43. Exhibit EC-2.

[21] Final Dumping Determination, pages 20 -22. Exhibit EC-2. In the case of the 20 x 20 cm size-category, when calculating normal value the DCD only relied on estimates of domestic prices taken from specialized publications.

[22] Final Dumping Determination, pages 30 -32. Exhibit EC-2.

[23] Exhibit EC-3A.

[24] Exhibit EC-3B.

[25] Preliminary Dumping Determination. Exhibit ARG-8.

[26] Preliminary Dumping Determination, p. 34. Exhibit ARG-8. Final Dumping Determination, p. 23. Exhibit EC-2.

[27] Final Dumping Determination, pages 23 -24 and p. 44. Exhibit EC-2. In the case of the 20 x 20 cm category, when calculating normal value the DCD only relied on estimates of domestic prices taken from price lists.

[28] Final Dumping Determination, pages 32-34 and p. 44. Exhibit EC-2. These import statistics referred to the period January-September 1998. We note that following the preliminary determina-

6.10 On 23 September 1999, the DCD issued an affirmative final determination. In this determination, the DCD relied predominantly on the information available on the record, other than that submitted by the exporters. Specifically, for each size category, the DCD determined two dumping margins. Both calculations used the same export price but different normal values.[29] The first normal value was an average domestic price drawn from the price lists and sale invoices referred to above.[30] This was the same pricing information used by the DCD for the purpose of the preliminary determination.[31] The second normal value was an average domestic price that reflected the same price lists and sales invoices, plus the pricing information submitted by the exporters, taken as a whole.[32] In the latter calculation, the pricing information submitted by the exporters received a weight of one third.[33] The DCD did not provide any justification for this approach of combining the information on normal value submitted by the exporters with the information on normal value filed by other parties.[34] The DCD simply stated that for its normal value calculations it was relying on the totality of the information at hand.[35] The final determination does not explain with clarity how the DCD calculated the export price.[36] However, from an annex to the Final Determination, we can conclude that the DCD calculated the export price by averaging the unit price drawn from official import statistics[37] and the import prices reported by two importers. The DCD did not explain why it had disregarded entirely the information submitted by the exporters with regard to the export price, even though for calculating normal value it had relied upon their data to some degree.

6.11 On 12 November 1999, the Ministry of the Economy, based upon the affirmative Final Determination regarding the existence of dumping issued by the DCD on 23 September 1999, and the affirmative Final Determination regarding the existence of injury and causality issued by the CNCE on 3 September 1999, imposed definitive anti-dumping measures on imports of ceramic tiles originating in Italy.[38] The measures were fixed for a period of 3 years and took the form of

---

tion, the DCD sent three letters to the exporters requesting that additional public information be provided. See Exhibits ARG-7, Exhibit ARG-10 and Exhibit ARG-11.

29 Final Dumping Determination, p. 45. Exhibit EC-2.

30 Final Dumping Determination, pages 44 - 45. Exhibit EC-2.

31 Final Dumping Determination, pages 44 and 24. Exhibit EC-2.

32 Final Dumping Determination, p. 45. Exhibit EC-2.

33 Final Dumping Determination, p. 30. Exhibit EC-2. As an exception, in the case of the 20 x 20 cm category, the pricing information submitted by the exporters received a weight of one-half, given that there was only one alternative source of information (price lists) for the calculation of normal value.

34 The DCD did not explain either why it considered the normal value information submitted by the exporters as a block, instead of considering that information by individual exporter (we recall in this connection the fact that the exporters filed individual questionnaire replies).

35 Final Dumping Determination, p. 30. Exhibit EC-2.

36 Final Dumping Determination, p. 37. Exhibit EC-2.

37 For the period October 1997-September 1998.

38 Exhibit EC-1.

specific anti-dumping duties applied in variable amounts. In particular, under this system importers are subject to an anti-dumping duty equivalent to the absolute difference between the FOB export price invoiced in any one shipment and a designated "minimum export value", also fixed in FOB terms, provided that the export price concerned is lower than the designated "minimum export value". The measures were established according to the three size categories described above. However, the notice of imposition of definitive measures does not explain which of the two normal values calculated by the DCD in its Final Determination for each size category was retained as "minimum export value" in each case, nor how the calculated normal values were converted into "minimum export values".[39]

D. *Claim 1: Facts Available under Article 6.8 And Annex II of the AD Agreement*

1. *Arguments of the Parties*

6.12 The **EC** argues that the DCD disregarded the information concerning normal value and export price provided by the four Italian exporters included in the sample and instead relied on information from other sources such as the petitioner and importers. The EC submits that under Article 6.8 of the AD Agreement, an investigating authority may make a determination on the basis of the facts available and resort to secondary source information only where the exporter: (i) refuses access to necessary information; (ii) does not timely submit the necessary information; or (iii) significantly impedes the investigation. The EC asserts that all four exporters included in the sample provided complete and timely responses to the questionnaires and agreed to the verification of the information submitted. Nevertheless, the EC submits, the Argentine authority discarded the information and made a dumping determination on the basis of facts available.

6.13 According to the EC, the DCD considered the exporters' responses on an equal footing with the information from the petitioner and eventually decided to rely on the latter. The EC submits that the DCD cannot pick and choose data from different sources in the establishment of the dumping margin, since this would render Article 6.8 and Annex II totally redundant. In particular, the EC points to paragraph 7 of Annex II which, according to the EC, explicitly recognises the hierarchy between primary and secondary sources. The EC argues that the primary source of information is the normal value and export price information supplied by the exporters concerned, and only under the specific circum-

[39] It would appear that the "minimum export values" are the FOB-adjusted normal values. However, as pointed out above, this is not clear in the text of the notice of imposition of definitive measures.

stances set out in Article 6.8 is an authority allowed to resort to secondary source information.

6.14 The EC further submits that the Argentine authority never informed the exporters that their responses had been rejected, nor did it explain why the information was rejected, as required by paragraph 6 of Annex II of the AD Agreement.

6.15 **Argentina** submits that the DCD was forced to resort to the use of facts available since the exporters significantly impeded the investigation and failed to provide the necessary information within a reasonable period, thereby *de facto* refusing access to necessary information. Argentina argues that all three of the conditions of Article 6.8 of the AD Agreement applied. Argentina identifies the following problems concerning the information supplied by the exporters included in the sample which, in its view, justified the use of facts available by the DCD. First, according to Argentina, the exporters did not provide sufficiently detailed non-confidential summaries for the confidential information in the questionnaire replies, thereby making it impossible for the DCD to rely on this confidential information in its public determination. Second, Argentina argues that the exporters failed to provide supporting documentation for the information they were supplying, in spite of being explicitly requested to do so by the DCD. Third, according to Argentina, the exporters failed to comply with a number of formal requirements set forth in the questionnaire, concerning translation of documents and the need to provide the information in US$. Argentina further asserts that the information was provided late, and proved to be incomplete. For these reasons, Argentina submits, the exporters significantly impeded the investigation and refused access to information which was necessary for the DCD's final determination of dumping. The DCD was therefore entitled to resort to facts available under Article 6.8 of the AD Agreement.

6.16 Argentina asserts that the DCD applied facts available so meticulously that it was willing to take the deficient exporter information into account as far as possible, thereby in fact reducing the margin of dumping. Argentina submits that the willingness to accommodate the exporters by extending deadlines and requesting additional information to complement the questionnaire replies show that the Argentine authorities complied with the requirement of paragraph 7 of Annex II to use secondary sources *with special circumspection.*

6.17 Argentina submits that the DCD informed the exporters on several occasions that they had not provided the necessary information. Argentina points to the DCD's letter of 30 April 1999 in which additional elements of proof and additional public information were requested. A further letter was sent to the exporters on 22 June 1999 with a request to withdraw the request for confidential treatment of certain information or to provide more detailed summaries. A third and final letter of a similar nature was sent on 3 August 1999 with regard to cost of production information. Argentina submits that these letters were warnings that the information provided was not sufficient.[40] Argentina argues that in any case, and even if we were to find that the DCD did not comply with the requirement to inform the supplying party that its information was rejected as set forth in paragraph 6 of Annex II, this constituted "harmless error" of a procedural nature which did not cause any prejudice to the exporters.

6.18 The **EC** refutes the procedural and substantive arguments presented by Argentina in defence of the DCD's decision to reject the exporters' information. The EC argues that the exporters fully cooperated with the DCD and provided very detailed non-confidential summaries. Moreover, the EC asserts, the exporters provided supporting documentation for the information submitted to the extent they were requested to do so by the DCD. Finally, the EC argues that the exporters' questionnaire replies were submitted in a timely manner and in accordance with domestic procedures. The EC therefore submits that the DCD was not justified in resorting to the use of best information available since none of the conditions of Article 6.8 of the AD Agreement applied.

2. *Analysis by the Panel*

6.19 In considering this issue, we first note that Article 6.8 of the AD Agreement governs the use by an investigating authority in an anti-dumping investigation of the "facts available". That article provides as follows:

> "In case any interested party refuses access to, or otherwise does not provide, necessary information within a reasonable period or significantly impedes the investigation, preliminary and final determinations, affirmative or negative, may be made on the basis of facts available. The provisions of Annex II shall be observed in the application of this paragraph".

6.20 It is clear to us, and both parties agree, that an investigating authority may disregard the primary source information and resort to the facts available only under the specific conditions of Article 6.8 and Annex II of the AD Agreement.[41] Thus, an investigating authority may resort to the facts available only where a party: (i) refuses access to necessary information; (ii) otherwise fails to provide necessary information within a reasonable period; or (iii) significantly impedes the investigation.

6.21 We recall that Article 6.8 provides that "the provisions of Annex II shall be observed in the application of this paragraph". Paragraph 6 of Annex II is highly relevant to the case before us. It provides as follows:

---

[40] Argentina refers to pages 29 and 39 of the DCD's Final Dumping Determination (Exhibit EC-2) in this respect.

[41] Argentina's answers to questions from the Panel at the first meeting, question 1, p. 1; EC's first written submission, para. 47.

> "6. If evidence or information is not accepted, the supplying party should be informed forthwith of the reasons therefor, and should have an opportunity to provide further explanations within a reasonable period, due account being taken of the time-limits of the investigation. If the explanations are considered by the authorities as not being satisfactory, the reasons for the rejection of such evidence or information should be given in any published determinations".

Accordingly, Article 6.8, read in conjunction with paragraph 6 of Annex II, requires an investigating authority to inform the party supplying information of the reasons why evidence or information is not accepted, to provide an opportunity to provide further explanations within a reasonable period, and to give, in any published determinations, the reasons for the rejection of evidence or information.

6.22 Argentina advances four bases for its decision to disregard certain information submitted by the exporters and to resort to the use of facts available. *First,* Argentina asserts that the exporters failed to provide complete non-confidential summaries of confidential information submitted by them, as required by Article 6.5.1 of the AD Agreement. *Second,* Argentina contends that the exporters failed to provide sufficient documentation in support of the information provided in their questionnaire responses. *Third,* Argentina contends that the exporters failed to comply with the formal requirements of the questionnaire, such as requirements to translate materials into Spanish and to express value in US$. *Finally,* Argentina contends that the exporters failed to provide requested information within a reasonable period.

6.23 The EC notes that the arguments presented by Argentina to justify the DCD's decision not to rely exclusively on information concerning normal value and export price provided by the exporters, are *ex post* justifications which are nowhere to be found in the DCD's Final Determination or in any other documents on the record. Argentina disagrees and asserts that all the arguments it is presenting are present in the DCD's determinations or other documents on the record.

6.24 Under the applicable standard of review of Article 17.6 of the AD Agreement, we are to examine whether the investigating authority properly established the facts and whether its evaluation of those facts was unbiased and objective. Our review of the measure is based on all the facts on the record, and we examined both the Final Determination[42] as well as other documents on the record in order to determine whether the evaluation of the DCD was unbiased and objec-

[42] In accordance with Article 12 of the AD Agreement this public determination of the authorities is to set out the finding on fact and law of the authority. Since we have not been asked to rule on the question whether the explanations provided in the DCD's Final Determination are sufficient under Article 12 of the AD Agreement, we will not make any findings as to whether the Final Determination as a public report complies with the requirements of Article 12 of the AD Agreement.

tive. Upon careful examination, we find that neither in the Final Determination nor in any other document on the record does the investigating authority explain its evaluation of the information that apparently led it to the conclusion that it was allowed to disregard the exporters' information and resort to the use of facts available. While it is true that the Final Determination contains a discussion of the use of confidential information as an insufficient basis for the public determination, and the subsequent request for additional non-confidential summaries, the report does not draw any conclusions from these or other considerations. With regard to normal value, the report also mentions certain factual considerations concerning supporting documentation, or problems relating to the reliability of the information provided. But again, the DCD does not draw any conclusions from these factual considerations in its report or in any other document on the record. It does not explain anywhere how it evaluated these facts and what weight it accorded to each of these factual considerations. The DCD merely states that: "subject to the qualifications mentioned in each item with respect to the merits of the evidence submitted in general and in particular the evidence set forth in the item on normal value in Italy, it is possible to establish the following percentage margins of dumping" [43] and then provides the two sets of margins of dumping mentioned above, one based in part on exporters' information concerning normal value mixed with petitioner and importer information, and a second one not using any of the information provided by the exporters. In both sets, the information from the exporters concerning export price is completely disregarded.

6.25 We are mindful of the Appellate Body's findings in the case of *Thailand - Anti-Dumping Duties on Angles, Shapes and Sections of Iron or Non-Alloy Steel and H-Beams from Poland ("Thailand - H-Beams")* that the procedural and due process provisions of Articles 12 and 6 should not be mistaken for the substantive provisions of the Agreement. However, it is important to recall that the legal issue before the Appellate Body was:

> "whether the terms "positive evidence" and "objective examination" in Article 3.1 require that "the reasoning supporting the determination be 'formally or explicitly stated' in documents in the record of the investigation to which interested parties (and/or their legal counsel) have access at least from the time of the final determination", and, further, that "the factual basis relied upon by the authorities must be discernible from those documents"". (footnotes omitted) [44]

6.26 We further note that the Appellate Body stated that:

> "[...] The "facts" referred to in Articles 17.5(ii) and 17.6(i) thus embrace "all facts confidential and non-confidential", made available to the authorities of the importing Member in conformity with

[43] Final Dumping Determination, p. 44. Exhibit EC-2.

[44] Appellate Body Report, *Thailand - H-Beams*, para. 107.

> the domestic procedures of that Member. Article 17.6(i) places a limitation on the panel in the circumstances defined by the Article. The aim of Article 17.6(i) is to prevent a panel from "second-guessing" a determination of a national authority when the establishment of the facts is proper and the evaluation of those facts is unbiased and objective. *Whether evidence or reasoning is disclosed or made discernible to interested parties by the final determination is a matter of procedure and due process. These matters are very important, but they are comprehensively dealt with in other provisions, notably Articles 6 and 12 of the Anti-Dumping Agreement.*
>
> 118. Articles 17.5 and 17.6(i) require a panel to examine the facts made available to the investigating authority of the importing Member. These provisions do not prevent a panel from examining facts that were not disclosed to, or discernible by, the interested parties at the time of the final determination".[45] (emphasis added)

6.27 The question before us, however, is not whether the evaluation of the authority is provided in a public document or not, but rather whether any such reasoning has been provided in any document on the record.[46] Under Article 17.6 of

---

[45] Appellate Body Report, *Thailand - H-Beams*, paras. 117-118.

[46] In the past, this has also been the view of panels reviewing the determination of injury by the authorities. We refer for example to the report of the Panel in the case *Mexico - Anti-Dumping Investigation of High Fructose Corn Syrup (HFCS) from the United States*, WT/DS132/R, adopted 24 February 2000, para. 7.140. The Panel stated as follows:

> "7.140 The final determination reflects no meaningful analysis of a number of the Article 3.4 factors: the Mexican sugar industry's profits, output, productivity, utilization of capacity, employment, wages, growth, or ability to raise capital.[610] Moreover, there is no analysis of the condition of the Mexican sugar industry during the period of investigation, or projected for the near future. It is therefore not possible, by reading the final determination, to understand the overall condition of the domestic industry with respect to the Article 3.4 factors. Yet without an understanding of the condition of the industry, it is not possible, in our view, for SECOFI to have come to a reasoned conclusion, based on an objective evaluation of the facts, concerning the likely impact of dumped imports. Such a conclusion must, in our view, reflect the projected impact of further imports on the particular domestic industry, in light of its condition. In order to conclude that there is a threat of material injury to a domestic industry that is apparently not currently injured, despite the effects of dumped imports during the period of investigation, it is necessary to have an understanding of the current condition of the industry as a background".
>
> ---
>
> [610] There is some information concerning some of these elements reflected in the determination. However, the mere recitation of data does not constitute explanation, or findings and conclusions, sufficient to satisfy the requirements of Article 12.2 of the AD Agreement. Mexico also pointed to certain working papers in the administrative file which contain information on certain of the Article 3.4 factors. However, unless consideration of a factor is reflected in the final determination, we do not take cognizance of underlying evidence in the record. See *Korea -*

the AD Agreement we are to determine whether the DCD established the facts properly and whether the evaluation performed by the DCD was unbiased and objective. In other words, we are asked to review the evaluation of the DCD *made at the time of the determination* as set forth in a public notice or in any other document of a public or confidential nature. We do not believe that, as a panel reviewing the evaluation of the investigating authority, we are to take into consideration any arguments and reasons that did not form part of the evaluation process of the investigating authority, but instead are *ex post facto* justifications which were not provided at the time the determination was made.[47]

6.28 We find that the DCD failed to provide any evaluation of the facts on the record that could have formed the basis for its apparent decision to disregard in

---

Resins Panel Report, paras. 210, 212, *Argentina - Footwear Safeguard Panel Report*, para. 8.126. Moreover, as discussed further below, SECOFI's references to this information are limited to a discussion of that part of domestic production of sugar sold in the industrial market.

[47] We note that our view is similar to that of the Panel in the case of *Guatemala - Cement (II)* which stated as follows:

"8.245. Before determining whether the Ministry was justified in having recourse to the "best information available" for the purpose of calculating normal value, we note that Guatemala's justification for the Ministry's use of "best information available" does not correspond to that provided by the Ministry in its final Resolution of 17 January 1997. In that Resolution, the Ministry considered that:

the information submitted by the exporter cannot be taken into account when calculating the normal value of the product investigated **because it could not be verified** and the technical accounting evidence submitted by the exporter on 18 December 1996 (confidential information) could not replace verification of the information by the Guatemalan investigating authority, as required by Article 6.6 of the Anti-Dumping Code (emphasis supplied, footnote omitted).

Thus, the Ministry clearly based its recourse to the "best information available" on its inability to verify the data submitted by Cruz Azul. The Ministry did not, according to its final Resolution, rely on the "best information available" because of Cruz Azul's failure to provide certain sales and cost data, as alleged by Guatemala in these Panel proceedings. Even if the additional factors identified by Guatemala before the Panel could justify the use of "best information available", such *ex post* justification by Guatemala should not form part of our assessment of the conduct of the Ministry leading up to the imposition of the January 1997 definitive anti-dumping measure. The issue before us is whether the Ministry complied with the AD Agreement. In examining that issue, we shall confine ourselves to the reasoning provided by the Ministry in its determinations. We note that this approach is similar to that adopted by the panel in *Korea - Definitive Safeguard Measure on Imports of Certain Dairy Products*, which ignored explanatory statements made in Korea's first submission to the panel that were not reflected in the Korean authorities' analysis at the time of the investigation". (footnotes omitted);

Panel Report, *Guatemala - Definitive Anti-Dumping Measures on Grey Portland Cement from Mexico ("Guatemala - Cement (II)")*, WT/DS156/R, adopted 17 November 2000, DSR 2000:XI, 5295, para. 8.245. We note that the Panel in this case nevertheless continued to discuss the *ex post* justifications given by Guatemala and found that even if its findings were to have been based on those justifications, the authorities would still not have been entitled to use facts available. (Panel report, *Guatemala - Cement (II)*, para. 8.254.)

large part the information provided by the exporters. We consider that on this basis alone we could have reached the conclusion that the DCD failed to perform an objective and unbiased evaluation of the facts. Nevertheless, for the sake of completeness, we will continue our analysis and discuss the arguments presented by Argentina in its submissions to the Panel in defence of the DCD's decision to disregard the exporters' information.

(a) Confidentiality of the Information Submitted and the Failure to Provide Non-Confidential Summaries

6.29 **Argentina** argues that in order to reach objective and valid conclusions, an investigating authority may base its determination on confidential information only if a sufficiently detailed summary of this information is provided in accordance with Article 6.5.1 of the AD Agreement.[48] According to Argentina, the exporters failed to provide complete non-confidential summaries. Argentina submits that the summaries provided for certain annexes of the questionnaire relating to normal value and export price information (Annexes VII-XI) were not sufficiently detailed so as to permit a reasonable understanding of the substance of the information, and could therefore not be used by the DCD as a basis for its final determination.[49] Moreover, Argentina asserts, even after the declassification of the information concerning product codes and cost of production, substantial information to determine normal value and export price remained confidential. Further, Argentina argues that the exporters failed to provide sufficiently detailed public summaries with regard to certain other essential questionnaire annexes (Annexes IV, V and VI).[50] According to Argentina, by failing to provide sufficiently detailed non-confidential summaries, the exporters withheld necessary information and significantly impeded the investigation, and the DCD was therefore allowed under Article 6.8 to resort to facts available.

6.30 The **EC** considers that the exporters fully cooperated with the investigating authority and, instead of merely providing a detailed non-confidential summary, even disclosed all of the relevant confidential information. The EC also takes issue with Argentina's argument that in the absence of a detailed non-confidential summary the authorities are not to rely on the confidential information submitted. In sum, the EC argues, the DCD was not entitled to resort to facts available for reasons relating to the confidentiality of the information supplied.

6.31 We note that, in effect, Argentina argues that an investigating authority may not base its determination on confidentially submitted exporter information. Argentina contends that unless a non-confidential summary is provided that is sufficiently detailed to permit the calculation of normal value, export price and

48 Argentina's answers to questions from the Panel at the first meeting, question 3, p. 15.
49 Argentina's oral statement at the first meeting, para. 18.
50 Argentina's first submission, paras. 19-21.

the margin of dumping[51] confidential information may not form the basis for the authority's determination.[52] Therefore, Argentina argues, the failure to provide such a detailed non-confidential summary amounts to a refusal to provide access to information that is necessary for the authority in the determination of a dumping margin determination.

6.32 In considering this question, we first look to the text of Article 6.5 of the AD Agreement, which is the key provision with regard to the protection of confidential information. Article 6.5 provides as follows:

> "6.5 Any information which is by nature confidential (for example, because its disclosure would be of significant competitive advantage to a competitor or because its disclosure would have a significantly adverse effect upon a person supplying the information or upon a person from whom that person acquired the information), or which is provided on a confidential basis by parties to an investigation shall, upon good cause shown, be treated as such by the authorities. Such information shall not be disclosed without specific permission of the party submitting it.[17]
>
> 6.5.1 The authorities shall require interested parties providing confidential information to furnish non-confidential summaries thereof. These summaries shall be in sufficient detail to permit a reasonable understanding of the substance of the information submitted in confidence. In exceptional circumstances, such parties may indicate that such information is not susceptible of summary. In such exceptional circumstances, a statement of the reasons why summarization is not possible must be provided.
>
> 6.5.2 If the authorities find that a request for confidentiality is not warranted and if the supplier of the information is either unwilling to make the information public or to authorize its disclosure in generalized or summary form, the authorities may disregard such information unless it can be demonstrated to their satisfaction from appropriate sources that the information is correct".[18]
>
> [17] Members are aware that in the territory of certain Members disclosure pursuant to a narrowly drawn protective order may be required.
>
> [18] Members agree that requests for confidentiality should not be arbitrarily rejected.

---

[51] Argentina's answers to questions from the Panel at the first meeting, question 7, page 17.

[52] According to Argentina, "confidentiality imposes a limit on the authority by preventing it from relying on public elements that can be invoked against the parties or third parties, particularly when the information in question is not accompanied by non-confidential summaries in sufficient detail to permit a reasonable understanding of the substance of the information submitted in confidence and hence to allow the determination reached, which must be public, to be backed". Argentina's answers to questions from the Panel at the first meeting, question 3, p. 16.

6.33 Article 6.5 of the AD Agreement thus requires an investigating authority to treat information which is by nature confidential or which is provided on a confidential basis as confidential information and prescribes that such information shall not be disclosed without specific permission of the party submitting it.

6.34 In our view, the presence in the AD Agreement of a requirement to protect confidential information indicates that investigating authorities might need to rely on such information in making the determinations required under the AD Agreement. The AD Agreement therefore contains a mechanism that allows parties to provide investigating authorities with such information for the purposes of making their determinations, while ensuring that the information is not used for other purposes. In accordance with the accepted principles of treaty interpretation, we are to give meaning to all the terms of the Agreement.[53] It would be contradictory to suggest that the AD Agreement creates a mechanism for the protection of confidential information, but precludes investigating authorities from relying on such information in making its determinations. If that were the case, then there would be no reason for the investigating authority to seek such information in the first place.

6.35 We find confirmation for this conclusion in Article 12 of the AD Agreement, which sets forth requirements regarding the contents of public notices:

> "12.2.1 A public notice of the imposition of provisional measures shall set forth, or otherwise make available through a separate report, sufficiently detailed explanations for the preliminary determinations on dumping and injury and shall refer to the matters of fact and law which have led to arguments being accepted or rejected. Such a notice or report shall, *due regard being paid to the requirement for the protection of confidential information*, contain in particular:
>
> (i) the names of the suppliers, or when this is impracticable, the supplying countries involved;
>
> (ii) a description of the product which is sufficient for customs purposes;
>
> (iii) the margins of dumping established and a full explanation of the reasons for the methodology used in the establishment and comparison of the export price and the normal value under Article 2;

---

[53] As the Appellate Body noted in the case of *United States - Standards for Reformulated and Conventional Gasoline*, "one of the corollaries of the 'general rule of interpretation' in the *Vienna Convention* is that interpretation must give meaning and effect to all terms of the treaty. An interpreter is not free to adopt a reading that would result in reducing whole clauses or paras. of a treaty to redundancy or inutility." Appellate Body Report, *United States - Standards for Reformulated and Conventional Gasoline*, WT/DS2/AB/R, adopted on 20 May 1996, DSR 1996:I, 3, p. 21.

(iv) considerations relevant to the injury determination as set out in Article 3;

(v) the main reasons leading to the determination.

12.2.2 A public notice of conclusion or suspension of an investigation in the case of an affirmative determination providing for the imposition of a definitive duty or the acceptance of a price undertaking shall contain, or otherwise make available through a separate report, all relevant information on the matters of fact and law and reasons which have led to the imposition of final measures or the acceptance of a price undertaking, *due regard being paid to the requirement for the protection of confidential information*. In particular, the notice or report shall contain the information described in subparagraph 2.1, as well as the reasons for the acceptance or rejection of relevant arguments or claims made by the exporters and importers, and the basis for any decision made under subparagraph 10.2 of Article 6". (emphasis added)

6.36 Thus, the transparency requirement which obligates the authority to explain its determination in a public notice is subject to the need to have regard to the requirement for the protection of confidential information of Article 6.5 of the AD Agreement. Confidentiality of the information submitted therefore limits the manner in which the authority explains its decision and supports its determination in a public notice. In sum, Article 12 implies, to our mind, that an investigating authority may rely on confidential information in making determinations while respecting its obligation to protect the confidentiality of that information.

6.37 We find support for our view in a recent Appellate Body Report on *Thailand - Anti-Dumping Duties on Angles, Shapes and Sections of Iron or Non-Alloy Steel and H-Beams from Poland ("Thailand - H-Beams")* which addressed the question of the use of confidential information by the investigating authority as a basis for its final determination. The Appellate Body stated that:

"An anti-dumping investigation involves the commercial behaviour of firms, and, under the provisions of the Anti-Dumping Agreement, involves the collection and assessment of both confidential and non-confidential information. An injury determination conducted pursuant to the provisions of Article 3 of the Anti-Dumping Agreement must be based on the totality of that evidence. We see nothing in Article 3.1 which limits an investigating authority to base an injury determination only upon non-confidential information".[54]

6.38 We are aware that, for the purpose of transparency, Article 6.5.1 obliges an authority to require the parties providing confidential information to furnish

[54] Appellate Body Report, *Thailand - H-Beams*, para. 107.

non-confidential summaries which shall be in sufficient detail to permit a reasonable understanding of the substance of the information submitted in confidence. We consider that this is an important element of the AD Agreement which reflects the balance struck by the Agreement between the need to protect the confidentiality of certain information, on the one hand, and the need to ensure that all parties have a full opportunity to defend their interests, on the other. However, we see nothing in Article 6.5.1, nor elsewhere in Article 6.5, that authorizes a Member to disregard confidential information solely on the basis that the non-confidential summary of that information contains insufficient detail to permit authorities to calculate normal value, export price and the margin of dumping.[55]

6.39 Consistent with our view that authorities may rely on confidential information in making their determination, the purpose of the non-confidential summaries provided for in Article 6.5.1 is to inform the *interested parties* so as to enable them to defend their interests. We do not consider that the purpose of the non-confidential summaries is to enable the *authorities* to arrive at public conclusions, as Argentina contends.[56] Thus, an authority would not in our view be justified in rejecting the exporters' responses simply because the information in the non-confidential summaries was not sufficient to allow the calculation of normal value, export price, and the margin of dumping.

6.40 Turning now to the facts of this case, we consider that, even if the DCD had been entitled under Article 6.8 to resort to the facts available in a case where the exporters failed to declassify confidential information concerning normal value and export price or to provide adequate non-confidential summaries thereof, we find no factual basis on the record for Argentina's assertion before us that the exporters did not respond fully to the DCD's request for the declassification of the confidential information and failed to provide adequate non-confidential summaries thereof.

6.41 The events concerning confidentiality of the information and the requests for non-confidential summaries are summarized in the DCD's Final Determination.[57] The DCD states that for most of the information provided in their questionnaire reply the exporters requested confidentiality. In its report, the DCD further explains that on 30 April 1999 the DCD sent letters to the firms in question requesting the exporting firms to consider providing a more detailed non-confidential summary than that already provided in the questionnaire replies, to

---

[55] We note that Article 6.5.2 of the AD Agreement specifically provides for a situation in which the authorities may disregard confidentially submitted information: in case the authorities consider that a request for confidentiality is *not warranted* and the supplier of the information is either unwilling to make the information public or to authorize its disclosure in generalized or summary form. We note, however, that the DCD considered the request for confidential treatment *was warranted* and treated the information as such. Argentina has not invoked Article 6.5.2 as a justification for the DCD's rejection of the exporters' information either.

[56] Argentina's answers to questions from the Panel at the first meeting, question 5, p. 16.

[57] Final Dumping Determination, pages 25-27. Exhibit EC-2.

elaborate on the information supplied, or to remove the requested confidentiality that had been granted by the investigating authority so that the authority would have the information it required to reach a public conclusion to the investigation. More specifically, information on sales in the Italian market (Annex VIII) and the cost structure of the goods in the domestic Italian market (Annex X) was requested. On 4 June 1999, the exporting firms submitted public and confidential information concerning domestic sales of the product concerned with conversion tables that were submitted as confidential information. On 7 June 1999, Bismantova and Casalgrande further submitted as confidential information sales invoices relating to the Italian domestic market. By its letters of 22 June 1999 and 3 August 1999, the DCD requested the exporting firms to reconsider the requested confidentiality of the information concerning product codes and the production costs or else to provide a sufficiently detailed non-confidential summary, so that the authority could issue a precise determination in its final report as to the existence of an unfair trade practice. The DCD's report acknowledges that the exporting firms agreed by letters of 23 and 24 June that the product code item could be made non-confidential. On 10 August 1999, the exporting firms further agreed to remove the confidentiality of the item concerning cost of production provided that the names of the companies relating to each cost structure were not revealed.

6.42 In light of the contradictory arguments presented by the parties before us, we sought further clarification of this matter. From the parties' replies to our questions, we conclude that the record shows that the exporters requested confidential treatment for most of the information provided in the questionnaire replies. In particular, confidential treatment was requested concerning information of a more general nature concerning the home market of the exporters and their sales performance both in volume and in value terms. This information contained in the following annexes of the questionnaire reply was presented in indexed form in a non-confidential summary submitted together with the confidential questionnaire reply:[58]

- the producers/exporters' home market (Annex IV);
- summary of producers/exporters' sales (physical volume) (Annex V);
- summary of producers/exporters' sales (value) (Annex VI).

6.43 In the course of the investigation, the DCD never suggested that it was dissatisfied with the information presented in indexed form, nor did it suggest that this summary was not sufficiently detailed.

6.44 The exporters also requested that the information concerning normal value, export price and cost of production be given confidential treatment. At the time of the original questionnaire reply on 10 December 1998, the exporters did

[58] The non-confidential summaries of these annexes were submitted by Argentina as Exhibit ARG-24.

not provide a meaningful non-confidential summary for the information concerning:

- list of importers (Annex III);
- exports to Argentina (Annex VII);
- sales made in the domestic (Italian) market (Annex VIII);
- exports to third countries (Annex IX);
- cost structure of products sold in the domestic market (Annex X);
- cost structure of products when exported (Annex XI).

6.45 In its preliminary determination of dumping, the DCD expressed the view that the confidentiality of the information was a limiting factor and that it implied a restricted and differential treatment of this information.[59] By letter of 30 April 1999, the DCD requested that a more detailed non-confidential summary be provided or that the request for confidential treatment with regard to these six annexes (III, VII, VIII, IX, X, XI) be waived. In a follow-up meeting of exporters with the case-handlers on 11 May 1999, it was agreed that more detailed summaries be provided for Annexes VII, VIII and IX.[60]

6.46 On 4 June 1999, the exporters submitted non-confidential summaries of the information of Annexes VII, VIII and IX, in the format agreed upon at the meeting of the exporters with the case-handlers on 11 May 1999, replacing the names of the products with a code and attaching a confidential conversion table in which the codes are explained.[61] On 7 and 10 June 1999, Bismantova and Casalgrande provided confidential copies of invoices of their domestic and export sales, as had been agreed during the meeting of 11 May 1999.

6.47 On 22 June 1999, the DCD sent a second letter to the exporters in which it requested that the product code information be declassified. On 24 June 1999, the exporters agreed to make the product codes public. On 3 August 1999, the DCD made an additional request to declassify or provide a more detailed summary of information on the cost structure of the domestically sold products (Annex X) and of the products when exported to Argentina (Annex XI). Such information was provided on 10 August 1999, as the exporters agreed to remove the confidentiality of the item concerning cost of production, provided that the names of the companies relating to each cost structure were not revealed.

6.48 The non-confidential summaries of Annexes IV, V and VI presented the information in indexed form, permitting a reasonable understanding of the substance of the confidential information. This appears also to have been the opinion of the investigating authority which, in the course of the investigation, never re-

---

[59] Preliminary Dumping Determination, pages 34-35. Exhibit ARG-8.

[60] Report of Ecolatina of the meeting with the case-handlers, Exhibit EC-10; EC's answers to questions from the Panel at the first meeting, question 6, para. 27.

[61] Exhibit EC-12 provides an example. We note that the information in the confidential and non-confidential documents appears identical apart from product codes and customer codes.

quested a more detailed public summary for these three annexes. The remainder of the confidential information (with regard to normal value and export price information as well as data concerning cost of production, Annexes VII-XI) was declassified by the exporters upon the request of the DCD and the only difference between the public and the confidential information related to the names of customers and the precise identity of the exporter whose cost of production information was being reported. We consider that such a non-confidential "summary" contained all the information the DCD would have needed to calculate normal value, export price and the margin of dumping, and therefore clearly permitted a reasonable understanding by the interested parties of the substance of the confidential information.

6.49 In conclusion, we find that following the preliminary determination the issue of non-confidential summaries was resolved by the positive replies of the exporters to the repeated requests for declassification of the information by the DCD. The facts on the record demonstrate that non-confidential summaries were provided for all the confidential information. Therefore, leaving aside the question of whether the failure to furnish non-confidential summaries which satisfy the requirements of Article 6.5.1 could in any case justify the application of the facts available under Article 6.8 of the AD Agreement, we find that, in this case, the exporters did provide such detailed non-confidential summaries and declassified most if not all of the confidential information concerning normal value and export price. Accordingly, we find that the DCD was not justified in law or in fact in disregarding in large part the information from the exporters for reasons relating to the confidentiality of the information.

6.50 We further recall our conclusion in paragraph 6.21 that Article 6.8 read in conjunction with paragraph 6 of Annex II, requires an investigating authority to inform the party supplying information of the reasons why evidence or information is not accepted, to provide an opportunity to provide further explanations within a reasonable period, and to give, in any published determinations, the reasons for the rejection of evidence or information. We find that the DCD never informed the exporters that their information was going to be rejected for this reason, as required by that provision. As discussed above, the requests for declassification of the information contained in the three letters sent by the DCD were all complied with, and the exporters could therefore legitimately have assumed that their information was not going to be rejected for reasons relating to the confidentiality of the information. Neither were the reasons for the rejection of such evidence or information given in any published determinations, as required by paragraph 6 of Annex II. We therefore find that the DCD also acted inconsistently with paragraph 6 of Annex II of the AD Agreement.

(b) Lack of Documentary Evidence

6.51 **Argentina** argues that the exporters failed to provide sufficient supporting documentation, in spite of being explicitly requested to do so on numerous occasions by the DCD both in the questionnaire and in subsequent letters to the exporters. According to Argentina, the exporters failed to meet even the minimum requirement of providing a statistically valid sample of invoices for their domestic sales' information.[62] Argentina submits that the DCD was allowed to resort to facts available since the required supporting documentation which was necessary to prove the reliability of the information and which was explicitly requested, was not provided by the exporters. In addition, Argentina argues, this refusal to provide the required documentary evidence significantly impeded the investigation.

6.52 The **EC** contests Argentina's argument that the exporters failed to provide the requested supporting documentation. The EC asserts that the exporters were not requested to provide any supporting documentation until very late in the investigation. According to the EC, the exporters were informed only towards the end of the investigation that no verification visit was going to take place and that the DCD required certain exporters to supply supporting documentary evidence instead.[63] The EC argues that the exporters complied with the request and that therefore the DCD was not justified in resorting to facts available for failure to provide supporting documentation.

6.53 The question before us is whether the DCD was entitled to resort to facts available because of the alleged failure of the exporters to provide sufficient supporting documentation.[64] We recall our view that, under Article 6.8, resort to the facts available is authorized only where a party refuses access to, or otherwise does not provide, *necessary* information, or where a party *significantly impeded* the investigation. Thus, the question before us is whether the DCD acted consistently with Article 6.8 by resorting to facts available on the grounds that the exporters allegedly failed to provide sufficient supporting documentation.

6.54 In considering this question, we first observe that a basic obligation concerning the evidence-gathering process is for the investigating authorities to indicate to the interested parties the information they require for their determination. This obligation is set forth in Article 6.1 of the AD Agreement which states as follows:

> "All interested parties in an anti-dumping investigation shall be given notice of the information which the authorities require and ample opportunity to present in writing all evidence which they consider relevant in respect of the investigation in question".

Article 6.1 of the AD Agreement thus requires that interested parties be given notice of the information which the authorities require. In our view, it follows

---

[62] Argentina refers in this respect to the lack of representativeness of the supporting documentation concerning domestic sales of the exporters which covered only 1.92 per cent of total domestic sales made by the sampled exporters. Final Dumping Determination, p. 29. Exhibit EC-2.

[63] The EC emphasizes that the exporters were willing to accept any verification visits of the DCD.

[64] We note that the facts on the record referred to by Argentina in support of its argument only relate to the lack of documentary evidence of the domestic sales information, and not with regard to the information provided by the exporters concerning export price. Nevertheless, as was noted above, the export price information supplied by the exporters was completely disregarded.

that, independently of the purpose for which the information or documentation is requested, an investigating authority may not fault an interested party for not providing information it was not clearly requested to submit.

6.55 This consideration is particularly relevant to the question of whether an authority is justified in resorting to the use of facts available under Article 6.8 of the AD Agreement. Paragraph 1 of Annex II of the AD Agreement on the "Use of Best Information Available in Terms of Paragraph 8 of Article 6" reiterates the obligation of Article 6.1. It states that:

> "1. As soon as possible after the initiation of the investigation, the investigating authorities should *specify in detail the information required* from any interested party, and the manner in which that information should be structured by the interested party in its response. The authorities should also ensure that the party is aware that *if information is not supplied within a reasonable time*, the authorities will be free to make determinations on the basis of the facts available, including those contained in the application for the initiation of the investigation by the domestic industry". (emphasis added).

Thus, the first sentence of paragraph 1 requires the investigating authority to "specify in detail the information required", while the second sentence requires it to inform interested parties that, if information is not supplied within a reasonable time, the authorities may make determinations on the basis of the facts available. In our view, the inclusion, in an Annex relating specifically to the use of best information available under Article 6.8, of a requirement to specify in detail the information required, strongly implies that investigating authorities are *not* entitled to resort to best information available in a situation where a party does not provide certain information if the authorities failed to specify in detail the information which was required.

6.56 We recall that the documentary evidence in this case appears to have been required in order to verify the information supplied by the exporters in their questionnaire replies since the DCD decided not to conduct any on-the-spot verification in Italy. In the context of this factual situation, we find further confirmation for the view that an investigating authority may not resort to facts available due to failure of a party to provide information that was not clearly requested in Articles 6.6 and 6.7 of the AD Agreement, which relate to the question of verification of information. They provide as follows:

> "6.6 Except in circumstances provided for in paragraph 8, the authorities shall during the course of an investigation satisfy themselves as to the accuracy of the information supplied by interested parties upon which their findings are based.
>
> 6.7 In order to verify information provided or to obtain further details, the authorities may carry out investigations in the territory of other Members as required, provided they obtain the agreement of the firms concerned and notify the representatives of the gov-

> ernment of the Member in question, and unless that Member objects to the investigation. The procedures described in Annex I shall apply to investigations carried out in the territory of other Members. Subject to the requirement to protect confidential information, the authorities shall make the results of any such investigations available, or shall provide disclosure thereof pursuant to paragraph 9, to the firms to which they pertain and may make such results available to the applicants".

6.57 Article 6.6 of the AD Agreement thus places the burden of satisfying oneself of the accuracy of the information on the investigating authority. As a general rule, the exporters are therefore entitled to assume that unless otherwise indicated they are not required to also automatically and in all cases submit evidence to demonstrate the accuracy of the information they are supplying. We note that in this case, all four exporters stated that they were willing to accept any kind of verification visits. The DCD decided however not to conduct such an on-the spot-verification.[65] We believe that if no on-the-spot verification is going to take place but certain documents are required for verification purposes, the authorities should in a similar manner inform the exporters of the nature of the information for which they require such evidence and of any further documents they require.

6.58 For the foregoing reasons, we conclude that an investigating authority may not disregard information and resort to facts available under Article 6.8 on the grounds that a party has failed to provide sufficient supporting documentation in respect of information provided unless the investigating authority has clearly requested that the party provide such supporting documentation.

6.59 In light of this conclusion, the first question we address is whether the DCD clearly informed the exporters that they were required to submit supporting documentation and the kind of information requested. We examined the requests to provide supporting documentation in the questionnaire on which Argentina bases its argument. We find that these requests are very vague and general in nature and are made in the general introductory part of the questionnaire setting out the goals and objectives of the questionnaire and in the section entitled "General Instructions".

6.60 In the section on goals and objectives, the questionnaire indicates that "the producer/exporter shall be required to reply to this questionnaire as precisely as possible, attaching supporting documents for its replies, or in case this is not pos-

---

[65] There does not exist a requirement in the Agreement to carry out investigations in the territory of other Members for verification purposes. Article 6.7 of the AD Agreement merely provides for this possibility. While such on-site verification visits are common practice, the Agreement does not say that this is the only way or even the preferred way for an investigating authority to fulfill its obligation under Article 6.6 to satisfy itself as to the accuracy of the information supplied by interested parties on which its findings are based.

sible, indicating the source of the information"[66] Similarly, the general instructions of the questionnaire state that: "1. The exporter is required to mention on each of the pages it presents, the case number, and is to reply to all questions in a detailed manner and to give information with regard to the sources used, attaching as a necessary condition to back up the veracity of the source, the corresponding documentation." A final reference to the need to provide supporting documentation is found in Section B of the questionnaire which relates to export price information. It requires the party supplying the information to provide "that information to be provided that assists the authority in getting a better understanding of the transaction be it through a buy order, sales contracts, commercial invoices, credit notes, ..., etc." [67]

6.61 We note that point 7 of the general instructions section of the questionnaire also provides that all information may be subject to verification by the authority. In this respect, the questionnaire provides that in the case where such verification takes place the exporters will be informed which documentation it will have to put at the disposal of the verification team. The exporters are requested to express their willingness to accept such verification visits. All exporters agreed to such verification visits.[68]

6.62 At the time of the preliminary determination, no supporting documentation (e.g. invoices, orders, price lists) had been submitted by the exporters. After the preliminary determination the DCD sent a letter to the exporting firms in the context of the above discussed need for additional public information. This letter of 30 April 1999[69] also mentions the question of supporting documents. It states that: "We therefore request the cooperation of the firm you represent, since it is of the utmost importance for the analysis being conducted by the DCD based on the inclusion of fresh evidence or the adaptation of the information already in the record in order to ensure that the implementing authority has information that enables it to reach a public conclusion on the matter at issue." [70]

6.63 Argentina refers to two other letters of 22 June 1999 [71] and 3 August 1999[72] which the DCD sent to the exporters with a request to declassify certain information in support of its argument that on several occasions throughout the investigation the DCD requested to be provided with additional supporting documents. We find however that these two later letters do not in any way refer

---

[66] We note that the questionnaire thus actually allowed exporters the choice of either providing supporting documentation or identifying the sources of the data reported (presumably to facilitate verification, see ARG-5, p. 2). We are aware of at least one exporter, Casalgrande, which complied with the second possibility, as it identified in its questionnaire response the sources of the information reported (Exhibit EC-4, pp. 16-17).

[67] Exhibit ARG-5.

[68] Exhibit ARG-5, p. 4.

[69] Exhibit ARG-7.

[70] Exhibit ARG-7.

[71] Exhibit ARG-10.

[72] Exhibit ARG-11.

to the need for supporting documents at all. They are requests for declassification.

6.64 The EC states that during the 11 May 1999 meeting with the case-handlers, the exporters were for the first time informed that the DCD was not going to conduct an on-the-spot verification. At that meeting, the EC asserts, the exporters or at least the two major exporters, Casalgrande and Bismantova, were requested to provide copies of the invoices covering an important number of sales.[73] The EC argues that, in response to this request, the exporters concerned submitted copies of invoices covering approximately 50 per cent of the sales in Italy and to Argentina and third countries.[74] Argentina, however, submits that the DCD, in its final determination, found that the supporting documentation provided by the four exporting companies with regard to the information supplied concerning domestic sales of the product concerned only covered about 1.92 per cent of the total volume of domestic sales made by these four sampled exporters. We requested further clarification from Argentina on how the DCD calculated this figure in light of the statement of the exporters that they were submitting a large number of sales invoices. Argentina argued that for reasons relating to the confidentiality of the information it was unable to provide the numerical calculations made.[75] After the submission of the invoices by the two largest Italian exporters, the DCD did not make any further request for additional supporting documentation.

6.65 We note that the DCD in its Final Determination stated that:

---

[73] EC's second written submission, para. 39. According to the report of this meeting by the representative of the Italian exporters in Argentina, Ecolatina (Exhibit EC-10), the following request was made: *"Additionally, this information must cover an "important" part of total sales in the domestic market (you said 50 per cent - I don't know, I guess that is largely enough), the coverage must be September 1997 - October 1998, and we have to present invoices (with confidential status) supporting this non-confidential version".*

[74] The DCD's Final Dumping Determination also reports that Bismantova and Casalgrande, on 7 June 1999 and 10 June 1999 respectively, submitted copies of invoices concerning sales in the domestic market as well as export sales. Final Dumping Determination, pages 26, 36. Exhibit EC-2. We note that the submission of the invoices is mentioned in the DCD report as part of the account of events concerning confidential information and the requests for more detailed non-confidential summaries or the declassification of the information.

[75] Argentina's answers to questions from the panel at the second meeting, question 8, p. 4. Argentina replied that "as already stated on several occasions, the implementing authority interrelated the information available in the questionnaires provided in the course of the proceedings, and concluded that the documentation supplied covered that percentage in relation to total sales on the Italian domestic market. Unfortunately, this is a good example of the limitations facing the implementing authority as a result of the request for confidentiality of the information provided. In this case, the Argentine authority is limited in the reply it can give to the question, in that it cannot reveal the numerical calculation made, but for the purposes of that calculation, it considered the information corresponding to the aggregate total amount of sales reported for the Italian domestic market by the four firms in relation to the total obtained from the documentation contributed by those firms during the proceedings".

> "The sample documentation relating to sales on the Italian domestic market supplied by all of the manufacturing export companies concerned in the case - and as affirmed at the time of their participation in the proceedings by the National Association of Italian Ceramic Tile and Refractories Manufacturers (Assopiastrelle), of which these firms are members, they are major representatives of the Italian *porcellanato* production market - covers no more than approximately 1.92 per cent of the physical volume (m^2) and 1.35 per cent of the total estimated value (Italian lire) of sales in the domestic market according to the information duly supplied".

This statement of fact in the Final Determination forms the basis for Argentina's argument that the DCD was justified to resort to the facts available under Article 6.8. We note that the DCD did not draw any conclusions from this factual consideration concerning the representativeness of the normal value information submitted by the exporters.[76]

6.66 In light of the ambiguity of the questionnaire regarding documentary evidence and given that the verification methodology to be used was not clearly indicated, some precision by the DCD as to what supporting documentation was expected from the exporters was necessary. We are of the view that the very general references to the need to provide supporting documentation in the introductory section of the questionnaire did not meet this requirement. Neither do we consider the one general reference in the letter of 30 April 1999 to the need for new probative elements expressed in the context of a request to declassify certain information or provide more detailed public summaries thereof to be a sufficient notice to the exporters to provide documentary evidence. Therefore, and especially in light of the complex nature of the kind of information that might be needed to demonstrate the accuracy of certain information, we do not consider that any clear request for supporting documentation was made to the exporters. We further do not believe that, independent of any clear request, an interested party is required to provide any particular number of documents to support the information supplied. At the meeting of 11 May 1999, the case-handlers requested at least some exporters to provide certain supporting documentation. The exporters concerned supplied the requested documentation and were never informed by the DCD that the documentation provided was insufficient or that their understanding of the DCD's request was incorrect. We therefore are unable to

[76] In its second submission to the Panel, Argentina summarized its conclusion of this para. of the DCD's report in the following manner: "We repeat that upon examining the supporting documentation - submitted late and at the DCD's specific request - the authority found that the firms making up the sample proposed by Assopiastrelle itself only represented approximately 1.92 per cent of the physical volume (m^2) and 1.35 per cent of the total estimated value (in Italian lire) of sales on the domestic market." Argentina's second written submission to the Panel, para. 25. Other explanations have been offered by Argentina in the course of the proceedings. In light of our finding on this issue in para. 6.65, we believe it is only necessary to understand that the DCD was not satisfied as to the completeness of the responses regarding sales in the Italian market.

accept Argentina's argument that the exporters significantly impeded the investigation or refused access to necessary information by not providing more supporting documentation. We find that the DCD was not justified in disregarding in large part the information supplied by the exporters for this reason.

6.67 We further recall our conclusion in paragraph 6.21 that Article 6.8 read in conjunction with paragraph 6 of Annex II, requires an investigating authority to inform the party supplying information of the reasons why evidence or information is not accepted, to provide an opportunity to provide further explanations within a reasonable period, and to give, in any published determinations, the reasons for the rejection of evidence or information. In this case, the exporters were never informed that in the absence of a certain number of supporting documents their information was going to be rejected, much less were they provided an opportunity to offer further explanations. Nor were the reasons for the rejection of such evidence or information given in any published determinations. We therefore find that the DCD also acted inconsistently with paragraph 6 of Annex II of the AD Agreement.

(c) Failure to Comply with Formal Requirements of the Questionnaire

6.68 **Argentina** argues that certain exporters provided information in Italian lire and not in US$ as requested by the questionnaire. Argentina further submits that three of the four exporters[77] failed to provide a Spanish translation of their balance sheets while the exporters were clearly informed both in the general instructions of the questionnaire and in the follow-up letter of 30 April 1999 that all their information needed to be translated into Spanish in order for it to be taken into consideration. Argentina submits that the unjustified refusals to provide the information in US$ and properly translated into Spanish significantly impeded the investigation. Finally, Argentina argues that two exporters, Caesar and Marazzi, refused to provide the requested information with regard to exports to third countries (Annex IX of the questionnaire), and that Marazzi also failed to provide any information with regard to the cost structure for the exported goods (Annex XI). Argentina submits that these firms thus refused to provide access to necessary information.

6.69 The **EC** argues that the exporters complied with all the formal requirements of the questionnaire. The EC acknowledges that certain individual exporters did not provide a translation of their balance sheets, but argues that this constituted a minor omission which could not have justified disregarding all of the exporters' information.

6.70 The facts on the record show that in fact only one exporting company, Bismantova, provided certain information in one annex of the questionnaire reply

---

[77] Marazzi is the only exporter that did provide such a translation of its balance sheet.

in Italian lire rather than in US$. This exporting company moreover provided the relevant exchange rates together with the information. The fact that this company did not provide the information directly in US$ as required, according to the questionnaire's instructions, in our view, does not amount to significantly impeding the investigation, nor did it constitute in this case a failure to provide necessary information.

6.71 We further consider that in general it is important that translations be provided whenever requested. However, the facts of this case indicate that what was not translated were certain lines of the balance sheets of three of the four exporting companies. We do not believe that this absence of translation of a balance sheet significantly impeded the investigation. We note that the translation which was provided by one of the exporting companies of its balance sheet was accepted while it contained only a minor translation from Italian into Spanish of two terms of the balance sheet.[78] We do not believe that the DCD was justified in disregarding the exporters' information because of this minor omission on the part of the exporters to translate certain parts of the balance sheets, as this did not significantly impede the investigation.[79]

6.72 With regard to the two exporters which did not provide information under certain of the questionnaire's annexes, we note that the questionnaire explicitly allowed the exporters not to provide such information if there existed sufficient domestic sales made in the ordinary course of trade. The two exporting firms concerned, Caesar and Marazzi, expressly relied on this possibility.[80] It appears that Marazzi did not refuse to provide information under Annex XI either (cost of production for the subject product when exported), but rather it replied that the costs for domestically sold and exported products did not differ, except for differences in selling expenses.[81] Based on the facts of this case, we find that an unbiased and objective evaluation of these facts would have led the authority to the conclusion that these omissions do not amount to a refusal to provide necessary information, nor that the exporters concerned can be considered to have significantly impeded the investigation.[82]

---

[78] Exhibit EC-13.

[79] We note that most of the information which the DCD used as the facts available also lacked any translations, which did not prevent the DCD from using this information as a basis for its determination.

[80] Preliminary Dumping Determination, pages 15 and 18. Exhibit ARG-8

[81] Preliminary Dumping Determination, p. 18. Exhibit ARG-8.

[82] We note that, in its last set of answers to questions from the Panel, Argentina for the first time appeared to argue that the information supplied by the exporters was not authenticated as allegedly required by the questionnaire. We note that there does not exist a factual basis for this argument in the record. In any case, it appears that Argentina itself does not consider that the DCD rejected the information for this reason, since it argues that "in spite of" this failure to have the information authenticated, the DCD proceeded to cross-check the information supplied. Argentina's answers to questions from the Panel at the second meeting, question 1.

6.73 We therefore find that the DCD was not justified in disregarding the exporters' information under Article 6.8 of the AD Agreement for reasons relating to the failure to comply with certain formal requirements.

6.74 We further recall our conclusion that Article 6.8 read in conjunction with paragraph 6 of Annex II, requires an investigating authority to inform the party supplying information of the reasons why evidence or information is not accepted, to provide an opportunity to provide further explanations within a reasonable period, and to give, in any published determinations, the reasons for the rejection of evidence or information. We find that the DCD never informed the exporters that their information would be rejected for having failed to comply with the formal requirements of the questionnaire, much less provided an opportunity to provide further explanations. Nor were the reasons for the rejection of such evidence or information given in any published determinations. We therefore find that the DCD also acted inconsistently with paragraph 6 of Annex II of the AD Agreement.

(d) Late Submission of the Information

6.75 **Argentina** argues that the exporters failed to provide the requested information within a reasonable period. Argentina asserts that, due to the many requests for extension of deadlines by the exporters, information which originally was supposed to be given by 30 November 1998 was submitted as late as 10 August 1999.[83] Argentina submits that the late submission of information towards the end of the investigation constituted a failure to provide the information within a reasonable period which significantly impeded the investigation and entitled the DCD to resort to facts available under Article 6.8 of the AD Agreement.

6.76 The **EC** submits that the exporters supplied the information in a timely manner. According to the EC, additional information was submitted late into the investigation because of the repeated requests for additional public information from the DCD. The EC stresses that in fact no new factual data was submitted, but rather confidential information provided at the time of the questionnaire response was declassified and supplied to the DCD together with supporting documentary evidence that was requested.

[83] We note that in its first written submission, Argentina argued that the submission of the questionnaire replies by the exporters was late by one day. In its answers to questions from the Panel at the first meeting (question 8, p. 17) Argentina admitted that in fact the questionnaire replies were submitted within the grace period provided by administrative Decree No. 1759/72, as amended by Decree 1883/1991. Article 25 of the Argentine Decree 1759/72, as amended by Decree 1883/1991 provides that information supplied within two hours of the day following the expiration of the deadline is considered to have been submitted in a timely fashion. Exhibit EC-8. The deadline for the questionnaire replies was 9 December 1998. The exporters supplied their questionnaire responses in the morning of 10 December 1998, and thus within the grace period provided in the Decree mentioned above.

6.77 We find that, according to the case record, the exporters requested an extension of the deadline for the submission of information on two occasions only. Both times the authority granted the request. An extension of the deadline for the filing of the questionnaire reply was requested from 30 November 1998 to 9 December 1998. This request was granted and the replies were submitted within the deadline during the morning of 10 December 1998.[84] On 30 April 1999, the DCD sent a letter to the exporters requesting additional public information to be provided within 15 days. The exporters requested an extension of the deadline on 14 May 1999. The request was granted and the information was submitted before the new deadline of 7 June 1999. Additional requests for declassification of the information made on 22 June and 3 August were almost immediately complied with.

6.78 In sum, all of the information was submitted in a timely manner. Additional requests for information implied that additional information, consisting of non-confidential summaries as well as supporting documentation, would of course be submitted long after the deadline for the submission of the questionnaire replies. In these circumstances, the exporters are not responsible for these additional requests for information. Therefore, the facts do not support Argentina's argument that the exporters were uncooperative and failed to submit the information within a reasonable period. We therefore find that the DCD was not justified in disregarding the exporters' information under Article 6.8 on this basis.

6.79 We further recall our conclusion that Article 6.8 read in conjunction with paragraph 6 of Annex II, requires an investigating authority to inform the party supplying information of the reasons why evidence or information is not accepted, to provide an opportunity to provide further explanations within a reasonable period, and to give, in any published determinations, the reasons for the rejection of evidence or information. We find that the DCD never informed the exporters that their information would be rejected for having failed to provide the information within a reasonable period, much less provided an opportunity to provide further explanations. Nor were the reasons for the rejection of such evidence or information given in any published determinations. We therefore find that the DCD also acted inconsistently with paragraph 6 of Annex II of the AD Agreement.

3. Conclusion

6.80 For the foregoing reasons, we find that the DCD acted inconsistently with Article 6.8 of the AD Agreement when it disregarded completely the exporters' information concerning export price and disregarded in large part the exporters' normal value information by mixing the primary source exporters' information with information from secondary sources such as the petitioner, importers and

[84] See footnote 83.

official statistics. We further find that the DCD acted inconsistently with Article 6.8 read in conjunction with paragraph 6 of Annex II, in that the DCD (i) did not inform the exporters why certain information supplied by them was not accepted (ii) did not provide the exporters an opportunity to provide further explanations within a reasonable period; and (iii) did not give, in any published determinations, the reasons for the rejection of evidence or information.

6.81 We are conscious that our finding that the DCD incorrectly disregarded the exporter's information and resorted to facts available in a manner inconsistent with Article 6.8 of the AD Agreement casts doubt on the entire final determination of dumping. In this respect, we recall the statements of the Appellate Body on "judicial economy" in the dispute on *United States - Measures Affecting Imports of Woven Wool Shirts and Blouses from India ("United States - Shirts and Blouses*") that "A panel need only address those claims which must be addressed in order to resolve the matter in issue in the dispute." [85] Nevertheless, as the Appellate Body stated in a subsequent dispute on *Australia - Measures Affecting the Importation of Salmon*, "[T]o provide only a partial resolution of the matter at issue would be false judicial economy. A panel has to address those claims on which a finding is necessary in order to enable the DSB to make sufficiently precise recommendations and rulings so as to allow for prompt compliance by a Member with those recommendations and rulings 'in order to ensure effective resolution of disputes to the benefit of all Members".[86] Mindful of the Appellate Body's comments in this respect, we will continue with our analysis of the other claims made before us "because it could prove of utility depending on any appeal"[87] and in order "to enable the DSB to make sufficiently precise recommendations and rulings so as to allow for prompt compliance with those recommendations and rulings" [88].

E. *Claim 2: Article 6.10: Requirement to Calculate Individual Margins of Dumping for All Exporters Included in the Sample*

1. *Arguments of the Parties*

6.82 The **EC** submits that the DCD did not determine an individual margin of dumping for each of the four exporters included in the sample, as required by

---

85 Appellate Body Report, *United States - Measures Affecting Imports of Woven Wool Shirts and Blouses from India ("United States - Shirts and Blouses")*, WT/DS33/AB/R, adopted 23 May 1997, DSR 1997:I, 323, p. 340.

86 Appellate Body Report, *Australia - Measures Affecting Importation of Salmon*, WT/DS18/AB/R, adopted 6 November 1998, DSR 1998:VIII, 3327, para. 223.

87 Panel Report, *United States - Anti-Dumping Measures on Stainless Steel Plate in Coils and Stainless Steel Sheet and Strip from Korea ("United States - Korea Steel")*, WT/DS179/R, adopted 1 February 2001, DSR 2001:IV, 1295, para. 5.11.

88 Appellate Body Report, *United States - Safeguard Measures on Imports of Fresh, Chilled, or Frozen Lamb Meat from New Zealand and Australia ("United States - Lamb Safeguards")*, WT/DS177/AB/R and WT/DS178/AB/R, adopted 16 May 2001, DSR 2001:IX, 4051, para. 194.

Article 6.10 of the AD Agreement, but rather calculated dumping margins for each of the three size categories of *porcellanato* and imposed the same duty rate on all imports irrespective of the exporter concerned. The EC argues that Article 6.10 of the AD Agreement requires that as a rule an individual margin be established for each exporter or, in the case this is not practicable because of the large number of exporters for example, an individual margin is to be established for each exporter included in the sample. The EC also points to Article 9.4 in support of its argument that an individual margin of dumping should have been established for each of the four Italian exporters that formed part of the sample.[89]

6.83 **Argentina** argues that the information provided by the four exporters included in the sample was not sufficient to allow an individual dumping margin to be established for each exporter. Argentina submits that the EC wrongly presupposes that it was possible to determine an individual margin for all four exporters included in the sample. Argentina recalls that the exporters themselves through their representative organization, Assopiastrelle, requested that the investigation be conducted on the basis of a sample to facilitate the task of the authority. However, Argentina submits, it proved impossible for the DCD to determine an individual dumping margin for each of the four exporters. According to Argentina, two producers, Caesar and Marazzi, did not provide price information for tiles in the size categories 30 x 30 cm and 20 x 20 cm. Argentina alleges that one exporter, Marazzi, did not even submit information with regard to the third size category (40 x 40 cm) either.[90] A third producer, Bismantova, reported that 56 per cent of its domestic sales for tiles in the category 30 x 30 cm and up to 93 per cent of the domestic sales in the 40 x 40 cm category were made to a related company, Rondine.

6.84 Argentina submits that the use of a sample in this case was justified in light of the large number of exporters. However, Argentina argues, the sample which was proposed by the exporters' association, Assopiastrelle, and accepted by the DCD, did not serve its purpose since the information provided by the exporters in the sample was deficient and insufficient. According to Argentina, the requirement to determine an individual dumping margin has to be read in light of the requirement under Article 2 of the AD Agreement to determine a dumping margin for the product subject to the investigation. Argentina submits that the product under investigation was ceramic tiles in all their sizes, and the DCD

---

[89] Article 9.4 of the AD Agreement relates to the determination of an anti-dumping duty for those exporters not included in the sample, which shall not exceed "the weighted average margin of dumping established with respect to the selected exporters or producers". The EC argues that this suggests that for those exporters included in the sample individual margins shall be established which may then be averaged in order to determine the rate for the exporters outside the sample. In other words, the EC submits that Article 9.4 and its reference to weighted averages and *de minimis* margins presupposes the determination of individual margins for exporters included in the sample.

[90] Argentina notes that the exporters replied to the questionnaires without making any objection concerning the use of size as the determining parameter and they should therefore have provided information with regard to all size categories, as requested.

from the outset calculated a dumping margin for each of the sizes that together formed the subject product (20 x 20 cm, 30 x 30 cm, 40 x 40 cm). According to Argentina, the exporters accepted this segmentation as they replied to the questionnaires without any objections in this respect. However, the exporters included in the sample failed to provide the necessary documents that would allow the DCD to determine such product/size specific margins. Argentina asserts that the DCD was therefore justified in looking for an alternative to supplement the missing necessary information. Argentina argues that in any case, even if the Panel were to find that the DCD acted inconsistently with Article 6.10 by not determining an individual margin of dumping for each exporter, this constituted a harmless error.

6.85 The **EC** takes issue with Argentina's argument that it was not practicably possible to determine an individual margin of dumping for each of the four exporters.[91] The EC argues that Argentina cannot, for example, claim that no margin could be established because information was not presented for all size categories if the exporter in question only exports tiles of a certain size (for example, 40 x 40 cm). Finally, the EC submits, it is not because a number of sales are made to related parties that no margin can be established. According to the EC, under the facts of this case, nothing prevented the DCD from calculating an individual margin of dumping for each of the exporters included in the sample, as required by Article 6.10 of the AD Agreement.

2. *Analysis by the Panel*

6.86 The DCD's Final Determination establishes a dumping margin for three size categories of *porcellanato* irrespective of the exporter.[92] According to the EC, the DCD thus failed to establish a dumping margin for each investigated exporter individually, as is required under Article 6.10 of the AD Agreement.

6.87 Article 6.10 provides as follows:

> "The authorities *shall, as a rule, determine an individual margin of dumping for each known exporter or producer concerned* of the product under investigation. In cases where the number of exporters, producers, importers or types of products involved is so large as to make such a determination impracticable, the authorities may limit their examination either to a reasonable number of interested parties or products by using samples which are statistically valid on the basis of information available to the authorities at the time of the selection, or to the largest percentage of the volume of the ex-

[91] The EC notes that in the case of Casalgrande no explanation is provided as to why this was not possible.

[92] Similarly, the *Resolución* which imposes the final anti-dumping duty also sets a minimum FOB export price for each size of ceramic tiles imported from Italy irrespective of the exporter concerned.

ports from the country in question which can reasonably be investigated.

6.10.1 Any selection of exporters, producers, importers or types of products made under this paragraph shall preferably be chosen in consultation with and with the consent of the exporters, producers or importers concerned.

6.10.2 In cases where the authorities have limited their examination, as provided for in this paragraph, they shall nevertheless determine an individual margin of dumping for any exporter or producer not initially selected who submits the necessary information in time for that information to be considered during the course of the investigation, except where the number of exporters or producers is so large that individual examinations would be unduly burdensome to the authorities and prevent the timely completion of the investigation. Voluntary responses shall not be discouraged". (emphasis added)

6.88 We consider also relevant in this respect Article 9.4 of the AD Agreement which provides as follows:

"When the authorities have limited their examination in accordance with the second sentence of paragraph 10 of Article 6, any anti-dumping duty applied to imports from exporters or producers *not included in the examination* shall not exceed:

(i) the weighted average margin of dumping established with respect to the selected exporters or producers or,

(ii) where the liability for payment of anti-dumping duties is calculated on the basis of a prospective normal value, the difference between the weighted average normal value of the selected exporters or producers and the export prices of exporters or producers not individually examined,

provided that the authorities shall disregard for the purpose of this paragraph any zero and *de minimis* margins and margins established under the circumstances referred to in paragraph 8 of Article 6. The authorities shall apply individual duties or normal values to imports from any exporter or producer not included in the examination who has provided the necessary information during the course of the investigation, as provided for in subparagraph 10.2 of Article 6". (emphasis added)

6.89 The first sentence of Article 6.10 of the AD Agreement sets forth a general rule that the authorities determine an individual margin of dumping for each known exporter or producer of the product under investigation. The second sentence of Article 6.10 permits an investigating authority to deviate from the general rule by permitting the investigating authorities to "limit their examination either to a reasonable number of interested parties or products by using samples ... or to the largest percentage of the volume of the exports from the country in question which can reasonably be investigated", in cases where the number of exporters, producers, importers or types of products involved is so large as to make such a determination impracticable. Article 9.4 provides that, where the authorities have limited their examination in accordance with the second sentence of Article 6.10, the anti-dumping duty applied to imports from exporters or producers *not included in the examination* shall not exceed an amount calculated on the basis of the margins of dumping for exporters or producers that were included in the examination. Finally, in cases where the authorities have limited their examination under Article 6.10, subparagraph 2 of Article 6.10 provides that the authorities shall nevertheless determine an individual margin of dumping for any exporter not initially selected who submits the necessary information in time for that information to be considered, except where the number of exporters is so large that individual examination would be unduly burdensome to the authorities and prevent timely completion of the investigation.

6.90 In our view, the general rule in the first sentence of Article 6.10, that individual margins of dumping be determined for each known exporter or producer of the product under investigation, is fully applicable to exporters who are selected for examination under the second sentence of Article 6.10. While the second sentence of Article 6.10 allows an investigating authority to limit its examination to certain exporters or producers, it does not provide for a deviation from the general rule that individual margins be determined for those exporters or producers that *are* examined. To the contrary, Article 9.4 provides that, where the authorities limit their examination under Article 6.10, the anti-dumping duty for exporters or producers that *are not* examined shall not exceed a level determined on the basis of the results of the examination of those exporters or producers that were examined. That Article 9.4 does not provide any methodology for determining the level of duties applicable to exporters or producers that *are* examined in our view confirms that the general rule requiring individual margins remains applicable to those exporters or producers. We find further confirmation in Article 6.10.2, which requires that, in general, an individual margin of dumping must be calculated even for the producers/exporters not initially included in the sample, if they provide the necessary information and if to do so is not unduly burdensome. If even producers not included in the original sample are entitled to an individual margin calculation, then it follows that producers that were included in the original sample are so entitled as well.[93] Indeed, the parties appear to agree that Arti-

---

[93] As the Panel in *EC - Anti-Dumping Duties on Imports of Cotton-Type Bed Linen from India ("EC - Bed Linen")* stated:

> "the fact that Article 2.4.2 refers to the existence of margins of dumping in the plural is a general statement, taking account of the fact that, as is made clear in Article 6.10 and 9 of the AD Agreement, individual dumping margins are determined *for each producer or exporter under investigation,* and for each product under investigation" (emphasis added). Panel Report, *EC - Anti-Dumping Duties on Imports of Cotton-Type Bed Linen from India ("EC - Bed Linen") EC - Bed Linen,*

cle 6.10 of the AD Agreement requires that as a rule an individual margin of dumping has to be determined for each exporter with regard to the product subject to investigation.[94]

6.91 Argentina argues, however, that, for substantive reasons relating to the reliability of the information as well as the absence of information with regard to sales by certain exporters included in the sample, it was simply not possible for the DCD to determine a margin of dumping for each exporter individually.

6.92 In considering Argentina's assertion, we first note that there is no explanation in the DCD's Final Determination or in any other document on the record as to why, in this case, it was not possible to determine an individual margin for each exporter that was investigated. We consider that the DCD failed to provide any evaluation of the facts on the record that could have formed the basis for such a conclusion. We consider that on this basis alone we could have concluded that the DCD failed to perform an objective and unbiased evaluation of the facts which, under the applicable standard of review, we are asked to review. Nevertheless, for the sake of completeness, we will continue our analysis and address the arguments presented by the parties in their submissions to the Panel.

6.93 We first observe that neither the DCD in its Final Determination nor Argentina in its submissions to the Panel provides any reasons why, with regard to the information provided by one exporter, Casalgrande, for which no discrepancies were noted, it was not possible to determine an individual margin of dumping.

6.94 We examined the arguments presented by Argentina with regard to the other three exporters included in the sample, Bismantova, Caesar and Marazzi. We find that there were no valid reasons for not determining an individual margin of dumping under Article 6.10 for each of these companies for the product subject to the investigation. Argentina argues that in the case of Bismantova it was not possible to determine an individual margin of dumping because, for a certain size of tiles, up to 93 per cent of its domestic sales were made to a related party. Caesar, as the EC acknowledges, only reported domestic sales information concerning tiles of the size 40 x 40 cm, and did not provide any data on domestic sales of tiles of the two remaining size categories, 20 x 20 cm and 30 x 30 cm. Argentina submits that it was for this reason that the DCD could not determine an exporter-specific margin of dumping for this exporter. According to the DCD's Final Determination, a third exporter, Marazzi, only provided lists of average prices without specifying total volumes sold or the total value of the sales. It was therefore not possible to determine an individual margin of dumping for this exporter either, Argentina contends.

WT/DS141/R, adopted as reversed in part by WT/DS141/AB/R, 12 March 2001, DSR 2001:VI, 2077, para. 6.118.

[94] Argentina's answers to questions from the Panel at the first meeting, question 17; EC's answers to questions from the Panel at the first meeting, question 17.

6.95 We understand Argentina's argument to be that, in the absence of reliable and useful information with regard to *each* of the size categories of the product subject of the investigation, no individual margin of dumping could be calculated for each exporter for the product under investigation, i.e. ceramic tiles in all sizes.

6.96 We consider however that while it may have been the case that Bismantova made an important part of its sales to a related party, this should not have impeded the DCD from determining an individual margin of dumping for this exporter. The issue of domestic sales to a related party may lead, in certain cases, to the use of a constructed normal value or third country export price under Article 2 of the AD Agreement.[95] The question of sufficient domestic sales in the ordinary course of trade does not, in our view, stand in the way of an individual margin of dumping determination under Article 6.10 of the AD Agreement, be this based on normal value information consisting of prices of sales made in the home market, on third country export prices, or a construction of the normal value as defined in Article 2.2 of the AD Agreement.[96] The basis of the normal value determination has no bearing on the ability to calculate an individual dumping margin for the producer whose normal value is in question.

6.97 With regard to the two other exporting firms, Caesar and Marazzi, we also fail to see why it was not possible for the DCD to determine an individual margin of dumping for each exporter. Based on the facts on the record, we understand that Caesar only exports tiles of the size 40 x 40 cm to Argentina and therefore only reported similar size domestic sales. In accordance with the DCD's own analysis concerning the requirement of making a fair comparison between normal value and export price by adjusting for size, it appears the DCD would have had to base its determination in any event on the information provided with regard to this one size category of 40 x 40 cm. Marazzi provided lists of average prices without any specification of the total amount sold or the total value of the sales. The DCD does not explain how this impeded it from determining an exporter-specific margin of dumping for Marazzi. If the DCD was dissatisfied with the information provided, it could have requested the exporter to provide additional and more specific information. It chose not to do so.

6.98 In effect, Argentina's argument in defence of the DCD's failure to determine an individual margin of dumping for all three exporters seems to be based on the fact that the DCD did not possess sufficient information for each size

---

[95] This is not to say that in this case we believe there existed such a need for the use of third country export price or to construct the normal value under Article 2.2.

[96] We believe that the provisions of Article 2 concerning the determination of dumping and Article 6.8 AD Agreement concerning facts available are intended to allow the investigating authority to complete the data with regard to a particular exporter in order to determine a dumping margin in case the information provided is unreliable or necessary information is simply not provided. It is precisely because of Articles 2 and 6.8, among others, that it will remain possible to determine an individual margin of dumping for each exporter on the basis of facts.

category to determine a separate margin of dumping for each producer for each of the size categories. The product subject to investigation was ceramic tiles "*en todas sus medidas*", i.e. in all sizes, or in other words, irrespective of size, and not ceramic tiles of 20 x 20 cm, 30 x 30 cm and 40 x 40 cm.[97] As a consequence, the DCD was required to determine an individual margin of dumping for each exporter with regard to this product as a whole and not just a section of the product or a certain size category. As the Appellate Body stated in the *EC -Bed Linen* case:

> "Having defined the product as it did, the EC was bound to treat that product consistently thereafter in accordance with that definition. ... We see nothing in Article 2.4.2 or any other provision of the AD Agreement that provides for the establishment of "the existence of margins of dumping" for types or models of the product under investigation. ... Whatever the method used to calculate the margins of dumping, in our view, these margins must be, and can only be, established for the product under investigation as a whole".[98]

6.99 In our view, it is important not to confuse the usefulness of grouping (by size, model, type) for the purpose of making a fair comparison under Article 2.4 and the requirement under Article 6.10 to determine an individual margin of dumping for the product as a whole. We consider that the use of types or models is a valid method of ensuring a fair comparison between normal value and export price under Article 2.4. We see nothing in the Appellate Body Report in the *EC - Bed Linen* case that suggests otherwise so long as the investigating authority goes on to determine a margin of dumping for the product *as a whole*. The product under investigation in the case before us is ceramic tiles of any size, and the authority was thus required to establish an individual dumping margin for each exporter for this product as a whole and not for each size category. Nor was the DCD entitled to invoke any problems it encountered with regard to the use of such models, such as lack of information concerning a certain size category, as a reason for not determining an individual margin of dumping for the product as a whole, in this case ceramic floor tiles of any size from Italy. Therefore, even if the DCD was entitled to disregard data concerning certain size categories for one reason or another, this should not have stopped the DCD from determining an individual margin of dumping for each of the exporters included in the sample for the product subject to the investigation.

6.100 Even if Argentina had been entitled to determine margins of dumping with respect to each of three sizes of tile rather than with respect to the product subject to investigation as a whole, we believe the DCD was not justified in not determining an individual margin for each exporter for each of the three sizes of tiles.

---

[97] Final Dumping Determination, p. 2. Exhibit EC-2.

[98] Appellate Body Report, *EC - Bed Linen*, para. 53.

In our view, even if the DCD were to have doubted the reliability of the information for one or two size categories in the case of Bismantova because of the significant quantity of sales made to a related party, this should not have impeded the DCD from determining an exporter specific margin of dumping for at least the one or two remaining size categories for which the DCD did not identify any problems. Similarly, in the case of Caesar, which only exported one size of tiles, this exporter should have at least received an individual margin for that size based on the information submitted.

3. Conclusion

6.101 We conclude that the DCD should have determined an individual margin of dumping for each of the four exporters included in the sample. Our conclusion holds, whether the product as defined by the DCD was in fact ceramic tiles in all their sizes or whether it consisted of three different categories of tiles distinguished from each other on the basis of size. We therefore find that the DCD acted inconsistently with Article 6.10 of the AD Agreement by not determining an individual margin of dumping for each of the four exporters included in the sample.

6.102 Argentina raises as a final defence the concept of harmless error, and argues that the EC failed to demonstrate that the Italian exporters were prejudiced by the failure to determine an individual margin of dumping. In its answers to questions from the Panel, Argentina asserts that the concept of harmless error - i.e., an error that does not cause injury or affect the rights of one of the parties[99] - has been accepted in WTO law. Argentina refers in particular to the Report of the Appellate Body in the *Korea - Dairy Safeguards* case.[100]

6.103 We note, however, that the Appellate Body Report in the *Korea - Dairy Safeguards* case, to which Argentina refers in support of its argument, dealt with the question of whether the request for establishment met the requirements of Article 6.2 of the DSU. The issue before the Appellate Body was whether Article 6.2 of the DSU was complied with or not. The Appellate Body, in deciding that question, concluded that one element to be considered was whether the defending Member was prejudiced in its ability to defend itself by a lack of clarity or specificity in the request for establishment. The Appellate Body did not address the question whether, once it had been established that a provision of the Agreement is violated, it needs in addition to be demonstrated that this violation had prejudiced the rights of the complaining party.[101] Thus, we do not agree that this Ap-

---

[99] Argentina's answers to questions from the Panel at the first meeting, para. 31, p. 23.

[100] Argentina's answers to questions from the Panel at the first meeting , para. 31, p. 23.

[101] Appellate Body Report, *Korea - Dairy Safeguards*, DSR 2001:I, 3, para. 127: "Along the same lines, we consider that whether the mere listing of the articles claimed to have been violated meets the standard of Article 6.2 must be examined on a case-by-case basis. In resolving that question, we take into account whether the ability of the respondent to defend itself was prejudiced, given the

pellate Body decision supports Argentina's argument that the concept of harmless error has been accepted in WTO law.

6.104 Quite the contrary is true. Article 3.8 of the DSU provides that:

> "In cases where there is an infringement of the obligations assumed under a covered agreement, the action is considered *prima facie* to constitute a case of nullification or impairment. This means that there is normally a presumption that a breach of the rules has an adverse impact on other Member parties to that covered agreement, and in such cases, it shall be up to the Member against whom the complaint has been brought to rebut the charge".

6.105 Article 3.8 of the DSU thus provides that there is a presumption that benefits are nullified or impaired - i.e., there is a presumption of "harm" - where a provision of the Agreement has been violated. Article 3.8 of the DSU also provides for the possibility that the Member found to have violated a provision may rebut the presumption. In light of the presumption of Article 3.8 of the DSU, the EC having established that Argentina has acted in a manner inconsistent with the AD Agreement, it is up to Argentina to show that the failure to determine an individual dumping margin has not nullified or impaired benefits accruing to the EC under the Agreement. Argentina has failed to adduce any evidence in this respect. Accordingly, we find that the presumption of nullification or impairment of benefits caused by the violation of Article 6.10 of the AD Agreement has not been rebutted by Argentina.[102]

F. Claim 3: Article 2.4: the Need to Make Adjustments for Differences in Physical Characteristics

1. Arguments of the Parties

6.106 The **EC** submits that the DCD failed to make due allowance for all the physical differences between the various models of *porcellanato* exported to Argentina and those sold domestically.[103] The EC argues that although the DCD acknowledged that differences in physical characteristics, not adjusted for, could have had a significant impact on price, it nevertheless, without any justification, rejected the exporters' request for a model-to-model comparison and failed to

---

actual course of the panel proceedings, by the fact that the panel request simply listed the provisions claimed to have been violated."

[102] We note that our view is similar to that of the Panel in the case of *Guatemala - Cement (II)*, (Panel Report, *Guatemala - Cement (II)*, DSR 2000:XI, 5295, paras. 8.22 and 8.111-112), and Panel Report, *Guatemala - Anti-Dumping Investigation Regarding Portland Cement from Mexico ("Guatemala - Cement (I)")*, WT/DS60/R, adopted as reversed on other grounds by WT/DS60/AB/R, 25 November 1998, DSR 1998:IX, 3797, para. 7.42.

[103] By way of example, the EC refers to a 100 per cent price difference between two types of unpolished 30 x 30 cm tiles, which was found in a price list relied upon by the DCD (Exhibit EC-5D) which the EC submits suggests that other factors apart from size impacted prices.

apply any alternative method for making due allowance for differences in physical characteristics affecting price comparability, thereby violating Article 2.4 of the AD Agreement. The EC argues that by failing to make the necessary adjustments, Argentina failed to make a fair comparison between normal value and export price as required by Article 2.4 of the AD Agreement.

6.107 **Argentina** submits that the DCD made due allowance for differences in physical characteristics affecting price comparability by distinguishing three types of ceramic tiles based on the one variable common to all models and types sold: size. Argentina argues that with 78 Italian producers selling a variety of models with different colours and designs, the DCD was justified to take into account the one parameter common to all models and on that basis the DCD distinguished three size categories. Argentina asserts that the exporters did not present any convincing reasons to invalidate the segregation of products on this basis and never objected to the determination of a margin of dumping per size category.

6.108 Argentina submits that, in light of the standard of review applicable to anti-dumping disputes set out in Article 17.6 of the AD Agreement, deference should be given to the national authority's methodology if it is based on a reasonable interpretation of the text of the Agreement. Argentina submits that Article 2.4 requires that the authority make due allowance for differences in physical characteristics *in each case on its merits*. Argentina argues that in this case, concerning a large variety of tiles of different colours and with so many different designs, the DCD distinguished between three different types of tiles based on the one physical characteristic common to all: size. This homogeneous standard used by the DCD, Argentina submits, is a reasonable basis for making due allowance for differences in physical characteristics affecting price comparability and the DCD's determination should therefore be upheld by the Panel.

6.109 Argentina emphasizes that when the DCD requested the exporters to identify the product by model/type or code the exporters merely referred to a catalogue containing an enormous number of models without any further explanation. In Argentina's view, this made any *a posteriori* adjustments, if at all required, practically impossible for lack of information. Argentina argues that the exporters also failed to give any market information per model or type of tiles and never submitted any concrete proposals for adjustments. Therefore, Argentina argues, the DCD's decision to distinguish the products on the basis of size was a reasonable and objective decision especially in light of the confidential nature and incomplete character of the information.

2. *Analysis by the Panel*

6.110 The EC's claim concerns the scope of the requirement of Article 2.4 of the AD Agreement to make due allowance for differences in physical characteristics affecting price comparability.

6.111 Article 2.4 of the AD Agreement provides as follows:

"A fair comparison shall be made between the export price and the normal value. This comparison shall be made at the same level of trade, normally at the ex-factory level, and in respect of sales made at as nearly as possible the same time. *Due allowance shall be made in each case, on its merits, for differences which affect price comparability, including* differences in conditions and terms of sale, taxation, levels of trade, quantities, *physical characteristics*, and any other differences which are also demonstrated to affect price comparability.[7] In the cases referred to in paragraph 3, allowances for costs, including duties and taxes, incurred between importation and resale, and for profits accruing, should also be made. If in these cases price comparability has been affected, the authorities shall establish the normal value at a level of trade equivalent to the level of trade of the constructed export price, or shall make due allowance as warranted under this paragraph. The authorities shall indicate to the parties in question what information is necessary to ensure a fair comparison and shall not impose an unreasonable burden of proof on those parties". (emphasis added)

[7] It is understood that some of the above factors may overlap, and authorities shall ensure that they do not duplicate adjustments that have been already made under this provision.

6.112 We recall our findings on claims 1 and 2 that the DCD was not justified in disregarding in large part the exporters' information and erred in failing to determine an exporter-specific margin of dumping. We are asked to rule now whether the DCD made due allowance for the physical differences affecting price comparability between the products sold in the domestic market and the products exported to Argentina. We recall that our task is to review the determination of the DCD and examine whether the DCD properly established the facts and whether it evaluated those facts in an objective and unbiased manner.

6.113 Article 2.4 places the obligation on the investigating authority to make due allowance, in each case on its merits, for differences which affect price comparability, including differences in physical characteristics. The last sentence of Article 2.4 provides that the authorities shall indicate to the parties in question what information is necessary to ensure a fair comparison. We believe that the requirement to make due allowance for such differences, *in each case on its merits,* means at a minimum that the authority has to evaluate identified differences in physical characteristics to see whether an adjustment is required to maintain price comparability and to ensure a fair comparison between normal value and export price under Article 2.4 of the AD Agreement, and to adjust where necessary.

6.114 We note that the DCD determined the export price of the product under investigation on the basis of information provided by the petitioner, as well as official import statistics. We note that these import statistics related to all products exported from Italy and not just to products of those four producers included in the sample. The DCD further calculated two normal values for each size, one based on petitioner and importers' information, a second one based on the two aforementioned sources together with information from the exporters. In general, the information on the record suggests that ceramic tiles may be distinguished on the basis of a number of characteristics, such as dimensions (length and width), colour, degree of processing (polished/unpolished), and quality, and that the price of the products differs as a function of these differences in physical characteristics. The record indicates that the DCD collected information concerning first-quality, unpolished tiles. The DCD also distinguished the product on the basis of differences in size within the various models of tiles sold on the domestic market and exported to Argentina.

6.115 In the Preliminary Determination, the DCD acknowledged that there existed a large variety of types and models of ceramic tiles with significant price differences between them.[104] In the Final Determination, the DCD further specifies that there existed significant price differences between various models of the same size, and that for certain models the smaller size tiles were sometimes more expensive than certain other models' larger size tiles.[105] We note that, in spite of this acknowledgement, the DCD failed to make any further adjustments for these apparent differences in price caused by factors other than size. Neither did the DCD indicate to the parties what information it required in order to make these further adjustments. Argentina argues that the DCD did in fact request the exporters to provide information per model in the questionnaire but that the exporters replied that such model specific information was not available. We note that the information requested in Annexes IV-VI of the questionnaire, to which Argentina refers in support of its argument, does not relate to information necessary to determine normal value and export price but concerns information of a more general nature concerning the domestic market of the exporters and their sales performance in general. If the DCD was dissatisfied with the information provided by the exporters concerning the technical characteristics of the models in their questionnaire responses, it could have and should have, according to Article 2.4, requested additional information. The DCD did not do so.

6.116 In addition to accounting for size differences, the DCD's methodology took account of two other physical differences affecting price comparability. As to quality, the DCD collected data only on first-quality tiles, thereby avoiding the need to make adjustments for tile quality. By the same token, the DCD's methodology made due allowance for the degree of processing, in that data were collected only on unpolished tiles.[106] In effect then, the DCD made due allowance within the meaning of Article 2.4 for three physical differences affecting price

[104] Preliminary Dumping Determination, p. 34, Exhibit ARG-8.

[105] Final Dumping Determination, p. 28. Exhibit EC-2.

[106] Moreover, when advised that one exporter, Marazzi, sold one model of tiles as a polished tile on the domestic market while this model was sold under the same name in Argentina as an unpolished tile, the DCD accepted the need to make an adjustment to account for this physical difference affecting price comparability.

comparability. Nonetheless, other important differences remained, as the DCD acknowledged in its final determination. We do not agree with Argentina's view that Article 2.4, through the qualifying language that due allowance shall be made "in each case" "on its merits", permits an investigating authority to adjust only for the most important of the physical differences that affect price comparability, even if making the remaining adjustments would have been, as the parties agree, complex. The DCD chose not to conduct a model-by-model comparison and it was then left to find other means to account for the remaining physical differences affecting price comparability. It did not do so.

3. Conclusion

6.117 In conclusion, we consider that, in light of the facts on the record, there were other factors significantly affecting price comparability. An objective and unbiased evaluation of the facts of this case would have required the DCD to make additional adjustments for physical differences affecting price comparability. We therefore find that the DCD acted inconsistently with Article 2.4 by failing to make adjustments for physical differences affecting price comparability.

G. Claim 4: Article 6.9: Failure to Inform the Exporters of the "essential facts" on which the Decision is Based

1. Arguments of the Parties

6.118 The **EC** submits that Argentina failed to disclose the essential facts under consideration which form the basis for the decision whether to apply definitive measures as required by Article 6.9 of the AD Agreement. The EC argues that Article 6.9 of the AD Agreement entails a positive action by the investigating authorities, and requires the authorities to actively disclose those essential facts on which the decision whether to apply definitive measures is based. According to the EC, Argentina merely invited interested parties to examine the public file.[107] The EC asserts that the public file of an anti-dumping investigation essentially consists of often contradictory questionnaire responses and allegations of different interested parties and thus clearly does not identify the "essential facts" on which the decision to impose a measure is based. The EC argues that in this case the final dumping determination (unlike the final injury determination) was not available in the public file. Nor did the public file contain any other document prepared by the DCD which identified the "essential facts" that would form the basis for the final dumping determination.

---

[107] Exhibit EC-7C. The EC asserts that if all that was required is to provide access to the public file, Article 6.9 would not add anything to the requirement of Article 6.4 to provide timely opportunities for all interested parties to see all information that is relevant to the presentation of their case. Argentina, on the other hand, argues that it complied with Article 6.9 by having provided an opportunity to view the complete file.

6.119 **Argentina** argues that the DCD complied with the requirement of Article 6.9 of the AD Agreement to inform the interested parties of the essential facts which form the basis for the decision whether to apply definitive measures by inviting the exporters to view the complete file. According to Argentina, the exporters viewed the file that contained all the information on which the determination was based, including the essential facts. Argentina argues that what is important is that the result envisaged by Article 6.9 is achieved, not how this result was achieved. Argentina asserts that the Ad Hoc Group on Implementation of the Committee on Anti-Dumping Practices has discussed the kind of information which needs to be disclosed under Article 6.9. Argentina submits that the fact that the Ad Hoc Group has not yet issued a recommendation on this matter demonstrates the diversity of criteria used by the Members in complying with this requirement. Finally, Argentina argues that in any case the exporters did not suffer any injury from this alleged lack of notification of the essential facts. In case the Panel were to find a violation of Article 6.9 of the AD Agreement, Argentina submits this constituted a harmless error.

6.120 The **EC** submits that the requirement concerning the disclosure of essential facts is not an empty formality, as Argentina seems to suggest, and therefore rejects Argentina's argument that the alleged failure to comply with Article 6.9 constituted a harmless error.

6.121 We also recall in this respect some of the arguments made by the third parties on this matter. **Japan**, as a third party, fully supports the EC position that the provisions of Article 6.9 of the AD Agreement must be read as imposing obligations that go beyond those in Article 6.4 of the AD Agreement to provide timely opportunities for interested parties to have access to all relevant information. Japan asserts that the requirement of Article 6.9 to disclose the essential facts that the authority will actually rely on is not satisfied by merely opening for inspection a file that includes both facts that will be relied upon and facts that will not be. **Turkey**, as a third party, also considers that the requirement of Article 6.9 goes beyond the obligation to provide timely opportunities to see all information as set out in Article 6.4 of the AD Agreement.

6.122 The **United States**, as a third party, does not take a position on whether, under the facts of this case, the measure is consistent with Article 6.9 of the AD Agreement. However, the United States agrees with Argentina that Article 6.9 requires only that interested parties be informed of the essential facts and that this requirement does not impose a particular means of disclosure. According to the United States, Members may implement the obligation under Article 6.9 in a variety of ways. In particular, the United States argues, Members may choose to establish an investigative process which allows interested parties to be presented with all of the facts as they are presented to the authority, as well as arguments made about those facts.

2. *Analysis by the Panel*

6.123 We note that there does not exist any disagreement between the parties concerning the relevant facts in respect of this claim. The record shows that the exporters were invited to view the information on the record, and made use of this possibility on 18 June 1999, 3 September 1999 and 21 September 1999. The EC submits, however, that by merely being given the opportunity to view the complete file the exporters were not informed of the essential facts under consideration which form the basis for the decision whether to apply definitive measures as required by Article 6.9 of the AD Agreement.

6.124 Article 6.9 provides that:

> "The authorities shall, before a final determination is made, inform all interested parties of the essential facts under consideration which form the basis for the decision whether to apply definitive measures. Such disclosure should take place in sufficient time for the parties to defend their interests".

6.125 We agree with Argentina that the requirement to inform all interested parties of the essential facts under consideration may be complied with in a number of ways. Article 6.9 of the AD Agreement does not prescribe the manner in which the authority is to comply with this disclosure obligation. The requirement to disclose the "essential facts under consideration" may well be met, for example, by disclosing a specially prepared document summarizing the essential facts under consideration by the investigating authority or through the inclusion in the record of documents - such as verification reports, a preliminary determination, or correspondence exchanged between the investigating authorities and individual exporters - which actually disclose to the interested parties the essential facts which, being under consideration, are anticipated by the authorities as being those which will form the basis for the decision whether to apply definitive measures. This view is based on our understanding that Article 6.9 anticipates that a final determination will be made and that the authorities have identified and are considering the essential facts on which that decision is to be made. Under Article 6.9, these facts must be disclosed so that parties can defend their interests, for example by commenting on the completeness of the essential facts under consideration.

6.126 The question before us is whether, under the facts of this case, the DCD complied with its obligation under Article 6.9 of the AD Agreement to inform the interested parties of the essential facts under consideration which form the basis for the determination whether to apply definitive measures. The DCD in this case invited the exporters to view the entire file.

6.127 In this case, the DCD relied primarily upon evidence submitted by petitioners and derived from secondary sources, rather than upon information provided by the exporters, as the factual basis for a determination of the existence of dumping. Thus, petitioner and secondary source information, rather than exporters' information, represented (with respect to the existence of dumping) the essential facts which formed the basis for the decision whether to apply definitive measures. We therefore examined the record in order to determine whether exporters were informed by the Argentine authority, through access to the file, that it was on these facts that the authority would primarily rely in its determination regarding the existence of dumping.

6.128 In considering this question, we observe that the file contained *inter alia* the Preliminary Dumping Determination, in which the DCD explained that it considered that the confidential nature of the information supplied by the exporters in the questionnaire responses concerning normal value and export price limited the use it could make of this information. In the Preliminary Determination, the DCD calculated the dumping margin without relying on any of the information supplied by the exporters in confidence. The file also contained the three letters the DCD sent to the exporters following the preliminary determination with the requests for declassification of the information discussed above in paras. 6.41 - 6.47. The exporters were further advised of the DCD's request for additional supporting documentation, as discussed above in paras. 6.59 - 6.65. We note in this regard that a meeting took place between the exporters' representatives and the case-handlers. As Argentina clarified, this was an informal meeting convened at the request of the exporters and no official record, which could have been included in the file, exists of what was agreed upon at that meeting. The exporters nonetheless supplied the invoices covering about 50 per cent of their reported domestic sales which they considered had been requested by the DCD.[108] We found above that the exporters also complied with the various requests for declassification of the information and never received any deficiency letters nor were any such deficiency notices put on the record. The file further contained a large variety of data from various sources such as the petitioner, importers and official registers.

3. *Conclusion*

6.129 In light of the state of the record, we find that the exporters could not be aware in this case, simply by reviewing the complete record of the investigation, that evidence submitted by petitioners and derived from secondary sources, rather than facts submitted by the exporters, would, despite the responses of the exporters to the DCD's information requests as summarized above, form the primary basis for the determination of the existence and extent of dumping. The DCD thus failed to put the exporters on notice of an essential fact under consideration. As a result, the exporters were unable to defend their interests within the meaning of Article 6.9, for example, by giving reasons why their responses should not be rejected and by suggesting alternative sources for facts available if their responses were nonetheless disregarded. Under these circumstances, we find that the DCD did not, by referring the exporters to the complete file of the investigation, fulfil its obligation under Article 6.9 to inform the exporters of the "es-

[108] Exhibit EC-10.

sential facts under consideration which form the basis for the decision whether to apply definitive measures".[109]

6.130 Argentina again raises the concept of harmless error as a defence. As discussed above, in our view it does not suffice to merely raise the issue of harmless error. Indeed, Article 3.8 of the DSU provides for a presumption that, in the case of an infringement of the obligations assumed under a covered agreement, the action is considered *prima facie* to constitute a case of nullification or impairment. Article 3.8 of the DSU also provides for the possibility that the Member found to have violated a provision may rebut the presumption. In light of the presumption of Article 3.8 of the DSU, the EC having established that Argentina has acted in a manner inconsistent with the AD Agreement, it is up to Argentina to show that the failure to determine an individual dumping margin has not nullified or impaired benefits accruing to the EC under the Agreement. Argentina has failed to adduce any evidence in this respect. Accordingly, we find that the presumption of nullification or impairment of benefits caused by the violation of Article 6.9 of the AD Agreement has not been rebutted by Argentina.

6.131 In conclusion, we find that the DCD acted inconsistently with Article 6.9 as it failed to inform the interested parties of the essential facts under consideration which form the basis for the decision whether to apply definitive measures thereby failing to allow the exporters to defend their interests.

VII. CONCLUSIONS AND RECOMMENDATION

7.1 In light of the findings above, we conclude

(a) that Argentina acted inconsistently with Article 6.8 and Annex II AD Agreement by disregarding in large part the information provided by the exporters for the determination of normal value and export price, and this without informing the exporters of the reasons for the rejection;

(b) that Argentina acted inconsistently with Article 6.10 AD Agreement by not determining an individual margin of dumping for each exporter included in the sample for the product under investigation;

(c) that Argentina acted inconsistently with Article 2.4 AD Agreement by failing to make due allowance for differences in physical characteristics affecting price comparability;

(d) that Argentina acted inconsistently with Article 6.9 AD Agreement by not disclosing to the exporters the essential facts under consid-

[109] In light of our findings under the facts of this case, we need not reach the larger question discussed by the Panel in the case of *Guatemala - Cement (II)* concerning the relationship between Article 6.9 and Article 6.4 of the AD Agreement.

eration which form the basis for the decision whether to apply definitive measures.

7.2 Under Article 3.8 of the DSU, in cases where there is infringement of the obligations assumed under a covered agreement, the action is considered *prima facie* to constitute a case of nullification or impairment of benefits under that agreement. Argentina has failed to adduce any evidence to rebut this presumption. Accordingly, we conclude that, to the extent Argentina has acted inconsistently with the provisions of the AD Agreement, it has nullified or impaired benefits accruing to the EC under that Agreement.

7.3 We recommend that the Dispute Settlement Body request Argentina to bring its measure into conformity with its obligations under the AD Agreement.